About the Editors

Jessie Carney Smith is University Librarian and William and Camille Cosby Professor in the Humanities at Fisk University, Nashville, Tennessee. As scholar, researcher, editor, and writer, she has published over 20 books. Her works include *Black Firsts,* 2nd ed., and *Black Heroes,* both published by Visible Ink Press; other works include *Notable Black American Women* (Books 1-3), *Notable Black American Men* (Books 1 and 2), *Encyclopedia of African American Business* (two volumes), *Epic Lives, Powerful Black Women,* and *Black Genealogy.* Her numerous honors include being the recipient of the Women's National Book Association Award, the Candace Awards in Education, *Sage* magazine's Anna J. Cooper Award, Black Women in the Academy's Distinguished Service and Leadership Award, Bennett College for Women's Bell Ringer Award, and the ACRL/Academic/Research Librarian of the Year Award. A native of Greensboro, North Carolina, Dr. Smith is a graduate of North Carolina A&T State University, Michigan State University, and Vanderbilt University; she received her Ph.D. degree from the University of Illinois.

Linda T. Wynn is the assistant director for state programs for the Tennessee Historical Commission and a faculty member in the history department at Fisk University. A graduate of Tennessee State University, she also earned M.S. degrees in history and in public administration from that institution. Devoted to teaching on the topic of civil rights, she helped to design the module "Civil Rights Movement in Nashville" for *The Beloved Community: Then and Now,* a collaboration course among American Baptist College, Fisk University's Department of History, and Lipscomb University. She edited *Journey to Our Past: A Guide to African-American Markers in Tennessee* and co-edited *Profiles of African Americans in Tennessee.* Other works include contributions to the *Tennessee Encyclopedia of Culture and History, Tennessee Women: Their Lives and Times, Notable Black American Men* (Book 2), *African American National Biography, The History of African Americans in Tennessee: Trials and Triumphs,* and *African American Almanac.* Wynn also served as a consultant and contributor for the *Encyclopedia of African American Business.*

Also from Visible Ink Press

Black Firsts, ISBN 978-1-57859-142-8
Black Heroes, ISBN 978-1-57859-136-7
The Handy History Answer Book, ISBN 978-1-57859-170-1

For a complete list of titles, please visit us at visibleink.com.

Freedom Facts and Firsts

400 Years of the African American Civil Rights Experience

Freedom Facts and Firsts: 400 Years of the African American Civil Rights Experience

Jessie Carney Smith and Linda T. Wynn

Copyright © 2009 by Visible Ink Press®

This publication is a creative work fully protected by all applicable copyright laws, as well as by misappropriation, trade secret, unfair competition, and other applicable laws.

No part of this book may be reproduced in any form without permission in writing from the publisher, except by a reviewer who wishes to quote brief passages in connection with a review written for inclusion in a magazine, newspaper, or web site.

All rights to this publication will be vigorously defended.

Visible Ink Press®
43311 Joy Rd., #414
Canton, MI 48187-2075

Visible Ink Press is a registered trademark of Visible Ink Press LLC.

Most Visible Ink Press books are available at special quantity discounts when purchased in bulk by corporations, organizations, or groups. Customized printings, special imprints, messages, and excerpts can be produced to meet your needs. For more information, contact Special Markets Director, Visible Ink Press, www.visibleink.com, or 734-667-3211.

Managing Editor: Kevin S. Hile
Art Director: Mary Claire Krzewinski
Typesetting: Marco Di Vita
Indexer: Larry Baker
Proofreaders: Amy Marcaccio Keyzer, Kenneth R. Shepherd
ISBN 978-1-57859-192-3

Cover photos: Maya Angelou, AP Photo/Charles Dharapak; Eleanor Holmes Norton, AP Photo/Adrian Keating; Barack Obama, AP Photo/Rick Bowmer,File; Angela Davis, AP Photo/Jeff Zelevansky; all others, AP Photo.

Library of Congress Cataloguing-in-Publication Data

Smith, Jessie Carney.

  Freedom facts and firsts : 400 years of the African American civil rights experience / Jessie Carney Smith and Linda T. Wynn.

     p. cm.

  Includes bibliographical references and index.

    ISBN 978-1-57859-192-3 (pbk.) — ISBN 978-1-57859-243-2 (ebook) 1. African Americans—Civil rights—History. 2. United States—Race relations—History. 3. Civil rights workers—United States—Biography. 4. African American civil rights workers—Biography. 5. African Americans—Biography. I. Wynn, Linda T. II. Title.

  E185.61.S636 2009   323.1196'073—dc22
                                                                                        2008041503

Printed in the United States of America

10 9 8 7 6 5 4 3 2 1

Freedom
Facts and Firsts

400 Years of the African American
Civil Rights Experience

Jessie Carney Smith and Linda T. Wynn, Editors

VISIBLE
INK
PRESS

Detroit

Contributors

Crystal Anne deGregory is a doctoral student in history at Vanderbilt University. She has contributed articles to *African American National Biography, Encyclopedia of African American Business,* and *Notable Black American Men* (Book 2).

Rebecca Dixon is assistant professor in the Department of Languages, Literature, and History at Tennessee State University. Her concentrations are in American, African American, and Caribbean literature. She has contributed articles to the *Encyclopedia of African American Business.*

Cheryl Jones Hamberg is assistant librarian for Technical Services at Fisk University and retired chief librarian from Meharry Medical College. Her writings are included in *Encyclopedia of African American Business* and *Notable Black American Men* (Book 2).

Mary N. Hernandez is a volunteer in the Fisk University Library and a retired librarian from the District of Columbia Public Library. She has contributed to *College and Research Libraries* and *Racial and Ethnic Diversity in Academic Libraries: Multicultural Issues.*

Helen R. Houston is professor of English at Tennessee State University. Her publications include *The Afro-American Novel, 1965–1975*

and articles in *Encyclopedia of African American Business, Notable Black American Women* (Books 1 and 2), *Notable Black American Men,* and the *Oxford Companion to African American Literature.*

Fletcher F. Moon is assistant professor and head reference librarian at Tennessee State University. He is active in research, editing, music/ministry, and in other areas, and has published articles in *Encyclopedia of African American Business* and *Notable Black American Men* (Book 2).

Victor Simmons serves as curator of Fisk University Galleries, adjunct art history instructor at Fisk, and as a commissioner for the Metropolitan Nashville Arts Commission. His work was recently included in the exhibition "Fragile Species: New Nashville Artists" at the Frist Center for the Visual Arts. Simmons co-authored *Building Your Future: Using Architecture in the Classroom.*

Frederick D. Smith is an information resource support specialist for the State of Tennessee, owner of the digital design company DigiDox, and a consultant in technology. He has contributed articles to *Encyclopedia of African American Business,* and *Notable Black American Men* (Books 1 and 2).

Contents

Introduction

Activists of the modern Civil Rights Movement inherited a revolution that began over 300 years earlier. While the players and the work that they did varied, the issues were, as previously, ones of equality, freedom, and justice. This struggle in America is never-ending. We acknowledge the overlap in this pursuit among different racial and ethnic groups. In one way or another, the struggle touches the lives of all people in America—black, white, Hispanic, Native American, Asian, and others of various racial and ethnic backgrounds. Notwithstanding the civil rights interests of these groups, we concentrate on the group that has been the one of the most tormented—African Americans.

Since 1619, when African Americans were first brought to this country, the public perception of their struggle toward equality, freedom, and justice has been one of ebb and flow. It has been characterized by a range of activities, from quiet disobedience to public agitation, and from organized direction that sometimes gained public support to public opposition and violent reaction. For three and a half centuries, African Americans have had a colorful and eventful past. We note the current surging interest on civil rights issues; thus, we chronicle here the struggle of African Americans and those who have supported their efforts in a convenient and timely work called *Freedom Facts and Firsts: 400 Years of the African American Civil Rights Experi-*ence. The earliest entry given is for African Americans at Jamestown in 1619. The most recent focuses on 2008, when Democratic Senator Barack Obama of Illinois became the first African American to become president of the United States.

Purpose

A trade source geared toward students, educators, organizations, and the general public, *Freedom Facts and Firsts* chronicles the struggle for freedom of African Americans, beginning with the earliest documented date to the present time. As the title suggests, many of the entries include contributions of those who fought for freedom, whether as abolitionists, activists, educators, preachers, politicians, organizers, or as demonstrators in the modern Civil Rights Movement. Since the abolishment of slavery did not bring full freedom to African Americans, we searched for the varied ways in which our forebears have worked to bring about the changes that we do see—whether perfect or flawed—in voting rights, housing, education, public accommodations, economic opportunity, and other areas affecting the quality of life for African Americans.

This encyclopedic work aims to increase the wealth of information on African Americans and their struggle for civil rights already published; it builds on such works by bringing together in one convenient volume topics and issues that may appear in different works. It profiles civil rights icons whose work we reintroduce. It also includes obscure figures, many of whom were only recently acknowledged for their work. When those of the latter group made their contributions, the effort might have seemed slight, but as we reexamine the movement toward freedom, we must acknowledge that acts of various magnitudes and scope were all aimed to change America for the better.

Scope

The scope of this work embraces slave uprisings, the work of anti-slavery societies, the familiar civil rights events of the 1950s and 1960s, and the nation's efforts to promote racial understanding and tolerance. We include the continuing struggles of churches, educational institutions, organizations, and local governments to ensure the civil rights of African Americans. There are entries on sports figures, education leaders, literary figures, the arts, organizations, movements, ideologies and strategies (e.g., Black Power Movement, Black Arts/Black Aesthetic Movement, nonviolent resistance/civil disobedience). These are described and focus on the significance of the cause, citing individuals associated with the cause. Areas that until now have received too little recognition, such as the work of women in the various civil rights movements, are developed here as well. Ella Josephine Baker, who helped to organize student leaders in the Student Nonviolent Coordinating Committee, said that "The movement of the '50's and '60's was carried largely by women" for it was church-centered and "sort of second nature to women to play a supportive role." As we "name names," we include that of Margie Jumper, who "took a stand by sitting down" on a streetcar in Roanoke, Virginia, 10 years before Rosa Parks refused to give up her seat to a white passenger on a Montgomery, Alabama bus. Not intended as a biographical work, *Freedom Facts and Firsts* gives only brief biographical sketches of popular as well as little-known figures who had their mind on freedom, along with historical items, speeches, and works that document civil rights activities in America.

Arrangement

Freedom Facts and Firsts is an encyclopedia work arranged under nine chapter headings, covering various aspects of the struggle for human justice. Cross-references are used but, in some cases, solely to guide the reader from one form of an entrant's name to the name popularly used.

The names of those profiled elsewhere in the various entries and chapters in this work are bold-faced, but within these entries are also mentioned people who might not otherwise have an entry; their names will appear within the index. In addition to people, the events and other items that have entries are also boldfaced when they appear in other entries. A bibliography at the end of the book provides readers with other useful sources for further research.

Uses

Freedom Facts and Firsts may be used as a quick ready-reference and a brief introduction to the history of African American freedom movements. Though primarily written in a popular style, it will engage a wide audience, ranging from school children to research scholars. Students may use it to determine term paper topics, and then search elsewhere for additional information to enrich and expand the specific topic. For example, the entry "Bridging the Racial Divide" may be expanded to determine how the divide is bridged in a wide context or extended to include other ethnic groups. Similarly, students may explore efforts of various abolition societies for commonalities of effort, or they may use some of the issues given to establish themes for debates. They may compare the various civil rights laws that have been enacted and then determine whether or how these laws have effected change. They may identify the various race riots in America and become curious to know their wide geographical locations and the range in dates of occurrence. The uses of the information discussed or compiled in this volume are legion. Public, school, college libraries, and collectors of freedom and civil rights information will add *Free-*

dom Facts and Firsts to their resources both
because of its quick reference and documentary
value and because it gives important facts never
before published or that have remained obscure.
This work helps to bring the contentious struggle for human justice in America to full circle.

Jessie Carney Smith
Fisk University

and

Linda T. Wynn
Tennessee Historical Commission and
Fisk University

Acknowledgments

Freedom Facts and Firsts is a product of the myriads of people who, in one way or another, were a part of the civil rights struggle throughout this nation's existence. We acknowledge their work and worth and all that they achieved to make life easier for those who followed. Since these acknowledgments are meant to deal with the "here and now," we take this moment to thank those who contributed to some aspect of this book.

First, we thank our contributors, beginning with Crystal deGregory, who helped us clarify some of the issues we faced as we deliberated over the list of entries and made agonizing decisions about who or what should be included and why. Cheryl Hamberg deserves special thanks for keeping a watchful eye for new sources that relate to our project and bringing them to our attention. Frederick "Rick" Smith deserves praise for scanning images for us. All of the contributors put aside other important matters to write multiple entries for this work. For those who came to our rescue again late in the project, when we thought our work was complete, and enabled us to fill the void in the sports chapter, we are grateful. Each of our contributors also called our attention to current developments related to our subjects, suggested people and events that should be added, and repeatedly helped us make important decisions about the book. We thank you again.

Works such as this are impossible to prepare without the assistance of libraries, particularly those with important civil rights materials in their collections. We acknowledge the support of many such libraries whose staff members responded to our requests for information or clarification on issues, who introduced us to local oral history interviews and historic civil rights sites, and who helped us fill in gaps in our research. Thank you Beth Howse, and the Special Collections Department at Fisk University's library, for pulling photographs and references needed to write the entries, and to library staffer Jason Harrison for retrieving and copying materials for us.

Our families have been especially understanding—and hopefully appreciative—of our untiring dedication to the project often at the expense of familial matters. We appreciate your support and your willingness to wait patiently or impatiently for our attention until the last item was sent to press.

To Roger Jänecke of Visible Ink Press, thank you for offering us the opportunity to develop this project, for guiding us throughout the stages of its development, and for the constant words of encouragement that you like to offer. We can probably never show enough appreciation to the staff of Visible Ink, especially editor Kevin Hile, who survived the project despite the problems that we know it (or we) created. Additional thanks to proofreaders Ken Shepherd and Amy Keyzer, designer Mary Claire Krzewinski, indexer Larry Baker, and typesetter Marco Di Vita.

The Editors

Foreword

The African American struggle for freedom, equality, and justice is emphasized by a number of civil rights anniversaries observed during the first decade of the twenty-first century. The modern civil rights movement had its roots in the long battle fought by African Americans as they sought inclusion in "We the People," as delineated in the 1787 Preamble to the Constitution of the United States. Despite the American Civil War and the abolition of slavery, African Americans continued to be excluded from "We the People" and regarded as second-class citizens. By 1896, under the U.S. Supreme Court's mandated system of racial apartheid, African Americans were sentenced to an existence under draconian justice. The omnipresent signs specifying segregation between blacks and whites punctuated the landscape of the American South. While *de jure* segregation discriminated against southern blacks, *de facto* segregation discriminated against northern blacks.

Although the movement for civil rights operated along a continuum among African Americans, it was not until the modern civil rights movement of the 1950s and 1960s captured the attention of everyday people that justice rolled down "like waters and righteousness like a mighty stream" (Amos 5:24)—at least to an extent. The modern movement relied upon the power of mass organization to convey the philosophy and attainable goals of equality, which in turn empowered the minds and spirits of ordinary people to take extraordinary actions to secure their rights as American citizens. As the chains of inequality and injustice were methodically broken, both the oppressed and the oppressor were released from the legally binding bonds of racial exclusivity.

Racial injustice in America was blatantly contradictory to the values of democracy that the nation's leaders espoused to the world. Images depicting separation of the races, lynching and other violence against blacks, active protests, and economic and social inequities were transmitted and published around the globe. Such philosophical hypocrisy, revealed in America's duplicitous perpetuation of the legalized caste system, caused international outrage and undermined America's image abroad. It also reinforced anti-American propaganda promulgated by the then-extant Union of Soviet Socialist Republics (USSR). The international attention given to the racial division solidly entrenched in the United States was both embarrassing and politically problematic. As affirmed by Mary L. Dudziak in *Cold War Civil Rights: Race and the Image of American Democracy*:

> Domestic racism and civil rights protest led to international criticism of the U.S. government. International criticism led the federal government to respond, through placating foreign critics by reframing the narrative of race in America, and through

promoting some level of social change. While civil rights reform in different eras had been motivated by a variety of factors, one element during the early Cold War years was the need for reform in order to make credible the government's argument about race and democracy.

The nonviolent black freedom struggle compelled America to live up to its professed democratic principles of freedom, equality, and justice for its black citizens. From civil rights organizations to everyday people, from dedicated workers to student activists, from organizers of the various local struggles to those who battled on the national front, all persevered. Despite violence, intimidation, and hostile governmental policies, all fought long and hard to ensure that African Americans gained their constitutional rights.

As discerned by a critical number of the movement's leadership, including the Reverend Dr. Martin Luther King Jr., non-cooperation and nonviolent insistence—the methods used in the modern Civil Rights Movement—were ways to try to awaken the moral truths in one's adversary and evoke the humanity that existed in both the oppressor and the oppressed. Despite the fact that racial segregation had been an ongoing injustice in the daily lives of American blacks for numerous generations, they gained the courage to cross the Red Sea of segregation and overcome the fear of retribution, even it became apparent that the movement might cost their lives.

What began with the Montgomery Bus Boycott in December of 1955 must be connected to the earlier, prolonged tradition of localized struggles against racial oppression. The media coverage given to the protests and demonstrations, including the bus boycott of 1955, the lunch counter sit-ins of the early 1960s, the Freedom Rides of 1961, the 1963 confrontations with the police in Birmingham (which at the time was reputed to be the nation's most segregated city), and the 1965 Selma-to-Montgomery March, as well as perpetrated acts of violence by white supremacists in between these events, played a substantial role in exposing racial injustices to public scrutiny.

These events, the participants, and the public outcry marshaled widespread support that pressured the administration of President John F. Kennedy to propose sweeping civil rights legislation. Under the subsequent leadership of President Lyndon B. Johnson, the U.S. Congress passed the Civil Rights Act of 1964, the Voting Rights Act of 1965, and the Fair Housing Act of 1968: three comprehensive acts that took African Americans a significant distance toward "We the People." These and other events, including the Brown v. Board of Education of Topeka decision in 1954, have been commemorated during the first decade of this century.

Due to the dedicated efforts of African Americans and their allies during the decade of the 1960s to secure the rights of freedom, equality, and justice within American society through nonviolent direct action, both philosophical and tactical, these commemorations were celebrated as reminders of the black freedom struggle. King and other practitioners of direct nonviolent resistance understood that the oppressor did not render freedom willingly. To overcome injustice with justice, freedom had to be demanded by the oppressed.

As a student at Fisk University in Nashville, Tennessee, where I first encountered racial segregation, I came to understand that basic to the civil rights struggle was the presentation of a way in which Africans Americans could affirm their sense of worth against laws and customs that abrogated human mutuality and, consequently, undermined their dignity as human beings. In order to "redeem the soul of America," there had to be an infusion of radical love. Using Christian precepts as the guiding force, Reverend James Lawson educated a core group of student and citizen activists in Nashville, of which I was a part, in the philosophy and strategy of nonviolent direct action. Our commitment was unwavering, even when the possibilities of violence and death loomed. Admittedly, some committed to nonviolence for tactical purposes, while others committed to it as a way of life. Yet we found a common ground in our shared struggle and ultimate vision for the forging of a better city, nation, and world.

Freedom Facts and Firsts: 400 Years of the African American Civil Rights Experience offers a wide-ranging historical narrative portraying African Americans as they struggled toward freedom, equality, and justice. However, it was not the struggle of African Americans alone; it also was America's collective struggle. This encyclopedic compendium will assist the reader in understanding the emotional, mental, physical, economic, familial, and social strains of men and women, boys and girls, blacks and whites, who courageously gave their hearts, minds, bodies, and, in some instances, their lives to the freedom struggle. The text acknowledges the veracity and timbre of the times for those who participated in the freedom movement, while available references for those who seek to learn from the freedom movement.

Although America has made societal progress from its days of overt racial intolerance and legal segregation, the true spirit of the civil rights struggle lives on in efforts to eradicate poverty; in campaigns for improvement of public education; in attempts to end unjust and disproportionate incarceration of blacks in the prison system; and in endeavors to obtain health care for every American. Until these and other civil rights are fulfilled, the struggle continues in every community, town, city, and state in our nation.

Diane Nash
August 2008

Arts and Entertainment

Movements

African American Art and the Civil Rights Movement

The Civil Rights Movement of the 1950s and 1960s was the most significant realignment of American democracy since the American **Civil War** of the 1860s. The movement asserted a rebirth and a reinvention of black identity and black consciousness as African Americans redefined themselves, while also forcing a reappraisal of white identity and America's democratic values. The landmark events, songs, speeches, poems, and literature of the period, spanning from the *Brown v. Board of Education* United States Supreme Court Decision of 1954 to the assassination of Reverend Dr. **Martin Luther King Jr.**, in 1968, are well known.

The art that grew out of the movement is also critical to understanding this tumultuous time. The struggle was waged on two fronts: in the streets and in the realm of images and ideas that proclaimed the awakening of a people in search of self-discovery, self-determination, and self-legitimization. Black artists asked themselves, "What kind of art should a black artist make in these times?" according to Lerone Bennett Jr., and they answered with various artistic respons-

es that embraced the struggle for social justice, racial pride, and the liberation of people of African descent everywhere.

The artwork, in large measure, resounded with propagandistic and reactionary messages. Even so, culturally as well as aesthetically important works were produced by black artists who are well known today, including Romare Bearden, Jacob Lawrence, Walter Williams, Betye Saar, Faith Ringgold, Elizabeth Catlett, Benny Andrews, Moneta Sleet, Raymond Saunders, Charles White, Marion Perkins, Richard Yarde, David Hammonds, Wadsworth Jarrell, Gordon Parks, Sam Gilliam, Jeff Donaldson, James Overstreet, and Nelson Stevens, among others. Important groups like *Spiral* in New York City and *AfriCobra* in Chicago embodied the spirit and aspirations of blacks and promoted Pan-Africanist ideals.

Much of the art produced by black artists of the period is only now emerging from the shadows of the iconic images of celebrity (Marilyn Monroe and Jacqueline Kennedy Onassis) and consumer goods (Campbell Soup Cans and Brillo Pads) favored by pop artists like Andy Warhol and Claus Oldenberg. African American artists responded, in the main, to the events of the period with an art that cast a critical eye on American democracy, much like Faith Ringgold's *The Flag is Bleeding* (1967), or addressed the matter of confrontation with authority as depicted in Jeff Donaldson's *Aunt Jemima and the Pillsbury Dough Boy '64* (1964). They also celebrated heroes and heroines who embodied in their personal story the struggle for social justice, as did Elizabeth Catlett-Mora in her iconic print *Malcolm Speaks for Us* (1969). Others, such as the photographer Moneta Sleet, chronicled the times in works like his *From Selma to Montgomery* (1965) that captured triumphs and tragedies of the period.

Much of the art produced by black artists of the period is only now emerging from the shadows of the iconic images of celebrity.

African American artists turned their easels, cameras, pencils, and pens not only to documenting the movement but also to producing an activist art that expressed and promoted the aspirations of black America. After World War II (1939–1945), African American artists witnessed, documented, and participated in the periodic but steady challenges blacks across the country waged against unjust political and social practices in America. Like all of black America, they witnessed the conflicts that erupted year after year throughout the American South, the legal challenges to racial segregation, the mass boycotts, the student sit-ins, and countless other events that called into question America's commitment to its democratic creed. And, like black Americans everywhere, they heeded the call for a new vision and a new way of life for black America, and

actively enlisted their art in the struggle for social and political change.

Victor D. Simmons

Black Arts Movement/Black Aesthetic Movement

In the same way that the Civil Rights Movement of the 1960s was launched to insure that black Americans received their rights as citizens, the Black Arts Movement, sometimes referred to as the Black Aesthetic Movement that operated alongside it, sought to define black Americans and the black experience on their own terms. The images that America had sanctioned as representative of black Americans were degrading, inaccurate, and racist. As long as these images were based on European criteria and racist notions, black Americans would never truly be able to enjoy their full rights as citizens.

The Black Arts Movement set out to create and promote a sensibility that embraced the beauty and truth of the black community, as well as the traditions and cultural ideas that enabled black Americans to survive in an environment that legally and socially relegated them to second-class citizenship. The Black Arts Movement created academic standards of analysis and criticism that had direct relationships to the black cultural experience. Acknowledging contributions and sacrifices in the creation of America while at the same time recognizing and respecting the traditions and culture of black Americans became paramount to the transformation of American society.

Artists of the Black Arts Movement offered works that were key in creating images which supported the manifesto that "black is beautiful." Black artists offered their own life experiences of struggle, survival, and accomplishment, as well as images of other members of the black community that had previously been denigrated or ignored. All artistic media were used to rail against white cultural perspectives, including art, music, poetry, fiction, drama, and literature in general. Many of the artists were also active in the Civil Rights Movement in various ways, including marches.

Leading artists of the movement included Amiri Baraka (also known as LeRoi Jones), Nikki Giovanni, Haki Madhubuti (also known as Don L. Lee), and Sonia Sanchez. Theorists and essayists included Larry Neal, Etheridge Knight, Addison Gayle Jr., and Maulana Karenga. Although the artists' works were often seen as anti-white, anti-middle class, and anti-American, their goal was to create a true image of black Americans in a social system that had either made blacks invisible or had promoted negative stereotypes of them. These artists' works changed the image of black Americans on a national and even global scale. Without the Black Arts Movement, the Civil Rights Movement would have lacked the framework to transform images and attitudes in order to bring about fundamental social change.

Lean'tin L. Bracks

New Negro Movement

The New Negro Movement is a term many scholars use to refer to the Harlem Renaissance; they feel that the phrase "New Negro" recognizes the shift in consciousness black writers had during the period and it recognizes that black literature proliferated at the time but did not undergo a renaissance. Several events serve as the precursors of the movement: the publication of *The Souls of Black Folks* (1903) by **W.E.B. Du Bois**, which delves into cultural history and helps define the problem of black identity and addresses the importance of black people in America; the organization of the **NAACP** (1909) and the **National Urban League** (1911); the Great Migration (beginning c. 1910) in which black people moved from the rural South to the urban North looking for employment and a better way of life; and the end of World War I (1918), which saw soldiers who had fought for foreign democracy returning home to find racism, unemployment, and poverty.

Individuals who were integral to the emergence of the New Negro included Charles Chesnutt and Paul Laurence Dunbar, who merged oral history and literary art by focusing their work on black folk traditions. **Marcus Garvey** raised the level of consciousness in black America by emphasizing the importance of African traditions; and **James Weldon Johnson**, who wrote *Autobiography of an Ex-Coloured Man* (1912) and *Fifty Years and Other Poems* (1917), worked for the American diplomatic service, had a career on Broadway, earned a law degree, and taught at Fisk University. Alain Locke edited the 1925 "Harlem Number" of the *Survey Graphic,* which set forth the ideas and characteristics of this new generation of artist and defined the movement. In the introduction Locke indicated that there was a new spiritual outlook and that in the book "the Negro [will] speak for himself." This self-definition was one of the characteristics of the "new" artists, whose work represented a new way of responding to the black man's position in America. Artists in the movement called for change, but they confronted the disparity in the way in which the American system was conducted, and not the system itself.

This artistic demand for action against the political and social situation can be seen in "If We Must Die" by Claude McKay, perhaps the first important writer of the period. It is also evident in periodicals such as *The Crisis* (the publication of the NAACP), *Opportunity* (the publication of the National Urban League), and *Fire!,* which was edited by Wallace Thurman and designed to replace the old way of presenting black life. Writers were attempting to define black art and who should judge it in such essays as Alain Locke's "The Legacy of the Ancestral Arts" and George Schuyler's "The Negro-Art Hokum." The literature of the period addressed urban life and its impact on the new arrivals; the question of color, passing, and responsibility; the response to oppression; identity; Africa in its romanticized view; and cultural heritage.

The New Negro Movement produced playwrights, actors, a black theater (both dramatic and musical) begun in Harlem around 1910, and serious and popular forms of music, painting, drawing, and sculpture. Many consider the end of the movement to be the 1929 Stock Market Crash and the Great Depression. This did lead to difficulty for many and required relocation, often resulting in a different thrust or form in the art, but it did not lead to a cessation of creative output. In fact, **Langston Hughes** lived and worked until 1967, and Dorothy West, who was considered the youngest member of the movement, was active until 1998.

Helen R. Houston

Bearden's lifelong achievements covered the range of human experiences intermingled with his own personal experiences.

Artists

Bearden, Romare (1912–1988)

Romare Bearden was one of the most original visual artists of the twentieth century. He experimented with different styles and mediums but is best known for his collages and photomontages. Bearden had spent nearly two decades using abstract subjects when, in the 1960s, he departed from this focus and moved to collages. He joined with twelve other African American artists who called themselves "Spiral." Inspired by the Civil Rights Movement, they sought to explore the identity and images of African Americans through the use of art. Bearden suggested the group participate in a collage project. After little interest from the other members, however,

Bearden moved ahead and began to make collages by himself. In 1964, he actively made collages consisting of images of African Americans taken from periodicals such as *Ebony, Look,* and *Life* magazine. He went on to reinterpret other forms and methods using African American cultural rituals, events, and history.

Bearden's work consisted of a grid system that resulted in arrangements that overlapped in both two-dimensional and three-dimensional space. He first presented his work at an exhibition entitled *Projections;* later, in October 1964, he had an exhibition at the Corcoran Gallery of Art in Washington, D.C. Through his exhibits Bearden gained enormous popularity during the 1960s and continued to present collages as a key part of his art. His images explored themes regarding the everyday lives of African Americans in the North as well as the South. Bearden's lifelong achievements covered the range of human experiences intermingled with his own personal experiences. He received legendary status for his collages, though he was never fully acknowledged in the records of American Art. Bearden died on March 12, 1988.

Lean'tin L. Bracks

Parks, Gordon (1912–2006)

Gordon Roger Alexander Buchanan Parks was born November 30, 1912, in Fort Scott, Kansas, and died March 7, 2006, in New York City. A renaissance man, Parks was born into poverty but blessed with a mother who taught him to use love and self-respect against racism— a lesson he not only internalized, but passed on through his works. Throughout his career, he opened doors that had previously been closed to black people. He became the first African American photojournalist for *Life* and *Vogue* magazines; he was a part of the *Life* staff from 1948 on into the Civil Rights Movement. During this time, he took some of the most telling pictures of racial strife and personalities in America. These included a Harlem gang, the **Black Panther Party, Malcolm X,** and the assassination of **Mar-**

tin **Luther King Jr.** These and his photograph "American Gothic," which depicts Ella Watson, a black cleaning woman with a mop and a broom standing in front of an American flag, provided a new way of seeing black people. This vision was reflected not only in his pictures, but also in his work producing and directing Hollywood films. He underscored to the public that race should be no cause for failure, that injustices in life are opportunities for self-help and not destruction, and that the weapons against the disparities in society can include cameras, pens, paintbrushes, pianos, and the desire to achieve.

Helen R. Houston

Entertainers

Belafonte, Harry (1927–)

Born Harold George Belafonte Jr., Harry Belafonte is best known as one of the most successful entertainers in American history. He was born in New York to parents of West Indian heritage and lived in Jamaica from the age of nine until he was thirteen. In addition to his work as an actor, Belafonte is worthy of admiration and respect for participating in and supporting the struggle for civil and human rights. He began participating in protests for civil rights in 1950, including a march in support of integrated schools. In 1956 Belafonte met **Martin Luther King Jr.** and was impressed by his commitment and sincerity. Using his influence with other entertainers, he encouraged many to perform at concerts to raise funds for civil rights. In 1963 Belafonte used his personal money to bail out workers of the **Student Non-Violent Coordinating Committee** (SNCC). When Martin Luther King was in the Birmingham jail, it was Belafonte who raised the $50,000 for King's release and later raised $90,000 when the need arose.

Belafonte worked diligently behind the scenes to raise funds and to serve as an intermediary for the struggle for civil rights. As a skilled mediator, he helped to ease the tension between

Harry Belafonte (Fisk University).

King and the SNCC, serving as King's negotiator in many instances. Over the years, he has influenced and supported these causes both in front of and behind the scenes.

Lean'tin L. Bracks

Cosby, Bill (1937–)

From an early age, Bill Cosby learned through his love of jazz how to take an idea and find new ways to express it. In his role as a comedian, entertainer, and philanthropist he has campaigned for a better world by using this approach. His ability to use comedy to express the common experiences between all persons began in the 1960s, when the Civil Rights Movement was in full force. He revolutionized comedy in 1963, when he came on the television scene with an act that did not use race as a subject. His goal was to talk about the similarities between people of all races and not the differences. He again made a historic impact in 1965, when he played alongside a white actor as his equal in the television series *I Spy*. Cosby's career in the entertainment field has supported a perspective of black Americans that lends itself to an equal share in the social and political opportunities open to all Americans. This idea is most poignant in his 1984 television show *The Cosby Show*, which broke many stereotypes about black Americans by allowing America to enter into the everyday lives of a middle-class black family. The similarities of experiences kept America watching this show from 1984 to 1992.

Cosby's commitment to education, which was a key factor in the struggle for civil rights, set the tone for his philanthropy, which supported many black colleges. He gave substantial contributions to Historic Black Colleges and Universities (HBCUs) such as **Fisk University**, **Howard University**, and **Morehouse College**, among others. He also gave to the United Negro College Fund, the **NAACP** and Operation PUSH. Cosby's view of life as presented through his work offers a more equal perspective of rights and opportunities that should be afforded all Americans regardless of race.

Lean'tin L. Bracks

Goldberg, Whoopi (1949–)

Whoopi Goldberg was born Caryn Elaine Johnson on November 13, 1949 (some sources say 1950 or 1955) in New York City. Her life experiences and work in the theater have been varied and met with various degrees of success. She has experienced and survived poverty, drug addiction, single parenthood, and welfare. These experiences have made it possible for her to see a side of life that needs to be explored and eradicated. She has been able to convert these issues into social commentary through comic entertainment and satire. Her one-woman performance *The Spook Show* is a satirical produc-

tion in which she plays several characters. Her outspoken observations in this comedy and other venues have made her a controversial figure. This has in no way silenced her, however; no subject or personality is off limits. Her work reflects her memory of her history, and she often pays tribute to legendary entertainers such as Moms Mabley. Goldberg has performed on numerous occasions at the annual *Comic Relief* shows on the Home Box Office television network, which raises money to assist the homeless. She received the Gay and Lesbian Alliance against Defamation Vanguard Award for her work. In 2003 she became a Goodwill Ambassador for UNICEF, with a focus on HIV/AIDS.

Helen R. Houston

Gregory, Dick (1932–)

Richard Claxton "Dick" Gregory overcame poverty to find early success in athletics and

Dick Gregory (Fisk University).

entertainment. He was born and reared in St. Louis, Missouri, began using comedy to relate to others, and worked odd jobs as a child to help support his family. In high school he won the state championship for the mile run in 1951 and 1952, and he received an athletic scholarship to Southern Illinois University, where he was named Outstanding Athlete in 1953. He was drafted into the U.S. Army in 1954, won a talent show, and transferred to the Special Services entertainment division. After his discharge in 1956, Gregory performed in Chicago, where he met and married Lillian Smith. They eventually became the parents of ten children. His first success was at the Chicago Playboy Club in 1961, but his activism hindered his entertainment career. Gregory also became politically active, running for mayor of Chicago in 1967 and for president in 1968 as a candidate of the U.S. Freedom and Peace party. He lectured widely, wrote several books, began advocating healthier lifestyles via his dieting, fasting, nutrition programs and products, and stopped performing in venues that allowed smoking and alcohol use. Respected as an elder statesman of the Civil Rights Movement, Gregory has received numerous awards and honorary doctorates in recognition of his service to humanity.

Fletcher F. Moon

Filmmakers

Grant, Joanne (1930–2005)

An important voice in the Civil Rights Movement, Joanne Rabinowitz Grant documented grass-roots efforts in the movement through her books, award-winning films, and articles in the *National Guardian*. She documented civil rights demonstrations and the work of organizations in rural southern towns that other publications ignored. While serving as a reporter for the *National Guardian,* her work took her to these towns to document the demonstrations that were taking place. She was a former assistant to

W.E.B. **Du Bois,** a member of the **Student Non-Violent Coordinating Committee,** and an organizer of benefits for social and political causes. "She was an important voice in the early writing on the civil rights movement," said Evelyn Brooks Higginbotham in the *New York Times*. In the same source, **Julian Bond** said that "she exposed and explained the Civil Rights Movement in ways that the daily press either couldn't or wouldn't." Some called her the "movement's publicist," who saw herself as a journalist and a civil rights advocate. Her works include *Black Protest* (1968), one of the first books to trace the Civil Rights Movement and its origin; *Confrontation on Campus* (1969), an account of the sit-in movement at Columbia University and elsewhere; and *Ella Baker, Freedom Bound* (1998), a biography of an unsung matriarch of the Civil Rights Movement. Her award-winning documentary film *Fundi: The Story of Ella Baker* (1981) was broadcast nationally on PBS.

Jessie Carney Smith

Lee, Spike (1957–)

Prominent American filmmaker Spike Lee is also widely recognized for his activism, work as an actor in commercials and his own films, and frequent media exposure as a devoted fan of the New York Knickerbockers. His success in the film industry created numerous opportunities for other African Americans behind and in front of the camera; he has inspired an entire generation of young filmmakers and media artists. Shelton Jackson "Spike" Lee was born in Atlanta, Georgia, the eldest of five children. His father was jazz bassist and composer William "Bill" Lee, and his mother, Jacqueline Shelton Lee, was an art teacher who nicknamed him "Spike" as a toddler. In 1959 the family moved to Brooklyn, New York, where he grew up and graduated from John Dewey High School. Spike followed his grandfather and father in attending **Morehouse College.** He graduated in 1979, before entering film school at New York University. His film successes include *She's Gotta Have*

Spike Lee (AP Photo/Mark J. Terrill).

It (1986), *School Daze* (1988), *Do the Right Thing* (1989), *Mo' Better Blues* (1990), and *Jungle Fever* (1991), but Lee is most noted for his epic film biography, *Malcolm X* (1992). He married attorney Tonya Lewis in 1993, and became the father of two children. Lee explored multiple phases of African American life in his commercial film productions, as well as documentaries on civil/human rights events, including the 1963 Birmingham church bombing, the **Million Man March** in 1995, and 2005's Hurricane Katrina.

Fletcher F. Moon

Films

Birth of a Nation (1915)

T*he Birth of a Nation* was first released on February 8, 1915. The film's depiction of African Americans as idle and brutish sparked a massive wave of protests from thousands of blacks. It was based on Thomas Dixon's 1905 melodramatic staged play, *The Clansman: An Historical Romance of the Ku Klux Klan,* the second volume in a trilogy that includes *The Leop-*

ard's Spots: A Romance of the White Man's Burden, 1865–1900 and *The Traitor.* Directed by D.W. Griffith, the film set off an explosive controversy that revealed Hollywood's power to reflect and shape public attitudes about race. It set the stage for a decades-long struggle to improve the portrayal of blacks on film and served as a stimulus for the birth of the black film movement. The subject matter of the film elicited immediate criticism from the **NAACP** for its racist portrayal of American blacks, its miscegenation, its pro-Ku Klux Klan stance, and its endorsement of slavery.

Riots broke out in major cities. Subsequent lawsuits and picketing tailed the film for years when it was re-released in 1924, 1931, and 1938. The resulting controversy only helped to fuel the film's box-office appeal, and it became a major hit. Even President Woodrow Wilson, during a private screening at the White House, was reported to have enthusiastically endorsed *Birth of a Nation*. Film scholars agree, however, that it is a key film in American movie history. It contains many new cinematic innovations and refinements, technical effects, and artistic advancements, including a color sequence at the end. It had a formative influence on future films and has had a recognized impact on the development of film as an art form. In addition, at almost three hours in length it was one of the longest film to date. Nevertheless, it still provokes conflicting views about the representation of African Americans during the Reconstruction era.

Linda T. Wynn

Eyes on the Prize (1987)

Winner of numerous Emmy Awards, a George Foster Peabody Award, an International Documentary Award, and a Television Critics Association Award, *Eyes on the Prize* is one of the most critically acclaimed documentaries on the African American struggle for civil rights in America. Derived from the song "Keep Your Eyes on the Prize," the 14-hour documentary series narrates the story of the modern civil rights era by giving voice to the everyday people whose exceptional actions launched one of the nation's most important social movements of the twentieth century. It conveys the struggle to end more than fifty years of racial discrimination and segregation. *Eyes on the Prize* is the story of the people—adults and children, men and women, northern and southern, black and white—who out of a sense of justice were obligated to right America's civil wrongs sanctioned by both law and custom. They worked to eliminate a society that racially restricted African Americans from cradle to the grave.

Narrated by **Julian Bond**, the documentary aired in two parts. Using first-person accounts and historical film footage, part one, which is six hours long, originally aired early in 1987 on the Public Broadcasting Service (PBS) as *Eyes on the Prize: America's Civil Rights Years (1954–1965)*, which covered *The Awakening* (1954–1956), *Fighting Back* (1957–1962), *Ain't Afraid of Your Jails* (1960–1961), *No Easy Walk* (1961–1963), *Mississippi: Is This America?* (1963–1964), *Bridge to Freedom* (1965), and *The Time Has Come*, (1964–1966). The remaining eight hours aired in 1990 as *Eyes on the Prize II: America at the Racial Crossroads* (1965–1985), which covered *Two Societies* (1965–1968), *Power!* (1966–1968), *The Promised Land* (1967–1968), *Ain't Gonna Shuffle No More* (1964–1972), *A Nation of Law?* (1968–1971), *Keys to the Kingdom* (1974–1980), and *Back to the Movement* (1979–mid-1980s). Henry Hampton (1940–1998), the founder of documentary film company Blackside (est. 1968), produced the series.

The series generated three books by noted journalists and historians. Juan Williams, an Emmy Award-winning radio and television correspondent, wrote *Eyes on the Prize: America's Civil Rights Years, 1954–1965,* published by Penguin Books in 1988, which serves as the series companion volume. In 1990, Bantam Books published Henry Hampton and Steve Fayer's *Voices of Freedom: An Oral History of the Civil Rights Movement from the 1950s through the 1980s,* and in 1991, Penguin Books published

The Eyes on the Prize Civil Rights Reader: Documents, Speeches, and Firsthand Accounts from the Black Freedom Struggle, 1954–1990, for which Clayborne Carson, David J. Garrow, Gerald Gill, Vincent Harding, and Darlene Clark Hine served as general editors.

Linda T. Wynn

During slavery, spirituals and work songs provided affirmation and strength in the face of a system meant to debilitate and degrade.

Music

Music of the Civil Rights Movement

African American music has been important to the lifestyle and survival of black people. Music is one of the most prominent areas of African retention in African American culture. Like the West African traditional role of art, music for African Americans during slavery served not only as an expression of morality and cultural values but also as a means of communicating social and political views. During slavery, spirituals and work songs provided affirmation and strength in the face of a system meant to debilitate and degrade. From the spirituals and work songs to the later forms of blues, jazz, R&B, and gospel, African American music from the time of slavery to the climax of the Civil Rights Movement in the 1950s and 1960s has inspired protest and progress.

During the 1950s and 1960s, a number of songs served to empower civil rights demonstrators. Some of these songs were performed by the Freedom Singers of Albany, Georgia, to raise money for protesters and the **Student Non-Violent Coordinating Committee**. The same songs performed and later recorded by the Freedom Singers were sung at marches and rallies to inspire protesters, giving them a common orientation and sense of purpose and direction. Prominent among the singers were Cordell Reagon and Bernice Johnson Reagon. According to Eilene Southern, "We Shall Overcome" was the theme song of the movement in its early days. **Martin Luther King Jr.** and other leaders of the movement commonly referred to that freedom song as a spiritual, probably because it resembled the nineteenth-century slave song "No More Auction Block for Me." Among other prominent songs of protest were "I Shall Not Be Moved," "Oh, Freedom," "Keep Your Eyes on the Prize," and "This Little Light of Mine."

The religious nature of some songs was modified at times to indicate a political agenda; the religious origin of the music, however, underscored the moral mission of the Civil Rights Movement. The music expresses the idea that the racial oppression and injustice visited upon African Americans was not only unfair but immoral, emphasizing the concept that their political mission was a spiritual one as well. Secular music also served to inspire change and encourage civil rights protesters. The dominance of Berry Gordy's black record label Motown and the ability of African American artists to win reputations in mainstream America suggest the determination of the Civil Rights Movement.

Singer, songwriter, and pianist Nina Simone, who was passionately committed to the Civil Rights and **Black Power Movements**, is said to have given musical expression to both. She contributed her talent to the movements by singing at benefits and marches. Her song "Mississippi Goddam" became a classic during the Civil Rights Movement. Sam Cooke's "A Change Gonna Come" and James Brown's song "I'm Black and I'm Proud" were two of the most well-known popular songs to inspire and serve the Civil Rights Movement. Some other R&B artists

who contributed inspiring messages to the movement include Curtis Mayfield and the Impressions, Marvin Gaye, and Martha Reeves and the Vandellas. The songs of the movement are variously recorded; a notable source is the Smithsonian Institution's three-volume collection released in 1980, *Voices of the Civil Rights Movement: Black American Freedom Songs 1960–66.*

Rebecca S. Dixon

Music Entrepreneur

Simmons, Russell (1957–)

Russell Simmons was born in Queens, New York, on October 4, 1957. He recognized the potential of rap music in the 1980s and the way in which it was being overlooked by the music industry. Thus, he began promoting the music and producing records. He later formed production companies and clothing lines that aided in moving this urban music and its artists into mainstream America.

In his endeavors, Simmons has not left the African American community behind. He has continuously provided ways in which youth can be empowered and has served as a role model for responsible use of that power, acting as a voice and a positive force in the community. Simmons established the Rush Philanthropic Arts Foundation that supports the arts, and The Rush Impact Mentorship Initiative, which seeks to give back to youth, especially urban youth. In 2001, he cofounded the Hip-Hop Summit Action Network (HSAN) with Benjamin Chavis. HSAN encourages political involvement; its programmatic strategy statement on its Web site indicates its focus is on "community development issues related to equal access to high quality public education and literacy, freedom of speech, voter education [and registration], economic advancement, and youth leadership development." He fought for and won the repeal of the Rockefeller Drug Laws in New York. On returning from a trip to Africa in 2007, he formed the Diamond

Empowerment Fund (DEF), a nonprofit program dedicated to economic and educational empowerment in diamond producing African countries. Simmons's endeavors reflect qualities necessary for strengthening the community in his efforts to empower, in his alliances with other individuals and groups, and his broad definition of community.

Helen R. Houston

Singers

Anderson, Marian (1902–1993)

Marian Anderson was born February 17, 1902, in Philadelphia and died there on April 8, 1993. She had a phenomenal contralto voice; her talent and love for singing were recognized at an early age. Because of her singing abilities, she performed in the United States and abroad before dignitaries and in such places as Germany, South America, and Austria. In spite of the barriers she faced as a black artist, she was instrumental in opening doors for and bringing acclaim and recognition to the black artist; but she was also denied many opportunities. In the United States, she found it difficult, if not impossible, to gain acceptance in the arenas her talent should have commanded. In fact, in 1939 the Daughters of the American Revolution (DAR) refused to allow her to perform at Constitution Hall in Washington, D.C. Eleanor Roosevelt, the wife of President Franklin D. Roosevelt and a member of the DAR, resigned in protest after that, and she arranged for Anderson to give an outdoor concert at the Lincoln Memorial. The DAR nevertheless again refused to let her perform in Constitution Hall.

Anderson persevered in the face of racial discrimination; she was the first African American to sing at the White House, to (finally) perform at Constitution Hall (1943), and to sing with the company of New York's Metropolitan Opera (1955). She sang at the presidential inaugurations of both Dwight D. Eisenhower and **John F.**

Kennedy; under the auspices of the State Department, she toured India and the Far East (1957); she was a delegate to the United Nations (1958), too. With quiet dignity, a superb contralto voice, and a demonstrated love for her people and her country, she fought for human rights.

Helen R. Houston

While Charles rarely made overtly political statements, the tenor and content of his music often conveyed his empathy for the suffering of black America.

Charles, Ray (1932–2004)

As one of the most influential American musicians of the twentieth century, Ray Charles possessed a talent that spanned most modern musical genres. By combining elements of jazz, gospel, and R&B, he pioneered a new genre known as soul and thus became known as the "Father of Soul Music." Born to Bailey and Aretha Robinson in Albany, Georgia, Charles was reared by his mother in an impoverished community of Greensville, Florida. At age five, he began to go blind and was completely blind by age seven. Determined to provide him with the skills to be independent, Charles's mother sent him to the St. Augustine School for the Blind. There, Charles learned to read and write music in Braille as well as play the piano, clarinet, and saxophone.

Orphaned at age 15, Charles began his career with country western road bands before touring with R&B bands. By his early twenties, he was a seasoned performer in the tradition of Nat King

Cole, but by the 1950s he had departed from traditional ballads. At Atlantic Records, his infusion of diverse musical forms was considered the mark of a genius. Throughout the decade, Charles's music increasingly appealed to white American youth, despite his refusal to compromise his musical style. While Charles rarely made overtly political statements, the tenor and content of his music often conveyed his empathy for the suffering of black America. In 1961, Charles famously refused to play to a sold-out audience in Memphis, Tennessee, because it was segregated, forcing the desegregation of the concert. The winner of 13 Grammy Awards, including lifetime achievement awards in 1987 and 1994, Charles was inducted into the Rock and Roll Hall of Fame in 1986. Immortalized in the biographical movie *Ray,* Charles died of acute liver disease at his Beverly Hills, California, home on June 10, 2004.

Crystal A. deGregory

Chuck D. (1960–)

Carlton Douglas Ridenhour is the given name of the innovative and socially conscious rapper known as Chuck D., who once called rap music "the black CNN." According to a review of his 1996 solo album, *Autobiography of Mistachuck,* "no one artist in hip-hop's history may have ever been simultaneously more well-respected and misunderstood." Ridenhour was born in Roosevelt, Long Island, New York, and graduated from Roosevelt High School and Adelphi University with a bachelor's degree in graphic design. He founded Public Enemy in 1982, which achieved critical acclaim as well as commercial success in the late 1980s and early 1990s with recordings such as "Yo! Bum Rush the Show," "It Takes a Nation of Millions to Hold Us Back," and "Fear of a Black Planet," which sold over five million copies. Public Enemy helped rap and hip-hop music become a major force in the music industry. With William "Flavor Flav" Drayton, Richard "Professor Griff" Griffin, Norman Lee "DJ Terminator X" Rogers, and DJ Lord, Chuck D. as front

man, lyricist, and lead singer, created "Fight the Power," a song that became an anthem for the hip-hop community. Chuck D. also defied the stereotype of rap and hip-hop artists through political activism offstage, including testifying before the U.S. Congress on music technology issues and serving as keynote speaker for the National Hip-Hop Political Convention in June 2004.

Fletcher F. Moon

Reagon, Bernice Johnson (1942–)

Born October 4, 1942, in Albany, Georgia, Bernice Johnson Reagon is the daughter of a Baptist minister. She grew up within the church community, and the church and the black community helped shape young Bernice. Fundamental to this life was the music that accompanied services. Having no piano, performers in her father's church sang *a cappella,* using their hands and feet to power the music with physical rhythms. She joined the local Youth Chapter of the **NAACP,** and by the time she was a senior in high school she was the organization's secretary. Around the same time, she auditioned for the head of the music department at Albany State College (now University), enrolling to study music in 1959.

Reagon continued her work with the NAACP and served as secretary while in school. When the **Student Non-Violent Coordinating Committee** (SNCC) came to Albany, she expanded her political activism by marching, singing, organizing, and whatever else was required. Because of her activities, she was arrested and expelled from Albany State in 1962. She then entered **Spelman College** in Atlanta, but soon withdrew and returned to work with the SNCC. **Cordell Reagon,** her future husband, organized the Freedom Singers for the SNCC and she became a member of the group, too. They sang together and traveled for a year while raising funds for the Civil Rights Movement and detailing the actions and issues for rallies and meetings.

Reagon married in 1963 and took time off for motherhood, but she still managed to be involved in the movement. In 1966 she founded the Harambee Singers, a woman's *a capella* group that was a part of the Black Consciousness Movement, and in 1973 she founded Sweet Honey in the Rock, a female *a capella* quintet. The name comes from the first song they practiced, which was based on a parable and spoke to the strength and sound of its message. The group has recorded albums and participated in various media events, earning international recognition and acclaim for its socially conscious renditions and the artistry of its sound.

Reagon retired from the group in 2004. She completed her degree at Spelman and earned her doctorate in history at **Howard University**. She has also served in a creative capacity in film, television, and recordings. Reagon received a MacArthur Genius Award in 1989. She then spent time studying African American sacred song and tradition, produced a 26-hour radio series called *Wade in the Water,* and worked on two documentaries. Now a curator emeritus at the Smithsonian Institution and professor emeritus at American University, she argues that it is impossible to know a community or a people without understanding its songs because music represents a people's way of thinking and their collective recorded history.

Helen R. Houston

Reagon, Cordell (1943–1996)

Cordell Hull Reagon was a founding member of the Freedom Singers. He was born in Nashville, Tennessee, in 1943 and died of a gunshot wound in his Berkeley, California, apartment in November 1996. Reagon became a civil rights leader at the age of 16. By the time he was 18 years of age, he was an experienced activist, having participated in sit-ins, freedom rides, voter demonstrations and workshops. He and Charles Sherrod were sent in 1961 to Albany, Georgia, to assist in the work of confronting and dismantling the thriving segregated system. Using non-violent tactics, they became involved in the Albany community and its fight in the

face of threats and violence. In 1962, as a means of raising money to support the work and goals of the **Student Non-Violent Coordinating Committee** and to tell the stories of the movement, the Freedom Singers group was founded by Reagon. Reagon, who had a strong tenor voice and experience with music as a force in Nashville, joined forces with Rutha Mae Harris and Bernice Johnson (who was to marry Reagon and later formed Sweet Honey in the Rock) of Albany, Georgia, as well as Charles Neblett, a civil rights demonstrator from Cairo, Illinois. They used the rich tradition of African American music to convey their message. They toured— not without threats and violence—the country, performing at colleges, universities, homes, jails, political rallies, and in the August 1963 **March on Washington**. The original Freedom Singers recorded an album and disbanded in 1963.

Helen R. Houston

Robeson, Paul (1898–1976)

Paul Leroy Bustill Robeson was born April 9, 1898, in Princeton, New Jersey, and died December 23, 1976, in Philadelphia, Pennsylvania. He was equipped with the principles, pride, and courage he needed to confront and surmount the racial barriers and racist treatment he received as a black renaissance man. In spite of the racism at Rutgers University at the time he attended, he earned a Phi Beta Kappa key, varsity letters in four sports, became first All-American in football, and graduated valedictorian. At Columbia University, he earned a degree in law; however, racism in the profession caused him to switch to the stage. His career flourished even though there were limited roles for black actors. He began to sing spirituals and work songs that reflected both the common man and the universal brotherhood of man. His travels led him to associate with a variety of organizations and ideologies. The 1930s saw him visiting the Soviet Union, an experience that marked a turning point in his life. He began to support communism and speak out against racism. However,

Paul Robeson (Fisk University).

Robeson's desire was to change America, not leave it. Thus, he led a delegation to Washington, D.C., as a part of the Anti-Lynching Crusade, urged Congress to lift the racial barriers in baseball, and was a founding member of the Progressive Party because he wanted to challenge the existing parties in the presidential election. Robeson's stances and rhetoric in the face of racism caused his concerts to be cancelled and his passport to be revoked.

Helen R. Houston

Literature

Literature of the Civil Rights Movement

African American literature is traditionally polemical and thus indicative of the political and social concerns of black people. This is evident in African American literature at the height of the Civil Rights Movement in the 1950s and 1960s, a time characterized by a rising consciousness of identity and self-affirmation. Beginning in the 1950s, writings by African Americans increasingly shifted from integrationist literature directed toward a primarily white audience to a literature that was reflective of intra-communal issues and the validation of black experiences. **Gwendolyn Brooks's** *Annie Allen* (1949), **James Baldwin's** *Go Tell It on the Mountain* (1953), Ralph Ellison's *Invisible Man* (1952), and **Lorraine Hansberry's** *A Raisin in the Sun* (1959) are among the most prominent works of the decade. These works are reflective of the concerns of the Civil Rights Movement. Unlike the naturalistic and social realist writings of the 1940s, this literature celebrated life in the black community, sometimes in relation to the white community, but more often not. These works revealed the humanity of black people, thus suggesting that the political and social rights of African Americans are an obvious extension of that humanity.

The 1960s marked a decidedly more pronounced shift in the literature. Like literature of the 1950s that focused on interpersonal and intra-communal issues of black people, the 1960s literature emphasized political and social awareness and black pride. The New York City literary organization called the Umbra Society held meetings in 1962 and 1963 that served as precursor to the Black Art Movement. Black writers Tom Dent, Askia Toure, David Henderson, and Calvin Hernton were among the writers who developed and attended Umbra meetings. At these meetings writers discussed their work, as well as social and political issues. Despite the efforts of the Umbra writers, the assassination of **Malcolm X**, and **Amiri Baraka's** establishment of the Black Arts Repertory Theatre School (BARTS) in 1965 are generally considered the beginning of the **Blacks Arts Movement**. Under the leadership of Amiri Baraka and Larry Neal, black writers sought to promote an aesthetic that was truly reflective of African artistic values and that celebrated the lives of black people. Amiri Baraka's essay "Black Art" and his poem

"Black Art," and Larry Neal's essay "The Black Arts Movement," all provide insights into the radical black aesthetic espoused by the most prominent writers of this period.

The movement largely produced poetry and drama. Some of the other dominant writers of the period included **Sonia Sanchez**, Etheridge Knight, Haki Mutabuti (Don Lee), Nikki Giovanni, Ishmael Reed, Alice Childress, Adrienne Kennedy, Ed Bullins, and Douglas Turner Ward. Larry Neal considered the literary movement the sister to the Black Power Movement because of its radical nature. Despite the empowering nature of the black aesthetic promoted by the writers of the Black Arts Movement, the efforts of the writers were marred by concerns of artistry being overshadowed by the didactic nature of the writing and problems of misogyny, vulgarity, violence, and a glamorization of an impoverished mindset and lifestyle. With the assassination of **Martin Luther King Jr.** and the decline of the Civil Rights Movement, the Black Arts Movement ended in the early 1970s.

Rebecca S. Dixon

Maya Angelou (AP Photo/Doug Mills).

Writers

Angelou, Maya (1928–)

Maya Angelou, born Marguerite Johnson in St. Louis, Missouri, spent her early years in Stamps, Arkansas. It was here that she learned the glaring need for change in the South. As the movement for civil rights began to build in the 1950s, Angelou became an active participant for change. Upon moving to New York in the 1950s to pursue a professional dancing career, Angelou joined the Harlem Writers Guild and became one of many artists who participated in the movement. Along with Godfrey Cambridge, she wrote a revue called *Cabaret for Freedom,* which was to be performed as a fundraiser for the **Southern Christian Leadership Conference** (SCLC). Between 1960 and 1961, Angelou served as the northern coordinator for the

SCLC. Just as her reputation began to grow as a writer and poet, she decided to move with her son to Africa with African freedom fighter Vusumzi Make. They lived for a while in Cairo, Egypt, then Angelou and her son moved to Ghana. In Ghana, Angelou met **Malcolm X** and they later corresponded. When she returned to the United States in 1964, her goal was to assist him in building a new organization. Malcolm X was assassinated shortly after Angelou's return, however, and this put an end to their plans. Angelou immersed herself in the Civil Rights Movement and again became a part of the SCLC. With the assassination of **Martin Luther King Jr.** in 1968, Angelou became more serious about her writing and wrote her first book, the award-winning *I Know Why the Caged Bird Sings.*

Lean'tin L. Bracks

Attaway, William Alexander (1911–1986)

William Alexander Attaway was born November 19, 1911, in Greenville, Mississippi, and died June 17, 1986, in Los Angeles, California. He was one of the first African Americans to write about the Great Migration and the impact of the new economic environment and industrialization on rural life and the spirit of minorities and the poor in America. His novels are peopled with the marginalized, not only African Americans but also Mexican Americans and migrant whites. Attaway's novels about these groups include *Let Me Breathe Thunder* (1939) and *Blood on the Forge* (1941). His treatment of the disenfranchised and the racial climate in which they lived has been

Baldwin was ever mindful of the need for the unity of humankind.

likened in some ways to the works of Richard Wright, with whom he became acquainted when they worked together on the Federal Writers Project during the Great Depression. Like many other African American writers, he found that polemical writings about the disenfranchised were not well received; following the publication of the novels and one short story, he therefore turned his attention to other genres. His second novel, *Blood on the Forge,* is his best known and most discussed work; it explores the causes and results of migration. It follows three African American half-brothers who flee a lynch mob in 1919 in Kentucky for the safety and security of the North, the Promised Land, only to find there are numerous forms of lynching and that the North has its own pitfalls. The brothers become trapped by the steel mills and

racial tensions of Pennsylvania. Attaway participated in the 1965 **Selma to Montgomery March** and continued his involvement in the fight for civil rights in his writing, emphasizing the black experience in works for television, radio, and motion pictures.

Helen R. Houston

Baldwin, James (1924–1987)

James Arthur Baldwin was born in August 2, 1924, in New York City and died December 1, 1987, in southern France. He was concerned with destroying the fantasies and delusions of a contented white America intent on avoiding reality. As a result of his candor, his writing is prophetic and prefigures the Civil Rights Movement. His works, especially the nonfiction *The Fire Next Time* (1963), emphasize the urgency of the civil rights initiative and the need for love. He rejects Christianity for the way it is practiced, but retains the belief that we must learn to live together in love. Baldwin was out of the country when the actual Civil Rights Movement began. His commitment to the struggle is seen in his writings and speeches in which he talks about race relations and his participation in social protest. He returned to America and participated in marches, met with black leaders, and even took part in a meeting with the U.S. attorney general. He visited the South in an attempt to understand the struggle, only to find the situation there mirrored by conditions in the North; the disenfranchisement of the populace in other parts of the world added to his certainty about his message. Baldwin was ever mindful of the need for the unity of humankind. He called for the oppressed and their oppressors to recognize the humanity in each other. Even though he seemed to despair in his early writings, and he was impatient with the slowness of change in society, in his works he continued to hold out hope for transformation in the world.

Helen R. Houston

Amiri Baraka was born LeRoi Jones in 1934 (AP Photo).

Baraka, Amiri (1934–)

Born Everett LeRoi Jones in October 7, 1934, in Newark, New Jersey, Amiri Baraka produced an oeuvre of diverse writings. He started as an integrationist, but has changed his black political and artistic thought reflecting society. Following a trip to China and a visit to Cuba, he became aware of the need for political involvement and active participation by artists in bringing about change. This ideological change is evident in his play *Dutchman* (1964) and his collection of social essays *Home* (1966), and it becomes even more apparent in his nationalist stance. He changed his name to Imamu Amiri Baraka (later dropping Imamu) and co-edited *Black Fire* (1968). Both his name and this work define his political vision and reflect the rejection of the integrationist thrust; he thereafter espoused a black nationalist political stance by young black writers and thinkers. With the 1965 assassination of **Malcolm X**, he and others moved further toward a black consciousness that manifested

itself in the **Black Arts Movement**. It calls for an art by, for, and about the black populace. He spoke as a black nationalist concerned with and addressing the political, social, and cultural needs of black people. His actions and speeches have made him a controversial figure. As a political activist in Newark and on the national scene, he served as chair of the Committee for a Unified Newark (1968–1975) and of the National Black Political Convention (1972). In 2003, the New Jersey General Assembly voted to eliminate the post of State Poet he held because of his poem on the 2001 World Trade Center attack.

Helen R. Houston

Bell, James Madison (1826–1902)

James Madison Bell was born April 3, 1826, in Gallipolis, Ohio, and died in 1902 in Toledo, Ohio. An active member of the African Methodist Episcopal Church, he is known as the "Poet of Hope" and the "Bard of Maumee." Bell's poetry, like much of the poetry of his day, was better recited than read and was often occasional. The poetry espoused human as well as his own political values. In fact, his poetry was a political tool to speak about the issues of the day (slavery, civil rights, and emancipation) from a black man's point of view. Consequently, his poetic concerns were more didactic and political than artistic. His themes were liberty, freedom, and hope. On November 9, 1847, he moved to Chatham, Ontario, Canada, and became active in the anti-slavery movement. Here he met and became friends with John Brown. He helped secure funds and support for Brown's 1859 Harpers Ferry Raid and was one of the signers of Brown's "Provisional Constitution and Ordinances for the People of the United States." In 1860, he moved to California, where he was a member of the Fourth California Colored Convention, which fought for suffrage rights. Later, he moved to Toledo and focused on the rights and education of newly freed slaves. He was a representative to the State Republican Convention and a delegate-at-large

James Madison Bell (Fisk University).

from Ohio to the 1868 and 1872 Republican National Conventions. He commemorated the **Fifteenth Amendment** with his ode "The Triumph of Liberty."

Helen R. Houston

Brooks, Gwendolyn Elizabeth (1917–2000)

Gwendolyn Brooks was born June 7, 1917, in Topeka, Kansas, and died December 3, 2000, in Chicago. Her writing can be divided into two parts: her early writings and her later work, which focused more on the social responsibility of both the artist and the artist's audience. Her early writing was recognized and praised by the establishment. It presented the plight of black America in an acceptable form and language. She won the American Academy of Arts and Letters Award and the Pulitzer Prize for Poetry during her early career. In 1968 she was named the Poet Laureate of Illinois. She published *The Bean Eaters* in 1960, which was a

more overtly polemical work than her earlier works and one that seemed to anticipate a brewing artistic rebellion.

The 1960s brought a parallel of the **Black Power Movement** with the **Black Arts Movement**. There was a call for black art to be written by black artists, about black people, and for a black audience; words were to be weapons and the language was to be accessible. In 1968 Brooks attended the Second **Fisk University** Writers' Conference in Nashville, Tennessee, where she heard one of the founders of the Black Arts Movement, LeRoi Jones (**Amiri Baraka**) speak; black poetry was redefined here, and the role of the black artist was discussed. This experience changed her direction so that she emphasized more audience awareness and artistic responsibility in her writing, while her commitment to the plight of black Americans remained firm. Following her experience at the conference, Brooks began to overtly support the black community, consciously deciding to use the term "black." She published her book of poems *In the Mecca* (1968). In Chicago, she started a workshop called the Blackstone Rangers, began mentoring young black writers, and supported black publishers. Brooks began publishing her works with publisher Dudley Randall's Broadside Press, which was committed to publishing young black poets; later, editor and publisher Haki Madhubuti also brought out her works.

Helen R. Houston

Brown, Sterling Allen (1901–1989)

As a civil rights activist Sterling Allen Brown took "the pen is mightier than the sword" approach to fight for racial equality. Brown worked with the likes of such Harlem Renaissance notables as **W.E.B. Du Bois**, **James Weldon Johnson**, **Langston Hughes**, and **Walter White** in the NAACP and served on its advisory board. As a journalist, he reported on social and racial issues of the day in such publications as *Crisis, Opportunity,* and *Phylon.* He addressed, among other topics, the effects of World War II

Gwendolyn Brooks (AP Photo).

following the Great Depression, the unethical restrictions of Jim Crow, the inferiority of black schools, and the political and social activities of the black church. Characteristic of Brown's writing as a journalist was his personal commentary. He often appealed to the conscience of white America relative to the quest to promote democracy: "If America is to indoctrinate the rest of the world with democracy, it is logical to expect that the American Negro will share it at home…. [S]egregation must be abolished before there will be true democracy at home." Brown is numbered among the "race men" of his day, and was a participant in the New Negro Movement–black intellectuals who were motivated by race consciousness and pride to advocate and demonstrate the superiority of black achievement. As national editor of *Negro Affairs* (1936–1940) for the Federal Writers Project, Brown brilliantly

showcased the achievements and contributions of black people in America.

Helen R. Houston

Hansberry, Lorraine (1930–1965)

Although Lorraine Hansberry had a short life, her fight for black civil rights and against racism and discrimination were reflected in her work and left a lasting impression on the overall struggle of blacks in America. Hansberry was confronted with racism early in her life. Her family moved to a white neighborhood when she was only eight years old. It was there that she experienced the physical violence and hatred associated with white supremacy and segregationist ideas. Because of this attack on her family, her father filed an anti-segregation case that was heard by the Illinois Supreme Court. In spite of Hansberry's victory in the court case, they were continually subjected to a hostile environment. This experience was the basis for Hansberry's 1959 play, *A Raisin in the Sun*.

The play is about a black family in Chicago who deals with their own dreams and hopes against a barrier of racism when they choose to buy a home and move to a white suburb. The play opened in 1959 and was a huge success; it brought attention to Hansberry as the first female African American playwright whose work was produced on Broadway. The play was later produced as a film in 1961. The Civil Rights Movement at this time had become intense, and Hansberry began to take a more active role in it. She was a field organizer for the **Congress of Racial Equality** (CORE) and helped plan fund raising events for the **Student Non-Violent Coordinating Committee** (SNCC) and other organizations.

Even though she was diagnosed with cancer of the pancreas in 1963, Hansberry continued to lend her support to the movement. She joined with artists such as **James Baldwin, Harry Belafonte**, and Lena Horne in a rally to raise funds for the SNCC. She left her sickbed to give a speech to the winners of the United Negro College Fund and attended a town hall debate challenging whites' criticism of the militant direction of the Civil Rights Movement. Hansberry died in 1965 at the young age to of 34, but her contribution to the movement offered a clear reflection of the challenges of being black in America.

Lean'tin L. Bracks

Hughes became a voice in the Harlem Renaissance ... that called for race pride and artistic independence.

Hughes, James Langston (1902–1967)

Langston Hughes was born February 1, 1902, in Joplin, Missouri, and died May 22, 1967, in New York City. Hughes's body of work, written in various genres, led to his being the most versatile African American writer of his day. Using free verse, black music, dialect, and prose, Hughes depicted black pride and life in America with candor, humor, and deceptively simple language. Through his writing and creation of characters, he pointed out the injustices in society and sought to effect social change and fair treatment for all people. His work is devoted to the grass-roots characters in both urban and rural America.

In the 1920s, Hughes became a voice in the Harlem Renaissance, one which espoused the manifesto of the period that called for race pride and artistic independence. In the 1930s, he wrote some leftist poetry that seemed pessimistic about America, such as *Good Morning Revolution* (1937), which would cause him trouble during U.S. Senator Eugene McCarthy's hunt for American communist sympathizers. The catalyst for his stance was his break with his patron, Charlotte Osgood Mason, and the plight of and

American response to the Scottsboro Boys, nine youths accused of raping two white women. One of the works that addresses the racial oppression in this case is *Scottsboro Unlimited: A One Act Play,* which was later published in *Scottsboro Limited: Four Poems and a Play* (1932).

In the 1940s, Hughes supported World War II, even though he understood whites were fighting for liberty abroad; but blacks were fighting for the same liberty in America, and he knew the fates of blacks and whites were interdependent. He created his feisty female character, Madam Alberta K. Johnson, who appeared in a number of his poems following the **Harlem Riots of 1943**. He encouraged black Americans to support the war and the government to provide the freedoms being fought for abroad to the citizens at home. Hughes's endorsement was voiced in a weekly column in *The Chicago Defender* through his character Jesse B. Semple (Simple). This character, often called an Everyman, needed encouragement to support the war; he develops into a character Hughes uses to explore the ironies of American black life and to emphasize both black race pride and nationalism. Through Simple, Hughes addressed the issues of the Civil Rights Movement in his columns and in his third collection of columns, *Simple Stakes a Claim* (1957) in which his claim to democracy is asserted.

Hughes supported the **NAACP** and the Urban League and worked openly to support civil rights efforts. He wrote pamphlets, such as *Freedom's Plow* (1943) and *Jim Crow's Last Stand* (1943) for the Civil Rights Movement. He participated in the rally for the **March on Washington**; followed assiduously the violence in the South and applauded the fearlessness of the student activists; attacked segregation through Simple; backed civil rights groups; and supported the rights of Louis Armstrong to vent his anger at events. However, he never became physically involved in the fight and viewed the civil rights struggle from a distance. With the onset of the **Black Arts Movement**, Hughes continued to be politically involved and nationalistic in his writing, but he rejected the language, style, and radical blackness of the movement. Consequently, he was attacked by younger black writers for not being true to his race.

Helen R. Houston

Johnson, James Weldon (1871–1938)

James William Johnson was the second child of James and Helen Louise Johnson. Born June 17, 1871, in Jacksonville, Florida, he developed the beliefs of a free thinker early; later in life, he changed his middle name to Weldon. James Weldon Johnson offered a unique and uncommon expression of who he was and what he would become. When Johnson graduated from Atlanta University in 1894 he attended the Chicago World's Fair and heard presentations by **Frederick Douglass** and Paul Laurence Dunbar. Douglass's commitment to uplift and Dunbar's mastery and respect for language, black speech, and culture reflected two aspects of Johnson's life and talent that would be consistent throughout his many professional successes.

James Weldon Johnson (Fisk University).

Johnson, who became principal of Stanton School in Jacksonville that same year, expressed his views on the conditions of blacks in the rural South and set about to educate the adult black community by founding the newspaper The *Daily American.* Finding he had further talents in the area of music, Johnson spent time on Broadway writing songs with his brother, John Rosamond Johnson.

Concerned about stereotypes prevalent in popular music, he took courses at Columbia University to further explore his literary interests. While serving as treasurer of the Colored Republican Club in New York, he accepted a diplomatic post in Puerto Cabello, Venezuela, in 1906 and later transferred to Corinto, Nicaragua, in 1909. He completed his novel *The Autobiography of an Ex-Coloured Man* (1912) while in Nicaragua and had it published anonymously. After resigning from diplomatic service in 1913, Johnson returned to the states.

Becoming an editorial writer for the periodical *New York Age,* he continued to advocate for equal rights. In 1916 Joel E. Spingarn, who served as chair and then president of the NAACP, offered Johnson a position as the NAACP's first field secretary. In this office, Johnson organized branches in the South and led protests against injustices. In 1919 he led a delegation to see President Woodrow Wilson to protest death sentences given to black soldiers after the Houston, Texas, race riots of 1917. Also in 1919, having proven himself an effective organizer and spokesman for the cause of civil rights, Johnson became general secretary of the **NAACP.** Johnson worked relentlessly, investigating injustices and championing voting rights. The overall demands of this position took a toll on Johnson, however, and he took a leave of absence on two occasions because of exhaustion.

Johnson resigned from the position as general secretary in 1930 and devoted himself to his writing on a full-time basis, while still championing the cause of civil rights. In his writings, he advocated integration as the solution to segregation and America's race problems. He saw the inequities in the American system and found his voice in the traditions of black culture to express and explore the history, experience, and opportunities deserved by black Americans. Johnson died on June 26, 1938, but he left a lasting legacy as a renaissance man with a vested interest in the rights of his people.

Lean'tin L. Bracks

McKay, Claude (1890?–1948)

Claude McKay is best known as a poet and writer of the Harlem Renaissance. McKay, a native of Jamaica, came to America in 1911 to earn a degree in agriculture. After transferring from the Tuskegee Institute to Kansas State College, he headed to New York in 1914 to pursue a literary career. Racial conflicts were happening more and more during that time as a response to the immigration of blacks from the South to the North. As a result there were as many as two dozen race riots that year across the country in which blacks were the victims. McKay wrote in *The Liberator* one of his most memorable poems, "If We Must Die," in response to a race riot in Chicago. He charged blacks to fight back against the forces that would destroy them. McKay's work celebrated the working class, represented blacks in America, sought to correct stereotypes prevalent in literature, and addressed political and social concerns such as racism.

Lean'tin L. Bracks

Sanchez, Sonia (1934–)

Sanchez's commitment to civil rights and the improved quality of life for African Americans permeates her work. Her interest in poetic expression to effect change began as early as six while she was under the care of her maternal grandmother. Her interest in verse continued through to college, when she took creative writing classes, and later postgraduate work at New York University, where she studied with Louise Bogan. Her poetic expressions during the 1960s gave voice to the turbulence of the time and the unjust treatment that was pervasive in the black community. Sanchez was an influential member of the Civil Rights Movement and the **Black Arts Movement**. While serving as an active member of the **Congress for Racial Equality (CORE)**, Sanchez met **Malcolm X**. She learned a lot about language from Malcolm X through his direct and truthful approach, later applying that knowledge to her poetry. Sanchez has published numerous works of poetry that address social and political concerns impacting civil rights and the quality of life for African Americans.

Lean'tin L. Bracks

Civil Rights

Cities and Towns

Black Migration to Northern States

Before the **Civil War** and the Emancipation Proclamation ended plantation slavery in the South, fugitive slaves in most cases headed north to seek freedom. The largest migration movements occurred in twenty-year cycles, beginning with the **Fugitive Slave Act** of 1850, which generated mass travel on the **Underground Railroad**. In 1870 the aftermath of the Civil War caused many to leave the South, while the Chicago World's Fair of 1893, World War I (1914–1918), and America's entry into World War II (1941–1945) also generated interest among blacks seeking industrial work in the North. The *Chicago Defender,* an African American newspaper founded by Robert Sengstacke Abbott in 1905, became a leading voice in promoting the "Negro Exodus" to northern states, described as the "promised land" and "New Canaan." The newspaper was also known for its strong attacks against racial prejudice and discrimination. When blacks moved north, they encountered densely populated urban environments and struggled for fair treatment in employment, housing, education, and other concerns. Northward migration continued to be a viable option until the Civil Rights Movement of the 1950s and 1960s brought major social changes to the South.

Fletcher F. Moon

Jamestown, Virginia

In August of 1619, twelve years after English colonists established the first permanent English settlement in North America, Jamestown received Africans as involuntary laborers. The 20 Africans who were put ashore by the captain of a Dutch ship were not slaves in the legal sense, but rather indentured servants, who, like their European counterparts, became free after their contractual period ended. The colony's inhabitants, however, did not appear to grasp the all-encompassing effect of the induction of Africans into the fledgling colony. As an institution, slavery did not exist in the colony. As an economic system the "peculiar institution," as slavery came to be called, developed gradually from indentured servitude to lifelong and heritable bondage as Virginia increasingly failed to meet its labor needs with Native Americans and indentured servants.

Once the Virginia colony recognized that blacks could not easily escape without being identified, could be strictly controlled and persecuted because they were not Christians, and seemed available in endless supply, the colony felt it had found the answer to its labor shortage problem. Like other colonies, Virginia had no statutes against the perpetual and inherited servitude of people from the continent of Africa or of African descent. While Jamestown, Virginia, was the first of the North America British colonies to receive Africans as involuntary laborers, it was not the first colony to codify the institution of slavery. Massachusetts preceded Virginia by twenty years when its code of laws, the Body of Liberties, recognized the enslavement of Africans as not only legal but also moral in 1641.

Virginia was evolving into a slave society with a racially based system of thralldom ...

Two decades later, the Virginia Assembly indirectly provided statutory recognition that blacks were to serve *durante vita,* or for life. Virginia was evolving into a slave society with a racially based system of thralldom subjugating all aspects of slaves' lives. In 1705 Virginia's planter-dominated House of Burgesses codified slave laws that sought to accomplish three things: confirm the perpetual and inherited bondage of people of African decent; establish an entirely separate penal code and judicial system for enslaved people; and create mandatory service in slave patrols by non-slaveholders to force them to protect the property rights of those who owned blacks. This last provision was designed to segregate the colony's black and white labor forces. The effort to accentuate racial diversity to the detriment of class unity was also manifested in the terms used by legislators to explicate and substantiate why the 1705 slave code was considered necessary.

Imbued with racially slanted language, it sought to debase humans of African descent and repudiate their humanity.

Linda T. Wynn

Rock Hill, South Carolina

This South Carolina community was the scene of several civil rights initiatives, beginning with the 1955 desegregation of St. Anne Catholic School, making it the first integrated school in the state. Rock Hill also launched a successful bus boycott in 1957 that was led by the Reverend Cecil A. Ivory, an African American Presbyterian minister and activist affiliated with the **Southern Christian Leadership Conference** (SCLC). Ivory provided leadership and guidance to local students participating in civil rights activities in sympathy with the **Greensboro, North Carolina sit-in** on February 1, 1960. The Rock Hill sit-in was the first in the state of South Carolina. It began on February 12, 1960, with 100 black students, mostly from Friendship Junior College. At the city's Woolworth's and McCrory's stores demonstrators were subjected to violent responses by unsympathetic whites. One black student was knocked off a stool at a lunch counter, and whites threw ammonia to cause eye irritation and further discourage other protesters. The stores closed the lunch counters down temporarily rather than change their policies, but when they reopened on February 23, the protesters returned to continue the demonstrations. Ivory coordinated mass meetings, organized and directed the demonstrations, and made national headlines when he was denied service at McCrory's despite being in his wheelchair. Demonstrations expanded to the bus terminals, resulting in 70 arrests, and continued into the following year. More student arrests resulted in the 1961 Rock Hill "Jail-In" (in which the students involved made a pact not to accept bail and to do hard time rather than submit to further discrimination) but the protests ultimately achieved success.

Fletcher F. Moon

Ruleville, Mississippi

Located in Sunflower County, Ruleville became the target of the Council of Federated Organizations (COFO), an umbrella organization of national and regional groups engaged in the freedom struggle in Mississippi. Established in 1962 to capitalize on the efforts of the **Student Non-Violent Coordinating Committee** (SNCC), the **Congress of Racial Equality** (CORE), and the **NAACP**, it focused on voter registration and education. The COFO targeted Ruleville, a town of approximately 1,100 people, because black Rulevillians were drawn to the Mississippi freedom struggle there that was the result racial oppression. It was also the target of the COFO because Ruleville was the home of Senator James Eastland, the ranking Democrat in the U.S. Senate.

As early as 1960, blacks attempted to register at the Ruleville courthouse, but the highway patrol turned them away. In 1962 local resident Celeste Davis started citizenship classes under the sponsorship of the SCLC; Ruleville's mayor quickly suggested that those attending the citizenship classes would be given a one-way ticket out of town. True to his word, Mayor Charles M. Dorrough fired Davis's husband, Ruleville sanitation worker Leonard Davis, because of her attendance at the citizenship classes. In addition, Marylene Burks and Vivian Hillet of Ruleville were later severely wounded when an unidentified assailant fired shots through the home of Hillet's grandparents, who were active in the voter registration drives.

Notwithstanding threats and physical abuse, women were prominent in the Mississippi freedom struggle. **Fannie Lou Hamer**, for one, is the best known woman leader out of Ruleville. On August 31, 1962, Hamer was fired from her timekeeping job on the Marlow Plantation outside of Ruleville, the same day she attempted to register at the Sunflower County Courthouse. After enduring a brutal jail beating, Hamer became the county supervisor for citizenship training and later an SNCC field secretary. In 1964 Hamer helped organize the Mississippi Freedom Democratic Party, which challenged the all-white Mississippi delegation at the 1964 Democratic Convention.

Linda T. Wynn

Freedom Celebrations

Black History Month/Negro History Week (est. 1926)

Negro History Week was first introduced in 1926 as a means of commemorating African American history when American history included primarily slavery as the participation of African Americans. **Carter G. Woodson** and several other colleagues saw a need to preserve the culture of their race and to make sure that persons were informed of the many contributions and accomplishments that were a part of their history. In 1912, Woodson formed the Association for the Study of African American Life and History. Shortly after the formulation of the group Woodson began publishing, in 1916, the *Journal of Negro History*. As Woodson worked on matters for the organization and served in various roles in academia, he acknowledged that the average African American knew very little about their history and culture. He also knew that whites saw little value in knowing African American history and African Americans also had little interest in their past due to the indoctrination of inferiority and the humiliation surrounding the experiences of slavery. To resolve this glaring concern, Negro History Week was initiated in 1926 as a time to celebrate and commemorate African American leaders. Because **Frederick Douglass**, Abraham Lincoln, and **Booker T. Washington** all had birthdates in February, a week was selected that was in close proximity to those dates. Materials were published by the association to support lectures, exhibits, and curriculum development for Negro History Week. The celebration was so well received that it gained national acclaim. In 1976, during the nation's bicentennial, Negro History Week was expanded to Black History Month. The annual celebrations focus on a specific theme; it 2008, that theme celebrated multiculturalism—a key concern that Woodson had early on.

Lean'tin L. Bracks

June 19 celebrations reinforce the idea that the Emancipation Proclamation did not bring immediate freedom to American blacks.

Juneteenth

A portmanteau of the words June and nineteenth, Juneteenth is considered one of the oldest known celebrations commemorating the end of the peculiar institution of slavery in America. Two years after President Abraham Lincoln issued the Emancipation Proclamation, also known as the Day of Jubilee, that became effective on January 1, 1863 (which theoretically freed only those slaves in states under the control of the Confederacy), Union General Gordon Granger's General Order Number Three finally emancipated approximately 250,000 slaves from thralldom in Texas. In addition to the slaves in Texas, those held in involuntary servitude in the states of Kentucky and Delaware were among the last to gain freedom. The few hundred slaves in Delaware and the tens of thousands of slaves in Kentucky had to wait until the **Thirteenth Amendment** to the U.S. Constitution was ratified in December 1865 before they were freed. This tardy emancipation gave rise to the enduring American black celebration of Juneteenth.

The news of their freedom was slow to reach many slaves; plantation owners read the procla-

mation to their slaves over the course of several months following the end of the **Civil War**. The news evoked a range of celebrations. In Austin, the state capital of Texas, Juneteenth was first celebrated in 1867 under the direction of the **Freedmen's Bureau**; it became part of the calendar of public events by 1872. Juneteenth in Limestone County, Texas, gathered "thousands" to be with families and friends. At one time 30,000 blacks gathered at Booker T. Washington Park in Limestone County, Texas (also known as Comanche Crossing), for the event.

The modern Civil Rights Movement of the 1950s and 1960s reinvigorated Juneteenth celebrations, as many African American youths linked the freedom struggle to the historical struggles of their ancestors. Student demonstrators involved in the Atlanta civil rights campaign of the early 1960s wore Juneteenth freedom buttons. In 1968 Juneteenth received another regeneration through the **Poor People's March on Washington**, when the Reverend **Ralph D. Abernathy** called for people of all races, creeds, economic levels, and professions to come to the nation's capital to demonstrate support for the poor. At the end of the 1970s, Representative Al Edwards, a Democrat from Houston, introduced a bill to make Juneteenth a state holiday. The Texas legislature passed the bill in 1979, and Republican Governor William P. Clements Jr. signed it into law.

Texas made Juneteenth an official holiday on January 1, 1980, and it became the first state to grant Juneteenth government recognition. Several states have since issued proclamations recognizing the holiday, but the Lone Star State remains alone in granting it full state holiday status. Today, Juneteenth is promoted not only as a commemoration of African American freedom, but also as an example of self-development and respect for all cultures. June 19 celebrations reinforce the idea that the Emancipation Proclamation did not bring immediate freedom to American blacks, but that true freedom was a protracted struggle lasting many generations.

Linda T. Wynn

Protests

Albany Movement (1961–1962)

The city became a focal point for one of the first large-scale community protests against segregation after the **Montgomery Bus Boycott**. These efforts involved a coalition of organizations, including the NAACP youth chapter at Albany State College, the Baptist Ministers' Alliance, the Federation of Women's Clubs, the **Student Non-Violent Coordinating Committee** (SNCC), and the **Southern Christian Leadership Conference** (SCLC) led by **Martin Luther King Jr.** The coalition tested the Interstate Commerce Commission ruling outlawing segregation in public transportation facilities at the Albany bus terminal on November 22, 1961. Albany State students attempting to use the "whites-only" waiting room and restaurant were arrested and jailed; two students were expelled from the college for their participation, leading to additional protests against school administrators. A second attempt was made on December 10 by an integrated group of SNCC activists who were also arrested. More protest rallies and marches led to mass arrests, but the subdued actions of Albany Police Chief Laurie Pritchett limited negative press coverage. King came to lend his support on December 15 and was also arrested. Protests continued through the spring and summer of 1962 with limited success. King and others learned important strategic lessons from the protests, however, and young activists such as **Cordell** and **Bernice Johnson Reagon** emerged from the Albany Movement.

Fletcher F. Moon

Atlanta Race Riot (1906)

This event was part of the larger context of violence directed toward blacks during the late nineteenth and early twentieth century. In Georgia, the racial climate was such that white supremacy values dominated the rhetoric and platform of the Democratic gubernatorial contest between Hoke Smith and Clark Howell. The five local newspapers controlled by whites published sensationalized and unsubstantiated reports of white women being raped by black men, as well as allegations of other destructive behavior by blacks against whites in the 18 months preceding the outbreak of violence. Black sections of the city were characterized as breeding grounds for vice and became the focus of a "crusade" against the supposed negative influences on the rest of the city. On September 22, 1906, a mob of whites gathered on Decatur Street in Atlanta, then moved toward the center of the city, attacking blacks and destroying their businesses on Auburn Street in the heart of the African American community, as well as other property owned and used by blacks in the immediate and surrounding neighborhoods. The violence continued until September 27, as the reported size of the mob grew from several dozen whites to as many as 5,000 and spread to Brownsville, a black middle class suburban area of the city.

Local police and state militia on the scene did little to restrain the violence.

Local police and state militia on the scene did little to restrain the violence, offering virtually no protection to the blacks being victimized and in some cases actually joining the mob in the mayhem and destruction. Twenty-five people died as a result of the riot, with hundreds more injured, thousands fleeing the city in fear, and an untold amount of property damage and loss. Hundreds of homes were burned, leaving over a thousand people homeless, while businesses were also looted by the mob before being subjected to other destructive actions. No mass arrests of whites took place during or after the riot, despite the numerous instances of mob violence and criminal behavior, much of which was done in the presence of law enforcement authorities. **Booker T. Washington** and some other black leaders gathered afterwards in Washington, D.C., to address the rebuilding of areas affected by the riot. **W.E.B. Du Bois**, an Atlanta resident at the time, channeled his anger and frustration into the creation of the poem "The Litany of Atlanta." Du Bois and many other African Americans saw the Atlanta riot and similar acts by whites as proof that racial intolerance would continue, that blacks did not receive "equal protection" under the laws of the land, and that the accommodation and self-help philosophy of Washington could not work in a climate of racial hatred.

Fletcher F. Moon

Back to Africa Movement

Efforts to move Africans and people of African descent in the United States back to Africa began in the early part of the nineteenth century and continued into the twentieth. Fostered by news and rumors of planned revolts, white Americans in the late eighteenth and early nineteenth centuries began to see free black people and newly freed slaves as a problem. Some white Americans believed, as did many African Americans, that black people could not achieve equality in the United States. While the majority of free African American leaders in the nineteenth century were against a movement back to Africa—also known as colonization—there were some African Americans in favor of emigration and the establishment of a new black homeland. The most prominent advocate of these efforts in the early nineteenth century was Paul Cuffe. A wealthy businessman, Cuffe transported 38 Africans from the United States to Liberia. In 1817 he met with an untimely death; this was the same year the American Colonization Society was established. This society was established by white Americans in an effort to solve the

"problem" of the free black presence through the establishment of a Liberian settlement. The most well-known champion of the back to Africa movement was black nationalist **Marcus Garvey**, a twentieth-century advocate. Garvey, like other proponents of the back to Africa movement, believed black people could not achieve equality in the United States. He claimed that all people should have their own homeland, and Africa belonged to black people. He hoped that his organizations, the **Universal Negro Improvement Association** and the Black Star Shipping Line, would help to make the dream of a mass emigration to Africa possible. However, once deported from the United States, his plans for the movement were never realized.

Rebecca S. Dixon

Birmingham Bus Boycott (1956)

The Birmingham Bus Boycott was one of the first actions of the **Alabama Christian Movement for Human Rights** (ACMHR), which was founded by the Reverend **Fred L. Shuttlesworth** when the **NAACP** was banned in the state of Alabama. Initially, it requested the hiring of black policemen for the black community. This request finally necessitated a lawsuit against Birmingham's Personnel Board to make civil service jobs available to all. Subsequently, all "white only" signs were removed, but no blacks were hired. Following the successful **Montgomery Bus Boycott** and the U.S. Supreme Court ruling that segregation was unconstitutional, the ACMHR decided to desegregate the Birmingham busses. Two hundred and fifty members of the ACMHR were to ride the buses on December 26, 1956. Before this happened violence broke out and the Reverend Shuttlesworth's home was bombed on December 25; the bed in which he slept was demolished, but he survived unscathed. He took his good fortune to mean that the boycott was sanctioned by God and that the fight for civil rights was to continue.

Twenty-one protesters were arrested during the bus ride on December 26, and the ACMHR filed a suit in federal court. Following this, Shuttlesworth and others made several attempts to desegregate other places, such as the railroad station and the all-white school. These attempts were met with varying degrees of violent resistance. Birmingham was known for its violence and frequent bombings in the black community; consequently, it had gained the name "Bombingham." Three months after the bus boycott, in 1957 there was another attempt to ride the segregated buses. Arrests were again made, and some 5,000 blacks gathered on the courthouse lawn in silent protest of the jailings. The riders were soon released on bond, and the ACMHR again filed another injunction against the city and the bus company. When the appeal reached the federal court, the law was repealed on October 14, 1958.

A new ordinance was passed, however, that authorized the Birmingham Transit System to enforce segregated seating. This was challenged by the ACMHR on October 20, 1958. Commissioner of Public Safety Eugene "Bull" Connor arrested 14 black challengers, including Shuttlesworth and three members of the **Montgomery Improvement Association**, who had arrived in the city to support the fight, charging them with vagrancy. Because of the dependency of the black populace on the city transit system, police brutality and intimidation, and the press blackout, the boycott failed. It was not until December 14, 1959, that desegregated seating on Birmingham buses was legalized.

Nevertheless, segregation and violence were so well entrenched in Birmingham in other aspects of daily life that it was felt that an organization with a national image and broader connections might provide the visibility needed to realize full equality for blacks. To this end, the Reverend **Martin Luther King Jr.** and the **Southern Christian Leadership Conference** were asked to come and lead workshops and demonstrations against Birmingham's racist practices. When they arrived, the strategic goals were to demolish segregation in Birmingham, to generate so much national awareness that the

Kennedy Administration would be forced to actively support civil rights for all citizens regardless of race, and to mobilize enough northern support to break the southern filibuster and pass a national civil rights act that would overturn segregation laws everywhere and outlaw all forms of discrimination.

Birmingham was known for its violence and frequent bombings in the black community.

The plan of action had the codename "Project C" for "Confrontation," and it was based at the **Sixteenth Street Baptist Church**. The confrontations began April 3, 1963, with sit-ins. Four days later, "Bull" Connor set police attack dogs and high powered water hoses on the demonstrators, effectively drawing national attention to the struggle. Demonstrators were arrested, an injunction was issued barring further demonstrations, and King and the Reverend **Ralph David Abernathy** were among those arrested on April 12, 1963, Good Friday. It was during this period that King wrote his "**Letter from the Birmingham Jail**" in response to eight white clergymen who accused him of agitating citizenry by addressing the subject of direct action. On April 26, 1963, all were convicted of criminal contempt and released on appeal, which resulted in the [Wyatt Tee] *Walker v. City of Birmingham* court case, in which it was determined that the city could put an injunction on protests, even though the parade ordinance it passed was constitutionally questionable.

With the release of King from jail, the third phase of the Birmingham campaign began. Children ages 6 to 16 participated as demonstrations began on May 2, 1963. The next day, Connor responded again with powerful fire hoses and German Shepard dogs; the citizens retaliated with bricks and rocks. During the confrontations there were mass arrests of children. The jails were so full by May 6 that Connor turned the stockade at the state fairground into a jail. President **John F. Kennedy** subsequently sent his assistant attorney general for civil rights to aid in the negotiation of the settlement that took place May 10, 1963.

Helen R. Houston

Black Power Movement (1960s)

The Black Power Movement of the mid-1960s was an outgrowth from the modern civil rights movement. However, the failure of legal and political decisions, and the non-violent movement for African American equality and justice in the American South to bring about significant transformation, resulted in a more militant posture against the prevailing white system of belief and the development of a distinctly African American ideology known as Black Power. Although the phrase had been used by African American writers and politicians for years, the expression gained currency in the civil rights vocabulary during the James Meredith March Against Fear in the summer of 1966, when **Stokely Carmichael** (later Kwame Turé), head of the **Student Non-Violent Coordinating Committee** (SNCC), used the expression as a means to galvanize African Americans. Later, Carmichael, in collaboration with Charles Hamilton, provided an explanation of its meaning in *Black Power: The Politics of Liberation in America* (1967). The Black Power Movement stressed racial pride, self-determination, economic independence, and social equality through the creation of black political and cultural institutions. Although the civil rights legislation was an effective attempt toward eliminating inequality between African Americans and whites, blacks were still encumbered by lower wages, police brutality, and racial discrimination. Later in 1966, **Huey Newton** and

Bobby Seale formed the **Black Panther Party** for self-Defense. By the late 1960s, the Black Power Movement had made a significant impact on American culture and society. Considered by some to be an affirmative and proactive force designed to help African Americans attain full equality with whites, others ostracized it as a radical, at times violent faction whose principal purpose was to further broaden the racial chasm. While the movement essentially disappeared after 1970, the concept of positive racial identity remained embedded in the African American consciousness.

Linda T. Wynn

Bloody Sunday (1965)

March 7, 1965, was called "Bloody Sunday" because of the violence directed toward civil rights demonstrators during an attempted march from **Selma to Montgomery**, Alabama, on that date. The purpose of the march was to protest against police brutality and the denial of voting rights; it was a continuation of earlier civil rights efforts in the Selma area that began in 1963. Participants included key leaders of the Civil Rights Movement, such as **John Lewis** and **Hosea Williams**, as well as many unsung heroes from the local community and outside supporters. **Martin Luther King Jr.** had been in the Selma area on several previous occasions, enduring arrest and physical as well as verbal attacks, including death threats. His decision not to participate in the march created some confusion, disagreement, and resentment among other activists, but King had delegated **Southern Christian Leadership Conference** (SCLC) representation and leadership to aides **Andrew Young**, **James Bevel**, and Williams. Lewis was the chairman of the **Student Non-Violent Coordinating Committee** (SNCC), but his decision to participate was personal, as his SNCC colleagues had also decided not to support the march.

The black community in Selma intended to move forward with or without the presence of King and other more high-profile leaders.

Lewis, a native of the state, felt he needed to show solidarity with fellow Alabamians and others involved in the effort. Alabama white leaders, including Governor George Wallace, Alabama Public Safety Director Al Lingo, Selma Mayor Jimmy Smitherman, Selma Public Safety Director Wilson Baker, and Dallas County Sheriff Jim Clark, were committed to preventing the march from being successful. An injunction was issued by Wallace in support of efforts to stop the march.

When the approximately 600 marchers left Brown Chapel African Methodist Episcopal (AME) Church, they were met at the foot of the Edmund Pettus Bridge by a large group of Alabama state troopers, many on horseback and wearing gas masks. They were joined by other groups of whites whom Clark had "deputized," some bearing large clubs and waving Confederate flags. A group of news reporters, photographers, and cameramen, as well as a small group of blacks, were also present to observe the event.

Williams and Lewis stopped the marchers and were told by Major John Cloud that their assembly was unlawful, so they would have to disperse. Before instructions could be given to the marchers, Cloud issued a command for the troopers to advance, attacking the demonstrators with clubs and tear gas. Lewis was among many who were wounded as a result of the attack, which continued as the marchers retreated in the direction of the church. The violence was recorded by the media, and the resulting international news coverage led to the overturning of Wallace's ban by a federal judge and a successful march led by King two weeks later.

Fletcher F. Moon

Boston Riot (1903)

This event took place in the context of a struggle between different approaches to racial progress for blacks at the turn of the twentieth century, epitomized in **Booker T. Washington's** "Tuskegee Machine" and **William Monroe**

Trotter, leader of the "Negro Radicals." Two years earlier Trotter and his colleague George W. Forbes founded the *Boston Guardian* newspaper which directly challenged Washington's ideas and methods. The actual confrontation between Washington and Trotter took place on July 30, 1903. At a meeting of the Boston branch of the **National Negro Business League**. Trotter and Forbes led a group of approximately 30 people to the African Methodist Episcopal (AME) Church and interrupted Washington's speech with a series of probing questions until police were called to the scene. Trotter was arrested, fined $50, and sentenced to 30 days in jail. The incident was exaggerated in the local press as the "Boston Riot," and Trotter was portrayed as a "martyr" by supporters for his willingness to openly challenge Washington and suffer the consequences of his actions. W.E.B. Du Bois was not present at the event, but he later joined Trotter and other radicals to establish the **Niagara Movement** as an alternative to Washington's power and influence.

Fletcher F. Moon

The black community in Selma intended to move forward with or without the presence of King.

Cambridge, Maryland, Demonstrations (1963–1967)

The racial and economic situation in this community for African Americans was bleak in 1963, with widespread poverty, discrimination, segregation, and high unemployment levels experienced by blacks, who made up a third of the city's 11,000 residents. In January of that year, college students from Baltimore and New York City began sit-ins and other protest activities. Local resident and **Howard University** graduate Gloria Richardson emerged as a leader, promoting black pride and taking a more militant stance than most established civil rights organizations did in addressing community issues and concerns. As boycotts, picketing, and marches continued, their efforts were met with strong opposition from angry whites and the local police. Demonstrations turned violent as some protesters chose to retaliate when attacked, instead of shielding themselves only and "turning the other cheek" in the manner of Mahatma Gandhi, **Martin Luther King Jr.**, and other civil rights leaders who advocated non-violent resistance. Numerous arrests were made, and on June 11 rioting broke out, with destruction of white-owned stores and other businesses and shooting of firearms.

Fires destroyed two city blocks, as white firemen refused to enter the area without protection.

A state of martial law was declared, as tensions remained high in black and white communities. After Richardson refused to meet with state officials, U.S. Attorney General **Robert F. Kennedy** became a part of efforts to end the violence and address the numerous community problems that led to the outbreak of violence. Kennedy promised that the federal government would intervene to establish desegregated accommodations in public venues, improve public housing, integrate the public school system, and develop a biracial commission to address employment/unemployment issues. Troops remained in the Cambridge area until May 1965, but problems in the community resurfaced in July 1967. The National

States Rights party and the Ku Klux Klan came to the city to protest school desegregation, and Richardson responded with a radio broadcast denouncing the two racist organizations.

The situation escalated when **Hubert Gerold "H. Rap" Brown**, a well-known young militant and **Black Power** advocate, came to Cambridge on July 24, 1967. Brown urged local blacks to "burn this town down" if their demands were not met. He was also widely quoted as saying "It's time for Cambridge to explode," as rioting broke out in the black section of the city that evening after a shooting was reported. Fires destroyed two city blocks, as white firemen refused to enter the area without protection from law enforcement officials. Maryland Governor (and future Vice President of the United States) Spiro T. Agnew ordered the state contingent of the National Guard into the city to restore order. Brown was arrested afterwards by Maryland authorities and charged with arson, inciting to riot, and disturbing the peace. The Cambridge incidents marked the shift from nonviolence to more militant civil rights activism.

Fletcher F. Moon

Chicago Freedom Movement (1966)

The Chicago Freedom Movement represented one of the most ambitious campaigns for African American civil rights in the North. An alliance of the **Southern Christian Leadership Conference** (SCLC) and the Coordinating Council of Community Organizations (CCCO), the Chicago movement attracted the attention of the national media and made the nation aware of racial problems African Americans faced under the system of *de facto* segregation in the northern region of the United States. The underpinning for the "northern" movement began in the summer of 1965, when the Chicago civil rights community asked **Martin Luther King Jr.** to lead a demonstration against segregation in education, housing, and employment. The CCCO, which was founded by the Chicago **Urban League**, the Chicago **NAACP**, and other activist organizations like the **Congress of Racial Equality** (CORE), sought to fuse the growing protest energies that emerged between 1963 and 1964, when African American parents protested against the city's inequitable educational system.

In 1964 activists Albert Raby called the CCCO together. During the summer of the following year, the CCCO staged daily marches against the school system's educational policies and urged Mayor Richard J. Daley to remove Superintendent Benjamin Willis. Chicago had never before experienced such a sustained demand for racial justice. In January 1966, King announced plans for the Chicago Freedom Movement, which signaled a shift from the South to the North. He appointed **Bernard Lafayette** to help plan and execute the campaign's direct non-violent action campaign. After the 1965 Los Angeles riots, it seemed critical to illustrate how the methods of nonviolence could be transported to the North, thereby bringing attention to how economic exploitation adversely affected northern blacks.

Considered a city impregnated with a southern mindset, Chicago practiced a brand of politics that made this appealing to many. Daley exerted a high degree of influence and power, which placed him in position to transform many of the racist practices that directly impeded black progress. The SCLC also initiated Operation Breadbasket, an enterprise under the direction of **Jesse Jackson** that was aimed at eradicating racist hiring practices by companies doing business in black neighborhoods. Despite its southern mindset, the "Windy City" also provided a supporting cast with substantial succor among black and white clergy and activists, who were in the struggle's forefront against racist hiring practices, police brutality and discrimination in housing and education. Later, that month King moved his family to Chicago where they resided in one of the slum areas on the city's west side. With that move, the Chicago Freedom Summer demanded an end to Chicago slums. Under the leadership of King and Raby, the Chicago Freedom Movement's

activities and polices were established by a committee made up of representatives of the city's diverse civil rights organizations.

Displeased at the prospect of King and others from the SCLC coming to his city, Daley made known that outside agitators were not welcome and declared there were no slums in Chicago. Drawing a line in the sand, he refused to meet with King. Reminiscent of southerners like Alabama's Theophilus Eugene "Bull" Connor, George Wallace, and Georgia's Lester Maddox, Daley exposed to the nation that there were southern counterparts in northern cities.

Chicago was set for a long hot summer. In the summer of 1966, the Chicago Freedom Movement staged numerous demonstrations in all-white neighborhoods protesting housing discrimination, a custom usually achieved by redlining (a form of mortgage discrimination directed against blacks or other minorities) and block busting (a means for real estate agents and speculators to trigger the turnover of white-owned property to African Americans; often characterized as "panic peddling," such practices frequently accompanied the expansion of black areas of residence and the entry of blacks into neighborhoods previously denied to them). Although the demonstrators were nonviolent, the communities were just the opposite. As the marches continued and gained momentum, riots erupted on Chicago's West Side in July. The viciousness and magnitude of the violence that met the marchers was unsurpassed by any previous attacks anywhere. On August 5, as marchers protested in an all-white community, black demonstrators were met with malevolence. Antagonists hurled a barrage of rocks, bottles, and other implements, causing bodily harm to the demonstrators. Although King was struck in the head with a rock, he kept marching.

Later, King told reporters that he had never seen such racial hatred, not even in such Klan strongholds as Mississippi. The violent response of local whites and the resolve of civil rights activists to carry on the movement for opening housing to all people captured the attention of the national press and caused Chicago's city hall to rethink its position. By late August, Daley backed down and was eager to find a way to end the demonstrations. He agreed to meet with movement leaders. After negotiating with King, various housing boards, and others, a 10-point agreement was signed that called for various measures to strengthen the enforcement of existing laws and regulations as they related to housing. However, the agreement did not satisfy everyone, and in early September activists marched on Cicero, Illinois, the town where a fierce race riot had previously occurred in 1951.

King told reporters that he had never seen such racial hatred, not even in such Klan strongholds as Mississippi.

Following the agreement, some members of the SCLC remained to help in housing programs and voter registration, and Jackson continued Operation Breadbasket. However, city officials failed to make good on their promises of the summit agreement. By 1967 the Chicago Freedom Movement ended as the **Black Power Movement** swept through Chicago, questioning interracial activism and non-violent direct action.

Linda T. Wynn

Danville, Virginia, Movement (1963)

The mill town of Danville, Virginia, saw the early efforts of an anti-segregation campaign that began with the opening of the public library to blacks. In 1960 a court order forced the facility to desegregate; instead, library leaders closed the building for several months. When it reopened as an integrated library, all seats had been removed and users were charged a fee for a library card. This campaign to deseg-

regate led to the founding of the Danville Christian Progressive Association (DCPA), later an affiliate of the **Southern Christian Leadership Conference** (SCLC). Local black leaders were displeased with the way the **NAACP** handled race matters: they were considered too slow to act because they did not want to disturb the status quo. By 1963, the DCPA's key aim was to bring about equal access to jobs in private enterprises and municipal jobs such as firemen, policemen, clerks, and meter readers. The aim, too, was to integrate lunch counters.

Martin Luther King Jr.'s visit to Danville in 1963 to address local blacks was followed by demonstrations from the black community. Worse than "Bull" Connor's order of fire hose attacks on protesters in Birmingham, Alabama, was Danville Mayor Julian Stinson's order to use dogs, fire hoses, and nightsticks on protesters who marched to oppose segregation in downtown public facilities. City officials deputized garbage collectors and used them to guard the police station complex. "We will hose down the demonstrators and fill every available stockade," Mayor Stinson declared. Local police also broke down church doors and arrested protest leaders and organizers. Some 65 protesters were injured. As a result of the brutality that blacks endured, June 10, 1963, became known as "Bloody Monday."

Danville officials remembered an 1831 statute that led to insurrectionist Nat Turner's hanging and its use to hang abolitionist John Brown in 1859. With this in mind, the municipal judge who heard the 1963 cases did so with a gun strapped to his waist. An attorney who tried to argue the protesters' case was arrested. Until then, the majority of the black community was afraid to join the protest. After Bloody Monday, however, the black community became solidified in its resolve.

Jessie Carney Smith

Detroit, Michigan, Race Riot (1943)

The black population in the city of Detroit increased greatly between 1910 and 1930, attracted to the industrial center by the need for automotive and other labor workers. World War II also drew blacks and others to Detroit from the South, as well as from other parts of the country and Canada, when automobile and other industrial plants began developing military vehicles and other equipment in support of the war effort. The influx into this urban setting created tension with whites who were also working in these industries, however. As early as August 1942 the potential for racial violence had been documented in local and national publications, as blacks experienced discrimination in housing, employment, and public accommodations. On June 20, 1943, a fight between blacks and whites took place on Belle Isle, where there was a segregated public beach and recreation area, and escalated into a riot. Local police were unprepared and ill-equipped to deal with the outbreak, but order was eventually restored with the help of military police. Twenty-nine African Americans and nine whites died, nearly 700 were injured, and close to 2,000 were arrested. One positive result was the formation of the nation's first interracial committee with authority to address discrimination issues.

Fletcher F. Moon

Detroit, Michigan, Race Riot (1967)

The summer of 1967 was marked by disturbances in several urban areas that suffered from poverty, racial discrimination, and other negative factors in the midst of increasing population density, as well as political turbulence connected with civil rights struggles and American involvement in the Vietnam War. In Detroit a single incident on July 23 triggered the outbreak of violence and destruction. After the police raided an "after-hours club" on 12th Street where illegal drinking was taking place, they arrested and handcuffed club patrons as a crowd of blacks gathered on the scene. Outnumbered police officers could not control the crowd, which began breaking into white-owned stores, looting merchandise, and destroying

property by setting fires and other means. As the riot continued over the next two days, even black-owned businesses were not spared from the violence. The National Guard restored order in the city on July 25, but by that time 43 African Americans had lost their lives, nearly 1,200 were injured, and well over 7,000 people had been arrested. The event became a symbol of urban problems and despair, with lasting negative implications for the city. Accelerated "white flight" to the suburbs and beyond caused additional economic problems for the inner city, and African Americans, who were soon to become the majority population, were left to address these and other issues largely by themselves.

Fletcher F. Moon

The event became a symbol of urban problems and despair, with lasting negative implications for the city.

Don't Buy Where You Can't Work (1930s)

Former prizefighter Bill Tate led a boycott of white merchants in Chicago in 1929 who refused to hire blacks, spearheading a strategy in the 1930s called "Don't Buy Where You Can't Work." It grew out of the "Double Duty Dollar" doctrine that African American ministers preached from the pulpit; churches promoted the strategy in mass meetings and through the newsletters. The primary aim was to help black businesses financially and to advance the race economically and socially. It spread to cities in other states, including Atlanta, St. Louis, Baltimore, Cleveland, Los Angeles, and Washington, D.C. There were branches in Richmond, Boston, and Pittsburgh, as well as in smaller cities, such as Evanston, Illinois, and Alliance, Ohio. Don't Buy was sustained from the 1930s to World War II.

The effort became variously known as the "Jobs for Negroes" movement, "Don't Spend Where You Can't Work" movement, and other titles. Organized mass meetings, trade pact agreements, boycotts, and block-by-block picketing advanced the purpose of the Don't Buy strategy. One of the larger movements took place in Harlem around 1930, when leaders sought clerical jobs for blacks in white-owned stores. After Sufi Abdul Hamid tried to follow his successful movement in Chicago in which blacks were placed in 200 jobs in two months, he moved his efforts to Harlem. Hamid and his Negro Industrial Alliance became so disruptive in their efforts that they helped to cause the Harlem Riots of 1935. White merchants in Harlem and in Maryland were unsuccessful in their legal maneuvers to end the pickets and boycotts. The Harlem network involved churches, fraternal groups, women groups, and social and political organizations.

Nearly a decade would pass before Harlem's black activists succeeded in their campaign to find jobs on a widespread basis. **Adam Clayton Powell Jr.** became a major player in Harlem's efforts. He organized a Citywide Coordinating Committee to find jobs for blacks. The diverse background of local black merchants caused some disparity, and many felt that, if the strategy worked, they would lose black customers to white businesses. Women agitators worked through organizations such as the Harlem Housewives League and urged women to patronize only those black grocery stores that belonged to the **Colored Merchants' Association**. The women also targeted the Atlantic and Pacific Tea Company (known as A&P). In time, the work of the women and Powell led to black employment in the New York Edison Electric Company, the New York Bus Company, the 1939 World's Fair, and elsewhere. Nationally, however, the plan led to no more than 2,000 jobs for blacks, but it tested the black commu-

nity's economic strength. The effects of the strategy were seen during the Civil Rights Movement of the 1960s, when African Americans deployed an economic boycott against white merchants who practiced racial discrimination in their businesses. The economic boycotts were short-lived, as most of the merchants readily changed their racial practices.

Jessie Carney Smith

Durham, North Carolina, Sit-ins (1960)

Although the **Greensboro, North Carolina, Sit-in** captured national attention in February 1960, it was preceded by the action of seven young African American Durhamites, who three years earlier entered the Royal Ice Cream parlor, sat in the whites-only section, and requested service. Because the Royal Ice Cream parlor was located in the African American community and those seeking service were required to enter by the back door and stand, it was selected as the protest site. Led by the Reverend Douglas E. Moore, the protesters included Mary Clyburn, Claud Glenn, Jesse Gray, Vivian Jones, Melvin Willis, and Virginia Williams. They entered the parlor on June 23, 1957, and were subsequently arrested and fined $25 each. It was their hope that their actions would test Durham's segregation laws. However, no redress came from the judicial branch, including the U.S. Supreme Court. Sit-ins in North Carolina had occurred as early as 1943, and, like the Durham sit-in of 1957, received little or no publicity. While the protesters' action did not result in a change of Jim Crow policy, it did signal the growing restlessness with America's system of racial segregation. The Reverend Moore, a classmate of **Martin Luther King Jr.** and pastor of the Asbury Temple Methodist Church, and **Floyd McKissick**, who headed the NAACP Youth Council, trained students to conduct sit-in protests. The 1957 Durham sit-in and its attendant court cases barely stoked the embers. However, in February of 1960, Durham and other cities across the South became hotbeds for sit-in protests. It was in

Durham that King made his 1960 "Fill Up the Jails" speech endorsing the sit-ins as a method of direct non-violent confrontation against the South's racial segregation laws.

Linda T. Wynn

East St. Louis, Illinois, Race Riot (1917)

This tragedy was considered one of the worst racial outbreaks in American history. The town of East St. Louis, Illinois, separated from St. Louis, Missouri, by the Mississippi River, experienced considerable racial tensions as blacks were drawn to the area to seek industrial employment. White union workers wanted restrictions placed on the number of blacks living in the town, as well as on working in local factories. Unsubstantiated rumors persisted that black men had harassed white women, further angering whites. After a white store owner was accidentally shot by a black man during a robbery, a white mob of more than 3,000 formed on May 28, 1917, and began destroying African American homes, businesses, and churches. Police and National Guard units called to the scene did nothing to stop the rioting, but rather searched black homes for concealed weapons. The violence reignited after July 1, when a "drive-by" shooting in a black neighborhood led to a response by blacks the next day that resulted in the accidental deaths of two undercover white police officers. Whites made a public show of the unmarked police car filled with bullet holes, and another mob sought revenge on the black community. Over 100 African Americans were gunned down by whites during the riot, including children, and more homes were burned.

Fletcher F. Moon

Economic Boycotts and Withdrawals (1950s–2000)

Economic boycotts and withdrawals as a strategy used by blacks during their mid-twentieth century struggle to secure civil rights

and liberties was not a modern-day approach. During the nineteenth century, African Americans used boycott methods to demonstrate against America's unjust treatment. Having staged several streetcar "ride-ins," abolitionist/feminist **Sojourner Truth** won a lawsuit against a streetcar driver who had forced her off his streetcar. Later, toward the century's end, journalist **Ida B. Wells-Barnett** seized upon the segregated transportation system with a public act of resistance by refusing to leave the white ladies' coach. At the dawn of the twentieth century, African Americans again employed the stratagems of economic boycotts and protests. From 1900 to 1906, African Americans in more than 25 southern cities organized boycotts of segregated streetcars. A half-century later, African Americans in Montgomery, Alabama, again instituted the boycott and economic withdrawals against the public transportation system. After decades of struggle, an open crusade by the people began in the 1950s against calcified racial intolerance and discrimination, a struggle that became a protracted fight.

Whites made a public show of the unmarked police car filled with bullet holes.

The **NAACP**, the **Congress of Racial Equality (CORE)**, the **Southern Christian Leadership Conference (SCLC)**, and the **Student Non-Violent Coordinating Committee (SNCC)** all employed an assortment of boycott and economic withdrawals to combat economic, social, and institutional injustices and inequities. Two years before the Montgomery movement captured America's attention and propelled the Reverend **Martin Luther King Jr.** into the modern Civil Rights Movement, in Baton Rouge, Louisiana, the Reverend T. J. Jemison initiated one of the first bus boycotts by American blacks in the country's South. Although short-lived, the Baton Rouge bus boycott served as a paradigm for similar protests throughout the South, including the 1955 **Montgomery Bus Boycott.**

African Americans also used protests to secure fair wages and better working conditions.

At the onset of the modern Civil Rights Movement, Montgomery, Alabama, was one of the first cities to employ economic pressure as a method of protest. Black Montgomery's yearlong boycott caused the bus company, downtown businessmen, and the city to lose approximately $1 million. As in Montgomery, when black Nashville leaders and students began their formal sit-in movement, they too added an economic assault that devastated downtown merchants and business owners. The Reverend **Kelly Miller Smith** and Vivian Henderson, a professor of economics at **Fisk University,** organized a boycott of downtown merchants just before Easter. Empowered by their stated motto, "No Fashions for Easter," the black community's economic withdrawal deprived store owners of incalculable amounts of business. The paucity of dollars flowing into the cash registers of city merchants and businessmen caused the walls of racial segregation in Nashville to fall.

African Americans also used protests to secure fair wages and better working conditions, as clearly established by the **sanitation workers' strike** in Memphis, Tennessee. While the primary impetus for the protest marches and demonstrations rested on the underpinning

of economics, they brought into focus other societal maladies, including blatant racial discrimination that manifested itself in the African American community. Throughout the 1960s and into the twenty-first century, African Americans boycotted and protested with their wallets where the remnants of racism remained covert rather than overt. They targeted such corporations as Texaco, Denny's, Coca-Cola, and Cracker Barrel, to name a few. Their use of boycotts and economic withdrawals made this methodology a compelling tool for constructive social change. African American activists and others would continue to use boycotts and protests to make American citizens more aware of, conscious about, and sensitive to all subjugated and oppressed groups.

Linda T. Wynn

Elaine, Arkansas, Race Riot (1919)

In the summer of 1919, black sharecroppers and tenant farmers in the area of Elaine, Arkansas, organized to receive fair wages for their labor in response to suspicions they were being cheated by white landowners. They created the Progressive Farmers and Householders Union (PFHU) and secured the services of a white attorney to negotiate on their behalf. On September 30, whites from the Missouri-Pacific Railroad fired on blacks attending a union meeting in a blatant attempt to disrupt and discourage the activities of the PFHU. The blacks returned fire, killing two whites; hundreds of other armed whites gathered to seek revenge. The white mob burned black homes and businesses. At least 200 blacks were killed during the riot, and 67 blacks were indicted for inciting violence. Hundreds of blacks who acted in self-defense were arrested by federal authorities, with many held in public school basements after jails were filled. Twelve black PFHU members were tried, convicted, and sentenced to death. In 1921 **NAACP** lawyers intervened, and six convictions were overturned by the Arkansas Supreme Court. The cases of the six other blacks were appealed to the U.S. Supreme Court, which ruled in 1923 that due process law was violated in convicting them, leading to their release in January 1925.

Fletcher F. Moon

Freedom Rides from Washington, D.C., to New Orleans, Louisiana (1961)

Fourteen years after the **Congress of Racial Equality** (CORE) attempted to desegregate interstate modes of public transportation, it would again test the South's compliance with rulings of the U.S. Supreme Court. The May 1961 Freedom Rides tested the 1960 Supreme Court decision in the *Boynton v. Virginia* case, which extended the *Morgan v. Commonwealth of Virginia* (1946) directive to all interstate transportation facilities, including terminals, waiting rooms, restaurants, and other amenities. The court's decision made it unconstitutional to racially segregate waiting rooms, restrooms, and lunch counters.

An interracial group of activists from CORE attempted to ride Greyhound and Trailways buses from Washington, D.C., to New Orleans, Louisiana, to test the Interstate Commerce Commission's ban on racially segregated buses and facilities on interstate routes. However, before they reached New Orleans, the Freedom Riders met with violence that caused CORE to terminate the excursion. Refusing to let violence override nonviolence, the **Nashville Student Movement** played a pivotal role in continuing the Freedom Rides to desegregate interstate transportation and auxiliary facilities. Although not the progenitors of the Freedom Rides of the 1960s, Nashville's student activists, under the leadership of **Diane J. Nash**, a member of the **Student Non-Violent Coordinating Committee** (SNCC), became their driving force. On May 4, 1961, CORE sent two buses and an assembly of 13 Freedom Riders (seven black men, three white men, and three white women) on what was supposed to be a two-week trip, traveling through the deep South from Washington, D.C., to New Orleans to test their right to intermingle blacks and whites in the region's bus stations. The group included **John Lewis**, a member of the Nashville student movement.

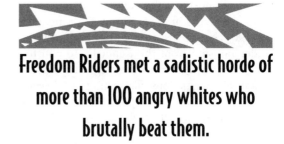

Freedom Riders met a sadistic horde of more than 100 angry whites who brutally beat them.

The interracial group encountered only a few problems during their first week of travel. However, when they reached Anniston, Alabama, on that fateful May 14 in 1961, the Freedom Riders met a sadistic horde of more than 100 angry whites who brutally beat them and fire bombed the bus. In Birmingham, a mob toting iron pipes and other weapons greeted the riders, who were battered, knocked unconscious, and hospitalized. Public Safety Commissioner "Bull" Connor knew that the Freedom Riders were coming and that hostile whites were awaiting their arrival. The following day, a picture of the burning Greyhound bus appeared in national and international news. While the violence garnered widespread attention, it also caused Farmer to terminate the ride.

On May 17, 1961, recruits left Nashville for Birmingham, Alabama. Three days later, they boarded a bus and traveled with a police escort to Montgomery, where the police abandoned them. Left to the mercy of a violent mob, several riders were beaten, causing the Kennedy Administration to call in federal marshals. On May 21 **Martin Luther King Jr.** flew to Montgomery to support the Freedom Riders. Three days later, 27 Freedom Riders left Montgomery for Jackson, Mississippi. Upon their arrival in Jackson, they were arrested for attempting to use the whites-only facilities. On May 26 the cadre of Freedom Riders were convicted and sent to **Parchman Farm Penitentiary**. The Nashville students' single-mindedness to carry on the Freedom Rides had major consequences for the southern Civil Rights Movement. The Freedom Rides continued for the next four months with student activists in the forefront. On September 22, 1961, in response to the Freedom Rides and under pressure from the Kennedy Administration, the Interstate Commerce Commission established regulations eliminating racial segregation in train and bus terminals. These regulations went into effect on November 1, 1961.

Linda T. Wynn

The 1964 Freedom Summer project was designed to draw the nation's attention to the violent oppression faced by African Americans in Mississippi.

Freedom Summer (1964)

Freedom Summer 1964 was an intensive voter registration project in the magnolia state of Mississippi. As a part of a larger effort launched by the **Congress of Racial Equality** (CORE) and the **Student Non-Violent Coordinating Committee** (SNCC), the goal was to increase the number of African American voters in the South. Initially started by SNCC activist **Robert Moses** in 1961, the 1964 Freedom Summer project was designed to draw the nation's attention to the violent oppression faced by African Americans in Mississippi when they attempted to exercise their constitutional rights and develop a grass-roots freedom

movement that could be sustained after student activists departed the state. By August 4, 1964, however, four people were killed, eighty were beaten, a thousand had been arrested, and 67 churches, homes, and businesses were set ablaze or bombed.

Although African American men were given the right of the franchise with the passage of the **Fifteenth Amendment** to the U.S. Constitution in 1870, almost a hundred years later many were still denied their constitutional right. Local and state functionaries used legal and extralegal methods to prevent this, such as poll taxes, literacy tests, and sinister methods such as beatings and lynchings. Even though SNCC activists had been striving to secure civil rights in rural Mississippi since 1961, they found that zealous and often vicious resistance by whites wanting to maintain the racial status quo in the state would not allow the direct action campaigns that proved successful in municipal areas like Montgomery and Birmingham.

In 1962 Moses became the director of the Council of Federated Organizations (COFO), an association of organizations that included CORE, the **NAACP,** and the SNCC. Responding to an upsurge of racial violence in 1963 that the **U.S. Commission on Civil Rights** described as a total collapse of law and order, he proposed that northern white student volunteers take part in a large number of simultaneous local campaigns during the summer of 1964. Moses and SNCC volunteers played the largest role in providing the majority of the funding and headquarters staff. The COFO sent letters to prospective volunteers alerting them to the possibility of arrest, the need for money to make bond and sustain themselves, and the necessity of obtaining Mississippi driver's licenses and tags for their cars.

The Freedom Summer project attracted more than a thousand volunteers, the majority of whom were affluent white northern college students. Training sessions attempted to prepare them to register African American voters, teach literacy and civics at Freedom Schools, and promote the **Mississippi Freedom Democratic**

Party's challenge to the all-white Democratic delegation at the Democratic National Convention in Atlantic City, New Jersey, which was to be held in August. On June 21, 1964, civil rights workers Andrew Goodman, **James Chaney**, and Michael Schwerner were reported missing after having left Meridian to investigate the burning of a black church near Philadelphia, Mississippi. The disappearance of Goodman and Schwerner, both white, captured the attention of the national media and the national government. While the abduction of Goodman, Chaney, and Schwerner deepened the volunteers' fear, the Freedom Summer project moved forward with the planned program of voter registration. Even though approximately 17,000 African Americans attempted to register to vote, local registrars honored only 1,600 voter applications, an action that demonstrated the necessity for federal voting rights laws. The efforts of the Freedom Summer volunteers and refusal of local registrars to accept registrants' applications cre-

ated momentum for the **Voting Rights Act of 1965**. As the lines of demarcation between the objectives of King and the younger, more revolutionary splinter group of the African American freedom struggle became more pronounced, Freedom Summer marked one of the last key interracial civil rights efforts of the 1960s.

Linda T. Wynn

Greensboro, North Carolina, Sit-ins (1960)

On February 1, 1960, Ezell Blair Jr., **Joseph McNeil**, Franklin McCain, and David Richmond, all students at **North Carolina Agriculture and Technical College** (now University), entered F.W. Woolworth's, purchased goods, and proceeded to the whites-only lunch counter and requested service. Denied service, the four students remained seated until the store closed. Sit-ins had taken place in the 1940s, and

The Greensboro Four returned to the Woolworth store on February 2, 1990, to commemorate their famous protest. Shown are (from left) Joseph McNeil, Jibreal Khazan (formerly Ezell Blair, Jr.), Franklin McCain, and David Richmond (AP Photo/Chuck Burton).

in 1958 and 1959 in Oklahoma City, Wichita, Kansas, and in St. Louis, Missouri, respectively. These protests demonstrated that the Civil Rights Movement was not just a southern phenomenon, but also a national one in its earliest days. The mass mobilization of student protesters emboldened by the action of the Greensboro Four, as they were called, was a new weapon in the African American struggle for freedom. The Greensboro students' attack against segregated public spaces in the South by direct non-violent resistance changed the spirit of the Civil Rights Movement. The simple request for a cup of coffee set off a chain of events that ultimately dismantled the remaining vestiges of *de jure* and *de facto* racial segregation.

The quartet returned each morning with other student protesters and occupied lunch counter seats. Within a week, sit-ins took place in **Durham**, Winston-Salem, Charlotte, and Raleigh, North Carolina. On February 10, 1960, Hampton, Virginia, became the first city outside of North Carolina to experience a sit-in, and by the end of the month sit-ins had occurred in more than 30 communities in 7 states. By the end of April, sit-ins had reached every southern state and attracted a total of as many as 50,000 students. The sit-ins that began in Greensboro and spread to other cities across the South gave birth in April 1960 to the **Student Non-Violent Coordinating Committee** (SNCC). Although the students at North Carolina A&T captured national attention, it was their counterparts in Nashville, Tennessee, who took over the leadership of the rapidly spreading student movement. Nashville students entered the movement 12 days after the Greensboro students. It did not hurt that in Nashville, *The Tennessean* covered the protest in detail: seventy stories within the next 14 weeks. While Greensboro began student demonstrations before Nashville, the Athens of the South began desegregating its lunch counters on May 13, 1960. Greensboro followed two months later and desegregated on July 25, 1960.

Linda T. Wynn

Hamburg, South Carolina, Race Riot (1876)

This event took place during the Reconstruction period after the **Civil War**, when freed blacks and radical Republicans held a number of elective offices and exerted significant political influence in South Carolina and other southern states. Ongoing tensions remained with former Confederates and other white Democrats who had been displaced from political power when the state's large black population was able to exercise voting rights. In South Carolina—and in Hamburg in particular—blacks not only exercised their constitutional right to bear arms, but had formed "colored militia" units. A confrontation between the Hamburg unit and two white men, Thomas Butler and Henry Getzen, took place on July 4, 1876. The unit was in military formation along a public highway and refused to break ranks to allow the passage of a white man's vehicle. An argument ensued between black militia captain "Doc" Adams and white general M. C. Butler on July 8. When Adams and the other blacks refused to surrender their guns, Butler and a mob of whites retaliated by attacking the outnumbered militia with artillery and other weapons. Seven blacks and one white man died in the riot, and according to one account four of the blacks killed had already disarmed and surrendered to Butler. Despite protests and mass meetings held by blacks in Charleston and efforts by white Republican governor Daniel H. Chamberlain to seek a fair and legal investigation, no people were prosecuted in connection with the incident.

Fletcher F. Moon

Harlem Race Riot (1935)

This violent event was attributed to factors including economic hardships during the Great Depression, police brutality in the black community, and job discrimination faced by African Americans. Ironically, the incident that triggered the riot involved a confrontation between a Latino boy and a white store owner in

Harlem on March 13, 1935. Ten-year-old Lino Rivera was accused of shoplifting and arrested after a fight with the store owner. Rumors circulated through Harlem that Rivera had been beaten or killed by the police after his arrest, and people in the community retaliated by destroying the storefront where the incident took place. The riot expanded to other white-owned property in Harlem, resulting in damage totaling over $2 million. Three lives were lost and over 200 people were wounded before order was restored.

Tension between white business owners and black residents already existed at the time because blacks were not being hired to work at the same stores they kept in business as customers. In 1933 African Americans started picketing and boycotting these establishments. By early 1935, however, the merchants secured an injunction from the city of New York to stop the protests. Efforts were made after the riot to investigate problems in Harlem and develop solutions, including the work of a biracial commission appointed by Mayor Fiorello La Guardia. African American intellectuals E. Franklin Frazier and Alain Locke were involved in these initiatives, which recommended ending discrimination in public services and hiring practices.

Fletcher F. Moon

Harlem Race Riot (1943)

Eight years after the 1935 riot, problems and tensions remained in Harlem and other large urban centers, even as the United States was in the midst of World War II. An incident involving confrontations between African Americans and police again led to widespread violence in the Harlem community, resulting in loss of lives as well as extensive property damage. On August 1, 1943, Marjorie Polite, a black woman, was alleged to have caused a disturbance at the Braddock Hotel in Harlem. She was subsequently arrested by New York City police and charged with the offense. An African American soldier in uniform, Robert Bandy, came to her defense and demanded her release from custody. It was

uncertain what happened next, as accounts indicated that Bandy either took a nightstick from an officer or hit the officer and fled the scene. Bandy was shot and wounded by the police, but rumors quickly circulated that he was killed while trying to protect his mother. An angry crowd of approximately 3,000 blacks surrounded the hotel, Sydenham Hospital, and the neighborhood police precinct, where they threatened the arresting officers. Later that evening the crowd began breaking windows and starting fires, and the violence escalated and continued until the next morning. By the time order was restored, six African Americans were dead, nearly 200 were injured, and at least 500 people had been arrested. Property damage was estimated between $500,000 and $1 million.

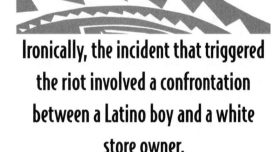

Ironically, the incident that triggered the riot involved a confrontation between a Latino boy and a white store owner.

Frustration was already high among Harlem blacks because of other problems involving the police, as well as from ongoing discrimination in jobs and housing. Bandy also represented the discrimination and disrespect faced by blacks in the military, even as America was fighting to preserve freedom in other parts of the world. Noted African American writer Ann Petry, a journalist in New York at the time, recorded her impressions of the riot and its implications in the novella *In Darkness and Confusion,* while **James Baldwin**, then a Harlem resident, reflected on the riot in his *Notes of a Native Son.*

Mayor La Guardia again joined black and white community leaders in efforts to defuse the immediate situation and downplay the racial overtones of the riot; he made attempts to address longstanding issues, too. The mayor held meetings of the Emergency Conference for Interracial Unity, created the Office of Price Administration to rein in price gouging by merchants, and even reopened the Savoy Ballroom in Harlem. The city had earlier closed the famous entertainment venue under questionable circumstances, which were widely believed to be unfair to the African American community. The actions of La Guardia helped him to gain additional respect and support from the sizeable number of constituents (and voters) in Harlem and other black neighborhoods in the city, but ongoing community problems would remain unresolved for the remainder of his tenure as mayor, and in succeeding years.

Fletcher F. Moon

Harlem Race Riot (1964)

Over 20 years after the 1943 riot, conditions in Harlem had continued to deteriorate as existing social and economic problems were compounded by the influx of illegal drugs in the community. Much of the black middle class had left the area by 1960, and rising addiction, infant mortality, and crime rates were further indicators of widespread health problems, poverty, and joblessness. In the context of the 1960s Civil Rights Movement, local activists such as **Malcolm X**, **Adam Clayton Powell**, Kenneth B. Clark, and others became national figures, but the work of these leaders and organizations such as the Nation of Islam, Harlem Youth Opportunities Unlimited (HARYOU), and the **Congress of Racial Equality** (CORE) could not completely rebuild Harlem after decades of decline. Once again, a single incident sparked a community uprising, but in this instance violence was not the immediate result.

On the evening of July 18, 1964, a peaceful demonstration involving CORE activists and community members took place to protest the fatal shooting of 15-year-old African American James Powell by a white police officer. The demonstration only turned violent after some protesters clashed with police, and the riot continued for the next two nights in Harlem, then spread to the predominantly black Bedford-Stuyvesant neighborhood in Brooklyn. Ironically, the **1964 Civil Rights Act** had just been signed into law by President Lyndon B. Johnson on July 2. While only one person was documented as being killed in the riot, hundreds were injured and arrested. Once the destruction and looting of property began, some merchants and shop owners posted signs indicating that they were "black" in attempts to prevent or minimize property damage and theft.

Another ironic circumstance related to the event (and a byproduct of civil rights activism) involved the number of African American reporters covering the event for mainstream news organizations such as the *New York Times* and *New York Post* newspapers, the Associated Press (AP) and United Press International (UPI) news services, *Time* and *Newsweek* magazines, and other national publications. Not only were they making history by their presence, in some instances they became "part of the story" when confronted by police themselves or while protecting non-rioting black bystanders and white press colleagues from random acts of violence. Even though the 1964 riot was smaller in comparison to previous Harlem uprisings, it foreshadowed other urban riots in Rochester, New York, and north Philadelphia during the summer of that year. The following year, major riots took place in the Watts community of Los Angeles, California, and two years later in Newark, New Jersey, and **Detroit**, Michigan, and in numerous cities nationwide after the 1968 assassination of **Martin Luther King Jr.** Television news coverage of these events brought the images, problems, and other realities of black urban life to national and international audiences, much as the broadcasts of southern civil rights demonstrations and violent responses from whites also highlighted American racial conflict and controversy.

Fletcher F. Moon

High Point, North Carolina, Sit-ins (1960)

Shortly after the **Greensboro sit-ins** began on February 1, 1960, High Point and neighboring cities in North Carolina and other states launched similar efforts. In the case of High Point, sit-ins began on February 11 after coordinated planning between local leader Reverend B. Elton Cox and other activists, such as **Floyd McKissick**, and the network of ministers in the **Southern Christian Leadership Conference** (SCLC). Cox also benefited from the presence of veteran civil rights activist Reverend **Fred Shuttlesworth** from Birmingham, Alabama. He had invited Shuttlesworth to High Point for a speaking engagement, not knowing that the students in Greensboro would take matters into their own hands and generate new energy for the Civil Rights Movement. Shuttlesworth in turn contacted Ella Baker at SCLC headquarters in Atlanta, and told her to inform **Martin Luther King Jr.** about the recent developments. Not only did Baker forward information to King, she also called contacts at other Historically Black Colleges and Universities (HBCUs) to urge widespread student activism. The protests at the downtown Woolworth's store led by Cox included 26 African American high school students the first day; it continued despite confrontations with whites opposed to changes in the store's lunch counter policy. One of the original high school student demonstrators, Mary Lou Blakeney, later co-founded the February 11 Association to commemorate the High Point sit-ins, and on February 11, 2008, she, Cox, and others unveiled a historical marker at the former site of the Woolworth store in the city.

Fletcher F. Moon

Houston, Texas, Race Riot (1917)

This violent outbreak involved African American soldiers in conflict with white police and other authorities. The riot took place on Thursday, August 23, 1917, only days after the violence in **East St. Louis**, Illinois, made national headlines and exposed American racial problems as the country was fighting World War I "to make the world safe for democracy." More than 3,000 black soldiers were stationed at Camp Logan, an Army base outside Houston. Most were from northern states and openly challenged the racial segregation practiced in the area. Several incidents caused commanding officers to attempt to head off potential trouble by imposing a curfew on the soldiers, allowing black women to visit the base, and permitting off-duty gambling and drinking, since the soldiers were not welcome in the "whites-only" bars and other establishments. After two black soldiers were beaten and arrested by white police officers in efforts to come to the defense of a black woman, word of the incident spread at the base. One of the soldiers had also been shot at, but the rumor spread that he had been shot and killed. In response a group of 600 black soldiers retaliated by arming themselves and going downtown to avenge the "murder." Before order was restored, one African American and 12 whites were dead, while 19 were wounded, including five black soldiers. Some involved in the incident were later subject to a military trial at Fort Bliss, outside El Paso, Texas.

Fletcher F. Moon

Lexington, Kentucky, Sit-ins (1950s–1960s)

The sit-ins of the 1950s and 1960s reached many cities and towns, including Lexington, Kentucky. It was the local and national press that carried the story of the sit-ins to the public and helped to preserve such activities in the annals of African American history. The press of Lexington, Kentucky, however, occasionally carried short stories about civil rights activities in town without providing important photographs to give a visual documentation of that history. Some scholars argue that *The Herald* (the morning paper) and *The Leader* (the afternoon paper) did irreparable damage to the

Civil Rights Movement at the time and damaged the historical record. As a result, readers missed one of the most important stories on civil rights of the twentieth century.

The weekly and peaceful sit-ins that black and white protesters held in Lexington, beginning in 1959 and extending into the early 1960s, targeted racially segregated lunch counters, hotels, and theaters. Top executives of *The Herald* and *The Leader,* papers that would later merge in the 1980s, gave strict orders to their reporters to bury coverage of the protests and were not encouraged to cover the protests at all. They were told to "play down the movement" and perhaps it would simply fade away. This was a stance that many southern newspapers took, thus censoring history. Some would question the racial attitudes of the late Fred Wachs, the publisher who set the policy on excluding the protests.

They were told to "play down the movement" and perhaps it would simply fade away.

Among the leaders in the protests was retired teacher Audrey Ross Grevious. Grevious reported in an article by James Dao that she attended an **NAACP** convention in New York City around 1960, and on her return train trip home became agitated because she and other blacks were required to move to a rear car once the train crossed the Mason-Dixon Line. Although she grew up in the segregated South, the reality of segregation finally hit home. She decided to organize demonstrations when she reached home. Grevious, over a period of several years, organized weekend sit-ins at lunch counters, movie theaters, and hotels. In retaliation, whites who opposed integration dumped garbage and

other waste on her lawn. Later, a patron in a local restaurant threw a beverage on one of her suits; she kept the suit as a "soiled souvenir." Negative reactions to her efforts continued; for several hours, the manager of one lunch counter swung a chain barrier into her legs and left her with chronic pain that lasted for years. Following the behavior of demonstrators elsewhere, Grevious refused to move.

The demonstrators were persistent with their efforts because they wanted to draw attention to the depths of segregation in Lexington. Unfortunately, the press published stories primarily to document the arrest of demonstrators, not the depths of their endurance. Among the published photographs available about the protests are those showing over 200 demonstrators marching in a solemn single file down Main Street to agitate against segregated stores and restaurants. Others show protesters on the steps of Fayette County courthouse; their heads are bowed in prayer, and a lone young lady is seated at a lunch counter that refuses to serve her. The Lexington sit-ins are important as much for the efforts of protesters as for the censorship that the local white press placed on African American history.

Jessie Carney Smith

Longview, Texas, Race Riot (1919)

This event was the second of 25 major U.S. racial conflicts during the "**Red Summer**" of 1919. The small northeast Texas community experienced racial tension earlier because black leaders Samuel L. Jones, a teacher, and Dr. Calvin P. Davis had urged black cotton farmers to bypass local white cotton dealers in selling their crops. Cotton did not cause the riot; rather, it was an article in the July 5 issue of the *Chicago Defender,* a weekly national black newspaper, defending the reputation of Lemuel Walters, a young black resident of Longview. Walters was arrested for reportedly having a white woman from Kilgore, Texas, fall in love with him. Walters was killed on June 17, when he was handed over to a white mob.

Jones, who was the local agent for the *Defender,* was held responsible for writing the July 5 article in defense of Walters, and he was attacked and beaten by three white men on the 10th, after the newspaper arrived in Longview. Whites were also angry because they had learned that Davis had formed the Negro Business Men's League, which aimed to stop whites from exploiting black cotton farmers. On July 11, a group of angry white men came to Jones's home, but they were fired upon and forced to retreat. One did not get away. He was beaten by a group of blacks who had come to defend Jones. The other whites gathered additional people, broke into a store to get guns and ammunition, returned to the black neighborhood, and set fire to the homes of Jones, Davis, and others. Local and state officials called in the Texas Rangers and the Texas National Guard, but Dr. Davis's father-in-law, Marion Bush, was killed on July 12. The area was placed under martial law between July 13 and 18. Whites and blacks were arrested, but no one was tried for their participation in the riot.

Fletcher F. Moon

March on Washington (1963)

Attended by an estimated quarter of a million people, this march was a peaceful demonstration to advance civil rights and economic equality. The August 28, 1963, March on Washington was one of the largest demonstrations ever witnessed in Washington, D.C., and it was the first to have extensive coverage by the electronic media. Successful in pressuring the administration of President **John F. Kennedy** to initiate a strong civil rights bill in the Congress, the marchers gathered at the Lincoln Memorial, 100 years after the signing of the Emancipation Proclamation. Not only did the March on Washington influence the passage of the **1964 Civil Rights Act** and the **Voting Rights Act of 1965**, it also galvanized public opinion. It was during this peaceful demonstration that **Martin Luther King Jr.** delivered his iconic famous "**I Have a Dream**" speech.

Far more complicated than the romanticized imagery remembered by most, the integrationist, non-violent, liberal brand of protest that the march represented was followed by a more revolutionary, combative, and race-conscious line of attack. However, because of the march's power of mass appeal, the 1963 March on Washington became the prototype for other social reforms, including the antiwar, feminist, and environmental movements. The 1963 March on Washington was not precedent-setting, though. Several marches or proposed marches occurred earlier. They included the proposed 1941 march called by **Asa Philip Randolph**, founder of the **Brotherhood of Sleeping Car Porters**, the May 1957 Prayer Pilgrimage for Freedom and the 1958 Youth March for Integrated Schools. The objectives of these marches still had not been implemented by 1963. African Americans continued to face high unemployment, systemic denial of the right to vote, and the omnipresent racial segregation code of the South. The government's failure to act on those goals prompted civil rights leaders to call for a march on Washington for economic, political, and social justice.

The civil rights leaders' developed goals were to pass an all-encompassing civil rights bill that negated Jim Crow public accommodation practices and to assure protection of the right to vote. They also wanted systems put in place to adequately address the breach of constitutional rights, a federal works program to train unemployed workers, and a Federal Fair Employment Practices Act banning discrimination in all employment. Commonly referred to in the press as the "Big Six," Randolph; Whitney Young, president of the **National Urban League**; Roy Wilkins, president of the **NAACP**; **James Farmer**, president of the **CORE**; King, the founder and president of the **SCLC**; and **John Lewis**, president of the SNCC were the major players in the March on Washington.

Bayard Rustin, organizer of the CORE's 1947 Journey of Reconciliation freedom ride, coordinated and administered the particulars of the

The 1963 March on Washington (Library of Congress).

march. Although women had played vital roles in the movement, they were thrust into the background of the August 28, 1963, march. No woman marched down Constitution Avenue with King, Randolph, Wilkins, and other male civil rights leaders; no woman went to the White House afterward to meet with President John F. Kennedy. However, because of **Anna Arnold Hedgeman**, the only woman on the march's planning committee, as a last-minute tribute the Negro Women Fighters for Freedom Award was given to Daisy Bates, **Diane Nash**, **Rosa Parks**, Gloria Richardson, Merlie Evers, and Mrs. Herbert Lee, the wife of the murdered farmer in Amite County, Mississippi.

A draft of John Lewis's prepared speech circulated before the march. Because of its militant tone against the Kennedy Administration, it was denounced by other march participants. In a meeting with King, Randolph, and the SNCC's James Forman, Lewis agreed to tone down his criticism of the federal government. Not all endorsed the march. Malcolm X and the Nation of Islam condemned it, and the executive board of the American Federation of Labor-Congress of Industrial Organizations (AFL-CIO) withheld its support, adopting a neutral position. President Kennedy originally discouraged the march, fearing that it might make Congress vote against civil rights laws in reaction to a perceived threat. Once it became clear that the march would go on, however, he became a supporter. The Civil Rights Act of 1964 and the Voting Rights Act of 1965> passed after Kennedy's assassination, and the provisions of each echoed the demands of the 1963 March on Washington. After the march, however, young African Americans increasingly turned to the **Black Power Movement**.

Linda T. Wynn

Memphis, Tennessee, Race Riot (1866)

One year after the **Civil War** ended, the city of Memphis suffered through the worst race riot in its history on May 1 and 2, 1866. Many whites, especially former Confederate soldiers, were angry about losing the war and resented the presence of large numbers of newly freed slaves and African American soldiers as part of the Union occupation of the city. The incident that sparked the riot was the killing of several white policemen by black soldiers after the attempted arrest of another black soldier. In response, Union General George Stoneman forced black soldiers to surrender their arms and confined them to quarters. This act left black settlements and neighborhoods unprotected from attacks by white mobs; 46 blacks and two whites lost their lives over the next two days. A congressional investigation documented that, in addition to the deaths, nearly a hundred were injured, hundreds of blacks were arrested, five women were raped, and numerous people fled the area. Almost a hundred homes, four churches, and eight schools were burned beyond repair, another hundred or so people were robbed, and $17,000 in Federal property was destroyed during the outbreak. The violence in Memphis impacted the movement toward Reconstruction, with radical Republicans passing a civil rights bill as well as the **Fourteenth and Fifteenth Amendments** to the Constitution, which guaranteed citizenship and equal protection under the law. Tennessee was forced to ratify the Fourteenth Amendment before being readmitted to the Union in July 1866.

Fletcher F. Moon

Million Man March and Day of Absence (1995)

The nation's first Million Man March and Day of Absence took place in Washington, D.C., on October 16, 1995. It occurred with parallel activities in cities and towns throughout the country; families were asked to stay at home from school and work during that "day of atonement" and to pray and fast. It provided an opportunity for black men to bear responsibility for their lives, families, and communities. They also were to show repentance for the ill treatment of black women. In the area of civil rights, the march aimed to bring whites and blacks together and spotlight national inactivity toward racial inequality.

Early in 1995 **Louis Farrakhan** of the Nation of Islam proposed the march. The Nation of Islam organizational efforts were supported by the National African American Leadership Summit. The planners garnered widespread support from religious, political, and business-oriented groups and leaders. Historically Black Colleges and Universities (HBCUs) offered their support

Thousands of black men from across the country gathered at the Capitol on October 16, 1995, in a show of unity and protest (AP Photo/Charles Tasnadi).

as well; they excused students from classes and chartered buses to take them to Washington for the event. Nonetheless, many white and black leaders opposed it from the start because of Farrakhan's involvement and denounced his anti-Semitic messages and inflammatory and nationalistic views. They called the march racially discriminatory. Some black women, in particular activist and teacher **Angela Davis**, opposed it too because women were involved in the planning but were excluded from the march.

In the mission statement for the march, organizers called the event significant for a number of reasons, including its challenge to black men and to the country in a time of increased racism, the call for black men to maintain hard-won gains, and the opportunity it offered to encourage operational unity. The organizers were concerned about the deteriorating social conditions in the black community and the trend in the country toward a turn to the right and the impact this would have on people of color, the poor, and the vulnerable. The statement also challenged followers to work beyond the spirit of the march, expand political gains, build and strengthen black united fronts, reaffirm and strengthen families, call for public admission and apology for the Holocaust of African Enslavement, work against violations of civil and human rights, support African-centered independent schools, reduce or eliminate negative media coverage, and build alliances with other people of color.

Notwithstanding opposition to Farrakhan and his supporters, marchers from all walks of life assembled at the Lincoln Memorial—the site of the historic **1963 March on Washington**—and near the Capitol Building. Among the speakers were **Dorothy Height** and the Reverend **Jesse Jackson**. Farrakhan gave the final address. Reports differ on the size of the march. Although the National Park Service claimed that 400,000 marchers were involved, leaders of the march, as well as participants, claim that a million people did, in fact, participate. Al Edwards, a member of the Texas State Legislature, said in *Crisis* magazine: "I took part in many marches during the Civil Rights Movement but the Million Man March had a feeling that was unexplainable. You could feel the warmth and the brotherly kindness.... The march helped to rejuvenate my commitment. It was just so energizing." Wendall Galloway of Largo, Maryland, said that "It felt good to be a Black man." Among the spin-offs and other demonstrations were a simulation of black voter registration and cross-theological gatherings. The event attracted national attention and was deemed a success. Its long-term success, however, is difficult to determine.

Jessie Carney Smith

Million Woman March (1997)

Over 300,000 African American women from all parts of the country met in Philadelphia and held the first Million Woman March on October 25, 1997. The purpose of the demonstration was to strengthen the bond between African American women from all elements of society and to bring about positive change. The women came to show solidarity and to address various issues confronting them, such as women in prison, independent schools for African Americans, hiring practices for African American women, crime, teen pregnancy, and the need to increase the number of black women in business and politics. Some were concerned that there were issues that many women's groups ignore, such as human rights abuses against blacks; they were also worried about what they felt was CIA involvement in the crack trade in black communities.

The event was modeled after the **Million Man March** held in 1995; women from all walks of life organized it. The daylong activities addressed the theme "Repentance, Resurrection, and Restoration" and began at the Liberty Bell with a prayer service; inspirational speeches and music followed. Some women had staked out their positions by 5:00 A.M. Speaking at the occasion were Congresswoman Maxine Waters;

Winnie Mandela, former wife of South African activist Nelson Mandela; and rapper Sister Soulja. During the breaks, the marchers chanted several phrases or messages, such as "MWM, MWM," for "Million Woman March." March cofounder and grass-roots activist and local entrepreneur Phile Chionesu told the crowd, "We are taking back our neighborhoods." Chionesu, a retired Chicago police officer, and Cheryl Thomas-Porter wanted the march to counteract the negative images of African American women so prominent in the media and popular culture. They called black women the epitome of strength in America and said that they "want to prepare our women, no matter what their status in life, to look at how we can begin to invest as black women and how we can begin to vote in blocs as black women."

Asia Coney, the first to recognize the need for a march, was cofounder of the event with Chionesu. She said in "Million Woman March Seen as Step Toward Unity" that, from the beginning of life for black women in this country, "We've taken care of white women, white men, white children … our own men, our own children. And now it's time that we take care of ourselves." The march ended at the Philadelphia Museum of Art. Estimates are that 2. 1 million people lined the march route along Benjamin Franklin Parkway by early afternoon, and law enforcement officers estimate that the crowd ranged in size from 300,000 to 1 million. The march officials estimated 2. 5 million people participated in the various activities and generated about $25 million in business for Philadelphia over a three-day period. The belief was that the march demonstrated the "capability and brilliance of African-centered self-determination and creativity."

On October 26 through 28, 2007, the Million Woman March Organization sponsored a reunion to celebrate the 10-year anniversary of the Million Woman March. Called "From March to Movement: The Resurrection," this celebration was also held in Philadelphia.

Jessie Carney Smith

Millions More Movement (2005)

A decade after the **Million Man March**, several leading African Americans, including **Louis Farrakhan** and then-U.S. Senator **Barack Obama**, planned another march on Washington called the Million More Movement that was to be a three-day affair. Planners aimed to mobilize black people to create a movement—not just a march—that would appeal to blacks to address the conditions of the poor. Issues included unity, spiritual values, education, economic development, political power, reparations, health, artistic/cultural development, and peace. The event was held in Washington, D.C., opening with a mass meeting at the National Mall on October 15, 2005; this was followed by a mass ecumenical service on October 16. Both the **NAACP** and the **Congressional Black Caucus** endorsed the event. The celebration called for a Day of Absence on October 14, meaning that black men should march instead of going to work. Those who did not march should stay at home and refuse to make purchases in order to demonstrate the significance of blacks on the economy. Farrakhan also called for women and youth to join in the movement. Economist Julianne Malveaux, who later became president of Bennett College for Women, was one who criticized the march of 1995 for its focus on black men, but she supported this new effort. In *Crisis* magazine, she said she saw the Millions More Movement in a different light and, after talking with Farrakhan, was assured that the new effort was an inclusive march and that "everyone was welcomed at the table." The movement called for unity in black leadership, too.

Jessie Carney Smith

Montgomery Bus Boycott (1955–1956)

The Montgomery Bus Boycott of 1955 marked the beginnings of mass protest among African Americans when **Rosa McCully Parks** refused to render her seat to a white man on the Cleveland Avenue bus driven by James F. Blake.

Arrested and sent to jail, Parks inspired African Americans, under the leadership of the Reverend **Martin Luther King Jr.**, to boycott Montgomery's public transportation system. A 13month boycott ensued after Parks's arrest and ended when the U.S. Supreme Court agreed that Montgomery's racial bus seating requirements were unconstitutional in the *Browder v. Gayle* case.

Before Parks's arrest, though, African American women, through the Women's Political Council (WPC), had focused their attention on the Jim Crow bus rules a year earlier. In 1954 **Jo Ann Robinson**, president of the WPC, met with W. A. Gayle, the mayor of Montgomery, and enumerated desired changes to the Mont-

gomery bus laws. The sought-after changes included: no one should have to stand next to empty seats; a decree that African Americans not be made to pay at the front of the bus and then enter from the rear; and a directive that required buses to stop at every corner in African American neighborhoods, just as they did in white neighborhoods. The March 1954 meeting yielded no changes, however, and Robinson followed up by sending Gayle a letter restating the WPC's requests and communicating the possibility of a citywide bus boycott.

A year later, buses remained segregated. On March 2, 1955, 15-year-old Claudette Colvin was arrested nine months before Parks, when

The bus where Rosa Parks staged her famous protest that sparked the Montgomery Bus Boycott is proudly preserved at the Henry Ford Museum in Dearborn, Michigan (AP Photo/Paul Warner).

she openly refused to surrender her seat to a white passenger. Seven months later, on October 21, 18-year-old Mary Louise Smith was arrested for the same violation. Neither of these cases galvanized the African American community like that of **Rosa Parks**. Following the December 1, 1955, arrest of Rosa Parks, Robinson printed flyers asking African Americans in Montgomery to stay off the city's buses on December 5, the day of Parks's trial. On that day, African American citizens of Montgomery complied with the request. Later in the day, the African American clergy and leaders decided to launch a long-term boycott. This meeting gave birth to the **Montgomery Improvement Association** (MIA) and brought the young Martin Luther King Jr. into the national spotlight.

Functionaries of the MIA met with city commissioners and bus company officials on December 8, 1955, and they issued a list of formal demands similar to those issued earlier by Robinson and the WPC. Both the city and the bus company refused to relinquish the Jim Crow seating rule on Montgomery buses. Black Montgomery continued the boycott. Following the paradigm set by the Reverend T. J. Jemison and the 1953 bus boycott in Baton Rouge, Louisiana, the MIA developed a carpool system to aid in the transportation needs of African Americans in Montgomery. Women played a critical role in sustaining the boycott, especially the anonymous cooks and maids who made long walks to and from home for a year to sustain the efforts of desegregation. After the U.S. Supreme Court refused to hear appeals in the *Browder v. Gayle* case, the MIA voted to end Montgomery's 381-day bus boycott. On December 21, 1956, blacks returned to riding a now-desegregated Montgomery public system of transportation.

Linda T. Wynn

NAACP Silent Protest Parade (1917)

The NAACP's Silent Protest Parade, also known as the Silent March, was held on 5th Avenue in New York City on Saturday, July 28, 1917, and was spurred by violence toward African Americans and race riots and outages in Waco, Texas; Memphis, Tennessee; and East St. Louis, Illinois. Typical of this unrest was the **East St. Louis Race Riot**, also called the East St. Louis Massacre, which drove almost 6,000 blacks from their burning homes, and left hundreds of blacks dead. **James Weldon Johnson**, then second vice president of the **NAACP**, became involved in that organization's reaction to the violence in East St. Louis. He was present when a number of organizations met at St. Philips Church in New York City to plan protest strategies. The group rejected the idea of a mass protest meeting in favor of a Silent Protest Parade.

The idea of a silent parade was first raised at the NAACP's Amenia, New York, Conference in August 1916 by Oswald Garrison Villard, when the association considered a protest for the rights of blacks. Now Johnson remembered Villard's call and suggested a silent parade to protest the current racial crisis in East St. Louis. As the NAACP's executive committee planned the march, they agreed that it would be an activity involving New York City's black citizens rather than the work of the association. Then a large committee comprised of pastors of leading churches and influential men and women was formed. The parade down 5th Avenue moved from 57th Street to Madison Square and brought out 9,000 to 10,000 blacks who marched silently to what Johnson called "the sound only of muffled drums." Children, some less than six years old and dressed in white, led the procession. Women—some of them aged—dressed in white followed, and men—some also aged—in dark suits brought up the rear. The marchers carried protest banners and posters proclaiming the purpose of the demonstration. The protesters also distributed circulars to the crowds that explained why they marched. "We march because we are thoroughly opposed to Jim Crow cars, … segregation, discrimination, disfranchisement, lynching, and the host of evils that are forced on us" is an example of what they displayed. Of the affair, Johnson wrote in his auto-

The NAACP stages a Silent Protest Parade in New York City on July 28, 1917 (Fisk University).

biography, "The streets of New York have witnessed many strange sites, but, I judge, never one stranger than this; certainly, never one more impressive. The parade moved in silence and was watched in silence. Among the watchers were those with tears in their eyes."

Jessie Carney Smith

Nashville Sit-ins (1959–1961)

In 1958, following the formation of the Nashville Christian Leadership Conference (NCLC) by the Reverend **Kelly Miller Smith Sr.** and others, African American leaders and students launched an attack on Jim Crow segrega-

tion. The NCLC utilized the concept of Christian nonviolence to stage the Nashville sit-in movement and combat racial segregation. The Reverend **James Lawson**, a devoted adherent of the Gandhi philosophy of direct non-violent protest, trained local residents in the techniques of nonviolence. In November and December of 1959, NCLC leaders and college students staged unsuccessful "test sit-ins" in an attempt to desegregate the lunch counters. Twelve days after the **Greensboro, North Carolina, Sit-in,** Nashville's African American students launched their first full-scale sit-ins on February 13, 1960.

Throughout the spring, Nashville students conducted numerous sit-ins and held steadfastly to the concept of Christian nonviolence.

Shortly before Easter, African Americans boycotted downtown stores, creating an estimated 20 percent loss in business revenues. As racial tension escalated, segregationists lashed out at civil rights activists. The April 19 bombing of **Z. Alexander Looby**'s home—he was the attorney for the students and a city councilman and leading figure in desegregation movements throughout Tennessee—caused thousands of blacks and some whites to silently march to City Hall, where Mayor Ben West conceded to **Diane Nash** of Fisk University that lunch counters should be desegregated.

On May 10, 1960, Nashville became the first major city to begin desegregating its public facilities. In November of that year, sit-ins resumed as racist practices still continued in most eating establishments and institutionalized racism remained intact. One of the best-organized and disciplined movements in the South, as noted by the Reverend **Martin Luther King Jr.**, the Nashville sit-in movement served as a model for future demonstrations against other violations of African American civil rights. Many of the student participants later became leaders in the national struggle for civil rights.

Linda T. Wynn

Nashville Student Movement

An outgrowth of the Nashville Christian Leadership Council (NCLC), which was founded by the Reverend **Kelly Miller Smith** on January 18, 1958, the Nashville Student Movement (NSM) produced a cadre of leaders in the modern Civil Rights Movement. These leaders included, but were not limited to **Marion Barry**, **James Bevel**, **John Lewis**, **Diane J. Nash**, **Bernard Lafayette Jr.**, the Reverends **James Lawson**, and **C.T. Vivian**, among others. **They actively participated and provided leadership in national civil rights organizations, including the** Congress of Racial Equality, Southern Christian Leadership Conference, **and** Student Non-Violent Coordinating Committee, **as well as leadership in several local efforts across the southeast**

to end racial discrimination. **In keeping with the SCLC, of which NCLC was an affiliate, the Nashville Student Movement adhered to** Martin Luther King Jr.'s **"beloved community" credo and to the precept of a city without a color line.**

The non-violent resister must be willing to accept suffering without retaliation and to exchange love for hate of the opponent.

The NCLC began holding workshops in March of 1958, the first of which was conducted by Lawson, Glen Smiley, and Anna Holden of the **Fellowship of Reconciliation** (FOR), at Bethel A.M.E. Church. Lawson, a student at Vanderbilt University's Divinity School, became a member of NCLC's board and projects committee chair. He and Smiley had frequently lectured and held workshops on black college campuses. Focusing on Christian nonviolence and love, workshop leaders presented the tenets of nonviolence as direct active resistance to violence. At the core of the nonviolence philosophy was the ethic of *agape* love: loving a neighbor for his own sake and not because of a person's friendliness. The non-violent resister must be willing to accept suffering without retaliation and to exchange love for hate of the opponent. Nonviolence, according to Lawson, denied the "segregationist power structure of its major weapon: the manipulation of law or law enforcement to keep the Negro in his place." Later, the workshops were moved to Clark Memorial Methodist Church, which was in proximity to Nashville's black colleges and universities.

Word of the workshops soon spread to **American Baptist College, Fisk University,**

Meharry Medical College, and **Tennessee A&I State University** (now Tennessee State University). Students from these educational institutions began attending the workshops. Among those who attended regularly were Peggy Alexander (Fisk), Marion Barry (Fisk), James Bevel (ABC), Angeline Butler (Fisk), Bernard Lafayette, Jr. (ABC), white exchange student Paul LaPrad (Fisk), John Lewis (ABC), and Diane Nash (Fisk). These students, under Lawson's tutelage, became workshop instructors for others who joined. In October 1959, the NSM formally came into existence with student participation from all four black institutions of higher learning. After having gone through months of training in the tactics and philosophy of direct **non-violent resistance**, the students were eager to transfer its values and beliefs into practical application.

In November and December of 1959, the NSM, with Nash as chair, and leaders from NCLC conducted experimental sit-ins at local department stores, three months before the **Greensboro, North Carolina sit-ins** of February 1, 1960, which captured national media attention. However, the Greensboro participants lacked the training, leadership, and organizational structure that the NSM possessed. Prepared to make Nashville a city without a color line, less than two weeks later the NSM began the process of dismantling the city's restrictive and exclusive racial culture. Although they endured physical abuse and incarceration, the students steadfastly remained committed to the principles of the beloved community and direct non-violent resistance. Considered by King to be one of the best organized and most disciplined student movements, the NSM, with its sit-ins, **boycotts**, mass demonstrations, and confrontation with then-Mayor Ben West after the bombing of attorney Z. Alexander Looby's home, helped Nashville become one of the first cities in the South to begin desegregating its lunch counters.

In the midst of the sit-in demonstrations and the economic boycott, the coterie of Nashville student leaders was among those students who

met in Raleigh, North Carolina, with **Ella Baker** of the SCLC, in April of 1960, to form the Student Non-Violent Coordinating Committee (SNCC). By the time the organizational meeting ended on April 17, the student delegation elected Marion Berry as their first chairman of the SNCC and Diane Nash as head of protest activities and chairman of the coordinating committee between students and adults. Over the next few years, as members of the SNCC, leaders of the NSM played a major role in keeping the CORE from aborting the **Freedom Rides** from Washington, D.C., after being met with violence in Anniston, Alabama. Leaders of the NSM also played a role in the 1963 **March on Washington** and Mississippi **Freedom Summer**.

Linda T. Wynn

National Welfare Rights Movement (1960s)

Numerous welfare rights organizations emerged in the 1960s and 1970s to challenge local, state, and national apathy toward programs to serve the needs of welfare recipients. Some of the groups had strong, assertive leaders who empowered welfare members to plan job training programs. Johnnie Tillmon, an African American and a resident of the Watts section of Los Angeles, was one such leader.

On the East Coast, the Brooklyn Welfare Action Council gained the attention of politicians as they sought endorsements from welfare groups. They also supported welfare rights activists. The National Welfare Rights Organization (NWRO), established in 1967, coordinated the efforts of these groups nationwide through a tightly organized structure. That organization emerged at the time when President Lyndon B. Johnson addressed the stark contradiction of poverty in affluent America. He developed a national antipoverty program to address the nation's seeming inability to combat poverty. To sustain itself, the NWRO was successful in obtaining funding from middle-class churches as well as the federal poverty program.

During the movement, welfare rights activists applied direct-action tactics by leading sit-ins at welfare departments and engaging in other protest activities. After that, welfare rolls swelled as many poor people learned more about their rights to benefits and insisted on relief. This forced many welfare agencies to change their demoralizing practices. Although a powerful anti-welfare backlash arose in the 1970s and caused the NWRO to lose financial support and file for bankruptcy, the organization had been successful in bringing together welfare rights and civil rights in a common struggle.

Jessie Carney Smith

New Orleans Race Riot (1874)

This event took place in the context of the post-**Civil War** Reconstruction era, when freed blacks and "radical Republicans" briefly held political power in the South. Defeated ex-Confederates reorganized into a group called the White League and dedicated themselves to restoring a "white man's government" through vigilante acts of violence directed at African Americans and white "carpetbaggers." On April 13, 1873, the White League launched an attack on the Louisiana militia, which was almost completely made up of black soldiers, and killed approximately 100 militiamen in Colfax, Louisiana. By the summer of 1874, the estimated membership of the White League was 14,000 strong. As they continued their reign of terror, President Ulysses S. Grant did not act to restrain the activities of the White League. On September 14, 1874, nearly 4,000 armed vigilantes assembled on Canal Street in New Orleans, intent on ousting Republican Governor William Kellogg. They were met by an equal number of

In addition to New Orleans race riots in 1874 and 1900, the earlier July 1866 riot caused great controversy, as this political cartoon by Thomas Nast, which is critical of President Andrew Johnson, shows (Library of Congress).

police and black militia, ironically under the command of ex-Confederate General James Longstreet. The one-hour fight became known as the "Battle of Liberty Place," with 38 killed and 79 wounded in the outbreak.

The White League prevailed, yet they restrained themselves from firing directly on Longstreet. They captured him, deposed Kellogg, installed John McEnery as governor, and maintained political control for three days. Grant finally ordered federal troops to New Orleans to force their withdrawal, the release of Longstreet, and the reinstatement of Kellogg as governor.

Fletcher F. Moon

New Orleans Race Riot (1900)

This event took place between July 24 and 28, 1900, and resulted from the actions of Robert Charles, an African American who took up arms in self-defense when confronted and attacked by white New Orleans policemen. Charles shot and killed two officers, wounded a third, and was wounded himself before fleeing the scene. He immediately became the object of a manhunt. Before he was killed in a shootout on July 28, varying reports indicate that Charles shot or killed up to 27 white people before losing his own life. In 1899 another black man, Sam Holt, had been lynched and dismembered in Newman, Georgia, and Charles was reported as "beside himself with fury" upon hearing of the incident. He had already proclaimed the right of blacks to defend themselves and carried a weapon for his own protection, based on previous encounters with whites in Mississippi before he moved to New Orleans. While Charles was an uneducated laborer, he was also an agent for the International Migration Society that encouraged blacks to emigrate to Liberia, West Africa. White mobs responded violently after hearing that a black man had dared to shoot white people, and so they began attacking African Americans and their property throughout the city. At least a dozen blacks were killed,

nearly 70 were injured, and the best city school for blacks was destroyed. Charles was alternately portrayed as a martyr and hero or violent murderer and desperado in the aftermath of the riot and violence.

Fletcher F. Moon

Newark, New Jersey, Race Riot (1967)

African Americans in the city had little political representation in the mid-1960s, despite being over half of the total population, and conditions were similar to those in other large urban areas. High crime and unemployment rates, political corruption, substandard housing, and police brutality led to increased community activism through organizations such as the **Congress for Racial Equality** (CORE), the Newark Coordination Council (NCC), and the Committee for a United Newark (CUN), the last formed in 1966 by writer and activist **Amiri Baraka**. In 1967 Baraka convened the first National Conference on **Black Power** in Newark, but still no meaningful progress had been made in addressing the city's problems. Tension and frustration exploded on July 12 after an incident of police brutality directed toward John Smith, an African American cab driver. Smith was arrested and severely beaten by police officers, but was taken to a hospital after civil rights leaders came to the police precinct. Rumors spread that Smith had died in police custody, leading to the outbreak.

The violence continued until July 17 and was described as "one of the bloodiest and most devastating racial insurrections in recent U.S. history." Between 23 and 26 people were reported killed during the riot, along with an estimated $10 million in property damage. Both the New Jersey State Police and the National Guard were called in to restore order, but problems and violence continued with another riot after the assassination of **Martin Luther King Jr.** in 1968.

Fletcher F. Moon

Non-Violent Resistance

The tactic of non-violent resistance was not a novel idea at the time of the modern Civil Rights Movement. American colonists employed it during the Revolution when they boycotted British imports and offered resistance to taxation without representation. A *modus operandi* of social change that employs strategies such as strikes, sit-ins, boycotts, and civil disobedience, non-violent resistance is a theory that was developed by Henry David Thoreau in his 1849 essay, *Civil Disobedience,* in which he argued that it was morally justifiable to peacefully resist unjust laws. Leaders such as **Asa Phillip Randolph**, **James Farmer**, **Bayard Rustin**, George Houser, and Abraham Muste advocated non-violent resistance in the black American struggle for freedom in the 1940s.

During the Civil Rights Movement of the mid-1950s through the 1960s, leaders such as the Reverends **Martin Luther King Jr.** and **James M. Lawson** also adopted this strategy in the crusade to combat racial discrimination. Perhaps the most noted adherents of non-violent resistance were Mohandas Karamchand Gandhi and Martin Luther King Jr. In 1906 at a protest meeting held in Johannesburg, South Africa, Gandhi adopted his methodology of *satyagraha* (devotion to truth), or non-violent protest, when he called upon his fellow Indians to defy a newly enacted law that compelled registration of the colony's Indian population by suffering the punishment rather than resisting by violent means. The adopted plan led to a seven-year struggle in which thousands of Indians were jailed, flogged, or shot for striking, refusing to register, burning their registration cards, or engaging in other forms of non-violent resistance. Notwithstanding his actions in South Africa, the story of non-violent resistance in colonial India is indistinguishable from the chronicle of Gandhi and the Non-Cooperation Movement. In addition to bringing Indian independence, he also assisted in improving the status of the Untouchables in Indian religion and society during the 1930s.

A civil rights activist in Brooklyn demonstrates the non-violent method of protest in 1964 (Library of Congress).

King captured America's attention with his philosophy of non-violent resistance. He believed that the only way to create a just society was to eradicate evil within that society. Putting this belief into action during the **Montgomery Bus Boycott**, King proved that non-violent resistance was an effective technique in fighting the unjust restrictions perpetrated upon American blacks. King understood that the oppressor did not render freedom willingly; freedom must be demanded by the oppressed in a non-violent fashion to overcome injustice with justice.

During the movement years, there were two different types of non-violent resistance practiced by leaders and participants: philosophical nonviolence and tactical nonviolence. Those who practiced philosophical nonviolence, like King, Lawson, **John Lewis**, **Bernard Lafayette**, and **Diane Nash**, were deeply grounded in the Gandhian credo and believed in taking action to counter injustice and converting the antagonist through redemptive suffering. For them, philosophical nonviolence was a lifestyle. Tactical nonviolence was a political strategy used in demonstrations to achieve specific goals. Adherents of tactical nonviolence believed that nonviolence was the best way to accomplish the goals of movement through political means. By 1963 many civil rights activists in the **Congress of Racial Equality**, the **Student Non-Violent Coordinating Committee**, and even the **Southern Christian Leadership Conference** were tactically non-violent rather than philosophically non-violent. Ultimately, in the late 1960s, those of the **Black Power Movement** overpowered the tactic of non-violent resistance.

Linda T. Wynn

King captured America's attention with his philosophy of non-violent resistance.

Northern Student Movement (1962)

Student sit-ins and other civil rights activism in the South generated interest and galvanized support from college campuses in northern states, leading to the formal organization of the Northern Student Movement (NSM) in 1962. Consisting primarily of young liberal whites who were sympathetic to the Civil Rights Movement, these students joined demonstrations and voter registration projects in southern states as well as assisted in community organizing efforts in northern urban cities. Along with Students for a Democratic Society (SDS), the NSM was labeled part of the "New Left," but NSM executive director William Strickland stated that the organization was not a continuation of socialist or communist philoso-

phy. They wanted to create new ideas and institutions, preferring to be called "New Democrats" or "New Realists." The NSM backed up its rhetoric with action, moving from campus fund raising for the southern Civil Rights Movement and tutorial programs for African American children in the North to involvement in direct action. The organization facilitated rent strikes in Harlem, Philadelphia, Boston, and Detroit. NSM activists from Swarthmore, Haverford, and Bryn Mawr colleges joined black students from Maryland State, Morgan State, **Howard**, and Lincoln University, the Civic Interest Group, and the Cambridge Non-Violent Action Committee (CNAC) in the Maryland Eastern-shore Project to address civil and voting rights issues during the summer of 1962. These successful efforts became the forerunner of more famous summer projects in succeeding years, such as the Mississippi "**Freedom Summer**" of 1964.

Fletcher F. Moon

Orangeburg, South Carolina, Massacre (1968)

This tragedy took place on February 8, 1968, less than two months before the assassination of **Martin Luther King Jr.** on April 4, but did not receive the same level of media coverage. The event involved a deadly confrontation between African Americans and law enforcement authorities on the campus of **South Carolina State College** (now University). State highway patrolmen fired into a crowd of African American students who had been protesting racial discrimination policies in Orangeburg, with three young black men losing their lives in the violence. Orangeburg's only bowling alley still refused to admit blacks, in defiance of the **1964 Civil Rights Act**, while other local businesses and facilities had changed their policies. Students from South Carolina State, Claflin College, and Allen University, all Historically Black Colleges and Universities (HBCUs) located in Orangeburg, began direct protests at the site on the evening of February 5. They were led by

John Stroman, a senior at South Carolina State and avid bowler who was tired of driving 40 miles to Columbia to another bowling alley that was open to African Americans. The owner, Harry Floyd, called local police who forcibly removed the students from the property. He previously changed the "For White Only" sign to "Privately Owned," and city authorities supported his contention that he had the right to choose customers for a "private establishment."

The students returned on February 6, but were met by local and state police. Some were arrested and then released into the custody of South Carolina State's Dean of Students Oscar Butler. Violence broke out while other students were returning to the campus, with a number of students and several officers injured or hospitalized. White-owned businesses in downtown Orangeburg were also vandalized. Activist Cleveland Sellers, a South Carolina native involved with the **Student Non-Violent Coordinating Committee** (SNCC) and organizer of the local Black Awareness Coordinating Committee (BACC), was accused of being an instigator of the outbreak. M. Maceo Nance, acting president of South Carolina State, visited students at hospitals and made the statement during a public meeting with city officials the next day that no property damage occurred until after "the young ladies were hit" by police officers. On the following Friday morning he issued a statement encouraging students to stay on the campus and in dormitories when not in class. South Carolina Governor Robert McNair appeared on television, stating that "outside agitators" (mentioning Cleveland Sellers in particular) had caused the problems in Orangeburg, and sent additional highway patrolmen and National Guard units to the city. Students became more angry and frustrated by the actions of the governor and other white officials; they gathered near the edge of the campus that evening. Shortly after 10:30 P.M., police officer David Shealy was injured, escalating the situation. Shots were fired, Samuel Hammond, Delano Middleton, and Henry Smith were killed, and 27 other male and female students

were seriously wounded. The historical marker at the site notes that this tragedy was "the first of its kind on any American college campus."

Fletcher F. Moon

The historical marker at the site notes that this tragedy was "the first of its kind on any American college campus."

Poor People's March on Washington (1968)

The **Southern Christian Leadership Conference** (SCLC), under the leadership of the Reverend Dr. **Martin Luther King Jr.**, shifted its strategies in 1967 and embarked on a campaign for poor people. It expanded its operational base in the South to a national focus. Economic inequities became the movement's target. The Poor People's Campaign was in response to the rioting that occurred in more than 180 cities during the summer of 1968. Based upon a survey conducted by the **NAACP** in Mississippi, it was noted that African Americans suffered from hunger, malnutrition, and starvation. In Chicago, the SCLC found an urban crisis of poverty embedded in racist economic structures. Even the Kerner Commission Report, released on February 29, 1968, called for jobs, housing, and economic development programs.

Because institutionalized racism did not capitulate to the strategies of resistance used against racial apartheid in the South, King and the SCLC began planning a new attack to focus the nation's attention on poverty in America. On June 19, 1968, more than 50,000 people assembled at the nation's capital to voice their support for the Poor People's Campaign for economic justice. King announced the Poor People's Campaign at an SCLC staff retreat in November 1967. Suggested to King by Marion Wright (now Marion Wright Edelman), director of the NAACP's Legal Defense and Education Fund in Jackson, Mississippi, that the Poor People's Campaign be staged in Washington, it was seen by King as the next chapter in the struggle for equality. Through non-violent direct action, King and the SCLC wanted to zoom the nation's lens on economic injustice and poverty.

The Poor People's Campaign was to be a movement for a wide range of people, including Native Americans, Mexican Americans, Puerto Ricans, and Appalachian whites.

During an early planning meeting in March 1968, King informed the gathering that this was an opportunity for poor people of all colors and backgrounds to gain their entitlement to a decent life. Contrasting his earlier campaigns for African American equality, the Poor People's Campaign was to be a movement for a wide range of people, including Native Americans, Mexican Americans, Puerto Ricans, and Appalachian whites. Many leaders of these communities pledged themselves to the Poor People's Campaign. King believed that economic deprivation caused the outbreak of urban riots throughout America and that capitalism was to blame for poverty. Some in the SCLC considered King's campaign too ambitious and his demands too nebulous. Others, such as civil rights activists **Bayard Rustin** and Roy Wilkins, questioned the advisability of a

poor people's march on Washington that might lead to violence. Government officials and organizations, ranging from the FBI to President Lyndon B. Johnson, instigated an out-and-out fight to disrupt the organizers.

In the midst of organizing, King went to Memphis, Tennessee, to support the city's striking sanitation workers. When the March 28, 1968, march, led by King, turned violent, 16-year-old Larry Payne, the only fatality of the day's mayhem, was killed by policeman L. D. Jones. Sixty others were injured. It seemed as though his nay-sayers were right. Determined to lead a peaceful demonstration, King returned to Memphis on April 2 and was assassinated on April 4, 1968. Because of King's assassination, support for the Poor People's Campaign gained momentum. The Reverend **Ralph Abernathy**, the new president of the SCLC, kept the movement going. On Mother's Day, May 12, 1968, thousands of women, led by King's widow, **Coretta Scott King**, formed the first wave of demonstrators. The next day, the first residents of **Resurrection City**, a temporary settlement, populated the National Mall in tents made from canvas and plywood. Each day the residents of Resurrection City marched to various agencies of the federal government and presented their economic bill of rights. Midway through the campaign, Senator **Robert Kennedy**, whose wife attended the Mother's Day opening of Resurrection City, was assassinated on June 5, 1968. Five days after the Solidarity Day mass demonstration on June 19, 1968, the U.S. Department of the Interior closed down Resurrection City after its permit to use the park expired. While the Poor People's March on Washington was only minimally successful, it did briefly focus the nation's attention on the plight of the poor.

Linda T. Wynn

Portsmouth, Virginia, Sit-ins (1960)

Civil rights actions in Portsmouth, Virginia, during 1960 were not well organized at the beginning, being unplanned and spontaneous student efforts in sympathy with the **Greens-boro sit-ins**. This led to the first violent confrontation between black demonstrators and white supporters of segregation, but later protests were more disciplined and successful in desegregating public facilities in the city. On February 12, 1960, several African American female high school students marked Abraham Lincoln's birthday by staging a sit-in at Rose's Variety Store in downtown Portsmouth. With no formal leadership, organization, or planning, they sat at the store's lunch counter and were refused service until the store closed at 5:30 P.M.

They continued the protest for the next few days, as other black students joined their efforts. Even without training, they applied the basic principle of non-violent protest by not responding to insults from white hecklers. Local media coverage began, documenting the violent outbreak on February 16, when young white hoodlums attacked the demonstrators, and some blacks retaliated after a flying object hit a black girl. On February 17, a crowd of over 3,000 blacks and whites gathered as the group attempted to continue the sit-in, and the blacks were attacked by police dogs. Gordon Carey, a white field secretary from the **Congress of Racial Equality** (CORE), arrived in Portsmouth on February 18 to train and organize the students into the Student Movement for Racial Equality, which achieved success in local civil rights efforts.

Fletcher F. Moon

Prayer Pilgrimage for Freedom (1957)

As the third anniversary of the 1954 U.S. Supreme Court decision in *Brown v. Board of Education* approached, little progress toward desegregation of public schools was evident. **Martin Luther King Jr.** and his colleagues in the recently formed **Southern Christian Leadership Conference** (SCLC) attempted to get President Dwight Eisenhower to make a public statement in support of the court decision and to confront segregationists for their resistance to federal law. When Eisenhower refused to act, King and asso-

ciates Thomas Kilgore Jr. and **Bayard Rustin** began to organize efforts for a prayer pilgrimage to the nation's capital on May 17. Veteran civil rights leader **A. Philip Randolph** saw parallels to his idea in 1941 for a March on Washington, and a planning meeting involving King, Randolph, **NAACP** president Roy Wilkins, Harlem Congressman **Adam Clayton Powell Jr.**, NAACP lobbyist Clarence Mitchell, and other leaders took place on April 5, 1957, at the Metropolitan Baptist Church in Washington.

They continued the protest for the next few days, as other black students joined their efforts.

Despites differences of opinion regarding strategies and objectives, Randolph, King, and Wilkins signed and issued a joint statement, the "Call to a Prayer Pilgrimage for Freedom," indicating that eight Southern states had made no good faith effort to move forward on school desegregation "with all deliberate speed" or with any speed at all. The statement also cited historic precedents, such as the Dred Scott decision exactly 100 years earlier and the 1863 Emancipation Proclamation issued by Abraham Lincoln, to dramatize the long wait of African Americans for freedom. Threats and violence directed toward black citizens and the NAACP were also cited, along with the intention to conduct a peaceful and orderly demonstration. Powel and Mitchell, among others, insisted that the event not become an open protest, which would embarrass the Eisenhower administration and hinder future government cooperation in civil rights and other political issues. On May 17, the anticipated number of participants and supporters was less than hoped for, but the estimated total of 25,000 to 30,000 who did attend presaged the much larger **March on Washington** that would take place in 1963. Legendary gospel singer Mahalia Jackson provided music, and a notable list of black leaders made speeches, including Randolph, Wilkins, Powell, **Howard University** president **Mordecai Johnson**, civil rights activist and minister **Fred Shuttlesworth** of Birmingham, Alabama, and Michigan Congressman Charles Diggs.

Race riots exploded in more than 25 cities across the nation.

It was King's speech, "Give Us the Ballot," however, that became the highlight of the event and elevated him to greater prominence, as it was his first address before a national audience. He had been virtually unknown outside of Georgia and Alabama, until his leadership during the **Montgomery, Alabama, Bus Boycott** drew national and international attention. Wilkins was not pleased when the press began touting King as the "top black leader" afterwards, especially with the NAACP underwriting a good portion of expenses for the gathering. The Prayer Pilgrimage provided valuable experience for leaders and organizers in the various civil rights organizations, in terms of working through differences, coordinating efforts and resources, and in preparing for future civil rights activities.

Fletcher F. Moon

Red Summer (1919)

The summer of 1919 was given the moniker Red Summer by **James Weldon Johnson** because it ushered in one of the greatest periods of interracial discord in U.S. history. Referring to the summer and fall of 1919, race riots

exploded in more than 25 cities across the nation, regardless of region. Some were large and others were small. All the racial riots were indicative of a complete meltdown in American race relations. Incited by racism, unemployment, and inflation, indigenous terrorist organizations such as the Ku Klux Klan urged the riots on by terrorizing African Americans into submission. Competition for employment also helped to inflame relations between the races. White Americans did not want to compete for jobs with African Americans. Additionally, the Red Scare fueled racial unrest, and African Americans who saw equality as a constitutional right were branded as radicals.

Among the riots that took place in 1919, the three most violent incidents occurred in Chicago (July 27), Washington, D.C. (July 19), and Elaine, Arkansas (October 1). Other cities of note where riots occurred in 1919 are: Charleston, South Carolina (May 10); Longview, Texas (July 13); Knoxville, Tennessee (August 30); and Omaha, Nebraska (September 28). Although rioting persisted for the next few years, not many of the racial eruptions equaled in proportion to those of 1919. In June 1921, interracial conflict broke out between Africans and whites in Tulsa, Oklahoma. Two years later, in January, a white mob from a neighboring community annihilated the predominately African American town of Rosewood, Florida, burning it to the ground. Those who escaped the Rosewood massacre did not break their silence until the early 1980s. In 1994 Florida's legislative body provided reparations of $150,000 to each of the survivors. Detroit joined the pandemic of racial unrest in 1925, when an African American physician purchased a home in a white neighborhood.

In the post-World War I environment, African Americans prepared to fight and die in their own defense introduced a new dynamic into America's most deep-seated societal dilemmas. No longer was it the case of one race intimidating another race into submission. In 1919 one of the Harlem Renaissance's outstanding poets, Jamaican Claude McKay, captured the feelings of many African Americans in his poem "If We Must Die," writing: "If we must die, let it be not like hogs hunted and penned in an inglorious spot.... If we must die; oh let us nobly die ... dying but fighting back." Unlike previous race riots that took place in American history, these riots were among the first to project an organized African American rejoinder. The **NAACP** conducted an investigation of the crimes committed against African Americans. In 1919 the NAACP published its findings in *Thirty Years of Lynching in the United States, 1889–1918*. The report indicated 3,224 people were lynched in the 30-year period. Of these, 702 were white and 2,522 were African American.

The Red Summer of 1919 galvanized the NAACP and its supporters to lobby for the passage of a federal law against lynching. Late in 1919, the NAACP took the first steps toward securing the passage of a federal law against lynching. Although the Dyer Anti-Lynching bill ultimately failed in Congress, its supporters succeeded in bringing attention to and generating greater condemnation of lynching. On June 13, 2005, Congress officially apologized for failing to pass anti-lynching legislation early in the twentieth century, when it passed a non-binding resolution introduced by two senators from the South: Democratic Louisiana Senator Mary Landrieu and Republican Senator George Allen of Virginia.

Linda T. Wynn

Reparations

The concept of reparations, which is compensation for injuries against a nation or people, was not a twentieth-century phenomenon among African Americans. Near the end of the nineteenth century, Callie House, a former slave from Tennessee, emerged as a leader in the movement to petition the U.S. government for pensions and reparations for African Americans formally held in involuntary servitude. Traversing the South, she organized the National Ex-Slave Mutual Relief, Bounty and Pension Association to build a reparation movement among

SNCC executive secretary James Forman issued the "Black Manifesto" insisting on reparations for African Americans (Fisk University).

former slaves. This movement met its demise after the U.S. attorney general charged House with using the mail to defraud people. Arrested in 1916 and later convicted, she was given a one-year prison term in 1917.

The death of House's movement did not terminate the call for redress for the inequities wrought by American slavery and Jim Crow laws, however. Reparations to blacks was a subject of debate in the early 1960s, when James Forman, executive secretary of the **Student Non-Violent Coordinating Committee**, issued his "Black Manifesto" to white churches, Jewish synagogues, and racist institutions. Near the end of the 1960s, remediation to Japanese Americans revived African Americans' demands to receive reparations for enslavement. In 1989 U.S. Representative John Conyers, an African American Michigan Democrat, introduced HR 40 to the House of Representatives; the bill would establish the Commission to Study Reparations Proposals for African Americans. It failed to pass then and in every session of Congress since it was first introduced. However, in 1994 the state of Florida allocated $2 million to nine black survivors of the 1923 Rosewood race riot. In addition, the Oklahoma Commission to Study the Tulsa Race Riot of 1921 recommended that survivors and their descendants be paid reparations. In 2000 Randall Robinson argued in *The Debt: What America Owes to Blacks* that the United States owes major reparations to the descendants of slaves. Two years later, attorneys filed a federal lawsuit on behalf of **Deadria Farmer Paellmann** against Fleet Boston Financial, the CSX Railroad firm, and Aetna Insurance Company, seeking reparations for the descendants of slaves in America. The suit charged the companies with conspiracy, human rights violations, unjust enrichment from their corporate predecessors' roles in the slave trade, and conversion of the value of the slaves' labor into profit. The concept of reparations, which had its beginnings in the nineteenth century to indemnify the descendants of American slaves, continues into the twenty-first century.

Linda T. Wynn

President Johnson ignored [Resurrection City] and Congress closed its governmental coffers.

Resurrection City (1968)

Resurrection City was a temporary shantytown constructed at the National Mall in Washington, D.C. It housed the citizens of the **Poor People's March on Washington**, which sought to place the problems of the poor at the seat of the federal government. The campaign was the **Southern Christian Leadership Conference's** (SCLC) last major initiative as it attempted to broaden the Civil Rights Movement to include an economic plank for all poor people regardless of race. Despite the death of the Reverend **Martin Luther King Jr.**, the SCLC under the leadership of its new president, the Reverend **Ralph D. Abernathy**, proceeded with the Poor People's Campaign. Approximately five weeks after King's assassination, Resurrection City was constructed for a multitude of protesters. The protest march for the poor departed from the Lorraine Motel, the site of Martin Luther King's assassination, on May 2, 1968. Led by **Coretta Scott King**, King's widow, teams of mules demonstrating the desperate plight of the rural poor pulled wagons full of people through Mississippi, Georgia, and Alabama, as they proceeded to the nation's capital. Tens of thousands gathered at Resurrection City. On May 12, 1968, Coretta Scott King led the **National Welfare Rights Organization's** Mother's Day mobilization. Staging a series of sit-ins and demonstrations at various government agencies, the protesters brought their concerns to the nation's attention. Protesters conducted a spirited demonstration on June 19, which was organized by Sterling Tucker and led by Abernathy and Coretta Scott King. However, torrential rains, conflicts between residents, and the June 6 assassination of Senator **Robert F. Kennedy** took their toll on Resurrection City. On June 24, 1968, Resurrection City came to an ignominious finale when Capitol Police cleared the site. While the Poor People's Campaign secured a few concessions from federal agencies, it cannot be considered successful. President Johnson ignored it and Congress closed its governmental coffers to the poor people's economic demands as the Vietnam War sapped the federal tax base.

Linda T. Wynn

Rochester, New York, Race Riot (1964)

This racial disturbance took place between July 24 and 26, 1964, sending shock waves through a city known for successful corporations and institutions such as Eastman Kodak, Xerox, and the Rochester Institute of Technology. The riot underscored social and economic differences between black and white communities and immediately followed a similar outbreak in Harlem on July 18 the same year. The event that led to the riot was the arrest of a 19-year-old African American man at a Friday night street dance in the city's Seventh Ward, in the area of Nassau Street and Joseph Avenue. Rumors spread that a child was attacked by a police dog and that a pregnant woman was hit by a police officer, and the crowd erupted into violence. Rochester Police Chief William Lombard attempted to get the crowd to disperse, but rioters overturned his car and threw objects at other police vehicles. By 3:30 A.M., on July 25, the crowd was estimated at 4,000, and a state of emergency was declared at 4:20 A.M. Despite a curfew and attempts by local African American leaders to discourage further violence, rioting in the city's Third Ward continued until the National Guard arrived in the city on Sunday, July 26. By the time order was restored on Sunday evening, four people were dead, nearly 400 were reported injured, from 800 to 1,000 had been arrested, and property damage was estimated at over $1 million.

Fletcher F. Moon

Rodney King Riot (1991)

On March 3, 1991, following a high-speed chase, African American motorist Rodney King was subdued with extreme force and arrested by officers of the Los Angeles Police Department (LAPD). The broadcast of a videotape by George Holliday of the King beating galvanized international attention on police brutality in Los Angeles. In a subsequent court trial, however, a predominantly white jury found the four officers not guilty of charges filed against them. The verdict ignited one of the worst race riots in the history of the United States. Later, the federal government indicted the officers on

charges that they had violated King's civil rights. Two of the officers were convicted and incarcerated. In response to this chain of events, Mayor Tom Bradley created an independent commission to investigate the LAPD. In July 1991, the Christopher Commission released its findings. Documenting the systematic use of excessive force and racial harassment in the department, the report called for structural reforms and the resignation of Los Angeles Police Chief Daryl Gates. The Christopher Commission found that minority communities in Los Angeles held the view that they were often treated differently from whites and that law enforcement officials engaged in the use of excessive force. Appalling and well-suited to the medium of television, the Rodney King beating only accentuated the image of police brutality. However, the beating in March 1991 and the attendant videotape produced sufficient violence and mayhem to alarm the national community. More than two decades after **Martin Luther King Jr.**'s assassination and the ensuing riots across the nation, the acquittal of Rodney King's assailants after videotape showed police beating him as he lay handcuffed on the ground caused reverberations of protest throughout America.

Linda T. Wynn

Sanitation Workers' Strike (1968)

The 1968 strike of sanitation workers in Memphis will forever be remembered in the context of the assassination of **Martin Luther King Jr.**, who had come to the city in support of these workers. After the King assassination on April 4, his widow, **Coretta Scott King**, courageously led another protest march in Memphis on April 8, one day before the funeral for her husband in Atlanta. National and union negotiators from the U.S. Department of Labor and the American Federation of State, County, and Municipal Employees (AFSCME) finally reached agreement with Memphis officials to end the strike one week later. African American sanitation workers in Memphis had endured racial discrimination in pay, staffing patterns, and other negative employment conditions for a number of years. Problems escalated after two black workers, Echol Cole and Robert Walker, were crushed to death when a garbage truck malfunctioned on February 1. Newly elected Mayor Henry Loeb had refused to replace worn-out equipment or pay overtime, and workers were forced to supplement their substandard wages with welfare and food stamps. The deaths of the two men galvanized other workers to press for fair treatment, but city officials still refused to make changes, so over 1,000 sanitation workers went on strike as of February 12.

Problems escalated after two black workers, Echol Cole and Robert Walker, were crushed to death when a garbage truck malfunctioned.

AFSCME officials met with Loeb, who refused to recognize the union and issued a back-to-work order effective February 15. After Memphis ministers also met unsuccessfully with the mayor, the **NAACP** endorsed the strike. Demonstrations continued into March, and the Reverend **James Lawson**, veteran activist and associate of King, helped create the Community on the Move for Equality (COME) to continue protests in support of the sanitation workers. King arrived on March 18, where he addressed over 25,000 strike supporters; he planned to return on March 22 to lead a city-wide protest. A snowstorm caused organizers to reschedule the event for March 28. The march began peacefully but ended after some demonstrators became violent. Memphis police attacked retreating demonstrators with clubs

and tear gas, and a black teenager was shot and killed by a police officer. Loeb declared martial law and brought in the National Guard, but striking workers continued their protest with signs reading, "I Am a Man."

King made his second and final trip to the city on April 3. At the evening rally in the Mason Temple Church of God in Christ, King delivered his final speech, "I've Been to the Mountaintop." The assassination of King at the Lorraine Motel on April 4 sparked violence nationwide. Lawson and other leaders attempted to calm the local African American community, but Loeb imposed a 7 P.M. curfew and added state police units to the National Guard soldiers already in the city. After the April 8 march led by Coretta Scott King and the intervention of U.S. Undersecretary of Labor James Reynolds, who had been sent to Memphis by President Lyndon B. Johnson, a resolution of the strike was finally reached on April 16, 1968.

Fletcher F. Moon

Selma to Montgomery, Alabama, March (1965)

In an attempt to bring the flagrant system of racial discrimination to the attention of the American nation, in 1965 leaders from the **Southern Christian Leadership Conference** (SCLC) and the **Student Non-Violent Coordinating Committee** (SNCC) targeted Selma, Alabama, to focus on the disenfranchisement of black voters. This was not the first time that black activists worked to gain access to the voting booth for blacks in Dallas County, Alabama. Between the 1920s and the 1940s, members of the Dallas County Voters League, in spite of resolute white resistance, struggled to register black voters.

In early 1965, the quest to gain the right of the ballot for blacks intensified on February 18, when during a peaceful march in Marion, Alabama, state troopers attacked peaceful demonstrators and shot Jimmie Lee Jackson, who was protecting his mother from the billy

Demonstrators in Harlem, New York, show their support of the Selma to Montgomery March in 1965 (Library of Congress).

club blows of the troopers. Jackson's death eight days later galvanized the protesters' resolve to bring national awareness to the need for a federal voter registration law. On March 7, 1965, approximately 600 marchers, led by **John Lewis** of the SNCC and **Hosea Williams** of the SCLC, walked from Browns Chapel to the Edmund Pettus Bridge, demonstrating for voter rights and remembering Jackson's ultimate sacrifice. Once they reached the bridge, the violence of "**Bloody Sunday**" erupted in full view of photographers and journalists, as armed state troopers and deputies led by Major John Cloud and Sheriff Jim Clark brutally battered the protesters. The televised events of Bloody Sunday triggered national outrage and the White House was inundated with calls and telegrams. Later, **Martin Luther King Jr.** and other civil rights

leaders decided to hold other marches. The second attempt was held on March 9, when King led the marchers despite Federal Court Judge Frank M. Johnson's restraining order against the journey to Montgomery. Just like the March 7 protest, state troopers again met the assembly of demonstrators head on. Rather than confront the awaiting state troops, King led the assemblage of protesters in prayer and led them back to Selma. However, the day did not pass without violence, as a group of white vigilantes beat the Reverend James Reeb, a white Unitarian minister, who died two days later.

Under the protection of the court and a federalized National Guard, a third march from Selma to Montgomery was held on March 21. Four days later, approximately 25,000 protesters arrived at the state capitol in Montgomery, and King delivered a victory speech. Again, however, death invaded the ranks of the civil rights workers when the Ku Klux Klan killed **Viola Liuzzo**, a white woman from Detroit, Michigan, in Lowndes County, Alabama. Nevertheless, the efforts of the civil rights organizations achieved their desired goal. On August 6, 1965, President Lyndon B. Johnson signed the **Voting Rights Act of 1965** into law. This act not only protects the rights of voter registration workers, it also proscribes discriminatory election measures that include land ownership as a prerequisite for voting, poll taxes, and literacy tests constructed to disenfranchise American black voters. Just as the mass demonstrations in Montgomery led to the **Civil Rights Acts of 1957** and 1960, and Birmingham served as the impetus for the passage of the **Civil Rights Act of 1964**, the mass protest march from Selma to Montgomery, Alabama, led to the passage of the Voting Rights Act of 1965. In 1996 the U.S. Congress, under the National Trail Systems Act of 1968, created the Selma-to-Montgomery Trail.

Linda T. Wynn

Springfield, Illinois, Riot (1908)

This outbreak of racial violence took place in August 1908, just as the city was preparing to celebrate the centennial of Abraham Lincoln's birth. The state capital was known for vice, political corruption, and negative racial attitudes toward its growing number of African Americans. In July a black man, Joe James, cut a white man, Clergy A. Ballard, who caught James in his daughter's bedroom. Ballard died from his wound, and James was beaten severely by a mob before going to jail. Things settled down until August 14, when local papers headlined his case and another crime with racial overtones. A black man, George Richardson, who was also arrested and jailed, had reportedly raped another white woman. Richardson, a working man with no previous record, was portrayed as being an ex-convict like James and a murderer. Irate whites gathered at the jail, and the crowd swelled to over 4,000 by late afternoon.

Local authorities diverted the crowd with fire engines and took the two black men away through the rear entrance. Word spread that white restaurant owner Harry Loper drove the men out of town, and the mob destroyed his business. Black neighborhoods were the next target, with two blacks lynched, others shot at or beaten, and black homes and businesses burned and destroyed. Four whites died from stray bullets before order was restored on Saturday, August 15, and the riot prompted a mass exodus of blacks from the city.

Fletcher F. Moon

Tallahassee Movement

Tallahassee's modern movement for civil rights began in May 1956, when Carrie Patterson and Wilhemina Jakes, students from Florida Agricultural and Mechanical University (FAMU), were arrested for sitting in the white section of a Tallahassee public transit bus. Their arrest and the subsequent cross burning at their rooming house sparked a citywide boycott of Tallahassee's public transit system. Because of the arrest and cross burning, at a mass meeting FAMU's students voted to boycott city buses. Patterson and Jakes's actions galvanized the black community and launched a desegregation campaign similar to the **Montgomery Bus Boycott**, which began in December 1955. Under the leadership of the Reverend **Charles K. Steele**, the Inter-Civic Council (ICC) coordinated the logistics of the mass demonstration. As the bus boycott continued, numerous people were arrested for giving car rides to the boycotters, which filled the jails to overcapacity.

On November 13, 1956, the U.S. Supreme Court affirmed the lower court ruling in the *Browder v. Gayle* case. Litigated by civil rights attorney **Fred Gray**, it held that bus segregation was unconstitutional. Later, the ICC suspended the boycott, and the transit system stopped enforcing racially segregated seating. However, refusing to acquiesce to the nation's highest tri-

Federal troops set up mess tents at the site of the 1908 Springfield, Illinois riots (Library of Congress).

bunal, nine white bus drivers and the company manager were arrested for allowing blacks to sit in the front of the bus in violation of the local segregation rules. Florida's Governor Leroy Collins suspended all bus service in Tallahassee. In January 1957, a federal judge ruled that all of the state's bus segregation laws were unconstitutional, so Collins allowed bus service to resume on a desegregated basis.

The Tallahassee Bus Boycott only foreshadowed the winds of change that were empowering the black community. Similar to other southern cities, Tallahassee was slow in surrendering its links to the Old South mentality and its resistance to a new racial order. After all, it was built on the presumption of white superiority and black inferiority. During the 1950s and 1960s, the Florida panhandle was as much a part of the Deep South as Alabama,

and as noncompliant with the change in race relations.

In the summer of 1959, Miami's chapter of the **Congress of Racial Equality** (CORE) conducted a workshop on direct nonviolence that was attended by FAMU students Priscilla and Patricia Stephens. Later, they organized a CORE chapter in Tallahassee on FAMU's campus and became key organizers of the student sit-in movement in Tallahassee. Tallahassee's chapter planned two sit-in demonstrations against segregated variety stores' lunch counters in February 1960. The first sit-in occurred on Saturday, February 13, in the downtown area at Woolworth's when Stephens and ten other students attempted to order food. Similar to what happened with the group of students in the **Nashville Student Movement**, their first attempt yielded neither service nor major incident. However, the second sit-in of February

20 led to eleven arrests and eight sentences of 60 days in jail or $300 in fines when students refused to move. Five students, including Priscilla and Patricia Stephens, chose to remain in the Leon County Jail for the full sentence. Like **Martin Luther King Jr.**, who penned the "**Letter from the Birmingham Jail**" three years later, during her 49 days of incarceration from March 18 to May 5, 1960, Patricia Stephens penned a "Letter from the Leon County Jail." Stephens's letter demonstrated that students across the sit-in movement were willing to accept incarceration as a tactic against segregation. Tallahassee's direct-action campaigns continued as Stephens led students in other forms of direct non-violent protests, including the freedom rides, voter registration, the desegregation of movie theatres and other public accommodations. They also worked with white students from neighboring Florida State University to begin the deliberate process of racial desegregation.

Linda T. Wynn

Hate groups such as the White Citizens Council and the Ku Klux Klan terrorized the makeshift city by firing shots into the tents.

Tent City (1960–1962)

In 1959 African Americans in Fayette and Haywood Counties in Tennessee fought for the right to vote. The concern for voting emerged as a byproduct of the absence of black jurors for the trial of Burton Dodson, an African American farmer in his seventies who was tried for the 1941 murder of a white man. By denying African Americans their rights to participate in the elec-

toral process, whites eliminated them from the pool of potential jurors. To combat this injustice, African Americans in the two counties organized the Original Fayette County Civic and Welfare League and the Haywood County Civic and Welfare League. Both leagues launched voter registration drives, and a number of blacks registered to vote during June and July. However, when the Democrats held their August primary, black registered voters were not allowed to cast their ballots. League members initiated the first legal action against a party primary under the **Civil Rights Act of 1957** when they filed suit against the local Democratic Party.

Whites in the west Tennessee counties used their economic advantage to penalize African Americans. Many blacks lost their employment, credit, and insurance policies. Whites circulated a list of those African Americans who had attempted to vote, and then white merchants refused to sell them goods and services; some white physicians even withheld medical care. In the winter of 1960, white property owners evicted hundreds of black tenant farmers from their lands. African American leaders did not surrender to the pressure tactics. With the support of black property owners, they formed makeshift communities known as "Tent Cities." Day-to-day existence proved strenuous for the "Tent City" residents. Hate groups such as the White Citizens Council and the Ku Klux Klan terrorized the makeshift city by firing shots into the tents. The U.S. Justice Department filed several lawsuits against landowners, merchants, and one financial institution for violating civil rights laws. On July 26, 1962, as noted in the July 27, 1962, Memphis *Commercial Appeal,* "landowners were enjoined from engaging in any acts … for the purpose of interfering with the right to vote and to vote for candidates in public office."

Linda T. Wynn

Tulsa, Oklahoma, Race Riot (1921)

The greatest period of racial conflict that the nation witnessed came in 1919, when approximately 25 race riots occurred in America's urban cities. The reign of terror continued beyond that time, though not in the same numbers as seen during the **Red Summer** of 1919. Prominent among these were the Tulsa Race Riot of June 1921, which set off what has been called the worst race riot in U.S. history. After a 19-year-old black man named Dick Rowland was falsely accused of assaulting a young white woman, other blacks armed themselves and went to the jail to ensure his safety. Later, as tensions mounted, black and white groups engaged in what some called a "race war." During the 16-hour clash, nine whites and 21 blacks were known to have lost their lives; over 800 people were injured and hospitalized and nearly 10,000 blacks were left homeless. The black community also lost churches, restaurants, stores, two movie theaters, a hospital, a bank, a post office, a library, and schools. The riot shattered the thriving black community known as the Deep Greenwood district, reducing it to ashes. After martial law was set up and the National Guard took control of Tulsa, most of the black residents were under guard; internment centers were set up for blacks, who were then held for civil prosecution. Many blacks deserted Tulsa for cities outside the state. About 20 black men were indicted after the riot, but no whites. No one was jailed. By the end of September 1921, the case against Rowland was dismissed. The Deep Greenwood district was rebuilt but never regained the economic status that it had enjoyed before the riot.

Jessie Carney Smith

Underground Railroad

The Underground Railroad, in the context of American history, refers to the secret, loosely organized network of people and the hiding spaces they used to guide slaves to freedom in the free states or Canada. While its legendary status during the antebellum period has become commonplace in American history, the history of the system actually dates back to the colonial period, when Native Americans aided the escape of African slaves on the frontier of planter society. Even so, the success of the Underground Railroad in securing the freedom of thousands of slaves during the plantation period stands as a testament to the strength of its participants and the enduring nature of its spirit.

The Seminole people of Florida provide the strongest example of furtive Native American and African slave cooperation. Based on religious principles, the Quakers, like the Native Americans, assisted the development of the second phase of early escape networks. As the third and most widely known phase, the secret network during the antebellum period was first given its name in print materials during the 1840s. Soon after, its elements assumed other railroad terminology. Those guiding escapees were dubbed "conductors," while escapees were called "passengers" and the homes in which they received shelter were called "stations." The network had numerous routes, called "lines," in at least 14 states that provided circuitous paths to confuse pursuers.

Escapees traveled mostly as individuals or in small groups and were generally middle-aged male field workers who often used their free status to raise the money to purchase freedom for their families. Supposedly guided by astrological constellations such as the Big Dipper and spirituals such as "Steal Away" and "Follow the Drinking Gourd," the system became more nuanced in defiance of the Fugitive Slave Acts that were passed to thwart abolitionists and the growing flow of blacks to the North. Among the Underground Railroad's most successful conductors were the Quakers and **Harriet Tubman**, who single-handedly guided at least 300 slaves to freedom using the Underground Railroad's routes. Dubbed the "Father of the Underground Railroad," **William Still** helped hundreds of slaves to escape to freedom, too, often hiding them in his Philadelphia home.

The perception that the Underground Railroad was a highly systemized operation of aboli-

An 1893 painting by artist Charles Webber depicts the hardships slaves faced as they fled on the Underground Railroad (Library of Congress).

tionists, however, does not accurately represent the courageous efforts of random people, both free and slave, black and white, who offered assistance to escaped slaves. The bravery and resourcefulness of escapees is also underestimated in conventional ideas of the Underground Railroad. In fact, fleeing slaves were mostly aided after they had already survived the most dangerous part of their escape. Despite perceptions of its effectiveness and operation in secret, exaggerated accounts of the Underground Railroad's success were commonly used as propaganda for both anti and proslavery causes in the North and the South. Conductors and fellow abolitionists used the accounts to raise support for anti-slavery causes by illustrating the evils of slavery, while slave owners pointed to the reports as evidence of the North's disobedience in the face of the **Fugitive Slave Act.**

Crystal A. deGregory

Voter Registration Projects

During the era of segregation, African Americans were denied voting rights by law in several southern states, and hindered from the free exercise of their Constitutional rights in other locations. Poll taxes, unfair literacy tests, "grandfather clauses" (prohibiting blacks from voting unless they could prove an ancestor of theirs could legally vote before 1857), and violence were used to prevent and discourage blacks from voting, especially in areas where they were a majority or large percentage of the population. Civil rights organizations began direct action and legal initiatives to challenge the existing order and secure voting rights. The **NAACP** launched several voter registration projects through branch affiliates beginning in the late 1950s.

Success was achieved in the Mississippi Gulf Coast region in 1960 and 1961 with leadership from Biloxi NAACP branch President Dr. Gilbert R. Mason, but efforts in other areas still met stern and sometimes violent opposition. Shortly after the creation of the **Student Non-Violent Coordinating Committee** (SNCC) in 1960, activist **Robert "Bob" Moses** was encouraged by mentor **Ella Baker** to travel to Mississippi, where he met local NAACP leader Amzie Moore. Moses was asked by Moore to increase the number of civil rights workers in the area, and to focus efforts on getting more black Mississippians to register and vote. The next year considerable numbers of black and white student activists came to McComb, Mississippi, to help with voter registration and basic literacy in black communities. Despite assaults, arrests, jailings, and murders of activists such as Herbert Lee (1961), and **Medgar Evers** (1963), voter education and registration efforts continued in the state.

In the fall of 1963, the Council of Federated Organizations (COFO) developed the Freedom Vote program to demonstrate black voting potential, and Moses expanded this concept into the "**Freedom Summer**" campaign of 1964. Despite the tragic murders of volunteers Michael Schwerner, Andrew Goodman, and **James Chaney** in June, Freedom Summer continued. Organizers established "freedom schools" and other community centers to address the educational, health, and legal needs of poor blacks; and they created the **Mississippi Freedom Democratic Party**, which challenged the legitimacy of the all-white Mississippi delegation to the 1964 Democratic National Convention in Atlantic City, New Jersey, led by activist **Fannie Lou Hamer**. These efforts dramatized the disenfranchisement of African American voters, and influenced the passage of the **Voting Rights Act of 1965**. As a result, numerous black candidates were elected to municipal, county, state, and national offices in southern states and other regions of the country. Mississippi changed from five percent of eligible blacks registered to vote in the 1950s to 66.5 percent by 1969.

Despite the increased number of black elected officials, their success did not immediately trans-

late into meaningful socioeconomic improvements for their constituents. **Jesse Jackson** inspired increased voter registration efforts during his presidential campaigns of 1984 and 1988, and Congress passed the National Voter Registration Act in 1993. A number of African American media personalities also used their celebrity status to encourage increased African American voter registration and participation in recent years.

Fletcher F. Moon

Poll taxes, unfair literacy tests, "grandfather clauses" ..., and violence were used to prevent and discourage blacks from voting.

War on Poverty (est. 1964)

On January 8, 1964, **President Lyndon B. Johnson** declared a "War On Poverty" during his State of the Union Address. In that address he called for the creation of a "Great Society." Johnson proposed an expansion in the federal government's role in domestic policy. During his administration, Congress enacted the **Civil Rights Act of 1964** and the **Voting Rights Act of 1965**, both of which were major civil rights acts. Succeeding to the presidency after the assassination of President **John F. Kennedy**, Johnson made poverty a national concern. His sensitivity to the issue, despite his personal wealth, rose with a growing national concern that was stimulated in part by Michael Harrington's now classic tome *The Other Americans: Poverty in the United States* (1962). Harrington detailed the deplorable living conditions for millions of Americans suffering in desperate poverty in the midst of the world's most affluent society. The destitute were everywhere, from decaying urban cities to rural areas such as Appalachia. More than one out of five Americans lived below the official poverty line and 70 percent of them were white.

Those who argued for a return to a homeland, nationalists, and separatists believed that there could be no equal treatment for men of color.

As a part of his Great Society Program, which was part of the administration's domestic policy, Johnson envisioned a federally directed application of resources that extended beyond social welfare to include education and healthcare. The Great Society programs were reminiscent of Franklin D. Roosevelt's New Deal program of the 1930s. Johnson and Congress passed several measures aimed at alleviating poverty. They increased the availability of money and food stamps through the Aid to Families with Dependent Children, raised Social Security benefits to senior Americans, and focused on improving educational opportunities. Along with the civil rights acts of 1964 and 1965, Congress passed the Economic Opportunity Act (1964) and two education acts (1965). In addition, legislation was passed that created the Job Corps, Operation Head Start, Volunteers in Service to America (VISTA), Medicaid, and Medicare.

The most effective measures of the War on Poverty provided federal funds for the education of children in low-income families through Title I of the Elementary and Secondary Education Act of 1965; Medicare for the nation's senior citizens; and Medicaid for individuals on welfare, which was created by the Social Security

Amendments of 1965. Although the Great Society programs made significant contributions to the protection of civil rights and the expansion of social programs, critics increasingly complained that the antipoverty programs were ineffective and wasteful. The economic and political costs of the Vietnam War, as well as the cost of the programs themselves, surmounted President Johnson's domestic initiatives. During the second term of President Richard Nixon, Congress replaced the Office of Economic Opportunity with the Community Services Administration and hastened the process in which favored parts of the antipoverty program were exported to established executive agencies, such as the Department of Health, Education, and Welfare. In 1981, President Ronald Reagan abolished the Community Services Administration, leaving only individual programs, such as legal services and Head Start, as the bureaucratic survivors of the War on Poverty.

Linda T. Wynn

Race Consciousness

Black Pride

Black Pride is an important concept in the struggle for freedom and civil rights, for it cannot exist without this belief. Since one tactic in the oppression of black people is to provide them with a negative sense of self-worth, the emergence of black pride fosters an urgency that serves as a catalyst or undercurrent for the struggle for equality. Black pride was a phrase that was popular during the Civil Rights Movement of the 1960s, but it is not limited to this period. It was a part of the thrust of educators and orators like Maria Stewart, **Frances Ellen Watkins Harper**, **Sojourner Truth**, and **Anna J. Cooper**, women who spoke in support of equality and fought for better treatment. Those who argued for a return to a homeland—nationalists and separatists—believed that there could be no equal treatment for men of color. Among adherents to this belief were **Henry Highland Garnet**, **Alexander Crummell**, **Martin Delany**, **Marcus Garvey**, and **Malcolm X**. Garvey encouraged pride in race and the beauty of black people, while Malcolm X preached independence and separatism. Even a personality like **Booker T. Washington**, who is often viewed as a conservative, said in *Up From Slavery* that he would rather be a member of the Negro race than any other. This celebration of self and of heritage is evident in the practice of changing one's name; following the emancipation, and especially during the 1970s, many black people changed their names to ones they felt were more reflective of their identity and freedom. Black pride is also in evidence in music, such as in James Brown's "Say It Loud, I'm Black and I'm Proud."

Helen R. Houston

Bridging the Racial Divide

Reconciling the races is a challenge that has permeated American society for centuries. There have been many initiatives to eliminate racial disparities over the years. The Center for Living Democracy (CLD) published the report *Bridging the Racial Divide: A Report on Interracial Dialogue in America* (1997), which explains what is occurring around the country and encourages open lines of communication and increased sensitivity towards interracial groups. The CLD report provides information on groups whose goal is to foster interracial communications and support, such as the Study Circles Resource Center, the Student Coalition Against Racism, and the Houston-based Center for Healing Racism, which are representative examples of what is taking place in America.

The national education project of the Southern Poverty Law Center, Teaching Tolerance, publishes the magazine *Teaching Tolerance* semiannually. Its aim is to support and aid Kindergarten through twelfth-grade teachers and others in promoting diversity. Organizations like the **NAACP**, **Southern Christian Leadership Conference**, and the **National Urban League** have

initiated programs like the Hip-Hop Summer Action Network (HSAN) Summit to promote understanding and collaboration among diverse groups. Russell Simmons and Ben Chavis founded the HSAN Summit, which, among other concerns, focuses on racial equity and empowerment. The Council of Bishops in the United Methodist Church has created dialogues to ascertain what can be done to eradicate racism within the church and the community. There are also groups that focus on bridging racial disparities in education, health issues, and technology. Reports like the CLD's show the need for these groups in the workplace, school, places of worship, the media, and in entertainment.

In addition to recognition on the part of organizations that there is a need for racial reconciliation, individuals have come to realize that they too can effect change. For example, Tim Wise, an activist and director of the Association for White Anti-Racist Education (AWARE) in Nashville, Tennessee, is the author of *Beyond "Diversity": Challenging Racism in an Age of Backlash* and a contributor to *White Men Challenging Racism: Thirty-Five Personal Stories*. He has lectured and held workshops on such topics as institutional racism, gender bias, and the growing gap between rich and poor in America. Racism, Wise believes, is a problem both whites and nonwhites must work together to solve.

Rabbi Marc Schneier and Joseph Papp are two other people active in bridging the racial gap. They founded the Foundation for Ethnic Understanding, which is "committed to the belief that direct face-to-face dialogue between ethnic communities is the most effective path towards the reduction of bigotry and promotion of reconciliation and understanding." The ongoing work of organizations and individuals such as these indicate that, even though the Civil Rights Movement resulted in laws such as the **Civil Rights Act of 1964**, there remain many racial, ethnic, and religious issues to solve in America.

Helen R. Houston

Speeches

Atlanta Compromise (1895)

The "Atlanta Compromise" is the common name given to **Booker T. Washington's** September 1895 address delivered at the opening of the Cotton States and International Exposition in Atlanta, Georgia, before a predominantly white audience. Because of his popularity as founder and principal of the Tuskegee Institute, his conservative views, and his rise as a black leader, Washington was asked to deliver the address. His speech was given at a time when

"With this faith we will be able to transform the jangling discords of our nation into a beautiful symphony of brotherhood."

violence and hostility toward blacks was intense and blacks were pushing for equality. The speech was a statement of his public philosophy on race relations, one that he espoused throughout his life. In his speech, he offered a compromise between the demands of whites for segregation and the demands of blacks for civil and political equality. Washington said, "The wisest among my race understand that the agitation of questions of social equality is the extremist folly," thereby allaying white concerns. He urged African Americans to "Cast down your buckets where you are" and to pursue economic enterprises, not to seek social relationships. "In all things that are purely social we can be as separate as the fingers." He advocated a gradual advancement of the race through hard work, economic improvement, and self-help. Even

though the speech addresses both races, it was seen as telling black people to maintain the status quo. Whites accepted Washington's speech in good spirits, and many blacks approved it, as well. It led to Washington being recognized as the spokesperson for black people.

Helen R. Houston

"I Have a Dream" (1963)

The Reverend **Martin Luther King Jr.**, minister, non-violent advocate for freedom, and the most prominent leader of the modern Civil Rights Movement, gave his famous "I Have a Dream" speech at the Lincoln Memorial, Washington, D.C., on August 28, 1963. Speaking before a crowd of 250,000 who joined the **March on Washington** in support of civil rights legislation, he said, in part: "Go back to Mississippi, go back to Alabama, go back to South Carolina, go back to Georgia, go back to Louisiana, go back to the slums and ghettos of our Northern cities knowing that somehow this situation can and will be changed. Let us not wallow in the valley of despair. I have a dream that one day this nation will rise up and live out the true meaning of its creed: 'We hold these truths to be self-evident; that all men are created equal. ' I have a dream that one day on the red hills of Georgia the sons of former slaves and the sons of former slave owners will be able to sit down together at the table of brotherhood; I have a dream—That my four little children will one day live in a nation where they will not be judged by the color of their skin but by the content of their character; I have a dream today. I have a dream that one day down in Alabama, with its vicious racists, with its governor having his lips dripping with the words of interposition and nullification, one day right there in Alabama little black boys and black girls will be able to join hands with little white boys and white girls as sisters and brothers; I have a dream today. I have a dream that one day every valley shall be exalted, every hill and mountain shall be made low, and rough places will be made plane and crooked places will be made straight, and the glory of the Lord shall be revealed, and all flesh shall see it together. This is our hope. This is the faith that I go back to the South with. With this faith, we will be able to hew out of the mountain of despair a stone of hope. With this faith we will be able to transform the jangling discords of our nation into a beautiful symphony of brotherhood. With this faith we will be able to work together, to pray together, to struggle together, to go to jail together, to stand up for freedom together, knowing that we will be free one day. This will be the day .... This will be the day when all of God's children will be able to sing with new meaning 'My country 'tis of thee, sweet land of liberty, of thee I sing. Land where my fathers died, land of the pilgrim's pride, from every mountainside, let freedom ring.' And if America is to be a great nation—this must become true. So let freedom ring—from the prodigious hilltops of New Hampshire, let freedom ring; from the mighty mountains of New York, let freedom ring—from the heightening Alleghenies of Pennsylvania!

Let freedom ring from the snowcapped Rockies of Colorado! Let freedom ring from the curvaceous slopes of California! But not only that; let freedom ring from Stone Mountain of Georgia! Let freedom ring from Lookout Mountain of Tennessee! Let freedom ring from every hill and molehill of Mississippi, From every mountainside, let freedom ring, and when this happens …

When we allow freedom to ring, when we let it ring from every village and every hamlet, from every state and every city, we will be able to speed up that day when all of God's children, black men and white man, Jews and Gentiles, Protestants and Catholics, will be able to join hands and sing in the words of the old Negro spiritual, 'Free at last! Free at last! Thank God almighty, we are free at last!'"

Education

Colleges and Universities

Alabama Agricultural & Mechanical University (est. 1875)

This higher education institution was organized after an 1873 act of the Alabama State Legislature and the efforts of William Hooper Council, an ex-slave who became its first principal and president. It opened on May 1, 1875, as the Huntsville Normal School with two teachers, 61 students, and an annual state appropriation of $1,000. During the early years the college received support from the Slater and Peabody Funds and private contributors. After successfully introducing industrial education in 1878, the legislature increased its state appropriation to $4,000 per year and changed the name to the State Normal and Industrial School at Huntsville. After the 1890 Morrill Act of the U.S. Congress, the school began receiving Federal support and changed its name again, this time to the State Agricultural and Mechanical College for Negroes, in 1891.

The additional support helped the college to grow. The campus moved to Normal, Alabama, and its name was changed to the State Agricultural and Mechanical Institute for Negroes in 1919. After the graduation of the class of 1920,

the college was designated a junior college; it resumed awarding bachelor's degrees in 1941 after authorization from the state board of education, and it became the Alabama Agricultural and Mechanical College in 1948. Its present name was adopted in 1969. The university now serves over 6,000 students in undergraduate and graduate degree programs, including offering Ph.D.s.

During the Civil Rights Movement, A&M's students participated in local sit-ins. This happened when white supremacists accelerated efforts to stamp out dissent activities in publicly supported institutions. Governor John Patterson complained that the school's president had allowed members of the **Congress of Racial Equality** (CORE) to enter the campus to solicit support. He claimed that one-third of the students who were arrested for sit-ins in Huntsville were A&M students. The governor responded by threatening the school's financial support. In an emergency session, the state's board of education ordered the president to take a year's leave of absence, followed by his retirement the next year.

Fletcher F. Moon

Alabama State University (est. 1867)

Originally the Lincoln School of Marion, the university was established by nine founders

Hiram R. Revels was a senator who became Alcorn State University's first president (Fisk University).

and original trustees who were former slaves: Joey P. Pinch, Thomas Speed, Nicholas Dale, James Childs, Thomas Lee, John Freeman, Nathan Levert, David Harris, and Alexander H. Curtis. The institution opened on November 13, 1867, with 113 students. In 1868 the name changed to Lincoln Normal School, and the school's title was transferred in 1873 after the Alabama State Legislature authorized funding for the first state normal school for blacks. George M. Card was selected as the first president, and the school's status as a public institution began in 1874. In 1878 William Paterson became the second president and oversaw the university's relocation from Marion to Montgomery, the state capital, in 1887. It grew from a junior college into a four-year degree institution (1928), and underwent several additional name changes: State Teachers College (1929), Alabama State College for Negroes (1948), Alabama State College (1954), and Alabama State University (1969). During the 1950s and 1960s people

affiliated with the institution became notable figures in the Civil Rights Movement, including alumnus **Ralph Abernathy** and faculty member **Jo Ann Gibson Robinson**. Presently, the university serves over 5,000 students in 47 undergraduate and graduate programs of study, including doctoral programs in physical therapy, microbiology, and forensic sciences.

Fletcher F. Moon

Alcorn State University (est. 1871)

The present-day Alcorn State University in Mississippi began on the site of Oakland College, a school for whites established by the Presbyterian Church. This school was closed at the beginning of the **Civil War** to allow its students to fight for the Confederacy. After the war, the property was sold to the state and renamed Alcorn University in 1871 to honor Mississippi Governor James L. Alcorn. Hiram R. Revels, the first African American senator, resigned from Congress to become the school's first president. There were eight faculty members and 179 students at the time. Early financial support included $50,000 cash for 10 consecutive years from the state legislature and $113,400 for agricultural and mechanical programs, making the school a land-grant college from its earliest days. The name of the institution was changed to Alcorn Agricultural and Mechanical College in 1878, as the state emphasized industrial training as the primary role for the institution. Originally intended for black men only, the college began admitting women in 1895. In 1974 university status was granted and the name was changed to Alcorn State University. During the 1960s many Alcorn students and alumni made great sacrifices to participate in the Civil Rights Movement. Conservative president J.D. Boyd dismissed over 700 students in April 1964 after a non-violent demonstration; former student Charles Moore was murdered during **Freedom Summer** of the same year, while Alcorn alumni Ernestine Denham Talbert, C.J. Duckworth, Professor N. R. Burger, and Ariel Burns were educators as well as key activists. In February 1968 Alcorn students Percell Rials and James Bishop were expelled by Boyd for supporting the congressional campaign of Charles Evers; subsequent protests led to beatings and shootings of other students when the Mississippi Highway Patrol was called to the campus. Two months later the campus erupted again after the assassination of Martin Luther King Jr., and the school closed for the remainder of the spring semester.

Fletcher F. Moon

American Baptist College (est. 1924)

American Baptist College in Nashville, Tennessee, formally opened its doors for the training of Christian workers as the American Baptist Theological Seminary on September 14, 1924. The curriculum contained both degree programs for high school graduates and non-degree programs for training those who had no high school degree. In 1937 the Southern Baptist Convention and the National Baptist Convention, USA, Inc. agreed to share in the operations of the college. In 1971 it became a four-year graduate Bible college under the name American Baptist College. In 1996 the Southern Baptist Convention withdrew its involvement and turned over the assets to the board of trustees of American Baptist College. The college is not well endowed, but it enrolls passionately committed students who want to make an impact on humanity. This is evidenced in its graduates who participated in the Civil Rights Movement in Nashville: the Reverend **James M. Lawson Jr.**, a divinity student at Vanderbilt University, organized nonviolence workshops where college students were trained; to these workshops were sent young, brilliant, idealistic students from the college by the Reverend **Kelly Miller Smith Sr.**, a popular professor at the seminary and an activist in the Nashville community. Among the leaders of the non-violent sit-in movement in Nashville was the Reverend **Bernard Lafayette**, former president of American Baptist College.

Helen R. Houston

Atlanta University (est. 1865)

The American Missionary Association, with support from the **Freedmen's Bureau**, founded Atlanta University. It became the first graduate institution serving African Americans. The school began granting bachelor's degrees by the late 1870s and supplied black teachers and librarians to public schools throughout the southern United States. **W.E.B. Du Bois** was a member of the Atlanta University faculty during the early years of the twentieth century. During his tenure, he helped to found the **NAACP**, as well as *Phylon*, a scholarly journal on race and culture, and agitated for civil rights after the **Atlanta race riot** of 1906. In 1929 Atlanta University offered its first programs of graduate study, expanding these to include library science (1941), education (1944), business administration (1946), and social work (1947). **Whitney Young Jr.** continued civil rights activism during his tenure as dean of the social work program. The institution also cooperated with **Morehouse College** and **Spelman College** within the Atlanta University System. In subsequent years Clark College, Morris Brown College, and the Interdenominational Theological Center joined to create the Atlanta University Center (AUC) in 1957. Students from AUC were active in March 1960 sit-ins to desegregate downtown Atlanta establishments. On July 1, 1988, Atlanta University merged with Clark College and became known as Clark Atlanta University. Walter Broadnax succeeded Thomas W. Cole Jr., the first president of the new institution, on August 1, 2002.

Fletcher F. Moon

Bennett College for Women (est. 1873)

Bennett College for Women was founded in 1873. The Freedmen's Aid Society took over the coeducational school in 1874, and oversaw its growth for 50 years. After a group of emancipated slaves acquired the present site in Greensboro, North Carolina, in 1878, the Women's Home Missionary Board of Education of the

Methodist Church oversaw its transition to a college for women. When four students at nearby Agricultural and Technical State University (A&T) sat at the "whites only" lunch counters in Greensboro on February 1, 1960, the student sit-in movement was born. Although public acknowledgement has gone to the young men, what is often unmentioned is the major contributions of Bennett College's administrators, faculty, and students. According to author Linda Brown, "One of Bennett College's finest hours was the historical moment of the Civil Rights Movement." It was characterized by three years of intense social activism for Bennett and others

Although public acknowledgement has gone to the [A&T students] ..., what is often unmentioned is the major contributions of Bennett College's administrators, faculty, and students.

involved. Their students joined others from A&T, three other colleges, as well as all-black Dudley High School and sought desegregation of lunch counters at S.H. Kress, F.W. Woolworth's, and the tea room at Meyer's department store. The demonstration increased and members of Greensboro's establishments were unsuccessful in persuading Bennett's president, Willa B. Player, to stop student participation. She also was the first person to return her credit card to Meyer's department store when it refused to desegregate its dining room. Bennett's students regularly attended organizational meetings at various sites, including their own campus. Player maintained close contact with organizers and gave them advice. These students, along with other protesters, were arrested during the sit-ins. At the apex of the struggle, about 40 percent of Bennett's student body was jailed and the college's participants numbered more than half of the total students from other colleges. In 1963 Player visited the students in the makeshift jail and later saw that they received toiletry supplies and class assignments so that their education would continue. She also ensured faculty protesters that their jobs were secure.

Jessie Carney Smith

Delaware State College (est. 1892)

As a result of the students of Delaware State College, as it was known then, challenging the laws of segregation, two local cases were later filed and subsequently included in the historic *Brown v. Board of Education* case of 1954. The black students of Delaware State College were dissatisfied that their college was not given equal services from the state, as was apparent from the numerous services offered at the University of Delaware, which was attended by white students. The separation of services, as supported by the laws of segregation, were challenged in court by the students. On August 9, 1950, *Parker v. University of Delaware* was filed and the Court of Chancery of Delaware ruled in favor of the plaintiffs (black students from Delaware State). The University of Delaware became the first public university, by court order, to admit black students. This victory made way for the cases of Ethel Belton and Shirley Bulah, who challenged segregation laws for local schools. Both cases received from the Delaware Court of Chancery, and affirmed by the Delaware Supreme court in 1952, a ruling in favor of the black students. Unfortunately, the decision only applied to schools in Delaware. The cases of Belton and Bulah were combined into the *Belton v. Gebhart* case, which was included among the five cases submitted under *Brown v. Board of Education* in 1954. The

Belton v. Gebhart case was the only case with a ruling in favor of the plaintiffs.

Lean'tin L. Bracks

Fisk University (est. 1866)

Since its founding on January 9, 1866, Fisk University has remained at the center of civil rights and race relations activities, becoming prominently known for its race relations institutes and its leadership in the sit-in movement. The school was founded six months after the **Civil War** ended and just three years after the Emancipation Proclamation was issued. The university's first five presidents were white; it was not until 1947 that sociologist and race-relations expert **Charles Spurgeon Johnson** (1893–1956) became the first African American president. He had a quiet but effective way of undermining segregation, and had a vision that would place the university in a prominent position as a leader in international race relations. Johnson led Fisk's first Race Relations Institute in 1942, offering a forum for blacks and whites from national and international arenas to come to Fisk and discuss issues of economics, education, governmental policy, housing, and employment. For the annual institutes that followed, Johnson brought to the campus great minds to discuss the phenomenon of racism, among them Ashley Montague, **Thurgood Marshall**, **Fannie Lou Hamer**, Hubert Humphrey, and Gordon Allport. The institutes continued intermittently after Johnson's death in 1956. The administrative unit, called the Race Relations Institute, is still functioning and offers a variety of programs during the year. **Angela Davis** and Bishop Desmond Tutu are among those who were brought to the campus for such programs.

Fisk joined in the modern civil rights struggle of the 1960s and became prominent in the Civil Rights Movement. In early 1960 the university was a moving force in the **Nashville Sit-in Movement**. Student protesters from Fisk and local institutions gained widespread support in the Nashville community; the sit-in movement that

Stephen J. Wright, Fisk University's second black president (Fisk University).

the students launched in 1960 was called one of the best organized of such movements. Stephen J. Wright, Fisk's second black president, supported the efforts to bring about positive change, declaring "This is the Fisk tradition." In the 1960s, in response to demands from its faculty and students, Fisk was one of the first Historically Black Colleges/Universities to develop a "black university" concept; it embraced black courses in the then-current curriculum in such disciplines as history, English, sociology, and art. Writers' workshops held at Fisk during the late 1960s brought to the campus numerous poets and writers who explored the fervor of the period and gave both young militants and realists a stage for expressing their views, many of which were in strong opposition to previous approaches to the "Negro problem." Led by John Oliver Killens, the workshops also helped emerging poets and writers to be heard, among them poet Nikki Giovanni, then a Fisk student who went on to enjoy international fame. Around this time as well, Fisk began to accelerate its practices of collecting African American art. The new items complemented the work of Harlem Renaissance artist Aaron Douglas, who had joined the faculty in 1937 and founded the art department. In the classroom the young art students created works that captured the unrest in the local and regional arenas; their productions characterized this era of protest.

Jessie Carney Smith

Hampton University (est. 1868)

The roots of Hampton Institute (now Hampton University) in the southeastern, coastal part of Virginia, literally began with a tree. The Emancipation Oak Tree (on land that became part of the campus) was the location for the first southern reading of the Emancipation Proclamation in 1863, and the first classes for newly freed Virginia slaves were taught under its branches by Mary Peake, daughter of a Frenchman and a black woman. The official founding of Hampton Normal and Agricultural Institute took place in 1868, with assistance from the **American Missionary Association**. General Samuel Chapman Armstrong, its first president, began the process of training young men and women "to go out to teach and lead their people." Its most famous graduate, **Booker T. Washington**, applied the principles of industrial education learned at Hampton to establish the Tuskegee Institute in Alabama and become the most influential black leader of his era. Other outstanding alumni of Hampton include composer R. Nathaniel Dett, Dr. Thomas Wyatt Turner (the first African American to receive a doctorate in botany), and Susan LaFlesche Picotte (the first Native American woman to earn the doctor of medicine degree). Along with its original mission as a Historically Black College/University (HBCU), from 1878 to 1923 Hampton also supported a formal education program for Native Americans, awarded its first baccalaureate degrees in 1922, formally changed its name to Hampton University in 1984, and now supports doctoral level graduate programs in nursing, physics, pharmacy, and

physical therapy. Alumnus Alonzo G. Morón became the first African American president of Hampton (1949–1959); he changed the emphasis of the school from industrial education to liberal arts. While he supported the 1954 *Brown v. Board of Education* decision and is credited with using his position and influence to push for civil rights and desegregation, Morón took the controversial position that Hampton and other HBCUs would no longer be needed after integration was achieved. This proved to be incorrect, as the school continued to thrive and maintain its identity under his successors, including recently elected president William B. Harvey.

Fletcher F. Moon

Howard University (est. 1867)

Founded in 1867 by congressional order, Howard University is one of the nation's oldest historically black universities. Named for **Freedman's Bureau** commissioner Oliver O. Howard, the university served as a leading center for black intellectual development and social activism during the twentieth century. As the home of black academicians Alain Locke, E. Franklin Frazier, and Ralph Bunche, Howard assembled a first-rate faculty by the mid-twentieth century and as the founding campus of five of the country's nine black Greek fraternities. While Howard received major improvements and additions following World War I, the school only rapidly expanded during the presidency of Wyatt Mordecai Johnson. Elected as the school's first African American president in 1926, Johnson oversaw the tripling of Howard's faculty, doubling of salaries, increase of congressional appropriations, and the production of half of the African American physicians in the country at its Freedmen's Hospital. By the time of Johnson's retirement thirty-four years later, Howard boasted 10 fully accredited schools and colleges. As a testament to Howard's enhanced academic status, its graduate programs were given the authority to grant Ph.D. degrees in 1955. Still, Johnson's most lasting achievement is its law school. With his support, law school dean **Charles Hamilton Houston** mentored a cadre of civil rights attorneys, including most notably **Thurgood Marshall**. As the site of the legal think tank for the landmark *Brown v. Board of Education* case, Howard's law school is credited with making an indelible mark on the emergent Civil Rights Movement. Howard University is currently a research institution with more than 10,000 students and more than 120 areas of study leading to undergraduate, graduate, and professional degrees.

Crystal A. deGregory

Jackson State University (est. 1877)

The American Baptist Home Mission Society in Natchez, Mississippi, founded Jackson State University, the urban university of the State of Mississippi, as Natchez Seminary in 1877; in November 1882, it moved to Jackson. It became Jackson College in March 1899. The state assumed support in 1940, changed its mission, and named it Jackson State College in 1956. The name was changed again, on March 15, 1974, to Jackson State University. On May 14 and 15, 1970, students there protested national issues, including the killing of four students at Kent State University, the beating death of a young black man in jail, and the shooting in the back and killing of another black person in Augusta, Georgia. Fears and tempers ran high; this was exacerbated by the routine racial intimidation and harassment of the Jackson community. When rumors surfaced that Mayor **Charles Evers**, brother of slain civil rights activist **Medgar Evers**, and his wife had been shot, a small group of students rioted. White motorists complained to the police that they had been attacked as they passed the campus; fires had been set and firefighters called. When they arrived, they were met with hostility and called for police backup. National Guardsmen, as well as heavily armed city and Mississippi State Police, responded. In the melee, two students died: Phillip Lafayette Gibbs, a 21-year-

old junior pre-law major, and James Earl Green, a 17-year-old high school senior. As a result, the president established the Commission on Campus Unrest, but this body found no reason for convictions or arrests.

Helen R. Houston

Before desegregation, Hubbard Hospital was the primary health care facility for African Americans in Nashville.

Meharry Medical College (est. 1876)

Located in Nashville, Tennessee, Meharry Medical College was founded in 1876 as the medical department of Central Tennessee College, with oversight from the Freedmen's Aid Society of the Methodist Episcopal Church, North (now the United Methodist Church). An early college catalog indicated "this is the only institution in the valley of the Mississippi, and, with a single exception, the only one in the United States that is designed especially for the education of colored physicians." A few years earlier, a young white man named Samuel Meharry received assistance from a family of freed slaves while traveling through Tennessee. His salt wagon slipped off the road into a swamp, and the black family provided him with food, overnight shelter, and help in recovering his wagon. Meharry had no money at the time, but promised, "When I can I shall do something for your race." In 1875 Meharry and his brothers donated $15,000 to help establish the college, which was originally located in south Nashville. While its first years produced small numbers of graduates, the school expanded to include departments of dentistry (1886) and pharmacy (1889).

In 1900 Central Tennessee College became Walden University, and in 1915 the medical department became Meharry Medical College. George W. Hubbard of the original faculty became the college's first president, serving until his death in 1921. The college subsequently relocated to north Nashville near Fisk University. Before desegregation, Hubbard Hospital was the primary health care facility for African Americans in Nashville and surrounding communities. Seay-Hubbard United Methodist Church and the Hubbard House (designed by African American architect Moses McKissack) remain as south Nashville historic landmarks. Eight men succeeded Hubbard in leading the institution, including Harold D. West, who became the college's first African American president in 1952; David Satcher, who went on to become U.S. Surgeon General; and Wayne J. Riley, who took office in 2006.

During the Civil Rights Movement in Nashville, some Meharry students took on the monumental task of participating in sit-ins and protests while continuing their medical studies, and Meharry faculty in several cases provided financial as well as professional assistance to civil rights activists who were injured and/or arrested for their activism. Meharry alumni have become political leaders from local to international levels, as well as pioneers in desegregating majority hospitals, medical school faculties, and professional organizations. For many years the college was the leading producer of African American medical doctors and dentists, and in the twenty-first century is still regarded as the second largest educator of black health care professionals. In partnership with the city of Nashville, Meharry operates the Metropolitan Nashville General Hospital, upholding with its mission to train professionals and provide health care to poor and underserved populations. In addition to the medical school, dental school, graduate school, and school of allied health, Meharry supports research centers for the study

of asthma and sickle cell anemia diseases, neurosciences, women's health, and HIV/AIDS. It publishes the *Journal of Health Care for the Poor and Underserved.*

Fletcher F. Moon

Morehouse College (est. 1867)

The only all-male Historically Black College/University (HBCU) was founded in Augusta, Georgia, in 1867 as the Augusta Institute by ministers William Jefferson White, Richard C. Coulter (a former slave), and Edmund Turney. Its first classroom was located in the basement of Springfield Baptist Church. The founders selected minister and physician Joseph T. Robert as its first president. The college moved to the basement of Friendship Baptist Church in Atlanta and was renamed the Atlanta Baptist Seminary in 1879. In 1885 the college relocated again, changing its name to Atlanta Baptist College in 1897. John Hope became its first black president in 1906, and in 1913 the school became Morehouse College. Sixth president Benjamin E. Mays led the college to international recognition and mentored **Martin Luther King Jr.**, the college's most renowned graduate; he counseled King during the early days of the Civil Rights Movement. Mays was succeeded by Hugh M. Gloster (1967–1987), the first of four alumni to lead the institution, and was followed by Leroy Keith (1987–1994), Walter Massey (1995–2007), and Robert M. Franklin Jr. (2007–). Other notable Morehouse alumni include Howard University president Mordecai Johnson; theologians Howard Thurman and Otis Moss Jr.; writer and editor Lerone Bennett; first black Atlanta mayor Maynard Jackson; U.S. Secretary of Health and Human Services Louis Sullivan; U.S. Congressmen Major Owens, Earl Hilliard, and Sanford Bishop; U.S. Surgeon General David Satcher; athletes Edwin Moses and Donn Clendenon; film artists Spike Lee and Samuel Jackson; and Nima Warfield, the first Rhodes Scholar from an HBCU. The college was well represented during the Civil Rights

Movement through its students who joined in protest those from area colleges, particularly Spelman, by participating in Atlanta's sit-ins and other desegregation struggles of the 1960s.

Fletcher F. Moon

North Carolina Agricultural and Technical State University (est. 1891)

North Carolina A&T State University, as the institution is popularly known, is a public research university and a land grant university located in Greensboro, North Carolina. It was founded during the time when North Carolina, like other southern states, was building its dual system of education. North Carolina was far more progressive than other southern states and continued to build other colleges for blacks until it had a total of five. James B. Dudley, the founding president, helped to shape the educational background of his students and also promoted black education, black economic development, and civil rights in the Greensboro community. A man who believed in passive resistance, he promoted racial cooperation in his public speeches and served on local committees, sometimes as the only black member. He may well have set the stage for the role that A&T would play in civil rights activities later on.

The university became prominent in the Civil Rights Movement of the 1960s, particularly for the role that its students played in sit-in demonstrations. On February 1, 1960, four freshmen students—Jibreel Khazan (Ezell Blair Jr.), Franklin Eugene McCain, **Joseph Alfred McNeil**, and David Lleinail Richmond—requested service at F.W. Woolworth's segregated lunch counter in downtown Greensboro, thus beginning the **Greensboro Sit-in Movement** and spurring similar movements by students in historically black colleges and universities throughout the South. The A&T students had no idea that their protest would reach historic proportions, touch off what would be called the sit-in movement, and help to shape civil rights movements around the world. Direc-

tives from the governor, who obviously had some control over the state institution, tempered the school's reaction to the activities of these students and others who joined them. To honor these students, A&T erected a bronze statue and unveiled it on February 1, 2001. It is appropriately named the February One Monument, honoring the date on which the students began their protest.

Jessie Carney Smith

[James B. Dudley] may well have set the stage for the role that A&T would play in civil rights activities later on.

Shaw University (est. 1865)

Located in Raleigh, North Carolina, this Historically Black College/University (HBCU) was founded in 1865. It claims the distinction of being the first HBCU established in the South. Nearly a hundred years later, participants in the first wave of student sit-ins and other activists met on the Shaw campus from April 15 through 17, 1960, resulting in the founding of the **Student Non-Violent Coordinating Committee** (SNCC). Shaw students were involved in Raleigh civil rights protests shortly after the **Greensboro sit-in** began on February 1, 1960, but this was not why it became the site of the Easter weekend meeting. Veteran activist **Ella Baker**, a 1922 graduate of Shaw working for the **Southern Christian Leadership Conference** (SCLC), convinced **Martin Luther King Jr.** to commit $800 from the SCLC budget for meeting expenses and secured an agreement from the school to host the conference. Over 200 people attended, including student activists from HBCUs and northern colleges and representatives from the **Congress of Racial Equality** (CORE), **Fellowship of Reconciliation** (FOR), National Student Association (NSA), and Students for a Democratic Society (SDS). King and the Reverend **James Lawson** were keynote speakers, but Baker encouraged the students to develop their own organization. This historic meeting enabled students to network, organize, and pursue objectives in cooperation with and independent of more established civil rights organizations such as the **NAACP** and SCLC. Baker believed that the students brought new energy and ideas to the movement, and she created a setting where they could empower themselves and others.

Fletcher F. Moon

Students from Spelman College and other schools in the Atlanta University community decided to write ... "An Appeal for Human Rights."

South Carolina State University (est. 1896)

Founded in 1896 as the only state-supported land grant institution for African Americans, this Historically Black College/University (HBCU) located in Orangeburg, South Carolina, has been the scene of historic and tragic events connected with the Civil Rights Movement. Students joined and led community protests and boycotts in 1956, sit-ins and marches between 1960 and 1964, and suffered deaths and injuries during the **Orangeburg Massacre of 1968**. The state legislature created and funded graduate and law programs at SCSU to prevent blacks from entering the University of South Carolina. Segre-

gation remained both law and custom until the 1954 *Brown v. Board of Education* decision, which spurred African American petitions for change in the Orangeburg community, where they were the majority (60 percent) of the population. Strong opposition came from local authorities and the White Citizens Council (WCC). SCSU student leaders supporting the 1956 community boycott were expelled from the school for their activism, and nearly 400 students from SCSU and Claflin College (another HBCU) were arrested after being attacked with tear gas and fire hoses during a 1960 march to downtown Orangeburg. Efforts gained momentum when an SCSU student launched the "Orangeburg Movement" in 1963, which continued into the next year. Despite success in desegregating most of Orangeburg, continued exclusion of blacks from the city's only bowling alley led to more student protests and the Orangeburg Massacre. On February 8, 2008, SCSU held a commemorative and memorial service to mark the fortieth anniversary of the tragedy.

Fletcher F. Moon

Spelman College (est. 1881)

Sophia B. Packard and Harriet E. Giles founded Spelman College in 1881 in Atlanta, Georgia. The school grew from small classes in the basement of the Friendship Baptist Church to become one of the most prominent colleges in the South in the later part of the twentieth century. While Spelman student participation in civil rights demonstrations was limited, those students who did participate were quite active. Most of the outstanding contributions to civil rights protests from Spelman students were from 1960 to 1964. Following the freedom rides and the sit-ins in the late 1950s and in 1960, students from Spelman College and other schools in the Atlanta University community decided to write in support of the civil rights protests. The document written by these students was called "An Appeal for Human Rights"; the primary author was the class president of the Spelman

Student Government Association, Roslyn Pope. The appeal was published in the Atlanta *Constitution* on March 9, 1960. Student leaders from Spelman, **Morehouse**, Clark, Morrison Brown, and **Atlanta University** signed the appeal. The appeal outlined the major areas of discrimination in Atlanta, including education, jobs, housing, voting, hospitals, movies, concerts, restaurants, and law enforcement. Students from these colleges in Atlanta participated in a sit-in on March 15, 1960. They remained active in marches and demonstrations organized by civil rights organizations such as the **Southern Christian Leadership Conference** (SCLC), **Student Non-Violent Coordinating Committee** (SNCC), and **Congress of Racial Equality** (CORE) in the 1960s. Ruby Doris Smith Robinson became active in SNCC while a student at Spelman College. Robinson was instrumental in SNCC protests in the Atlanta area in the early 1960s. Eventually, she became the executive secretary for the organization and helped organize pickets of Woolworth's, A&P grocery, Grady Hospital, and other local Atlanta businesses. Her work with the SNCC ended in 1966 when she was diagnosed with terminal cancer.

Helen R. Houston

Talladega College (est. 1865)

Talladega College, in Talladega, Alabama, was conceived November 20, 1865, by former slaves William Savery and Thomas Tarrant of Talladega, who met with a group of freedmen in Mobile. Savery and Tarrant immediately began to carry out their commitment to education, aided by General Wager Swayne of the **Freedmen's Bureau**. Swayne persuaded the **American Missionary Association** to buy Baptist Academy, which was being sold and had been built by Savery, Tarrant, and other slaves. The school was renamed Swayne School and opened in November 1867. In 1869 Swayne School was reissued a charter as Talladega College. In keeping with the original commitment to the preservation of liberty, Talladega took an activist role in the Civil

Rights Movement. The demonstrations in Talladega took place almost two years after the **Greensboro, North Carolina, sit-ins**. The demonstrations and repercussions strengthened the ties between the campus and the black community. Everett McNair, former dean of the chapel at Talladega, was a participant in the first demonstrations in Talladega; he was arrested and jailed with students at Landham's store in April 1962. The students made two sit-in attempts, and on April 22 (Easter Sunday) held a kneel-in; they were arrested on each occasion. The newspaper reports in the Talladega *Daily Home,* the Talladega newspaper founded in 1909, detailed the arrests, trials, attempts to appeal the cases, and measures taken by the city to obtain a permanent injunction. All of the sit-in cases, which had been tried in Circuit Court in March 1963, were appealed. In July 1963, all of the students were found guilty.

Helen R. Houston

Tennessee State University (est. 1909)

Tennessee State, in Nashville, Tennessee, originally opened as Normal School in 1909, and in 1912 it was renamed the Agricultural and Industrial State Normal School at Nashville. It became a degree granting institution in 1924, and in 1927 its name was changed to Tennessee Agricultural and Industrial (A&I) State Teachers College. By 1958 it was a full-fledged, land-grant university; in 1968 "A&I" was dropped from its name, and it became Tennessee State University. That same year Rita Sanders (Geier), a student faculty member, filed suit alleging a dual system of higher education existed based on race; there were two four-year public institutions in Nashville: Tennessee State and the University of Tennessee at Nashville. In 1979, as a result of the Geier case, the former University of Tennessee at Nashville was merged into Tennessee State, creating two campuses: this was the first merger of its kind. In the late 1950s, Tennessee State students, along with other students in the city, began training and participating in the non-violent workshops held by the Reverends **James Lawson Jr.** and **Kelly Miller Smith**. Students were involved in the movement's **Freedom Rides** and sit-ins. Initial forays into the latter had begun by the fall of 1959, and by February 13, 1960, the **Nashville Student Movement** commenced. Students were threatened, arrested, and in the initial days of the demonstration some from Tennessee State were expelled. The community rallied to support the students with attorneys and bail money; however, 81 of the students rejected bail and chose to remain in jail. The university awarded honorary degrees to 17 of the expelled students in May 2008.

Helen R. Houston

The college has demonstrated a social awareness and commitment to the improvement of race relations in Mississippi.

Texas Southern University (est. 1947)

Originally established in 1947 as the Texas State University for Negroes in Houston, TSU gained its current name in 1951. It was an institution of higher education for black students. It became the first Historically Black College and University (HBCU) to house a law school. The university has since grown in both physical size and scope. The Texas Legislature designated it a "special purpose institution for urban programming" in 1973. The university's community involvement and concern for the civil rights of the citizenry are not only evident in its graduates, but also in the actions of its students. Following the **Greensboro Sit-ins**, the

students at Texas Southern, on March 4, 1960 and under the leadership of law student Elderway Stearns, began sit-ins and boycotts of Houston's downtown stores. However, due to behind-the-scenes negotiations by a group of older black citizens led by Bob Dundas, lunch counters were integrated without media coverage. Next targeted were hotels, which were also desegregated without incident or publicity. However, the restaurants and movie theaters resisted. One hundred students prepared to disrupt the nationally televised tickertape parade for astronaut Gordon Cooper; again, a behind-the-scenes, quiet negotiation resulted in the integration of public accommodations. On the 48th anniversary of the sit-ins, students at Texas Southern commemorated their contribution to the integration of the city of Houston and to the Civil Rights Movement.

Helen R. Houston

Tougaloo College (est. 1871)

A private, historically black, four-year liberal arts college and a church-related institution, Tougaloo College is located in Tougaloo, Mississippi, just outside Jackson. It started when the **American Missionary Association** of New York purchased land for the training of young African Americans. In 1871 the Mississippi State Legislature granted it a charter as "Tougaloo University"; it became Tougaloo College in 1916. In 1954 Tougaloo College merged with Southern Christian Institute and became Tougaloo Christian College. The name was again changed in 1962 to Tougaloo College. The college has demonstrated a social awareness and commitment to the improvement of race relations in Mississippi since its original inception. That emphasis continued into the 1950s and 1960s, when Tougaloo's students became actively involved in the Civil Rights Movement in Mississippi.

Students began protesting in Jackson and led a boycott of restaurants that refused to serve blacks. Students were arrested for protesting and trying to attend white churches and concerts. The university's president, Adam Beittel, supported the students' action and often bailed them out of jail. The students led a campaign to encourage white entertainers not to participate in segregated performances in Jackson. In the 1960s, **Robert "Bob" Moses** and the **Reverend James Lawson** held voter registration and non-violence workshops on the campus. Nevertheless, violence erupted on the campus, there were threats to both students and faculty, and the state of Mississippi was successful in having the board of trustees remove Beittel as president. Tougaloo played a vital role in the Mississippi Civil Rights Movement.

Helen R. Houston

University of Maryland, Eastern Shore (est. 1886)

This institution was founded in 1886 as the Delaware Conference Academy of the Methodist Episcopal Church even though it is considered a Historically Black College/University (HBCU) located in Princess Anne, Maryland. It was also known as the Industrial Branch of Morgan State College and Princess Anne Academy in early years. The state of Maryland assumed control in 1919 and took formal ownership of the campus in 1926. Maryland State College was the name of the institution from 1948 until 1970, when it became the University of Maryland, Eastern Shore (UMES). In 1988 UMES officially was identified as a campus of the University of Maryland System, which subsequently changed its name to the University System of Maryland.

Maryland originally acquired the college to maintain the exclusion of African Americans from its flagship campus in College Park, and gave it 1890 land-grant institution status. Away from the campus, eastern shore communities such as Cambridge, Salisbury, Easton, and Chestertown maintained segregation policies well into the 1960s. Maryland State College students joined activists from the Baltimore-based Civic Interest Group (CIG), Cambridge Non-

Violent Action Committee (CNAC), **Student Non-Violent Coordinating Committee** (SNCC), **Northern Student Movement** (NSM) and the **Congress of Racial Equality** (CORE) in sit-ins and freedom rides during 1961 and 1962. Maryland State College student Bill Henry was a leader of the Maryland Eastern-shore Project in the summer of 1962, and students from the college remained active during efforts in subsequent years to end segregation in the area.

Fletcher F. Moon

Virginia State University (est. 1882)

Located in Petersburg, Virginia, this Historically Black College/University (HBCU) was founded on March 6, 1882, as the Virginia Normal and Collegiate Institute, but opposition and a lawsuit delayed its actual opening until October 1, 1883. This marked the beginning of a long pattern of struggle for both the institution and other public education for African Americans in the surrounding area, continuing into the civil rights era of the 1950s and 1960s before significant change was achieved. In 1902 the Virginia legislature curtailed the college program and changed the name to Virginia Normal and Industrial Institute, and in 1920 land-grant status was moved from Hampton Institute (now University) to the school. The college program was restored in 1923, and the name changed again in 1930 to Virginia State College for Negroes. A two-year branch located in Norfolk was established in 1944, eventually growing into an independent, four-year HBCU, Norfolk State College, while the parent institution was renamed Virginia State College in 1946. The present name of Virginia State University (VSU) won legislative approval in 1979. The school's first president was **John Mercer Langston**, the only black elected to Congress from Virginia (in 1888) until 1992 and great-uncle of famed African American writer **Langston Hughes**. Fifth president Robert P. Daniel demonstrated great courage and leadership during his tenure at VSU, supporting independent elementary and secondary education for black Virginians when all public schools in **Prince Edward County** were closed between 1959 and 1963 in opposition to desegregation.

Fletcher F. Moon

Integration of Colleges and Universities

University of Alabama and Vivian Malone Jones (1942–2005)

A trailblazer during the modern civil rights era, Vivian Malone Jones was one of two African American students who in 1963 broke down racial barriers at the University of Alabama; the other was James Hood. Their arrival on campus attracted national attention due to the efforts of Alabama's Governor George Wallace to block their entrance by standing in the schoolhouse door. After that, National Guard troops escorted the two students to the school and through the halls to registration. Quoted in the *Washington Post,* she said of her approach to the school: "I didn't feel that I should sneak in. I didn't feel I should go around to the back door." After the U.S. Supreme Court's landmark decision *Brown v. Board of Education* in 1954, Alabama was the first Southern university ordered to comply, but it refused to do so until 1963. Jones graduated in 1965, having studied

Vivian Malone Jones broke down racial barriers at the University of Alabama in 1963; here, she is led into Foster Auditorium at the University of Alabama in Tuscaloosa, Ala., in 1963 (AP Photo/Montgomery Advertiser).

previously at the historically black **Alabama Agricultural and Mechanical College** (now University). She was the school's first African American graduate. Her experiences at the university were mixed—some painful, some not. Some of her fellow students were openly hostile, while others were supportive and extended a hand of fellowship. After graduation, she remained mindful of the importance of the Civil Rights Movement and became active in it and organizations such as the **NAACP** and the **Southern Christian Leadership Conference**. Jones and Wallace had a conversation in 1996, at which time she asked him why he took the doorway stand back in 1963. According to the *Washington Post,* "He said he did what he felt needed to be done at that point in time, but he would not do that today." Jones also spoke of forgiveness in the article.

Jessie Carney Smith

Curriculum

Black Studies

Black Studies is an activist-based discipline. It emerges out of the conscious determination that education about the history and circumstances of African Americans can be used to elevate their status. Early proponents of Black Studies believed that learning of the contributions of people of African descent to human history and progress would encourage a positive self-concept among African Americans while also challenging racist distortions used to justify discrimination and oppression. While some attempts at creating Black Studies curricula were made before the twentieth century, the idea of studying black people in a traditional setting to inspire social and political progress for African Americans was not initiated until the early part of the twentieth century. The work of **Booker T. Washington**, advocating black pride and agency, and the founding of **Carter G. Woodson**'s Institute for the Study of

Negro Life and History are in part responsible for the conscious demand for courses on black culture and history at American universities. **W.E.B. Du Bois** is recognized among those who formed early attempts to establish Black Studies programs. At **Atlanta University** in the 1930s, Du Bois taught a Black Studies curriculum. However, the actual establishment of Black Studies programs and departments came in response to student protests in the 1960s. These students were inspired by the protests of the Civil Rights Movement; in particular, they were encouraged by the radical shift in the movement in the late 1960s that demanded black pride, black power, and black self-awareness. These students led demonstrations on predominantly white college campuses across the United States. They argued that the development of such programs was necessary for black students at white institutions. The first program was established at San Francisco State University and led by Black Studies advocate, activist, and sociologist Dr. Nathan Hare.

Helen R. Houston

Educators

Appiah, Kwame Anthony (1954–)

As a prolific scholar, writer, and teacher, Kwame Anthony Appiah experienced a life that crossed the boundaries of race, culture, gender, and geography. This has made him a highly regarded and widely respected intellectual in African and African American literary and cultural studies. Kwame Anthony Akroma-Ampim Kusi Appiah was born in London, England, on May 8, 1954. However, he spent his early years in Kumasi, Ghana. His Ghanaian father, Joseph Emmanuel Appiah (1918–1990), was a lawyer and politician, while his English mother, Peggy Cripps Appiah (daughter of statesman Sir Stafford Cripps), was a novelist and children's book writer. The young Appiah returned to England for undergraduate and graduate studies at

Clare College of Cambridge University, earning the B.A. and Ph.D. in philosophy. Appiah has taught at leading American institutions, including Yale, Cornell, Duke, Harvard, and Princeton, where he recently was named Laurance S. Rockefeller University Professor of Philosophy at the University Center for Human Values. He has also lectured at universities in England, France, Germany, Ghana, and South Africa; he has published extensively, authoring several philosophy texts and novels. Appiah collaborated with his mother to produce a volume of African proverbs, and with Henry Louis Gates on multivolume and multimedia versions of an Africana encyclopedia, completing a project first envisioned by W.E.B. Du Bois in 1909.

Fletcher F. Moon

[Derrick Bell] supervised over 300 school desegregation cases in Mississippi.

Bell, Derrick (1930–)

The first black tenured professor of Harvard University's law school, Derrick Albert Bell Jr. gained national attention for his work as an activist for the rights of black and other minorities. Whether a mentor to minority law school students at Harvard, at other academic institutions, or in his legal practice, he has consistently refused to compromise his principles. The Pittsburgh native became a staff attorney in the Civil Rights Division, U.S. Department of Justice—the only black among 1,000 staff lawyers. Claiming that his **NAACP** membership represented a conflict of interest with his civil rights work, the Department of Justice demanded that he resign his membership. Bell refused and resigned from

the department instead. Bell continued to work in the area of civil rights, as first assistant council for the NAACP Legal Defense Fund. Under the leadership of **Thurgood Marshall**, he supervised over 300 school desegregation cases in Mississippi; he also led James Meredith's efforts to desegregate the University of Mississippi. In 1969 Bell joined Harvard's law school. There he introduced a course in civil rights law. He engaged in various protests while serving as the first black dean at the University of Oregon Law School and later at Stanford University. Returning to Harvard in 1986, he protested the school's refusal to appoint and tenure a black woman visiting professor. He left and Harvard reacted by dismissing him from his tenured position in June 1992. Then he joined the law school at New York University. Bell has written major works on racism and racial justice.

Jessie Carney Smith

Berry, Mary Frances (1938–)

The first African American woman to chair the U.S. Commission on Civil Rights, Mary Frances Berry's most perceptible contribution has been in the civil rights arena. An assistant secretary for education in the Department of Health, Education, and Welfare under President Jimmy Carter, Berry was appointed by Carter in 1980 to the U.S. Commission on Civil Rights, an independent agency established by the **Civil Rights Act of 1957**. During her tenure with the commission, Berry became involved in legal disputes with President Ronald Reagan. Because of their disagreements over civil rights policies, in 1984 Reagan removed her from the commission. According to Berry, Reagan wanted to transform the commission from a regulator of civil rights to a servile subject of the administration. She sued President Reagan and won reinstatement by the federal district court. In 1993 President Bill Clinton named her chair of the U.S. Civil Rights Commission. Six years later, Berry was reappointed to a six-year term.

Throughout her term as commission chair, Dr. Berry issued significant reports on numerous issues, including the 2000 Florida Presidential Elections, police brutality in New York, environmental justice, percentage plans and affirmative action, church bombings, and conditions on Native American reservations. Her activism in civil rights spread abroad as a founding member of the Free South Africa Movement, which instigated protests against apartheid at the South African Embassy.

The second of three children born to George and Frances Berry, Mary Frances Berry was born in Nashville, Tennessee, where she received her primary and secondary education. She received her undergraduate (1961) and graduate (1962) degrees from Howard University, and a terminal degree in history (1966) and a law degree (1970) from the University of Michigan. A member of the District of Columbia Bar and an academician, Berry was the first African American women to head a major research university in America (as chancellor of the University of Colorado at Boulder). Recently named the Geraldine R. Segal Professor of American Social Thought at the University of Pennsylvania, she has served on the faculties of numerous universities and colleges. An acclaimed author and scholar, Professor Berry has produced numerous works in the field of history and constitutional law. Elected by her peers as a vice president of the American Historical Association and President of the Organization of American Historians, she has received over thirty honorary doctorate degrees and numerous awards for her public service and scholarly activities. She is one of the 75 women photographed in the book *I Dream a World: Portraits of Black Women Who Changed America.*

Linda T. Wynn

Bethune, Mary McLeod (1875–1955)

❝We cannot accept any excuse that the exclusion of Negro representation was an oversight.... We are incensed!❞ This was the response of Mary McLeod Bethune when black women were excluded from membership in an

advisory council to the War Department in October 1941. The uncompromising Bethune was born in 1875 near Mayesville, South Carolina, and met many challenges because of her race and gender. In spite of these obstacles, she possessed a missionary spirit toward helping others. Bethune, desiring to provide more opportunities for educating black children, opened a school in Daytona, Florida, for Negro girls. Through her determination, keen business skills, and ingenuity the school evolved into the Bethune-Cookman College for boys and girls. As an active member of the community and a member of the **NAACP**, she was also the only invited black guest at the National Council of Women's luncheon in 1927. Bethune worked hard to achieve social justice for black Americans. The NAACP acknowledged her leadership and success as an educator when she was awarded the organization's highest honor, the Spingarn Medal.

"We cannot accept any excuse that the exclusion of Negro representation was an oversight.... We are incensed!"

In an effort to open doors for young black women, Bethune founded the National Council of Negro Women in 1935 and was also appointed by President Franklin Delano Roosevelt to the advisory board of the National Youth Administration (NYA). She was able to bring national attention to issues of race, women, education, and justice. Bethune was considered the preeminent leader on racial issues from 1936 to 1945. One example of her influences and political connections came when she brought together the Department of Labor and the Secretaries of Commerce and Agriculture with the **Black Cabinet** and the most important African American leaders of the day for a conference on January 6 through 8, 1937. The conference addressed the most pressing issues confronting black Americans at that time. After Bethune became director of the Negro Division of the NYA, she helped many youths and women secure employment during the Great Depression. Bethune continued her campaign for social justice until May 18, 1955, when she died of a heart attack.

Lean'tin L. Bracks

Brown, Charlotte Hawkins (1883–1961)

The granddaughter of slaves, Charlotte Eugenia Hawkins Brown founded Palmer Memorial Institute in Sedalia, North Carolina, opening the school on October 10, 1902. She became a driving force in preparatory education for African American youth, attracting students from across the nation. Although she focused primarily on her students and the mission of her school, Brown was a social activist as well. In 1909 she helped to found the North Carolina State Federation of Negro Women's Clubs and served as president of the organization from 1915 to 1926. Her interest in black women and youth continued when she established the Efland Home for Wayward Girls. An advocate for racial harmony and mutual understanding, she founded the Commission on Interracial Cooperation in 1919. She was a non-violent activist who challenged the South's Jim Crow standards. For example, she refused to ride in segregated elevators, was removed from Pullman car berths on trains that were restricted to whites only, and filed lawsuits to oppose discriminatory practices in public transportation. Brown's reputation as an educator and orator, as well as her school's reputation, brought her numerous speaking engagements at churches, interracial groups, and college campuses such as Mount Holyoke, Smith, Radcliffe, and elsewhere. Wherever she spoke, she remained an advocate for

Charlotte Hawkins Brown (Fisk University).

interracial understanding. Furthermore, she earned recognition from the Council of Fair Play, which in 1944 presented her with its Second Annual Award for Racial Understanding.

Jessie Carney Smith

Chambers, Julius L. (1936–)

For more than four decades, Julian Chambers has been on the front line of the nation's legal struggle to secure civil rights. During the mid-1960s he became the first intern with the new NAACP Legal Defense Fund (LDF). Later, as the owner of his own legal practice in North Carolina, Chambers championed diversified workplaces when his firm became the first to integrate in the state. Both as an attorney in private practice and as director-counsel of the LDF, Chambers's influence in landmark state and federal legislation to secure school desegregation, as well as employment and voting rights, are legendary. Born and reared in North Carolina, Chambers is a graduate of North Carolina Central University, University of Michigan, University of North Carolina at Chapel Hill, and Columbia University Law School. Following his internship with the LDF in 1964, Chambers opened his firm later the same year. With his partners, James E. Ferguson II and Adam Stein, and the LDF, Chambers helped shape the legal arguments that won several important U.S. Supreme Court cases. Among his most salient victories was the *Swann v. Charlotte-Mecklenburg Board of Education* (1971), which led to federal mandated busing. He left his firm in 1984 to become the LDF's director-counsel, leading the organization's continued fight for civil rights legislation and affirmative action programs. In 1993 Chambers became chancellor at his alma mater North Carolina Central, where he launched a $50 million capital fund raising campaign and established its first 10 endowed chairs, including a $1 million chair in honor of Charles Hamilton Houston at the School of Law, before retiring in 2001.

Crystal A. deGregory

Clark, Septima Poinsette (1898–1987)

Septima Poinsette Clark was best known for her untiring efforts to promote her race; she was an activist in areas such as literacy, voter registration, civil rights, and women's rights. She saw racism first hand in 1916 on Johns Island near Charleston, South Carolina, where she taught school and witnessed vast discrepancies between schools for whites and those for blacks. After teaching assignments elsewhere, in 1947 she returned to Charleston and was fired after she refused to drop out of the **NAACP**. In 1952 she began her affiliation with **Highlander Folk School** in Monteagle, Tennessee, where she attended an interracial institute in two consecutive summers. The school became well known for its interracial training programs, attracting civil rights workers from across the South. By 1954 Clark began to focus on voting rights and

persuaded Charleston's activists to attend Highlander. Next, she and Esau Jenkins, a former student from Johns Island, set up a Highlander-sponsored adult literacy training program on Johns Island to help blacks prepare to register and vote. She also hosted at Highlander the first regional conference comprised of students in the sit-ins. In 1959 Tennessee began successful efforts to close Highlander and the **Southern Christian Leadership Conference** (SCLC) took on its literacy work. Clark traveled the South promoting the program. For ten years (1960–1970) she implemented the SCLC's citizenship programs and worked with other groups, such as the **Student Non-Violent Coordinating Committee**, in preparing blacks to register and vote. After her retirement in 1970, Clark lectured widely on civil and women's rights.

Jessie Carney Smith

Cleaver, Kathleen Neal (1945–)

Perhaps best known as the wife of **Black Panther Party** leader **Eldridge Cleaver**, Kathleen Neal Cleaver is an activist in her own right. A former member of the **Student Non-Violent Coordinating Committee** (SNCC), Cleaver worked as a grass roots organizer in the party alongside her then-husband. She has since become a respected lawyer and college professor who brings her unique prospective on race, gender, and class issues to her work.

Kathleen Neal was born in Dallas, Texas, to a middle-class family. Both Ernest and Juette Johnson Neal were college educated. Her father's work as a college professor led the family to relocate in Tuskegee, Alabama, and later to several countries after he joined the Foreign Service. Neal returned to the United States alone; she graduated from the George School near Philadelphia in 1963, before attending Oberlin College in Ohio. In 1966, shortly after transferring to Barnard College in New York, Neal dropped out of college to work full-time with the SNCC as its secretary. After she met and married **Eldridge Cleaver**, she joined the

Panthers and became the first woman to serve on its central committee. Cleaver fled the country with her husband following a series of violent conflicts in 1968. While in Algeria, the Cleavers founded the international wing of the party together, but infighting forced its expulsion from the party. Cleaver's work on her husband's defense fund helped him to be granted bail in 1976. She later graduated from Yale University in 1983. Cleaver divorced in 1987 and graduated from Yale Law School two years later.

Crystal A. deGregory

Cruse went on to help create the Center for Afro-American and African Studies at the University of Michigan.

Cooper, Anna J. (1858?–1964)

Anna J. Cooper used her education and scholarship as a platform for her women's rights and civil rights activism. As the fourth African American to earn a doctoral degree in the United States, she is the author of *A Voice from the South* (1892), which not only advocated self-determination through education and social uplift, but also was among the earliest works to address feminism among black women.

Anna Julia Haywood was born in Raleigh, North Carolina, to Hannah Stanley Haywood, an enslaved woman, and her master, George Washington Haywood. In 1868 she attended St. Augustine's Normal School and Collegiate Institute on a scholarship. After finishing the school's "Ladies Course," Haywood worked there as an instructor. In 1877 she married St. Augustine's alumnus A. C. Cooper, an Episcopal minister whom she assisted as a teacher's aid

after her marriage barred her from teaching classes at the school. Widowed at 21, Cooper attended Oberlin College in Ohio and graduated with her bachelor's degree in 1884; this was followed by a master's degree in mathematics three years later. She served for a time as the principal of Washington Colored High School in Washington, D.C., one of the nation's leading academic high schools for African Americans. While working full-time, Cooper pursued doctoral studies at Columbia University and at the University of Paris, which awarded her a Ph.D. in 1925. Cooper continued her intellectual and social activism throughout her life as an author and as a participant in the Colored Women's League of Washington, D.C., the first Pan-African Congress, and the Colored Women's YMCA. She died in her sleep at age 105.

Crystal A. deGregory

Cruse, Harold (1916–2005)

Harold Cruse used the power of the written word from an artistic perspective to offer critical and often searing explorations of issues of social justice and equality. After serving in the military during World War II, he spent several years as a member of the Communist Party and attended the City College of New York, but he never graduated. He became fascinated with the relationship between art and social change and went on to write several plays. In 1960 he co-founded, along with Leroi Jones (**Amiri Baraka**), the Black Arts Theater and the School in Harlem. Cruse is most remembered for his book *The Crisis of the Negro Intellectual* (1967). Cruse's book analyzes leadership in the black community, as well as philosophies of integration, separatism, and other cultural issues of the time. This text placed Cruse in the forefront of critical discussions in the black community; Cruse saw himself as a dissenter of all American sensibilities and philosophies. After receiving much attention for his book, he was invited to lecture at the University of Michigan in 1968 and later became a tenured professor of history without ever having received a college degree. Cruse went on to help create the Center for Afro-American and African Studies at the University of Michigan. He continued to voice his dissent on matters such as the boycotting of Gershwin's folk opera *Porgy and Bess* (1935) because its music was "stolen" from Harlem nightclubs; the 1954 *Brown v. Board of Education* decision, which he saw as ultimately making unemployed a generation of experienced black educators; and a rejection of *Raisin in the Sun* by **Lorraine Hansberry** in 1959 as representative of working class Chicago black life. Cruse continued to author critical texts about both white and black American society until his retirement in 1980. He died in 2005 at the age of 89.

Lean'tin L. Bracks

Du Bois, W.E.B. (1868–1963)

Arguably the greatest African American scholar-intellectual of the twentieth century, William Edward Burghardt Du Bois employed his research and training to further the causes of social uplift and the educational and professional development of African Americans. His 1903 publication, *The Souls of Black Folk,* is among the most influential texts of the twentieth century, while his "Talented Tenth" theory countered **Booker T. Washington's** accommodationist platform. As a founder of both the **Niagara Movement** and **NAACP**, Du Bois was a pioneer of the modern Civil Rights Movement. He dedicated his life to ending colonialism, exploitation, and racism worldwide.

Born into a small community of blacks in Great Barrington, Massachusetts, Du Bois was reared by his mother, Mary Sylvina Burghardt. His father, Alfred Du Bois, had disappeared soon after Du Bois's birth, leaving his son with little knowledge of him. Poverty stricken, his mother struggled to meet the family's needs. Fortunately, she was assisted by her extended family. In school Du Bois experienced little racial discrimination and outperformed his white counterparts to become Great Barrington High School's first African American valedictorian. Awarded a

W.E.B. Du Bois (Fisk University).

scholarship to college, he arrived at the all-black **Fisk University** in Nashville, Tennessee, in 1885. The school not only offered Du Bois greater exposure to African American culture, but also helped to politicize his thinking.

By the time he graduated with a baccalaureate degree in 1888, Du Bois had already established himself as a critic of racism and social injustice during his tenure as writer and chief editor of the *Fisk Herald.* He entered Harvard University that same year as a junior and earned a second B.A. In the spring of 1891, Du Bois received his master's degree, before furthering his studies at the University of Berlin from 1892 to 1894. Following his time in Berlin, Du Bois became the first African American to earn a Ph.D. from Harvard with his doctoral thesis, *The Suppression of the African Slave Trade to the*

United States of America, 1638 to 1870. After his marriage to Nina Gomer in 1896, Du Bois taught variously at Wilberforce University (1894–1896) and the University of Pennsylvania (1897–1899), where he wrote the landmark sociological study *The Philadelphia Negro* before arriving at **Atlanta University** (AU).

Throughout the 1950s, Du Bois's criticism of American capitalism, imperialism, and racial inequality firmly tied him to leftist causes.

Following the publication of *Souls,* Du Bois helped to organize the Niagara Movement that, despite its failure, led to the founding of the NAACP in 1909. Du Bois became editor of the organization's *Crisis* magazine. As a trumpet against all forms of racism, the publication soon became the authoritative resource for black America with circulation reaching 30,000 by 1913. He began to tie Pan-Africanism to socialism, which led to a break with *Crisis's* executive committee and his eventual resignation as editor. Du Bois taught for a time at AU before serving another four-year stint with the NAACP (1944–1948).

Du Bois was also the author of *The Star of Ethiopia.* An Afrocentric history pageant, The *Star of Ethiopia* was presented on three occasions. It reflects Du Bois's belief in the possibilities for serious black theatre, given the richness of available subject matter, black actors, and black writers. He saw in this a way of educating both black audiences to the richness and meaning of its history and talent, and white audiences to a recognition and knowledge of black people. Du Bois's interest in Ethiopia and all it symbolizes is evident in much of his writing; it

is apparent in the language and the props utilized in the pageant. The pageant was first presented in 1913 as part of the New York's commemoration of the fiftieth anniversary of the Emancipation, and it played before an interracial audience of around 14,000 people. It was again presented in Philadelphia's Convention Hall at the African Methodist Episcopal church's hundredth anniversary general conference in May 1916. The final presentation was at the Hollywood Bowl in 1925.

The *Star of Ethiopia* commemorated blackness, had hundreds of actors, was three hours long, and was divided into a prologue and five scenes: The Gift of Iron, The Dream of Egypt, The Glory of Ethiopia, The Valley of Humiliation, and The Vision Everlasting. The music for the pageant included two pieces from Giuseppe Verdi's *Aida,* and the remainder was by black composers Bob Cole, Rosamond Johnson, Samuel Coleridge Taylor, and Charles Young. It was considered for film adaptation, but the prospect of a movie proved too costly. David Levering Lewis said it was "the most thoughtful, ambitious theatrical response to [Thomas] Dixon and [D.W.] Griffith's racist epic," *The Birth of a Nation* (1915).

Throughout the 1950s, Du Bois's criticism of American capitalism, imperialism, and racial inequality firmly tied him to leftist causes, including chairing the Peace Information Center. He and the center's refusal to register as foreign agents led to his indictment. While he was soon exonerated, his passport was revoked and Du Bois settled in Ghana with his second wife, Shirley Graham, in 1961. He joined the American Communist Party and became a citizen of Ghana, where he died one day before the famous **March on Washington**.

Crystal A. deGregory and Helen R. Houston

Duncan, Gladys (1896–2005)

A formidable career civic activist, Gladys Duncan helped break down racial barriers in Washington, D.C., and in the Democratic Party. At first an elementary school teacher, she later became a protestor and supported the work of her husband, singer Todd Duncan, the first black member of the New York City Opera. Spurred by her activism, he refused to sing to white-only audiences in Washington; as a result, theaters in the district and vicinity were desegregated. Active in the Democratic Party, Duncan was first a volunteer; then, in 1955, she joined the Woman's National Democratic Club and was its first black member. She walked picket lines in the city, with the aim of desegregating such businesses as the People's Drug Store. Duncan revealed a favorite trick that she used to integrate eating establishments in Washington—a city filled with diplomats: "If you could speak another language, they were afraid not to serve you because they thought you might be diplomats," she once said. Duncan served the Democratic National Committee as a delegate to presidential nominating conventions in 1956, 1960, and 1964. She took advantage of that role to fight for civil rights. She protested against the racist seating arrangement of Mississippi's delegation in 1956, and in 1964 joined others who advocated seating the integrated **Mississippi Freedom Democratic Party.**

Jessie Carney Smith

Foster, Autherine Juanita Lucy (1929–)

Born to Milton and Minnie Hosea Lucy in Shiloh, Alabama, on October 5, 1929, Foster attended Alabama's public schools. Shortly after graduating from Linden Academy in 1947, she matriculated at Selma University and earned a bachelor's degree in English from Miles College in Birmingham. After her 1952 graduation, she wanted to further her education. With the assistance of the **NAACP**, she and Pollie Myers were accepted at the all-white University of Alabama, until school officials learned they were not white.

Attorneys **Thurgood Marshall, Constance Baker Motley,** and Arthur Shores began court proceedings on their behalf in July 1953. In June

1955, the NAACP attorneys won a court order prohibiting the University of Alabama from denying Foster or any other person admission based on race. After three and a half years of legal work to prove racial discrimination, on February 3, 1956, Autherine Lucy (she married Hugh Lawrence Foster in April 1956) became the first black student admitted to the University of Alabama. She enrolled in the graduate School of Library Science at the main campus in Tuscaloosa, Alabama. Myers, however, was denied admittance because she was an unwed mother. The university claimed that rendered her an unfit student. A riot broke out following Foster's admittance to the University of Alabama. She was met with violent anti-desegregation demonstrations, cross burnings, and a riotous mob of students, townspeople, and Ku Klux Klan members who shouted, "Kill her!" "Kill her!"

Because of the riot, university officials suspended Lucy "for her own safety." Again, the NAACP sued on Lucy's behalf and won. However, the decision was thwarted by her expulsion on the grounds of making "false" and "outrageous" statements about the school. The federal government failed to enforce either the 1954 *Brown v. Board of Education* decision or the court order against the University of Alabama. Although Lucy attended the university for less than a week, her short tenure at the University of Alabama was a significant signpost in the Civil Rights Movement. Her case became an emblematic battleground for pro-segregationists and anti-segregationists alike. Blacks were not able to penetrate the University of Alabama's barrier of segregation until 1963, when the National Guard had to escort James Hood and **Vivian Malone Jones** to class registration.

While Foster was the first black to desegregate the University of Alabama, Jones was its first black to graduate. In April of 1988, at the behest of several faculty members, the University of Alabama officially overturned Autherine Lucy Foster's expulsion. A year later, she enrolled in the university's graduate program in elementary education. She and her daughter,

Grazia, graduated in the spring of 1992 with a master's degree in education and an undergraduate degree in corporate finance, respectively.

Linda T. Wynn

Franklin, John Hope (1915–)

John Hope Franklin was an accomplished professor who believed that it was the obligation of historians like himself to become involved in the activism of his day. Franklin, who was born in Rentiesville, Oklahoma, entered **Fisk University** in Nashville, Tennessee, in 1931; he was determined to follow his father's example and pursue a career in law. After being introduced to history by a white professor at Fisk, Franklin saw his future was not in law. Franklin went on to earn a Ph.D. in history from Harvard, and along the way he confronted the challenges of racism and segregation. After being barred from the University of Oklahoma's graduate program in history, he testified in the case of Lyman Johnson, who was seeking entry into the all-white graduate history program at the University of Kentucky.

In the 1950s Franklin served on the **NAACP** Legal Defense team led by **Thurgood Marshall** by writing historical essays and working with other researchers. Franklin provided research that helped in developing the case that led to 1954's *Brown v. Board of Education,* which desegregated public schools. Franklin assisted Marshall in responding to the U.S. Supreme Court's question regarding the original intent of the **Fourteenth Amendment**. Franklin's research with the NAACP further supported his view of the historian as an activist and the importance of that relationship to the development of public policy. Franklin was in England during the 1963 **March on Washington**, but he joined the **Selma to Montgomery March** led by Martin Luther King Jr. in 1965. He joined with many other historians in protesting racism and inequality in the United States. Franklin spoke out, too, against the Supreme Court nominations of Robert Bork in 1987 and Clarence Thomas in 1991. Franklin,

John Hope Franklin (Fisk University).

who lent his voice to many civil rights and affirmative action causes, received the Presidential Medal of Freedom in 1995 from President Bill Clinton. In 1997 President Clinton appointed him as chair of the advisory board to the **President's Initiative on Race**. The board held dialogues on race across the nation and then counseled the president on improving race relations.

Lean'tin L. Bracks

Hobson, Julius W. (1922–1977)

An uncompromising civil rights activist, Julius W. Hobson was instrumental in breaking down racial barriers in Washington, D.C., including the elimination of *de facto* segregation of its public schools. He was a founder and chair of **Act Associates** and worked through that organization to effect policy changes concerning school funding. The Birmingham native was a graduate of Tuskegee Institute (now University), an educator, and an economist with the U.S. Department of Housing and Urban Development for twenty years. He retired on April 1, 1970. From 1961 to 1964 he was president of the **Congress of Racial Equality** (CORE). He led over 80 picket lines before 120 downtown retail stores and was active in many other local desegregation protests. Hobson also served on his local school board until 1969, when he was defeated in an election. Hobson was elected to the Washington, D.C., City Council in 1974 on the Statehood ticket. An acknowledged Marxist, in the mid-1960s he had an ambiguous but confidential relationship with the FBI and was an informant. Although he was markedly different from other charismatic figures such as **Martin Luther King Jr.** and **Malcolm X**, many consider him to have been important in breaking down racial barriers in Washington, D.C.

Jessie Carney Smith

Horton, Myles Fall (1905–1990)

A trailblazer in the cause of social justice within America's southern region, Myles Horton was an activist and a founder and director of both the **Highlander Folk School** and the Highlander Research and Education Center. Interested in advancing new ideas about class and race, Horton's programs contributed to the labor and Civil Rights Movements. A controversial individual in Tennessee and the South in general, Horton was the oldest of four children born in Savannah, Tennessee, to socially active parents who taught him the core values of love, work, service, and education. As he grew into adulthood, Horton adhered to the advice of his mother, Elsie Falls Horton, and sought to fashion his life around the principle of being of service to others and building a community based on recognizing the humanity in all people. It was through his experiences in the work place and in education that Horton further refined his personal and organizational ethos for social change.

Because education beyond the secondary level was not available in Savannah, Horton left home at 15 to attend high school. He supported himself by working in a saw mill and later a box factory, where he garnered an understanding about the strength of organizing and the power of collective action. In 1928 Horton received his undergraduate degree from Cumberland University. He later attended Union Theological Seminary, where he studied under Reinhold Niebuhr, an outspoken advocate of socialist principles in social and economic matters. He then matriculated at the University of Chicago and toured the folk schools of Denmark, which were a populist education experiment. While in Denmark, he decided to establish a school where students and teachers could dwell together in an unceremonious atmosphere of proposing and resolving problems. It was his belief that the basic experience of existing in an intellectually stimulating environment of debate would be the primary instructor.

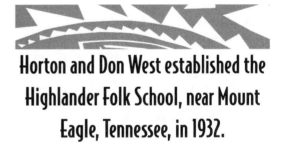

Horton and Don West established the Highlander Folk School, near Mount Eagle, Tennessee, in 1932.

Upon his return to his native state, Horton and Don West established the Highlander Folk School, near Mount Eagle, Tennessee, in 1932. Throughout the 1930s and 1940s, the school became a center of labor education in the American South. Through extension programs, Horton and his colleagues aided striking coal miners, woodcutters, mill hands, government relief workers, and union members. Because of its activities, Highlander became the educational arm of the Congress of Industrial Organizations (CIO) union, and in 1937 Horton joined the

CIO staff and organized one of its first local chapters in the southern textile industry. Realizing the similarities between workers' rights and civil rights, he grasped that as long as the races remained segregated, labor would never be free. With that understanding, Horton organized and designed workshops to decimate the Jim Crow system. Because of his belief and promotion of interracial unionism, Horton and the CIO parted ways in the 1940s.

A year before the U.S. Supreme Court's decision in the *Brown v. Board of Education* case, Horton began conducting workshops on school desegregation. Over the next two decades, Highlander's founder devoted his energy to creating programs that aided leaders and participants in the African American struggle for civil rights. For many years, Highlander was the only place in the South where white and African American citizens lived and worked together, defying local laws against such multiracial cooperation. Later, Horton extended the programs to Appalachia, hoping to build a multiracial alliance that would revolutionize America's economic, social, and political structure. In 1982 Horton and Highlander were nominated for the Nobel Peace Prize. Myles Horton, a catalyst for social change, educator, and author, died on January 10, 1990. That year, Doubleday Press published his autobiography, *Long Haul,* and Temple University Press published his *We Make the Road by Walking: Conversations in Education and Social Change.*

Linda T. Wynn

Johnson, Charles Spurgeon (1893–1956)

The contributions of Charles Spurgeon Johnson to the field of race relations and sociology spanned three decades. His path-breaking research in these fields began in Chicago, where he first examined the poverty and racial discrimination prominent in the African American community. There he did studies of the **black migration to the northern states** and race relations in the industrialized North. He was in Chicago in

Charles Spurgeon Johnson (Fisk University).

1919 during of the horrible race riots of **Red Summer.** Afterward, he worked as associate executive secretary for the Chicago Race Relations Commission, which examined race matters after the riot. The publication *The Negro in Chicago: A Study of Race Relations and a Race Riot* (1922) was largely his work; it concentrated on problems of housing, social service, employment, and education. As research director for the national office of the National Urban League (NUL) in New York City from 1921 to 1929, he conducted many more studies similar to his Chicago work. Johnson was editor of *Opportunity,* the NUL's official magazine. Through the magazine, he exposed racial stereotypes, discrimination, and prejudice. He also aided rising young black artists and writers who were in New York during the Harlem Renaissance period of the 1920s by connecting them to publishers who produced their works. In 1919 he moved to **Fisk University** in Nashville, Tennessee, and built a solid sociology department and founded the Social Science Research Institute; he produced innumerable research studies on race relations, too. Works such as *Shadow of the Plantation* (1934) and *Patterns of Negro Segregation* (1943) are examples of his landmark studies. In 1942 he established the Race Relations Institute, which brought together leaders to engage in dialogues on race. He spent his last ten years (1946–1956) as president of Fisk—the first black person to hold that post.

Jessie Carney Smith

Josey, Elonnie J. (1924–)

The first African American male to be elected president of the American Library Association (ALA), Elonnie J. Josey, known as "E. J.," took his activist spirit with him when he accepted that high office. He has spoken out against racism in the library profession and in society as a whole. A native of Norfolk, Virginia, Josey studied at **Howard University**, where he came under the influence of intellectual black giants such as Sterling Brown, **John Hope Franklin**, E. Franklin Frazier, Alain Locke, and Rayford Logan. Josey has a lifelong devotion to human rights and supported students at Savannah State College and **North Carolina Agricultural and Technical College** who held sit-ins at lunch counters and led other demonstrations to protest racial segregation. In 1964 and 1965, Josey urged the American Library Association to honor its commitment to its black members in Alabama, Georgia, Louisiana, and Mississippi by admitting them to librarian positions. During the stormy 1960s and 1970s, he participated in debates that resulted in the ALA's responsiveness to the needs of blacks. In 1970 Josey became a founder of the Black Caucus of the American Library Association, whose purpose was to address many issues that the ALA had ignored, such as institutional racism, poverty, and lack of opportunities for blacks and other minorities. A committed community servant, Josey has continued to demonstrate his dedication to the Civil Rights Movement. In 1980 he was elected vice president of the Albany, New York, branch of the **NAACP**, and in 1981 he was elected branch president. He led fights in the interest of affirmative action and helped to organize minority contractors in the area.

Jessie Carney Smith

[Elonnie J. Josey was the] first African American male to be elected president of the American Library Association.

Just, Ernest Everett (1883–1941)

One of the few African Americans with professional training in the life sciences during his era, Ernest Just was internationally recognized for his scientific achievements, especially in the field of marine biology. He also became the first winner of the **NAACP**'s Spingarn Medal, which he received in 1915. Just was born in Charleston, South Carolina, received his early education at his mother's school, and at age 13 entered the academy of South Carolina State College. He left South Carolina in 1899 and continued his studies at Kimball Union Academy and Dartmouth College, majoring in history and biology, and graduating *magna cum laude* and Phi Beta Kappa in 1907. At **Howard University** he taught English, rhetoric, and sciences, and helped found the College Dramatic Club and Omega Psi Phi fraternity. Just began graduate study at the Marine Biological Laboratory (MBL) in 1909, married and published his first scientific research in 1912, and earned a Ph.D. in zoology from the University of Chicago in 1916.

Although the MBL offered him an opportunity to expand his research interests, he also experienced both thinly disguised and overt racial prejudice there. Some scientists showed little regard for his expertise and intellect. Social gatherings connected to the laboratory often excluded him, and he felt the sting of racial slurs from those in his workplace. Despite this, from 1912 to 1941 Just held the posts of professor and head of Howard's Department of Zoology. Just received research grants from philanthropist Julius Rosenwald and others, accelerated his rate of research publishing, participated in scientific organizations, and traveled extensively for scientific activities. His frequent absences caused professional and family problems, however, despite his international success. He divorced and remarried in 1939. World War II caused him to abandon plans to live in Europe. Financial and health issues forced Just to return to America and Howard, but his health declined, resulting in his death from cancer on October 27, 1941. He is celebrated, especially during **Black History Month**, as an outstanding achiever in the field of life sciences.

Fletcher F. Moon

Although skeptical at first about the espoused Gandhian philosophy of non-violence, Nash became a passionate supporter of its protest ideology.

Nash, Diane (1938–)

Diane J. Nash entered the perilous and uncertain era of the modern Civil Rights Movement, called the "Second Reconstruction" by some historians, at a crucial moment. The movement started in 1954 when *Brown v. Board of Education* dismantled segregated public education, but 1960 can generally be considered

the end for America's apartheid system of racial segregation. Nash, a native of Chicago, Illinois, transferred from **Howard University** to **Fisk University** in 1959, where she personally experienced the South's brand of racial segregation. Her move to Nashville, Tennessee, projected her into the African American struggle for equality, justice, and social change. Seeking to rectify the South's code of racial segregation, the young college student began attending non-violent workshops conducted by the Reverend **James M. Lawson**, under the alliance of the Nashville Christian Leadership Conference, an affiliate of **Martin Luther King's Southern Christian Leadership Conference** (SCLC).

Although skeptical at first about the espoused Gandhian philosophy of non-violence, Nash became a passionate supporter of its protest ideology. Beginning in November and December of 1959, Nash was among those who "tested" Nashville's racial code of segregated lunch counters. Elected chair of the Student Central Committee, she played a pivotal role in **Nashville's Sit-in Movement**. Twelve days before Nashville students could stage their first full-scale sit-in, four **North Carolina Agricultural and Technical State University** male students—Ezell Blair, Jr. (now known as Jibreel Khazan), Franklin E. McCain, **Joseph Alfred McNeil**, and **David Leinail Richmond**—staged a sit-in on February 1, 1960, in Greensboro, North Carolina. When the Nashville sit-ins began, the non-violent army of students from the city's four predominately black colleges and universities (**American Baptist College, Fisk University, Meharry Medical College**, and Tennessee Agricultural and Industrial State University [now **Tennessee State University**]) elected their own leaders.

Because of Nash's clarity of thought and increasing dedication to non-violent, direct action, they elected her the chair of the Student Central Committee. Intrepid and hardworking, she exhibited strong leadership and exceptional communication skills that manifested themselves early during the Nashville movement. As the Nashville sit-in continued, violence erupted, students were arrested and tried, and the home of their attorney, **Z. Alexander Looby**, was bombed. The bombing of Looby's home caused approximately 3,000 active and passive supporters to silently march to the city's courthouse for a face-to-face meeting with Mayor Ben West. Nash's leadership abilities and communications skills were evident on this day, when she caused West to affirm that Nashville's lunch counters should be desegregated.

Later in April 1960, Nash became a cofounder of the **Student Non-Violent Coordinating Committee** (SNCC); she was among the first group of SNCC students, including Ruby Doris Smith, arrested in the **Rock Hill, South Carolina**, protest for desegregation. In May of 1961, Nash became the driving force behind the resumption of the **Congress of Racial Equality's** (CORE) aborted **Freedom Rides** of 1961; and later she directed SNCC's Direct Action Division. She was a key strategist for the Selma Right to Vote movement and worked with others to bring about the **Civil Rights Act of 1964** and the **Voting Rights Act of 1965**.

After 1965, Nash brought her same zeal and level of involvement to issues such as underclass oppression and the Vietnam War. On May 7, 2007, Fisk University awarded Nash with an honorary doctor of humane letters degree for her unyielding pursuit of justice for African Americans crippled by state-sponsored segregation and for her never-ending quest to contribute to the moral enlightenment of America.

Linda T. Wynn

Reason, Charles Lewis (1818–1893)

Charles L. Reason was an abolitionist and educator who believed that industrial education was crucial, but classical education was the means toward self-sufficiency and an escape from the servile roles of the past. Reason's passion for activism regarding rights and opportunities for blacks was displayed early on when he joined the Young Men's Convention in 1837 to protest suffrage restrictions for blacks in New York state. In 1840, as secretary to the New York State Convention for Negro Suffrage, he, along with Henry Highland Garnet and George Downing, launched a petition for black suffrage. An active abolitionist, Reason was a member of the Vigilance Committee, which supported the Underground Railroad. In 1841 he founded the New York Political Improvement Association, which won the right of a jury trial for fugitive slaves. As the pending **Civil War** brought issues of colonization and the place of free blacks in America, colonization became a topic of political discussion. Reason was an adamant opponent of black colonization and spoke out against the American Colonization Society and the African Civilization Society, which supported the colonization of blacks to Africa. Reason promoted his ideas by serving on the New York Citizens Civil Rights Committee for the expansion of black civil rights. After the Civil War, he served as vice president of the New York State Labor Union. He firmly believed in education for blacks, and after earning his degree from Central College in McGraw, New York, he became the first black professor at a predominately white institution in 1849. He continued his advocacy for black civil rights and education throughout his life, and in 1873 he headed the movement to end racial segregation in the New York public school system. Reason retired in 1892, having held the longest tenure in the school system's history.

Lean'tin L. Bracks

Smith, Angeline Bailey (1908–1991)

A crusader for civil rights and other humanitarian causes for 50 years, Angeline Bailey Smith left a legacy in Greensboro, North Carolina, that dates back to the early 1940s. Her activist work began when she campaigned against the racially segregated rest rooms and water fountains in Greensboro in the 1940s and, in time, saw the signs come down. In the 1940s and 1950s, she also worked to integrate Greensboro's Young Women's Christian Association. A powerful and outspoken voice against racial segregation, she worked through a local group known as the Interracial Committee that visited white merchants and implored them to curtail their racially biased policies.

When four students from **North Carolina Agricultural and Industrial State University** decided to take direct action against segregated lunch counters in Greensboro, they first sought the counsel of Angeline Smith, who carefully and deliberately guided them. Thus, when the sit-ins began on February 1, 1960, at the whites-only lunch counter in Woolworth's, the students were armed with the wisdom, courage, and tenacity that Smith taught them. Contrary to what the press and others believed for so long, their work was neither spontaneous nor lacking in guidance from seasoned civil rights protesters. Smith's behind-the-scenes work with the students became an important catalyst in the success of the sit-ins. The articulate high school English teacher was rewarded with citations from organizations such as the **NAACP**, the National Conference of Christians and Jews, and the General Assembly of North Carolina.

Jessie Carney Smith

Terrell, Mary Church (1863–1954)

Mary Church Terrell devoted her life to civil rights causes and worked to improve the social, economic, and political conditions of African Americans. She fought for women's suffrage, and for the rights of black women in particular. When she was 93 years old, she led and won a fight to desegregated public facilities in Washington, D.C. The Memphis native, who came from the prominent Church family, attended Oberlin College in Ohio, which, at that time, was one of the few racially integrated institutions in the nation. Terrell held various teaching positions but entered the political and professional arena after the 1892 lynching of her lifelong friend, Tom Moss, in Memphis. That year, she became head of the Colored Women's League in

Mary Church Terrell (Fisk University)

the District of Columbia. After that group, the Federation of Afro-American Women, and other black women's organizations merged to form the **National Association of Colored Women** (NACW), Terrell was elected founding president.

Terrell became well known for the NACW's primary cause: the fight for equal rights for women, particularly black women. Beginning in 1895, she was appointed to the District of Columbia's school board. She was reappointed at various times and continued to serve until 1911. She was one of the first black women in the country to hold such a position. The segregated school system in the District troubled her; thus, she fought for equal treatment of black students and black teachers. The racial disturbance in Brownsville, Texas, in 1906 distressed Terrell; she joined in protest and asked Secretary of War William H. Taft to withhold action against the black troops involved to allow for a fair hearing. Although the request was granted, the case was later dismissed.

In 1949 Terrell was elected chair of the Coordinating Committee for the Enforcement of District of Columbia Anti-Discrimination Laws. The laws had been passed in 1872 and 1873 and never repealed; nonetheless, segregation in the District's public facilities continued and blacks who tested the law were jailed. Terrell and her committee challenged the laws; she joined in several demonstrations and targeted Thompson's Restaurant, which denied service to the group. The case finally went before the U.S. Supreme Court, which ruled in their favor, thus initiating desegregation in the District.

In addition to her work in Washington, D.C., Terrell was active in national and international programs for interracial cooperation. She was a charter member of the **NAACP**, founded in 1910. A prolific writer and noted public lecturer, she often wrote and spoke on themes dealing with racism and its impact on African Americans. Her personal struggles against racism were published in her autobiography, *A Colored Women in a White World* (1940). Terrell died on July 24, 1954, just two months after the *Brown v. Board of Education* decision.

Jessie Carney Smith

Booker T. Washington (Fisk University).

Washington, Booker T. (1856–1915)

Booker T. Washington towered over American race relations as the leading black educator, political figure, and institutional head of his era. As the founder of the Tuskegee Institute in Tuskegee, Alabama, he led the charge for vocational training of black Americans as a means to upward mobility. His 1895 "**Atlanta Compromise**" address sparked an intense debate between himself and leading black intellectual **W.E.B. Du Bois**. At the turn of century, Washington also notably founded the **National Negro Business League** to encourage African American business development.

Born a slave on a West Virginia farm, his mother, Jane, was owned by James Burroughs, and his father is believed to have been a white man. Reared in a single-room slave cabin along with his siblings, Booker (his only name at the time) was put to work as a slave during his ado-

lescence. Prohibited from attending school, the young Booker did not even own a pair of shoes until he was eight years old. At the close of the **Civil War** in 1865, his stepfather, an ex-slave named Washington Ferguson, settled in Malden, West Virginia, where he began working in Kanawha Salines's salt furnaces. The family joined Ferguson there the same year, and soon after Booker began working alongside him in the furnaces. Later, he was forced to work in the coal mines, but he remained excited about the possibility of receiving an education.

It was in Malden that he first received classroom instruction and declared himself Booker Washington. While at work, he overheard a conversation about the Hampton Institute (now **Hampton University**) and began making plans to attend the school. After working as a houseboy for the furnace's owners, General Lewis and Viola Ruffner, and with the financial aid of several local blacks, Washington enrolled at Hampton in 1872. The virtues of thrift, industry, and hard work were encouraged at the all-black school and by its founder, General Samuel

Chapman Armstrong. By the time he finished paying his own way through the school in 1875, those principles stayed with him.

After teaching in Malden, Washington returned to work for Chapman as an instructor at Hampton. In 1881 Washington founded Tuskegee as a training school for black teachers with just $2,000 in state grant money for salaries. The school opened in a meager church the following year, and Washington later borrowed enough money to purchase a plantation for the school's permanent site. Over the course of the next two decades, the school's self-help platform gained the support of both races and the financial backing of northern white industrialists. His 1895 address at the Cotton States and International Exposition catapulted him to national prominence. The school's graduates, his connections to the federal government, and his part ownership of the *New York Age* solidified Washington's place as the country's black power broker. The establishment of the National Negro Business League in 1900, followed by his invitation to the White House by President Theodore Roosevelt one year later, signaled the height of his prominence. Despite the decline of his prominence in the face of criticisms by **William Monroe Trotter**, Du Bois, and several other black leaders, Washington died in 1915 as one of the most beloved African American leaders of his life and times.

Crystal A. deGregory

West, Cornel (1953–)

Cornel Ronald West grew up surrounded by the activism of the 1960s and was greatly influenced by black leaders such as **Malcolm X**. While in high school, he marched in civil rights demonstrations and in protests to bring **black studies** classes to his high school in Sacramento, California. At 17 West entered Harvard University, earned his B.A. in just three years, and went on to receive his Ph.D. from Princeton University in 1980. Focusing on philosophy, race and ethics, history, and social thought,

West aligned himself with causes that championed social justice. He participated in breakfast programs for low-income children while in college, and then demonstrated for divestment from South Africa while he was assistant professor at Yale University. West spent time as director of the African American studies program at Princeton from 1988 to 1994, leaving to become director of the African American studies program at Harvard with a joint appointment in the School of Divinity. After public differences between West and Harvard's president Lawrence Summers, West left Harvard in 2001. He returned to Princeton, where he has continued his scholarship, focusing on the struggles for racial equality. He has written many books and has been the recipient of the National Book Award and numerous honorary degrees. Among his organizational involvements are his roles as a member of the Democratic Socialists of America and as a board member of the International Bridges to Justice. As an internationally recognized scholar, a social and political philosopher, and activist, West has continued to challenge the issues of racial equality and justice.

Lean'tin L. Bracks and Linda T. Wynn

Williams, Jamye Coleman (1918–)

Jamye Coleman Williams was born in Louisville, Kentucky, on December 15, 1918, to the Reverend Frederick Douglass Coleman Sr. and Jamye Harris Coleman. A multifaceted and multitalented woman, Jamye Williams fought tenaciously to terminate racial and gender discrimination. As an educator and community and denominational activist, Williams was profoundly concerned about the withheld rights of equality and justice for African Americans. Molded by her parental rearing and the protest paradigm of the African Methodist Episcopal (AME) Church, she penned pedagogical writings that reflected her profound interest in the civil and social reform movements of the 1960s. She was active in the Nashville, Tennessee, branch of the **NAACP**, for which she served on the executive committee. Williams was among those who provided active adult support to the Nashville student demonstrators during the sit-in and freedom ride movements. Additionally, she aided sharecropping African Americans in West Tennessee's Fayette and Haywood counties, when white land owners forced them off the land. Because these sharecroppers dared to register to vote, they were banished and forced to live in the makeshift **Tent Cities** during the winter of 1960. Further emboldened by her concern for the rights of voters, Williams was a member of and secretary for the Tennessee Voters Council from 1969 to 1985. A major principal in the AME Church, Williams, the first woman elected as a major general officer in the denomination's 197-year history, blazed a trail through her activities of reform, opening up a new line of denominational reasoning that helped to elect the first woman as a bishop in the AME Church. The editor of the *AME Church Review,* the oldest black journal in America, from 1984 to 1992, Williams settled in Georgia with her husband, McDonald Williams.

Linda T. Wynn

Young, Jean Childs (1933–1994)

Jean Childs Young was born on July 1, 1933, in Marion, Alabama, and died on September 16, 1994. She married **Andrew Young**, an activist, minister, and politician, in 1954. After living and teaching in New York for a short period, the Youngs moved to Atlanta, Georgia, where Andrew Young was active in the **Southern Christian Leadership Conference** (SCLC) and Jean Young taught. Her commitment to the Civil Rights Movement was demonstrated through her hospitality and charity to those activists and civil rights workers she allowed into her home. In 1961 she participated in boycotts and marches in Birmingham, Alabama. She was an active participant in other major civil rights marches, including the **March on Washington** of 1963, the march from **Selma to Montgomery**, Alabama, in 1965, and the **Poor People's March on**

Washington in 1968. Jean Young was recognized as a leader in education in Atlanta and was appointed coordinator for school programs in the Atlanta system. President Jimmy Carter recognized Young's efforts to benefit child welfare in 1978; he appointed her chair of the U.S. Commission on the International Year of the Child. As chair of the commission, Young worked to gain support from the business sector as well as other government and social organizations for child welfare programs. Young's work as an educator and advocate for children was furthered by her involvement in educational, cultural, and social welfare organizations, such as the Atlanta Task Force on Education, UNICEF, Families First, and Habitat for Humanity.

Rebecca S. Dixon

The ferocious opposition to desegregation in Little Rock was the first major test of the United States's resolve to enforce African American civil rights.

School Desegregation

Central High School, Little Rock, Arkansas

In the fall of 1957, Little Rock became the symbol of state resistance to school desegregation. Arkansas Governor Orval E. Faubus questioned the sanctity of the federal court system and the authority of the U.S. Supreme Court's desegregation ruling. The ferocious opposition to desegregation in Little Rock was the first major test of the United States's resolve to enforce African American civil rights despite massive southern resistance following the *Brown v. Board of Education* decision in 1954. Forced to deploy federal troops to secure the rights of African American students to attend the previously all-white Central High, President Dwight D. Eisenhower became the first president since the post-Reconstruction era to use the military to support African Americans' civil rights when nine black students attempted to attend the school.

On May 22, 1954, the Little Rock School Board stated it would act in accordance with the *Brown v. Board of Education* decision, but only after the court outlined the method and time frame for implementation. The board directed Superintendent Virgil Blossom to formulate a plan for desegregation. In May 1955, the school board adopted the Phase Program Plan of gradual desegregation known as the Blossom Plan. As originally envisioned, the desegregation process was to begin at the elementary school level. However, as white parents of elementary school students became some of the most outspoken opponents against integration, district officials decided to begin token desegregation in the fall of 1957 at Central High School. This would then be expanded to the junior high level by 1960 and, tentatively, to the elementary school level by 1963. The Little Rock chapter of the **NAACP**, under the presidency of Daisy G. Bates, watched this process with some trepidation. As time passed, it was decided to sue in order to expedite the process of desegregation. However, before the NAACP could file suit, African American parents attempted to register their children at white schools in January 1956. School officials refused to admit the children.

In February, 33 children, represented by the NAACP, filed the *Aaron v. Cooper* suit in federal court for the Eastern District of Arkansas, alleging that school officials were conspiring to deny black children their constitutional rights by maintaining segregated schools and fashioning a gradual plan for school desegregation. Resis-

tance to school desegregation grew across the southern region. Its manifestation reached an apex when 19 U.S. senators and 81 congressmen, including all eight members from Arkansas, signed the 1956 Southern Manifesto denouncing the Supreme Court's decision and urging Southern states to resist implementing school desegregation.

In Little Rock, the Capital Citizens' Council, a local version of the white citizens' councils that were emerging across the South, was established in 1956 and promoted public resistance to desegregation. Central High School attracted national attention on September 4, 1957, when nine African American students, under the tutelage of Bates, attempted to begin their classes at the school. Two days earlier, Governor Oval Faubus called out the Arkansas National Guard. Despite the intimidation, bomb threats, and other disruptions, the only senior among the Little Rock Nine, Ernest Green, became Central High's first African American graduate on May 27, 1958. His graduation, however, did not signal an end to the Little Rock crisis. The NAACP continued to press for continued desegregation through the federal courts. Racial separatists and moderate whites began a struggle to gain control of local schools, a struggle that would not end until the public high schools closed for the duration of the 1958 to 1959 academic year, reopening in the fall of 1959.

Linda T. Wynn

Clinton, Tennessee, Schools

Located in Tennessee's eastern region in Anderson County, Clinton entered the Civil Rights Movement shortly after World War II, when African American parents demanded more equitable school facilities for their children. The building where their children attended school had no cafeteria, no gymnasium, no indoor restrooms, and no high school classes. Between 1947 and 1948, local functionaries expanded the Clinton Colored School by adding indoor restrooms and a cafeteria. In 1950 African Americans filed suit against Anderson County because school officials refused to admit four black students eligible to attend Clinton High School. Attorneys **Z. Alexander Looby** of Nashville, **Avon N. Williams,** and Carl A. Cowan of Knoxville, and **Thurgood Marshall** of the NAACP's Legal Defense Fund filed the suit that became *McSwain et al. v. County Board of Education of Anderson County, Tennessee,* the state's first school desegregation case. Two years later, Judge Robert L. Taylor heard the case in the U.S. District Court of Knoxville. In his ruling of April 1952, Taylor denied the lawsuit and sided with the county school board. He refuted the line of reasoning that it violated the *Plessy v. Ferguson* decree of separate but equal for African American students to attend high school in another county.

By 1954, the U.S. Supreme Court had dismantled the Jim Crow doctrine of separate but equal with its unanimous ruling in the *Brown v. Board of Education* decision. Two and a half weeks later, the U.S. Court of Appeals, Sixth Circuit, reversed Taylor's 1952 ruling and returned *McSwain et al. v. County Board of Education* to federal district court for a new decision. In January of 1956, Judge Taylor was forced to overturn his earlier ruling and mandated that Clinton High School desegregate by the fall semester of that year. On August 26, 1956, Clinton High School became Tennessee's—and the South's—first public, all-white high school to desegregate when 12 black teenagers enrolled.

Two days before classes began, however, Frederick John Kasper, executive secretary of the Seaboard White Citizens Council, arrived in Clinton and called for massive resistance from segregationists. On Labor Day weekend, September 1 and 2, 1956, full-scale rioting erupted in the East Tennessee town. The rioting white crowd overwhelmed Clinton's small police force. City officials requested assistance from Governor Frank G. Clement. Unlike Arkansas Governor Orval Faubus, who a year later used the National Guard in an attempt to prevent school desegregation, Clement activated the National Guard to maintain peace. With the arrival of

approximately 600 guardsmen, the worst of the violence ended. The use of the National Guard by Clement was another first in the Civil Rights Movement. The National Guard stayed in Clinton for the rest of September to keep order.

The use of the National Guard by Clement was another first in the Civil Rights Movement.

In December 1956 and January 1957, journalists from across the country documented the progress in Clinton. Edward R. Murrow of the Columbia Broadcasting System (CBS) TV produced one of his famous "See It Now" programs on Clinton titled "Clinton and the Law." Throughout the spring of 1957, the process of school desegregation in Clinton captured the nation's attention, as well as that of the international community. Like the **Little Rock Nine** who succeeded them a year later, the Clinton Twelve faced angry protests and violence. The same year that Little Rock's **Central High School** desegregated, Robert "Bobby" Cain Jr., the Clinton group's only senior, became the first American black to graduate from a public high school in the South. He graduated on May 17, 1957, three years to the day after the *Brown* decision.

Crystal A. deGregory and Linda T. Wynn

Nashville, Tennessee, Schools

Responding to the U.S. Supreme Court's school desegregation ruling in the 1954 *Brown v. Board of Education* case, 16 black six-year-olds and their parents ended the era of segregated education in the "Athens of the South" on September 9, 1957. In Nashville, like Arkansas's Little Rock Nine and **Clinton, Ten-**

nessee's "Clinton Twelve," they too walked past protesting whites into seven of the city's previously all-white elementary schools. Nashville's school desegregation was in response not only to the *Brown* decision but also to the *Kelley v. Board of Education* case, which Nashville black families filed in 1955. Nashville attorneys **Z. Alexander Looby** and **Avon N. Williams Jr.**, joined by **Thurgood Marshall**, legal director of the **NAACP**'s Legal and Educational Fund, filed suite against the Nashville public schools in federal district court to bring the city into compliance with the *Brown* decision.

16 black six-year-olds and their parents ended the era of segregated education.

The lead plaintiff in the Nashville case was Alfred Z. Kelley, a Nashville barber whose son Robert had to commute to the all-black Pearl High School even though the white East High School was within walking distance of his home. Judge William E. Miller decided in favor of the plaintiff and ordered the Nashville School Board to desegregate the public schools and submit to the court a desegregation plan by January 1957. In the spring of 1957, the court accepted the board's plan to desegregate the first grade in the fall and one grade a year thereafter. Meanwhile, white resisters led by the Ku Klux Klan, the White Citizens Council, the Parent School Preference Committee, and the Tennessee Federation for Constitutional Government (TFCG) fought school desegregation. Vanderbilt University English professor Donald G. Davidson, one of the noted Fugitives group of literary scholars, who defended racial segregation, led the TFCG.

Despite their protests, the school desegregation process in Nashville had been set in motion. Nineteen six-year-old students registered to attend the first grade, desegregating the all-white Buena Vista, Jones, Fehr, Bailey, Glenn, Emma Clemons, and Hattie Cotton schools. But because of "improper transfer papers," three students were unable to attend opening day. Still, 16 black students braved the crowd of white resisters and desegregated the Nashville Public School System. Black students successfully entered Buena Vista (Errol Groves, Ethel Mai Carr, and Patricia Guthrie); Jones (Barbara Jean Watson, Marvin Moore, Richard Rucker, Charles E. Battles, and Cecil Ray Jr.); Fehr (Charles E. Ridley, Willis E. Lewis, Bobby Cabknor, Linda McKinley, and Rita Buchanan); Glenn (Lajuanda Street, Jacqueline Griffith, and Sinclair Lee Jr.); Emma Clemons (Joy Smith, daughter of the Reverend **Kelly Miller Smith**); and Hattie Cotton (Patricia Watson) schools.

For all practical purposes, the first day of school desegregation appeared to have been a peaceful success, unlike **Central High School** in Little Rock, Arkansas, where Governor Orval Faubus called out the Arkansas National Guard. Resistant forces shattered the city's process, however. In the early hours of the following morning, Hattie Cotton School was dynamited. Frederick John Kasper, an outside agitator from the North, incited the cowardly deed. Despite Kasper's intended intimidation of the young trailblazers and their families, his actions only served to reinforce the resolve of the students and their families and supporters to end racial segregation in Nashville's public schools. After many disputes, litigants finally settled the *Kelley v. Board of Education* case in 1998, which was Tennessee's longest school desegregation lawsuit.

Linda T. Wynn

Prince Edward County, Virginia, Schools

Formed in the Virginia Colony in 1754, Prince Edward County is widely known as the subject of *Davis v. County School Board of Prince Edward County,* the only public desegregation case initiated by students. While the case was eventually incorporated into the **NAACP**-led *Brown v. Board of Education*, the Virginia General Assembly still passed a series of laws in 1956 to implement massive resistance. Since the close of the **Civil War**, racial inequality persisted in the county's educational system, including rundown facilities and salary inequities between black and white teachers. Efforts to fend off potential litigation by the NAACP resulted in the founding of the all-black Robert Russa Moton High School in 1939, which nevertheless lacked a gymnasium, cafeteria, and teachers' restrooms. In 1951 inadequate classroom space and supplies, as well as repeated denials by the all-white school board for additional funding, led Barbara Johns, the niece of the activist Reverend **Vernon Johns**, to lead a walkout in protest of the school's conditions. Following the *Brown* decision and subsequent changes in state law, tuition grants had allowed whites to enroll in private schools, which reinforced the segregated school system. In response, the county's board of supervisors refused to appropriate any funds for the county's school board, effectively closing all of the county's public schools because white officials refused to desegregate them. For five years the county's public schools remained closed until they were forced to reopen in 1963.

Crystal A. deGregory

Protest Training School

Highlander Folk School (est. 1932)

Myles Horton and Georgian Don West established Highlander Folk School in Monteagle, Tennessee, in 1932, to help workers and organized labor in the South. Horton saw education as a tool for social change and therefore all leadership courses and classes were racially integrated. Horton loosely modeled the school on the Danish folk school model, which provided adult education in history and government to instill pride and raise the consciousness of its students. Highlander teachers began offering workshops in 1953 on public school desegregation for black and white community leaders and students. These endeavors grew from a focus on public schools to encompass communitywide integration. In 1957 Highlander sponsored a Citizenship Project on the South Carolina Sea Island and taught thousands of black adults in Tennessee, Georgia, and Alabama to read and write as preparation for voting.

The philosophy of the school was to develop an awareness in students that they were part of the government; they were empowered individuals who could actively participate in societal change. Highlander became the educational center of the Civil Rights Movement during the 1950s and early 1960s. Both **Rosa Parks** and **Martin Luther King Jr.** attended Highlander workshops before participating in the Montgomery demonstrations. Some of the student leaders met at Highlander to discuss issues confronting them before the meeting at Shaw University and the formation of the **Student Non-Violent Coordinating Committee** (SNCC). Myles Horton was still the director of Highlander and the director of education was **Septima Poinsette Clark**.

In 1960 and 1961, when sit-in protests began to spread across the South, student activists met at Highlander to explore possible directions for this new era of black protest. There were workshops to identify and train leaders, who were then sent back into the community. The emphasis was on the practical. Here they learned new freedom songs, and adapted other traditional songs like "We Shall Overcome." As Highlander's impact became more evident, there was a growing and sustained assault against the school; both the ideology and pedagogy were attacked, with some accusing it of being a communist training school.

After a barrage of legislation, investigations, propaganda campaigns, and trials, Tennessee officials revoked Highlander's charter and confiscated its property. However, a new institution, with essentially the same goals, was chartered: Highlander Research and Education Center. It was located for a brief period in Knoxville, but is now in New Market, Tennessee. It continues to support the Civil Rights Movement. Myles Horton allowed the State Library and Archives of Tennessee to copy the original audiotapes in the *Highlander Folk School Audio Collection 1953–1963*. The majority of the collection spans the growth and development of the Civil Rights Movement and voices of students who participated in the movement on such topics as voter registration, the impact of certain tactics on both the black and white communities, the **Southern Christian Leadership Conference**, **NAACP**, **Student Non-Violent Coordinating Committee**, and the **Congress of Racial Equality**.

Helen R. Houston

Journalism

Journalists

Barnett, Ida B. Wells. *See* Wells-Barnett, Ida B.

Baskin, Inez J. (1916–2007)

Women news reporters of the 1950s and 1960s were rare, but rarer still were African American women journalists. Inez J. Baskin began to make a place for herself as early as the 1950s, when she rose from typist for the *Montgomery Advertiser*'s weekly "Negro News" section to reporter, covering events such as cross burnings and, later, sit-ins and the **Montgomery Bus Boycott**. In so doing she joined other women of the modern civil rights era whose work influenced the outcome of the movement but who, for so long, remained obscure in the pages of history. Baskin put herself in the middle of hostility and danger as she gathered news for her stories and documented many of the tumultuous moments in American history. Whatever the big civil rights stories of the day in Alabama, Baskin held a front-row view and gave the community information that it might not have known otherwise. Her experiences included riding on a bus to cover the **Freedom Riders** and witnessing a terrifying late-night chase by the Ku Klux Klan. She attended strategic planning meetings of civil rights groups and was often the only women present. Baskin would later witness and record events of a historic day in 1956, when **Martin Luther King Jr.** took the first ride on a Montgomery bus after the boycott ended and sat in a seat previously reserved for whites. She held a seat in front of King and reported it all. She realized her dream of becoming a reporter, later working as a stringer for *Jet* magazine and contact with the **Associated Negro Press**.

Jessie Carney Smith

Bibb, Henry Walton (1815–1854) and Mary Elizabeth Miles Bibb (1820?–1877)

Near the middle of the nineteenth century, Henry and Mary Bibb aided fugitive slaves who fled the United States and settled in Canada. Henry Bibb was a fugitive slave himself and had been labeled incorrigible when he was in bondage in Kentucky and later in New Orleans. His flight was successful in 1841, when he settled in Detroit. There he engaged in anti-slavery and Liberty party activities. Along with **Frederick Douglass**, **William Wells Brown**, and **James W.C. Pennington**, he became an accomplished abolitionist speaker.

His work brought him in contact with Mary Elizabeth Miles, whom he married. When the **Fugitive Slave Act** of 1850 was passed and Henry Bibb's freedom was at risk, the Bibbs moved to Canada West and for a while settled in Sandwich, and later in Windsor, Ontario. There they worked in the interest of fugitive slaves and harbored many in their home and elsewhere. They also provided for the slaves' subsistence. Determined to keep anti-slavery sentiments alive, in 1851 Henry Bibb founded and edited *The Voice of the Fugitive*; Mary Bibb gave the paper its polished editorial style. The paper reached audiences in Canada West and in the United States as well, especially Ohio, Michigan, New York, Pennsylvania, and the New England states.

Women news reporters of the 1950s and 1960s were rare, but rarer still were African American women journalists.

The Bibbs were also active in the Refugee Home Society (RHS), established to meet the needs of the numerous destitute Canadian fugitives. *The Voice of the Fugitive* newspaper became the RHS's official organ. The Bibbs also carried their fight to anti-slavery societies that they joined, such as the Anti-Slavery Society of Windsor, of which Henry Bibb was founding president and Mary Bibb was a member.

Jessie Carney Smith

Brown, Tony (1933–)

William Anthony "Tony" Brown has made a considerable impact on media in America through his advocacy and involvement in various media formats. Over more than forty years, Brown has worked in television, film, radio, and print journalism on issues affecting African Americans and other disenfranchised communities.

Brown was born on April 11, 1933, in Charleston, West Virginia. He became an entrepreneur at an early age, excelled in academics, athletics, and theater, and graduated from Garnet High School in Charleston, West Virginia. After U.S. Army service, Brown earned a bachelor's degree in sociology and a master's degree in psychiatric social work from Wayne State University. His first media employment was for the *Detroit Courier* newspaper until 1968, when he began work for public television station WTVS. Brown was also credited with coordinating the largest civil rights march ever led by Martin Luther King Jr.

Tony Brown's Journal was recognized as the longest-running black news program in television history. Brown also became founding dean of the Howard University School of Communications and dean of the Scripps Howard School of Journalism and Communications at Hampton University; he established Black College Day in 1980. Brown has received numerous awards and honorary doctorate degrees, yet he continues to use his multiple platforms to communicate to and for African Americans.

Fletcher F. Moon

Cornish, Samuel Eli (1795?–1858)

Noted for helping to establish *Freedom's Journal,* the first black newspaper in the United States, Samuel Cornish was born of free black parentage in Sussex County, Delaware. He challenged slavery and colonization through participation in reform movements, ministry, and writings. Cornish studied for the Presbyterian ministry after 1815 with John Gloucester, pastor of the First African Presbyterian Church in Philadelphia. He served as minister there after Gloucester became ill, receiving his preaching license in 1819. The following year he did missionary work in Maryland, and then he moved to New York City in 1821.

Cornish was ordained in 1822 and developed the first black Presbyterian church in the city. He married Jane Livingston in 1824, and they became the parents of four children. In 1827 Cornish represented the New York African Free Schools and joined **John B. Russwurm** in editing *Freedom's Journal,* which first appeared on March 16 that year. Cornish continued the paper by himself in 1829 after Russwurm resigned, and changed the name to *The Rights of All.* Eight years later Cornish became editor of the *Colored American,* remaining in that post until 1839. Although Cornish was a leader in several reform organizations as well as churches, his frequent disagreements with others created problems throughout his personal and professional life.

Fletcher F. Moon

Fortune, T. Thomas (1856–1928)

T. Thomas Fortune was born October 3, 1856, in Marianna, Florida, and died June 2, 1928, in New York City. Fortune had little formal education, but was enthralled by the newspaper business and learned the trade. He became a printer, a publisher, and an outspoken and militant journalist. Like his father, he became actively involved in politics. Fortune came to be known as the dean of African American journalism: he worked for, owned, and published several newspapers. His ideas appeared not only in his journalistic writing, but also in his book *Black and White: Land and Politics in the South* (1884).

While editor of the *New York Age,* Fortune conceived of ideas that led to the formation of the **Afro-American League,** which became defunct in 1893; in 1898 he was asked, however, to aid in the development of the Afro-American Council, which had almost the same concerns as the league. Many of these same issues are seen in the **Niagara Movement** and the **NAACP.** Fortune worked with civil rights

T. Thomas Fortune (Fisk University)

organizations and leaders in addition to his editorial efforts for civil rights. He was well acquainted with **Booker T. Washington** with whom he shared many ideas.

Fortune became the editor of the *Negro World,* the organ of **Marcus Garvey's** Universal Negro Improvement Association, supported black women activists, and aided in the efforts of **Ida B. Wells** with information, employment, and her lecture engagements. The methodologies and proposals in Fortune's editorial writing foreshadow the direction of twentieth-century civil rights.

Helen R. Houston

Garvey, Amy Jacques (1895–1973)

While she is most widely remembered as the second wife to black nationalist **Marcus Moziah Garvey,** Amy Jacques Garvey rose to prominence in her own right as a race activist and a pioneering African American female journalist and publisher. Having assumed the leadership of the **Universal Negro Improvement Association** (UNIA) during her husband's imprisonment, Garvey assured the prominent legacy of the UNIA as one of the twentieth century's most important movements for black equality.

Garvey stood by her husband's side throughout his imprisonment, becoming his main propagandist.

Born in Kingston, Jamaica, to George Samuel and Charlotte Henrietta South Jacques, Amy Jacques emigrated to New York in 1917. After hearing an address by Marcus Garvey the following year, she became involved in the UNIA and its *Negro World* newspaper. In 1919 she assumed responsibility for proselytizing the organization as its secretary general, a position she held for more than half a century. Just one year after she and Garvey married in July 1922, he was tried for mail fraud and imprisoned. Garvey stood by her husband's side throughout his imprisonment, becoming his main propagandist and the driving force behind the UNIA. As his personal representative, she pushed the publication of *Philosophy and Opinions* (1967), two volumes of Garvey's writings and speeches, to raise money and support for his defense. She also traveled across the country to UNIA chapters to lead the organization's official business and planning along with other UNIA officers and public officials.

From 1924 to 1927, she served as associate editor of the *Negro World* and added a page for women called "Our Women and What They Think." The page was a vehicle for Garvey to advance her nationalist and feminist platforms and featured black women's contemporary profiles, international news, and historical informa-

tion. Following her husband's release and deportation in 1925 and 1927 respectively, Garvey returned with him to Jamaica but continued to work as a contributing editor to the *Negro World* until 1928. Together, the couple then toured England, France, and Germany during the spring and summer of 1928, impressions of which she reported in the UNIA newspaper. In 1930, the couple welcomed their first child, Marcus Moziah Garvey, Jr., and a second son, Julius Winston Garvey, was born in 1933.

When her husband moved to England the following year, Garvey remained in Jamaica with their sons. Reunited only for a short time before her husband's death in London in 1940, she continued her commitment to the struggle they led together. Throughout the 1940s Garvey actively contributed as editor of the Harlem-based, black nationalist journal the *African,* and she was founder of the African Study Circle of the World in Jamaica. In 1963 she published a work of her own, *Garvey and Garveyism,* and in 1968 she published two collections of essays: *Black Power in America: The Power of the Human Spirit* and *The Impact of Garvey in Africa and Jamaica.* Garvey produced her final work, *Philosophy and Opinions of Marcus Garvey: Volume III* in 1969, and later died in Kingston.

Crystal A. deGregory

Jarrett, Vernon D. (1921–2004)

A radical and fiery career journalist and an aggressive agitator, Vernon D. Jarrett used journalism to ensure that the achievements of blacks would be recognized. He also used the media to promote race matters, politics, urban affairs, and the history of his race. He was articulate and persuasive in his presentations in print and non-print media.

Born on June 19, 1921, in the small town of Saulsbury, Tennessee, near the Mississippi border, he was the son of Annie Sybil Jarrett and William Robert Jarrett, the children of former slaves. He graduated from historically black

Knoxville College in Tennessee in 1941 and continued his education at Northwestern University, where he studied journalism. From there he moved to the University of Kansas in Missouri in 1956, studying television writing and producing. Still later, in 1959, he studied urban sociology at the University of Chicago.

By now he was well prepared for the positions that he would hold. Although Jarrett taught at Northwestern University and at City College of Chicago, as time passed his primary interest was journalism. In 1946 he joined the *Chicago Defender* as general assignment reporter. The *Chicago Tribune* hired him in 1970, making him its first black syndicated columnist. He was also a columnist and a member of the editorial board for the *Chicago Sun Times,* posts that he held from 1983 to 1996.

Jarrett then became a talk-show host, producer, and commentator for WLS-TV, ABC's station in Chicago. Now he was in position to broadcast his views, which he did on the show *Black on Black,* serving as first moderator. Renamed *For Blacks Only* and then *Face to Face with Vernon Jarrett,* the hour-long program gained popularity. Chicago's only black-owned radio station, WVON-AM—for which he was part owner— aired his *Jarrett's Journal* beginning in 1996.

The elder statesman was a part of numerous national and international media productions, and in 1992 the *MacNeil Lehrer Report* selected Jarrett to analyze the final debate between President George H.W. Bush and presidential candidates Bill Clinton and Ross Perot. Jarrett was also a featured commentator for four of the five shows in the British Broadcasting Corporation's *The Promised Land*—a television series on black migration to the North after World War II.

Jarrett was instrumental in promoting black journalists and their work. He founded the Chicago Association of Black Journalists in 1976; in 1975 he was one of the founders of the National Association of Black Journalists (NABJ) and was its second president from 1977 to 1979; in 1977 he was a founder of the Trotter

Group at Harvard University. He was a constant presence at the NABJ convention and charged those presidents who succeeded him to keep advocacy for black journals at the head of the association's goals. In founding the Trotter group, he commemorated the work of **William Monroe Trotter**, journalist and an elite militant integrationist who in the early twentieth century was an important black spokesperson.

Jarrett was instrumental in promoting black journalists and their work.

He further demonstrated his interest in race during the years from 1977 until his death, serving as a member of the advisory board for the Race Relations Institute at **Fisk University**. One of his prized activities was the Afro Academic, Cultural, Technological and Scientific Olympics (**ACTSO**), which he founded and chaired. The program recognizes the academic and artistic talents of young blacks in grades nine through twelve in a manner similar to that given to star athletes. In 1977, the **NAACP** adopted ACTSO as one of its major programs. With NAACP support and Jarrett's devotion to activities for young people, the program is active in over 1,000 cities across the country. Commenting on Jarrett's legacy, Marsha Eaglin wrote in an NABJ article that "he made such a difference in using his expert skills as a journalist to herald the causes and issues that concerned the African American community."

Jessie Carney Smith

Lampkin, Daisy (1884–1965)

Daisy Lampkin was born in 1884 in Washington, D.C., and came of age at a time when most women were not very politically active. After graduating from high school in her home town of Reading, Pennsylvania, she moved to Pittsburgh and married William Lampkin in 1912. It was during this time that she became active regarding issues that were important to her as an African American house-wife, but more specifically as an American citizen. Women's rights and civil rights for African Americans were causes Lampkin championed all her life. After joining the Negro Women's Equal Franchise Federation she became president of the organization in 1915 and held the post for forty years.

After winning a contest for selling the most newspaper subscriptions, Lampkin began a life-long association with the *Pittsburg Courier* and its editor **Robert L. Vann**, a noted publisher, politician, and attorney. She later became vice president of the Pittsburg Courier Corporation and wrote stories and articles for the paper. Once women gained the right to vote in 1920, Lampkin moved into the political sphere and on two occasions served as an alternate delegate at large to the National Republican Party Convention. Lampkin's leadership and fund raising ability gained her attention during World War I. She received considerable recognition for leading the campaign for the sale of Liberty Bonds for the Allegheny county black community, which resulted in their raising over $2 million.

Lampkin, as the national organizer and chair of the executive board of the **National Association of Colored Women** (NACW), had established herself as a national figure by the 1920s. In 1924 she was the only woman in a delegation of a dozen or more African American leaders to meet with President Calvin Coolidge; they were seeking justice for black soldiers in the 1917 **Houston race riot**. In 1930 Lampkin became the first regional field secretary for the **NAACP**, and in 1935 she became the national field secretary. Lampkin was very effective in her role, as reflected in her almost single handedly arranging the 1931 national convention, and her promotion of various campaigns such as the lynching button campaign of 1937. (The 1937 anti-

lynching button campaign was aimed at supporting the Costigan-Wagner Act. The act called for federal intervention when local authorities failed to respond to lynching of African Americans). She remained field secretary for the NAACP until 1947, when she became a member of the board of directors.

Lampkin remained active in the National Council of Negro Women (NCNW) and the NACW throughout the years. She contributed to numerous other organizations, as well, and worked tirelessly to promote the cause of civil rights. In 1964 Lampkin was still campaigning for civil rights when she collapsed on stage after giving a rousing speech. She died on March 10, 1965.

Lean'tin L. Bracks

McGill, Ralph Emerson (1898–1969)

Ralph McGill was born February 5, 1898, in Igou's Ferry, Tennessee, and died February 3, 1969, in Atlanta, Georgia. McGill, the editor and publisher of *The Atlanta Constitution*, dubbed by many "the conscience of the South," exhibited social consciousness throughout his career. His style contained enough of the down home turn of the phrase and biblical cadence to remain true to the southern tradition. He supported the civil rights of all, believed in separate but equal as long as there was real equality, and encouraged following the law, reasoned action, and nonviolence.

McGill enrolled in Vanderbilt University in Nashville, where he showed a keen interest in the humanities and was exposed to the Fugitives, a band of literary scholars who helped establish the New Criticism through their journal "The Fugitive" in the 1920s. While there, he worked part-time as a writer for the *Nashville Banner*, the evening paper and a conservative voice on the issue of race. He was expelled from the university because of a fraternity prank and a column in which he questioned the university's handling of funds that had been left to the university for a specific purpose.

McGill became a full-time sports editor at the *Nashville Banner,* but his ambition was to be involved in more challenging reporting. In 1929, he joined the staff as an assistant sports editor and columnist and moved through the ranks. He was named associate editor in 1938, editor in 1942, and publisher in 1960. He was mentored and supported by former publisher Clark Howard, whose policy had been moderation on racial issues and support for modern industry and technological policies, which McGill expanded with a degree of candor, logic, and intelligence that made them frequently confrontational and morally moving. His columns were varied in their focus and did not always address racial or moral issues. With support given by his friend Robert W. Woodruff, president of the Coca-Cola Company, and James M. Cox, the Ohio owner of the *Constitution,* McGill was free to respond to civil rights issues and confront racist politicians, regardless of the controversial nature of his columns.

McGill applied and won a Rosenwald Fellowship and spent six months in 1938 in Europe writing columns for the paper. While abroad, he witnessed Adolf Hitler's rise to power in Germany, experienced racism, and began to see parallels between what happened to black people and what happened to him overseas. In 1953 he wrote an article titled "One Day It Will Be Monday." Here he cautioned readers that there would come a day when the U.S. Supreme Court would make a decision about school desegregation and that they needed to face this fact and be prepared to act with responsible leadership, not with violence or anger that solves nothing. He encouraged journalists to be fair but to have opinions and not to be muzzled by objectivity. Following James Meredith's University of Mississippi enrollment experience, he admonished the Jackson papers for allowing the political and oppressive power structure to act without limitation and scoffed at the whole idea of states' rights. By the 1960s, he was saying we should be wary of the dual school system. Adhering to the law, he warned, would lead to

the acceptance of segregation. The inequities of segregation have carried a private weight of guilt, he said, and the movement's success would free white people as well as black.

Helen R. Houston

McGill was free to respond to civil rights issues and confront racist politicians, regardless of the controversial nature of his columns.

Poston, Theodore (1906–1974)

Born in Hopkinsville, Kentucky, Theodore "Ted" Roosevelt Augustus Major Poston grew up with parents who were teachers. His father, Ephraim Poston, was also a newspaper publisher. The younger Poston attended the local segregated schools and worked as a copy clerk for his father's newspaper, until racism forced the paper out of town because of its controversial nature. After graduating from college, Ted Poston became a writer for the Alfred E. Smith campaign for the Democratic nomination for the U.S. presidency. Later he became a columnist for the *Pittsburgh Courier,* and in 1929 for the *New York Amsterdam News.*

While in New York, Poston worked with **A. Philip Randolph** in his efforts to unionize black railroad workers. In the late 1930s, Poston became the first African American to write full time for a big, white-owned daily—the *New York Post.* Soon he witnessed racism firsthand in the journalism industry. When he covered New York's City Hall, white reporters shunned him at first; he scooped them on stories, however, and they began to accept him and his talent.

Poston soon protested segregation and used the press to cover racial issues and promote civil rights. On leave from his position at the *Post* from 1940 to 1945, Poston became a New Deal publicist under President Harry Truman's administration and maintained a close relationship with the president. Among his duties, he was head of the Negro News Desk in Washington's Office of War Information. He was given assignments in the South that were dangerous and life-threatening. In order to cover the Scottsboro trial in Alabama, in which a white woman falsely charged that a group of young black men raped her, Poston dressed shabbily and posed as an itinerant preacher. His news coverage included the **Montgomery Bus Boycott,** *Brown v. Board of Education,* and Little Rock school integration. While visiting activist Daisy Bates's home in Little Rock, he nearly lost his life from a would-be assassin's bullet.

A pioneer journalist, Poston used the press to protest race matters; he also helped other African American journalists advance in their work. He was known as the dean of "black journalism" and was honored for his work and for the risk-taking ways that he covered accounts of racism in the South.

Jessie Carney Smith

Ruggles, David (1810–1849)

At an early age, David Ruggles knew that he would fight against the injustices of slavery. When Ruggles was 17, he moved to New York and became secretary of the New York Committee of Vigilance. He was a steadfast advocate for escaped slaves and assisted them in their struggle for freedom. The most famous fugitive who found refuge with Ruggles was **Frederick Douglass**. While in hiding at Ruggles's home, Douglass married Anna Murray before continuing his escape. By this time in 1838 Ruggles was already a notorious abolitionist. After an article he wrote in *Colored American* accusing John Russell, a black lodge owner, of helping to kidnap blacks, the paper was sued for libel and Russell won.

Samuel Cornish, the owner of the paper and a member of the Vigilance Committee, saw Ruggles's behavior as objectionable. This, along with other radical acts, resulted in Ruggles having to resign from the committee in 1839.

As a journalist, Ruggles produced numerous pamphlets and articles about the condition and situations of blacks at that time. He strongly disagreed with the American Colonization Society, which advocated black relocation, and in response published his own pamphlet, *Extinguished,* in 1834. Ruggles continued to publish in abolitionist journals as his health deteriorated to the point that he was nearly blind. He was fearless in his confrontation with legal and political forces that supported slavery. Eventually, Ruggles left New York for Massachusetts in 1841, and he later felt his health improve by using certain water cures. By 1845, he had regained his health and continued to write about the abolitionist movement. Ruggles's return was shortened when he succumbed in 1849 from a severe bowel infection. He was considered a true warrior for the cause of abolition.

Lean'tin L. Bracks

Russwurm, John (1799–1851)

John Brown Russwurm, who was born in Port Antonio, Jamaica, to a white American merchant father and a slave mother, was raised as a free person. He is best known as one who fought for the abolition of slavery and supported the colonization of blacks. Russwurm was educated in Québec, Ontario, and Maine and graduated from Bowdoin College in Brunswick, Maine, in 1826. In 1827, Russwurm went to New York and later founded the first black newspaper in America, *Freedom's Journal.* With prominent abolitionist **Samuel Cornish** as senior editor and Russwurm as editor, the paper sought to vocalize the abolitionist demands to end slavery in the South and give equal rights and opportunities to blacks in the North. The paper's first issue came out on March 16, 1827; it rejected the colonization of blacks as advocated by the American Coloniza-

John Russwurm (Fisk University).

Mary Ann Shadd (Fisk University).

tion Society. When Russwurm became sole editor in September of 1827, he reversed this opinion and spoke out in support of colonization, which advocated black emigration to Africa. He made this statement formally on March 7, 1829. As a result, he resigned 14 days later in a farewell editorial. Russwurm subsequently accepted a position in Liberia as superintendent of schools and arrived in Monrovia, Liberia, in November of 1829. Although abolitionists in America continually rejected him, his role in Liberia was important in establishing positive communications with neighboring countries. Russwurm died in 1851 and a monument was erected at Cape Palmas in recognition of his service.

Lean'tin L. Bracks

Shadd, Mary Ann (1823–1893)

Critical issues of the nineteenth century, especially abolition, women's suffrage, and equal rights, were of primary concern to Mary Ann Shadd. She was a talented figure whose voice was heard in her editorial work, lectures, and legal and educational activities. Born in Wilmington, Delaware, she saw runaway slaves protected in her home. She was exposed to the work of her abolitionist father, who sought parity for blacks. After the **Fugitive Slave Act of 1850** was passed, many blacks who had lived free for some time in the North were forced back into slavery. To avoid this fate, many emigrated to Canada. Black luminaries moved there as well.

Shadd gave up teaching and moved to Windsor, Canada West, in 1851 to aid in the black cause. There she helped black immigrants by teaching in segregated schools that the **American Missionary Association** supported. Her goal, however, was to see schools integrated. In 1852, Shadd published a pamphlet that aimed to help the fugitives. *A Plea for Emigration, or Notes on Canada West, in Its Moral, Social and*

Political Aspects gave them information on the moral, social, and political atmosphere in Canada West. Meanwhile, she continued to fight for fugitive slaves in the *Provincial Freeman,* which she edited. The first edition appeared in March 1853, and it became Canada West's first official anti-slavery organ. In the paper, Shadd declared war on slavery and all-black settlements. From 1855 to 1856 Shadd was in the United States, lecturing in Michigan, Ohio, Pennsylvania, and Illinois on race matters.

Although she relinquished editorial responsibility for her journal, she continued to write letters to the paper and report on race matters. Shadd became the first woman to enroll in the law department at **Howard University** in Washington, D.C., graduating in 1883. Then she became a suffragette while continuing her advocacy for racial equality.

Jessie Carney Smith

Trotter, Geraldine Pindell (1872–1918)

Geraldine Pindell Trotter (Fisk University).

Geraldine "Deenie" Pindell Trotter, who came from a family of Boston militants, moved within Boston's elite black militant society as a staunch supporter of activism. In the 1850s, her uncle had led a movement to integrate public schools in Boston. Both Geraldine and her partner and husband, **William Monroe Trotter,** were dedicated to the cause of equal rights. She became society editor for the *Boston Guardian,* a journal that promoted equal rights for African Americans. It was founded by Monroe Trotter, **W.E.B. Du Bois,** and other black militants and anti-**Booker T. Washington** supporters.

When the **NAACP** was founded in 1909, Geraldine Trotter became a member. She had joined the failing **Niagara Movement,** but resigned due to internal conflict. It soon lost influence to a new organization, the **NAACP.** Monroe Trotter's illness around 1916 and subsequent imprisonment catapulted Geraldine Trotter to a higher leadership role at the paper. Then she saw firsthand the realities of racial agitation. Beyond the *Guardian,* Geraldine Trotter had a number of civic interests, including supporting the Saint Monica's Home for elderly black women. Later on, she formed a woman's anti-lynching committee and joined the National Equal Rights League that Monroe Trotter had helped to establish. During World War I she spoke before black soldiers at Camp Devens and she continued other efforts on behalf of the men. Her friend Du Bois said at her death that she "died as one whom death cannot conquer."

Jessie Carney Smith

Trotter, William Monroe (1872–1934)

Even though he grew up in comfortable circumstances in the predominantly white area of Hyde Park in Boston, Massachusetts, where he was the only black student in his classes throughout his educational career, William Monroe Trotter (who went by his middle

William Monroe Trotter (Fisk University).

a means toward progress for the black race as promoted by **Booker T. Washington** was one topic that Trotter discussed in his paper. He disagreed with Washington's view of accommodation in that it ignored the development of blacks' intellectual abilities. The disagreement between the two worsened to the point that, in 1903, Trotter confronted Washington. Washington was giving a speech at the Columbus Avenue African Methodist Episcopal Church when Trotter stood on a chair and proceeded to read off a list of questions for Washington's response. Trotter was arrested and spent 30 days in jail and paid a $25 fine.

To provide a forum about race matters on a national scale, Trotter organized the National Equal Rights League in 1908 as an alternative to the **NAACP** that had white financiers. Throughout his life, Trotter railed against racism in issues ranging from the 1915 film *The Birth of a Nation,* to the treatment of black soldiers in World War I, to ending segregation in the District of Columbia.

Lean'tin L. Bracks

name), was adamant about challenging the racism that he encountered as he entered into a career. In a tribute to Trotter at his death, **W.E.B. Du Bois** said that his lifelong philosophy was "intense hatred of all racial discrimination and segregation."

Once receiving his Harvard degree in June of 1844, along with his election into the Phi Beta Kappa honors society, he found that racist attitudes ignored his accomplishments and subjected him to a climate of disrespect despite his educational accomplishments. "He thought that Boston and America would yield to clear reason and determined agitation," wrote Du Bois, but they did not. In response, Trotter and other elite blacks formed the Boston Literary and Historical Society in 1901 to discuss race matters. He also started a weekly newspaper, *The Guardian,* as a forum to express the cause of equal rights. The issue of accommodation as

Vann, Robert L. (1887–1940)

Activist Robert L. Vann used the newspaper that he edited, the *Pittsburgh Courier,* as an advocate for social change for African Americans. Born in North Carolina, he studied for a while at Virginia Union University in Richmond and became disturbed over deteriorating racial conditions in the South. He was affected by **Booker T. Washington's** autobiography, *Up from Slavery,* which helped to shape his ideas on racial pride and economic self-help for African Americans. Vann relocated to Pittsburgh where he continued his studies. After completing his law degree, he became one of only five black attorneys in Pittsburgh. By 1910 he was editor of the *Pittsburgh Courier.* He used the paper to crusade for improvement in areas of housing, health, education, employment, crime, and other issues that affected African Americans.

Vann urged blacks to form their own financial institutions. He wanted more blacks to become medical doctors and pleaded for a hospital to serve the needs of the black community. The crafty journalist also worked to dispel negative images of blacks that the white press had promoted. He provided blacks with positive news on the local community—facts that the mainstream presses disregarded. The new black immigrants from the South were able to use the *Courier* to read news about their home states. He had a temperate attitude toward the **riots in Houston** (1917) and in Chicago (1919). Vann, once a supporter of **A. Philip Randolph** and the **Brotherhood of Sleeping Car Porters**, was a critic of both by 1928. His work with the *Courier* demonstrated his continuing interest in promoting racial pride and self-respect.

Jessie Carney Smith

Vann urged blacks to form their own financial institutions [and] ... wanted more blacks to become medical doctors.

Wells-Barnett, Ida B. (1862–1931)

One of the first African American women to serve as an investigative reporter, Wells began her fight at the age of 22, when she brought legal action against the Chesapeake, Ohio, and Southwestern Railroad Company. Through written and spoken communication, she made known the stark atrocities of lynchings in America. Ida B. Wells was born a slave on July 16, 1862, in Holly Springs, Mississippi, to James and Elizabeth (Warrenton) Wells. The oldest in a family of four boys and four girls, she

attended Shaw University (later Rust College) in Holly Springs; after her move to Memphis, Tennessee, she attended summer sessions at Nashville's **Fisk University**. The yellow fever epidemic of 1878 claimed the lives of Wells's parents and youngest brother, and in the 1880s she moved to Memphis. While preparing for the teachers' exam for the Negro Public Schools of Memphis, she taught in Woodstock, Tennessee, outside Memphis.

In May 1884 Wells purchased a first-class ticket on a local Memphis-to-Woodstock line. Taking a seat in the white ladies' coach and refusing to move to the segregated "smoker" car as instructed by the conductor, Wells was ejected from the train. She subsequently filed suit against the railroad company. In December of 1884, the Memphis circuit court ruled in her favor and awarded her $500 in damages, a decision that the Tennessee Supreme Court reversed in 1887. Using the story of her suit against the railroad and its outcome, Wells contributed to the publication *The Living Way* under the pseudonym "Iola." She also wrote regularly for the African American press throughout the country. Known as the "Princess of the Press," she became the editor of and partner in the *Free Speech and Headlight*, a militant journal that served as a voice of the African American community.

Wells's 1891 editorials critical of the Memphis Board of Education and its unequal distribution of the resources allotted to the segregated Negro schools led to her dismissal as a teacher. The lynchings of Thomas Moss, Calvin McDowell, and Henry Stewart, three young African American proprietors of the People's Grocery Store, on March 9, 1891, caused Wells to declare journalistic war on lynching. Because of her prickly penned editorials about the issue of lynching, she was banished from Memphis. Exiled from the South, Wells persisted in her struggle against racial injustice and lynching as a columnist for the New York *Age* and intensified her campaign against lynching through lectures, newspaper articles, and pamphlets. Works from this period include *Southern Horrors: Lynch*

Law in All Its Phases (1892); *A Red Record: Tabulated Statistics and Alleged Causes of Lynching in the United States, 1892, 1893, and 1894* (1895); and *Mob Rule in New Orleans* (1900). In addition to investigating and reporting on the execution of blacks without due process of law, she lectured on the subject and made her findings known throughout the Northeast, England, Scotland, and Wales. Three years after she was expelled from Memphis, on June 27, 1895, Ida B. Wells married attorney Ferdinand L. Barnett, editor and founder of the Chicago *Conservator.*

In 1918, in her unremitting crusade against racial violence, Wells-Barnett covered the race riot in **East St. Louis, Illinois,** and wrote a series of articles on the riot for the *Chicago Defender.* Four years later, she returned to the South for the first time in 30 years to investigate the indictment for murder of 12 innocent farmers in Elaine, Arkansas. She published and distributed 1,000 copies of *The Arkansas Race Riot* (1922), in which she recorded the results of her investigation. Wells-Barnett, who was also a cofounder of the **NAACP,** died on March 25, 1931, in Chicago, at the age of 68.

Linda T. Wynn

Withers, Ernest C. (1922–2007)

Trained as a photographer during World War II, Ernest C. Withers documented over 60 years of African American history. His visual images were devoted to the Civil Rights Movement, the negro baseball leagues, and the blues and R&B performances that he witnessed on Beale Street in his Memphis hometown. While serving in the war, he was trained by the Army Corps of Engineers to be a photographer. When the war ended, he returned to Memphis and established a commercial studio. He served the black newspaper industry, working as a freelance journalist for such newspapers as the *Tri-State Defender* and the old *Memphis World.*

In 1955 two white men were accused of killing a black teenager from Chicago, Emmett Till, for supposedly whistling at the wife of one of the defendants. The men were acquitted, but much later admitted that they committed the crime. Withers covered the trial in Sumner, Mississippi, and published the photographs that he took in a booklet. The booklet led to other assignments for Withers. The black press, including the *Chicago Defender, Jet,* and the *Baltimore African American,* gave him assignments, as did mainstream outlets such as the *New York Times, Life, Time,* and the *Washington Post.* As the Civil Rights Movement progressed, Withers captured key moments of activities in the South. Among his subjects were **Martin Luther King Jr.** and **Ralph Abernathy** riding a bus in Montgomery, Alabama; the photo was taken on December 21, 1956, the first day that desegregation of the buses occurred. In 1957 he chronicled the integration of Little Rock's **Central High School** in Arkansas, and James Meredith's entrance into the University of Mississippi in 1962. He documented the funerals of **Medgar Evers** in 1963 and King in 1968, as well.

Jessie Carney Smith

Ernest C. Withers documented over 60 years of African American history.

Magazines

Aframerican Women's Journal (est. 1940)

The major advocate for black women by the mid-twentieth century, the National Council of Negro Women, published the *Aframerican Women's Journal* to articulate the needs of black women who had been denied their rights in many arenas. From its founding, the NCNW has focused on such issues as health, employment, family life, citizenship, public affairs, religion, consumer education, and rural life. The journal was established to target legislation affecting women, particularly black women; it published the organization's projections for the future, as well. Also included were articles noting the accomplishments of individual black women who, until then and for many years that followed, were ignored in most published sources. Sue Bailey Thurman (1903–1996), a religious worker, lecturer, and community servant, was the founding editor of the journal, supervising it from 1940 to 1944 under educator **Mary McLeod Bethune**'s administration. Bethune founded the NCNW organization in New York City on December 5, 1935. The journal's name was changed in 1949, when it became known as *Women United.* Copies of the publication are in the National Archives for Black Women's History, located in Washington, D.C.

Jessie Carney Smith

Writings of all kinds, graphic works, and fine arts found a supporter in *The Crisis.*

The Crisis (est. 1910)

The official magazine of the **NAACP**, *The Crisis* magazine began publication in November 1910 with **W.E.B. Du Bois** as founding editor. Its title grew out of informal discussions in July and August 1910 of the NAACP's board concerning the new magazine. Founding member Mary White Ovington mentioned James Russell Lowell's poem "The Present Crisis," when a board member responded, "There is the name for your magazine." It was to be "A Record of the Darker Race" and for many years carried that subtitle. Du Bois, who served as edi-

tor until 1934, said in his first editorial that *The Crisis* would "be first and foremost a newspaper"; following that, it would give a review of opinion and literature.

From the start, *The Crisis* published information on race and other news of the day considered important to black people. The first issue was about seven by ten inches in size and consisted of sixteen pages. There were six contributors in addition to the editor. They were Oswald Garrison Villard of the *Evening Post;* Charles Edward Russell, a well-known magazine writer; author and critic Kelly Miller; Mary Dunlop Maclean, staff writer for the *New York Times;* J. Max Barber, former editor of *The Voice of the Negro;* and poet and writer William Stanley Braithwaite. The inaugural issue, with a print run of 1,000 copies, expressed the objectives of the journal: "To set forth those facts and arguments which show the danger of race prejudice, particularly as manifested today toward colored people." Assuredly, it aimed to be primarily a news organ. Further, it would publish brief articles, reviews of opinion, literary reviews, and editorials that upheld the rights of people regardless of color or race.

Since the first issue was so successful, the Committee on Publications that oversaw the journal recommended that it double in size. This occurred with the second issue, as did the beginning of a series of articles on women called "Talks about Women." The articles dealt with the status of women in education, business, and the professions. The author, Mrs. John E. Milholland, urged black women to expand their efforts beyond their small circles and their race and embrace the larger movement, where there was a struggle for women's rights and the ballot. Later on, contributors included Jane Addams, **Mary Church Terrell**, and **Ida B. Wells**. Circulation reached 30,000 by 1913, and the magazine had become so popular that readers eagerly anticipated the publication of each issue. By 1917, circulation had reached 50,000, and two years later it was 100,000.

Writings of all kinds, graphic works, and fine arts found a supporter in *The Crisis.* During the

Harlem Renaissance of the 1920s, the journal offered a series of prizes to creative young African American poets, writers, and artists, and awarded the Amy Spingarn Prizes in Literature and Art. One of the oldest black journals, the monthly magazine maintains its early mission and as "the NAACP's articulate partner" in the struggle for the rights of black people. It also continues to focus on race and present issues of economic, political, social, moral, and ethical concern. It publishes reports of the NAACP's annual conventions, as well.

Jessie Carney Smith

Opportunity (1923–1949)

Opportunity, the official journal of the **National Urban League** (NUL), was first published in January 1923, with **Charles S. Johnson** as editor. At that time, Johnson headed NUL's Department of Research and Investigation. The magazine was intended as a factual account of elements of black life, including employment, urban life, the labor market, housing, health, and a wide range of topics. Johnson believed that the magazine could speed up activities in the cycle of race relations. The Carnegie Corporation underwrote the cost of the publication through a five-year grant that it provided. By 1927, however, Carnegie believed that NUL should be able to support its own publication and refused to renew the grant. At the beginning of 1927, *Opportunity* was comparable in quality to any other magazine of similar character published in America at the time. It was influential and had impressive standards. When circulation peaked in 1928, its sales had reached no more than 11,000 copies. Forty percent of these sales went to white subscribers.

Opportunity published works by Harlem Renaissance writers and artists. This was especially important because it came at a time when mainstream presses refused to print works by African American writers. Johnson also provided a forum for arriving artists and

writers in Harlem and, beginning in May 1925, rewarded them at an elaborate banquet by giving prizes for outstanding creative achievement. By the Great Depression, *Opportunity* focused on unemployment, housing, and crucial issues of that time. It remained a financial burden to the NUL, however, and ceased publication in 1949.

Jessie Carney Smith

News Services

Associated Negro Press (1919–1964)

Founded in Chicago in March 1919, the Associated Negro Press (ANP) was the first and largest national news service for African Americans, providing news stories, opinions,

Journalist Claude A. Barnett established the Associated Negro Press in 1919 (Fisk University).

book reviews, essays, and other information of interest to black newspapers. Its symbol was an owl holding a scroll inscribed with the slogan "Progress, Loyalty, Truth." Claude A. Barnett was a journalist and publisher who established the news service to exchange national news among black publishers and advertisers throughout the United States. For an initial fee of $25, many organizations subscribed to the ANP. Staff writers wrote many of the stories and news items based on information that stringers provided. Correspondents and stringers were based in major centers where black people lived. Many of these staffers represented the ANP in high places, thus contributing to the service's popularity. In time, the ANP brought on writers who worked without pay but were able to give national exposure to their ideas.

The Atlanta Constitution was well known as one of the most prominent and responsible newspapers of the South.

As the ANP became an effective organization for publishing the latest news and trends about the African American community, it became an important newsgathering network long before the mainstream press was receptive to such news. The service helped to raise black self-esteem well before the civil right movement was able to do so. The ANP never became a commercial success, but the information it gathered documented the vast experiences of black people. As its debts climbed and Barnett devoted less time to its operations due to health reasons, the service ceased operation in midsummer 1964.

Jessie Carney Smith

Newspapers

Atlanta Journal-Constitution

*T*he *Atlanta Constitution* was first published in 1886, and *The Atlanta Journal* was established in 1883. The two papers then merged in 1950, when *The Atlanta Constitution* was purchased by James M. Cox, who was the owner of *The Atlanta Journal*. The papers ran separately until they were published as one paper in 2001. *The Atlanta Constitution* was well known as one of the most prominent and responsible newspapers of the South. In 1938 journalist **Ralph Emerson McGill** became executive editor of *The Atlanta Constitution*. Under McGill's leadership, the newspaper became one of the first to recognize that Negro, as a designation of race and ethnicity, should be written was a capital "N," rather than a lower case "n." This practice was thought to be progressive. McGill's positions on race at times appeared conservative; however, as the Civil Rights Movement grew, his stance on race issues was viewed to be more liberal. It was under McGill's leadership as editor and publisher, from the 1940s through the 1960s, that *The Atlanta Constitution* documented the Civil Rights Movement. In 1959 McGill won the Pulitzer Prize for his writing in the *Atlanta Constitution* on integration and in response to violence against black churches and schools. In 1968 Harmon Perry was the first African American journalist to work for *The Atlanta Journal-Constitution*. Perry wrote about the assassination of **Martin Luther King Jr.** and other turbulent events in the struggle for civil rights in the late 1960s and early 1970s.

Helen R. Houston

Charlotte Observer

*T*his newspaper was established shortly after the end of the **Civil War**, beginning publication on January 25, 1869, as the *Carolina Daily Observer*. Even during the Reconstruction period, the city of Charlotte, North Carolina, was a leading location for business enterprises and maintained a significant black population (approximately 42 percent). Former slave Anthony Rivers was credited with being an outstanding pressman involved in the mechanical production of the first issues of the paper. Blacks in Charlotte and the surrounding Piedmont region should have been considered a vital part of the newspaper's readership and customer base, but they were mostly ignored or taken for granted by the four Confederate veterans who were the paper's first publishers and editors. This changed somewhat after 1872, when new owner/editor Johnstone Jones and writer Joseph Caldwell toned down its blatant racism while still supporting the existing system of segregation. The earlier editions provided little news of interest to the African American community, but the new staff fairly reported incidents, such as the first execution of a white man for the murder of a black. In subsequent years, the paper reported on black churches, businesses, the Biddle Institute (later Johnson C. Smith University), and civil rights activities, including the 1960 student sit-ins that began in North Carolina. The paper hired its first black reporters, Jacob "Jake" Simms and Shirley Johnson, in the late 1960s.

Fletcher F. Moon

Commercial Appeal

The largest circulating newspaper in North Mississippi and the dominant newspaper in Memphis, Tennessee, the *Commercial Appeal* was established in 1894. There is a long history behind the paper that made it what it is today. It began as Henry Van Pelt's publication *The Appeal,* a weekly newspaper founded in 1841. During the **Civil War,** the paper was pro-Confederacy, and when the Union Army arrived it was decided it would be more expedient to move the presses from Memphis and work elsewhere in 1862. During this period, it published from cities in Alabama, Georgia, and Mississippi, returning to Memphis in 1865 after the war.

In the 1870s the yellow fever epidemic greatly impacted the newspaper industry, and in 1890 the *Appeal* purchased its rival, *Avalanche,* whose first publication was in 1858; the paper came to be known as the *Appeal-Avalanche.* In 1894 *The Daily Commercial Appeal* purchased the *Appeal-Avalanche* and it became known as the Memphis *Commercial Appeal.* It gained respect for its reporting, was nationally known, opposed prohibition, supported women's suffrage, and won a Pulitzer Prize for its campaign against the Ku Klux Klan. In 1936 the newspaper was bought by the Scripps-Howard Syndicate. During the Civil Rights Movement, the racial news was often downplayed, and it often took the stance that educational opportunities for African Americans should be expanded, but that these opportunities should not be achieved at the expense of the *status quo* for whites. The editor often gave credence and news space to known white supremacists and articles on race that demonstrated fallacious reasoning.

Helen R. Houston

Herald-Leader

Over 40 years after the modern civil rights demonstrations of 1959 and the 1960s, including the 1960s sit-ins in Lexington, Kentucky, the *Herald-Leader* published accounts of these activities for the first time. Although protesters held weekly sit-ins at Lexington's segregated lunch counters, hotels, and theaters, the top newspaper executives ordered their staffs to suppress the news coverage, if they covered the events at all. In a few instances, coverage was given, but buried within the papers. The aim was to "play down the movement" with the hope that it would go away. By 1964 most of the places targeted had desegregated and the city experienced little violence. As a result, some claim that their censorship hurt the movement at the time, caused irreparable damage to historical records, and forced readers to miss one of the most important accounts of the century. On July 4, 2004, the paper published a front-page exposé, sidebar articles, and a full page of photographs and accounts of the **Civil Rights Movement** in Lexington. *The Herald* (the morning paper associated with Democrats) and *The Leader* (the afternoon paper associated with Republicans) merged in the 1980s and later became a part of the Knight Ridder newspaper chain—a group with an interest in diversity.

Jessie Carney Smith

News of events and black individuals were ignored, downplayed, or ridiculed and sensationalized in a pejorative way.

Jackson Clarion-Ledger

The largest circulating newspaper in North Mississippi, the *Jackson Clarion-Ledger* had its beginnings in 1837 with *The Eastern Clarion Ledger* in Jasper County. The paper was sold and relocated to Meridian. Following the **Civil War**, it relocated again to its present site, Jackson, Mississippi, but it had not completed its mergers and name changes yet. It merged with *The Standard* to become *The Clarion,* and in 1888 it combined with the *State Ledger* to become the *Daily Clarion-Ledger.* In 1920, Thomas and Robert Hederman bought *The Clarion-Ledger.* The Hederman family dated its connection with the paper back to 1871 and established a bastion of power that dominated the tenor of the news and much of the political life of the region.

It was this newspaper that reported on and manipulated many people and events during the Civil Rights Movement of the 1950s and 1960s. On August 24, 1937, *The Clarion-Ledger* and the *Jackson Daily News* incorporated under

a charter for the purpose of advertising. The family consolidated the two newspaper plants in 1954. The two papers were consolidated under the title *The Clarion-Ledger* in 1989, when it was published by the Gannett Company. The newspaper's reporting reflected a segregationist and Confederate mindset. News of events and black individuals were ignored, downplayed, or ridiculed and sensationalized in a pejorative way. In short, the paper was not known for its in-depth research or objective reporting of civil rights issues.

Helen R. Houston

Jackson Daily News

The *Jackson Daily News* came into being around 1907. It was the result of a post-**Civil War** merger between *The Standard,* which came to be known as *The Clarion,* and the *State Ledger,* to become the *Daily Clarion-Ledger.* In 1882 four young men who had been adversely impacted by the merger pooled their finances and began publishing the *Jackson Evening Post;* in 1907 Fred Sullens bought an interest in the paper, and soon after it became known as the *Jackson Daily News.* The *Jackson Daily News* and the *Clarion-Ledger,* owned by Thomas and Robert Hederman, were incorporated on August 24, 1937, under a charter issued to Mississippi Publishing Corporations for joint advertising. In 1954 the Hederman family bought the paper and consolidated the two newspaper plants. By purchasing the paper and adding to their numerous other business enterprises, the Hederman family represented a major political and media power base. The *Jackson Daily News,* which had never been considered one of the strongest deliverers of the news, took on the biases of the publishers; there was little if any separation between news and opinions, and it was known to carry editorials and news stories by both the Citizen's Council (the white supremacist organization formed to prevent the **Brown v. Board of Education** decision from being implemented) and the FBI.

Helen R. Houston

Tennessean

The *Tennessean* had its origins in the Nashville *Whig,* which was begun by Joseph and Moses Norvell in 1812. Later, it became known as the Nashville *American,* and Colonel Luke Lea issued the first edition of the *Tennessean* on May 12, 1907. Three years later, the two newspapers merged as the *Nashville Tennessean.* In 1963 publisher Amon Carter Evans changed the paper's name to the *Tennessean.* Later, Evans hired John Seigenthaler as managing editor. Seigenthaler worked for the newspaper from 1948 to 1961 before serving as administrative assistant to U.S. Attorney General **Robert Kennedy** from 1961 to 1962. During the **Nashville Sit-in Movement,** while the *Tennessean* did not back the sit-ins in its editorial column it did cover the student protests. One of the reporters assigned to the sit-in movement was David Halberstam. He was close in age to the non-violent contingent of students and he was sympathetic to their cause. Halberstam connected with the students and took their calls. He also wrote stories for *The Reporter* that further defined the students' protests and their non-violent philosophy. However, Nashville's evening paper, *The Nashville Banner,* published by staunch segregationist James Stahlman, refused to cover the student protest. Stahlman used his position on the Vanderbilt University board of trustees to force the university into expelling the **Reverend James Lawson,** one of the architects of the Nashville student movement and a divinity student at Vanderbilt. During the 1950s and 1960s, several reporters who worked for the *Tennessean* went on to outstanding careers elsewhere. They included David Halberstam, Tom Wicker, Fred Graham, and Wallace Westfeldt, who wrote, "Settling a Sit-in," a report prepared for the Nashville Community Relations Conference.

Linda T. Wynn

Law and Government

Attorneys

Davis, John Aubrey Sr. (1912–2002)

John Aubrey Davis Sr. was a celebrated veteran of landmark civil rights confrontations from the 1930s until his death. His fight for equal rights began while he was a young academic at **Howard University** in Washington, D.C., and through his leadership of the **New Negro Alliance**, a group known for protest against racial injustice. In the mid-1930s a hamburger restaurant with a black clientele in Washington fired its black employees to make room for whites. Davis responded by setting up a picket line to promote "buy where you can work" among the black community. The movement was similar to the **"Don't Buy Where You Can't Work"** protest movement that, around this time, served the black community well in various parts of the country. Davis's protest brought immediate and positive results, and the black employees were rehired within two days.

Davis was so pleased with the response that he organized the New Negro Alliance, whose purpose was to pressure those businesses located in Washington's black neighborhoods—but were not black owned—to make their employees reflect the community's racial character.

While the businesses sought to enjoin the group against such actions—and the lower courts ruled against the alliance—in 1938 the U.S. Supreme Court decided that the group had a right to picket. In the case of *New Negro Alliance v. Sanitary Grocery Company Inc.,* **Thurgood Marshall**, later a U.S. Supreme Court Justice, served as one of the group's lawyers. The two civil rights attorneys also worked together in the landmark school desegregation case **Brown v. Board of Education** that in 1954 ended the separate-but-equal doctrine for public schools. Davis led the research team that collected historical and legal facts for the NAACP's Legal Defense and Education Fund, providing documentation that Marshall, the lead counsel, needed to support his argument.

Jessie Carney Smith

Farmer Paellmann, Deadria (1965–)

Deadria Farmer Paellmann left a promising legal career to become one of the nation's leading researchers in the campaign for slave reparations. Her fascination with the connections of American corporate interests to the slave trade began as a research paper while in law school in the late 1990s. Her continued investigation revealed that Aetna, the country's largest insurance company, offered life insurance polices on slaves to their owners. The revelation not only forced a public apology from the company's officials but also signaled the beginning of a comprehensive Farmer Paellmann-led effort to sue several major American corporations that profited from slavery in the years prior to the **Civil War**.

Reared by a divorced mother of six, Farmer Paellmann was a gifted pianist in adolescence but opted for a degree in political science from Brooklyn College, and a master's degree in lobbying and political management from George Washington University, before completing a law degree from New England School of Law in 1999. As a freelance legal researcher and a reparations activist since that time, Farmer Paellmann is well acquainted with the criticisms of her detractors. The basis for reparations, she argues, was not challenged in the case of Jewish Holocaust survivors and is supported by the federal government's failure to deliver on the promise of 40 acres and a mule to African American freedman following the close of the Civil War. In 2002, as the executive director of Restitution Study Group, Inc., Farmer Paellmann filed a federal lawsuit against Aetna, Fleet-Boston Financial, and railroad firm CSX on behalf of 35 million descendants of slaves, with the promise to add up to 100 additional corporations in time.

Crystal A. deGregory

Gibbs, Mifflin (1823–1915)

Long before Mifflin Wistar Gibbs became a rising star in the Republican Party, he was an ardent abolitionist and a pioneer in the settlement of California and British Columbia. His business acumen and political savvy secured him impressive offices, including as the first African American to be elected a municipal judge, and culminating with an appointment as a consul in Madagascar. Born in Philadelphia to Methodist minister Jonathan Clarkson Gibbs and Maria Jackson Gibbs, Gibbs had to abandon his formal education when he was only eight

because of his father's sudden death. Following a stint in a free school, he was put to work as a stable hand and in a series of other odd jobs throughout adolescence. At 16 he apprenticed with James Gibbons, an ex-slave and carpenter who built several of the nation's black churches.

All the while Gibbs busied himself by studying independently. He joined the Philomatheon Institute, a black literacy society where he encountered many of the city's most influential African Americans. Under the influence of men such as Isaiah West and Robert Purvis, Gibbs became a devoted abolitionist. Following the completion of his apprenticeship, he became active in the **Underground Railroad** and was invited by **Frederick Douglass** to join him on a speaking tour following the National Antislavery Convention in Philadelphia in 1849. Shortly thereafter, Gibbs joined the Gold Rush to California. Upon his arrival he assumed various menial jobs after white carpenters barred blacks from working in the field. His successful partnership with Peter Lester, a fellow Philadelphia native and abolitionist, ended abruptly after Gibbs witnessed Lester being assaulted by a customer. Since California laws prohibited African Americans from offering testimony against whites, Gibbs joined an 1851 petition in protest and subsequently participated in a string of state conventions further protesting the status of blacks in California.

As a member of the San Francisco Athenaeum, the city's black intellectual center that was founded in 1853, Gibbs helped to establish *Mirror of the Times,* a black newspaper, just three years later. Still, the city's black community became increasingly attracted to the possibilities of emigration. While an attempt to bar African Americans from immigrating to California was narrowly defeated, it served to reinforce the prevailing racist attitudes that existed there. Conversely, Vancouver Island welcomed between 400 and 800 African American migrants to its capital of Victoria. Among this number was Gibbs, who used his business acumen to amass a small fortune.

Mifflin Gibbs (Fisk University).

Following his organization of a black militia in 1861, he was elected to the town council and reelected again in 1867. He eventually settled in Arkansas after marrying and studying law at a business college in Oberlin. In 1872 he opened a private law office with Lloyd G. Wheeler and attended the Republican National Convention that same year. The following year he assumed the post of municipal judge, making him the first African American to do so. In 1877 Gibbs was appointed registrar for the Little Rock district in the U.S. Land Office, a post he held for twelve years under successive Republican presidents. After a series of other impressive political appointments, Gibbs served as U.S. Consul to Madagascar from 1891 to 1901. His work in the Republican Party did not blind him to the inequalities in American society, but instead empowered him to push for the continuing advancement of blacks in the nation.

Crystal A. deGregory

Gray, Fred D. (1930–)

Fred D. Gray served as counsel for **Rosa Parks**, the Reverend **Martin Luther King Jr.**, the **Montgomery Bus Boycott**, the Tuskegee Syphilis Study, the desegregation of Alabama schools, the **Freedom Riders**, and the **Selma to Montgomery March**. He began his solo law practice at the age of 24 and was in the legal forefront of modern civil rights as one of America's leading civil rights attorneys. With a calm manner, impassioned resolve, and an undisclosed promise made during his college years, Gray became an attorney, returned to his native state, and set about the task of destroying the vestiges of Jim Crow. An agent for change, he made numerous strides in altering the social contours of America as they relate to desegregation, constitutional law, racial discrimination in voting, housing, education, jury service, farm subsides, medicine and ethics, and in the main, humanizing the nation's judicial system.

In 1970 citizens from Barbour, Bullock, and Macon Counties elected attorney Gray to the Alabama State Legislature (1971–1975) as a representative from Tuskegee, where he became one of the first two African Americans to serve since Reconstruction. An ordained minister of the Church of Christ, Gray served as an assistant or part-time minister at several churches in Alabama, Kentucky, and Tennessee. In 1979 President Jimmy Carter nominated Gray for the position of U.S. District Judge for the Middle District of Alabama. However, because of opposition, in the late summer of 1980 Gray asked President Jimmy Carter to withdraw his name from nomination. Attorney Myron Thompson, another African American, was later confirmed and seated in his stead.

Gray is the author of the books *Bus Ride to Justice: The Life and Works of Fred Gray* (1995) and *Tuskegee Syphilis Study: The Real Story and Beyond* (1998). The youngest of five children, he was born to Abraham and Nancy Jones Gray in Montgomery, Alabama. He attended schools there until 1943, when his mother arranged for him to complete his education at the Nashville Christian Institute (NCI) in Nashville, Tennessee. An African American secondary school operated by the Church of Christ, the NCI placed emphasis on teaching young men to become preachers. After graduating, the young Gray returned to his home state and entered Alabama State College for Negroes, where he earned an undergraduate degree in 1951. In September of the same year, he entered Case Western Reserve University Law School. He received his law degree three years later and returned to Alabama with a stated purpose, which was to "destroy everything segregated [he] could find. "

Gray made his mark and ... brought America closer to principles of freedom, equality, and justice for all.

In the post-*Brown v. Board of Education* era, it did not take Gray long before he started to make good on his promise. He defended Claudette Colvin and **Rosa Parks** against charges of disorderly conduct for refusing to give up their seats to white passengers. He also filed a petition that challenged the constitutionality of Alabama state laws mandating racial segregation on buses, which resulted in the *Browder v. Gayle* case. In November 1956, the U.S. Supreme Court ruled that racial segregation of public means of conveyances was unconstitutional. Another notable case in which Gray was involved was *Gomillion v. Lightfoot,* which challenged the Alabama legislature after it redrew the boundaries of the city of Tuskegee, Alabama, to exclude black neighborhoods, thereby denying African Americans the right to vote in municipal elections. The *Williams v. Wallace* case resulted in the court ordering Governor Wallace and the State of Alabama to protect marchers as they marched

from **Selma to Montgomery, Alabama,** to present grievances for being denied the right to vote. These actions led to the enactment of the **Voting Rights Act of 1965.** Gray also was a lawyer for the *Pollard v. United States of America* case that resulted because of the Tuskegee Syphilis Study (1932–1972), in which black men were not informed of or treated for syphilis. The federal government was ordered to continue its treatment program.

These are just a few cases where Gray made his mark and in the process brought America closer to principles of freedom, equality, and justice for all. The senior partner in the law firm Gray, Langford, Sapp, McGowan, Gray & Nathanson, in July 2002 Gray became the first African American to hold the position of president of the Alabama Bar Association. The recipient of numerous awards, Gray, as a civil rights attorney for more than a half century, kept his promise to destroy the bastions of racial segregation not only in his native state but also throughout America.

Linda T. Wynn

Grimké, Archibald (1849–1930)

Archibald Grimké, a civil rights activist of the nineteenth and twentieth centuries, was born to Nancy Weston and her white slave master, Henry Grimké, a member of a socially prominent, slaveholding South Carolina family. While his father was alive, Archibald and his family did not live a slave existence. Even when Henry Grimké died in 1852, the family lived comfortably, with his sisters, Archibald's aunts, providing for them. However, the elder Grimké had willed Archibald and his family to Montague, his son by his white wife, who preceded him in death. A few years after his father's death, Montague enslaved his three half brothers and their mother.

These circumstances groomed Archibald Grimké to become a force who fought relentlessly for racial equality and civil rights. His biracial existence complicated matters for him, with his life changing dramatically when his half brother enslaved his family. Archibald decided to run away and was hunted as a fugitive slave. In later years he would meet his father's sisters: Angelina Weld Grimké and Sarah Moore Grimké, suffragettes and staunch abolitionists. These women would have a profound impact on Archibald's life. After attending Lincoln University and graduating from Harvard Law School, he knew the advantages of being well educated, socially refined, and positioned to make significant differences in society, politics, and the individual lives of others. Grimké's intellectual prowess and his ongoing fight for civil rights attracted him to both the black elite social class and upper crust of white society. Noteworthy was his membership in the **American Negro Academy**, the first national African American learned society, which was co-founded by his brother Francis in 1897; Archibald served as its president for 16 years. Grimké was also numbered among the Committee of Forty, the governing body of the National Negro Conference formed in 1909 by abolitionists and black leaders to address increased lynching activities and other race engendered problems. This organization was the forerunner to the **NAACP**; he was a founding member and served as president of the Washington, D.C., chapter.

Grimké's fight for the inalienable rights of black people was complemented by his fight for women's rights. He chaired the Massachusetts Woman Suffrage Association, but in whatever organization Grimké belonged, he was a strong voice and held powerful positions. As a civil rights activist, Grimké was outspoken and an independent thinker. Initially, he was a strong proponent of the Republican Party when it was "the party of emancipation." However, when its focus shifted to anti-black and anti-civil rights, Grimké became a Democrat. His allegiance was always to the people and party who put race before party business. Grimké openly challenged **Booker T. Washington** in a series of speeches known as the "great debate" when he

disagreed with Washington's leadership of compromise and accommodation regarding the race issue. Grimké pursued a vigorous fight for racial equality and justice until he became too ill to engage in the battle.

Helen R. Houston

Grimké's fight for the inalienable rights of black people was complemented by his fight for women's rights.

Hastie, William Henry (1904–1976)

William Hastie was born in Knoxville, Tennessee, to William Henry and Roberta (Child) Hastie on November 17, 1904. He received his primary education in the Knoxville public schools and in the schools of Washington, D.C. After graduating from Dunbar High School in Washington, Hastie entered Amherst College. He later was elected president of Amherst's Phi Beta Kappa chapter. First in his class, Hastie completed his A.B. at Amherst College in 1925. Following this, he joined the staff of New Jersey's Bordentown Manual Training School, where he taught until 1927. Three years later, he earned an LL. B. degree from Harvard University, where he served on the staff of the *Harvard Law Review.*

Hastie joined the faculty at Howard University Law School, and in 1931 he was admitted to the District of Columbia Bar. He entered private practice in association with the law firm of Houston & Houston. Following the 1932 election of President Franklin Delano Roosevelt, Hastie achieved high visibility as a race relations advisor to the Roosevelt administration. In 1933 he left private practice to accept the position of assistant solicitor of the Department of the Interior. Next, in 1937, President Roosevelt appointed Hastie judge of the Federal District Court in the Virgin Islands. Confirmed on March 26, 1937, he became the nation's first African American federal magistrate. Although the Virgin Islands were 90 percent black, no person of African descent before Hastie had been appointed to a federal judgeship. Judge Hastie served on the bench for two years before resigning his judgeship to return to Howard University's School of Law as dean and professor of law.

During this civil rights era, Hill's team filed more civil rights suits than all other southern states combined.

From 1941 to 1943, Hastie served as civilian aide to Secretary of War Henry L. Stimson. On January 15, 1943, he resigned this to protest the government's racial policies of segregation and discrimination in America's armed forces. Later that year, Hastie was awarded the **NAACP's** prestigious Spingarn Medal "for his distinguished career as jurist and as an uncompromising champion of equal justice." In 1944, Hastie supported the position of the National Committee to Abolish the Poll Tax, demanding senatorial authorization of the proposed law to enjoin the levy in elections.

On May 7, 1946, he was inaugurated as the first African American governor of the Virgin Islands. On October 15, 1949, President Harry S. Truman nominated him judge of the Third United States Circuit Court of Appeals. It was the highest judicial position attained by an African American at that time. He served on the appellate court bench for 21 years. In 1968 he

became chief judge, and in 1971, the year of his retirement from the bench, Hastie was senior judge. Hastie died on April 14, 1976. Funeral services were held on April 17 at the Temple University Baptist Chapel in Philadelphia.

Linda T. Wynn

Hill, Oliver W. (1907–2007)

A lawyer for the **NAACP** Legal Defense Fund (LDF), Oliver W. Hill became prominent for his efforts to desegregate the nation's public schools. The LDF filed a series of lawsuits in 1954 to break down racial barriers in public schools. Hill's efforts at racial justice were noticed first in 1940, when he and LDF lawyers **Thurgood Marshall**, William H. Hastie, and Leon Ransom were successful in the case *Alston v. School Board of Norfolk, Virginia,* which brought equal pay for Virginia's black and white teachers. In 1951 Hill argued on behalf of black students at R.R. Moton High School in Farmville, Virginia, who protested the deplorable conditions at their school. Known as *Davis v. County School Board of Prince Edward County,* this case became one of five included in the **Brown v. Board of Education** landmark decision of 1954. When Spottswood Robinson was named special NAACP counsel in Virginia in 1948, he and Hill filed suit against dozens of school districts in the state. At times there were as many as 75 cases pending. During this civil rights era, Hill's team filed more civil rights suits than all other southern states combined, covering such areas as jury selection, voting rights, employment protection, and access to school buses. His family endured a cross burning on his lawn in 1955 as well as threats on their lives. Hill was awarded the Presidential Medal of Freedom on August 11, 1999. When President Bill Clinton presented the award, he said: "Throughout his long and rich life, he has challenged the laws of our land and the conscience of our country. He has stood up for everything that is necessary to make America truly one, indivisible and equal."

Jessie Carney Smith

Hollowell, Donald L. (1917–2004)

The work of civil rights attorney Donald L. Holloway placed him at the center of historic events. He was a lead lawyer in the desegregation of public schools in Atlanta in the 1950s and 1960s. Hollowell helped free **Martin Luther King Jr.** from state prison in Georgia in 1960, when King was jailed in Reidsville Prison on a DeKalb County traffic charge. The next year Hollowell represented Charlayne Hunter and Hamilton Holmes Jr. in their successful efforts to integrate the University of Georgia. His firm, Arrington & Hollowell, worked to desegregate buses in Augusta and schools in Macon, Georgia. In a landmark case, his firm also broke down racial barriers at Atlanta's Grady Memorial Hospital, requiring the facility to place black doctors and dentists on staff. He was regarded by many as Georgia's preeminent civil rights attorney who, case by case, "helped Atlanta to save its soul," according to his former law partner Marvin Arrington in an *Atlanta Journal-Constitution* article. Prominent attorney and presidential adviser Vernon Jordan and federal judge Horace Ward are among the host of young black attorneys whom he mentored. President **Lyndon B. Johnson** appointed Hollowell in 1966 as Southeast Regional Director of the then-newly created Equal Employment Opportunity Commission.

Jessie Carney Smith

Houston, Charles Hamilton (1895–1950)

A groundbreaking civil rights lawyer and law professor, Charles Hamilton Houston is credited with laying the legal foundations of the Civil Rights Movement. His landmark cases were among the most lasting achievements of the decades preceding the mass movement activism of the 1950s and 1960s. Houston led the NAACP's fight to dismantle state-sanctioned segregation. The only child of William and Mary Ethel Houston, Houston was born into a

Charles Hamilton Houston (Fisk University).

comfortably middle-class family in Washington, D.C. His father was a lawyer and his mother was a school teacher. Insulated from the ugliness of racist America, young Houston was pushed by his parents to revere education; he attended Dunbar High School before graduating from Amherst College Phi Beta Kappa and magna cum laude in 1915.

A college valedictorian, Houston then taught at **Howard University**, an all-black college in Washington, D.C., for two years. There, he witnessed the growing inequalities of American society. This new awareness led Houston to enlist in World War I in 1917. He served in Europe as a second lieutenant in field artillery until 1919. After the war he enrolled at Harvard Law School. His admission was a remarkable achievement given that only a handful of blacks were admitted to the college at the time. In recognition of his academic achievement, Houston was elected to the editorial board of the

Harvard Law Review in 1921. The appointment made Houston the first ever African American member.

Following his graduation with honors in 1924, Houston participated in a one-year fellowship in Madrid, Spain. Upon his return, he worked in his father's law practice while teaching part-time at Howard. Five years later, Houston left the practice to become a full-time law professor and later served as the institution's dean from 1932 to 1935. First as a professor and then as dean, Houston helped turn the law school into a center for training future civil rights leaders. By revitalizing the school's curriculum and faculty, as well as tightening its admissions standards, Houston helped Howard strengthen its commitment to nurturing a generation of emerging lawyers who would later assume the mantle of leadership. In 1934 the NAACP retained Houston to lead its legal charge.

With the assistance of his protégé and future U.S. Supreme Court Justice, **Thurgood Marshall**, Houston worked tirelessly to dismantle the legal basis of the *Plessy v. Ferguson* ruling that established the "separate but equal" standard. He led the NAACP's first victory in the U.S. Supreme Court and was involved in virtually all of its causes from the 1930s through the 1940s, including *Missouri ex rel. Gaines v. Canada* (which successfully challenged the "separate but equal" ruling as applied to public education by asserting that states that provide a school to white students must provide in-state education to blacks as well) and *Shelley v. Kraemer* (which set a precedent for elimination of race as an element in denying individuals the right to purchase property). Satisfied that Marshall could successfully continue as his intellectual heir, Houston left the NACCP in 1940 to return to private practice. He still remained a member of the NAACP's national legal committee and argued two cases that struck down discriminatory practices by railroads.

Appointed by President Franklin D. Roosevelt to the Fair Employment Practices Committee (FEPC) in 1944, Houston resigned from the agency to protest the Capital Transit Company's discriminatory hiring practices. After a long battle with heart disease, Houston died in Washington, D.C., four years before Marshall succeeded in forcing the desegregation of American society in the *Brown v. Board of Education* case of 1954.

Crystal A. deGregory

Jones, Scipio Africanus (1863?–1943)

Despite being born in the antebellum period, Scipio Africanus Jones rose to the upper echelons of the early twentieth century American legal world. For a half century, he operated out of his private practice in Arkansas, using his legal acumen to secure civil rights in labor relations, voting rights, and educational opportunities. As the first African American lawyer to have command over a major **NAACP** case, Jones most famously defended 12 black men who were sentenced to death following the racial tensions during the **Red Summer** that erupted in the Elaine Race Riots of 1919.

Jones is believed to have been born around 1863. His father was a white man and his mother, Jemmima Jones, was a slave. Reared by his mother and stepfather, Horace Jones, in Tulip, Arkansas, he attended local schools before enrolling in Bethel College's (now Philander Smith College) preparatory department in Little Rock. He then attended Shorter College, from which he graduated in 1885. Notwithstanding the segregation of the University of Arkansas, Jones nurtured his interest in law by studying privately under white attorneys, all the while teaching school to support himself.

Admitted to the bar in 1889, Jones's popularity grew steadily shortly after he opened a private practice. A capable litigator, he represented numerous black fraternal organizations while lending his business acumen to companies such as the Arkansas Realty and Investment Company and the People's Ice and Fuel Company. Elected as a special judge to the Little Rock Municipal Court in 1915, Jones was also active

Scipio Africanus Jones (Fisk University).

in Republican politics, where he worked hard to secure the inclusion of African Americans in the party's local, state, and national platforms.

After successfully ameliorating racist prison work contracts, Jones led the fight to bar the passage of a "grandfather" voting clause, exposed the illegality of excluding blacks from jury service, and helped secure state appropriation for blacks to seek professional training at out-of-state schools because Arkansas's schools were closed to blacks. It was not until joining the NAACP defense of the 12 men convicted in the aftermath of the Elaine race riots, however, that Jones was catapulted to national acclaim. Working alongside George W. Murphy, a former Confederate solider and the representative of the local Citizens Defense Fund Commission, Jones helped secure a new trial for six of the men. While the Arkansas Supreme Court upheld the sentences of the remaining six, Jones

was left to defend the other half alone following the death of Murphy only a short time later. Despite receiving death threats, Jones defended the men, but to no avail. They were again condemned to death.

After repeated appeals and subsequent trials over the course of four years, the NAACP attorney successfully argued for the extension of the **Fourteenth Amendment** to cover the conduct of state criminal trials, which released the six not previously granted a new trial. Subsequently, the governor conditionally pardoned the six remaining men. In addition to securing their freedom, Jones had helped to initiate an important modification in constitutional law and inspired a generation of African Americans to invest their time and money into the NAACP as a viable institution for the advancement of black social justice and equality.

Crystal A. deGregory

Jordan, Barbara Charline (1936–1996)

Barbara Jordan was a political trailblazer in her native state of Texas. Traversing the revolutionary changes brought by the Civil Rights Movement, in 1966 she became the first woman—and the first American black since 1883—elected to the Texas senate. Later, in 1972, she became the first black woman from the South elected to serve in the U.S. House of Representatives. The same year that she won election to Congress, Jordan became president *pro tempore* of the Texas state senate, making her the first black woman in the United States to preside over a legislative body. Other breakthroughs for Jordan came when she was the first black state senator to chair a major committee—Labor and Management Relations—and was the first freshman senator named to the Texas Legislative Council.

As a state senator and U.S. Representative, she sponsored bills that promoted the concerns of the poor, people of color, and the disadvantaged. A strong advocate for these causes, during her tenure in the Texas State Senate she sponsored and passed the Workman's Compensation Act, which increased the maximum benefits paid to injured workers. State Senator Jordan also worked on legislation that dealt with the environment and eradicating racial favoritism in business contracts. Later, as a U.S. Representative from Texas's 18th Congressional District, she sponsored legislation to expand the **Voting Rights Act of 1965** to cover Mexican Americans and extended the law's authority to those states where minorities were denied the right to vote or had their voting rights abridged by inequitable registration practices.

In 1974 the Watergate scandal brought Jordan into the national spotlight. As a member of the House Judiciary Committee during President Richard M. Nixon's impeachment hearings, Jordan captivated the nation with her powerful oratory, adroit interpretation of American history and constitutional law, and her conscientious commitment to ethical standards in politics and society. Through the televised proceedings, Representative Jordan let it be known that she intended to be more than a casual observer. An active participant and a skillful attorney who steadfastly believed in the principles of the U.S. Constitution, she refused to contribute to the further diminution, subversion, and destruction of the nation's guiding document. Her speech before the Judiciary Committee and the nation captured media attention as one of the most powerful speeches delivered during the impeachment hearings.

Two years later Jordan would again command media and national attention as one of the Democratic Party's most eloquent and persuasive speakers. Awed with Jordan's oratorical skills and growing prominence in the party, the Democrats selected her to give the keynote address at the 1976 Democratic national convention. The first woman and the first African American to deliver the Democratic Party's keynote address, Jordan addressed the themes of unity, equality, accountability, and American ideals. Two years after that, Jordan ended her

tenure in the House of Representatives when she decided not to seek reelection. Upon leaving Congress in 1979, Jordan rejected offers to practice corporate law. Instead, she accepted a teaching position at the University of Texas in Austin, where she taught at the Lyndon Baines Johnson School of Public Affairs.

The recipient of numerous honorary degrees and awards, including the **NAACP**'s Spingarn Medal for service to the African American community, she was only finally silenced when she passed away on January 17, 1996. Her remains were interred in the Texas State Cemetery. In 2001 the Austin City Council approved the placement of a Jordan statue in the Austin-Bergstrom International Airport at the Barbara Jordan Passenger Terminal.

Linda T. Wynn

Langston, John Mercer (1829–1897)

In 1890 John Mercer Langston became the first black U.S. congressman elected from his native state of Virginia, and he soon took his seat in the 51st Congress. Although he is best known for that accomplishment and for his post as U.S. Minister Resident and Consul-General to Haiti, he had important experiences in civil rights early on. While living in Cincinnati in the summer of 1841, he experienced the mounting racial tensions that erupted in a white mob's attack on homes and businesses in the areas where he lived. Although blacks successfully defended their homes and families, he saw black codes at work (which tried to restrict the movement and freedom of blacks in the same way that slave codes had done during slavery) and the efforts of blacks to comply with them. He also came in contact with some of the best oratory and anti-slavery rhetoric, which benefited him later. Langston returned to Chillicothe, Ohio, and later graduated from Oberlin College. He planned to study law; for a while, however, he turned his energies to black protest and reform during the time of a growing Ohio black convention movement. Among various concerns, the

John Mercer Langston (Fisk University).

movement sought to repeal the Black Codes and bring about the enfranchisement of blacks. As a respected lawyer and orator, in 1855 he became town clerk in Brownhelm Township, Ohio, making him the first black person elected to public office in the United States. In the early 1850s he lectured before the American Anti-Slavery Society, the Ohio Anti-Slavery League, the Colored National Convention at Rochester (New York), and the State Convention of Colored Citizens of Ohio. He gained wide recognition for his work in anti-slavery causes.

Jessie Carney Smith

Lee, J. Kenneth (1923–)

The modern civil rights era in North Carolina was shaped in large measure by the work of John Kenneth Lee, who helped to integrate the law school at the University of North Carolina,

Chapel Hill, and served as a lawyer for over 1,700 civil rights cases across the state. He is especially recognized for defending students in **Greensboro's sit-in** movement during the 1960s. His contribution to the wellbeing of local blacks also extended to his pioneer work as an entrepreneur, opening doors that had been previously closed. He had experienced racial segregation in North Carolina, and knew that the military was segregated as well. While serving in the U.S. Navy, he saw separate sleeping quarters and dining facilities for black and white men. After college, he learned that racial segregation continued to surround him in his home state as he sought and was denied employment as an engineer. He saw a variety of racially segregated acts in the community, including separate seating on buses and college-educated blacks relegated to jobs far below their qualifications. Conditions to him were like "hell certified by law," he once said in the *News and Record*.

Lee was so conflicted by the legal system and its impact on society that he decided to become a lawyer and seek solutions to the problem through the courts. For blacks, North Carolina offered a law degree at North Carolina College for Negroes (NCC; North Carolina Central University) and for whites at the University of North Carolina (UNC) at Chapel Hill. The **NAACP**, however, was already involved in the *McKissick, et. al. v Carmichael* lawsuit against UNC, but the process was long and slow. Lee enrolled at NCC, but promptly became a plaintiff in the NAACP's case file, while **Floyd McKissick** and other blacks were in NCC's law school. After graduating, Lee became a plaintiff in 1948. **Thurgood Marshall**, later a U.S. Supreme Court Justice, was chief counsel for the NAACP's Legal Defense Fund (LDF) and worked with a team of over two dozen blue-ribbon lawyers, among them Spottswood Robinson, **Constance Baker Motley**, and Jack Greenberg of the LDF.

A judge who acknowledged that blacks should be admitted to UNC's law school nevertheless denied the case. The court ruled in favor of the plaintiffs on appeal, and then the U.S.

Supreme Court refused to hear the case. *McKissick et. al. v Carmichael* attracted widespread attention and marked the integration of law schools in the South. Lee and Harvey Beech of nearby Kinston, North Carolina, enrolled at UNC in June 1950. Given the racial tension at the time, armed white law enforcement officers escorted the two on their campus journey until their interest waned. Lee and Beech, nevertheless, still faced racism at football games, in law school courses, and elsewhere. In one class, for example, white students were addressed as "mister," while blacks were never addressed, only pointed to when the professor wanted their attention. Lee passed the state bar examination before he graduated in the summer of 1952, and by September he was licensed.

Lee was so conflicted by the legal system and its impact on society that he decided to become a lawyer.

The courtrooms where he began to argue cases throughout the state were hostile; jurors, judges, and his fellow lawyers all showed Lee disrespect. The cases that he argued helped to fuel the racial fire, though. He said in his family history that legal work for defendants in civil rights cases was a "hazardous occupation." As the sit-in movement spread across the state, numerous civil disobedience cases followed in the courts. In Greensboro, he often sat on the side of the local jail with **Jesse Jackson**, who was then a student at Agricultural and Technical State University (A&T).

Soon activities associated with the movement became personal. A local member of the Ku Klux Klan, Clyde "Hammer" Webster, clearly respected Lee's wisdom but not his race. Hearing his plea for a job, Lee had hired Webster as a carpenter for construction on his new home when no one else would do so. Lee was called to testify in an appeals case for Webster, who had been convicted of vandalism. After that, according to a *News & Record* report, Webster told him, "You and me ain't gonna never agree on race," however, he respected the attorney and addressed him as "Mr. Lee." The relationship between the two was, to Lee, an "unholy alliance."

Lee's career as a civil rights lawyer came to an abrupt end when black students took the lead in integrating local theaters. "I was elated that after 175 years of segregation, I had finally been a part of bringing it to an end," he said in his family history. After that, he entered a number of business ventures that aided local blacks who wanted to build sizeable homes but, until then, were denied loans large enough to do so. His work in civil rights will be preserved, at least in part, in the civil rights museum at the old Woolworth's building in downtown Greensboro, where the 1960s sit-in movement began.

Jessie Carney Smith

Looby, Zephaniah Alexander (1899–1972)

Z. Alexander Looby was born in Antigua, British West Indies, on April 8, 1899, the son of John Alexander and Grace Elizabeth Joseph Looby. After the death of his father, Looby emigrated to the United States in 1914. He received a bachelor's degree from **Howard University**, a bachelor of law degree from Columbia University, and a doctor of juristic science from New York University. In 1929 Looby was admitted to the Tennessee bar. Later, he became an integral part of the African American Civil Rights Movement.

In 1946, the **NAACP** hired Looby, Maurice Weaver, and Thurgood Marshall to represent the African Americans charged with murder following the Columbia, Tennessee, race riot. Looby's legal defense helped acquit 23 of the defendants. He crisscrossed the state in the company of other black lawyers, arguing against Jim Crow practices. In 1950 Looby and attorneys **Avon Williams Jr.** and Carl Cowan of Knoxville filed the Anderson County School desegregation case, the first public school case in Tennessee. This case, *McSwain v. Board of Anderson County, Tennessee,* resulted in the U.S. Supreme court-ordered desegregation of Tennessee public high schools. In 1955 Looby and Williams filed the Nashville school desegregation case (*Kelley v. Board of Education*) on behalf of A.Z. Kelley, whose son Robert had been denied access to a nearby white school.

During the sit-in demonstrations and civil rights marches of the 1960s, Looby and other black attorneys defended local college students who were arrested and jailed. Because of his civil rights activities, on April 19, 1960, his home was targeted and destroyed by dynamite. After a long and distinguished career in law and politics, Looby died on March 24, 1972.

Linda T. Wynn

Thurgood Marshall (Fisk University).

Marshall, Thurgood (1908–1993)

Thurgood Marshall was born July 2, 1908, in Baltimore, Maryland, and died January 24, 1993, in Bethesda, Maryland. Upon being denied admission to the law school at the University of Maryland, he enrolled at **Howard University**, where he studied under **Charles Hamilton Houston**, dean of the law school and the first black lawyer to win a case before the U.S. Supreme Court. Houston encouraged his students to fight discrimination and injustices against black people and to change the image of the black lawyer. From 1933 to 1936, Marshall was in private practice, and many of his cases dealt with discrimination or injustice. In 1935 Marshall successfully sued the University of Maryland to admit a young black student. The next year, he became assistant special Counsel for the **NAACP**, working with his mentor, Houston. Upon Houston's resignation, Marshall assumed the post. In 1939 the NAACP established the Legal Defense Fund; he served as its director-counsel until 1939.

In his capacity at the NAACP as a legal warrior against segregation and discrimination, Marshall traveled, investigated, raised money, decided which cases to pursue, oversaw the preparation of briefs, and coordinated appeals to higher courts. He, the NAACP, and its legal staff won 29 of the 32 cases argued before the U.S. Supreme Court. They began to work against the separate but equal practices exercised at graduate schools, and with each victory they moved closer to focusing on secondary and elementary schools. Meanwhile, cases were won that overthrew the South's "white primary" system (which restricted black voters from participating in party primaries), struck down the legality of racially restrictive covenants keeping blacks and other minorities out of some neighborhoods, and won the Supreme Court decision that interstate passengers entering the South could not be forced into segregated seating on public transportation.

Marshall led the NAACP's first victory at the U.S. Supreme Court, and from 1930 on he was involved in virtually all of its cases that preceded *Brown v. Board of Education* in 1954, including *Missouri ex rel. Gaines v. Canada* and *Shelley v. Kraemer*. Marshall and the NAACP legal staff fought in various venues to ensure that the decision was enforced. They represented students trying to enter schools, such as the Little Rock Nine, Autherine Lucy, and college students arrested for their attempt to peacefully integrate public places. In 1961 President **John F. Kennedy** appointed Marshall to the U.S. Court of Appeals for the Second Circuit. There was strong opposition of his nomination from southern senators; he served as a recess appointee until 1962, when he was confirmed. From 1961 to 1965, Marshall wrote over 120 opinions on topics such as tax and constitutional issues, none of which were reversed. Several of his opinions became majority opinions by the Supreme Court. From 1965 to 1967, he was appointed Solicitor General by President **Lyndon Johnson** and won 14 of the 19 government cases he argued. And in 1967 Johnson nominated Marshall to the U.S. Supreme Court, making him the first African American to hold this post. Marshall served on the court until 1991, when he retired. During his tenure he made a lasting impact in the area of constitutional law.

Helen R. Houston

McKissick, Floyd (1922– 1991)

Floyd McKissick sought to bring substance to the rhetoric of "black power" by pursuing economic, political, and social initiatives. He challenged patterns of segregation and discrimination through legal work and activism, and attempted to develop a model community of successful integration called "Soul City." Floyd Boyce McKissick was born in Asheville, North Carolina; his parents were a hotel bellman and a seamstress, despite being graduates of Livingstone College in Salisbury, North Carolina. McKissick experienced racial discrimination during his boyhood, and this stimulated his interest in becoming a lawyer. He attended **Morehouse College**, but joined the army during World War II and received a Purple Heart and other military awards. After the war he returned to North Carolina, worked for the **NAACP** and the **Congress of Racial Equality** (CORE), and participated in the first "Freedom Ride" in 1947. McKissick was denied admission to the University of North Carolina (UNC) law school, filed suit with help from the NAACP Legal Defense Fund, and won his case. He thus received his law degree from UNC in 1951 and began practicing law. McKissick worked with North Carolina student activists during the 1960 sit-ins and continued work with CORE as national chairman and national director, but in the 1970s he became a Republican and shifted his interests to economic development. Although he secured nearly $30 million in federal and state funding, "Soul City" was never completed.

Fletcher F. Moon

Mitchell, Juanita Jackson (1913–1992)

As she grew up in Baltimore, Maryland, Juanita Mitchell became committed to weapons of protest that she would use successfully—the ballot, public opinion, and the legal system. She also saw Baltimore as a city mired in unemployment and racial segregation practices. Her protest in 1942, a march on the state capitol in Annapolis, led to the beginning of the governor's Interracial Commission, the addition of African American law enforcement officers, and investigations into police brutality charges. She had been refused admission to the University of Maryland's law school 23 years earlier, but her challenge to the school's racial barriers finally gained her admission; she graduated in 1950. This made her the school's first African American graduate.

Mitchell committed herself to work on behalf of African Americans through litigation. In 1950 she began her fight to integrate municipal and state beaches and swimming pools, winning before the U.S. Supreme Court in 1955. She then continued her fight against racial injustice, this time in the local school system. As counsel in suits that desegregated Baltimore's schools, she argued a 1954 case before the Supreme Court that ruled that such systems were unconstitutional. In 1965 she won a case to desegregate Maryland's restaurants. Mitchell continued to protect the rights of African Americans as she aided homeowners in proceedings to enjoin local police from searching private homes without a search warrant. She was also devoted to the ballot, and in 1957, 1958, and 1960 led voter registration drives in Baltimore that placed over 50,000 new registrants on the books.

Jessie Carney Smith

Motley, Constance Baker (1921–2005)

Pioneering African American woman lawyer Constance Baker Motley was at the forefront of the civil rights struggle in America and was an effective legal advocate for the movement. Her groundbreaking achievements include becoming the first African American woman elected to the New York state senate in 1964 and becoming a U.S. federal judge in 1966, and then senior judge in 1986. In 1965 she was also the first woman of any race to serve as president of one of New York's five boroughs—Manhattan. For over 20 years she was highly involved in legal victories for the **NAACP**'s Legal Defense and Educational Fund. Motley won nine of the ten civil rights cases that she argued before the U.S. Supreme Court.

Motley's awareness of racial discrimination was aroused as she grew up in New Haven, Connecticut. After she was denied admission to a skating rink and later to a swimming pool, she determined that she would become a civil rights attorney. During her last year in law school at Columbia University, she was selected as a law clerk for **Thurgood Marshall**, who was then chief counsel for the NAACP Legal Defense

Fund and later a U.S. Supreme Court justice. Her travels through the United States during the course of her work with the NAACP gave her full appreciation of the state of racial and gender prejudice in America. She appeared before state and federal courts arguing cases related to public school desegregation, public and publicly aided housing, transportation, recreation, and sit-in cases.

Mitchell committed herself to work on behalf of African Americans through litigation.

The key link between African American lawyers of an earlier generation and those of the 1950s and 1960s was Motley. In addition to Thurgood Marshall, she had worked with A. Leon Higginbotham and James Nabrit as they planned a legal attack on racial segregation in the 1950s, as well as the Civil Rights Movement of the 1960s. She was a chief legal adviser to **Martin Luther King Jr.** and helped him to win the right to march against racial segregation in Birmingham and Albany. As well, she represented **Ralph Abernathy**, **Fred Shuttlesworth**, and other civil rights protesters.

Her most important achievement, however, came when she served on the legal team that won the historic *Brown v. Board of Education* in 1954. Motley drafted the original complaint and Thurgood Marshall argued it in court. The Brown decision drastically changed society and, according to Motley, provided the impetus for other successful movements, such as the poor people's movement, the women's rights movement, and other movements of public concern. In 1956 Motley was involved in the **Central High School** case in Little Rock, Arkansas, when black children were denied access to the school. She was lead counsel for James Meredith in his petition for admission to the University of Mississippi in 1962 and for Charlayne Hunter (Gault) and Hamilton Holmes in their suit to enroll in the University of Georgia. She was involved in countless legal cases throughout the South that prompted political cases and other forms of civil disturbances.

Jessie Carney Smith

Murray, Pauli (1910–1985)

Pauli Murray was a woman with many successful careers. Through each of them, however, she was steadfast in her concern for civil and women's rights. She helped to reorder the national agenda by insisting on conciliation among all peoples. Murray was born in Maryland, but grew up in the segregated South in Durham, North Carolina. She had to deal with the conflict of tolerating racial codes while accepting pride, strength, and the blend of races and cultures in her ancestry. Murray studied at Hunter College in New York, where she honed her writing skills and associated with the giants of the Harlem Renaissance, including Countee Cullen and **Langston Hughes**. By the late 1930s, she was an innovator in movements to bring about racial and gender equality. It has been said that her activism in the Civil Rights Movement was so intense that it could be considered one of her careers.

Murray's urge to protest came when she was a young child and chose to walk to school rather than ride the segregated city buses. In 1938 she was denied admission to the University of North Carolina's graduate school because of her race. Her case received national attention and prompted black students all over the country to seek admission to southern white universities. In 1978 UNC offered Murray an honorary degree, but she refused because the school was delinquent in implementing an adequate desegregation plan. Her activism was demonstrated again in March 1940, when she and a friend

were en route to Durham on a Greyhound bus. They were arrested in Petersburg, Virginia, and charged with disorderly conduct because they refused to move toward the rear of the bus to a broken seat. They were jailed three days and fined. That action prompted her to work on larger efforts to remove all segregation laws; she rejoiced in 1946 when the *Morgan v. Virginia* case concerning interstate travel was passed.

Murray's agitation continued and helped lead to the abolition of the Virginia poll tax. She also joined the **Congress of Racial Equality** (CORE) and worked through the organization to fight racism using Gandhian techniques. While a law school student at **Howard University**, she led sit-in demonstrations in Washington, D.C., aiming to desegregate local restaurants. By 1962 Murray was well acknowledged as a legal scholar, educator, and activist with civil rights groups. She was elected to the Committee on Civil and Political Rights set up by the President's Commission on the Status of Women. She was one of 32 women who, in October 1966, founded the National Organization of Women.

Murray became an ordained minister in the Episcopal Church and received her Master of Divinity degree in 1976—the last decade of her life. On January 8, 1977, she was ordained an Episcopal priest at Washington's National Cathedral, the first black women to reach this stature in the 200-year history of that church. She wrote a number of books, including autobiographies and legal works, such as *Proud Shoes: The Story of an American Family* (1956), *Song in a Weary Throat: An American Pilgrimage* (1987), and *States' Laws on Race and Color* (1951).

Jessie Carney Smith

Norton, Eleanor Holmes (1937–)

Eleanor Holmes Norton, a fourth generation Washingtonian, has demonstrated a lifelong commitment to civil rights and human rights issues. Her engagement with civil rights began with her membership in the **Student Non-Vio-**

Eleanor Holmes Norton (AP Photo/Charles Tasnadi).

lent **Coordinating Committee** (SNCC). She was a participant in the Mississippi Freedom Democratic Party and in 1963 was a part of the national staff that orchestrated the **March on Washington**. After completing her B.A. from Antioch College in 1960, and her M.A. in American history from Yale University in 1963, Norton focused on law as a means to continue her commitment for civil rights. In 1965 she received her J.D. from Yale University and worked for the American Civil Liberties Union (ACLU) in New York. Norton was appointed in 1977 by President Jimmy Carter as the first female chair of the Equal Employment Opportunity Commission (EEOC). She held that position until 1981. She took her commitment to

civil rights into the political arena when she campaigned and was elected in 1990 as a Democratic delegate to the House of Representatives for the District of Columbia. Norton has since continued her work seeking full voting representation and the democratic process for the people of D.C. and all citizens.

Lean'tin L. Bracks

Obama, Barack (1961–)

Barack Obama was elected to the U.S. Senate from the state of Illinois in November 2004 and sworn into office on January 4, 2005. The same year that he was elected to the U.S. Senate, he gave the keynote address at the Democratic National Convention in Boston, Massachusetts. A presidential candidate, who won the Democratic Party's nomination in 2008, he serves on the Health, Education, Labor and Pension Committee; the Foreign Relations Committee; and the Veterans' Affairs Committee. Before entering the U.S. senatorial race to replace Republican Peter Fitzgerald, Obama served eight years in the Illinois State Senate, where he represented the Thirteenth Legislative District. Elected in 1996, during his tenure in the Illinois State Senate, Obama worked with his fellow senators on both sides of the aisle. With this coalition of Democrats and Republicans, he passed bills that increased funding for AIDS prevention and care, expanded early childhood education, and introduced legislation to curb racial profiling. After numerous inmates on Illinois's death row were found innocent, Obama enlisted the support of law enforcement officials to draft legislation requiring the videotaping of interrogations and confessions in all capital cases.

Prior to entering the political arena, Obama, a graduate of Columbia University (1983) and Harvard Law School (1991), where he became the first African American president of the *Harvard Law Review*, worked with a church-based organization in Chicago, Illinois, that focused on the city's economically distressed environs. He later became a community organizer in the Altgeld Gardens public housing development on Chicago's South Side. A civil rights attorney, he practiced law with the Miner, Barnhill & Galland firm, where he dealt with voting and employment-rights cases. As an activist, he directed the Illinois Project Vote campaign that registered over 100,000 voters; this facilitated the election of President William Jefferson Clinton and U.S. Senator Carol Moseley Braun, the first African American woman elected and second African American elected to the U.S. Senate since Reconstruction. The same year that he graduated from Harvard Law School, he accepted the position of senior lecturer in constitutional law at the University of Chicago Law

Barack Obama (AP Photo/Rick Bowmer).

School. Before successfully running for the U.S. Senate, in 2000 Obama ran unsuccessfully for Illinois's First Congressional District against Bobby Rush, the sitting four-term U.S. Representative and founder of the Illinois chapter of the **Black Panther Party**.

Born in Honolulu, Hawaii, Barack Obama is the son of Barack Obama Sr. (1936–1982), a native of Nyangoma-Kogelo, Siaya District, Kenya, and Stanley Ann Dunham (1942–1995), a native of Wichita, Kansas, and a descendant of Jefferson Davis, the President of the Confederate States of America. Obama is the author of *Dreams from My Father: A Story of Race and Inheritance* (1995), *The Audacity of Hope: Thoughts on Reclaiming the American Dream* (2006), and *Barack Obama in His Own Words* (2007), among titles. As Illinois's junior senator, he worked to promote civil rights and fairness in the criminal justice system throughout his career. As a civil rights attorney, he litigated cases against employment discrimination, housing discrimination, and voting rights cases. One of the leading advocates for protecting the right to vote, he helped to reauthorize the **Voting Right Act of**

1965 and led the opposition against discriminatory barriers to voting.

In January 2007, Senator Obama announced that he was forming a presidential exploratory committee as the first step towards seeking the office of the presidency. A month later, he announced his intentions to run in the election. Only the fifth African American elected to the U.S. Senate, and the only African American senator in the 110th U.S. Congress, Obama campaigned with a message of change that resonated with many Americans. Defeating Republican Senator John McCain, on November 4, 2008, Obama made history when he became the first African American elected as president of the United States of America. Forty years after the assassination of the Reverend Dr. **Martin Luther King Jr.**, citizens of all hues felt that America had finally come of age. Obama's election not only impacted the nation, it reverberated globally.

Linda T. Wynn

Redding, Louis L. (1901–1988)

The first African American lawyer licensed to practice in Delaware, Louis L. Redding was best known as a desegregation lawyer with deep connections to *Brown v. Board of Education*. He first attacked segregation in Wilmington, where in the late 1920s his agitation against separate seating for whites and blacks, and in the courtroom he broke down that unlawful practice. At first he practiced law statewide, and then in 1950 joined Jack Greenberg, the **NAACP's** Legal Defense and Educational Fund lawyer, in pursuing the *Parker v. University of Delaware* case that resulted in desegregating the University of Delaware on August 9, 1950. By court order, the university became the first public institution to admit black students. The legal victory became a part of 1954's *Brown v. Board of Education*. In 1952 eight black students who had been denied admission to white public schools in the state were permitted to enroll, thanks to Redding's work. Thus, Delaware became the first state in the nation to have court-ordered desegregation of public

schools. Although the state appealed, the U.S. Supreme Court ruled in the Brown case that separate-but-equal schools for the races was unlawful and called for public schools to desegregate. Outside the courtroom, Redding helped to develop a number of strategies for boycotts and sit-ins but was not a visible participant. As far as the public was concerned, the courtroom was his workplace; his record there was stellar, for he never lost a desegregation case. He did, however, participate in the **March on Washington** in 1963, where he and other civil rights leaders came together.

Jessie Carney Smith

Ruffin, George Lewis (1834–1886)

George Lewis Ruffin was born December 16, 1834, in Richmond, Virginia, and died November 20, 1886, in Boston. The impetus for Ruffin's activism was his education at Chapman Hall School in Boston, Massachusetts, where he was introduced to the Republican Party, and the 1857 *Dred Scott* decision. He was unable to serve in the **Civil War** but worked in the Home Guard and the Sanitary Commission. He earned a reputation for his critical reviews in the *Anglo-African*, a weekly published in New York; and in 1864, as a delegate to the National Negro Convention, he supported Abraham Lincoln for reelection and demanded Negro suffrage. He was admitted to Harvard Law School and earned a bachelor of law degree in 1869. That same year, on September 18, he was admitted to the Suffolk County Bar, one of the first blacks admitted to practice law in Boston. He then joined the firm of Harvey Jewell. Both he and Jewell were elected to the Massachusetts Legislature, and Ruffin was later reelected. Politically, he focused his attention on violence in the South, attended Negro Conventions, was a delegate and presided over the 1872 Negro Convention in New Orleans, and in 1876 and 1877 was elected to the Boston City Council. His law practice and political life flourished. In 1883 he was appointed by Massachusetts Governor Benjamin Butler to be judge of a municipal court in Charlestown.

Also in 1883, he was appointed consul resident in Boston for the Dominican Republic.

Helen R. Houston

Sandifer, Jawn A. (1914–2006)

A civil rights attorney who later became a New York state judge, Jawn A. Sandifer argued a case before the U.S. Supreme Court that went on to become a precedent for the *Brown v. Board of Education* decision of 1954 barring segregation in public schools. Sandifer, a lawyer for the **NAACP**, successfully argued the 1950 case *Henderson v. U.S. Interstate Commerce Commission and Southern Railway*. The victorious decision meant that railroads that ran across state lines were forbidden from barring passengers from dining cars because of their race. The ruling declared "The denial of dining service to any such passenger subjects him to a prohibited disadvantage," adding that "The right to be free from unreasonable discriminations belongs to each particular person." Sandifer said in a 1995 interview concerning his client Elmer W. Henderson, "Even if a black person bought in New York a first-class ticket on a train that included dining privileges, once that train left Washington and went south he or she could not eat in the dining car." Even though seats in the car could be empty, there was no room for black passengers, except behind a curtain. The case became important in the U.S. Supreme Court rulings of the 1940s and 1950s, especially since it was a precedent for *Brown*. After becoming a judge, Sandifer continued to oppose discrimination. When he was a state supreme court justice assigned to Manhattan, in 1986 Sandifer declared that women were discriminated against in a civil service test for sanitation workers. His ruling allowed them to become sanitation workers for the city.

Jessie Carney Smith

Williams, Avon Nyanza, Jr. (1921–1994)

A von Williams was born on December 22, 1921, in Knoxville, Tennessee, the fourth of Avon and Carrie Belle Williams's five children. He received his primary and secondary education in the public schools of Knoxville and earned an A.B. degree from Johnson C. Smith University in 1940. He later entered Boston University's School of Law, where he received the L.L.B. degree in 1947 and the L.L.M. degree in 1948. In April and August of 1948, he was admitted to the bars of the states of Massachusetts and Tennessee, respectively. Attorney Williams interned with Nashville attorney **Z. Alexander Looby** and then returned to Knoxville to set up his own law practice. Early in his legal career, Williams demonstrated an interest in civil rights cases. He had been in practice less than a year when he filed suit on behalf of four African American male students applying to the University of Tennessee's graduate school. When the case of *Gray v. the University of Tennessee* reached the U.S. Supreme Court, the university capitulated and admitted the young men. In 1950 Williams, along with attorneys Looby and Carl Cowan of Knoxville, filed the Anderson County School desegregation case, the first public school case in the Volunteer State. *McSwain v. Board of Anderson County, Tennessee* resulted in the Supreme court-ordered desegregation of Tennessee public high schools. In 1955 Williams and Looby filed the Nashville school desegregation case (*Kelly v. Board of Education*) and ultimately assisted in every school desegregation case in Tennessee, except in Shelby County.

During the turbulent decades of the 1950s and 1960s, Williams involved himself, without remuneration, in various civil rights suits—many of which reached the state and federal supreme courts. These cases involved such issues as school desegregation, public accommodations, employment and housing discrimination, and police brutality. In 1972 Williams became involved in the Tennessee State University/University of Tennessee at Nashville merger suit as attorney for the plaintiff interveners. He successfully persuaded the court that UT Nashville should be merged into TSU. It was the first time a major white university had been merged with a black one, Williams died on August 29, 1994. Later, he was buried in Nashville's Greenwood Cemetery.

Linda T. Wynn

Civil Rights Commission

National Advisory Commission on Civil Disorders

In 1968 the National Advisory Commission on Civil Rights released the Kerner Report, which was named for Illinois Governor Otto Kerner, chair of the commission. President **Lyndon B. Johnson** appointed the 11-member commission on July 28, 1967, after numerous riots in major northern and western cities, including Los Angeles (1965), Chicago (1966), **Detroit** (1967), and Newark (1967). Johnson charged the commission with answering three questions: What happened? Why did it happen? What can be done to prevent it from happening again? The race riots that swept through urban areas during the 1960s demonstrated the deep-seated frustrations of northern African Americans, for whom the civil rights struggles in the South had no real impact. African Americans in the North did not need the federal government to grant them entrance to public facilities or give them the right to vote. In the country's northern region, however, they lacked political power, encountered excessive force from law enforcement officials, and the jaws of destitution gripped them in an economic vice.

The summer of 1967 again brought racial disorder to American cities. The worst came during a two-week period in July, centered first in Newark and then in Detroit. Each set off a sequence of reactions in neighboring communities. Johnson sent federal troops to Detroit and Newark to reinstate order, much as he and other presidents had acted before to suppress racial disturbances in Arkansas, Alabama, and Mississippi. Established by Executive Order 11365,

the Kerner Commission was created to investigate the problem. Commonly known as the Kerner Report, the commission's 1968 report concluded that the nation was "moving toward two societies, one black, one white—separate and unequal." The commission collected evidence on a multiplicity of problems that befell African Americans, including not only overt discrimination but also chronic poverty, high unemployment, poor schools, inadequate housing, lack of access to health care, and systematic police bias and brutality.

The summer of 1967 again brought racial disorder to American cities.

The Kerner Report was the nation's first comprehensive look at race issues in the United States, and it was the federal government's first official document that said racism existed and was a problem. It warned that unless solutions were found, the country faced a major crisis within its major cities. Commissioners delivered an indictment of "white society" for isolating and neglecting African Americans and urged legislation to promote racial integration and to enrich slums—primarily through the creation of jobs, job training programs, and decent housing. In response, President Johnson ignored the commission's findings. In April 1968, one month after the release of the Kerner Report, rioting broke out in more than a hundred cities following the assassination of civil rights leader **Martin Luther King Jr.** The urban riots of the 1960s were catalyzing events: a violent postscript to an earlier period of attempts at peaceful revolution and change. The devastation of the disturbances and the underlying causes continue to plague the nation's cities. Events, including riots following the arrest of Rodney King (1992) and racial violence in Benton Harbor, Michigan, only prove evidence that resolving the economic and social inequities, which in many ways are at the heart of urban violence, remain among America's greatest domestic challenges.

Linda T. Wynn

[President] Johnson declared that affirmative steps must be taken to close the gap between blacks and whites.

Civil Rights Laws and Cases

Adams v. Richardson (1973)

In the fall of 1970, the **NAACP's** Legal Defense and Education Fund filed a class action suit in the federal district court in Washington, D.C., on behalf of 31 people. As the agency historically assigned responsibility for enforcing Title VI, the suit was against the Office for Civil Rights (OCR), or the former Department of Health, Education and Welfare (HEW) for failing to enforce the legislation against the state of North Carolina. The ruling approved a district court order requiring federal education officials to enforce Title VI of the **1964 Civil Rights Act** (which bars discrimination by recipients of federal funds) against state universities, public schools, and other institutions that receive federal money. Named after Kenneth Adams, a black parent whose name appeared first in the alphabetical list of plaintiffs, and Elliot Richardson, the secretary of HEW, as the defendant of OCR and HEW, *Adams v. Richardson* eventually underwent several name changes to reflect the new HEW and Department of Education secretaries. In his memorandum opinion, Judge John

H. Pratt declared that the "HEW has not properly fulfilled its obligation under Title VI ... to eliminate the vestiges of past policies and practices of segregation in programs receiving federal assistance." The ruling remains extremely important in the fight for equality. It demanded the dismantling of all state-operated dual systems in higher education that created Traditionally White Institutions (TWI) and Historically Black Colleges and Universities (HBCU). By the late 1970s, the OCR and Department of Education found that numerous states, including Alabama, Delaware, Kentucky, Missouri, Ohio, South Carolina, Texas, and West Virginia, still had "vestiges of segregation" and ordered them to submit plans to desegregate. Failed efforts to meets the demands of the *Adams* decision resulted in numerous discrimination cases over the course of the decades that followed.

Crystal A. deGregory

Affirmative Action

Affirmative action has its roots in the Civil Rights Movement. On March 6, 1961, President **John F. Kennedy** signed Executive Order 10925, which established the President's Commission on Equal Employment Opportunity. The order stated that contractors doing business with the government "will take affirmative action to ensure that applicants are employed, and employees are treated during their employment, without regard to their race, creed, color, or national origin." However, President **Lyndon B. Johnson** developed the concept and idea of affirmative action into public policies. In his **Howard University** commencement address on June 4, 1965, Johnson declared that affirmative steps must be taken to close the gap between blacks and whites. "This is the next and more profound stage of the battle for civil rights," Johnson stated. "We seek ... not just equality as a right and a theory, but equality as a fact and as a result." In September of the same year, President Johnson issued Executive Order 11246, requiring government contractors to "take affirmative action" to recruit and hire qualified minority employees in all aspects of hiring and employment and to document such efforts. Two years later, the order was amended to cover discrimination based on gender.

President Richard M. Nixon was the first to implement federal policies designed to guarantee minority hiring. In response to continuing racial inequalities in the work force, in 1969 his administration developed the Philadelphia Plan that required contractors on federally assisted projects to set specific goals for the hiring of minorities. In 1970 and 1971 the federal courts upheld this plan. Affirmative action policies faced a storm of controversy from their inception. Critics argued that racially sensitive solutions practiced "reverse discrimination" against whites and were an affront to the meritocratic paradigm that each individual be judged by his or her qualifications. They further attacked the notion that blacks were entitled to special consideration because of their membership in a racial group and insisted that charges of discrimination be investigated on an individual basis. Neo-conservatives condemned affirmative action and felt that it resulted in an increased consciousness of the significance of group membership, an increased divisiveness based on race, color, and national origin, and widened the divide of resentment among disfavored groups against the favored groups.

Advocates retorted that discrimination is, by definition, unfair treatment of people because they belong to a certain group. They further contended that affirmative action policies were the only way to ensure an "integrated" society in which all segments of the populace had an opportunity to share in jobs, education, and other benefits. They argued that numerical goals for hiring, promotions, and college admission were necessary to open fields traditionally closed to minorities and women because of racial and gender discrimination. In 1971 the U.S. Supreme Court struck a positive chord for affirmative action in the *Griggs v. Duke Power Company* case when it ruled that "neutral"

employment tests were not valid if they preserved the effects of prior prejudicial employment practices. The justices placed the burden on employers to substantiate that an employment exam that operated to rule out persons of African heritage in America was connected to job performance.

By the late 1970s, while the Supreme Court continued to uphold affirmative action polices, it placed certain restrictions on their implementation, beginning with the *Regents of the University of California v. Bakke* case. In this case, the court held it was unconstitutional for the medical school of the University of California at Davis to establish a rigid quota (16 of 100 spaces were set aside for entering minorities) system by reserving a certain number of places in each class for minorities. Later, in the *Ward's Cove Packing Company v. Antonio* case, those employees filing discrimination suits demonstrated that specific hiring practices had led to racial disparities in the workplace. In essence, the burden of proof shifted from the employer to the employee. Those charging racial discrimination could no longer depend on statistics of numerical imbalance in the work place to substantiate discrimination; rather, they had to provide proof that "a specific employment practice" illicitly injured minority employment.

Cases continued to challenge affirmative action into the last decade of the twentieth century. In response to the Supreme Court rulings, the U.S. Congress passed the Civil Rights Act of 1991, which reinforced anti-discrimination laws and essentially overturned the Ward's Cove Packing Company decision. During the decade of the 1990s, affirmative action became a highly charged legal and political issue. Appointments to the Supreme Court by Presidents Ronald Reagan and George H.W. Bush signaled an ideological change. In the *Adarand Constructors v. Pena* case, which looked at a federal statute that said that "not less than 10 percent" of funds provided for highway construction for small business should be owned by "socially and economically disadvantaged individuals," the court ruled that affirmative action programs based on race were constitutional only if they were "narrowly tailored" to serve a "compelling government interest." The following year, in the *Hopwood v. State of Texas* case, the 5th U.S. Circuit Court of Appeals upheld the claim of four white students who felt that they had been denied admission to the University of Texas Law School because of racial preferences given to supposedly less-qualified African American and Hispanic applicants. Consequently, the University of Texas Law School was proscribed from "any consideration of race or ethnicity" in its admission policies.

Cases continued to challenge affirmative action into the last decade of the twentieth century.

In 1996, Governor Pete Wilson and Ward Connerly, a conservative African American and member of the University of California Board of Regents, pushed for and got passed Proposition 209, which ended all state-sponsored affirmative action programs. Two years after Connerly led California's Proposition 209, he successfully led Washington State's Initiative 200, which also eradicated affirmative action. The Supreme Court again addressed the issue of affirmative action on June 23, 2003, when it upheld the use of race as a factor in promoting educational diversity as long as the University of Michigan did not consider it in a "mechanical way." Consequently, the Supreme Court justices approved the University of Michigan's Law School plan for affirmative action for operating in a "holistic way." However, it rejected Michigan's undergraduate plan that placed too much emphasis on race as a determining factor in its admissions

policies. On November 7, 2006, Michigan voters approved a referendum calling for an end to race-sensitive admission at the University of Michigan. By a margin of 58 to 42 percent, voters approved the public referendum that banned the use of race or sex by any agency of state government, including the state's university system, employment, or contracting. Affirmative action has been a highly contentious and divisive issue since its inception. With state legislatures, the public, and the courts at variance, its continued status is uncertain.

Linda T. Wynn

Bailey v. Alabama (1911)

This case was brought before the U.S. Supreme Court, whose ruling helped to end the practice of peonage. This process in particular had victimized blacks after emancipation, as they lacked employment, land, and other resources. White former slave owners still needed labor, and so they took unfair advantage by entering into exploitative contractual agreements with blacks to perform labor and/or live on parcels of land, with their work paying debts to landowners. These arrangements were devised to keep black labor in debt to support the sharecropping system that replaced plantation slavery in the South. Alonzo Bailey, an illiterate black man, was arrested and brought to trial by his employer for violating an Alabama state law that supported peonage. He had received a small advance for a 12-month labor contract, but left the job before the year ended without repaying the advance. The state law stipulated that his actions were taken with intent to defraud, and Bailey was convicted of the offense in state court. Bailey's attorneys appealed to the Supreme Court in 1908, arguing that the Alabama law violated his **Thirteenth Amendment** rights under the U.S. Constitution. In the first hearing of the case, the Supreme Court remanded the case to lower courts, but later struck down the Alabama law.

Fletcher F. Moon

Bates v. Little Rock, Arkansas (1960)

Daisy Lee Gaston Bates, a civil rights activist, newspaper publisher, and president of the Arkansas branch of the **NAACP**, was arrested in late October 1957 for failure to adhere to a recently amended Little Rock city ordinance. Codified in 1957, the ordinance required all organizations operating within the city to turn over, upon request, a list of their members and donations made to the organization, including dues. It also stipulated that the list would be open for public inspection. Likewise, the City of North Little Rock amended its occupation tax ordinance with the identical language. The language of the ordinance opened the door of fear and intimidation for members of the NAACP. As Justice Potter Stewart noted in the *Bates* decision, some refused to renew their membership because of "fear of community hostilities and economic reprisals." In fact, members of the NAACP, like Bates, who were publicly identified as members, were subjected to harassment and threats. It was the opinion of many that the ordinances targeted the NAACP.

The Little Rock and the City of North Little Rock ordinances resulted in court cases against the officers and custodians of the NAACP's records because they refused to furnish city officials with a list of names of the members of the respective local branches. The arrest of NAACP officials culminated in court cases that reached the U.S. Supreme Court. As an officer and custodian of the records of the NAACP's local branch, Bates surrendered all pertinent information; however, she refused to relinquish to city officials the names of members who belonged to the organization's local branch. Her counterpart in the City of North Little Rock also refused to give over to city officials a listing of members. Subsequent to her arrest, Bates was tried, convicted, and fined for violating the occupational license tax ordinance. Bates's counterpart in the City of North Little Rock was also arrested for not surrendering the names of NAACP members.

When the cases reached the Arkansas Supreme Court in 1958, the petitioners' convic-

tions were upheld and the cases were consolidated. Arkansas's highest court ruled that compulsory disclosure of the membership lists was not an unconstitutional invasion of the freedoms guaranteed. Two years after Bates's arrest, the case was argued before the nation's highest court on November 18, 1959. Attorneys Robert L. Carter and George Howard Jr. represented the plaintiffs. A first amendment case, at issue was whether the City of Little Rock's license tax ordinance that required the compulsory disclosure of any organization's membership list in order to verify its tax-exempt status unconstitutionally burdened the freedom of association of an organization's members. On February 23, 1960, in enunciating the unanimous decision of the U.S. Supreme Court in the *Bates v. Little Rock, Arkansas* case, Justice Stewart denounced and overturned the convictions based upon the Constitution's First Amendment. He concluded that Little Rock and North Little Rock failed to demonstrate a controlling justification for the deterrence of free association which disclosure of the membership list would cause. He further stated that the petitioners could not be punished for refusing to produce information, which the municipalities could not constitutionally require. Once again, the NAACP had prevailed in assisting African Americans in Arkansas in their pursuit of equality and justice.

Linda T. Wynn

Boynton v. Virginia (1960)

In 1958 Bruce Boynton, a law student from historically black **Howard University** in Washington, D.C., took a Trailways bus from Washington to his hometown of Montgomery, Alabama. When he reached the terminal in Richmond, Virginia, he had a 40-minute stopover, which he used to seek food in the segregated restaurant. He was asked to move to the "colored" section, but he refused on the grounds that he was an interstate passenger and was protected by federal law. Boynton was arrested, charged with trespassing, and fined $10. Boynton appealed to the Hustins Court of Richmond, admitting that he remained in the white section of the restaurant but repeating his federal right. Further, Boynton claimed that his presence was not "unlawful," as he was charged and that he remained within "authority of law." The Virginia Supreme Court heard the case, held that his conviction was "plainly right," and rejected Boynton's petition. The **NAACP**, with **Thurgood Marshall** as chief lawyer for the case, appealed to the U.S. Supreme Court, which on December 5, 1960, in a seven-to-two decision, ruled in Boynton's favor and held that bus transportation was related to interstate commerce, and that racial segregation in public transportation, including terminals, was illegal and violated the Interstate Commerce Act. In writing the majority opinion, Justice Hugo L. Black added that "Interstate passengers have to eat," and they have a right to

Redding agreed to take the case because Bulah and her family "were the ideal standard-bearers for the fight."

expect such service "without discrimination." As a non-violent direct action test of the *Boynton v. Virginia* case, the **Freedom Rides** were put in place on May 4, 1961.

Jessie Carney Smith

Brown v. Board of Education of Topeka, Kansas (1954)

On May 17, 1954, a unanimous U.S. Supreme Court overturned the *Plessy v. Ferguson* doctrine with its ruling in the *Brown v. Board of*

Education of Topeka, Kansas case and require the desegregation of schools across the nation. While the Court's decision did not abolish racial segregation in other public arenas or required the desegregation of public schools by a specific date, it did affirm that the permissive or *de rigueur* segregation, which existed in a number of states, was unconstitutional. The importance of the *Brown* case comes not from what the justices' opinion stated but from an awareness of what it expected to eradicate: an American social, political, economic, and legal system that prior to the end of slavery treated its African American populace as chattel property. When the maniacal institution of slavery ended, state legislators constructed a legal system built upon a set of lawful stratagems that racially segregated African Americans from the rest of American society. That Jim Crow structure relegated and rendered African Americans second-class citizens.

When the history of civil rights policies is analyzed, the most grave wrongs endured by African Americans, including thralldom, racial segregation, and unwarranted lynchings, have not been enough, in and of themselves, to obtain redress from either the executive, judicial, or legislative branches of the nation's government. Rather, relief has only come when policymakers accept that such covenants will afford a coherent and cogent benefit for the nation or a portion of the populace. Refusing to be bound by the opinions of the nineteenth-century court, the justices ruled that segregated public places of learning were "inherently unequal" and therefore violated the Equal Protection Clause of the **Fourteenth Amendment**. It looked not to the perceptible aspects but to the outcome of racial segregation itself on public education.

Although known as the *Brown v. Board of Education* case, this case actually consisted of four other cases: *Briggs v. Elliott* (South Carolina); *Davis v. County School Board of Prince Edward County, Virginia*; *Gebhart v. Belton* (Delaware); and *Boiling v. Sharpe* (Washington, D.C.). By the time these cases reached the Supreme Court, the nation's social and political context had changed dramatically since 1927, when the justices considered the question in the *Gong Lum v. Rice* case. That case stated that states could define racial classifications for schools, thereby adhering to the 1896 logic as enunciated in the Plessy decision. Considered one of the most significant cases on race in American history, the *Brown v. Board of Education* decision led to more than a dozen unanimous decisions by the U.S. Supreme Court. Additionally, it also helped the African American community to begin the healing process. This was necessary because of the **Dred Scott v. Sanford** (1857) decision, which asserted that persons of African decent had "no rights which the white man was bound to respect," and the *Plessy v. Ferguson* conclusion that the Fourteenth Amendment to the U.S. Constitution was not intended to abolish distinctions based upon color, or to enforce racial equality.

Linda T. Wynn

Bulah v. Gebhart (1952)

A forerunner to *Brown v Board of Education* (1954), *Beulah v Gebhart* was begun by Sarah Beulah. A school bus for white children passed her Hockessin, Delaware, house daily, while she had to drive her daughter, Shirley, two miles each way to the "colored" school. Beulah took her case to court, with civil rights attorney **Louis L. Redding** leading the fight, and won. Redding agreed to take the case because Beulah and her family "were the ideal standard-bearers for the fight," said Bradley Skelcher in the *New York Times*. The family had neither ulterior motives nor animosity toward whites. "They were fighting because it was the right thing to do." On August 1, 1952, the Delaware Court of Chancery ruled that the white high school in Claymont and Wilmington, Delaware's black high school were not equal and Claymont had to admit the plaintiffs. On appeal, the Supreme Court of Delaware on August 28, 1952, upheld the decision and declared that racially separate schools had to be equal. Young Shirley became

one of the first black children to attend a whites-only Delaware school. Her case was combined with several others from around the country and the action that followed led to the historic *Brown v Board of Education* case of Topeka, Kansas. The ruling in that suit declared segregated public schools unconstitutional. Shirley Beulah Stamps died on May 28, 2003, at age 59.

Jessie Carney Smith

Civil Rights Act of 1875

U.S. Senator Charles Sumner and Representative Benjamin Franklin Butler, both of whom were anti-slavery advocates, introduced the Civil Rights Act of 1875 to Congress in 1870. However, the act did not become law until March 1, 1875, when it was signed by President Ulysses S. Grant. As written, it protected Americans, regardless of race, in their access to public accommodations and facilities, as well as the right to serve on juries. Neither President Grant nor his successor, Rutherford B. Hayes, devoted much effort to enforcing the act, and relatively few private lawsuits resulted in the years immediately following its enactment.

Constitutional challenges to the Civil Rights Act of 1875 reached the U.S. Supreme Court in a group of cases decided in 1883 under the collective name the *Civil Rights Cases*. Justice Joseph P. Bradley wrote the Court's opinion, finding the act unconstitutional because it did not regulate state action but rather actions by private companies operating hotels and theaters. Therefore, the Court affirmed that Congress did not have the power to regulate the conduct and transactions of individuals.

The next federal statute intended to protect civil rights did not become law until 1957, three quarters of a century after the 1875 Civil Rights Act. In addition to the Civil Rights Act of 1875, Congress passed three other major Civil Rights Acts during the Reconstruction era (1866–1877). The first of these is the Civil Rights Act of 1866, which passed over President Andrew Johnson's veto on April 9, 1866. It overturned

A lithograph by E. Sachse & Co. titled "The Shackle Broken — by the Genius of Freedom" depicts important scenes and people related to the Civil Rights Act of 1875 (Library of Congress).

the 1857 **Dred Scott** decision in which the Supreme Court ruled that African Americans were not citizens of the United States. The law declared all persons born in the United States to be citizens, except for unassimilated Native Americans, and defined and protected all citizens' civil rights.

Because of constitutional criticism leveled against the 1866 Civil Rights Act, Congress relied upon the implementation powers of the Fourteenth and Fifteenth Amendments to the U.S. Constitution and passed the Civil Rights Act of 1870, also known as the 1870 Enforce-

ment Act. The main thrust of the 1870 Enforcement Act was to put in place sanctions against interference with African American suffrage, which was granted under the Fifteenth Amendment. However, the act's third and fourth sections were declared unconstitutional in 1876 in *United States v. Reese*; in 1903, the fifth section was declared unconstitutional in the *James v. Bowman* case; and three years later, the sixteenth section was declared unconstitutional in the *Hodges v. United States* case.

The Second Enforcement Act of 1871, more commonly known as the Civil Rights Act of 1871 or the Ku Klux Klan Act, followed the 1870 Enforcement Act. Passed by Congress to overturn state laws preventing African Americans from voting in the South, the 1871 amendment sought to eliminate registration fraud. It also instituted federal procedures for supervising elections in the South, upon petition to the federal circuit court. An act to enforce the provisions of the Fourteenth Amendment, section two of this decree was also found to be unconstitutional in two cases: *United States v. Harris* (1883) and *Baldwin v. Franks* (1887). In 1896 the U.S. Supreme Court ruled in *Plessy v. Ferguson* that designating separate railroad cars for African Americans and whites was constitutional as long as the facilities were "equal." The Supreme Court doctrine of "separate but equal" stood for more than a half century, until the Court reversed itself in *Brown v. Board of Education* in 1954.

Linda T. Wynn

Civil Rights Act of 1957

In 1957 the U.S. Congress passed the first civil rights legislation since the **Civil Rights Act of 1875**. The Act established the U.S. Justice Department as a guarantor of the right to vote. In his presidential response to the political divisions wrought by the unanimous Supreme Court decision in the 1954 *Brown v. Board of Education* case, Dwight D. Eisenhower sought a centrist agenda for civil rights. President Eisenhower, encouraged by Attorney General Herbert Brownell, in his 1956 State of the Union address adopted the 1947 recommendations of President Harry S. Truman's Civil Rights Committee. Brownell introduced legislation that sought to provide federal protection of basic citizenship rights and an independent Civil Rights Commission, a Department of Justice civil rights division, and authority to enforce civil rights and voters' rights and other civil rights infringements. Many southern senators went against the administration. However, through the efforts of House Speaker Sam Rayburn and Senator **Lyndon B. Johnson**, a compromised version of the legislation passed.

Under the sway of the Civil Rights Act of 1957, the Commission of Civil Rights was established.

Eisenhower signed the Civil Rights Act of 1957 into law on September 9, 1957, five days after the Little Rock Nine desegregated **Central High School** in Little Rock, Arkansas. Under the sway of the Civil Rights Act of 1957, the Commission of Civil Rights was established with the authority to investigate allegations that citizens were being denied their constitutional right to the franchise. It also called for the appointment of an assistant attorney general to oversee the new civil rights division of the U.S. Justice Department. In 1958 the Civil Rights Division gathered information on voter discrimination in Tuskegee, Alabama, where the Tuskegee Civic Association (TCA), an organization founded by Charles Gomillion (1900–1995) in the 1940s to foster voter registration, shared its extensive records that documented voter discrimination. Consequently, the commission held televised hearings where witnesses disclosed the deceptive strategies used by registrars to proscribe black voter registration. Ultimately, Gomillion became the lead plaintiff in the landmark 1960 civil rights case of *Gomillion v. Lightfoot* (1960) litigated by attorney **Fred Gray**. The case was brought against the city of Tuskegee for redrawing its political boundaries to exclude black voters. In its 1960 unanimous decision, the Supreme Court declared gerrymandering (redrawing district borders to favor certain voter outcomes) unconstitutional. The *Gomillion v. Lightfoot* case proved to be a significant step in advancing federal examination of state voting practices.

During its inaugural two years, the Civil Rights Division brought forth only three enforcement hearings in the states of Alabama, Georgia, and Louisiana. The division, under the leadership of Burke Marshall and John Doar, furthered voting rights during President **John F. Kennedy**'s administration and signaled further action in the area of civil rights laws in the 1960s. Three years after the passage of the 1957 Civil Rights Act, Congress again addressed the issue of black voter registration and voting with much debate and consternation by southern Democrats. The Civil Rights Act of 1960 established federal inspection of local voter registration polls and introduced penalties for anyone who obstructed an individual's attempt to vote or even register to vote. It also permitted federal courts to appoint voting referees to conduct voter registration following a judicial finding of voter discrimination.

Beneficiaries of the American black struggle for freedom included women, the disabled, gays and lesbians, the elderly.

The Senate debate over the passage of the bill began on February 29, 1960. However, because 18 southern Democrats divided into three teams of six to create a filibuster, the debate over the Civil Rights Act of 1960 became one of the longest filibusters in the history of the U.S. Congress. Lasting for 125 hours and 31 minutes, minus a fifteen-minute break before Lyndon Johnson, then the Senate Majority Leader, called it off, the filibuster did not prevent the act from being signed by President Eisenhower on May 6, 1960. Although the Eisenhower administration enacted two civil rights acts that targeted the rights of American blacks to register and/or vote, only an additional three percent of

black eligible voters were added to the electoral roll during the 1960 election, as southern states continued to ignore national enactments.

Linda T. Wynn

Civil Rights Act of 1964

The Civil Rights Act of 1964 was one of the most important pieces of domestic legislation of the post–World War II era. Congressional concern for civil rights lessened after Reconstruction and the U.S. Supreme Court's decision in 1883 to nullify the constitutionality of the **Civil Rights Act of 1875**. The U.S. Congress did not address the issue again until 1957, when it was under pressure from the modern Civil Rights Movement, and then it was only a feeble attempt to redress civil wrongs. The passage of the **Civil Rights Act of 1957** was a modest statute that created the Civil Rights Commission with the authority to investigate civil rights violations; however, it lacked enforcement provisions and it was a weak corrective for voting rights violations.

Congress enacted the Civil Rights Act of 1960, which only slightly reinforced the voting rights provision. However, when it came to addressing civil rights at the federal level, advances had been limited mostly to the judicial branch of the government. The **NAACP** Legal Defense and Education Fund brought forth numerous victories that declared racial discrimination to be unconstitutional when engaged in by government. With the Supreme Court's *Brown v. Board of Education* decision in 1954, the Legal Defense Fund succeeded in overturning *Plessy v. Ferguson*'s doctrine of "separate but equal," which had consequences far beyond educational arenas.

In 1963 the compelling images of the South's racial system of apartheid was made known both in the print and electronic media, as Birmingham, Alabama, steadfastly held to the Old South ways in an attempt to maintain segregation. Images of Eugene "Bull" Connor's use of attack dogs and fire hoses against peaceful civil

At the signing of the 1964 Civil Rights Act, Martin Luther King watched as President Lyndon B. Johnson signed the document surrounded by other congressional and civil rights leaders (AP Photo).

rights activists, including children, were shown nationally and begged the question: would the American principle of equality and justice for all incorporate black Americans in the nation's southern region?

In May 1963, President **John F. Kennedy** proposed a new civil rights act that languished in the House of Representatives until Kennedy's assassination (November 22, 1963), when President **Lyndon B. Johnson** adopted the civil rights agenda as his own commemoration to Kennedy. He enlisted assistance from the NAACP and the Leadership Conference on Civil Rights. The civil rights legislation passed the U.S. House of Representatives on February 10, 1964. However, it ran into strong opposition in the U.S. Senate, where southern senators mounted a filibuster. Overcoming the filibuster, the act finally won approval in the Senate. President Johnson signed the civil rights act into law on July 2, 1964.

The 1964 Civil Rights Act had eleven main provisions or titles. Several strengthened the Civil Rights Commission and the voting rights provisions of the Civil Rights Acts of 1957 and 1960, including a provision authorizing the U.S. attorney general to sue states that violated voting rights. However, the act's other provisions were far more important. They dealt with discrimination in public accommodations and employment and with discrimination by agencies, both public and private, that received federal funds. The Civil Rights Act of 1964 is among the Civil Rights Movement's most enduring legacies. While the legislation was directed specifically at removing barriers to equal access and opportunity that affected American blacks, it greatly extended the reach of federal protection. It led to a major restructuring of the nation's sense of justice and expanded legal protections to other minority groups. Beneficiaries of the American black struggle for freedom included women, the disabled, gays and lesbians, the elderly, and others who experienced discrimination. However, concerned that the issue of voting rights would defeat the legislation, the president and his allies in Congress deferred action on that matter.

Linda T. Wynn

Rarely did whites, northern or southern, capitulate to blacks who sought housing in their communities and neighborhoods.

Civil Rights Act of 1968

President **Lyndon B. Johnson** signed the 1968 Civil Rights Act on April 11. Also known as the Fair Housing Act, it bans discrimination in the sale, rental, or financing of housing based on race, religion, national origin, sex, and (as amended) handicap and family status. The last of the 1960s enactments on civil rights, it was designed to eliminate systemic discrimination that resulted in the unrelenting segregation of American blacks and other minorities that isolated them to the ghet-

tos in the country's major cities. Before passage, the act faced a long and arduous journey in the U.S. Congress. From 1966 through 1967, the nation's legislative body regularly considered the fair housing bill to no avail. However, after the assassination of the Rev. Dr. **Martin Luther King Jr.** on April 4, 1968, and the release of the **National Advisory Commission on Civil Disorders** report on racial discrimination and pervasive unrest that manifested itself before and after King's death, Johnson urged Congressional approval. King's name had been associated with fair housing since 1966, when he staged marches in Chicago. Additionally, the act prohibited advertising with discriminatory preferences and banned municipalities and county governments from legislating zoning laws to exclude or discriminate against minorities. It also empowered the U.S. Department of Housing and Urban Development and the United States Attorney General to enforce its terms, to assist victims of discrimination, and authorized the federal courts to order the payment of damages to victims of discrimination.

Even after the passage of the 1968 Fair Housing Act which barred racial discrimination in the sale, rental, or financing of most housing units, there was no significant reduction in housing segregation during the ensuing years. Rarely did whites, northern or southern, capitulate to blacks who sought housing in their communities and neighborhoods. Although the law did little to eliminate housing discrimination, it was another device that those who felt impinged upon could use in the courts to fight discrimination on the basis of race, gender, or disability. Albeit, three times in five years, Johnson and the Congress shattered barriers of racial equality that had persisted for more than a century. The 1968 Civil Rights Act was expanded in 1974 to prohibit discrimination based on sex. Fourteen years later, it was expanded and prohibited discrimination based on disability and familial status.

Linda T. Wynn

Declaration of Independence (1776)

The document agreed upon by the Continental Congress on July 4, 1776, during the Revolutionary War, the Declaration of Independence proclaimed the separation of the 13 American colonies from Britain. While New York's delegation was forced to abstain from voting on the act until July 15, the statement endures as both a declaration of the colonies' freedom and independence as well as the embodiment of the fledgling nation's founding principles. Drafted by future American president Thomas Jefferson, the Declaration of Independence encompasses both American constitutional theory and the republican theory of government. Written in four parts, it begins with a preamble, which unveils its purpose as a justification for the colonies' separation from the Crown. Secondly, it alleges the right of the

people to overthrow tyrannical governments. Third, it offers a list of grievances against King George III (1738–1820). Finally, the last section declares the colonies to be "free and independent states." Many of the constitutional, legal, and policy offences leveled at George III were, at best, dubious in nature.

Jefferson's initial draft included indictments against the slave trade; however, the Second Continental Congress mandated the involvement of a committee on the issue, including John Adams and Benjamin Franklin among its members. While his condemnation of slavery was omitted from the adopted draft, Jefferson acknowledged that his work was not novel but instead represented the culmination of preceding political thought, such as that of John Locke, Emerich de Vattel, and Jean Jacques Rousseau. Among its most memorable passages is "We hold

The signing of the Declaration of Independence is depicted in this Currier & Ives print. African Americans would have to wait generations before the ideals of freedom expressed in this famous document were applied to them (Library of Congress).

these truths to be self-evident: that all men are created equal; that they are endowed, by their Creator, with certain unalienable rights; that among these are life, liberty and the pursuit of happiness. That to secure these rights, governments are instituted among men, deriving their just powers from the consent of the governed; that when any form of government becomes destructive of these ends, it is the right of the people to alter or abolish it, and to institute a new government." Despite its basis on the theory of natural rights, the declaration guaranteed no such rights to the thousands of slaves held in bondage in the former colonies. The rights it implicitly endorsed would not begin to be realized for them until the adoption of the Thirteenth and Fourteenth Amendments, which were the result of the combined efforts of slaves who themselves rebelled, ex-slaves who documented their slave experience, anti-slavery activists, and the victory of the Union in the **Civil War**.

Crystal A. deGregory

Dred Scott v. Sanford (1857)

One of three cases that severely impinged on the rights of African Americans in the United States—and second only to the *Brown v. Board of Education* decision in its impact on race relations—the Dred Scott case was the most far-reaching judicial opinion of the nation's highest tribunal in the nineteenth century. This case set the stage for the **Civil War**. Scott first went to trial to sue for his freedom in 1847. Ten years later, after a decade of appeals and court reversals, his case was finally brought before the U.S. Supreme Court. The issues in the case involved the constitutionality of the Missouri Compromise of 1820 and the legal right of African Americans to become citizens of the United States.

Dred Scott was a slave owned by John Emerson, an army surgeon stationed temporarily in Illinois. In 1836 Emerson took Scott to Fort Snelling in what is now Wisconsin; slavery was forbidden there, as well as in Illinois, according

Dred Scott's desire to be free sparked a key U.S. Supreme Court case on slavery and state laws (Fisk University).

to the terms of the 1820 Missouri Compromise. While in free territory, Scott married one of Emerson's other slaves. Later, Scott and his wife were summoned by their master to return to Missouri, which they did, apparently not knowing that they could have made a case for their freedom while living up North. After Emerson died, Scott made a bid to obtain freedom for himself and his wife. In 1846, after a failed attempt to buy his freedom, Scott and his attorneys filed suit in the state court, arguing that residence in a free territory released him from slavery. The Supreme Court of Missouri, however, ruled (in 1852) that after being brought back to Missouri, where slavery was legal, Scott's status returned to that of a slave; consequently, he had no standing before the court.

Two years later, the U.S. Circuit Court in Missouri upheld the decision of the Supreme Court of Missouri. After Scott lost in the U.S.

Circuit Court, the case was appealed to the U.S. Supreme Court, where it was argued at length in 1855 and 1856, and finally decided in 1857. Of the nine justices on the Supreme Court, seven were appointed by pro-slavery presidents from the South, five of whom were from slave-holding families. On March 6, 1857, Chief Justice Roger Brooke Taney, a staunch supporter of slavery, wrote the court's majority opinion. It stated that because Scott was black, he was not a citizen and therefore had no right to sue. The decision also declared the Missouri Compromise of 1820, legislation that restricted slavery in certain territories, was unconstitutional.

The case, and particularly the court's decision, provoked acrimony among abolitionists, further intensified the divide between the North and the South, and helped draw the nation closer toward the Civil War. After the Civil War, the **Thirteenth and Fourteenth Amendments** to the U.S. Constitution superseded the U.S. Supreme Court's decision. Enacted and ratified in 1865 and 1868 respectively, the Thirteenth Amendment abolished slavery and the Fourteenth Amendment guaranteed full citizenship and rights regardless of race. However, before the nineteenth century ended, the U.S. Supreme Court would again assail the rights of African Americans with its 1896 decision in the *Plessy v. Ferguson* case that sanctioned legal racial segregation.

Linda T. Wynn

Fifteenth Amendment to the U.S. Constitution. *See* Reconstruction Amendments.

Fourteenth Amendment to the U.S. Constitution. *See* Reconstruction Amendments.

Fugitive Slave Act of 1850

Passed by the U.S. Congress on September 18, 1850, the Fugitive Slave Act was the result of the Compromise of 1850, which attempted to avert secession by the South by ensuring balance between the free and slave-holding states. Written as a follow-up to the Fugitive Slave Act of 1793, the 1850 act mandated the arrest and return of any escaped slave to his or her owner. While the 1793 act included a clause to enforce the section of the U.S. Constitution that ordered the return of escapees, the authorities in free states often failed to return fugitives to their masters. The act's enforcement only lessened as more northern states abolished slavery. Slavery advocates in the South increasingly resented the North's passage of both emancipation and liberty laws, which guaranteed a trial before a jury before alleged fugitives could be returned to slavery. In repeated instances, several northern states demonstrated a commitment to preserving the freedom of these quasi-free blacks (who had liberated themselves without being freed by their owners) by fighting slave hunters' attempts to seize them, as well as refusing to convict them. Southern resentment culminated with the 1850 act, which not only denied a fugitive's right to a jury trial but also mandated that citizens assist in the recovery of fugitive slaves. With the assistance of additional federal marshals to ensure its enforcement, the law impeded the attempts of many free and quasi-free blacks to build new lives in the North. With no right to trials, free blacks were also captured and sent to live in servitude. Virtually defenseless, an estimated 20,000 blacks fled to Canada over the next decade. Using the **Underground Railroad**, abolitionists responded by strengthening their resolve to end slavery. Both laws were repealed by Congress in 1864.

Crystal A. deGregory

Geier v. Tennessee (1968)

This landmark court case in the desegregation of higher education was initiated in 1968 and not officially resolved until 2006. Over its nearly 40-year history the case was known by a number of names. Initially, when **Tennessee State University** (TSU) faculty

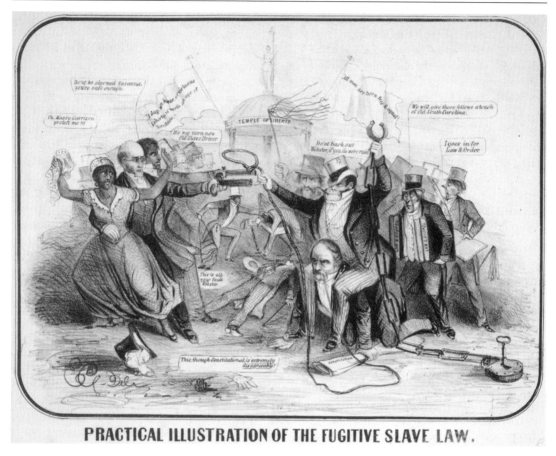

An 1851 political cartoon depicts the tension between abolitionists and supporters of the Fugitive Slave Act (Library of Congress).

member Rita Sanders filed the original lawsuit on May 16, 1968, it was known as *Sanders v. (Tennessee Governor Buford) Ellington,* and involved the attempt to block the construction of a new facility for the University of Tennessee at Nashville (UTN). George Barrett, a white attorney, represented Sanders and was joined by numerous other legal professionals during the decades of court proceedings, rulings, and appeals. The premise behind the case was that the presence and expansion of UTN created direct competition between two state institutions in the same city for students, faculty, and state funding, and would hinder efforts to desegregate not just TSU, the only public historically black college/university (HBCU) in the

state, but also traditionally white institutions (TWIs), "perpetuating a dual system of public higher education in Tennessee."

Despite the lawsuit, the UTN campus was expanded in downtown Nashville near the state capitol as part of the University of Tennessee system, while TSU languished with inadequate resources in the northwest part of the city as part of the Tennessee Board of Regents system. Sanders, meanwhile, married and became Rita Sanders Geier. As a result, the case's name changed several times, as new governors of Tennessee were elected and became legal defendants in the suit. The case was also documented as *Geier v. Dunn, Geier v. Blanton,*

Geier v. Alexander, Geier v. McWhorter, and *Geier v. Sundquist,* until its final resolution as *Geier v. Bredesen* during the administration of Tennessee Governor Philip Bredesen. In 1972 Federal Judge Frank T. Gray allowed TSU professors Sterling Adams, Raymond Richardson, and 100 other black Tennessee citizens to enter the case. They were represented by **Avon Williams Jr.**, a leading African American civil rights attorney and state senator. Gray ruled in 1978 that UTN must be merged under the authority of TSU.

When the merger took effect on July 1, 1979, it marked the first time that a HBCU and TWI were combined, with the HBCU as the surviving institution. UTN and TSU faculty member H. Coleman McGinnis and others also secured legal representation and became plaintiff interveners in the case. In 1984 Judge Thomas Wiseman revised the merger agreement to include the "Stipulation of Settlement," which imposed racial quotas on TSU to increase "other-race" (white) enrollment, while other state schools were to increase their minority (nonwhite) populations. Over $100 million in much-needed and long-overdue capital improvements were made to the TSU campuses. In 1986 the TSU downtown campus was officially renamed the Avon Williams Campus in recognition of his legal and legislative career. Federal mediator Carlos Gonzalez facilitated negotiations that led to final dismissal of the case by Wiseman on September 21, 2006.

Fletcher F. Moon

Guinn and Beal v. United States (1915)

In the Guinn and Beal case, the U.S. Supreme Court held that voter registration requirements containing "grandfather clauses," which made voter registration in part dependent upon whether the applicant was descended from men enfranchised before enactment of the **Fifteenth Amendment**, violated that amendment. The Supreme Court found that the Oklahoma law was adopted in order to give whites, who might

otherwise have been disfranchised by the state's literacy test, a way of qualifying to vote that was not available to blacks. The **NAACP**, through attorney Moorefield Storey, the organization's first president, submitted an *amicus curiae* brief (a document offering information from a party not involved in the case) on the behalf of Frank Guinn and J. J. Beal. The civil rights organization's participation had historical implications within itself, since the Guinn and Beal case represented its first major entrance into the struggle for African American civil rights.

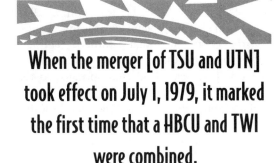

When the merger [of TSU and UTN] took effect on July 1, 1979, it marked the first time that a HBCU and TWI were combined.

After it was argued before the court on October 17, 1913, Chief Justice Edward Douglas White delivered the court's decision on June 21, 1915, which nullified Oklahoma's grandfather clause. For the first time a unanimous Supreme Court invalidated a state law disenfranchising African Americans. However, within a year Oklahoma found another way to continue discriminating against African American voters. A special session of the 1916 Oklahoma legislature enacted a new statue that "grandfathered" in all those who had registered in the 1914 election. This blatant defiance of the court's intention went unpunished for years. Not until 1939 did the court strike down the Oklahoma law with its ruling in the *Lane v. Wilson* case. However, it was not the **Voting Rights Act 1965** that African American voting rights truly became established throughout the nation.

Linda T. Wynn

Henderson v. U.S. Interstate Commerce Commission and Southern Railway (1950)

Civil rights activist Elmer W. Henderson (1913?–2001) filed a suit before the U.S. Supreme Court ending segregation in railway dining cars. He experienced segregation during a trip from Washington to Birmingham while he was a field representative for President Franklin D. Roosevelt's Committee on Fair Employment Practices. Blacks and whites were separated by a curtain or a partition; sometimes dining cars allowed 10 tables for whites and just one or two for blacks. When whites had filled their tables, at times they moved to the black section. In 1942 Henderson filed a complaint with the lower court, but the court ruled that Southern Railway's revised rules met the separate but equal tenet of *Plessy v. Ferguson*. Henderson appealed to the U.S. Supreme Court, which likewise questioned the constitutionality of *Plessy*. The court held that Henderson had been denied equal access due to the use of partitions, curtains, and signs that called for a difference in treatment. The Supreme Court ruled on June 5, 1950, that segregation in dining cars violated the Interstate Commerce Act. After that success, Henderson targeted segregated waiting rooms in railroad and bus companies.

Jessie Carney Smith

Segregation on interstate buses was legally sanctioned until 1946.

Morgan v. Virginia (1946)

Segregation on interstate buses was legally sanctioned until 1946, when the U.S. Supreme Court declared a Virginia state law invalid and segregation in interstate buses illegal. The case grew out of Irene Morgan (Kirkaldy)'s courageous stand. In July 1944, as Morgan traveled on an interstate bus from Virginia to Baltimore, she sat in the rear section and refused to give her seat to a white person in Gloucester, Virginia; she was subsequently thrown in jail. She was also fined $100 for resisting arrest, having kicked the Middlesex County sheriff who removed her and scratching the deputy when he took her to jail. Morgan declared that the Virginia law, effective since 1930 and requiring segregated seating rows, did not apply to her interstate journey. The Baltimore resident was on a return trip home when the incident occurred. The **NAACP** and its lawyer **Thurgood Marshall**, later the first black U.S. Supreme Court Justice, took the case *Morgan v. Commonwealth of Virginia* all the way to the Supreme Court, which ruled on June 3, 1946, that segregation in interstate travel was unconstitutional. In many southern states the victory was at best a moral one for African Americans and the NAACP, for they refused to enforce the law and continued their Jim Crow practices for some time. It was not until the Civil Rights Movement of the 1960s, when **Freedom Riders** successfully brought down the racial barriers, that southern states observed the law. For her work in this civil rights case, in 2001 President Bill Clinton awarded Irene Morgan Kirkaldy the Presidential Citizens Medal.

Jessie Carney Smith

Plessy v. Ferguson (1896)

American blacks' political rights were affirmed by the **Thirteenth, Fourteenth, and Fifteenth Amendments** to the U.S. Constitution and numerous laws passed by Congress during the Reconstruction era. **The Civil Rights Act of 1875** attacked racial discrimination. This act made it a crime for any individual to be denied equal enjoyment of any accommodations at inns, public conveyances on land or water, and theaters and other places of public amusement. The law was subject only to the conditions and limitations established by law and applicable alike to citizens of every race and color. However, in 1883 the U.S. Supreme Court struck down the 1875 act, ruling that the Fourteenth Amendment did not give Congress authority to prevent discrimination by private individuals. Consequently, the ruling instructed those victimized by the perpetrators of racial discrimination to seek relief not from the federal government, but from the states. Unfortunately, state governments were passing legislation that codified inequality between the races. Laws requiring the establishment of separate schools for children of each race were most common; however, segregation was soon extended to encompass most public and semipublic facilities.

Racial segregation developed in the American South as early as 1875, when Tennessee became the first state to enact the first Jim Crow legislation segregating public transportation. Six years later, the state amended its 1875 Jim Crow statute to mandate separate train cars for black passengers. Florida, Mississippi, and Texas passed similar laws later in the decade, and in the 1890s and 1900s other southern states followed their lead. These measures were unpopular with the railway companies that bore the expense of adding segregated cars. Segregation of the railroads was even more objectionable to black citizens, who saw it as a further step toward the complete refutation of the constitutional amendments.

When the Louisiana legislature proposed a segregation bill in 1890, the black community of New Orleans protested vigorously. Despite the presence of 16 black legislators in Louisiana's assembly, the law passed. It required either separate passenger coaches or partitioned coaches to provide segregated accommodations for each race. Passengers were required to sit in the appropriate areas or face a $25 fine or a 20-day jail sentence. However, in the case of black nurses attending to and caring for white children, the statute allowed them to ride in white compartments. In 1891 a group of concerned black men from New Orleans established the Citizens Committee to Test the Constitutionali-

ty of the Separate Car Law. After raising funds, they hired Albion W. Tourgee as their legal representative. The committee decided to bring forth a test case on intrastate travel. With the cooperation of the East Louisiana Railroad, on June 7, 1892, Homer Adolph Plessy, a mulatto who was one-eighth black, seated himself in a white compartment. The conductor challenged his seating. Consequently, Plessy was arrested and charged with violating the state law.

Racial segregation developed in the American South as early as 1875, when Tennessee became the first state to enact the first Jim Crow legislation.

In the Criminal District Court for the Parish of Orleans, Tourgee argued that the law requiring separate but equal accommodations was unconstitutional. When Judge John H. Ferguson ruled against him, Plessy applied to the Louisiana State Supreme Court to review the lower court's decision. In 1893, although the state supreme court upheld the state law, it granted Plessy's petition for a writ of error that enabled him to petition the case to the U.S. Supreme Court. On May 18, 1896, the U.S. Supreme Court ruled against Plessy. Justice Henry Billings Brown of Michigan delivered the majority opinion of the court that upheld the Louisiana law requiring racial segregation. He noted that the law did not violate either the Thirteenth or Fourteenth Amendments. In giving the majority opinion, he observed that the Thirteenth Amendment applied only to slavery and the Fourteenth Amendment was not intended to give blacks social equality but only political and civil equality with whites. While

Brown, a northerner, justified racial segregation, Justice John Marshall Harlan, a southerner from Kentucky, delivered the lone, reverberating, prophetic dissension. Noting that the U.S. Constitution is color blind and neither recognizes nor tolerates classes among the citizens of the United States, Harlan voiced a dissension that became the dominating theme in the unanimous *Brown v. Board of Education* case of 1954. Until then, however, the majority decision in the *Plessy v. Ferguson* case served as the organizing legal foundation and justification for separating the races for almost 60 years.

Linda T. Wynn

Reconstruction Amendments

The Thirteenth, Fourteenth, and Fifteenth Amendments to the U.S. Constitution were ratified between 1865 and 1870, the years immediately following the **Civil War**. Although President Lincoln's 1863 Emancipation Proclamation symbolically freed American blacks held in those states under Confederate control, it did not free those held under the control of the Union. Consequently, slavery still existed in the United States. The Thirteenth Amendment to the Constitution was passed by the U.S. Senate on April 8, 1864, and by the House on January 31, 1865. On February 1, 1865, President Lincoln approved the

A circa 1870 lithograph and watercolor published by Thomas Kelly illustrates some of the newly granted rights for African Americans (Library of Congress).

Congressional Joint Resolution and submitted the proposed amendment to the state legislatures. The necessary number of states ratified the amendment by December 6, 1865. The Thirteenth Amendment provides that "Neither slavery nor involuntary servitude, except as a punishment for crime whereof the party shall have been duly convicted, shall exist within the United States, or any place subject to their jurisdiction." With the ratification of the Thirteenth Amendment the United States found a definitive constitutional resolution to the question of slavery.

The Fourteenth Amendment was proposed on June 13, 1866, and was ratified by the necessary number of states on July 9, 1868. Providing a broad definition of U.S. citizenship, the Fourteenth Amendment superseded the U.S. Supreme Court's 1857 *Dred Scott v. Sanford* decision, which excluded slaves and their descendants as citizens. It declared that all persons born or naturalized in the United States and subject to its jurisdiction are citizens thereof. It forbids the states to abridge the privileges or immunities of citizens of the United States, or to deprive any person of life, liberty, or property without due process of law. It was used in the mid-1950s to dismantle racial segregation in the United States.

The Fifteenth Amendment granted American black males the right to vote, declaring "the right of citizens of the United States to vote shall not be denied or abridged by the United States or by any state on account of race, color, or previous condition of servitude." Although it passed the Congress on February 26, 1869, it was not ratified until February 3, 1870. However, black and white women were not allowed the right of the franchise until the 1920 passage of the Nineteenth Amendment. Through the use of grandfather clauses, poll taxes, literacy tests, and other extralegal stratagems, southern states continued to effectively disenfranchise American blacks. It would take the **Voting Rights Act of 1965** to grant blacks unobstructed access to the voting booth.

Linda T. Wynn

Sipuel v. Board of Regents of the University of Oklahoma (1948)

Despite the *Plessy v. Ferguson* "separate but equal" precedent handed down by the U.S. Supreme Court in 1896, schools and colleges for African Americans and whites were nowhere near equal by the mid-twentieth century. In the 1930s, the issue of the inequality between black and white colleges came to the forefront in a series of cases litigated before the U.S. Supreme Court, beginning with the 1938 *Missouri ex rel. Gaines v. Canada* case. Because of his race, Lloyd Gaines, an African American, was refused admission to the University of Missouri's law school. The Supreme Court ruled that any state offering legal education for whites must offer it to blacks as well; however, the court did not stipulate that such education must be offered in the same facility.

Ada Lois Sipuel, an African American, had graduated summa cum laude with an undergraduate degree in political science. In 1946 she applied to the University of Oklahoma Law School. Sipuel, despite her excellent academic qualifications, was denied admittance based on her race. Attorneys **Thurgood Marshall** and Amos T. Hall argued her case before the Oklahoma District Court, asking that the university be required to admit Sipuel. The court ruled in favor of the university. A year later, Oklahoma's State Supreme Court upheld the district court's decision. In 1948 Marshall and Amos took the *Sipuel v. Board of Regents of the University of Oklahoma* case to the U.S. Supreme Court. The nation's highest tribunal reversed the lower courts and held that the state was required to provide African Americans with equal educational opportunities as soon as such facilities were available to whites. Notwithstanding the court's decision, the later *McLaurin v. Oklahoma State Regents for Higher Education* (1950) case damaged the "separate but equal" doctrine beyond repair. *McLaurin v. Oklahoma* reversed a lower court decision upholding the efforts of the state-supported University of Oklahoma to adhere to the state law requiring Africans Americans to be provided instruction on a segregated basis. The nation's highest tribunal ruled that a public institution of higher learning could not provide different treatment to a student solely because of race as doing so deprived the student of his/her **Fourteenth Amendment** rights of equal protection. This prevented any state school from discriminating against a graduate student on the basis of race.

Linda T. Wynn

"There is no Negro Problem. There is no Southern Problem. There is no Northern Problem. There is only an American Problem."

Thirteenth Amendment to the U.S. Constitution. *See* Reconstruction Amendments.

Voting Rights Act of 1965

The march from **Selma to Montgomery, Alabama**, marred by the violent deaths of **Viola Liuzzo** and the Reverend James Webb, persuaded American functionaries that additional federal legislation was needed to guarantee the voting rights of American blacks. On March 15, 1965, President **Lyndon Johnson** addressed a joint session of the Congress and requested a new voting law. "There is no Negro Problem. There is no Southern Problem. There is no Northern Problem. There is only an American Problem ... we are ... here as Americans to solve that problem," stated Johnson in his address to Congress. Two days later, he sent the Voting Rights Act to Congress.

Before 1965, Congress passed civil rights legislation in 1957, 1960, and 1964 that contained voting-related provisions. The **Civil Rights Act of 1957** created the Civil Rights Division within the U.S. Department of Justice and the Commission on Civil Rights; the Civil Rights Act of 1960 permitted federal courts to appoint voting referees to conduct voter registration following a judicial finding on voting discrimination; and the **Civil Rights Act of 1964** contained minor voting-related provisions. However, before Congress addressed issues pertaining to the African American struggle to obtain the right to vote, the U.S. Supreme Court had intervened in a number of voting rights cases. The Supreme Court held in the case of *Guinn and Beal v. United States* (1915), that voter registration requirements containing "grandfather clauses," which made voter registration in part dependent upon whether the applicant was descended from men enfranchised before enactment of the **Fifteenth Amendment**, violated that amendment. The Supreme Court found the Oklahoma law was adopted in order to give whites, who might otherwise have been disfranchised by the state's literacy test, a way of qualifying to vote that was not available to blacks.

Twelve years later, the Supreme Court handed down a unanimous decision in *Nixon v. Herndon* (1927), which overturned a Texas law that forbade blacks from voting in the Texas Democratic primary. Immediately, Texas enacted a new provision to continue restriction on voter participation that granted authority to political parties to determine who should vote in their primaries. In 1944 the Supreme Court held in *Smith v. Allwright* that the Texas "white primary" violated the Fifteenth Amendment.

The southern states experimented with numerous additional restrictions to limit black participation in politics, many of which were struck down by federal courts over the succeeding decades. In the *Gomillion v. Lightfoot* (1960) case, the Supreme Court struck down the Alabama legislature's effort to gerrymander the city boundaries of Tuskegee, Alabama, which removed all but a handful of the city's black registered voters from eligibility. The Supreme Court ruled that by doing so Alabama had violated the Fifteenth Amendment. Although court decisions and civil rights enactments made it more problematical, at least in theory, for states to keep black citizens disenfranchised, the litigious stratagem proved to be of very limited success and it did not prompt voluntary compliance among jurisdictions that had not been sued.

Two months after President Johnson sent the Voting Rights Act of 1965 to Congress, the Senate passed the bill on May 11 and the House passed it on July 10, 1965. After the bills passed by the House and Senate were resolved in a conference committee, the House passed the Conference Report on August 3, and the Senate followed suit on the following day. President Johnson signed the act into law on August 6, 1965. Extended in 1970, 1975, 1982, and 1992, it codified and made permanent the Fifteenth Amendment's guarantee that throughout the United States no person shall be denied the right to vote because of his or her race or color. Outlawing the requirement that voters in the United States take literacy tests to vote, the 1965 Voting Rights Act also provided oversight by the Department of Justice and its approval for any change in voting laws by districts that previously used a device to limit voting.

Although most provisions of the Voting Rights Act are permanent, key provisions such as Section 5, which requires "pre-clearance" of voting changes for covered jurisdictions, and Section 203, which requires voting materials in non-English languages for certain jurisdictions, expired in the summer of 2007. In addition to making certain amendments to the Voting Rights Act, House Resolution 9 reauthorized the expiring provisions for an additional 25 years. On July 27, 2006, President George W. Bush signed the extension into law. Named the **Fannie Lou Hamer**, **Rosa Parks**, and **Coretta Scott King** Reauthorization and Amendments Act of 2006, the act includes the following: Section 5, which requires jurisdictions with a history of

discrimination in voting to get federal approval of any new voting practices or procedures; Section 203, which ensures that American citizens with limited English proficiency get the help they need at the polls; and Sections 6 through 9, which authorize the attorney general to appoint federal election observers where there is evidence of attempts to intimidate minority voters at the polls. The 1965 Voting Rights Act is considered one of the most successful pieces of civil rights legislation enacted by the U.S. Congress.

Linda T. Wynn

Executive Order

President's Initiative on Race, Executive Order No. 13050 (1997)

President Bill Clinton had a vision of one America in the 21st century—a diverse and democratic community in every sense of the word. He wanted people to celebrate their differences as well as embrace a shared vision that would unite America. The President's Initiative on Race was established as an effort to move the country closer to the stronger, unified, and more just America that the president envisioned. It was to offer everyone fairness and a chance to become a part of a great national conversation on racial diversity. President Clinton asked all Americans to become a part of a national effort to speak openly and fairly about race. So committed to this purpose was President Clinton that, on June 13, 1997, his Executive Order No. 13050 established a seven-member President's Advisory Board to the President's Initiative on Race. It would counsel the president on ways to improve the quality of race relations in America.

Headed by historian **John Hope Franklin**, the board reflected at least some of the ethnic diversity in America. The team's charge was "to promote national dialogue on race issues; increase the nation's understanding of the history and future of race relations; identify and create plans to calm racial tension and promote increased opportunity for all Americans; and address crime and the administration of justice." The board also examined issues of race and immigration, the impact of media on racial stereotyping, and the enforcement of civil rights laws already in effect. To meet the full charge, the board reached out to the nation to involve the public in conversations about race. It held a series of meetings across the country, reviewed the charge, and wrote its findings. The Advisory Board traveled, deliberated, held dialogues, worked for 15 months to discharge its duty, and in its September 18, 1998, report presented its findings and recommendations to the president.

The President's Initiative on Race was established as an effort to move the country closer to the stronger, unified, and more just America.

The report, "One America in the 21st Century: Forging a New Future," noted that the final document was not a definitive analysis of racial matters in this nation. "We were engaged in the task of assisting with the initial stages of this new America's journey toward building a more just society in the 21st century," the board wrote. The report stated that the challenges to race matters in America continue to grow, and so does the complexity of giving meaning to a promise for America. By seeking input from communities across the nation and identifying the diverse points of view about race, the board was able to frame those challenges, show opportunities that exist, and recommend action to be taken. The report concluded that the board had simply laid a foundation for the work that needed to be

done to build one America. No single group could accomplish that task; rather, the report said that its work "has provided the Nation with the chance to identify leaders in many given parts of the country, working in numerous fields, who will promote a vision of a unified, strong, and just society." It affirmed the efforts of those who have or will bring meaning to "justice," "equality," "dignity," "respect," and "inclusion."

Jessie Carney Smith

Federal Commission

U.S. Commission on Civil Rights

Established by the Civil Rights Act of 1957, the U.S. Commission on Civil Rights was originally a six-member bipartisan commission responsible for investigating complaints alleging that citizens are being denied their civil rights. Since its inception, the scope of the commission's responsibilities also included reporting and offering recommendations on civil rights problems. Reauthorized and reconfigured by the Civil Rights Acts of 1983 and 1991, and the Civil Rights Commission Amendment Act of 1994, the commission studies and collects information, appraises federal laws and policies, serves as a national clearinghouse for information, submits reports, findings, and recommendations, and issues public service announcements regarding discrimination. In its early years, the commission investigated allegations of racial discrimination in Montgomery, Alabama, and held hearings on the execution of the *Brown v. Board of Education* decision in Nashville, Tennessee, as well as on housing discrimination in Georgia, Chicago, and New York. The commission's findings served as the foundation to the nation's most salient civil rights legislation, including the **Civil Rights Acts of 1960 and 1964**, the **Voting Rights Act of 1965**, and the Fair Housing Act of 1968. After more than a decade, Clarence M. Pendleton became the commission's first African American chairman in 1981, but he opposed both busing as a means of school desegregation and **affirmative action** programs. Other influential African American chairs included **Arthur Fletcher** and **Mary Frances Berry**. Currently, the commission is composed of eight commissioners, four of whom are appointed by the president, two by the president pro tempore of the Senate, and the remaining two by the Speaker of the House of Representatives.

Crystal A. deGregory

Federal Officials and Intervention

Johnson, Lyndon B. (1908–1973)

Marred by the failures of the Vietnam War, and obscured by the martyrdom of his predecessor, **John F. Kennedy**, Lyndon Baines Johnson championed most of the twentieth century's most salient pieces of American civil rights legislation. A consummate politician, Johnson helped persuade President Dwight Eisenhower to achieve some of his social reform measures. Chief among these successes was the passage of the **Civil Rights Act of 1957**, the first legislation of its kind in the twentieth century, and the Civil Rights Act of 1960. Despite being an unlikely candidate, Johnson accepted Kennedy's offer to share his ticket. As Kennedy's successor following his assassination, Johnson worked with civil rights leaders to prevail over southern resistance to secure the passage of the **Civil Rights Act of 1964** and the **Voting Rights Act of 1965**. Johnson used the political influence he secured during his time in the U.S. Senate to advance his Great Society initiatives.

Johnson was born in rural Texas to Samuel Ealy Johnson Jr. and the former Rebekah Baines. After graduating from Southwest Texas State Teachers College in 1930, he briefly taught in Texas public schools. Soon after, he became secretary to a Texas congressman in Washington, D.C. There, he became an admirer of Franklin D. Roosevelt and his New Deal programs. Elect-

Protesters urged President Lyndon Johnson to get more directly involved in the Selma to Montgomery march. During his presidency, Johnson signed two important pieces of civil rights legislation (Library of Congress).

ed to Congress as a New Deal Democrat in a special election in 1937, Johnson remained in the House until 1949. In 1948, he won election as a senator, becoming Democratic whip in 1951, then minority leader in 1953. The following year, Johnson became the second youngest man ever to be named Senate majority leader.

Using the power of persuasion, which he had come to master, Johnson used leveraged political connections to ensure the passage of the 1957 and 1960 Civil Rights Acts. In 1960 Johnson lost his bid for the Democratic Presidential nomination to Kennedy. In an effort to win the South, Kennedy surprisingly offered Johnson the vice presidency, which Johnson accepted. In addition to overseeing the country's burgeoning space program, Johnson served as chair of the President's Committee on Equal Employment

Opportunity and the Peace Corps Advisory Council. Due in large part to Johnson's encouragement, Kennedy framed civil rights in moral terms for the first time during a national address in June 1963, just five months before his assassination on November 22. Under the banner of his Great Society programs, Johnson signed the Civil Rights Act of 1964 with **Martin Luther King Jr.** standing behind him. However, a month later, he initially refused to recognize the integrated delegation of the Mississippi Freedom Democratic Party (MFDP) at the Democratic National Convention of 1964 for fear that he would lose Southern votes in the upcoming election. Later, the brutality of white law enforcement during the **Selma to Montgomery March** led Johnson to send the Voting Rights Act of 1965 to Congress. The legislation not only protected the voting rights of blacks in the South but also tripled the number of black registered voters within three years and changed the makeup of the Democratic Party.

Kennedy was reluctant to meet the call of black leaders for political enfranchisement and social equality.

While he and King later diverged on the issues surrounding the Vietnam War, Johnson had once viewed King as a natural ally for his vision of the Great Society. Less than a week after King's assassination, Johnson invoked his memory when he signed into law the **Civil Rights Act of 1968.** Despite his efforts to secure peace in Vietnam during his last year in office (1968-69), Johnson died of a heart attack at his Texas ranch on January 22, 1973, before this goal was achieved.

Crystal A. deGregory

Kennedy, John F. (1917–1963)

Arguably the most beloved American president of the twentieth century, John Fitzgerald Kennedy helped guide the nation through the Cold War and the struggle from civil rights at home. Despite being portrayed as having a strong commitment to civil rights in the wake of his assassination in 1963, Kennedy was reluctant to meet the call of black leaders for political enfranchisement and social equality. He did, however, set up the President's Committee on Equal Employment Opportunity and regularly lent his support to his brother **Robert F. Kennedy,** who served as attorney general. In 1961 the brothers reluctantly ordered 600 federal marshals to Alabama to protect the "**Freedom Riders.**" The following year, they also notably authorized the intervention of 5,000 federal marshals to quell rioting at the University of Mississippi, after James Meredith became the first black man to desegregate the university.

Born in Brookline, Massachusetts, to business executive Joseph P. Kennedy and Rose Fitzgerald Kennedy, Kennedy was educated at the Choate School, the London School of Economics, and Harvard University. Upon graduation, he served in the navy from 1941 to 1945, during which time he was decorated for his bravery and hailed as a hero for helping rescue crew members in 1943. He began his campaign for the U.S. House of Representatives in 1946, and was reelected twice before winning a U.S. Senate seat in 1952.

Despite suffering nagging illnesses that detracted from his overall effectiveness, Kennedy won a Pulitzer Prize in 1955 for *Profiles in Courage,* a series of biographies of American politicians that he wrote while convalescing after a spinal operation the previous year. After a failed attempt at the vice presidency in 1956, Kennedy was reelected to the Senate. Four years later, his charm and vigor helped him narrowly defeat Richard Nixon to become the country's first Catholic president. In his acceptance speech, Kennedy announced the nation's "New Frontier" and promised "to get America moving again." Kennedy's New Frontier went beyond his encouragement of space exploration. He wished to address the unsolved problems of peace and war, unconquered pockets of ignorance and prejudice, and unanswered questions of poverty and surplus. The "New Frontier" was concerned with all of the problems facing Americans in the 1960s. Kennedy focused his attention domestically on improving health care and helping the working poor, rather than on advancing civil rights legislation. During his presidential campaign, he interceded when **Martin Luther King Jr.** was arrested in Atlanta, Georgia, for a probation violation after participating in a sit-in. On the recommendation of his brother Robert Kennedy, the president famously called Coretta Scott King, King's wife, to lend his support.

Kennedy's relationship to civil rights can only be described as cautious at best. During his second term as senator, he voted against President Dwight Eisenhower's **Civil Rights Act of 1957.** The civil rights legislation he supported during his presidency took a back seat to his role in the Cuban Missile Crisis and issues surrounding the Cold War. It was consistently stalled in Congress. Kennedy initially expressed ambivalence towards the Freedom Rides and the Albany movement before pushing for his administration's participation in the Voter Education Project of 1962 and involving federal troops in the desegregation of the University of Mississippi the same year. Following the brutality of the 1963 Birmingham Campaign, Kennedy introduced a comprehensive civil rights bill that remained filibustered in Congress even after the **March on Washington** and the bombing of the 16th Street Baptist Church in Birmingham, Alabama. Kennedy had not signed any civil rights legislation at the time of his assassination on November 22, 1963. Eight months later, his successor **Lyndon B. Johnson** signed the **Civil Rights Act of 1964.**

Crystal A. deGregory

Kennedy, Robert F. (1925–1968)

For more than 25 years, Robert Francis Kennedy was involved in most of the mid-twentieth century's most important political and legal developments. He was famously the younger brother of President **John F. Kennedy** in whose cabinet he ultimately served. Arguably more committed to civil rights than his elder brother, Kennedy encouraged the president to become more involved in the Civil Rights Movement. As attorney general, he dispatched federal troops to the South to protect activists in many of the region's bloodiest confrontations, including the **Freedom Rides** in 1961 and the

Attorney General Robert F. Kennedy, brother of President John F. Kennedy, talks outside the Justice Department building in Washington, D.C., in July 1963 (Library of Congress).

rioting at the University of Mississippi, after James Meredith became the first black man to desegregate the university in 1962. Following his brother's assassination in 1963, he resigned his post to run for the Senate, where he was an advocate of social reform.

Born on November 20, 1925, in Brookline, Massachusetts, "Bobby" Kennedy, as he was affectionately known, was the son of Joseph P. Kennedy and Rose Fitzgerald Kennedy. He graduated from Milton Academy and attended Harvard before interrupting his studies to serve in World War II as a U.S. Navy lieutenant. In 1946 he returned to Harvard after being honorably discharged and earned his bachelor's degree two years later. Kennedy earned his law degree from the University of Virginia Law School. In 1951 he was admitted to the Massachusetts bar. The following year, he served as his brother's campaign manager for U.S. Senate.

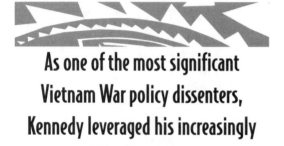

As one of the most significant Vietnam War policy dissenters, Kennedy leveraged his increasingly liberal position.

For the next six years, Kennedy served as counsel to a series of congressional subcommittees. In 1960 he acted as campaign manager for John F. Kennedy's successful campaign for the presidency. During the campaign, Robert Kennedy encouraged his brother to call Coretta Scott King following her husband, **Martin Luther King Jr.**'s, arrest in Atlanta, Georgia, for a probation violation after participating in a sit-in. When the president appointed his brother attorney general, there were widespread accusations of nepotism, but the elder Kennedy remained

resolute. As his brother's closest adviser, Robert Kennedy helped guide the president throughout foreign policy crises in Cuba and Vietnam, as well as the domestic unrest over civil rights.

Kennedy was devastated by his brother's assassination in 1963. He continued to serve in President **Lyndon B. Johnson**'s Cabinet and helped him secure the **Civil Rights Act of 1964**. However, Kennedy was disappointed that Johnson did not choose him as his vice presidential candidate in 1964. The same year, he resigned to run for the Senate from New York. Kennedy increasingly disagreed with the administration on foreign policy, especially regarding Vietnam. However, he backed Johnson's Great Society program and supported civil rights initiatives that desegregated busing and integrated public facilities, as well as advocating the **Voting Rights Act of 1965**. In 1966 Kennedy toured South Africa, championing the cause of the anti-apartheid movement. As one of the most significant Vietnam War policy dissenters, Kennedy leveraged his increasingly liberal position to declare his candidacy for the Democratic nomination in 1968. When King was assassinated on April 4 of the same year, Kennedy gave an impassioned speech in the inner city of Indianapolis, which helped to quell anger in the city, despite rioting in 60 other cities. Just two months later, after winning primaries in Indiana, Nebraska, and California, Kennedy was shot at a campaign function on June 5, 1968, and succumbed to his injuries the next day.

Crystal A. deGregory

The Military

Buffalo Soldiers

During the mid- to late-nineteenth century, the regular U.S. Army was composed of 65 regiments, six of which were to be made up of black troops led by white officers. In 1869 a further reorganization of the regiments occurred, and the black regiments were reduced to four:

the 9th and 10th Calvary and the 24th and 25th Infantry. These regiments played an important role in settling the West, particularly the Texas frontier, the Indian Territory, New Mexico, and Arizona. For the black regiments as a whole, their nickname "Buffalo Soldiers" came from the Native Americans, who saw their short, curly hair as similar to the hair on a buffalo's neck. Their bravery and fighting skill were also seen as similar to that of a buffalo. To the native tribes, however, this was a term of respect and endearment. The men served with distinction, and 14 of them earned the Congressional Medal of Honor in combat against the Apaches, Comanches, and Utes. The regiments also fought in the Spanish-American War, the Philippine Insurrection, and the raids against Poncho Villa. Later, these regiments were stationed in the South, where racial tensions were high and the military was still segregated. When faced with racial prejudices, sometimes they responded with violence, as seen, for example, in the racial outbreaks that occurred in Tampa (1898), Brownsville, Texas (1906), and Houston (1917). After segregation in the military was eliminated in 1952, the black regiments were disbanded or integrated into the rest of the armed forces. A monument honoring the Buffalo Soldiers was unveiled at Fort Leavenworth, Kansas, in 1992, and a Buffalo Soldier National Museum was established in Houston, Texas, in 2000.

Civil War (1861–1865)

As the most costly war ever fought on American soil, the Civil War claimed the lives of an estimated 620,000 soldiers. The conflict between the nation's federal government and 11 southern states that attempted to secede from the Union arose out of longstanding differences over the issues of states' rights to continue slavery and to control trade and tariffs. Despite once being invested in the institution of slavery, the North emerged as the center of anti-slavery sen-

A photo from 1890 of the Buffalo Soldiers taken by Chr. Barthelmess at Fort Keogh, Montana (Gladstone Collection, Library of Congress).

timent in the late 1830s through the 1850s. With the election of Abraham Lincoln to the presidency, southern unease erupted into secession from the Union and the formation of the Confederate States of America (CSA) in February 1861, two months before Lincoln even took office. While Lincoln himself was adamant that the issue of slavery was not at the heart of the conflict, but rather his opponents' insistence in maintaining a free association of sovereign states, the Civil War forced the signing of the **Emancipation Proclamation**, and the Union's victory enabled the passage of the Thirteenth and Fourteenth **Reconstruction Amendments**.

[The Emancipation Proclamation] cemented slavery as the central issue of the war in the minds of many northerners.

Elected as the nation's first Republican president in 1860, Lincoln was considered by southerners to be associated with his party's free labor ideology. Led by South Carolina, seven states, including Alabama, Georgia, Florida, Louisiana, Mississippi, and Louisiana, founded the CSA, electing former Secretary of War Jefferson Davis as its president. Despite Lincoln's promise not to interfere with slavery where it existed, his insistence that he would "hold, occupy, and possess" all federal property would result in conflict.

On April 12, 1861, the Confederate artillery fired on Fort Sumter in Charleston, South Carolina, beginning the war. With both sides quickly raising armies, the Union had the benefit of a population twice as large as that of the Confederacy. Still, the Confederate forces seemed to get the better of the Union during the first two years of

the engagement. Led by Robert E. Lee, the Army of Northern Virginia won or obstructed Union army forces in a series of battles in northern Virginia and Maryland, including the First Battle of Bull Run on July 21, 1861. The defeat of 30,000 of its troops shocked the Union, which began an aggressive campaign to recruit 500,000 soldiers. By the following February, Ulysses S. Grant had begun to chip away at the Confederacy's western defenses. His joint army-navy attacks took Kentucky's Fort Henry and Tennessee's Fort Donelson, but his forces suffered high casualties while fending off an attack near Shiloh.

The following year, 1862, proved to be a decisive one for the war. As a military measure, Lincoln signed the Emancipation Proclamation, freeing slaves in Confederate territories as of January 1, 1863. Its passage cemented slavery as the central issue of the war in the minds of many northerners, and discouraged Britain from offering any aid to the Confederacy. With thousands of blacks joining its ranks for the first time since 1820, the Union boasted several colored regiments, including the **Massachusetts 54th Volunteer Infantry**. Despite Lee's failed attempt to bring the war to a peaceful end by launching an offensive strike at the Battle of Gettysburg, the engagement was the war's largest and most consequential. Following the taking of Vicksburg, Mississippi, on July 4, 1863, Grant, who was promoted to general-in-chief, successfully orchestrated attacks on Richmond, Virginia, and Atlanta, Georgia, before approving General William Tecumseh Sherman's March to the Sea. On April 9, 1865, at Appomattox Court House in Virginia, Lee surrendered the Army of Northern Virginia, effectively ending the war, although the last of the Confederate forces would not surrender until April 26. The Union had prevailed over the South, and in the process of doing so had abolished slavery.

Crystal A. deGregory and Jessie Carney Smith

Davis, Benjamin O., Sr. (1877–1970)

Benjamin Oliver Davis Sr. was born July 1, 1877, in Washington, D.C., and died November

26, 1970, in Great Lakes Nursing Hospital in Washington. He was the first black American general in the U.S. Army. This was in spite of the segregation, racial discrimination, and obstacles facing soldiers in his day. Having been denied admission to West Point, he nevertheless built a successful military career. In 1898 he enlisted as a volunteer soldier during the Spanish-American War (1898–1901). In 1899 Davis enlisted as a private in the regular army and was assigned to the 9th Calvary at Fort Duchesne, Utah. He advanced rapidly through the ranks due to his education, previous experience, and exemplary military service. By 1901 he had been promoted to second lieutenant in the 10th Calvary. In 1915 he was assigned to Wilberforce University, where he spent 14 years as an officer in a noncombatant post. Racial discrimination and governmental hypocrisy towards black soldiers both in and out of the military delayed his promotion to colonel until 1929. After 42 years as a soldier, he was promoted to brigadier general, retiring in 1941. Because of discrimination in the military, he was recalled to duty when America entered World War II to monitor and aid in race relations, equal opportunity, and racial uplift and recognition. Davis was a major force in the efforts to change the U.S. military's policies of segregation. He was awarded the Distinguished Service Medal for his untiring work to combat segregation in the armed forces.

Helen R. Houston

Flipper, Henry Ossian (1856–1940)

Henry O. Flipper was born March 21, 1856, in Thomasville, Georgia, and died May 3, 1940, in Atlanta. He was selected to enter West Point in 1873 and became the first African American to graduate from the academy (1877). He received his commission as a second lieutenant and was assigned the next year to the all-Negro 10th Calvary Regiment, one of the four regiments that made up the **Buffalo Soldiers**. He performed his duties well, but due to racism and jealousy, he was falsely accused of conduct

unbecoming an officer. After a court martial on November 4, 1881, he was dismissed from the service. There was a fruitless effort on the part of some to restore his rank, and from that time until his death Flipper tried to appeal the verdict. It was not until 1976—36 years after his death—that he was acquitted and granted an honorable discharge. Following dismissal, Flipper stayed in the West and worked as an engineer, surveyor, and translator. He served as surveyor for American companies and opened his own mining and engineering office. Because of his familiarity with Spanish and Mexican law, he served as a special agent for the Private Land Claims department formed by the Justice Department; he also translated *Spanish and Mexican Land Laws,* published by the U.S. government in 1895. He continued to work as an oil engineer in Mexico and New Mexico until 1930. Flipper is remembered for his historical place in West Point history and his autobiography of his time in the Academy, *The Colored Cadet at West Point* (1878).

Helen R. Houston

Racial discrimination and governmental hypocrisy towards black soldiers ... delayed his [Davis's] promotion to colonel.

Massachusetts 54th Volunteer Infantry

Most commonly known for its immortalization in the Academy Award-winning 1989 motion picture *Glory,* the 54th Massachusetts Infantry was one of the earliest regiments to be formed during the **Civil War**. Organized in March 1863 by John A. Andrew, Governor of

Massachusetts, the regiment's bravery and courage demonstrated their ability as capable fighters, silencing their critics and encouraging scores of other blacks to join their ranks. Despite being paid less than their white counterparts, they sprung into action following the passage of the Emancipation Proclamation and exhibited nothing less than valor during their service in battle. U.S. Secretary of War Edwin M. Stanton mandated that black units such as the 54th be placed under the command of white officers. As the organizer of the unit, Robert Gould Shaw, the son of a prominent abolitionist family, was promoted to colonel and personally selected each officer.

They [the Triple Nickels] were ... the first African American unit to be integrated into the regular army during that war.

The 54th included both free blacks and ex-slaves from Massachusetts and neighboring states, including several from New York and Pennsylvania. Among the regiment's most well-known recruits were Lewis N. and Charles Douglass, the sons of former slave and famed abolitionist **Frederick Douglass**. Following their training, the unit's recruits were generally restricted to performing manual labor tasks before they were dispatched to Hilton Head, South Carolina. After being ordered to participate in a successful raid on Darien, Georgia, in May 1863, the 54th gallantly held Confederate troops back during combat on July 16 on James Island, South Carolina. The victory, however, was not without casualties: 42 men died in the battle. Two days later, the regiment led an attack

on Fort Wagner near Charleston, South Carolina. This battle secured their legendary fame. While being assailed by Confederate gunfire, 600 of the 54th charged the fort. With more than one hundred casualties, including Colonel Shaw, nearly half the regiment was killed, wounded, or captured. Then-23-year-old sergeant William Harvey Carney received the Medal of Honor on May 23, 1900, nearly forty years later, for carrying the U.S. flag across the battlefield and, despite being repeatedly wounded, returning the flag to his regiment and the Union. As he handed off the flag before falling to the ground he cried out, "Boys, the old flag never touched the ground!" For his bravery, he became the first African American to be awarded the medal, the nation's most prestigious military decoration.

Under the command of Edward N. Hallowell, the 54th participated in other battles in Charleston throughout the remainder of 1863. The following February, they assisted forces in Jacksonville, Florida, before rendering similar service in the Battle of Olustee, where they fought on the front lines alongside the 35th United States Colored Troops. In November 1864, the 54th participated in an unsuccessful attack at the Battle of Honey Hill and served in the April 1865 Battle of Boykin's Mill, one of the war's last engagements. The regiment disbanded soon after the war. Tributes to their courage abound, including a monument on the Boston Common, where Shaw and the 54th are memorialized. Today, the 54th continues to be the most widely recognized African American Civil War regiment.

Crystal A. deGregory

Triple Nickels

America's first African American paratrooper unit, the 555th Parachute Infantry Battalion, popularly known as the "Triple Nickels" (sometimes spelled Nickles), was called to duty on December 19, 1944, by the Army Ground Forces Headquarters. On December 30, the unit was officially activated at Fort Benning, Georgia. They were also the first African American unit to be integrated into the regular army during that war. At the time of the 555th's founding, the U.S. Army was still following its tradition of relegating African Americans to menial jobs. Sometimes black troops were assigned to tasks that placed them at a high risk for failure.

After several weeks of training, the group relocated to Camp Machall, North Carolina, and was reorganized as Company A, 555th Parachute Infantry Battalion. This made them officially the world's first black paratroopers. Walter Morris was the first black enlisted paratrooper, while Bradley Biggs was the first black officer accepted for paratroop duty in the army. Eventually, there were more than 1,300 Triple Nickels. The battalion was never deployed overseas; instead, after jump training the men went to the west coast to watch for possible Japanese attacks. There were brush and forest fires in the area, which some suspect Japanese saboteurs had set. They engaged in dangerous "fire-jumping duty" and made over 1,000 jumps to put out forest fires in Oregon and California. For this assignment they were also called the "Smoke Jumpers."

The 555th was renamed the 505th Airborne Infantry Regiment in 1947 and its troops assigned to the 82nd Airborne Division. The original African American group formed an organization known as the 555th Parachute Association; they made charms of their logo—three stacked buffalo nickels. They set as their motto, "Before us there weren't many, after us there weren't any."

Jessie Carney Smith

Tuskegee Airmen

The segregated U.S. Army Air Force reluctantly opened its ranks to blacks and formed four fighter squadrons comprised solely of black men. The squadrons were known as the Tuskegee Airmen, named for Tuskegee, Alabama, where they took their training. Because the military expected—and hoped—that these men would fail, the training program was called the "Tuskegee Experiment." Of the four squadrons, the 99th Pursuit Squadron was the first group to enter American military aviation. While in aerial combat, these pioneer black units compiled impressive records and later led the air force toward racial parity.

When World War II came, the tradition of maintaining a racially segregated military force was justified as a simple adherence to accepted practices. In particular, the military could not allow blacks to break into what was considered the glamorous branch of service—the U.S. Army Air Corps. This would be a shift in the prevailing view that blacks should be relegated only to menial positions. In military aviation, however, they would be highly visible and would prove that they could master complex machinery. Thus, the pressure to integrate the air corps came from black Americans.

When civilian aviation arrived on the scene in 1939, the government-sponsored Civilian Pilot Training Program (CPTP) accepted blacks and set the stage for opening the air corps to them as well, but only on a segregated basis. On January 9, 1941, the War Department approved plans for an all-black pursuit squadron that the Army Air Corps organized. Blacks officially entered the air corps on July 19, 1941, when twelve blacks were inducted into military aviation training. The new air-training center was located near Tuskegee Institute in Tuskegee, Alabama. The cooperative program originally called the 99th Pursuit Squadron was renamed the 99th Fighter Squadron in May 1942. On October 13, 1942, the 332nd Fighter Group was activated at Tuskegee Army Air Field. It consisted of the 100th, 301st, and 302nd fighter squadrons, and later on the pioneering 99th was added.

The 332nd, known as the "Red Tails" because of the all-red tail surfaces of their P51's, was the only black fighter group in World War II. Some blacks opposed the segregated pilot unit, among them the National Airmen's Association and **William Hastie**, civilian aide on Negro affairs to the secretary of war. Later, Hastie was a judge on

A photo taken in 1945 in Ramitelli, Italy, of some of the members of the Tuskegee airmen (Library of Congress).

the U.S. District Court in the Virgin Islands and governor of the islands. The Tuskegee area was the site selected due to the presence of a veterans' hospital nearby as well as the facilities that Tuskegee Institute offered. The War Department provided money to purchase land located in Chehaw, Alabama, some six miles from the school, to build an air base consisting of hangars, repair shops, dormitories, and space for other facilities. Black architects Hilyard Robinson, McKissack & McKissack, Alexander Repass, and landscape architect David Augustus Williston were involved in the project. The first 75 recruits, who were to become airplane mechanics, received technical instruction at Chanute Field in Illinois, then transferred to Tuskegee to serve the fledgling 99th. Captain Benjamin O. Davis Jr. was appointed military instructor and flight commander.

In July 1941, the training center was dedicated. The black pilots entered aerial combat in the European theater and compiled impressive combat records. While many assumed that the men were of limited capability, what had been ignored was the fact that they were an elite

group, the cream of black youth, and held college degrees. In combat, they saved many bombers and their crews. They engaged in famous battles in Rome, southern France, Greece, the Balkans, and Germany as they fulfilled their "right to fight." The 99th also fought in North Africa. According to Stanley Sandler in *Segregated Skies,* "much of the racial progress in the U.S. Air Force in the post-World War II years can be traced to the pioneer 99th Pursuit Squadron and the 332nd Fighter Group." The Tuskegee Airmen became highly acknowledged, especially in the African American community, and formed an organization by that name to perpetuate the memory of their success.

Jessie Carney Smith

Prisons

Parchman Farm Penitentiary

The Mississippi State Penitentiary at Parchman, which was founded during the period of Reconstruction after the **Civil War**, is widely known for its role as a horrendous maximum-security detention center where civil rights workers and leaders were detained after being arrested during the **Freedom Rides** in the spring of 1961. The penal complex's guards forced the Riders to parade around the cell block naked and tortured them with electric cattle prods, fire hoses, and wrist-breaker cuffs. Because the Reverend C.T. Vivian refused to accept being called "boy," Parchman guards beat him. Others who refused to follow the guards' orders were placed in solitary confinement, which they termed the hot box. Those incarcerated in Parchman also experienced inhumane and humiliating acts at the hands of their jailers. In response to this treatment, the detainees answered with hunger strikes and audacious renditions of freedom songs, which kept their spirits high and strengthened their resolve to continue the fight against white supremacy.

Women activists, such as Ruby Doris Smith, were not exempt from Parchman's horrendous physical abuse. As wardens prepared the women for showers, Smith refused to shed her clothes. Consequently, they took her clothes off and for 20 minutes scrubbed her with a wire brush. As Wesley Hogan noted, prison and incarceration became a central experience to the freedom struggle. Undeniably, during the civil rights years the infamous Parchman Prison was one of the most horrific penal institutions for movement workers and leaders. Like other strongholds of Jim Crowism, Parchman Farm fell when four inmates sued in federal court to put an end to the abusive conditions. The case, *Gates v. Collier,* was decided in 1972 by federal judge William C. Keady, who found that Parchman Farm was an outrage to the prevailing values of civility. He ordered an immediate end to all unconstitutional conditions and practices.

Linda T. Wynn

Resolutions

Anti-lynching Resolution (Senate Resolution 39;2005)

On June 13, 2005, the U.S. Senate passed a non-binding anti-lynching resolution that apologized for its failure to enact such federal legislation in the past. Eighty of the U.S. Senate's 100 members signed on as cosponsors of the resolution. Ironically, Senators Trent Lott and Thad Cochran from the state of Mississippi, where the most incidents of lynching were reported, were not signatories to the resolution. This marked the first time that America's legislative branch formally apologized for the treatment of African Americans. Democratic Senator Mary Landrieu from Louisiana and Republican Senator George Allen from Virginia introduced Resolution 39,

having been motivated after reading the book *Without Sanctuary: Lynching Photography in America* by James Allen. More than a century after Congressman George H. White, an African American from North Carolina, introduced the first anti-lynching bill, the resolution was stalled by opponents on the Judiciary Committee who wished to prevent it from being heard by the full U.S. House of Representatives.

This marked the first time that America's legislative branch formally apologized for the treatment of African Americans.

During the first fifty years of the twentieth century, the lower chamber of the U.S. Congress passed three anti-lynching bills, all of which failed in the Senate. These bills included the Dyer Anti-lynching Bill (1922), which was in response to the **Red Summer** of 1919. More than 20 governors, 39 mayors, 29 college presidents and professors, 30 editors, and a large number jurists and lawyers supported the legislation and urged Senate passage. In 1935 and 1940, the U.S. House passed the Costigan-Wagner and Wagner-Gavagan bills, respectively. Referencing Billie Holiday's 1938 song "Strange Fruit," Senator Landrieu noted there may be no other injustice in American for which the Senate so uniquely bears responsibility.

Linda T. Wynn

Organizations

Groups

Act Associates (est. 1965)

Black activists who were dissatisfied with the established black leadership formed a quasi-functional organization called the Act Associates in 1965. They were opposed to civil rights bills, claiming that they provided little or no help to urban blacks. The group also wanted school systems, which practiced *de facto* segregation, to cease unequal expenditures and other inequities. As a result of their suit against the Washington, D.C., school board, U.S. District Judge J. Skelly Wright of the U.S. Court of Appeals declared on June 19, 1967, that the *de facto* segregation system was unconstitutional. The historic decision banned discrimination in educational funding as well as policy. When local judges avoided becoming involved in political issues affecting the schools, Congress granted the District its first elected school board in nearly 100 years. Although the exact number of Act Associates groups is unclear, it is known that one group, located in Chicago and headed by Nahaz Rogers, remained active for some time. There were 12 founding members of Act, including Jesse Gray, Milton Galamikson, and chair **Julius W. Hobson**. Hobson was the one who initiated the lawsuit and was known as an uncompromising civil rights activist; he was elected to the school board later on.

Jessie Carney Smith

Afro-American League (est. 1890)

The Afro-American League was launched under the leadership of **Timothy Thomas Fortune**, the editor of the newspaper *The New Age*. Delegates representing 23 states met in Chicago in October of 1890, officially forming the League, which grew from the ideas that Fortune espoused in his newspaper. The League's aim was to fight for the civil and political rights of Negroes and full citizenship for all Americans. It espoused racial solidarity, self-help, and confrontation in the face of racial oppression and revolution. These goals were in response to rising discrimination, including: the overturning by the U.S. Supreme Court of the **Civil Rights Act of 1875** by declaring it unconstitutional; the weakening of the **Fourteenth and Fifteenth Amendments**; lynchings; and other practices of disenfranchisement.

Branches of the League were located in 40 cities. J.C. Price, the president of Lincoln University, was elected the League's president. As a vehicle for the fight for civil rights, the League was initially active for only four years. However, it reemerged in 1898 as the Afro-American Council, established by Timothy Thomas Fortune and Alexander Walters, an African American Episcopal Bishop, and advocating and supporting aggressive action and direct challenges to racial practices. The League ceased to exist in 1908. Other organizations, such as the Afro-American Council, **Niagara Movement**, and **NAACP** filled the vacuum it left behind.

Helen R. Houston

By 1960 the ACMHR was lending its full support to the student sit-in movement.

Alabama Christian Movement for Human Rights (est. 1956)

Four black ministers of righteous discontent—the Reverends **Fred L. Shuttlesworth**, Edward Gardner, R.L. Alford, and N.H. Smith—founded the Alabama Christian Movement for Human Rights (ACMHR) in May 1956. Shuttlesworth suggested that the organization include "Christian" in its name, and that it should be "first, foremost, and always Christian." He also emphasized human rights, saying, "We believe that any 'FIRST RIGHTS' IS 'HUMAN RIGHTS. '" The need for the organization was made clear after Alabama's attorney general ordered the **NAACP** to cease operations in the state. After that, the ACMHR, with Shuttlesworth as president, became Birmingham's premiere civil rights organization. Although social and economic barriers divided black Birmingham, the organization reached all black residents equally.

The ACMHR participated in major demonstrations from 1956 to 1965, including boycotts

of businesses and challenges to the legal system. Its first major task in 1956 was to challenge the racially segregated bus system in Birmingham in December, and again in October 1958. The organization sought to integrate local schools and the railroad station in 1957. By 1960 the ACMHR was lending its full support to the student sit-in movement, including the 1961 protests of the **Freedom Riders**. It had the support of the **Southern Christian Leadership Conference** due to Shuttlesworth's affiliation with that organization. The next task was to lead the Birmingham Confrontation in the spring of 1963. That same year, the organization carved a path for **Martin Luther King Jr.** to lead the **March on Washington**. Shuttlesworth left the presidency in 1969, and longtime first vice president Edward Gardner took up the leadership post until the 1990s.

Jessie Carney Smith

American Anti-Slavery Society (1833–1870)

Co-founded in December 1833 in Philadelphia by William Lloyd Garrison and Arthur Tappan, the American Anti-Slavery Society (AAS) led the campaign for the denunciation of slavery as immoral and demanded its immediate abolition. Two years earlier, the society began an abolitionist journal called *The Liberator*. Its impressive propaganda campaigns included printing pamphlets containing the testimony of former slaves and holding public meetings where personalities such as **Frederick Douglass** and **William Wells Brown** offered vibrant condemnations of slavery. By 1838 the organization boasted more than 1,000 chapters and a membership of approximately 250,000.

Despite its early inception, the society was not the first of its kind. As early as 1775, anti-slavery sentiment among the Quakers (also known as the Society of Friends) culminated with the founding of the Society for the Relief of Free Negroes Unlawfully Held in Bondage. This society disbanded during the Revolutionary

War, but it was reconstituted in 1784 with Benjamin Franklin as its first president. Combined with the efforts of other like-minded groups such as the Pennsylvania Antislavery Society and the New York Manumission Society, the gradual emancipation of slaves began in northern states in 1799 in New York. Nine years later, the official prohibition on the importation of slaves marked another significant milestone in the anti-slavery movement. Even so, efforts to sabotage the movement became increasingly apparent by the 1830s, when the AAS was founded. Violent mobs invaded meetings, attacking speakers and burning presses in the process. The U.S. postmaster refused to mail their pamphlets, while southerners burned them. Ironically, their opponents' acts of terror only served to strengthen the abolitionists' case.

In the late 1830s, the movement split because ideological differences surfaced between Garrison, who denounced the U.S. Constitution and advocated sharing organization leadership with women, and more conservative members like Tappan. Despite the departure of the antifeminists, who went on to establish the Liberty Party, the influence of the anti-slavery movement grew through the localized organizations and the growing political nature of the question of slavery. Voting with the Free-Soil and Republican parties, abolitionists also became increasingly involved in the **Underground Railroad** following a series of restrictive slave laws in the 1850s. Following the **Civil War** and the eventual signing of the **Emancipation Proclamation**, the AAS was formally dissolved in 1870.

Crystal A. deGregory

American Missionary Association (est. 1846)

While the American Missionary Association (AMA) was formally established on September 3, 1846, the organization's beginnings can be traced back to 1839, when a committee from the **American Anti-Slavery Society** (AAS) was formed to assist in the defense of African slaves involved in the mutiny against the Spanish owners and crew of the *Amistad* slave ship. The "*Amistad* Committee" included liberal whites Lewis Tappan, Simeon Smith Jocelyn, and Joshua Leavitt, with Tappan in particular credited as being the driving force behind the creation of the AMA. Their group merged with other missionary anti-slavery societies such as the Union Missionary Society (UMS), led by escaped slave James William Charles Pennington, a Congregationalist pastor in Hartford, Connecticut.

The original goal of the AMA was to establish overseas missions for freed slaves, but the organization soon turned its efforts to abolitionist and educational activities in the United States. As well as being promoters of the Christian faith, the "evangelical abolitionists" of the AMA were African Americans and whites who opposed slavery as well as colonization efforts designed to return blacks to Africa. Most were associated with the Congregational or Presbyterian Church and believed in the equality of the races and in integration. From 1850 until the end of the **Civil War** the AMA put its beliefs into practice by establishing a number of churches and more than 500 schools for blacks and whites in the South, as well as by involving African Americans at every level in the organization. Four blacks were members of the first AMA board, including Pennington, Charles Bennett Ray, **Samuel Ringgold Ward**, and Theodore S. Wright. In later years distinguished African Americans such as **Henry Highland Garnet** and Samuel E. Cornish were AMA board members, with Wright and Cornish serving until their respective deaths in 1847 and 1858. **Frederick Douglass** lauded the group for its policies of fairness and inclusion, and he received publishing support from the AMA, while **Mary Ann Shadd** Cary challenged the organization's commitment to integrated schools but later worked at the AMA-supported Lincoln School in Washington, D.C.

During the Reconstruction period, the AMA focused its resources and efforts in creating and supporting higher education institutions for African Americans. The list of Historically Black Colleges/Universities (HBCUs) that were founded by the AMA or received early support from the organization includes the **Hampton Institute** (now University), **Fisk University**, **Howard University**, **Atlanta University**, Straight (now Dillard) University, **Tougaloo College**, **Talladega College**, LeMoyne (now LeMoyne-Owen) College, Avery Institute, and Tillotson (now Huston-Tillotson) College. African Americans were represented among the first AMA teachers in the South, including Mary Smith Peake, who is credited with being the first teacher at a school for freed slaves. Until her death in 1862, she taught at Brown Cottage in Virginia, which became the foundation for the establishment of Hampton Institute.

During the Reconstruction period, the AMA focused its resources and efforts in creating and supporting higher education institutions for African Americans.

The original archives and documents of the AMA were housed at Fisk University until 1969, when they were moved to the Amistad Research Center in New Orleans for microfilming and other preservation initiatives.

Fletcher F. Moon

American Negro Academy (est. 1897)

From 1897 until 1928, the American Negro Academy (ANA) was the first scholarly organization created by and for African American intellectuals. Clergyman and scholar Alexander Crummell led efforts to launch the organization with John Wesley Cromwell, Paul Laurence Dunbar, Walter B. Hayson, and Kelly Miller. Dunbar suggested the name, and the group decided that the membership would be by invitation only, male only, and limited to 50 black intellectuals. The first ANA meeting was held on March 5, 1897, in Washington, D.C., with the goal of seeking to provide alternatives to the philosophy and influence of **Booker T. Washington**. ANA objectives were to offer a "defense of the Negro against vicious assaults, publication of scholarly works, fostering higher education among Negroes, formulation of intellectual taste, and the promotion of literature, science, and art." Founding members Crummell, Cromwell, and other prominent intellectuals such as **W.E.B. Du Bois**, **Archibald H. Grimké** and Arthur Schomburg all served as presidents of the academy over the years. The elitism and small size of the ANA, however, made it difficult to meet financial obligations and led to its demise. Many ANA ideas and strategies were continued through independent work and in other institutions and organizations.

Fletcher F. Moon

Association for the Study of African American Life and History (est. 1915)

Often called the "Father of Black History," Carter G. Woodson was one of several men who, on September 9, 1915, in Chicago, founded what was then called the Association for the Study of Negro Life and History. The organization was the first learned society devoted to the study of black history. Its mission is "to promote, research, preserve, interpret, and disseminate information about black life, history, and culture to the global community." From the time he founded the association, Woodson promoted the history of black people and saw to it that people of all races and from all walks of life had an opportunity to learn the history of African Americans. He used his expertise as a historian and writer to demonstrate to the world that his people did, indeed, have a rich and glorious history.

The association enjoyed the financial support of the Carnegie Corporation, the Rockefeller Foundation, and other organizations, but in the 1920s these donors had withdrawn their support. After that, it was supported largely by blacks. In 1926 the association launched Black History Week, which later became Black History Month to extend the celebration and recognition of black history. By 1950 Woodson reexamined the American identity and expressed concern about racial and ethnic diversity; he thus became known as a pioneer of multiculturalism. In 1972 the organization changed its name and became the Association for the Study of African American Life and History. It publishes the *Journal of African American History* (previously known as the *Journal of Negro History*), and the *Black History Bulletin* (formerly the *Negro History Bulletin*).

Jessie Carney Smith

Association of Southern Women to Prevent Lynching (1930)

Founded in Atlanta by Jessie Daniel Ames, of Palestine, Texas, the Association of Southern Women to Prevent Lynching (ASWPL) came to be as a result of prodding from the Woman's Committee of the Commission on Interracial Cooperation. The Woman's Committee of CIC was organized in 1919. Once founded, black members of the CIC worked hard during the 1930s to persuade the ASWPL to support anti-lynching legislation; however, Ames refused. State branches of the organization, joined by other women's groups such as the Woman's Missionary Council of the Methodist Church South did, in fact, join forces with the Anti-Lynching Crusaders' drive for legislation. Southern black women, notably Lugenia Burns Hope and **Ida Wells-Barnett**, reminded southern progressive white women that they, too, were racists. Nevertheless, unified support was

needed to call for a national bill prohibiting lynching. They wanted the bill to prosecute local officials who served in areas where lynching occurred. The ASWPL favored state laws prohibiting lynching and thought that success might be achieved easier at that level. As the ASWPL worked, they drew threats and hostility from those who opposed their mission. They collected thousands of signatures petitioning anti-lynching legislation. Their efforts extended to alter public opinion and to educate youths on the evils of racism. Although the national lynching campaigners were unsuccessful in their bid to push such legislation through the U.S. Congress, the agitation managed to arouse national sentiment to make lynching a federal offense.

Jessie Carney Smith

Black Cabinet (1930s)

This network of African American advisers to President Franklin Delano Roosevelt represented black interests and concerns during the Great Depression and the New Deal economic recovery programs of the 1930s. Previously, no African Americans had served in an official advisory capacity to a U.S. president. The **NAACP**, the Julius Rosenwald Fund, and other organizations lobbied the Roosevelt administration to appoint blacks as advisers to federal agencies and New Deal programs. Even with the support of First Lady Eleanor Roosevelt, the administration was hesitant to act because of the potential backlash from powerful southern Democrats in Congress. After considerable political maneuvering, Robert C. Weaver received an appointment as an assistant adviser on Negro affairs in the Interior Department. Other African American appointees followed, increasing to 45 the number of black advisers in U.S. government agencies. The network called itself the Federal Council on Negro Affairs, but the press called it the Black Cabinet or Black Brain Trust. The group met regularly at the home of **Mary McLeod Bethune** and worked to influence progressive civil rights developments in politics, government, economic issues, and social welfare. The Black Cabinet also provided a model of successful coalition-building for leaders and organizations during the Civil Rights Movement of the 1950s and 1960s.

Fletcher F. Moon

[T]he administration was hesitant to act because of the potential backlash from powerful southern Democrats in Congress.

Black Panther Party (est. 1966)

The Black Panther Party for Self-Defense was founded by **Huey Newton** and **Bobby Seale** in Oakland, California, in October 1966; it later became known as simply the Black Panther Party (BPP). It was influenced by **Malcolm X** and the writings of Franz Fanon, Che Guevara, Mao Zedong, and Karl Marx. The party advocated a restructuring of American government and called for equality of opportunity and an end to police brutality. The Panthers advocated support for black businesses, the right to bear arms for self-defense, and the right to monitor police actions. These goals, which grew out of their experiences, reading, and consultation with members of the community, were articulated in a Ten Point Program that addressed the needs of the people and the responsibilities of party members. These encompassed a broad definition of self-defense, including self-empowerment and protection against systemic obstacles to equal opportunity and access. The party grew to over 40 domestic chapters, as well as expanding to chapters in England, Israel, Australia, and India. The official newspaper of the party, *The Black Panther,* sold over 100,000 copies a week. The slogans of the BPP most commonly used were "Power to the People" and "Off the Pig"; FBI Director J. Edgar Hoover identified the BPP as "the greatest threat to the internal security of the country"; he established a counter-intelligence program, COINTELPRO, to target the party and its community programs. Police repression, FBI infiltration into the party, and internal conflict contributed to the decline of the BPP, which virtually disappeared by the late 1980s.

Helen R. Houston

Brotherhood of Sleeping Car Porters (est. 1925)

George Pullman created the Pullman sleeping car in the late nineteenth century, and along with it the job of Pullman Sleeping Car porter. He conceived the job as being ideal for black workers. True to the views of the late nineteenth century on the limited roles black people could play in American society, Pullman purported that African Americans were well suited for this service; thus, he sought out black men for the job. Since the nineteenth century, black men generally occupied the profession of Pullman porter. By the 1920s, the Pullman Company was one of the largest employers of black men.

The organization of the Pullman porters was one of the first attempts to unionize black men. Socialist and champion of worker's rights **Asa Philip Randolph** led the union. As co-founder and editor of *The Messenger Magazine,* Randolph was known for his radical political views. While Randolph had made other attempts to unionize workers to fight against exploitation, his most successful venture began in 1925, when he began uniting Pullman porters and other railroad workers. Once the union was established and Randolph was its president, he changed the subtitle of his magazine *The Messenger.* Initially, the magazine's subtitle was "The Only Radical Negro Magazine in America"; once the union was founded, the magazine served to discuss issues pertinent to the union and the workers.

Thus, the subtitle became "The Official Organ of the Brotherhood of Sleeping Car Porters."

By the late 1920s, Randolph's organization represented half of all railroad workers, and in the 1930s the Brotherhood of Sleeping Car Porters represented the railroad workers in negotiations with management. Although founded in 1925, the union was not officially recognized by the Pullman Company until 1937, and the Brotherhood was then able to negotiate for better hours and increases in salary. The Brotherhood was 18,000 members strong by 1950 and became a part of the American Federation of Labor (AFL). In 1957 Randolph became vice president of the newly merged American Federation of Labor and the Congress of Industrial Organizations.

Rebecca S. Dixon

Colored Farmers' National Alliance and Cooperative Union (est. 1886)

The Colored Farmers' Alliance was founded in Houston County, Texas, in December 1886 as an appendage to the southern white Farmers' Alliance movement of the post-bellum period. Its mission was to train African American farmers in agricultural sciences. It also supported black rights, brotherhood, and programs for black farm families. Since it had a connection to the white farmers' organization, it was led by whites who had a paternalistic attitude toward them. These leaders nevertheless worked to keep the black farmers oppressed; they also discouraged any black assertiveness. The black farmers, however, defied them and founded a newspaper called the *National Alliance,* formed a network of farmers' cooperatives, and encouraged their white general superintendent, R.M. Humphrey, to support black farmers' strikes and protests. Whites refused to yield to the black farmers' demands and activism. Protests led to a strike in 1891 by cotton pickers in Arkansas during which several people died. Those black farmers who were thought to be instigators of the strike were lynched. The next year, white resistance destroyed the Alliance.

Jessie Carney Smith

Colored Merchants' Association (est. 1928)

Among the various cooperative movements that took place in the African American community was the Colored Merchants' Association (CMA). The association aided in the development of black-owned grocery stores. In addition to grocery stores, the early cooperatives involved department stores, shoe stores, and other enterprises. The CMA's purpose was to stimulate black business, effect cost savings for customers, and provide jobs for blacks. Founded on August 10, 1928, in Montgomery, Alabama, by local grocer A.C. Brown, the organization soon spread to other states and adopted the slogan "Quality, Service, and Price." The voluntary chain would operate under the banner "C.M.A. Stores," displaying the proprietor's name below the CMA designation. The association promoted cooperative buying and intensive selling—a pronounced difference between the CMA and other cooperatives. CMA taught its members to move their merchandise quickly in an effort to increase profit. Each week the member stores advised each other and promoted their businesses in weekly newspapers, taking care to promote special bargains. The advertisements were reprinted and distributed in black homes within the stores' communities.

CMA stores also worked to enhance business practices; thus, a uniform accounting system was established in each store. After the success of the initial stores, Albon L. Holsey, national secretary of the **National Negro Business League** (NNBL), became involved, visited some of the stores, and was so impressed with the "Montgomery Plan," as he called it, that he recommended that the NNBL support the project. The league did so and Holsey became its national organizer. He would advance the CMA's objectives of promoting modern methods of selling and the psychology of the black consumer, and he united local jobbers and wholesalers. Around the same time, the plan spread to Winston-Salem, North Carolina, in May 1929, making it the second city to open a CMA store.

Holsey helped the plan expand even more, and soon CMA stores were seen in most major American cities, including Dallas, Tulsa, Atlanta, Nashville, Louisville, and Richmond in the South; and Omaha, Detroit, Philadelphia, New York, and Brooklyn outside the South. Most transactions were for cash, with greater sales coming on Fridays and Saturdays. As Holsey moved the plan to Harlem, he emphasized the necessity of training in modern merchandizing methods under the tutelage of experts. Membership grew rapidly, reaching a total of 23 stores in two years. Even the stock market crash of 1929 did not affect the CMAs. By 1936, however, many CMA stores withdrew membership, some claiming that the chain was white owned, others claiming that members intentionally oversold each other on the "specials" that were offered, and still others preferring to sell different chain brands. Despite its eventual failure, the CMAs had benefited from "oneness of action," witnessed the purchasing power of blacks, provided jobs for blacks, and promoted black pride in business ownership.

Jessie Carney Smith

The CMA's purpose was to stimulate black business, effect cost savings for customers, and provide jobs for blacks.

Commission on Interracial Cooperation (1918–1944)

Founded in December 1918, the Commission on Interracial Cooperation was incorporated eleven years later in Atlanta. Membership included prominent blacks and whites who were willing to address the social, political, and economic ills of black Americans. According to historian **John Hope Franklin**, its goal was "to quench, if possible, the fires of racial antagonism which were flaming … with such deadly menace in all sections of the country." White Methodist minister Will W. Alexander led the organization for 25 years. A Department of Women's Work was established in 1920, which enabled black and white women to share their problems in a forum. The commission worked primarily in the South, establishing a program of education in race relations at state and local levels. To train blacks and whites as leaders in promoting interracial work, several 10-day schools were set up. In addition, local interracial committees were formed. When interest was demonstrated, state committees were established, resulting in a state committee in every southern state. The commission spoke against discrimination and violence but did not attack segregation. Through its monthly publication, *The Southern Frontier,* and other mediums, the organization sought justice in government welfare programs, to abolish lynching, to provide for equal justice under the law, and to provide a ballot for all citizens. The commission conducted research on problems of the South, including agriculture, health, and education. Financial difficulties beset the organization by the 1940s, however, when northern philanthropists withdrew their support. On February 16, 1944, the organization was dissolved and then succeeded by the Southern Regional Council.

Jessie Carney Smith

Congress of Racial Equality (est. 1942)

Founded by a group of students in Chicago in 1942, the Congress of Racial Equality (CORE) is an American civil rights organization dedicated to securing equality for all people throughout the world. Influenced by the teachings of Henry David Thoreau and Mahatma Gandhi, its founders and early members were also members of the Chicago branch of the **Fellowship of Reconciliation** (FOR), a religious-pacifist organization. As one of the first organizations in the country to employ Gandhian tactics of coercive non-violent strategy, CORE sponsored a two-week "Journey of Reconciliation" from Virginia to Kentucky to test the 1946 U.S. Supreme Court ruling in the *Morgan v. Virginia* case that banned segregation in interstate travel. More than a decade later, CORE sponsored a similar journey in 1961 that it dubbed the **Freedom Ride**. Over the course of the decade CORE worked hand-in-hand with other civil rights organizations to force the most salient legislative changes in American society.

Led by University of Chicago students **James Farmer** and George Houser, CORE was initially an interracial and nonhierarchical, decentralized organization that was entirely funded by the voluntary contributions of its members. In the same year of its founding, the group organized sit-ins to protest segregation in public accommodations, and Farmer, accompanied by FOR field secretary **Bayard Rustin**, traveled the country to recruit activists at FOR meetings. While the early ranks of its membership were almost entirely limited to middle-class white college students from the Midwest, CORE helped to pioneer the tactical use of coercive nonviolence in the United States. The CORE-sponsored Journey of Reconciliation began on April 9, 1947. Against the advice of **NAACP** leaders, the team of 16 riders, including eight black and eight white men, ventured into the Deep South, where they faced the brutality of white mobs. However, the group only gained national attention when four riders were arrested in Chapel Hill, North Carolina, and three, including Rustin, were sentenced to work on a chain gang.

In 1953 Farmer became the national director of CORE. As the organization spread south, its membership became increasingly comprised of working-class blacks. CORE's initiatives reflected this change. In 1960 CORE officials helped guide the sit-in campaigns of black college students across the region. Modeled after its earlier Journey of Reconciliation, the group organized Freedom Rides the following year. Following the fire-bombing of one of the buses and the

beating of its passengers by a white mob in Birmingham, Alabama, CORE officials called off the rides. Having witnessed their sacrifice, members of the **Student Non-Violent Coordinating Committee** (SNCC) took over the protest. By 1961 CORE had 53 chapters across the United States. Two years later, it helped organize the **March on Washington**. That same year, CORE helped to organize the **Freedom Summer**, a campaign to enfranchise thousands of African Americans in the Deep South. Concentrated in Mississippi, the program resulted in the founding of the **Mississippi Freedom Democratic Party** (MFDP) before its leadership assumed a black nationalist posture in the mid-1960s, following the election of **Floyd McKissick** as national director.

Crystal A. deGregory

Against the advice of NAACP leaders, the team of 16 riders ... ventured into the Deep South.

Congressional Black Caucus (est. 1971)

After passage of the **Civil Rights Act of 1964** and the **Voting Rights Act of 1965**, African American representation in Congress increased. The common concern for the interests of their race led Representative Charles Diggs (D-Michigan) to form the Democratic Select Committee. The committee, comprised of the nine African Americans already in Congress, became active immediately. They fought judicial nominations of judges who were opposed to civil rights legislation, and investigated killings in 1969 of members of the **Black Panther Party** in Chicago, calling the crime racially motivated. The Congressional Black Caucus (CBC) grew out of this committee and was formally established on

June 18, 1971. Diggs became the first chair. In 1976 Yvonne Braithwaite Burke (a California Democrat), became the first woman chair. Early on, the CBC's goals were to promote legislation to bring about racial parity in domestic and international policies.

Since it was founded, the CBC has held an annual Legislative Weekend, a series of meetings devoted to the discussion of timely and important issues related to African Americans. Its town hall meetings, seminars, and forums attract thousands of participants from across the nation. Topics of discussion ranged from housing discrimination to the impact of technology on African Americans. The CBC addresses legislation that affects the poor, women, health care, welfare reform, crime, civil rights, and other issues that impact African Americans and other underrepresented groups. The organization remains successful in the significant legislative issues that it promotes, ranging from the Full Employment Act of 1977 to the celebration of a national holiday to celebrate and honor **Martin Luther King Jr.**. The CBC's goals, activities, and the national priorities are promoted in its various publications. It maintains contact with black elected officials and organizations nationwide, and has become one of the most influential voting blocks in Congress.

Jessie Carney Smith

Delta Ministry (est. 1964)

The National Council of Churches established the Delta Ministry in 1964 to help with the extreme economic depression and lack of opportunity in the black community in the state of Mississippi. Jon L. Regier and a staff of five led the ministry. The National Council of Churches did not envision Delta Ministry as a civil rights organization; however, the primary goals of the organization were similar to those of civil rights organizations of the time. The organization, like the **Student Non-Violent Coordinating Committee** (SNCC), hoped to provide financial relief and education and to

promote self-help and community development. The goals of the ministry included economic development, the establishment of Freedom City, voter registration, community organization, and establishing local black leadership. The organization offered civil and job training, too; it also offered literacy programs and financial assistance in housing and education. Many of the members of the Delta formed close ties with the SNCC and the **Congress of Racial Equality** (CORE). The central office for the ministry was located in Greenville, Mississippi.

One of the ministry's main projects was Freedom City; the program provided housing for agricultural workers who were without adequate housing. Black people formerly living in substandard housing were moved into Freedom City. The ministry stated that Freedom City's primary mission was to promote self-determination among African Americans; Freedom City was to serve as an ideal example for other black communities in Mississippi to follow. In the 1970s, financial difficulties would not allow the ministry to continue to support Freedom City.

Rebecca S. Dixon

Fellowship of Reconciliation (est. 1914)

English and German pacifists founded the Fellowship of Reconciliation (FOR) in 1914, after World War I began. The next year a branch of FOR was opened in the United States. Devoted to social justice, it consistently advocates non-violent direct action to end whatever programs it is protesting, but especially to end wars, fight racism, and combat economic injustice. To FOR, peace means more than absence of war; it necessitates unity and harmony among all people, races, and classes. The organization worked to keep the country out of World War I; it was also sympathetic to conscientious objectors of the war. FOR had been supportive of several well-known organizations, such as the American Civil Liberties Union that it helped to found in 1916. Then its aim was to support conscientious objectors. Since then it has protested the U.S. military actions and the nuclear arms buildup. During the 1920s, its members included **James Weldon Johnson** and Will W. Alexander, who were active in interracial activities. In 1942, the **Congress of Racial Equality** (CORE) was created by FOR as part of its continued commitment to social justice.

Among CORE's field secretaries were **James Farmer** and **Bayard Rustin**, who practiced the non-violent resistance that FOR advocated. The "Freedom Rides" of 1947, which CORE initiated, also had FOR's endorsement. FOR continued its support of social justice groups that emerged during the 1950s and 1960s, including the **Southern Christian Leadership Conference** and the **Student Non-Violent Coordinating Committee**. Although FOR's membership boomed before World War I, since the 1960s its membership has declined. It is the oldest peace organization in the country and continues to support non-violent resistance.

Jessie Carney Smith

Freedmen's Bureau (1865–1872)

The Bureau of Refugees, Freedmen, and Abandoned Lands, or the Freedmen's Bureau, was established by an act of the U.S. Congress on March 3, 1865. As a federal agency in the aftermath of the **Civil War**, the bureau was designed to guide the transition of newly freed slaves from slavery to freedom. Its vast array of services ranged from establishing schools and conducting military courts to negotiating the terms of former slaves' employment and providing emergency food, clothing, and shelter in the aftermath of the war. Arguably the most salient initiative of the Reconstruction period, the bureau was a source of hope for a generation of African Americans and is credited with helping to establish many of the country's historically black colleges.

Organized under the War Department, the bureau was directed by Major General Oliver O. Howard, who served as its commissioner.

Known as the "Christian General," Howard was given command of the Army of Tennessee in 1864 and assisted General William T. Sherman in the 1864 to 1865 March to the Sea campaign. During the five-week, 285-mile raid from Atlanta to Savannah, Howard visited the South Carolina coastal islands, which had been seized by slaves once planters abandoned them in 1861. The success of slaves in farming small holdings of former large plantations led Congress to envision a similar sharing of other abandoned lands in 40-acre units to slaves across the South under the supervision of the bureau. President Andrew Johnson, however, soon reneged on Congress's plan for land redistribution. By exploiting the privilege of presidential pardons, he returned former white slave and land owners almost all the land that was appropriated for redistribution to freed slaves.

The organization [Fellowship of Reconciliation] worked to keep the country out of World War I; it was also sympathetic to conscientious objectors of the war.

Howard had divided the former slave states, as well as the border slave states that had remained in the Union, into 10 districts. While Congress did not even appropriate money for the salaries of field agents, Howard appointed an assistant commissioner to each district to supervise their work. Although the bureau's initial purpose was to provide food, housing, and medical aid to ex-slaves, the return of land to former slave owners forced the bureau to also develop an alternative plan to help freedmen support themselves. The bureau's new scheme included convincing ex-slaves to enter into labor contracts with former slaveholders in field gangs or as tenant farmers or sharecroppers.

Intended to be a temporary agency, the bureau's original authorization was only for one year. In 1866 President Andrew Johnson vetoed a bill that would have indefinitely extended its life and significantly increased its powers. Despite signaling the beginning of the president's long and unsuccessful fight with the radical Republican Congress over Reconstruction, the bill was passed in a slightly different form over Johnson's veto later the same year. During its seven years of existence, the bureau appropriated more than $15 million for food and other aid to freed slaves. Among its most lasting contributions to African American life was the support of black education. The bureau spent over $6 million for schools and educational work, and by 1871 it had helped found 11 colleges and universities and 61 normal schools. The bureau closed in 1872.

Crystal A. deGregory

Greensboro Bicentennial Mosaic Partnerships Project (est. 2004)

Concerned about the distrust between the white and black races in Greensboro, North Carolina, in September 2004 Mayor Keith Holliday announced a program that would begin in November to ease that distrust and other racial tensions. The aim was to repair the racial divide before the city's 200th birthday in 2008. "I continue to be concerned about many of our citizens living and working in their 'comfort zones,'" Holliday said in the *News and Record.* While relations between the city's blacks and whites had improved since the civil rights movement, local residents still lived and worked without interacting with each other at the time the mayor made his announcement. Consequently, they find it hard to trust each other. Local residents have difficulty talking about race relations, too. The new program, as

well as the existing Greensboro Truth and Community Reconciliation Project, have similar goals but employ different approaches to the problem. Some members believe that the wounds of the past must be healed before progress can be made. They remember a 1979 anti-Ku Klux Klan march through a public housing project in Greensboro that left race relations tense. The Greensboro Bicentennial Mosaic Partnership Project is comprised of 180 top civic leaders across racial lines. The program was deliberately limited to leaders because they set examples for those under their charge. They meet monthly in small groups and socialize as well as discuss racial issues. As they share experiences with the Greensboro Truth and Community Reconciliation Project, the two may become friends.

Jessie Carney Smith

Housewives' League of Detroit (est. 1930)

Blacks who migrated from the South to northern cities beginning in the mid-1920s, and especially during the Great Depression of the 1930s, met a fierce struggle for employment, housing, education, and treatment as equal partners in society. As conditions worsened, black women in Detroit established an organization to provide mutual aid, promote self-determination, and address economic needs. Having experienced the success of black women's organizations that they had founded earlier, they put their organizational skills to work. Fifty black women met on June 30, 1930, to plan for the organization that grew out of the initial meeting: the Detroit Housewives' League. It grew quickly and by 1934 membership reached 10,000. Various neighborhoods in the city had their own chapters. Chapters were developed elsewhere, too, including Baltimore, Chicago, the District of Columbia, and the Harlem section of New York. The main purpose of the league was to support black businesses, encourage members to buy black products, patronize black professionals, and ensure that black residents kept their money in the black community. The women promoted black family life and encouraged white and black businesses to hire black youths as clerks or stockpersons. They offered their patronage to those who did. They organized lectures across various cities, planned displays for state fairs, reviewed picketing and boycotting strategies, and distributed information on black economic self-help. So effective was the work of the various chapters that, during the Great Depression, many black businesses survived. The Detroit league faded from view in the late 1960s.

Jessie Carney Smith

Mississippi Freedom Democratic Party (est. 1964)

Members of the **Student Non-Violent Coordinating Committee** (SNCC) founded the Mississippi Freedom Democratic Party (MFDP) in 1964. The party was formed as a part of the initiatives of the Mississippi Summer Project. It was intended to encourage black people to register to vote despite the violent intimidation visited upon black Mississippians by hostile white racists. SNCC recognized that the Democratic Party did not adequately represent the large population of African Americans in Mississippi. The MFDP's mission was therefore to serve the political interest of the African American community in that state. Founding member **Fannie Lou Hamer** was instrumental in the development of the party. Hamer, a native of Montgomery County, Mississippi, had been active in the founding of **Delta Ministry** and worked as field secretary for the SNCC. Key members such as Hamer, Unita Blackwell, Victoria Gray, Ruby Hurley, and Winnie Hudson organized meetings and people from 40 counties; they attended meetings to select 68 delegates to represent Mississippi. The MFDP intended to attend the Democratic Presidential Convention in Atlantic City, New Jersey, and be seated in place of the all-white Democratic delegates who supposedly represented Mississippi. Instead, the Democratic Party stated that two members of the MFDP could serve in place of the elected white delegates. The MFDP rejected the offer and challenged the appointments of five of Mississippi's U.S. Congressmen. They claimed that those elected officially had not been elected fairly, since black citizens had not been allowed to register and vote. In 1964 Fannie Lou Hamer ran unsuccessfully for Congress, representing the MFDP.

Rebecca S. Dixon

Montgomery Improvement Association (est. 1955)

Black ministers and community leaders formed the association on December 5, 1955, four days after the arrest of **Rosa Parks**, who refused to give up her seat on the Cleveland Avenue bus, driven by James F. Blake in Montgomery, Alabama. Under the leadership of **Martin Luther King Jr.**, as president, the MIA was instrumental in guiding the **Montgomery Bus Boycott** that focused national attention on the racially segregated South and catapulted King into national prominence. Other officers included: Roy Bennett, the first vice president; Moses W. Jones, second vice president; Erna Dungee, financial secretary; U.J. Fields, recording secretary; E.N. French, corresponding secretary; Edgar Daniel Nixon, treasurer; C.W. Lee, assistant treasurer; and A.W. Wilson, parliamentarian. Subsequent to the MIA's initial meeting, the executive committee drafted the demands of the boycott, which included: courteous treatment by bus drivers; first-come, first-served seating, and the employment of African American drivers. The executives agreed that the mass protest would continue until the city met their stated demands. Over the course of the next year, the MIA organized carpools and held weekly mass meetings to keep the African American community mobilized against Montgomery's transit company.

After a successful fund-raising campaign, the association hired the Reverend R.J. Glasco as King's executive secretary. Officers of the MIA negotiated with Montgomery's functionaries, supported the boycott financially, solicited support from civil rights organizations, and, with the NAACP, coordinated legal challenges to the city's segregated bus ordinance. However, the organization's vision covered more than just the abuse African American passengers experienced on Montgomery's buses; its mission also included the overall improvement of race relations and bringing down the wall of Jim Crowism.

[The Montgomery Improvement Association's] vision ... included the overall improvement of race relations and bringing down the wall of Jim Crowism.

Early in 1956, the MIA suffered a setback when Alabama officials were determined to defeat the Montgomery bus boycott movement. On February 21, 1956, King and 89 others were indicted for violating the state's anti-boycott law of 1921, which prohibited boycotts against businesses. Represented by eight attorneys, including local attorney **Fred Gray**, King endured a trial that began on March 19 and ended on March 22, when Judge Eugene W. Carter found him guilty and fined him $500, as well as another $500 for court costs. King chose to appeal his verdict rather than pay the fine.

Despite the legal troubles of the MIA's president, the Montgomery Bus Boycott continued. On November 13, 1956, the U.S. Supreme Court upheld a federal district court's ruling in the *Browder v. Gayle* (1956) case that ended segregated seating on public buses. Brought on behalf of Aurelia S. Browder, Susie McDonald, Claudette Colvin, Mary Louise Smith, and

Jeanatta Reese (who later withdrew from the case), the *Browder* case affirmed that segregation on Alabama's intrastate buses was unconstitutional. The Supreme Court rejected both city and state appeals to reconsider its decision on November 17.

One month after city and state officials received the decree, King and the MIA voted to end Montgomery's 381-day bus boycott. On December 21, 1956, African Americans returned to riding the Montgomery public system of transportation. The following month, the MIA became one of the founders of the **Southern Christian Leadership Conference** (SCLC). Three years after establishing the SCLC, in 1957 King returned to Atlanta. Under the leadership of **Ralph David Abernathy**, Solomon Seay, and Johnnie Carr, the MIA continued campaigns into the 1960s, focusing on voter registration, local school desegregation, and the desegregation of public facilities and accommodations.

Linda T. Wynn

NAACP, the National Association for the Advancement of Colored People (est. 1909)

Founded in 1909, the National Association for the Advancement of Colored People (NAACP) has been at the helm of the American freedom struggle since the turn of the twentieth century. An interracial group of white progressives and black militants formed in response to the Springfield, Illinois, race riot of August 1908 as an outgrowth of the **Niagara Movement**. As the nation's first integrated institution of its kind, the NAACP had a militant platform that demanded civil rights as well as educational and political equality for all Americans.

Relying on the courts as a means to secure these objectives, NAACP officials focused on eradicating inequalities in public education up until the mid-twentieth century. Its most salient victories include the now legendary *Brown v. Board of Education* (1954) ruling, which arguably signaled the beginnings of the modern Civil Rights Movement. Despite its philosophical differences with groups like the **Congress of Racial Equality** (CORE) and **Student Non-Violent Coordinating Committee** (SNCC), which primarily focused on direct-action protest, the NAACP enjoyed successes second to none among American civil rights organizations.

Following the 1908 Springfield riot, an eminent interracial group including Niagara Movement founder **W.E.B. Du Bois** and member social worker Mary White Ovington sent out "The Call" for a national conference on black rights. The meeting was planned for the centennial of Abraham Lincoln's birthday, February 12, 1909. In May of the same year, more than 40 people attended the organization's conference in New York and formed the National Negro Committee. During the group's second conference in May 1910, they formally renamed the organization the NAACP, which was incorporated the following year. Its mission was to promote equality, eradicate class and race prejudice, and to advance the interest of colored citizens by securing truly universal suffrage, justice under the law, and education for all children.

As the sole African American on the NAACP's founding board, Du Bois also served as the founder and editor of the organization's official publication, *The Crisis* magazine, a current affairs journal showcasing black literature, history, and culture. While its leadership remained white well into the mid-twentieth century and the organization did not elect its first black president until 1975, the NAACP tackled the nation's pressing issues of mob violence and lynching, as well as pushed for the commissioning of African Americans as officers in World War I within 10 years of its founding. Over the course of the next three decades its membership grew steadily as the NAACP championed additional causes, including the abolition of restrictive tests that typically disenfranchised blacks, the nullification of Jim Crow housing ordinances, and the desegregation of public education.

By 1950 the NAACP had already amassed an impressive record of successful litigation efforts due in part to the leadership of **James Weldon Johnson**, who served as the organization's executive secretary, and **Charles Hamilton Houston**, who was dean of the **Howard University** Law School. Together, with his mentee **Thurgood Marshall**, Hamilton helped the NAACP win the cases that led to the desegregation of American public education. Over the course of its history, the NAACP has been led by such notables as Roy Wilkins, **Myrlie Evers-Williams**, **Julian Bond** and, more recently, **Kwesi Mfume**. Today, the NAACP continues to fight for social justice to ensure that the voices of African Americans are heard.

Crystal A. deGregory

While its leadership remained white well into the mid-twentieth century ..., the NAACP tackled the nation's pressing issues of mob violence and lynching.

National Association of Colored Women (est. 1896)

The National Association of Colored Women (NACW) was established in Washington, D.C., in 1896, when the National League of Colored Women and the National Federation of Afro-American Women merged. When the united NACW was established, it also welcomed African American women from various social and political women's organizations. The founders of the NACW announced that their mission was to provide evidence that the "moral, mental and material progress" of

African Americans was made possible by black women. They believed that black women were responsible for the promotion of the ethical standards of their communities. The NACW's early efforts focused on education, lynching protests, and eliminating discriminatory practices in the judicial system. The first president of the organization was **Mary Church Terrell**.

Like other women's organizations of the period, the NACW championed temperance, self-help, and political rights for women.

Like other women's organizations of the period, the NACW championed temperance, self-help, and political rights for women. The members of the organization espoused middle-class values. Their main emphasis, however, was on the home and education. Many of the women helped develop educational programs, including kindergartens. These kindergarten programs also included instruction for mothers on child care and health. The NACW also was committed to care for the elderly, orphaned and abandoned children, and the indigent. **Mary McLeod Bethune** served as director of NACW in the late 1920s. In 1935 Bethune, with the support of the NACW, established the National Council of Negro Women (NCNW). In many ways this actually weakened the influence of the NACW, and after the 1930s its membership declined.

Rebecca S. Dixon

National Dental Association (est. 1900)

The National Dental Association began in 1900 with the increase in the number of trained dentists and the need to have a professional organization. It took several local and regional organizations before the national group was established. Initially there was the Society of Colored Dentists in the District of Columbia (founded in 1900); this became the Robert T. Freeman (first black dental college graduate) Dental Society in 1907. With the urging of Dr. D. A. Ferguson of Richmond, Virginia, a national organization was formed on May 1, 1901, but it lasted only five years. In 1913 Dr. Ferguson succeeded in establishing the first regional organization of black dentists, Tri-State Dental Association; these dentists were from Virginia, Maryland, and the District of Columbia, and by 1918 the group had grown to include 14 states. This expansion emphasized the need for a program of national scope, and in 1918 it was reorganized to become the Interstate Dental Association. In 1932 in Bordentown, New Jersey, the Commonwealth Dental Society of New Jersey and the Interstate Dental Association joined to form the National Dental Association. The association set out to strengthen its organizational structure, increase and educate its members, and define its mission. The association, the largest organization of minority oral health professionals, continues its commitment today in advancing the rights of those in the dental profession, as well as serving disenfranchised minorities, children, the indigent, the elderly, and the disabled. Its publications are *Flossline,* a quarterly newsletter that reports association activities, and the *Journal of the National Dental Association,* which reports technical and scholarly information.

Helen R. Houston

National Equal Rights League (est. 1864)

Historically, organized efforts to promote the civil rights of African Americans have been numerous. The National Equal Rights League (NERL) was one such effort. It was founded in 1864 with John Mercer Langston, its first president. A second league was formed in early 1908, with William Monroe Trotter as a founder. The

NERL was a forerunner of the **Niagara Movement** that **W.E.B. Du Bois** organized to protest **Booker T. Washington**'s conservative views. It was also a forerunner of the **NAACP**, formally founded in 1910. For a number of years, Trotter worked through the organization to agitate for the rights of black people. Those who were unable to accept the principles of the NAACP had as an alternative the NERL. Trotter and his followers did not fully embrace the NAACP. The two organizations also competed with each other for members. The NAACP, with its moderate approach to matters of race, grew in importance and membership numbers. Trotter, however, employed discordant tactics, which made his organization less successful. He openly criticized Republican William Howard Taft's election to the presidency, attacked President Woodrow Wilson's racial policies, and met with presidents Warren G. Harding and Calvin Coolidge to attack the federal government's racial practices. By the 1920s, when he unsuccessfully tried to form a relationship between the NERL, Marcus Garvey's **Universal Negro Improvement Association** movement, as well as the African Blood Brotherhood, the league folded in the 1920s.

Jessie Carney Smith

National Medical Association (est. 1895)

The National Medical Association (NMA) was established in 1895 as a response of African American physicians and other health professionals to their denial of membership in the American Medical Association. At the Cotton States and International Exposition held in Atlanta, Georgia, the NMA was established at the First Congregational Church. The initiators of the meeting of professionals that led to this were Dr. Miles V. Lynk of Memphis, Tennessee, and Dr. Robert F. Boyd of Nashville, who was subsequently elected as the association's first president. The association was opened to all, but its focus was on African Americans' health and the elimination of disparities in health and professional medical care before World War II. Following the

war, the emphasis expanded to include ways of addressing the health needs of a growing population, increasing the number of minority physicians, and improving the overall health of the black population. In keeping with its concern for an informed and educated body of medical professionals, it began publishing the *Journal of the National Medical Association* in 1909, edited by Dr. Charles V. Roman. It was a quarterly scholarly publication that provided information on research and findings. In 1957 the NMA, along with the **NAACP**, the **National Urban League**, and the Medico-Chirurgical Society of the District of Columbia, sponsored the first Imhotep National Conference on Hospital Integration. In 1960 the NMA participated in activism by advocating civil rights. The results of its involvement can be seen in government-funded health programs, Medicare, and Medicaid. Today, the NMA continues its fight for parity.

Helen R. Houston

National Negro Business League (est. 1900)

Controversy surrounds the history of the National Negro Business League (NNBL). **W.E.B. Du Bois** is said to have called for such an organization "in every town and hamlet" where blacks lived in 1899, but was unable to follow through with his plan. Credit has been given to Tuskegee Institute president **Booker T. Washington** for actually bringing the organization to life. He visited African American businesses all over the country, observed their struggles, noted that banks denied them loans, and concluded that a league was needed to work together on their behalf. He wanted the group to be political and thought that many wealthy black business leaders could work collectively to benefit many areas of American life. He also called for representation from every business in which black men and women were involved. The first meeting of the league was held in Boston, with 300 delegates present. They elected Washington president, an office he held until he died in

1915. He saw the organization as an instrument for a new emancipation that could come about through black economic independence. After Washington died, leaders from Tuskegee continued to head the organization until 1945. Until 1923 the NNBL was actually based at Tuskegee. The organization is still in existence. Its mission is to encourage African American business leaders and youth to become entrepreneurs. Since its founding, the NNBL has closely adhered to that mission. Among its various initiatives, it helps blacks establish new ventures, promotes youth business developments, and encourages African Americans to buy from members of their race.

Jessie Carney Smith

National Urban League (est. 1911)

As one of the earliest organizations of its kind, the National Urban League has been a grass-roots leader in the twentieth-century struggle to secure African American civil rights and economic opportunity. Founded as the Committee on Urban Conditions Among Negroes on September 29, 1910, by Ruth Standish Baldwin, the widow of railroad magnate and philanthropist William H. Baldwin Jr., and by **Fisk University** and Columbia University graduate George Edmund Haynes, the league was fostered through the consolidation of the Committee for Improving the Industrial Condition of Negroes in New York (founded 1906) and the National League for the Protection of Colored Women (founded 1906). Renamed the National Urban League in 1911, the interracial organization was not only committed to securing economic and social parity for blacks, but also advocated integration. Its goals were particularly geared toward northern populations of blacks who had migrated during the **great black migration** in search of economic opportunity only to find that racism also pervaded the North and often reduced them to manual labor. The league quickly emerged as a leader in the fight for blacks in urban settings. Through its artful

George Edmund Haynes was co-founder of the National Urban League, along with Ruth Standish Baldwin (Fisk University).

mastery of negotiation and persuasion, the league successfully pushed for better educational and employment opportunities for African Americans for almost a century.

The Great Depression was a difficult period in the history of United States. Its effects on black communities, however, were particularly amplified. Consequently, the league worked aggressively to have African Americans included in federal relief and recovery programs, encouraged boycotts of businesses that refused to employ blacks, and forced the desegregation of labor unions. In response to the boom in the defense industries during the 1940s, the league pressed for an end to discrimination and demanded the desegregation of the U.S. armed forces. In 1941, under the leadership of Lester Granger, the league rallied around A. **Philip**

Randolph and **Bayard Rustin**'s efforts to organize a March on Washington.

In the educational sector, the league pressured schools to expand vocational opportunities, all the while pursuing its strategy of "education and persuasion." Throughout the 1960s, it kept pace with the efforts by other groups that demanded African American civil rights during the modern Civil Rights Movement. With the election of **Whitney M. Young** as the organization's president in 1961, the league was able to extend its fundraising ability and become more involved with its cohorts, who primarily focused on direct action as a means to achieving racial equality. In 1963 the league participated in the planning of the Randolph and **Martin Luther King Jr.**-led **March on Washington**. While his 10-year tenure was tragically cut short when he died in a swimming accident off the coast of Lagos, Nigeria, in 1971, Young's vision for the closure of economic racial disparities and commitment to health, job training, and educational services to communities was extended by subsequent directors. Among these is **Vernon E. Jordan Jr.** and, more recently, through the leadership of president and chief executive officer Marc H. Morial, a former mayor of New Orleans.

Crystal A. deGregory

New Negro Alliance (est. 1933)

John Aubrey Davis, Belford Lawson, and M. Franklin Thorne, who worked with Ralph Bunche, **Thurgood Marshall**, William Hastie, James Nabrit, and other activists formed this group to improve accommodations, fair treatment, and employment of African Americans in Washington, D.C., during the period preceding World War II. The alliance participated in a boycott of the Hamburger Grill in Washington after it fired black employees in August 1933. Using the slogan "Don't Buy Where You Can't Work," they mobilized support from black Washingtonians in the academic, legal, and religious communities, and the boycott was successful. The New Negro Alliance (NNA) was formally organized in 1935 for direct action to secure black economic rights, but they should not be confused with Alain Locke and the "New Negro" cultural movement of the 1920s. The NNA achieved its greatest success in *New Negro Alliance v. Sanitary Grocery Company* (1938). Lawson, Marshall, Hastie, and Nabrit were on the NNA legal team that argued the case before the U.S. Supreme Court on March 5, 1938, which was decided in their favor by a 62 vote of the justices on March 28. This legal victory led to Executive Order 8802 by President Franklin Delano Roosevelt on June 25, 1941, mandating fair treatment of employees in agencies of the federal government, and establishing the Fair Employment Practices Committee (FEPC). Davis began work with the FEPC, and the NNA soon ceased to exist in the 1950s after he left.

Fletcher F. Moon

Niagara Movement (1905–1910)

As the first American civil rights organization of the twentieth century, the Niagara Movement arguably influenced all modern civil rights initiatives that followed. Founded in 1905 by **W.E.B. Du Bois** and **William Monroe Trotter** and comprised of the leading African American intellectuals of the time, the organization was established as a challenge to **Booker T. Washington**'s accommodationist stance. While the movement disbanded soon after its founding, its commitment to affecting legal change and its efforts to address issues of crime, economics, religion, health, and education were reborn in the **NAACP**, which many of its members helped to establish.

While a closed-door meeting at New York's Carnegie Hall in 1904 created the Committee of Twelve for the Advancement of the Interest of the Negro Race, infighting led the group to disband. The following year, Du Bois and Trotter extended invitations to 59 leading African Americans who opposed Washington to attend a meeting in western New York that summer. In addition to being the nation's eighth largest city,

Buffalo had historically been associated with the struggle for freedom from slavery, and western New York was considered an important crossing point on the **Underground Railroad** for runaways headed to safety in Canada. However, a Buffalo hotel refused to accommodate the attendees, forcing them to move their organizational efforts to the Canadian side of Niagara Falls. Twenty-nine African American businessmen, writers, teachers, and clergy met from July 11 to 14, 1905, to form the Niagara Movement. Its name honored the place of its founding and acted as a constant reminder of the "mighty current" of protest its founders wished to unleash on American society. Du Bois was named general secretary of the organization.

[The] Niagara Movement arguably influenced all modern civil rights initiatives that followed.

While the founders divided responsibilities among state chapters, the organization had only 170 members at the end of its first year. Despite its relatively small membership and financial constraints, members continued to distribute pamphlets and lobbying against Jim Crow. They sent circulars and protest letters to President Theodore Roosevelt after the Brownsville affair in 1906. The Niagara Movement held its second conference at Harper's Ferry, West Virginia, in the summer of 1906. In the years that followed, the group held its annual meetings at other sites that represented the freedom struggle, including Faneuil Hall in Boston. However, Washington's determined opposition barred virtually all white assistance to the Niagara Movement and limited its effectiveness. It was not until a violent race riot in Springfield, Illinois, in 1908, that the

Niagara Movement effectively paved the way for the creation of the more powerful, interracial NAACP in 1909.

Crystal A. deGregory

Oval Table Gang (1960s)

Civil rights activities in Raleigh, North Carolina, during the 1950s and 1960s included organized efforts of a group of local and influential black leaders who for two decades, beginning with the early 1960s, gathered around June Elizabeth Kay Campbell's kitchen table. They called themselves the "Oval Table Gang" and took their name from the oval-shaped table with a cast iron base and glass top that June Campbell bought. The exact date of the group's founding is unclear. The table became historic and represented the behind-the-scenes, grassroots activism that often occurred during the Civil Rights Movement. The gang saw themselves as a black think tank and worked to desegregate Raleigh's school system, support black candidates for office, organize demonstrations (including sit-ins at Woolworth's, pickets of the Ambassador movie theater, and boycotts), and fight redistricting that threatened to dilute black political power.

June Campbell (1925–2004) opened her home to the group, presided over the meetings, and became known as the matriarch of Raleigh's civil rights struggle. Most of the members held important leadership positions, such as superior court judge, minister, state senator, and county commissioner. The gang also included Campbell's sons: Ralph Campbell, who became North Carolina's state auditor and the first black elected to the Council of State, and William "Bill" Campbell, mayor of Atlanta from 1994 to 2002. June Campbell is documented in a 1960 photograph, which shows her leading her young son Bill through a group of hostile white onlookers to Murphey School in Raleigh on September 7. This was his first day at the school he integrated. She took the challenge of walking with her son because her husband, civil rights activist and postal worker Ralph Campbell Sr., had been threatened with the loss of his job if he escorted Bill to school. At his mother's death, Bill Campbell said that "most of the women in the civil rights movement were seen through the prism of their more celebrated spouses. But those ladies were on the front lines, just like my mother, marching every day." After Ralph Campbell Sr. died in 1983, the meetings ceased. Though barely visible on the political scene, the gang was one of Raleigh's most powerful civil rights groups.

Jessie Carney Smith

People United to Serve Humanity (est. 1971)

This organization, better known by the acronym PUSH, was founded by **Jesse Jackson Sr.** in 1971 to address economic issues and problems faced by African Americans. It replaced Operation Breadbasket, the economic arm of the **Southern Christian Leadership Conference** (SCLC). Its acronym originally stood for People United to Save Humanity, but changed later to mean People United to Serve Humanity. From its base in Chicago, PUSH organized boycotts of businesses and corporations that were unfair to black consumers and/or were lacking in minority employment and advancement opportunities. Jackson used his charismatic personality to draw media attention to targeted companies, enter into negotiations with corporate boards and executives, and secure agreements favorable to African American employees and customers. PUSH also highlighted black-owned and black-managed business enterprises, and encouraged more interactions and business opportunities with mainstream America and Wall Street.

In the late 1970s, the organization also focused its attention on education for African Americans through its PUSH for Excellence program (later known as PUSH/EXCEL), but this effort was less successful because of administrative problems. In the 1980s Jackson turned to more direct human rights and political

involvements including the anti-apartheid movement, securing the release of African American Navy Lt. Robert Goodman from Syria, and two unsuccessful presidential campaigns in 1984 and 1988. As a result, he withdrew from official leadership of PUSH (which had received Federal support) to organize the Rainbow Coalition political organization. He returned to a more active role in PUSH during the 1990s, and in 1996 merged the two organizations into the Rainbow/PUSH Coalition.

Fletcher F. Moon

Southern Christian Leadership Conference (est. 1957)

The impetus for the founding of SCLC was the success of the non-violent **Montgomery, Alabama Bus Boycott** that took place from December 5, 1955, until December 21, 1956. This sparked a chain of boycotts across the South. It became apparent at a meeting with **Martin Luther King Jr.**, **Ralph David Abernathy**, **Fred Shuttlesworth**, **Bayard Rustin** and others that there was a need for a central coordinating body for these boycotts. Thus, from January 10 through 11, 1957, 60 disparate regional groups from 10 states met in Atlanta, Georgia, and formed the Southern Leadership Conference on Transportation and Non-Violent Integration. Its initial objectives were to use non-violent tactics and appeal to the moral conscience of America. They asserted at the meeting that civil rights are a basic part of democracy, that segregation should end, and that it was incumbent upon all black people to oppose segregation.

At the next meeting, held on February 14, 1957, at the Reverend A.L. Davis's Baptist Church in New Orleans, Louisiana, the name was changed to the Southern Leadership Conference and the members of the executive board were elected. They included Dr. Martin Luther King, Jr., president of the board; Dr. Ralph David Abernathy, secretary-treasurer; Reverend C.K. Steele of Tallahassee, Florida, vice president; Reverend T.J. Johnson of Baton Rouge, Louisiana, secretary; and Attorney I.M. Augustine of New Orleans, Louisiana, general consul. This group represented the many local community groups throughout the South and not individuals; it adopted a non-violent strategy, and resolved to be open to all regardless of race, religion, or background. Because the church played an integral role in the lives of black people, the SCLC's leadership was composed mainly of well-trained ministers from large urban churches; it added "Christian" to its name in August 1957 during the first convention in Montgomery, Alabama.

[The SCLC's] initial objectives were to use non-violent tactics and appeal to the moral conscience of America.

The SCLC's first major campaign was the 1957 Crusade for Citizenship, which assisted in voter registration with the establishment of citizenship schools, registered citizens to vote, raised the consciousness of citizens, and established workshops for training in non-violent tactics. Voter registration for the disenfranchised and consciousness raising continues to be part of the SCLC's main work. In the 1960s, the SCLC worked with local groups to coordinate campaigns such as the ones in Albany, Georgia, and Birmingham and Selma, Alabama. The media coverage of these campaigns and the voter registration endeavors served to move the nation towards the passing of the **Civil Rights Act of 1964** and the **Voting Rights Act of 1965**. It was involved in organizing the **March on Washington** for Jobs and Freedom in 1963, when Martin Luther King Jr. delivered his "**I Have a Dream**" speech.

In addition to its southern thrust, the SCLC also made forays into the northern inner cities in an attempt to address the issues of poverty

and violence; toward this end it founded Operation Breadbasket in Atlanta and Chicago. In 1971 the SCLC founded the quarterly *SCLC National Magazine,* which serves as an educational and recruiting link between the headquarters in Atlanta, Georgia, and its affiliates.

Helen R. Houston

Student Non-Violent Coordinating Committee (1960–1970)

The Student Non-Violent Coordinating Committee (SNCC), a youth political organization, was organized under the leadership of **Ella Baker**, a founder and executive director of the **Southern Christian Leadership Conference** (SCLC). Baker saw a need for students to become involved in the fight for equal rights, anticipating that they would need to organize and coordinate their efforts. She invited students to a meeting held from April 15 to 17, 1960, at **Shaw University** in Raleigh, North Carolina, her alma mater. Over 200 college and high school students came from 13 states, though most were from Nashville, Tennessee. This meeting followed a smaller meeting held at **Highlander Folk School**, where a number of the issues considered at Shaw were discussed. Although many concerns had been discussed, it was at Shaw that the fight for civil rights gained a new organization, the SNCC. It was independent of other civil rights groups even though these groups wanted them to affiliate. At the urging of Baker, they determined to have a decentralized leadership, maintain strong local leaderships, and keep the lines of communication open among campuses and students. The group asserted its commitment to "the philosophical or religious ideal of nonviolence." The first elected chair was **Marion Barry**, a graduate of **Fisk University** and a prominent participant in the Nashville sit-ins. The SNCC concentrated on direct action and voter registration, with an emphasis on the power of the ballot. It saw itself as a movement against injustice and not racially exclusive in membership or focus.

Helen R. Houston

Universal Negro Improvement Association (est. 1914)

Black Nationalist **Marcus Garvey** founded the Universal Negro Improvement Association (UNIA) in 1914. Garvey initially organized the UNIA in Kingston, Jamaica. However, when he came to the United States in 1916, the organization developed a more extensive following. The UNIA had members from around the world. There were 996 branches of the organization in 43 countries. During the early 1920s, the association had grown larger than any other black organization in U.S. history. The UNIA served as the basis for Garvey's Black Nationalist and consciousness-raising movement. The motto of the organization was "One God! One Aim! One Destiny!" The organization's agenda included racial pride, self-help, and racial segregation. The establishment of a black homeland in Africa and black economic independence were considered natural extensions of that agenda.

Marcus Garvey was a controversial figure who was attacked by other black leaders because of his views on civil rights for African Americans in the United States. Garvey and his UNIA questioned whether black people could achieve equality in a white majority country. The UNIA, therefore, promoted migration of people of African descent back to Africa. As a part of the organization's emphasis on self-help and black economic enterprise, the UNIA established the Negro Factories Corporation. Black-owned grocery stores, restaurants, as well as other service-oriented businesses, were a part of the corporation. The UNIA also established the Black Star Shipping Lines.

The UNIA also organized several conventions in the 1920s. The conventions consisted of inspiring and elaborate parades by the UNIA that included members of auxiliary groups such as the African Legion and the Black Cross Nurses. There were religious services and speeches given that were meant to rally support for the movement. During one of the conventions it was announced that a Negro Declaration of

Rights would be written that would be designed to support African peoples worldwide. While Garvey and followers of the UNIA did not believe they would gain equality in the United States, the organization helped to foster racial pride, unity, and a commitment to the progress of all African peoples.

Marcus Garvey was a controversial figure who was attacked by other black leaders because of his views on civil rights.

In 1924 Garvey was indicted on federal charges of income tax evasion and mail fraud. While the income tax charges were later dropped, Garvey was convicted of the fraud charge. After a brief stay in prison, he was deported. After this, the organization lost many of its members. Garvey moved his headquarters to London, England, and continued to work toward his goals there. His organization never fully recovered in terms of membership or productivity, however, and its goal to establish a black homeland in Africa was left unfulfilled.

Rebecca S. Dixon

Leaders

Baker, Ella Josephine (1903–1986)

Ella Baker had a deep sense of social responsibility, contributed to human freedom, and fought on the front lines of the freedom movement in the United States. She was best known as national director of the **Southern Christian Leadership Conference** (SCLC) and as founder and advisor to the **Student Non-Violent Coor-**

dinating **Committee** (SNCC). Although born in Norfolk, Virginia, she grew up in a rural and racially segregated community in North Carolina, where she developed a strong sense of community ties. She moved to New York City after graduating from college in 1927, but, as a black woman, had few opportunities for work after she finished school. She refused to teach and, for several years, worked in positions where she learned about tenant and consumer rights.

Carr ... became an important link between the black community and activists Martin Luther King Jr., Ralph Abernathy, and Edgar D. Nixon Sr.

Baker's work with the **NAACP** began in 1941 and continued until 1946; it took her throughout the country, especially the South, where she was assistant field secretary and then a director of branches. Among her responsibilities was organizing local campaigns such as those against lynching and for job training for black workers and equal pay for black teachers. Considering the NAACP too bureaucratic, Baker left her post in 1946. She took with her, however, an understanding of how people work collectively to fight oppression. Now that she knew how to empower people for social change by encouraging their direct participation, by 1957 she went to Atlanta to set up the SCLC and organize its voter registration program in the South—the Crusade for Citizenship. **Wyatt Tee Walker** succeeded her at the SCLC in April 1960.

From the beginning of the student sit-in movement in 1960, Baker became a full supporter. She understood the significance of non-violent protests and the need for students from various colleges and universities to communicate with each other. The SCLC contributed $800 to a student leadership conference held over the 1960 Easter weekend (April 16–18) at Shaw University in Raleigh—Baker's alma mater. One hundred students were expected but over 300 came. SCLC officials **Martin Luther King Jr.**, **Ralph Abernathy**, and Wyatt Tee Walker wanted the organization to have oversight over any formal group that grew out of the conference. Baker protested, the SCLC officials backed off, and on April 17, the SNCC was established. She resigned from the SCLC after the Easter conference, and in August began her work with SNCC.

Baker became a mentor to the SNCC's civil rights workers. She was active in the training programs at **Highlander Folk School** in Monteagle, Tennessee, and helped to balance the view of activists who supported political action with those who advocated non-violent direct action. After the SNCC organized the **Mississippi Freedom Democratic Party** (MFDP), and thousands of blacks registered to vote, she set up an MFDP office in Washington, D.C. Baker also gave the keynote address at the party's state convention in Jackson. She supported the dozen or more projects that SNCC undertook between 1961 and 1964, including those in Fayette County, Tennessee, and in other rural and urban communities across the South. In her role as movement teacher, she left generations of activists the intellectual and political wherewithal to continue.

Jessie Carney Smith

Carr, Johnnie Rebecca Daniels (1911–2008)

Activist Johnnie Carr is considered "one of the three major icons of the civil rights movement," alongside **Martin Luther King Jr.** and **Rosa Parks**. Quoted in the *Tennessean*, Morris Dees of the Southern Poverty Law Center in Montgomery, Alabama, said: "When the final history books are written, she'll be one of the few people remembered for that terrific moment." The Alabama native grew up outside Montgomery and later relocated to that city. She enrolled in the all-black Montgomery Industrial School, also called Miss White's School, where she met Rosa McCauley (later Parks); they became lifelong friends. Carr became a practical nurse while Parks became a seamstress. In 1944 she married Arlam Carr, who supported her work in local black causes. She was a member of the Montgomery chapter of the **NAACP** and worked on membership drives. Her connection to Rosa Parks continued after Carr became youth council director of the local NAACP and Parks's secretary.

Carr was active in the **Montgomery Bus Boycott** of 1955, which catapulted Rosa Parks into public view for refusing to give her seat to a white man. Carr remained at the forefront of the boycott until the U.S. Supreme Court declared bus segregation unconstitutional in November 1956. She became an important link between the black community and activists Martin Luther King Jr., **Ralph Abernathy**, and **Edgar D. Nixon Sr.** They worked through the **Montgomery Improvement Association** (MIA), the organization behind the boycott. Carr led initiatives to improve race relations, engaged in economic boycotts, protested segregated public accommodations, and led movements for open housing. In 1967 she succeeded King as president of the organization, becoming its first woman president. Johnnie and Arlam Carr Sr. filed suit on behalf of their son, Arlam Jr., in 1964, which eventually led to the desegregation of the Montgomery County school system. She remained president of the MIA and continued her civil rights activism until her death in 2008.

Jessie Carney Smith

Farmer, James (1920–1999)

James Farmer was born in Marshall, Texas, on January 12, 1920. After completing high school at the age of 14, he went on to college at **Howard University** and earned a bachelor of divinity degree in 1941. Farmer, who became a

James Farmer (Fisk University).

pacifist, refused to serve in the U.S. military during World War II, particularly because of its segregationist policies. After becoming an ordained minister he chose to travel and speak about racial equality instead of pursuing his own ministry.

While fighting racial segregation, Farmer became involved in an interracial housing situation that manifested in civil disobedience and protest. As a result, in 1942 he and a group of students founded the Committee of Racial Equality (CORE), which sought to end racial segregation in America. CORE began as a committee of the nondenominational organization the **Fellowship of Reconciliation** (FOR), which rejected violence and war. Farmer became the first leader of CORE, which later became the **Congress of Racial Equality**. Farmer left the organization in 1945 to work for a union organizer with the goal of affecting the practice of giving only menial jobs to blacks. He remained as an organizer until 1959, when he became the program director of the **NAACP**. This position put Farmer at the heart of many of the southern civil rights battles.

In 1961 Farmer was encouraged by Roy Wilkins to accept the position of national director of CORE. The organization had lost its effectiveness and needed someone to confront the issues of the day. One of Farmer's first acts was to renew attempts to test the interstate laws of segregation. CORE and the **Student Non-Violent Coordinating Committee** (SNCC) formed a group Farmer named the **Freedom Riders**. The group departed on May 4, 1961, for the Deep South. The violence and brutality that whites inflicted on the Freedom Riders brought them national attention and placed Farmer in the forefront of the Civil Rights Movement. Farmer resigned from CORE in 1966 at a time when a more militant and nationalist sentiment was becoming prevalent. He was offered and accepted from President Richard Nixon the post of Assistant Secretary of Health, Education, and Welfare in 1969. Farmer retired from politics in 1971. He went on to speak on the lecture circuit and teach at various colleges. In 1998 President Bill Clinton awarded Farmer the highest civilian honor, the Presidential Medal of Freedom.

Lean'tin L. Bracks

Forman, James (1928–2005)

As a program director of the **Student Non-Violent Coordinating Committee** (SNCC), James Forman was responsible for guiding young activists through the turmoil of 1960s non-violent activism. A veteran of the Korean War, Forman used his maturity and life experiences to organize many of the SNCC's most successful initiatives, including the "**Freedom Summer**" of 1964. Born in Chicago, he spent his early years on a farm in Mississippi with his grandmother, who stressed the importance of education. He studied at Roosevelt and Boston universities, then served in the U.S. Air Force for four years. Forman also attended Middlebury College before returning to Chicago, where he worked as a reporter for the Chicago *Defender*.

The *Defender* sent him to western Tennessee to research black farmers who were being evicted by their white landowners for registering to vote.

In 1961 Forman became the director of the SNCC's Atlanta office. The following year, he led an interracial group of SNCC activists on the **Freedom Rides**, which they took over after violence forced **Congress of Racial Equality** (CORE) activists to abandon their efforts. In 1964 Forman became the SNCC's executive secretary. That summer, he helped organize "Freedom Summer," a campaign to enfranchise thousands of African Americans in the Deep South. Despite their success, SNCC leaders increasingly disagreed about the organization's direction, strategies, and tactics. After serving as executive secretary for two years, Forman left the SNCC in 1968 to seek economic development opportunities for black communities. Forman remained active in promoting black causes while earning a master's degree in African and African American Studies at Cornell University in 1980 and a doctorate from the Union of Experimental Colleges and Universities in Washington, D.C., in 1982.

Crystal A. deGregory

Garvey, Marcus (1887–1940)

As founder of the **Universal Negro Improvement Association** (UNIA), Jamaican-born black leader Marcus Moziah Garvey led one of the most powerful movements of the twentieth century. With Garvey's Black Star Shipping Line as its flagship asset, his Pan-Africanist "Back to Africa" Movement captivated thousands of blacks across the African Diaspora and inspired future generations of black intellectuals.

Garvey was born in St. Ann's Bay, Jamaica, to Sarah Jane Richards, a domestic worker, and Marcus Moziah Garvey Sr., a mason from whom he inherited his love of books. At the age of 14 he moved to Kingston, where he worked in a print shop. Having seen firsthand the plight of the city's poor black masses, Garvey soon became involved in public activities that promoted social reform. In 1907 he helped found

Marcus Garvey (Fisk University).

the Printers Union, the island's first trade union, and subsequently began a newspaper called *The Watchman*. In 1910 his fundraising efforts took him to Central and South America. After witnessing the deplorable working conditions of West Indians, Garvey became incensed by the rampant poverty in his native country. After briefly returning to Jamaica to establish himself as a politician, he traveled to England in 1912 to gain support for his cause. Upon his return to Jamaica in 1914, he co-founded the UNIA and the African Communities League (ACL) with his future wife, Amy Ashwood. Two years later, he traveled to the United States to raise money and gain support for his organization.

Garvey, who had been in communication with **Booker T. Washington** after reading his *Up from Slavery,* was greeted with the news of Washington's death the previous year. Undaunted, Garvey bellowed his opinions through the streets of Harlem during evening street meetings. The founding of the New York branch of the UNIA soon followed, signaling the beginning of a wave of local chapter foundings across the United States, the Caribbean, and Central and South America. In August 1918, the organization began publishing the *New World* in English, Spanish, and French, with Garvey as its editor. The same year the UNIA founded the Black Star Line as well as the Negro Factories Corporation. In 1920 the UNIA boasted four million members with 1,100 divisions in more than 40 countries. It also held its International Convention in New York, which opened with an elaborate parade down Lenox Avenue; an audience of 25,000 filed into Madison Square Garden to listen to Garvey's address.

He married fellow nationalist Amy Jacques in 1922, but soon after faced financial challenges. Coupled with investigations from the U.S. State Department and infighting among African American and Afro-Caribbean leaders, the UNIA began to decline. In 1923 Garvey was convicted of mail fraud under the pretense that he used the postal service to defraud his shipping line investors. After several unsuccessful attempts at an appeal, Garvey began serving his sentence in February 1925. Despite the eventual commutation of his sentence by President Calvin Coolidge in November 1927, Garvey was deported to Kingston. He moved to London in 1934, where he died in virtual obscurity after a stroke. His remains were exhumed and ceremoniously reinterred in Jamaica's National Heroes Park.

Crystal A. deGregory

Hamer, Fannie Lou (1917–1977)

A former Mississippi sharecropper, Fannie Lou Hamer made history during the 1960s when she worked as the field secretary of the **Student Non-Violent Coordinating Committee**

(SNCC). Not only did Hamer labor tirelessly to help local blacks become enfranchised, she also helped found the Council of Federated Organizations (COFO), which planned the **Freedom Summer** of 1964. Perhaps most notably she is remembered for her role in the founding of the **Mississippi Freedom Democratic Party** (MFDP) and for delivering a moving testimony for the party on national television.

Born into dire poverty in Montgomery County, Mississippi, Fannie Lou Townsend was the twentieth and youngest child of Mississippi sharecroppers Jim and Lou Ella Townsend. She was reared in Sunflower County from age two, residing there for the rest of her life. At age six, Townsend began picking cotton and could pick at least 200 pounds a day by age 13. The family's poverty forced her to end her formal education after the sixth grade. While working as a sharecropper on a neighboring plantation owned by the Marlowe family near Ruleville, Mississippi, in the 1940s, Townsend worked at various times as a sharecropper, timekeeper (keeping track of workers' time on the plantation), and domestic. In 1944 she married fellow plantation worker Perry "Pap" Hamer. The couple supplemented their income by running a small salon and making liquor.

Already in her mid-forties at the time of SNCC's founding in 1960, Hamer joined the organization just two years later. Convinced that African American powerlessness was largely due to fear of white retribution, Hamer tried unsuccessfully to pass the voter registration test; this resulted in violent threats against her and the loss of her job. In 1963 Hamer nevertheless became a registered voter, as well as the field secretary for the SNCC. Earning $10 a week, Hamer organized a poverty program and educated her community about the right to vote. In April of 1964, she was instrumental in the founding of the MFDP, an organizational alternative to the all-white Mississippi Democratic Party. Elected vice chair at the MFDP's national convention, Hamer was a part of the party's official delegation to the 1964 Democra-

tic National Convention (DNC). Her candid testimony outlined the brutality faced personally and collectively by blacks in Mississippi. Her address forced President **Lyndon B. Johnson** to offer blacks two at-large delegate seats and a pledge that segregated delegations would not be seated in the future.

Hamer continued her activism throughout the remainder of her life. In 1965 she participated in the march from **Selma to Montgomery**, Alabama, and later traveled to Africa as a part of a SNCC delegation. In 1968 she received a standing ovation after taking her seat at the DNC as a part of the renamed Mississippi Loyalist Democratic party. She later served on the DNC and was a plaintiff in a class action lawsuit to desegregate Sunflower County in 1970. She died of cancer in Mound Bayou, Mississippi.

Crystal A. deGregory

Hedgeman, Anna Arnold (1899–1990)

Anna Arnold Hedgeman was involved in several civil rights activities of historic significance. In 1941 she helped **A. Philip Randolph** plan his March on Washington but the plan disintegrated when President Franklin D. Roosevelt issued Executive Order 8802 forbidding discrimination in employment in certain government jobs. Since she was experienced in race relations activities, had joined the civilian defense of Roosevelt's administration, and served as assistant in race relations through a New York office, she was well equipped for the task that followed. Now that the threat of the march brought about some changes, Hedgeman left civilian defense in February 1944 to become executive director of the National Council for a permanent Fair Employment Practices Commission that resulted from negotiations with President Roosevelt and federal authorities.

An impressive public speaker, Hedgeman spoke out on civil rights and helped to plan strategies for the changes that the FEPC envisioned. Before long, however, Congress eliminated the commission. Civil rights remained central to her work, and she became a major architect of the civil rights **March on Washington** held in 1963. It was through her persistence that women were added to the official program and received recognition for their tremendous contributions to the movement. Hedgeman was assistant director of the National Council of Churches' Committee on Race Relations. In that post she worked to get the U.S. Senate to pass the **Civil Rights Act of 1964**. She continued her activism, dabbled in politics, and agitated for women's rights for the rest of her life.

Jessie Carney Smith

Height, Dorothy Irene (1912–)

Dorothy Height has advised some of the most powerful men and women of the twentieth century, coordinating everything from international movements to voter registration drives to multi-city black family reunions. Because of her contributions to American society, in 1994 President Bill Clinton awarded Height the Presidential Medal of Freedom (the same year as **Barbara Jordan**). Ten years later, President George W. Bush, on behalf of the U.S. Congress, presented her with the Congressional Gold Medal. Beginning as a civil rights activist in the 1930s, Height gained prominence through her resolute efforts to promote interracial schools, to register and educate voters, and to enhance the visibility and standing of women. A consultant on civil and human rights to Eleanor Roosevelt, she emboldened President Dwight D. Eisenhower, under whose administration the **Civil Rights Acts of 1957** and 1960 were passed, to desegregate public schools across the nation and urged President **Lyndon B. Johnson** to appoint American black women to sub-cabinet posts.

Born to James Edward and Fannie Borroughs Height on March 24, 1912, in Richmond, Virginia, Height was reared in Rankin, Pennsylvania. She attended New York University, where she earned bachelor's and master's degrees. Height furthered her education by doing post-

graduate work at Columbia University and the New York School of Social Work. While working with New York's Department of Welfare, Height was among the first American blacks named to deal with the 1935 **Harlem riots** and became one of the leaders of the National Youth Movement of the New Deal era. It was during this period that her career as a civil rights advocate unfolded, as she worked with others to prevent lynching, desegregate the U.S. Armed Forces, reform the criminal justice system, and guarantee access to public accommodations.

An impressive public speaker, Hedgeman spoke out on civil rights and helped to plan strategies for the changes that the FEPC envisioned.

In 1937, as assistant director of the Harlem YWCA, she escorted First Lady Eleanor Roosevelt into the National Council of Negro Women's (NCNW) meeting. **Mary McLeod Bethune**, founder and president of the NCNW, had herself recruited Height. Two years later, her work with the YWCA led her to relocate to Washington, D.C., where she served as the executive director of the Phillis Wheatley House. Her appointment to the presidency of the NCNW in 1957 gave Height a forum in which to weave together all of her passions and expertise.

During the 1960s, Height focused the organization's attention on issue-oriented politics and sponsored "Wednesdays in Mississippi," where interracial groups of women helped out at Freedom Schools promoting voter education drives in the North and voter registration drives in the South. She also influenced the YMCA to become involved in the Civil Rights Movement and worked within the association to desegregate all levels of the organization. Height was one of the few women who participated at the highest levels of the Civil Rights Movement. Working with **A. Philip Randolph, Martin Luther King Jr., Roy Wilkins, Whitney Young,** and others, she was on the platform during the **1963 March on Washington,** when King delivered his "**I Have a Dream**" speech.

Open Wide the Freedom Gates: A Memoir was published in 2003. Here, Height covers her life's work over seven decades. Two years later, her memoir gave birth to the musical stage play *If This Hat Could Talk.* The recipient of numerous awards, including but not limited to the **NAACP's** Spingarn Award; the **John F. Kennedy** Memorial Award from the National Council of Jewish Women; the **William L. Dawson** Award by the **Congressional Black Caucus;** the Citizens Medal Award for distinguished service presented by President Ronald Reagan; and the Franklin D. Roosevelt Freedom Medal awarded by the Franklin and Eleanor Roosevelt Institute, Height enjoyed a career of public service that has aided the progress of America, as well as the global society.

Linda T. Wynn

Hope, Lugenia Burns (1871–1947)

Widely remembered as the wife of celebrated Atlanta Baptist (now **Morehouse**) College president John Hope, Lugenia Burns Hope made a name for herself as a social reformer. As the founder of Atlanta's Neighborhood Union, Hope's community service not only improved the lives of Atlantans but also served as a model for the social and civic ethos of the future civil rights movement. Born into a comfortably middle-class family in St. Louis, Missouri, she worked for several charitable entities as an adolescent. These experiences served as an inspiration for her lifelong commitment to social service. From 1890 to 1893, Hope studied at the Chicago Art Institute, the Chicago School of Design, and the Chicago Business College. In

1897 she married Georgia native and educator John Hope. A Ph.D. student at the University of Chicago, Hope accepted a position at Atlanta Baptist College a year later. Arriving at Atlanta Baptist in September 1898, the Hopes might have been surprised to find that city slums surrounded the growing campus. While her husband busied himself with his teaching duties and frequent speaking engagements, Lugenia Hope immersed herself in the development of social programs for the underprivileged in the surrounding community.

Following her husband's appointment to the presidency of the college in 1906, Hope employed the college's students in her efforts to provide community development programs. Founded two years later as the first female-run social welfare agency in the city, the Neighborhood Union has been heralded for its commitment to community building and gender equality. Hope also worked with the city's Young Christian Women's Association's (YMCA's) War Work Council and was a founding member of the Atlanta Branch of the **National Association of Colored Women.** A lifelong reformer, Hope participated in efforts to end segregation within the YWCA nationally and advocated for the unconditional black enfranchisement as the vice president of the local **NAACP** chapter.

Crystal A. deGregory

Jacob, John Edward (1934–)

The social and economic progress of African Americans and other minority groups has been a primary concern of John E. Jacob's. Beginning in 1965 he worked with the Washington, D.C., Urban League as director of education and youth incentives. By 1967, when summer rioting occurred in the District, he managed its Project Alert program and helped inner city youths gain leadership positions; he also helped local residents deal with tensions arising from the riots. Then Jacob moved up in rank to become national president of the **National Urban League** (NUL). In these positions he addressed critical issues that affect African Americans, such as education, housing, health care, and job skills. Jacob often made controversial public remarks about the indifference of America's political system to the needs of the disadvantaged. He was determined to make a difference at the NUL, and criticized President Ronald Reagan for several actions that hampered the ability of African Americans to make racial gains.

Jacob also sought private funding for job training programs and other activities to support the poor, regardless of race. While he joined other African American leaders in favoring self-help neighborhood programs, he maintained that federal assistance was needed for training programs to thrive. In 1994 Jacob left the NUL to take a leadership post with Anheuser-Busch Companies. Still, he continued to promote his concerns for low-income black and Hispanic communities. He criticized his own company's ad campaigns that targeted these communities with sales programs that promoted alcohol consumption.

Jessie Carney Smith

King, Coretta Scott (1927– 2006)

Coretta Scott King has earned national acclaim as a leading voice in the cause of civil rights. Her early role in the movement began as the wife of esteemed non-violent civil rights leader **Martin Luther King Jr.** As the wife of a minister, rearing their four children, and the commitment they both made to civil rights, Coretta Scott King was indeed a busy person. In her own right, she dedicated herself to the cause of civil rights and walked beside her husband in his many campaigns for justice. She often traveled abroad with him, gave speeches on his behalf when he could not attend a function, and gave concerts to help raise funds for the movement. She gained the release of her husband from a Georgia prison in 1960 by appealing to presidential candidate **John F. Kennedy**, and she met with **Malcolm X** in 1965 shortly before his assas-

sination. In 1962 King was a delegate for the Women's Strike for Peace and attended the Disarmament Conference in Geneva, Switzerland.

With the death of her husband in 1968, King dedicated herself to keeping his memory alive. Just four days after his assassination, King stepped in and led a march of 50,000 people on behalf of the sanitation workers striking in Memphis, Tennessee. She kept a speaking engagement scheduled for her husband at an anti-Vietnam war rally in New York and helped with the **Poor People's March on Washington**. In 1969 King became the first woman to speak at London's St. Paul Cathedral and at Harvard University's Class Day exercise. She published her autobiography, *My Life with Martin Luther King Jr.,* that year, as well, and began her campaign to build an exhibition hall that became the Martin Luther King Jr. Center for Non-Violent Social Change located in Atlanta, Georgia.

With the death of her husband in 1968, King dedicated herself to keeping his memory alive.

King's involvement and commitment to civil rights made her one of the most influential African American leaders of her time. In 1983 she helped to bring more than a half million people together to commemorate the twentieth anniversary of the 1963 March on Washington. Over the years she worked diligently by writing newspaper columns, speaking out against apartheid, and helping to establish the national holiday in honor of her husband. King worked tirelessly for almost four decades, actively contributing to numerous women's organizations and community groups, as well as dialoging with heads of state, presidents, and popes, all for the cause of civil rights and her husband's dream of non-violent social change. King died January 31, 2006, following a stroke and mild heart attack.

Lean'tin L. Bracks

Mitchell, Clarence M., Jr. (1911–1984)

For more than 30 years, Clarence M. Mitchell Jr. worked tirelessly as the chief lobbyist for the **NAACP** as he battled for the end of segregation. Dubbed the "101st Senator" in recognition of his unrivaled influence in the U.S. Senate, Mitchell was a fixture in the halls of the U.S. Congress. He worked with both Democrats and Republicans to secure the passage of many of the nation's most salient civil rights laws, including the **1957**, 1960 and **1964 Civil Rights Acts** and the **1965 Voting Rights Act** and the 1968 Fair Housing Act. In honor of his life's work, President Jimmy Carter presented him with the Presidential Medal of Freedom in 1980.

Born in Baltimore, Maryland, Mitchell was educated at Douglass High School and Lincoln University in Oxford, Pennsylvania. He later returned to Baltimore, where he went to work for the *Afro-American* as a reporter. While on the Eastern Shore in 1933, Mitchell witnessed the lynching of a black man, which led him to testify before Congress and to commit his life to public service. In 1937 he became secretary of the Urban League of St. Paul, Minnesota, before working with the National Full Employment and Practices Commission in 1941. Four years later, Mitchell became first labor secretary of the NAACP and in 1950 was named head of the Washington office. His career with the NAACP ended in 1978, when he retired from public service.

Crystal A. deGregory

Moon, Mollie (1908–1990)

A pioneer in the Civil Rights Movement, for nearly 50 years Mollie Moon worked through the elite milieu in programs aimed at bringing about equal rights and racial uplift. In 1942, she founded the **National Urban League Guild** in New York City. As guilds were established in cities throughout the nation, their work helped to meet Moon's goal to bring the races together for social interaction. This, she believed, would advance the cause of racial equality and social justice. Already prominent in New York City, in the 1940s Moon was called to help the National Urban League overcome its financial difficulties. League president Lester B. Granger asked her to assemble a group of volunteers to meet that mission, and she responded by crossing racial lines in her fundraising activities. Soon she established her reputation as one concerned for community unity. The guild that she founded held its first benefit early in 1942: a Victory Cocktail Party. It was so successful that it became a tradition each February and attracted entertainers, movie stars, business leaders, and others of prominence. Through her efforts the Council of Urban League Guilds, which she also established, raised over $3.4 million to support the Urban League's initiatives. Mollie Moon preserved the civil rights legacy by working to establish the Henry Lee Moon Civil Rights Library, which was located at the **NAACP**'s headquarters in Baltimore. The library honors her husband, who had been a longtime public relations director for the NAACP and editors of its *Crisis* magazine.

Jessie Carney Smith

Newton, Huey P. (1942–1989)

Born in Monroe, Louisiana, Huey Newton grew up in Oakland, California, where he attended Merritt College and was influenced by **Malcolm X** and other revolutionaries. He also met **Bobby Seale** while at Merritt, and began efforts to change course offerings at the college to reflect their political interests. Newton and Seale formed the **Black Panther Party** for Self-Defense in 1966. He coauthored the party's manifesto, including demands for land, physical necessities (food, clothing, and housing), justice, and peace. The Panthers exercised the right to bear arms, patrolling black neighborhoods to deter not only crime but police brutality, and generated controversy and widespread media coverage in May 1967, when armed members appeared at the California Legislature in Sacramento. The party expanded into other parts of the country, but their actions led to many hostile confrontations with authorities. Several Panthers were killed by the police, while Newton was arrested and charged with the murder of a police officer on October 28, 1967, and became a celebrated political prisoner. "Free Huey" rallies drew thousands and continued until his release in 1970. Newton left for Cuba in 1974, but returned to America in 1977. He received a Ph.D. in social philosophy from the University of California, Santa Cruz, in 1980, but experienced personal and drug problems after the Panthers disbanded in 1982. Newton was killed in Oakland, California, in 1989 in what was reported as a drug-related incident.

Fletcher F. Moon

A. Philip Randolph (Fisk University).

Randolph, A. Philip (1889–1979)

Arguably the greatest African American trade unionist of the twentieth century, Asa Philip Randolph was the most important civil rights leader to emerge from the American labor movement. As the cofounder of the *Messenger,* organizer of the **Brotherhood of Sleeping Car Porters**, and the director of the 1941 March on Washington, Randolph pressured presidents and compelled companies to end racial injustices. During the last two decades of his 90-year life, younger Civil Rights Movement leaders such as **Martin Luther King Jr.** displaced Randolph as an influential figure. Even so, there was a time when Randolph commanded the support of thousands of black workers and when the *New York Times* dubbed him "the most dangerous Negro in America."

The grandson of slaves, Randolph was born in Crescent City, Florida, to the Reverend James Williams, an African Methodist Episcopal

Church minister, and Elizabeth Robinson Randolph. After graduating from Jacksonville's Cookman Institute in 1911, he moved to Harlem, New York, against the will of his parents. Here he worked by day and studied by night at City College. Already exposed to the intellectual works of Karl Marx and **W.E.B. Du Bois**, Randolph joined the Socialist Party at age 21 and co-founded the *Messenger* with Chandler Owen in 1917. A monthly magazine, the *Messenger* campaigned against racism, discouraged African American involvement in World War II, and encouraged trade unionism.

In 1925 Randolph organized the Brotherhood of Sleeping Car Porters. As the country's first African American trade union, the Brotherhood struggled to secure certification from the Pullman Company, the country's then-largest employer of African Americans. Randolph and the Brotherhood claimed a sizeable victory in 1937, when they signed the first-ever contract between a white employer and a black labor leader. In addition to leading the new National Negro Congress and serving as vice president of the American Federation of Labor and Congress of Industrial Organizations, Randolph notably helped to force the signing of two Executive Orders during the 1940s. In 1941 he planned the nation's first March on Washington and projected its attendance to be as much as 100,000.

When his attempts at subverting Randolph failed, President Franklin Delano Roosevelt issued Executive Order 8802, which banned discrimination in the defense industry less than a week before the scheduled demonstration. Critics not only charged that the president fell short of providing the means to enforce the legislation, but also that Randolph was a sellout for canceling the march. In 1948 President Harry Truman issued Executive Order 9981 to enforce desegregation in the armed forces. Nine years later, Randolph organized the Prayer Pilgrimage to Washington to support the emergent civil rights struggle in the South; he organized a Youth March for Integrated Schools the following year. While the **Civil Rights Movement** had less of a focus on economic disparity than Randolph, he leant his support to the movement as an elder who helped organize the now-famous 1963 **March on Washington**, which boasted of an attendance of more than 250,000 people.

Crystal A. deGregory

Robinson, Jo Ann Gibson (1912–1992)

As president of the Montgomery, Alabama, Women's Political Council during the 1950s, Jo Ann Gibson Robinson was one of the several significant originators of the 1955 to 1956 **Montgomery Bus Boycott**. An undergraduate of Fort Valley State College, she earned her master's degree in English from Atlanta University. In 1949 Robinson joined the faculty of Alabama State College as a professor of English. Later, she joined Montgomery's Dexter Avenue Baptist Church and the Women's Political Council (WPC), founded by Mary Fair Burks.

Established to protest racial abuse, the WPC developed a program of political action, including protest demonstrations of African American abuse on Montgomery City buses. Because she and others came face-to-face with the debasing effects of racism from drivers of Montgomery city buses, Robinson and the WPC targeted the racial seating practices. A year and a half before **Rosa Parks** refused to give up her seat, Robinson, in May of 1954, corresponded with Mayor W.A. Gayle and alluded to the possibility of a bus boycott by African Americans if the abuses did not end. After Parks's arrest on December 1, 1955, she played a prominent role in the Montgomery bus struggle. Noting that the WPC would not wait for Parks to consent to a call for a boycott of Montgomery's buses, Robinson issued a call for the boycott to take place on December 5, 1955. She prepared a one-page boycott flyer that was distributed to African Americans in Montgomery. A member of the executive board of the Montgomery Improvement Association (MIA), Robinson, who wrote the organization's newsletter, was largely responsible for organizing the Montgomery Bus Boycott. Robinson's 1987 memoir, *The Montgomery Bus Boycott and the Women Who Started It,* took her and other middle-class women from a footnote status in history to one of centrality within the narrative for open seating on the buses of Montgomery. Robinson died five years after the publication of her memoir.

Linda T. Wynn

Robinson, Randall (1941–)

As the director of the Washington, D.C., based lobbying organization TransAfrica, Inc., Randall Robinson dedicated almost two decades to fighting for the rights of colored people around the world. Under his leadership, TransAfrica was at the forefront of United States policymaking decisions with African and Caribbean countries. The 1984 yearlong protest of the South African embassy in Washington, D.C. that he helped to organize was instrumental in initiating the end of South African apartheid. Ten years later, Robinson staged a 27-day fast to protest the country's policy toward Haitian refugees, forcing the hand of then-President Bill Clinton to intercede in Haiti's escalating violence.

The son of Maxie and Doris Robinson, Robinson was born and reared in Richmond, Virginia. Educated in the city's public schools, he enrolled in historically black Virginia Union University. However, he was drafted into the army in 1963. He returned to Virginia Union after his military service to graduate in 1967; he then earned a law degree from Harvard University in 1970. After pursuing a Ford Fellowship in Tanzania, Robinson returned to Boston to work as a civil rights attorney for a legal aid project. His commitment to the underserved became a lifelong passion by the mid 1970s. Following the founding of TransAfrica in 1976, Robinson advocated for increased minority representation in high-ranking international affairs. In 1981 he helped found the TransAfrica Forum to influence U.S. foreign policies with black nation states. While his work with South Africa and Haiti was undoubtedly climatic, Robinson continues to fight for Third World debt relief and American slave reparations.

Crystal A. deGregory

Ruffin, Josephine St. Pierre (1842–1924)

The diverse ethnic heritage that characterized Josephine St. Pierre Ruffin was mirrored in her appearance. She left her native Boston to attend private, integrated schools in Charleston and Salem, and then returned to Boston in 1855 to attend the now-integrated Bowdoin School. She became active in community and national reform and joined the freedom struggle before the **Civil War**. Ruffin and her husband, George, were recruited for the 54th and 55th Colored Regiments of Massachusetts. After the war Josephine Ruffin organized the Kansas Relief Association and aided southern blacks in their exodus to Kansas. She was well connected in Massachusetts and worked with several volunteer organizations. Ruffin also served in women's organizations, such as the Massachusetts School Suffrage Association. Ruffin organized the Woman's Era Club in February 1893 to promote the interests of blacks and women; membership was open to all, regardless of race. The club became highly active and was the most representative organization for New England blacks.

Robinson advocated for increased minority representation in high-ranking international affairs.

Ruffin's interest and work in the women's club movement led her to national prominence and to forge a national organization. As she moved in that direction, she criticized black women for being silent too long and urged them to protest against stereotyped images of themselves. Under Ruffin's leadership, the first national conference of black women was held in Boston in 1895, out of which the National Federation of Afro-American Women was formed. Other strong black women's clubs were inclined toward national unity as well, and in 1896 they organized the **National Association of Colored Women**. It, too, carried forth Ruffin's concern for racial uplift. Ruffin continued to work for racial and gender equality for the rest of her life.

Jessie Carney Smith

Seale, Bobby (1936–)

Born Robert George Seale in Dallas, Texas, Bobby Seale helped create the **Black Panther Party**, one of the most well-known radical organizations of the 1960s and 1970s. He endured numerous arrests, imprisonment, and unfair treatment during highly publicized trials before leaving the organization in 1974. In later years he became a community activist, lecturer, author, and food entrepreneur.

His parents moved to Oakland, California, where they raised Seale, his brother, and sister. At 18, Seale joined the U.S. Air Force and became a sheet metal mechanic before being dishonorably discharged after a dispute with an officer. He then returned to Oakland and worked several jobs before entering Merritt College, where he met **Huey Newton**. Seale and Newton established the Black Panther Party in 1966, attracting the attention of local and federal authorities. Seale and other Panthers were arrested in May 1967 for carrying weapons in Sacramento, California. After confrontations with police left several Panthers dead, Seale was arrested and tried as part of the "Chicago Eight" (who disrupted the 1968 Chicago Democratic Convention) and the "New Haven Nine" (in which members of the Panthers were accused of torturing a fellow Panther they suspected of informing for the FBI) cases. After his release, Seale attempted to change the image of the Panthers and even tried to enter politics, nearly winning election as mayor of Oakland in 1973.

Bobby Seale (AP Photo).

He later settled down into family life, worked with youth organizations, wrote his autobiography (1978) and a cookbook (1988), marketed his own barbeque sauce, and lectured widely on the history of the Black Panther Party.

Fletcher F. Moon

Smith-Robinson, Ruby Doris (1942–1967)

Despite dying when she was just 25 years old, Ruby Doris Smith-Robinson left an indelible mark on the Atlanta Student Movement as well as the **Student Non-Violent Coordinating Committee** (SNCC). From the SNCC's founding in 1960 to her premature death, she served as a critical organizer in the Atlanta central office. Elected as the successor to James Forman in 1966, Smith-Robinson was the only woman ever to serve as the executive secretary of the SNCC. Born in Atlanta, Georgia, to J.T. and Alice Smith, young Ruby was reared in Atlanta's Black Summerhill neighborhood. Largely insulated from white racism in the segregated black community, she quickly became involved in the Atlanta student movement after entering **Spelman College** in the fall of 1959. Along with other student activists, she protested and picketed local businesses in an effort to desegregate the city. By 1961 her local acclaim led her to the national scene when she became involved in the early efforts of SNCC. As a volunteer on the 1961 SNCC-resumed **Freedom Rides**, Smith-Robinson was also one of the earliest architects of the SNCC's jail-no-bail policy.

Her courage became legendary throughout the organization's ranks. By 1963 she had become a full-time member of the central office staff. Three years later, she was elected to the post of executive secretary. As a student, activist, wife, and mother, Smith-Robinson juggled her endless administrative and activist duties with her family responsibilities. In 1964 she married Clifford Robinson and the couple welcomed a son, Kenneth Toure Robinson, the following year. Although she earned a bachelor's degree in physical education in 1965, the totality of her responsibilities took a heavy toll on her health. Months after her health began precipitously declining in January 1967, Smith-Robinson was diagnosed with terminal cancer. She succumbed to the illness in October of the same year.

Crystal A. deGregory

Springer-Kemp, Maida (1910–2005)

Maida Springer-Kemp was an activist whose work benefited labor unions, including the International Ladies Garment Worker's Union (ILGWU), which brought benefits to thousands of African American women garment workers who had been discriminated against due to their race and gender. Her work raised the standard of living for these women, beginning with those in Harlem, New York. Springer-Kemp knew well the problems of the urban ghetto of Harlem, where the black exodus from the rural South brought many unskilled and poorly educated people in search of housing, jobs, and a new life. There was also a growing West Indian population competing for the same resources. By 1933 Springer-Kemp, herself a West Indian immigrant who came to America when she was seven, joined the ILGWU. Soon she became a union lobbyist and sought minimum wage for workers who were poorly paid. Although she was pleased with some of the union's progress, she was aware of its continuing practices of racial and gender discrimination. For those women who worked in New York City's suburbs, she knew that as domestic day workers they would receive greater benefits as union rather than nonunion workers.

In 1942, when World War II was in progress, Springer-Kemp became education director of Local 132 and designed a program to meet the needs of incoming workers. The male work force was being depleted as men left for the war. Thus, she addressed the needs of women who were refugees from war-torn countries, black women migrants from the South, or newly released pris-

oners. Her program focused on improving wages and work conditions. She also supported the work of **A. Philip Randolph**, who worked on behalf of the **Brotherhood of Sleeping Car Porters** and now threatened a March on Washington to help force a change in federal laws dealing with discrimination in the workplace.

Maida Springer-Kemp died in Pittsburgh on March 29, 2005. In her honor, the ILGWU established the Maida Springer-Kemp Fund, which supports the needlework schools, provides scholarships for workers' children, and gives women financial aid to start home-based enterprises.

Jessie Carney Smith

Smith-Robinson was ... one of the earliest architects of the SNCC's jail-no-bail policy.

Taylor, Susie King (1849–1912)

Born a slave but dying a free woman, Susie Baker King Taylor chronicled her life in *Reminiscences of My Life in Camp* (1902). The work is more than an autobiography, however; it is also a personal account of the nation's struggles during the **Civil War**. Taylor wanted the book to awaken a social consciousness in the United States and to see a harmonious unification of the races. She grew up in segregated Savannah, Georgia, and became a camp nurse during the Civil War. For eight months in 1863, Taylor worked with nurse Clara Barton, founder of the American Red Cross. She saw the devastation of racial segregation in the military and among the veterans once the war ended. She also witnessed a lynching during a railroad trip to Louisiana. In 1886 she found-

Susie King Taylor (Fisk University).

ed Corps Sixty-Seven, Women's Relief Corps, which was an auxiliary to the Grand Army of the Republic; she held several offices in the organization, including as president. Taylor saw racism as a national problem but found it more pronounced in the South. On racism, she wrote: "I wonder if our white fellow men realize the true sense or meaning of brotherhood? ... Was the war in vain?" Taylor noted the horrors that blacks faced in the "land of the free" and that the nation did nothing to protect them. "We cannot sing, 'My Country 'tis of thee, Sweet land of Liberty,'" she concluded. Although she died alone and unknown, she left a legacy as a woman of peace and love who simply wanted a better world for everyone.

Jessie Carney Smith

Walker, Maggie Lena (1867–1934)

Maggie Lena Walker is best known for her role as the first woman to become president of a local bank, but she also devoted much of her life to creating opportunities and employment for African Americans and, in particular, African American women. While Walker served as president of the St. Luke Penny Savings Bank of Richmond, Virginia, she continued to get involved in both local and national organizations. Walker was a part of a group of prominent African American women who were invited to start the International Council of Women of the Darker Races. She served as an active member of the Janie Porter Barrett's Virginia Federation of Colored Women's Club that raised funds for the operation of an Industrial School for Colored Girls. In 1912, as founder and president of the Richmond Council of Colored Women, she helped raise $5,000 for the operation of the

Maggie Lena Walker (Fisk University).

Industrial School. Walker was a member of the National Association of Wage Earners, the National Urban League, and the Virginia Interracial Committee. She co-founded the Richmond branch of the **NAACP** and was one of the founders of Virginia's Negro Organization society whose goal was to get African American organizations involved in the struggle for education and health care. Her dedication to public service was relentless; she even customized her car to accommodate her wheelchair so she could continue to work in her later years. During that time she became known as the Lame Lioness. Walker died on December 15, 1934, of diabetes gangrene after giving a lifetime of service to the African American community.

Lean'tin L. Bracks

White, Walter (1893–1955)

In spite of his Anglo features of white skin, blue eyes, and blond hair, Walter Francis White firmly identified himself as an African American. In the race riots of 1906, White experienced first hand the violence of racial hatred. His commitment to changing the attitude of hatred and the laws of segregation was formalized when Atlanta's black community formed a local **NAACP** branch in 1916. While secretary of the local branch, White met **James Weldon Johnson**, who later offered him a position as assistant secretary in the NAACP's New York office. White took the post in New York, which consisted of clerical and office work, on January 31, 1918. In February of that year, he volunteered to go out and investigate a lynching scene with Johnson. He proved to be a valuable and skilled agent, and from that point on White investigated numerous lynchings and traveled extensively. White worked closely with Johnson, and much of the data he collected was publicized.

In 1930 Johnson resigned from the NAACP; White became executive secretary and Joel E. Spingarn was president. When Spingarn resigned in 1935 and his term ended in 1939, White became the primary force in the organiza-

tion. Due to White's efforts, the NAACP received a grant in 1935 that allowed them to hire **Charles Hamilton Houston**, who developed a campaign for dismantling legal segregation. White was an ongoing presence among members of the U.S. Congress and was notorious in his resistance to compromises. This can be seen in his rejection of a deal offered by President Franklin D. Roosevelt on an anti-lynching bill. White was considered a great statesman who initiated important changes in public attitudes and created considerable change for the cause of civil rights in the first half of the twentieth century.

Lean'tin L. Bracks

In spite of his Anglo features of white skin, blue eyes, and blond hair, Walter Francis White firmly identified himself as an African American.

Wilkinson, DeLois Jackson (1924–2005)

Called "Miss Civil Rights," DeLois Wilkinson played a major part in the **Nashville sit-in movement** by joining other women in aiding the protesting students. **Diane Nash**, **John Lewis**, **Bernard Lafayette**, **Marion Barry**, and **James Bevel** were among those aided by Wilkinson, who helped them with plans, provided food, and ran supportive errands. Wilkinson, however, was primarily a behind-the-scenes person. The group and their leader, **James M. Lawson**, wanted to rid the city of segregation and began to agitate against racial discrimination in Nashville by targeting downtown lunch counters. Wilkinson and other local black women attended one of Lawson's early training workshops and were astonished that Lawson knew nothing about the segregated downtown. Suddenly, as if in chorus, the women poured out their pent-up black rage, telling of segregated rest rooms or no restrooms at all for blacks, stores with salespeople who called black women "Auntie" or would not allow blacks to try on clothes, and stores that accepted money from blacks but refused to allow them to eat in their restaurants. Wilkinson knew first-hand the pain of being denied service at the lunch counters. "Her young son had desperately wanted to stop and eat, and she had to tell him again that they did not have time, that they were in too much of a rush," wrote David Halberstam in *The Children*. "She hated it all, not being able to enjoy the small pleasures of a shopping trip the way that white people did, and worse, hav-ing to lie to her son about what she was doing."

Wilkinson was a crusader for justice, having participated in civil rights marches in Washing-ton in 1963 and again in 1983. She devoted her life to civil rights causes. One of eight children, she was born in 1924 in Fayette County, Ten-nessee, and reared in Helena, Arkansas. She was the daughter of John Wesley and Ada Jackson. She graduated from the historically black LeMoyne College in Memphis and from North-western University, where she studied to become a physical therapist. After moving to Nashville, she became a physical therapist at historically black Meharry Medical College. She was married to Fred D. Wilkinson and they had five children.

Jessie Carney Smith

Woodson, Carter Godwin (1875–1950)

The impact of Carter G. Woodson's work on African American culture and civil rights can't be overestimated. Known as "the Father of Black History," the Virginia native and son of former slaves spent part of his life as a teacher and college administrator. He devoted much of his life to writing, editing, and promoting African American history. In 1915 Woodson was a cofounder of the Association for the Study of Negro Life and History, since 1972 known as the **Association for the Study of African Amer-**ican Life and History (ASAALH). He was prac-tically obsessed with the association and its work. In 1916 he established the *Journal of Negro History* (JNH) and was its editor for life. He used the journal to promote black scholar-ship and to make public the scholarly writings on black themes. Woodson appreciated the importance of publishing and in 1921 organized the Associated Publishers, a subsidiary of ASAALH. It became known as the most impor-tant African American-owned publishing com-pany for the next 35 years. Of Woodson's works that the publisher issued, his most famous is *The Mis-Education of the Negro* (1933). Wood-son became so concerned that young people and laymen lacked information on black culture that he decided that churches, schools, and organizations should devote one week each year to the commemoration of black people and events of historical significance to their people. Thus, in February 1926 he established Black History Week to coincide with the birthdays of Booker T. Washington, Abraham Lincoln, and Frederick Douglass. Now known as Black His-tory Month, the celebration is widely observed in the United States.

Jessie Carney Smith

Young, Whitney M., Jr. (1921–1971)

Whitney Moore Young Jr. was born July 31, 1921, in Lincoln Ridge, Kentucky, and died March 11, 1971, in Lagos, Nigeria. Young was frequently criticized by black people for his moderate views, but he made a major impact during the height of the Civil Rights Movement. He joined the U.S. Army with the intention of studying medicine; however, his experiences in a segregated army and his mediation efforts between black enlisted soldiers and white offi-cers caused him to change his goals from medi-cine to social work. He earned degrees in social work, and spent seven years with the Urban League branch offices in Minnesota and Nebras-ka. In 1954 he became the dean of the School of Social Work at **Atlanta University** (now Clark

Atlanta). While in Atlanta, he became more involved in the Civil Rights Movement and worked for civil rights initiatives; he was co-chair of the Atlanta Council on Human Relations and one of the founders of Atlanta's Committee for Cooperative Action.

In 1961 Young became executive director of the **National Urban League**. Under his leadership, the number of branches grew and funding increased; the attempt to win over corporate America resulted in support for black causes and employment, and the traditionally conservative league assumed a more assertive role in the fight for civil rights and justice. The league took part in the **March on Washington** and in other major civil rights activities. He organized the Community Action Assembly to fight poverty in black neighborhoods, proposed a domestic Marshall Plan to increase opportunities for black citizens, and started the New Trust program to attack the problems of poor housing for blacks, inadequate health care, and limited

Young was frequently criticized by black people for his moderate views, but he made a major impact during the height of the Civil Rights Movement.

educational opportunities. Young was a consultant to corporate leaders, local black groups, and three presidents: **Lyndon B. Johnson** (who used part of his Marshall Plan in his War on Poverty), **John F. Kennedy**, and Richard M. Nixon.

Helen R. Houston

Political Activists

Abolitionists

Allen, Sarah (1764–1849)

Sarah Allen experienced slavery early in life. However, by age eight she was brought to Philadelphia and was freed by 1800. Some, but by no means all, of her work was connected to that of her husband, Richard Allen; together they purchased and then he founded Mother Bethel Church in Philadelphia. He is known as the father of the African Methodist Episcopal (AME) Church. Through her work as missionary, Sarah Allen created the first official role of women in the church. In addition to her church and missionary work, Sarah Allen was devoted to the **Underground Railroad** and played an important part in its operations. She was located in Philadelphia, an important hub of the underground network. The area provided a haven for runaway slaves, for it was strategically located and connected those from the South and Southeast to the North and Canada. The Allens provided food, clothing, and temporary quarters for runaways; Mother Bethel Church was similarly used. Sarah and Richard Allen raised a considerable amount of money to enable the slaves to continue their run. Those who decided to settle in the Philadelphia area received the Allens' support as well. Descen-

dants of some of the slaves continue to worship at historic Mother Bethel Church.

Jessie Carney Smith

Bibb, Mary Elizabeth Miles. *See* Bibb, Henry, and Mary Elizabeth Miles Bibb in "Journalism"

Brown, William Wells (1814–1884)

William Wells Brown was born sometime in 1814 and died November 6, 1884, in Chelsea, Massachusetts. He was born a slave, escaped from his master in 1834, and gained a middle name from the Quaker Wells Brown, who aided his escape. After his successful bid for freedom, he began to educate himself and started a family. Brown moved to New York and began working on steamer ships, which allowed him free movement; by 1836 he was an active abolitionist, taking advantage of his employment aboard ships to help slaves travel the **Underground Railroad**; he also made his home one of the rest stations for those on the run.

Brown was also active in the temperance society in Buffalo, New York. In 1843 he became a lecturer for the New York Anti-Slavery Society. He then moved to Farmington, Massachusetts, where he associated with major figures of the

William Wells Brown (Fisk University).

abolitionist movement. In 1848, Brown published a collection of poems, *The Anti-Slavery Harp*. In July 1849 he went to Europe as a representative of the American Peace Society at the International Peace Congress in Paris, later traveling to Britain to promote his book *Narrative of William W. Brown, a Fugitive Slave, Written by Himself*. He also lectured for the anti-slavery crusade in the United States. Because of the **Fugitive Slave Act of 1850**, he could not return to the United States until 1854, when he became a free man. He then continued working for the abolishment of slavery until the **Civil War**.

Helen R. Houston

Coker, Daniel (1780–1846)

Fugitive slave Daniel Coker, whose freedom was later purchased, figured prominently in founding the African Methodist Episcopal (AME) Church in the first quarter of the nine-

teenth century. He was more successful as an abolitionist than in his church affiliations, and was inspired by the efforts of black ship builder Paul Cuffe Sr., who developed a plan to transport free blacks to Sierra Leone. The Maryland Colonization Society tapped him to accompany the first shipload of free blacks who repatriated to Africa. Their relocation led to the founding of Liberia. The ship *Elizabeth* departed for Liberia on January 31, 1820, under the financial support of the U.S. government. Coker recorded his journey in the *Journal of Daniel Coker* (1820).

The independent settlement was to be established in Sherbro Island, which meant that the colonists were relocated from British Sierra Leone. Coker replaced the white agent on the mission, who had died, and became the society's acting agent. He thus had full responsibility for the new settlers, as well as the property that belonged to the society and the government. The new settlement had its problems, mostly due to heavy rains and diseases. When the settlers left Liberia to return to Sierra Leone on

Daniel Coker (Fisk University).

March 8, 1821, Coker was left behind because the Maryland Colonization Society only wanted to use white agents. Coker was so determined to see Liberia established that he and his family remained in the British colony, founded a church, and lived there until he died. Although black Americans were divided in their views of colonization societies, Coker held fast to his support of their anti-slavery efforts and in his zeal to build strong black institutions.

Jessie Carney Smith

Craft, Ellen. *See* Craft, William, and Ellen Smith Craft.

Craft, William (1824–1900) and Ellen Smith Craft (1826?–1897?)

The account of William and Ellen Craft's daring 1848 escape from slavery in Georgia to freedom in Philadelphia and then Boston was a well-publicized event that overshadowed the contributions they made later on as educators. Ellen, who had a fair complexion, posed as a crippled white man, while William acted as her servant; they traveled by train, ferry, and steamer as they made their way from the South to the North. The **Fugitive Slave Act of 1850** put them at risk of being returned to slavery; consequently, they settled in London, England, around 1852. Their successful escape encouraged them to further the cause of freedom for their race. Thus, in London, where they remained for 16 years, William Craft became an effective anti-slavery worker. He joined abolitionist **William Wells Brown** on the lecture circuit for six months, and both lashed out against slavery. While William spent some time in Africa conducting pioneering work to open trade with America, Ellen remained in London and supported the abolitionist movement and the newly formed Women's Suffrage Society. The Crafts returned to the United States in 1868 and settled in South Carolina two years later. There they opened an agricultural cooperative and established a school for adults and

another for children. Once again they felt the sting of racism, however, as night riders set their house and barn afire, causing them to move near Savannah, Georgia, in 1871. There they established an industrial school for black youths. The Crafts never lost their uncompromising concern for helping blacks in the South after the **Civil War**; however, their efforts to do so were largely unsuccessful.

Jessie Carney Smith

Delany, Martin R. (1812–1885)

The author of several tracts and a novel, Martin Robinson Delany is widely considered a pioneer of Black Nationalism. An intellectual and writer, he insisted on civil rights and was an advocate of the emigration of blacks to Africa. As a lecturer, Delany's unconditional enthusiasm for all things black was enjoyed by live audiences and readers alike. Delany was born in Charles Town, Virginia (now West Virginia), to Samuel Delany, a slave, and Pati Peace Delany, a free woman of color. Both parents had a history of resistance, which resulted in his mother relocating with her children to Chambersburg, Pennsylvania. Taught

Martin R. Delany (Fisk University).

to read by his mother, Delany was educated there until moving to Pittsburgh in 1831. The city provided new opportunities for Delany's growing interest in activism, as well as educational instruction at a night school. By 1836, a doctor's tutoring allowed him to practice as a cupper, leecher, and bleeder (someone who bleeds patients using leeches, a common practice at the time for treating wounds). Married in 1843, he founded the weekly newspaper *Mystery,* and later became a contributor to **Frederick Douglass's** *North Star.*

By the 1840s, Delany became increasingly convinced that African Americans should emigrate. Throughout the following decade, he visited Canada, Great Britain, Liberia, and Nigeria in an effort to establish a colony. During the **Civil War,** Delany recruited troops and became a major in the U.S. Army. He worked for the **Freedmen's Bureau** as an officer but remained a critic of Reconstruction failures. Delany continued to research and write about black people, both at home and abroad. He made several unsuccessful bids for political office in the 1870s and published *Origin of Races and Color* in 1879. Delany later died in Xenia, Ohio.

Crystal A. deGregory

Douglass, Frederick (1818–1895)

The beloved leader of black America in the nineteenth century, Fredrick Douglass was the most influential African American of his day. As a pioneer of the anti-slavery movement, Douglass was a charismatic speaker and writer who commanded the respect of audiences and readers alike. His *Narrative of the Life of Frederick Douglass* (1845) has long been revered as the canon in African American literature.

Douglass was born Frederick Augustus Washington Bailey on Maryland's eastern shore to a slave mother named Harriet Bailey and a white father whom he never knew; his exact date of birth is unknown, however. Separated from his mother at an earlier age when he was just eight, Douglass was sent to Baltimore by Thomas Auld, his master's son-in-law. Sent to

Frederick Douglass (Fisk University).

Auld's brother, Douglass was offered reading lessons by his new mistress until her husband forbade them. But Douglass continued teaching himself how to read and write, and this was his earliest act of resistance. Returned to the former Auld in 1833, Douglass was allowed to hire himself out under Edward Covey's supervision. The increasingly vicious beatings he suffered at the hands of Covey, led the teenager to attempt an escape from slavery in 1836.

Following his first botched attempt, Douglass was sent to work in the Baltimore shipyards. Two years later, using a sailor's protection papers, Douglass escaped to New York. Once there, he married a free black woman and changed his last name to Douglass in honor of the hero of poet Walter Scott's "The Lady of the Lake." He settled in New Bedford, Massachusetts, and quickly became involved in the anti-slavery movement there. Hired as a lecturer by the Massachusetts Anti-Slavery Society, he proved to be a forceful speaker whose prose was eloquent by all accounts. Following the publication of his autobiography, Douglass went on a 21-month lecture tour in England, Ireland, and Scotland. He returned to the United States in the spring of 1847 to launch the *North Star* against the advice of William Lloyd Garrison and other cohorts. While Douglass's decision caused a chasm to form between him and Garrison, the paper and its successors were successfully kept in print until 1863.

Despite only having been an acquaintance of abolitionist John Brown, Douglass was forced to flee Rochester, New York, for Canada in the aftermath of the Harper's Ferry raid in 1859 that was led by Brown. After the **Civil War** began, President Abraham Lincoln solicited Douglass to recruit soldiers for the Union Army in 1863. Douglass successfully lobbied Lincoln for better treatment of African American soldiers in the Union Army; he then began a crusade for African American enfranchisement and was rewarded for his loyalty to the Republican Party with an appointment as federal marshal and recorder of deeds for the District of Columbia, president of the **Freedmen's Bureau** Bank, consul to Haiti and *charge d'affaires* for the Dominican Republic.

After discovering that American businessmen were using his position to exploit the Haitian government, Douglass resigned his positions in Haiti and the Dominican Republic. Following the death of his wife in 1882, Douglass married Helen Pitts, a white woman who had been his secretary, in 1884. His real estate investments allowed him and his family to comfortably live in Union Town, Washington, D.C., during the last two decades of his life. After a lifetime of accomplishments, including publishing two additional autobiographies, Douglass died in Washington, D.C., in 1895.

Crystal A. deGregory

Douglass, Grace Bustill (1782–1842)

Born into a prominent, free, and interracial Philadelphia family, Grace Bustill Douglass knew well the evils of slavery and the work of abolitionists who sought its legal end. Douglass

The beloved leader of black America in the nineteenth century, Fredrick Douglass was the most influential African American of his day.

became known for her abolitionist work in 1833, when she became a founder of the racially integrated Philadelphia Female Anti-Slavery Society. Among those black women who signed the charter were Douglass, **Charlotte**, **Margaretta**, and **Sarah Louisa Forten**, and Sarah McCrummell, all of whom became well-known abolitionists. The organization was instrumental in the abolition of slavery and in women's suffrage as well. When its sessions were held in New York in 1837 and 1839, Douglass was elected a vice president of the Anti-Slavery Convention of American Women. Its members represented anti-slavery societies that existed in the free states. Her daughter, **Sarah Mapps Douglass**, became an abolitionist as well. Through the organization, Douglass helped to raise money to build an anti-slavery hall, circulated anti-slavery materials, and petitioned against slavery in Washington, D.C. The society had other areas of interest, too, such as gender discrimination and the education of African American children. The organization saw fewer reasons to exist after 1865, however, when the **Thirteenth Amendment** to the U.S. Constitution abolished slavery in 1865, and after the **Fifteenth Amendment** was passed in 1870 to abolish discrimination against voters, it was disbanded.

Jessie Carney Smith

Douglass, Sarah Mapps (1806–1882)

While she was still a young woman, Sarah Mapps Douglass joined the Philadelphia

Female Anti-Slavery Society, which her mother, **Grace Bustill Douglass**, helped to found in 1833. She had witnessed segregation in Philadelphia involving the Quakers, of which she was a member. Their meeting houses held separate "Negro seats" or pews that were located in a corner or under stairs to ensure that black and white members did not mix, even though membership in the society was interracial. Joined by the prominent Grimkés, who were also black and Quaker, Douglass challenged the segregated seating practices at the Arch Street Meeting site in Philadelphia. Douglass and her family endured incidents of subtle and overt racial discrimination and oppression for some time. Their friendships with activists led to an outrageous act when a mob burned down the society's recently constructed headquarters building and set afire to the Shelter for Colored Orphans. The Quakers themselves were slow to eliminate discriminatory practices, but in time they relented. Douglass had received an usually fine education and became a teacher. In the 1820s, she established a school for black youth that in 1838 received funding from the Philadelphia Anti-Slavery Society. By this time, Douglass was serving the society by attending conventions and as a member of the board of directors, the committee on fairs, librarian, corresponding secretary, and the education committee. After the **Civil War**, Douglass worked with freedmen's aid groups located all over the North. She also became vice chair of the Woman's Pennsylvania Branch of the American Freedmen's Aid Commission.

Jessie Carney Smith

Forten, James (1766–1842)

James Forten was born to Thomas and Sarah Forten, free blacks from Philadelphia. Through hard work and considerable abilities, Forten became a very wealthy man. His first exposure to organized abolitionists was in 1785, when be came into contact with Granville Sharp and Thomas Clarkson in England. Returning to America in 1786, he became an apprentice to Robert Bridges, a sail maker. By 1798 Forten was able to buy out Bridges to become the owner of the company. In 1800 Forten was among the first African Americans to sign a petition to the U.S. House of Representatives protesting the Fugitive Slave Act of 1793 and the slave trade. He wrote pamphlets protesting racism and laws that limited free blacks, as well as protesting the continuation of the slave trade. By the 1830s, Forten was very active in the abolitionist movement. He believed in the equality of the races and was a strong voice against African colonization, even though early on he privately shared the views of those who supported colonization.

Forten founded the American Moral Reform Society. He became the organization's first president, addressing both state and national issues. Forten's commitment extended itself to housing other abolitionists, such as L. Maria Child and William Lloyd Garrison, helping to raise funds for Garrison's newspaper, *The Liberator,* and making his home a stop on the **Underground Railroad**. Forten made contributions to many abolitionist causes, even purchasing the freedom of a number of slaves; in addition, he opened a school for black children. Forten left a strong legacy, and his work was continued by his family long after his death in 1842.

Lean'tin L. Bracks

Forten, Margaretta (1815–1875)

Margaretta Forten was the daughter of James and Charlotte Vandine Forten, one of the most prominent black families in Philadelphia, Pennsylvania, in the 1800s. The Fortens were active abolitionists and their home was open to many visitors who supported their cause. This greatly influenced Margaretta's involvement and commitment to the cause for freedom. With the establishment of the American Anti-Slavery Society by her father, which denied membership to women, Margaretta Forten and others saw a need for an organization to support female activism for the cause of abolition. Forten, along with her mother and sisters, Harriet Louisa and **Sarah**, helped to establish the Philadelphia Female Anti-Slavery Society in 1833. The organization was open to whites as well as blacks and drew its black members from the city's elite. Forten served as recording secretary and policy maker while also spearheading programs. Her service to the organization and the cause of freedom spanned almost four decades. In 1870 Forten offered the last resolution of the Philadelphia Female Anti-Slavery Society that heralded the post-**Civil War** amendments as a success in the cause of the organization. Forten actively supported the women's rights movement by aiding in petition drives and speaking out for the movement. In 1863 she and other members of the Female Anti-Slavery Society helped to obtain signatures for a Women's National League. In her role as an educator, Forten, after teaching in the 1840s at a school operated by **Sarah Mapps Douglass**, opened her own school in 1850. She remained single and used her sharp business sense in helping to manage her father's estate after his death. She remained in Philadelphia, residing in the family home on Lombard Street, until her death on January 28, 1875.

Lean'tin L. Bracks

Forten, Sarah Louise (1814–1883)

Sarah Louise Forten was one of five children born to **James** and **Charlotte Forten**, who were members of a prominent free black activist family in Philadelphia, Pennsylvania, known for its abolitionist commitments. All five of the Forten children were greatly influenced by the sentiments and activities in their home regarding slavery and civil rights. At the age of 17, Sarah Forten first expressed her views as an anti-slavery author in the January 29, 1831, issue of the *Liberator* newspaper. Through essays and poems such as "The Slave Girl's Address to Her Mother," "The Slave," and "The Abuse of Liberty," Forten challenged the hypocrisy of a nation built on individual liberty while denying the humanity and rights of the enslaved and of black citizens.

The Fortens were active abolitionists and their home was open to many visitors who supported their cause.

In 1833 Forten joined her mother and sisters, Harriet and **Margaretta**, as charter members of the Philadelphia Female Anti-Slavery Society and was an active member throughout the 36-year history of the organization. She participated in policy making, fundraising, and petitioning. Forten served on various committees such as the education committee to improve opportunities for children. Through the committee, the society allocated annual funds to finance a school taught by **Sarah Mapps Douglass**, an educator and abolitionist from a prominent free black family in Philadelphia. From 1835 to 1838, she worked on a campaign to end slavery in the District of Columbia that resulted in submission of petitions for abolition from the Female Philadelphia Anti-Slavery Society to the U.S. Congress. In 1838 Sarah married Joseph Purvis, the older brother of **Robert Purvis**, who married Sarah's sister Harriet in 1832. While married, Sarah devoted less time to her activities in the anti-slavery society, but remained a dedicated member to the cause. In 1857 her husband died and she moved back into the home of her parents. Forten continued to work for the abolition of slavery and for the cause of civil rights until the time of her death in 1883.

Lean'tin L. Bracks

Forten Grimké, Charlotte (1837–1914)

Charlotte Forten Grimké was reared in a family of activists and leaders who worked diligently for the abolition of slavery and for civil rights. Her father and mother, Robert

Bridges and Mary Woods Forten, were members of the Forten-Purvis family, a prominent Black family of Philadelphia. Her grandfather was **James Forten Sr.**, a successful abolitionist and sail-maker. Greatly influenced by her heritage, Charlotte Forten Grimké became a member of the Philadelphia Female Anti-Slavery Society. She spoke out about abolitionist issues and promoted the organization through fundraising and making contact with many prominent persons. Forten Grimké was familiar with notable abolitionists such as William Lloyd Garrison, Wendell Phillips, and William Wells Brown. Forten also used her skills as a poet to support the cause. She wrote poems that addressed abolition that were subsequently published in periodicals such as the *Liberator* and *Anti-Slavery Standard*. In 1878 Charlotte Forten married **Francis J. Grimké** a promising Presbyterian minister who was a strong advocate for civil rights; he was the nephew of abolitionists Sarah and Angelina Grimké and the brother of Archibald Grimké. Forten Grimké was active in her role as a minister's wife while she continued her lifelong advocacy for black civil rights.

Lean'tin L. Bracks

Forten also used her skills as a poet to support the cause.

Hall, Prince (1735?–1807)

From unknown beginnings, Prince Hall became the founder and master of the first black Masonic lodge—African Lodge No. 459, in Boston, Massachusetts—during the period of the American Revolution. Hall became the most prominent black in the Boston area, despite his lack of a formal education. Records indicate Hall was the slave of Boston leather craftsman

William Hall, and he learned his father's trade; he joined the Congregational Church in 1762 and married in 1763, while still a slave. After his first wife's death, Hall was freed and remarried in 1770. He then established his own successful leather business, the Golden Fleece, and worked as a caterer. Denied membership in a Boston lodge in early 1775, Hall and 14 other free blacks joined a British Army lodge and gained permission to organize separately. On July 3, 1775, African Lodge No. 1 was founded, with Hall as its first master. Hall led petitions to end slavery in Massachusetts until it was abolished in 1783. African Lodge No. 1 had no permanent charter, so Hall requested and received a charter with a new number on April 29, 1787. Hall also lobbied for African colonization, provided education for black children, expanded African lodges into other cities, and married for a third time in 1798. After his death, his supporters renamed the organization in his memory as the Prince Hall Masons.

Fletcher F. Moon

Harper, Frances (1825–1911)

Born in Baltimore on September 24, 1825, Frances Ellen Watkins Harper died on February 20, 1911 in Philadelphia. Although Harper was one of the most prolific and best-known writers of the nineteenth century (she wrote in almost every genre), she was versatile in other activities as well, including teaching and lecturing. She integrated her oratorical, intellectual, and writing skills into her polemical stance against the dehumanization of any group. She was influenced by her uncle, William Watkins, a religious and politically active minister who ran a school for free blacks in Baltimore that was attended by Harper.

Early in Harper's career she was a teacher, but she found the work too taxing and her health too precarious to continue. She still sought ways, however, in which to help her race. She felt her writings, which often addressed the plight of black people, were not enough. Around 1853, when Maryland law made free blacks entering the state from the North liable for enslavement, she became committed to the anti-slavery cause. She published works in anti-slavery publications such as *Frederick Douglass's Paper* and the *Liberator*. Because of the law, she could not return to Maryland because of these activities, and therefore relocated to Philadelphia, where she lived in an environment alive with social and political activism and became an active member of the anti-slavery movement.

In 1854 Harper was hired as a lecturer for the Maine Anti-Slavery Society based on her oratorical skills, and she thus became the first black female abolitionist lecturer. In her lectures and writings, she appealed to the conscience of white America. In 1854 she also published a polemical collection of poetry, *Poems on Miscellaneous Subjects,* which contains poems on abolitionist themes, on women's rights, and equal rights. Between 1854 and 1860, she traveled extensively for the Pennsylvania Society, speaking on the evils of slavery. She married in 1860, but four years later her husband died and she returned to her fight against slavery. She toured the South with her message of racial uplift, moral reform, and women's rights, and spoke for the Women's Christian Temperance Union.

Following the **Civil War**, her advocacy work was aimed at equal rights for newly freed slaves. The double oppression of racism and sexism in the United States was a constant concern. She joined with Susan B. Anthony, **Frederick Douglass**, and Elizabeth Cady Stanton in the campaign for women's rights. She attended conventions of the American Woman Suffrage Association (1875 and 1877), as well. Among other organizations, she participated in the First Congress of Colored Women in the United States and was a member of the meeting that resulted in the formation of the National Council of Negro Women. Harper continued to write about racism and sexism and to counter the negative images portrayed in society throughout her life. Her novel *Iola Leroy, or Shadows Uplifted* (1892)

addresses many of the issues she had been voicing in her lectures.

Helen R. Houston

The double oppression of racism and sexism in the United States was a constant concern [for Harper].

Jones, John (1816–1879) and Mary Jane Richardson Jones (1816–1910)

Born free in the South, John Jones and Mary Jane Richardson Jones lived in Chicago, beginning in 1845. Here they were in direct contact with anti-slavery societies, the Liberal party, and **Underground Railroad** activities. Although many people in Chicago were hostile to anti-slavery activities and blacks in general, there were prominent white abolitionists who lived there and assisted the Joneses. Because of the success of John Jones's tailoring business, they became affluent and recognized as among the most outstanding blacks in the Midwest. Their home became a station on the Underground Railroad; and they helped to arrange safe havens for escaping slaves in churches, including Quinn Chapel, and other black homes in the city. As was the case with other black abolitionists, the Joneses became concerned about the implications of the **Fugitive Slave Act of 1850**, which threatened the success of their work. In 1853 the Illinois legislature passed a law restricting the immigration of free blacks to the state. Such laws spurred on John and Mary Jones and other abolitionists, including **Frederick Douglass**, who had visited the city, to rally blacks statewide and lobby against these new laws. Fugitive slaves flooded Chicago in the 1850s and early 1860s, making

John Jones (Fisk University).

Mary Jane Richardson Jones (Fisk University).

it more imperative that the Joneses and their supporters intensify their efforts. At a mass meeting held at Quinn Chapel, John Jones was elected head of the Chicago Common Council, which would challenge the constitutionality of Illinois's new law. The group also set up patrols that kept vigilant watch for slave catchers. The Joneses continued their work, with Mary serving as housemother to hundreds of fugitives. The general superintendent of the Michigan Central Railroad provided the abolitionists a railroad car stocked with rations to further aid the slaves' journey. John and Mary Jones thus helped hundreds of fugitives escape to Canada.

Jessie Carney Smith

Jones, Mary Jane Richardson. *See* **Jones, John, and Mary Jane Richardson Jones.**

Martin, John Sella (1832–1876)

A recognized and constant advocate for the freedom and rights of his people, John Sella Martin was an outspoken abolitionist. Born a slave in Charlotte, North Carolina, Martin escaped to Chicago in 1856. There he came into contact with black abolitionists **Mary Ann Shadd** and H. Ford Douglas and became involved in abolitionist circles. After studying for the ministry, he pastored at churches in Boston, New York City, and Washington, D.C. While pastor of Joy Street Church in Boston, in 1859 he gave various addresses on Nat Turner that appealed to large audiences. He joined such abolitionists as **William Wells Brown** and **William C. Nell** in expressing to President Abraham Lincoln opposition to colonization. In April 1865 Martin became an agent in Great Britain for the **American Missionary Association** (AMA). He helped to craft an arrangement between the AMA and the British Freed-Man's Aid Society that led to effective fund raising for the latter organization. He was also the AMA's delegate to the Paris Anti-Slavery Convention on August 27, 1867, where he presented a lecture on various themes. He spoke out in support of freedmen to dispel the mistaken notion that blacks were cowards and too degraded to want to fight for their freedom. Further, he argued against the idea that blacks were lazy and would not work. As relations between Martin and the AMA became strained, in early August 1868 he returned to America and fought for a variety of issues, such as the full participation of women in the Colored National Labor Union and schooling for blacks in Washington, D.C.

Jessie Carney Smith

Nell, William C. (1816–1874)

William C. Nell was born into a privileged black family, but this did not allow him to escape the harsh realities of racism. Nell early on demonstrated an ability for speaking and writing that positioned him to serve as errand boy for William Lloyd Garrison's newspaper, the *Liberator*. Garrison taught Nell the skill of printing, which aided Nell in securing work and having access to express his opinion about issues of the day. Nell began to study law, but he did not complete his studies when he found out he had to swear allegiance to a Constitution and a nation that supported slavery. Between 1840 and 1843, Nell worked for the **American Anti-Slavery Society** but left when funds were no longer available to support the organization.

In 1840 Nell campaigned for the end of segregated schools in Massachusetts and was successful in the spring of 1855, when legislation was passed. He was honored for his work in achieving this goal. Nell also worked for equal access for blacks on transportation and to all public places; he founded the Freedman Association in 1842 to help fugitive slaves. In 1847, after moving to Rochester, New York, Nell became a printer for the *North Star* and had his name on the

masthead, along with **Martin R. Delany** and the founder, **Frederick Douglass**. When Douglass broke with Garrison and his abolitionist philosophies, Nell maintained his allegiance to Garrison. He did not believe in segregated organizations of any kind. The relationship between Douglass and Nell remained strained and at times even hostile after that, and it segregated him from other more radical black abolitionists. Although Nell did disagree with Garrison's anti-political stance for blacks, he remained loyal and wrote a tribute to Garrison in the last issue of the *Liberator* in 1865. Nell became a U.S. postal worker in 1861, and after the last issue of the *Liberator* he became less visible in the struggle for black equality and opportunities.

Lean'tin Bracks

Paul, Susan (1809–1841)

Born into a family of abolitionists in New England, Susan Paul had ties with prominent white women abolitionists, especially those loyal to William Lloyd Garrison. While most known abolitionists of the antebellum period were men, a number of women made their mark in this movement as well. There are claims that as many as one-fourth to one-third of these freedom fighters were women, often working behind the scenes and raising money to support the cause. Susan Paul became an officer in the Boston Female Anti-Slavery Society, founded in February 1832. She also joined other anti-slavery societies. Thus, she became one of the first women of her race who, from 1834 through 1840, gained popularity in the movement. Beginning in 1833, Paul held life membership in the New England Anti-Slavery Society, and two years later she held life membership in the Massachusetts Anti-Slavery Society. In 1838 she was one of two black women delegates from Boston chosen as an officer in the Second Annual Anti-Slavery Convention of American Women held in Philadelphia. She held the post of vice president. Paul continued her work with such groups for many years, becoming a counselor of the Boston Female Anti-Slavery Society. As her membership in these groups suggests, Paul had a keen interest in racial as well as gender equality; she often lectured to women's rights groups and the women's movement of that time. She and women such as **Sarah Mapps Douglass** were tactful in their approach to gender rights, though, and refused to challenge male authority or the work of male abolitionists. In fact, they often praised these men and their work.

Jessie Carney Smith

Pennington, James W.C. (1807–1870)

An escaped slave and one of the leading abolitionists of the first half of the nineteenth century, James W.C. Pennington secured an education and became an effective writer and persuasive speaker. These skills helped him in his work in Hartford, Connecticut, and in New York City. In Hartford he became prominent in the Foreign and **American Anti-Slavery Society** in 1840, and the next year he became founding president of the Union Missionary Society, which was founded by blacks. In 1846 that organization joined other groups to form the **American Missionary Association**, an organization that figured prominently in the life and welfare of black people. The Connecticut Anti-Slavery Society in 1843 appointed Pennington a delegate to the World Anti-Slavery Convention held in London. So impressive was his address before the convention that he attracted widespread attention in anti-slavery circles and received invitations to lecture throughout Great Britain. Now a celebrated fugitive slave, Pennington feared for his continued freedom when the **Fugitive Slave Act of 1850** was passed. In 1849 he returned to Great Britain to agitate against the American Colonization Society and continued to protest the society for some time. He ended an effort to buy his freedom, which he initiated in 1844, by paying his former owner in Maryland $150. He also published an account of his slave life and escape in *The Fugitive Black-*

James W.C. Pennington (Fisk University).

smith (1850). Pennington returned to New York in 1852 and continued to lecture widely on anti-slavery and civil rights causes. Long a member of the **Underground Railroad** and one of its agents in Hartford, Connecticut, he helped to raise money for the cause. Although best known as an abolitionist, Pennington worked several pastorates, as well, and he saw evangelism and education as important for his people.

Jessie Carney Smith

Purvis, Robert (1810–1898)

Robert Purvis was an ardent abolitionist who believed in the rights of blacks in America. Being light skinned and wealthy would have allowed Purvis to "pass" as white; instead, he embraced the anti-slavery sentiments of his father and the influences of **James Forten Sr.**, who was like a father to him. Purvis stepped on the abolitionist platform in 1827 to give his first speech. He immersed himself in the movement as a lecturer and leader and became a founding member of the **American Anti-Slavery Society** of Philadelphia in 1833, which included activists such as William Lloyd Garrison. He was also the only black member of the older Pennsylvania Society for Promoting the Abolition of Slavery, founded in 1775. Purvis's home outside of Philadelphia was also a stop on the **Underground Railroad**.

Purvis was president of the Vigilance Committee of Philadelphia from 1839 to 1844, but when the organization ceased to function, he continued to aid escaped slaves. A subsequent organization was established and Purvis served as its president for four terms. He actively sought to maintain the rights for free blacks when many states sought to limit their rights. With the arrival of the **Civil War**, Purvis remained dissatisfied with the government and saw no positive changes until the Emancipation Proclamation of 1863. At the end of the Civil War, he was asked to head the **Freedmen's Bureau**, but he refused. He feared this was a ploy by President Andrew Johnson to keep black support while attempting to destroy the bureau. In early February 1866, the Republican Congress passed the Freedmen's Bureau Bill. It called for the distribution of land to the freedmen, provided schools for their children, and set up military courts in southern states to protect freedmen's rights. But to the dismay of Republicans and the joy of most white southerners, President Johnson vetoed the bill. He called it unconstitutional and too expensive.

Purvis continued to work on behalf of education, temperance, and women's rights. With the passing of the **Fifteenth Amendment** in 1870, he argued that enfranchisement for black men should not be passed unless it included women.

Lean'tin L. Bracks

Purvis, Sarah Louisa Forten (1811?–1898?)

The evils of racial prejudice did not elude Sarah Forten Purvis, who grew up in a wealthy family and was insulated from the worse effects that prejudice offered during her childhood. Her family taught her to oppose slavery and to do what she could to help eradicate its presence. Her most powerful tool was the verse that she wrote. Writing under the name "Ada," her first poem, "The Graves of the Slave," appeared in William Lloyd Garrison's journal, the *Liberator,* on January 22, 1831. Her message was that the slave would only find rest from his labors through death. She reminded slave owners that, in death, the master and slave were equal. Purvis followed with other poems with the recurring theme of the slave or slavery. Her protest efforts against abolition were not confined to her poetry, however. Purvis and her older sisters Harriet and **Margaretta Forten** signed the charter establishing the Philadelphia Female Anti-Slavery Society in December 1833. For some time Purvis was on the society's board of managers and campaigned to abolish slavery in the District of Columbia. She also fought against efforts to annex Texas—an effort that would only benefit slave owners. While Purvis lived in Philadelphia, anti-slavery activities remained central to her work. She attended local anti-slavery meetings, as well as the Female Anti-Slavery Convention in New York. She also helped to entertain visiting abolitionists and enjoyed the company of black and white friends who were abolitionists. Leaving Philadelphia early in 1838, she married the wealthy Joseph Purvis, but later the Purvises lost their fortune and Sarah died a poor widow.

Jessie Carney Smith

Remond, Charles Lenox (1810–1873)

Charles Remond was born February 1, 1810, in Salem, Massachusetts, and died December 22, 1873, in Boston. It is speculated that he was a part of the original **American Anti-Slavery Society** since his mother and sisters founded the Female Anti-Slavery Society. Because of his oratorical skills, in 1838 the Massachusetts Anti-Slavery Society hired him as a lecturer. He

Charles Lenox Remond (Fisk University).

was adamant in his support of abolition and his rejection of separate black organizations, schools, and institutions. He spoke for the rights of all and pushed for immediate equality. He espoused William Lloyd Garrison's philosophy that moral suasion was the only way to end slavery; this philosophical agreement led to many positions in the Garrison camp. In 1840 Remond was chosen by the American Anti-Slavery Convention as a delegate to the first World Anti-Slavery Convention in London. Upon arrival, however, he found that women could not be seated; he and other American delegates therefore boycotted the meeting and joined delegate Lucretia Mott in speaking on the convention topics outside. He remained in London and for over a year lectured on temperance, slavery, and racial prejudice. In 1824, in an address before the Massachusetts House of Representatives, he helped secure legislation favoring free black travel. He was among those who rejected **Henry Highland Garnet's** support of slave

revolts in 1843. By 1848, he had become militant and aided the anti-slavery Free Soil Party, going so far as to call for the dissolution of the Union in 1858.

Helen R. Houston

Remond, Sarah P. (1826–1894)

Sarah P. Remond lectured widely throughout America and Great Britain on the issues of slaves' and women's rights during the mid-1800s. She also advocated equal education opportunities for all races. Growing up in a prominent family in Salem, Massachusetts, she saw her family host important abolitionists, suffragists, fugitives, radicals, and other rights advocates. She witnessed firsthand the racially segregated schools in Salem, which prompted her family to move to Newport, Rhode Island, and enroll their children in a private black school.

Remond became involved in interracial politics in 1853, when she and her friends refused to sit in the segregated gallery of the Howard Athenaeum in Boston during a concert. After authorities ejected her and caused her to fall, she sued the Salem police and won an important legal and moral victory, as well as $500 in damages. Remond first became an official anti-slavery agent in 1856; she joined a lecture circuit in New York State for the **American Anti-Slavery Society**. In 1858 Remond was a member of the National Women's Rights Convention's platform group at its New York City meeting. She spread her message abroad, and by 1859 began an extensive lecture tour in Scotland, England, and Ireland. In Liverpool, England, she spoke to a predominantly female audience. While in London, she attended a meeting that led to the founding of the London Emancipation Committee, of which she was a member. She also was a member of the Freedman's Aid Association. After the **Civil War** ended, Remond spent about a year in the United States, where she joined **Frederick Douglass** and other members of the American Equal Rights Association in the fight for universal suffrage. Then she returned to London, where she studied medicine before settling in Italy for the rest of her life.

Jessie Carney Smith

Smith, James McCune, (1813–1865)

Smith was born April 18, 1813, and died November 17, 1865, in Williamsburg, Long Island. As a student at the African Free School, he was exemplary; however, he could not pursue an advanced education in America. A black Episcopalian rector aided his attendance at Glasgow University, Scotland, where he earned a bachelor's, a master's, and a doctorate in medicine degrees. While in Scotland, he participated in the Scottish anti-slavery movement as an officer of the Glasgow Emancipation Society. Upon his return to the United States, he established a medical practice and supported the **Underground Railroad**. Smith spoke and wrote against acts that denied the equal rights of black people. He was against the American Colonization Society, wrote for both the *Emancipator* and *Colored American* (serving as an editor for a period of time), opining on such subjects as slavery and the Haitian Revolution. Smith recognized that the aims for black abolitionists and those of white abolitionists were often not the same. As time passed, he came to recognize the need for a narrower gap between black leadership and the black masses, and that blacks had to be more forceful in taking matters of liberation into their own hands. At the 1847 National Negro Convention, Smith and **Alexander Crummell** pushed for the creation of a black college. Throughout his life, he demonstrated intellectual excellence, concern for and a willingness to fight for the equal rights of all humans, and an ability to articulate the disparities in America.

Helen R. Houston

Still, William (1821–1902)

William Still was an advocate of black civil rights and did all he could to make freedom available to those who sought to attain it.

William Still (Fisk University).

Still was born of escaped-slave parents. In 1844 he left home and secured a position in the office of the Pennsylvania Society for the Abolition of Slavery in Philadelphia. With his position as clerk and janitor, he often gave aid and comfort to escaped slaves as they journeyed north to Canada. In 1852 the society created the General Vigilance Committee to specifically support the work of the **Underground Railroad**. This committee, which included Still as secretary and four other members, was charged with fundraising and record keeping; more importantly, the duties of aiding escaped slaves had placed them in defiance of federal law. Still stated in his own records that he learned that one of the fugitives, Peter Still, was a brother of his who his mother had been unable to take with her when she escaped slavery. In 1872 Still published the material he had collected in a book entitled *The Underground Railroad*. The book offered vital information about the people who had escaped and offered a perspective different from those of white abolitionists who portrayed fugitives as passive and submissive. Still's book pictured the fugitives as people who were strong, brave, and determined to gain their freedom in spite of tremendous odds. The book also has excerpts from newspapers, legal documents, and biographical sketches. Still was active in all aspects of abolition and black rights. He continued his commitment to the Abolition Society well after the **Civil War**, when he served as head of an employment office for freed slaves in 1862 and again as vice president of the organization from 1896 to 1901.

Lean'tin L. Bracks

Truth, Sojourner (1797?–1883)

Sojourner Truth rose from the brutality of slavery to become one of the most commanding anti-slavery and feminist orators of the nineteenth century, despite being illiterate. An itinerant preacher and speaker, Truth worked as a domestic servant and championed the cases of slaves and of women. Standing at reportedly almost six feet tall, Truth commanded the attention of her audiences. In 1851 she famously bore her breast during her "Ain't I a Woman?" speech before the delegates of the Ohio Women's Rights Convention. The salvo was typical of those she would continue to offer throughout her life as an evangelist and civil and women's rights advocate.

Truth was born Isabella Baumfree around 1797 on a plantation in Ulster County, New York. Little is known of her early childhood in the Dutch household before she was sold to John Neely in 1806. She suffered violent beatings from the Neelys and was sold four years later to the Dumonts. She married a fellow slave, with whom she had five children. Together, the family excitedly awaited their freedom following New York's passage of an emancipation act in 1827, which forced emancipation the following year. That same year, her owner's refusal to grant them their freedom prompted her to escape with only her youngest child to live with the Van Wageners, a Quaker family whose name she took.

After relocating to New York City, she worked as a domestic and held other odd jobs.

Sojourner Truth (Fisk University).

While working in the home of religious zealot Robert "Matthias Kingdom" Matthews, Truth emerged as a leading street-corner preacher and mystic. A captivating storyteller and singer of the spirituals, Truth developed and exhibited a remarkable knowledge of the Bible, despite being illiterate. Disenchanted with Matthews, she assumed the names Sojourner, for the journey she had undertaken to discover God, and Truth, because she felt ordained to spread the truth of God's Word. The renown of Truth's religious work was easily equaled by her activism in the anti-slavery and women's rights movements. She had embraced moral reform along with evangelical religion in the 1840s and had since emerged in anti-slavery circles among William Garrison and his cohorts.

The incorporation of religious and moral convictions, as well as her social activism, made Truth a much sought-after speaker. Her stature and distinct Dutch-English speech helped her to repeatedly draw large audiences of listeners. At the beginning of the **Civil War**, Truth worked to gather supplies for black volunteer regiments. She continued to aid the troops with gifts during the war and used the money raised from her lectures to assist fugitive slaves in securing employment and housing. In 1864 she began working for the National Freedman's Relief Association in Washington, D.C. President Abraham Lincoln received her in the White House in October of the same year. Truth also notably attempted to force the desegregation of Washington's streetcars the following year. She moved to Battle Creek, Michigan, in the late 1860s, which served as her base of operations until her death there in 1883.

Crystal A. deGregory

Tubman, Harriet (1820?–1913)

Following her escape from slavery in 1849, Harriet Tubman guided hundreds of American slaves to freedom along the series of loosely organized agents called the **Underground Railroad**. Returning to the South at least 19 times, Tubman personally led more than 300 men, women, and children to freedom in the North and Canada at the risk of losing her own life. Dubbed the Moses of her people, she also served as a nurse, scout, and spy in the Union Army during the **Civil War**, and in her later years became a champion of the elderly and the poor.

Originally Araminta Ross, she was one of eleven children born to Benjamin and Harriet Green Ross in Dorchester, Maryland. Despite her slave status, young Ross defiantly changed her name to Harriet as a child. She was rented out to neighboring plantations during her adolescence, denied an education, and punished severely for the smallest infraction. A particularly severe beating she received at age 15 caused narcoleptic episodes for the duration of her life. Married to a free black man named John Tubman in 1844, she escaped slavery three years later following his threats to sell her into slavery in the Deep South. The free status she enjoyed in Philadelphia was

Harriet Tubman (Fisk University).

jeopardized, however, by the passage of the 1850 **Fugitive Slave Act**, which authorized the enslavement of northern blacks regardless of their legal status. Soon after, Tubman became associated with the Philadelphia Vigilance Committee.

She coordinated her first escape plan with the organization in 1851, before moving to St. Catherine's, Canada. For the next six years she guided runaways north before coordinating the 1857 escape of her parents to freedom. Employing drugs to quiet babies and disguises to trick slave patrols, she went so far as to threaten to shoot any escapee who attempted to turn back because it would have jeopardized the others. In this way, Tubman helped hundreds to freedom before her last trip in 1860.

Arguably the most successful conductor of the **Underground Railroad**, Tubman was well known to the country's foremost abolitionists and was a regular speaker at anti-slavery and women's rights meetings. A friend of John

Brown, only illness prevented her from participating in his failed attack on Harper's Ferry in 1859. Throughout the 1860s, Tubman worked in the South, where she assisted escapees who volunteered for the Union. She traveled to South Carolina as a nurse and teacher for the abandoned Gullah people, as well as to Florida, where she taught newly freed blacks how to become self-sufficient. In 1863 Tubman became the first woman to lead U.S. troops when she guided the soldiers of the 2nd South Carolina Regiment up the Combahee River. Despite her gallantry, the U.S. government repeatedly denied her military wages and benefits. A member of the **National Association of Colored Women** and the National Federation of Afro-American Women, Tubman supported the suffrage movement and was an advocate of the elderly. Her lifelong dream, a Home for the Aged and Indigent Colored People, opened in 1908. In 1911 Tubman began living there before dying of pneumonia two years later.

Crystal A. deGregory

Tubman was well known to the country's foremost abolitionists.

Vashon, John Bathan (1792–1854)

A man of courage, John B. Vashon was faithful to the cause of black emancipation. The Norfolk, Virginia, native was the son of a mulatto mother and a white father of French ancestry. In 1822 he became a seaman on the *U.S.S. Revenge,* served in the War of 1812 in an engagement on the coast of Brazil, and was held prisoner for a while. When released from captivity, he returned to Virginia, settling in Fredericksburg and subsequently in Leesburg. There he volunteered to aid in the defense of his country and

helped to prevent the British from moving up the Potomac River. Vashon relocated to Carlisle, Pennsylvania, and in 1823 assisted in establishing a mutual improvement association—the Lay Benevolent Society—and served as its treasurer. After he moved to Pittsburgh in 1829, he became active in the anti-slavery movement and was associated with abolitionist William Lloyd Garrison, serving as an agent for Garrison's paper, the *Liberator*. A loyal supporter of Garrison, Vashon followed him to Boston and witnessed the Boston riot in 1835 in which Garrison was attacked and a rope put around his neck. Of this experience, William C. Nell notes: "The old soldier, who had helped to preserve his country's liberty ... had lived to witness freedom of speech and of the press stricken down by mob violence, and life itself in jeopardy." In Pittsburgh, Vashon organized the first anti-slavery society west of the Appalachian Mountains. In 1834 he was elected president of the Temperance Society and president of a Moral Reform Society. Vashon was also elected a vice president of the National Convention of Colored Men at its meeting in Rochester, New York, in July 1853.

Jessie Carney Smith

Walker, David (1785–1830)

D avid Walker was born free on September 28, 1785, in Wilmington, North Carolina, and died June 28, 1830, in Boston. Growing up, he found little difference between the life of a freedman and that of a slave. This resulted in a strong antipathy for slavery and prejudice and caused him to leave the South. He eventually settled in Boston in 1826, where he became a businessman known for his benevolence and for aiding fugitives. He contributed to newspapers and to civil rights organizations and lectured against slavery. His major contribution to the fight against slavery was his publication in September 1829 of the pamphlet *David Walker's Appeal in Four Articles: Together with a Preamble to the Coloured Citizens of the World, But in Particular, and Very Expressly, to Those of the United States of America.* This was the most bitter and fiery condemnation of white racism that had been published up to that time. His primary target was white racism, but he also attacked black complicity; he used a writing style that echoed the Constitution of the United States and underscored the discrepancy between words and actions. He drew upon religion, history, and politics to provide a well-reasoned argument. Walker called for black men to fight prejudice and injustice, emphasizing black pride and unity in the cause. The *Appeal* went through three editions within several months and frightened southerners to the point that it was banned in some states. In addition, after its publication free blacks were no longer allowed in some states to gather in large numbers. A reward was offered for Walker's capture, and even many abolitionists were against his *Appeal* because of its incendiary nature.

Helen R. Houston

Ward, Samuel Ringgold (1817–1866?)

Astaunch abolitionist, Samuel Ringgold Ward was uncompromising in his demand for a prompt end to slavery. Whether engaged in religious activities or in editing a newspaper, he lashed out against slavery at every opportunity. He was born on Maryland's eastern shore to slave parents who escaped and settled in New Jersey, then in New York City. Samuel Ward began work in the anti-slavery movement in 1833, while he clerked for an inventor and later for black abolitionist David Ruggles. His commitment to the movement became more intense after a mob beat him while he was leaving an anti-slavery meeting; the attackers were later freed. In 1836 Ward began to teach school in Newton, New York, and by 1839 he was licensed to preach as well. He became a traveling agent of the **American Anti-Slavery Society** that year, and later on for the New York Anti-Slavery Society. He was a highly respected orator, with skills that some said equaled those of abolitionists **Frederick Douglass**, James Pennington, **Henry Highland Garnet**, and Alexander Crummell.

In 1844 Ward campaigned for the anti-slavery Liberty Party, and by 1849 he was editing *The Impartial Citizen*. Ward became involved in the "Jerry rescue," the case of fugitive slave Jerry McHenry, who had lived in Syracuse, New York, and was seized, rescued, and rearrested. After 12 blacks and 14 whites were indicted in the case, nine of the blacks escaped to Canada. Ward and prominent black abolitionist Jermain W. Loguen were among those who escaped. The passage of the **Fugitive Slave Act** in 1850 spurred him to lecture throughout the North. The Anti-Slavery Society of Canada hired him in 1851 and engaged him in a strenuous speaking and writing venture. In 1855 Ward published his slave narrative, *Autobiography of a Fugitive Negro*. He is remembered for his moving and powerful oratorical and writing skills, and for protesting the unrelenting racism that surrounded him.

Jessie Carney Smith

Abu-Jamal remained on death row for more than 25 years, yet he maintained his innocence.

Civil Rights Activists

Abu-Jamal, Mumia (1954–)

Political activist and journalist Mumia Abu-Jamal attracted international media attention after his arrest, conviction, death sentence, imprisonment, and near-execution for the 1981 murder of Philadelphia policeman Daniel Faulkner. Abu-Jamal remained on death row for more than 25 years, yet he maintained his innocence, pursued legal appeals, and continued to research, write, publish, and broadcast on social justice issues while in prison. Born Wesley Cook

Mumia Abu-Jamal (AP Photo/Jennifer E. Beach).

and reared by his mother in Philadelphia after his father died when he was nine years old, he joined the **Black Panthers** as a high school journalist, changed his name, and continued his education at Goddard College and California State University. He returned to Philadelphia, where he worked as a radio journalist and joined the MOVE organization led by John Africa. Abu-Jamal intervened when police stopped his younger brother, William Cook; both Faulkner and Abu-Jamal were shot at the scene. Faulkner died, while Abu-Jamal, who had been beaten, was hospitalized and charged with first-degree murder. Support for Abu-Jamal came from organizations such as the **NAACP** Legal Defense Fund. As a result, two death warrants signed by Pennsylvania Governor Tom Ridge in 1995 and 1999 were stayed through legal appeals. Abu-Jamal is the author of four books, including *Live from Death Row; Death Blossoms: Reflections from a Prisoner of Conscience; All Things Censored;* and *Faith of Our Fathers: An Examination of the Spiritual Life of African and African-American People.*

Fletcher F. Moon

Al-Amin, Jamil Abdullah. *See* Brown, Hubert.

Allen, Mark (1962–)

The involvement of Mark Allen in social issues spans more than twenty years of service in private and public sectors, primarily working from his birthplace and home base of Chicago, Illinois. His activism began when he served as an assistant and national co-director for Citizen Action-Midwest Academy in 1986, the same year he received his bachelor's degree from Western Illinois University. Allen became project director of the Chicago office of **People United to Serve Humanity** (PUSH), a branch of the national PUSH organization led by **Jesse Jackson**. In 1988 he became national youth coordinator for the Jesse Jackson presidential campaign, but returned to PUSH in 1989 as interim chief of staff and special projects coordinator. The experience and expertise Allen gained led to other positions as a voter education and government relations specialist with the Chicago Urban League, where he worked until 1992, and as field coordinator for the Chicago Rehabilitation Network in 1993. In 1994 Allen began work as a human rights investigator for the Illinois Department of Human Rights; this was followed by service as field director for Rainbow/PUSH and A.J. Wright and Associates. Allen received honors and community service awards for his work in leadership development and political empowerment, and he was also influential through his consulting and media involvements, such as television appearances and writing newspaper columns.

Fletcher F. Moon

Barry, Marion Shepilov, Jr. (1936–)

Marion Shepilov Barry Jr. was born on March 6, 1936, in Itta Bena, Mississippi. He later moved to Memphis, Tennessee, where he grew up, excelled academically, and earned a B.S. in chemistry (1958) at LeMoyne College (now LeMoyne-Owen). At LeMoyne, he helped organize and served as president of the college's chapter of the **NAACP**, and he spearheaded an effort to force a white trustee of the college to retract a derogatory racial statement. Upon graduation, Barry enrolled at **Fisk University** in Nashville, Tennessee, and earned an M.S. in chemistry. He participated in a workshop on nonviolence and the first lunch counter sit-ins in Nashville. Barry and other students involved in non-violent practices responded to a call by **Ella Baker**, one of the founders of the **Student Non-Violent Coordinating Committee** (SNCC), in 1960 to meet at the "Southwest Student Leadership Conference on Non-Violent Resistance to Segregation." Out of this meeting grew the SNCC; Barry was elected its first chair. In the early part of the 1960s, he worked with the SNCC, and in 1964 he left to complete a Ph.D.; he then established a Washington, D.C., chapter of the SNCC. In Washington, he continued fighting for racial equality, and his advocacy for the working class was one of the reasons for his success in politics. He eventually served three terms as mayor of Washington, D.C., from 1979 to 1991 and again from 1995 to 1999. His tenure in office was fraught with successes and controversy. In his third mayoral term, Barry faced drug charges, resigned his office, and was sentenced to prison, serving six months. Following his release, he successfully ran for mayor, returning to office from 1995 to 1999. In 2004 he was elected Ward 8 Council Representative in the District of Columbia. His political achievements permeate the District and influence his popularity with his constituents.

Helen R. Houston

Bond, Julian (1940–)

Julian Bond was born on January 14, 1940, in Nashville, Tennessee. He began his activism at an early age by refusing to sit in the section reserved for African Americans in the Newtown movie theater. Bond entered **Morehouse College** in 1957, assisting Lonnie King, another student, in organizing discussions of the black sit-in movement and forming Atlanta's Committee on Appeal for Human Rights whose agenda was to

stage a sit-in. They executed the sit-in and Bond was among the students arrested; the group participated in other non-violent activities. In 1960, he and other students were called together at Shaw University where the **Student Non-Violent Coordinating Committee** (SNCC) was formed. James Forman hired Bond as SNCC's director of communication. He immediately inaugurated the photographically illustrated *Student Voice*, SNCC's newsletter. He participated in voter registration activities in Georgia, Alabama, Mississippi, and Arkansas. He left Morehouse in 1961 to work on the protest newspaper, *The Atlanta Inquirer,* and later became its managing editor.

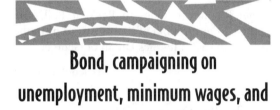

Bond, campaigning on unemployment, minimum wages, and fair housing, was elected to the Georgia House of Representatives.

In 1965, Bond, campaigning on unemployment, minimum wages, and fair housing, was elected to the Georgia House of Representatives; however, he was not seated because of his voiced opposition to the Vietnam War. He was again elected in 1966, again denied seating, but the U.S. Supreme Court ruled the Georgia House had violated his rights. Ultimately, he served four terms in the House and six in the Senate. He became the first black chair of the Fulton County Senate Delegation, chairman of the Committee on Consumer Affairs, and a member of the Committee on Human Resources. In the Georgia General Assembly, he sponsored more than 60 bills that became law and organized the Georgia Legislative Black Caucus. In 1968, Bond was nominated for vice president of the United States, but had to withdraw because of his youth. In 1971, when Morris Dees and Joseph J. Levin Jr. founded the Southern Poverty Law Center, Bond became its first president, later served as president emeritus, serves on its board of directors, and narrated two of its videos: "A Time for Justice" and "Shadow of Hate." In 1986, he retired from the state senate to run for a seat in the U.S. House of Representatives, but lost to former SNCC member **John Lewis**. He has served four terms on the NAACP Board. He has been a commentator, writer, and narrator on television and radio programs, videos, and documentaries. Among these are *America's Black Forum*, "Rush Toward Freedom," "Eyes on the Prize," "A Time for Justice," and "Crossing the Color Line: From Rhythm 'n Blues to Rock 'n Roll." He received the 1985 Bill of Rights Award from the American Civil Liberties Union of Georgia.

Helen R. Houston

Boyd, John W., Jr. (1965–)

A poultry farmer near South Hill in Baskerville, Virginia, John W. Boyd Jr. watched U.S. Department of Agriculture officials throw his loan application in the trash can without further discussion. On other occasions, his application for farm support was delayed past the time to be helpful for his purposes. In 1991, Boyd filed a discrimination complaint with the U.S. Department of Agriculture. His suit was settled after five years of legal wrangling, but he lost his poultry business and declared bankruptcy. In 1995 Boyd founded and became president of the National Black Farmers Association (NBFA). The organization united black farmers who had similar encounters. The NBFA set as its motto, "We have our mule, now we're looking for our 40 acres." The group made its voice heard in Washington, D.C., in 1996 at a meeting with the Secretary of Agriculture, attesting to its solidarity.

The next year the group met with President Bill Clinton, after which he included in his 1999 agricultural budget funds for direct operating loans to minority farmers. The NBFA's first rally in Washington spurred USDA officials to hold a series of "listening sessions" across the country in early 1997. The aim was to investigate alleged abuse in the agency's programs of the farmers' civil rights, resulting in the publication of "Civil Rights at the United States Department of Agriculture." This special report concluded that systematic civil rights abuses had occurred for three decades, and gave 92 recommendations for change. In April 1997, the NBFA and over 200 black farmers protested outside the White House. After that, the Secretary of Agriculture proclaimed that the agency's top challenge was the problem of civil rights. Boyd and the NBFA achieved a major breakthrough for minority farmers, who then received compensation, loans, and benefits that they were due provided they filed claims by a certain date. Many farmers did not know there was a deadline and received no compensation. By 2007 the farmers' lawsuit was reopened and awaited approval of Congress and President George W. Bush.

Jessie Carney Smith

Brown, Elaine (1943–)

Elaine Brown became the first woman to chair the **Black Panther Party**, making her the highest-ranking woman in the organization, second only to **Huey P. Newton**. Newton and **Bobby Seale** founded the Panthers in Oakland, California, in 1966. The group was organized to protect local communities from police brutality and racism. Brown was born on March 2, 1943, in Philadelphia, Pennsylvania, to Dorothy Brown, a working-class mother. Her father, Dr. Horace Scott, never publicly acknowledged his daughter. She received her education from the Thaddeus Stevens School of Practice and Philadelphia High School for Girls. Brown attended the Philadelphia Conservatory of Music and, for a short time, Temple University. In 1965 she left Philadelphia for Los Angeles, California, to pursue a career as a songwriter. Soon after arriving in Los Angeles, Brown was introduced to the ideas of the **Black Power Movement**. Later she began writing for *Harambee* (which in Swahili literally means "pulling together"), the organ of the Los Angeles Black Congress, an assembly of black organizations whose objective was to serve the needs of the black community.

By 1967 Brown had become acquainted with the Black Panther Party, and in April of 1968 she joined the party's Southern California chapter. By the following year, Brown became the chapter's minister of information. In 1974, with the expulsion of cofounder Bobby Seale, Brown was named chair of the Black Panther Party, a position she held until 1977, when she left the party and migrated to France with her daughter, Ericka Suzanne Brown. During Brown's tenure as party chief, the Panthers sought power through political channels. One of the party's objectives was to elect a black mayor in the city of Oakland. The Panthers registered 90,000 black Democrats toward this goal. Because of this political activity, Black Panther candidate Lionel Wilson was elected the first black mayor of Oakland, California, in 1976. A political activist, singer, and author, Brown's autobiography, *A Taste of Power: A Black Woman's Story* was published in 1992. Moving to Atlanta, Georgia, Brown founded Mothers Advocating Juvenile Justice. In addition to her memoir, she is the author of *The Condemnation of Little B: New Age Racism in America* (2002).

Linda T. Wynn

Brown, Hubert (1943–)

H."Rap" Brown was born in Baton Rouge, Louisiana, on October 4, 1943. In 1960 Brown attended Southern University in Louisiana. Two years later, after visiting his brother, Non-Violent Action Group (NAG) leader Ed Brown, in Washington, D.C., he joined his brother in working for NAG. By 1964 he was serving as the director of NAG. He also became immersed in the work of the **Student Non-Violent Coordinating Committee** (SNCC). In 1966

Brown was named Alabama project director and helped to register voters in the South. The next year, he was appointed the national director of the SNCC and also became an active member of the **Black Panther Party**. **Stokely Carmichael** called Brown a "bad man," and Brown's leadership was considered radical and aggressive. Under Brown's leadership, the SNCC emphasized separatism, black power, and agency. He encouraged self-defense and even violence. The police therefore often harassed Brown. In 1970 he was indicted for inciting a riot in Maryland and went into hiding. He was imprisoned in 1973 on burglary charges in New York and paroled three years later. During his stay in prison, he became a Muslim and changed his name to Jamil Abdullah Al-Amin. He moved to the West End area of Atlanta and became active in the community, helping to fight against crime. In 2000 he was arrested again and charged with the murder of a sheriff's deputy; he was subsequently sentenced to life without parole.

Helen R. Houston

Bunche, Ralph (1904–1971)

Ralph Bunche learned early on the importance of education and thus succeeded in earning a Ph.D. from Harvard University in 1934. From 1928 until 1950, he was a professor of political science at Howard University. In his service to the U.S. government and the United Nations, Bunche received many accolades and earned the Nobel Peace Prize in 1950 for his successful negotiation of a peace armistice between Israel and Arab states. He was the first African American to receive this honor. Politically, Bunche was seen as a moderate who often criticized the American system. He co-founded the National Negro Congress in 1935, which focused on labor coalitions and economic rights. Drawing on past experiences, including his role as co-director of the Institute of Race Relations at Swarthmore College, Bunche wrote the book *A World View of Race* (1936). He clearly saw that segregation and the denial of voting rights and political power to African Americans was incompatible with democracy. While working in government, Bunche continued his involvement in race matters and was a member of the **Black Cabinet**, but he later refused the position of assistant secretary of state in protest of racist policies regarding housing in Washington, D.C. Bunche often viewed black organizations as elitist in their policies and too passive in their actions. During the 1955 **Montgomery bus boycott** in Alabama, Bunche was a supporter not only of the boycott but also of the work of **Martin Luther King Jr.** In 1963 he spoke before King at the **March on Washington** and later joined King during the **Selma to Montgomery March** in 1965. He provided his support on many advisory levels but never aspired to a leadership role. Bunche never saw civil rights as a domestic issue, but rather as a part of the larger struggle for worldwide human rights and dignity.

Lean'tin L. Bracks

Carmichael was beaten and arrested, but he continued to work on SNCC projects.

Carmichael, Stokely (1941–1998)

Also known as Kwame Toure, Carmichael gained notoriety for popularizing the "Black Power" slogan in 1966. He worked with several civil rights organizations, most notably as a member and chair of the **Student Non-Violent Coordinating Committee** (SNCC). He influenced the shift of the SNCC from nonviolence to militancy, and in later years was affiliated with the **Black Panthers**, Pan-African, and Marxist organizations. Stokely Standiford Churchill Carmichael was born in Port of Spain,

Trinidad, and emigrated to New York City in 1952. He graduated from Bronx High School of Science in 1960, and earned a bachelor's degree in philosophy from **Howard University** in 1964. During the 1961 **Freedom Rides**, Carmichael was beaten and arrested, but he continued to work on SNCC projects. After replacing **John Lewis** as the SNCC chair in 1966, he coauthored the book *Black Power* with Charles V. Hamilton and joined the Black Panther Party in 1967. In 1969 he became a Pan-Africanist and Marxist, changed his name, married singer Miriam Makeba, and moved to Conakry, Guinea. He wrote another book, *Stokely Speaks,* in 1971, divorced in 1978, remarried and was divorced again by 1992, and remained in Guinea until his death from prostate cancer at age 57.

Fletcher F. Moon

Chaney, James Earl (1943–1964)

James Chaney was murdered during the desegregation and voter registration drives in Mississippi, during the **Freedom Summer**. The Freedom Summer project was designed to draw America's attention to the violence against blacks in Mississippi and to develop a grass-roots freedom movement that could be sustained after student activists left the state. Freedom Summer is often remembered for the deaths of three young civil rights workers in Mississippi. Chaney, who was then 21, and his two white comrades from New York, Michael Schwerner (24) and Andrew Goodman (20), disappeared on Sunday, June 21, 1964. They had gone to visit Mt. Zion Methodist Church, which the Ku Klux Klan had firebombed because the church was going to be used to house Freedom School. Their disappearance attracted the national news media and hundreds of searchers to Neshoba County. The trio's burned-out station wagon was found the next day in the Bogue Chitto swamp. Rescuers found their bodies 44 days later buried 15 feet in an earthen dam. While the search for the missing civil rights workers in Mississippi continued, the

Civil Rights Act of 1964 was passed by the U.S. Congress.

Chaney, the son of Ben and Fannie Lee Chaney, was born in the racially exclusive and economically depressed town of Meridian, Mississippi, where he received his primary and secondary education. An apprentice plasterer working for his father, Chaney, a civil rights activist, joined the **Congress of Racial Equality** (CORE) in 1963. A year later, the Council of Federated Organizations (COFO) launched a massive desegregation and voter registration drive in Mississippi, and Chaney became an active participant in black Mississippians' struggle for equality and justice. On June 21, 2005, in Philadelphia, Mississippi, a jury convicted 80-year-old Edgar Ray Killen, a former member of the Ku Klux Klan, of manslaughter in the murders of Chaney, Goodman, and Schwerner. Their tragic deaths during Freedom Summer inspired the 1988 film *Mississippi Burning*.

Linda T. Wynn

Shirley Chisholm (AP Photo).

Chisholm, Shirley (1924–2005)

Chisholm early on had role models of strong black women and a strong academic background that helped prepare her for her role as a politician for the people of New York. She became the first African American woman elected to the U.S. Congress and the first African American to run for president of the United States. Throughout her career she campaigned diligently for civil rights and for the rights of women. Shirley Chisholm, born Shirley Anita Saint Hill, was greatly influenced by her maternal grandmother during the six years that Chisholm and her sisters lived with her in Barbados. It was also during this time that Chisholm received the strong academic foundation that prepared her for higher education. Embracing teaching as her initial career goal, as few other opportunities were open to women, Chisholm went on to receive a college degree from Brooklyn College in 1946 and then pursued her master's degree at Columbia University. It was during this time that she

got involved with the local political organization the Seventeenth Assembly District Democratic Club. It is through this experience that Chisholm learned the potential power of the black vote and women's vote.

With no key black elected officials and women only in the role of organizers, Chisholm saw a need for change. In 1960 she started the *Unity Democratic Club*. One goal of the club was to encourage black and Hispanic voters to exercise their right to vote. Chisholm ran for the New York State Assembly in 1964 and won, which eventually led to her winning a seat in Congress in 1968 representing New York's 12th Congressional District. The Congressional seat made Chisholm the first African American woman elected to Congress. During her years in Congress, Chisholm spoke out for civil rights, women's rights, and for the poor and uneducated. Setting no limitations on her aspirations Chisholm announced her candidacy for president of the United States on January 5, 1972. She received little support from white, women-led organizations or black, male-led organizations, however, nor did male opponents see her as a serious challenger. In spite of these concerns, Chisholm remained in the race until the Democratic convention, where she received more than 150 votes on the first ballot. Although she did not win the nomination, Chisholm continued to serve. She retired from the House of Representatives in 1983.

Lean'tin L. Bracks

Cleaver, Eldridge (1935–1998)

Most famously remembered for his tenure as the Minister of Information for the **Black Panther Party**, Eldridge Cleaver was the face of America's most militant black nationalist organization during the late 1960s. His 1968 book, *Soul On Ice,* secured his national prominence

and became a standard for Civil Rights Movement participants. Born in Wabbaseka, Arkansas, to Leroy and Thelma Cleaver, Leroy Eldridge Cleaver was reared in the Watts section of Los Angeles, California. His adolescent petty crime record devolved into a full-fledged criminal career by the time he reached his early twenties, resulting in his imprisonment. During a two-and-a-half year stint at the California State Prison that began in 1954, Cleaver completed his high school education. After he was convicted of assault in 1957, he decided to give up crime. He was influenced by the Black Muslims and was a proponent of their teachings, until he became a committed follower of **Malcolm X**. Following his 1966 parole, he worked for *Ramparts* magazine. He began a new life as political activist and married fellow activist Kathleen

Eldridge Cleaver with his wife, Kathleen (AP Photo/Preston Stroup).

Neal the following year. In 1968, the same year he helped to found the Black Panther Party, a number of political controversies, including his insistence on criticizing the injustices black America faced, resulted in his being ordered to return to jail. In his legal struggle to remain free, Cleaver fled the country. While in Algeria, the Cleavers founded the international wing of the Panther party, but arguments forced a break with the party in America. He returned to the United States in 1976. Now a political conservative, he rejected his former views and eventually joined the Mormon Church. Throughout the 1980s, he struggled with substance abuse and made several unsuccessful bids for public office. Cleaver died of prostate cancer in Pomona, California, at age 62.

Crystal A. deGregory

Davis, Angela (1944–)

Angela Yvonne Davis was emboldened by her mother and grandmother to fight for civil rights. Once on the FBI's most wanted list, Davis is often associated with the **Black Panthers** and the black power politics of the late 1960s and early 1970s. Arrested as a conspirator in the abortive attempt to free George Jackson from a courtroom in Marin County, California, on August 7, 1970, Davis was active with the **Student Non-Violent Coordinating Committee** (SNCC) before she moved on to the Black Panthers. She joined the Communist Party after **Martin Luther King Jr.**'s assassination in 1968. A promoter of women's rights and racial justice, while pursuing her career as a philosopher and professor at the University of Santa Cruz and San Francisco University, Davis was tenured at the University of California at Santa Cruz, despite Governor Ronald Reagan's admonition that she would never teach again in the University of California system.

In 1970 Davis's political activism earned her international attention. An advocate for black political prisoners, she spoke in defense of inmates known as the Soledad Brothers. When

Angela Davis (AP Photo).

the brother of prisoner George Jackson attempted to free an inmate from a courthouse in Marin County, California, four people were killed in the process with guns owned by Davis. She was charged with kidnapping, conspiracy, and murder, even though she was nowhere near the vicinity. Davis went underground. Found two months later in New York, she was extradited to California and incarcerated without bail. During her incarceration, a massive international "Free Angela Davis" campaign was organized, leading to her acquittal in 1972.

Davis, the youngest child of B. Frank and Sallye E. Davis, was born in Birmingham, Alabama, on January 26, 1944. Her political activism was fashioned while an undergraduate attending Brandeis University (1961-65) and by her studies at the Sorbonne in Paris, where Algerian students provided her with a universal perspective on the struggle against colonialism and oppression. Davis's political commitments intensified in 1963, when on September 15, Denise McNair (11), Addie Mae Collins (14), Carole Robertson (14), and Cynthia Wesley (14), whom she knew, were killed in the **Sixteenth Street Baptist Church** bombing in her native city of Birmingham, Alabama. In 1980 and 1984, she ran for the office of Vice President of the United States on the Communist Party ticket.

Never forgetting the racial discrimination she endured as an actress, Davis was ... fierce, forceful, and eloquent in her lectures.

A student of philosopher Herbert Marcuse, Davis has written numerous works on race, class, and gender. She has more recently worked as a professor at the University of California, Santa Cruz, where she teaches courses on the history of consciousness. Professor Davis has lectured in all 50 states, as well as in Africa, Europe, the Caribbean, and the former Soviet Union. Her articles and essays have appeared in numerous journals and anthologies and she is the author of several books, including *Angela Davis: An Autobiography* (1975); *Women, Race, and Class* (1982); *Women, Culture, and Politics* (1988); *Blues Legacies and Black Feminism: Gertrude "Ma" Rainey, Bessie Smith, and Billie Holiday* (1998); *The Angela Y. Davis Reader* (1998); and *Are Prisons Obsolete?* (2003).

Linda T. Wynn

Davis, Henrietta Vinton (1860–1941)

Although widely known as an actress, Henrietta Vinton Davis was also a revolutionary and a radical who contributed significantly to

Marcus Garvey and his **Universal Negro Improvement Association** (UNIA). Her theatrical work took her to the West Indies, where she met Garvey supporters and became attracted to the UNIA. She met Garvey in 1919, while the UNIA was in its infancy. He invited her to speak at the Palace Casino in Harlem. Her theatrical career was in full swing by then; however, she left it behind, isolated herself from her friends, and began work with Garvey and the UNIA. A staunch nationalist, Davis placed race and support of Africa at the cornerstone of her philosophy. Among other advocacies, she urged blacks to emigrate to Africa and to take pride in their race; she preferred the term "Negro" over "colored," as blacks were called during that period.

Never forgetting the racial discrimination she endured as an actress, Davis was so fierce, forceful, and eloquent in her lectures that she had no difficulty promoting the philosophies of the UNIA. Thus, in 1919 she was named the UNIA's first international organizer. Davis became a loyal Garvey supporter and helped build the movement. She spoke in various cities where her reputation as an actress was firmly established, giving her a readymade audience. She became a part of a delegation to Africa in 1924 to aid in founding a colony in Liberia. In time, however, Davis became alienated from Garvey and moved to head a splinter rival group.

Jessie Carney Smith

Dawson, William L. (1886–1970)

William Levi Dawson was an active member of the Democratic Party and a powerful influence on Chicago politics from 1943 to 1970. A graduate of **Fisk University** in Nashville, Tennessee, and Northwestern University School of Law in Evanston, Illinois, along with other educational accomplishments, he was admitted to the Illinois bar in 1920. He started a law practice and became an active participant in local politics. After serving as state central committeeman, alderman for the second ward, and Democratic committeeman, he ran for U.S. Congress, winning a seat in 1942. Dawson was an effective representative for his constituents because he maintained contact with them throughout his political terms. He advocated for the removal of the poll tax and was credited with defeating the Winstead Amendment, which allowed military personnel to decide if they wanted to serve in units that included blacks. Dawson became the first African American chosen to chair a standard congressional committee. In 1960, when President John F. Kennedy offered Dawson an appointment as postmaster general as a reward for his work during the election campaign, he refused because his commitment to his constituents would be better served if he remained in the House of Representatives. Dawson remained in the House until his death in 1970.

Lean'tin L. Bracks

Denby, Charles (1908–1983)

A native of Lowndes County, Alabama, Charles Denby was born Simon Peter Owens to a family of farmers. After migrating to the North during the Great Migration, the then–17-year-old Denby found work as an auto assembler on the production lines in 1924. His experiences as a Detroit autoworker led him to labor union activism. In the 1940s and 1950s, Denby emerged as a militant and labor organizer, associating with Marxist intellectuals C.L.R. James and Raya Dunayevskaya, the founder of the Marxist Humanism philosophy in the United States. In the midst of the Great Depression black unemployment soared at rates that exceeded those of whites. After being repeatedly laid off, Denby sought work as a day laborer but eventually returned to the South, where he worked as a chauffeur for nearly a decade. Back in Detroit in 1943, a citywide riot got him involved in strikes and organizing black workers. As a participant in the critical struggles that led to the development of the United Auto Workers (UAW), Denby witnessed interracial and class infighting that convinced him that

gains for the working classes could not be made unless unions addressed systemic racism.

In the wake of his involvement, Denby became immersed in leftist organizations, including the Trotskyist movement and the Socialist Workers' Party (SWP). In 1952 he published the first volume of his autobiography, *Indignant Heart: A Black Worker's Journal,* with the second volume not appearing until 1978. Three years later, he and Dunayevskaya founded the Marxist newspaper *News & Letters,* for which Denby served as editor. The paper featured Denby's column "Worker's Journal" in every issue until his death in 1983. Like his autobiography, the column and newspaper recorded the struggles of the working class and reported the rank-and-file's activist experiences.

Crystal deGregory

Dukes, Hazel Nell (1932–)

A career political and social activist, Hazel Nell Dukes was inspired early on by **Rosa Parks**, her neighbor in Montgomery, Alabama. Parks's words "to be somebody one day" helped her to set her sights on advancing civil rights when she relocated to New York City. Long a member of the **NAACP**, she protested in more than 100 marches, resulting in six arrests. She was president of the NAACP from 1990 to 1992. While in office, she was adamant in her views on the plight of the poor in American society and she challenged the White House for what she felt was its lack of regard on this matter. She blamed President Ronald Reagan for the lack of progress in civil rights. Her tenure as national president was steeped in controversy due to her views on the impact of immigrants on the employment prospects of blacks, as expressed in statements that she said were taken out of context, when all the while her concern was with the work ethic of blacks. Turmoil within the organization led to her departure from the post, however. As head of the New York State Conference of the NAACP, she kept her indomitable spirit and the support of her local constituents. Dukes has been cited for her work in social justice, as seen, for example, in the awards received from the New York Human Rights Commission and the New York State Black and Puerto Rican Legislative Caucus.

Jessie Carney Smith

[Dukes] blamed President Ronald Reagan for the lack of progress in civil rights.

Elliott, Daisy L. (1919–)

As the sponsor of more than 80 bills during her 17-year tenure in the Michigan State House of Representatives, Daisy L. Elliott was one of the state's most influential legislators during the 1960s and 1970s. In 1977 she notably cosponsored the Elliott-Larsen Civil Rights Act, which was the most comprehensive civil rights legislation adopted by any state at the time and resulted in the creation of the Michigan Department of Civil Rights. Born Daisy Elizabeth Lenoir in Filbert, West Virginia, her father, Robert Lenoir, was a coal miner and her mother, Daisy Dorum Lenoir, was a housewife who stressed the value of education. Reared and educated in Beckley, West Virginia, Lenoir graduated high school in 1936 and married soon thereafter. During the 1940s, she studied at Wayne State University and Vallejo College, before graduating from the Detroit Institute of Commerce in 1950.

Over the course of the next decade, she became active in a number of civic and political organizations, including the **NAACP** and the League of Women Voters. Elected as a Democrat with strong interracial labor union support, Elliott served in the Michigan State House of Representatives from 1963 to 1978 and again

from 1981 to 1982. The Elliott-Larsen Civil Rights Act of 1977 bars discrimination in employment, housing, public services, and accommodations based on an individual's religion, race, color, national origin, age, sex, height, weight, familial status, or marital status. Around the same time, she also founded *CAPITOL: Woman,* a newsletter that focused on issues concerning women. Appointed to a number of powerful house committees, Elliott helped to guide legislation affecting labor, education, and minorities, as well as the young and old. Even when an unsuccessful defense against a charge of purchasing a stolen vehicle effectively ended her political career in 1982, Elliott continued to serve as a public advocate through her work at the Detroit Housing Commission well into the 1990s.

Crystal A. deGregory

Evers, Charles (1922–)

Charles Evers, like his brother Medgar, learned well the lessons his father taught. He understood to never be afraid of whites and that the problems they had were often a result of elected officials. In 1940, after serving in the U.S. Army during World War II, Charles and his brother returned to Mississippi. After trying to register to vote in the 1946 election campaign, they were turned away from the polling station by angry whites. Both Charles and Medgar successfully graduated from Alcorn Agricultural and Mechanical College in 1952. Charles Evers continued to do organizing for the **NAACP**, and by 1954 he was the NAACP's State Voter Registration Chairman. After two years in this office, he was driven out of Mississippi by angry whites. Evers moved from Philadelphia, Pennsylvania, to Chicago, Illinois, and took on various jobs and economic dealings. After his brother Medgar was assassinated in 1963, Evers took over his position as state field secretary for the NAACP's Mississippi chapter and actively established groups to assist blacks in registering to vote. He also led numerous demonstrations for black civil rights. Evers was highly motivated to carry on his brother's work because he believed that if he had been there to protect his brother the assassination might not have happened. In 1969 Evers was elected mayor of Fayette, Mississippi, becoming the first black to hold a mayorship in the state since Reconstruction ended. He served in this position until 1981, and again from 1985 to 1989. He has also served as an advisor to politicians such as Presidents **John F. Kennedy, Lyndon B. Johnson,** Richard Nixon, and Ronald Reagan, and to Senator **Robert Kennedy,** and Governor George Wallace.

Lean'tin L. Bracks

Evers, Medgar (1925–1963)

Medgar Evers was the third of four children born to James and Jessie Evers of Decatur, Mississippi. Medgar and his older brother Charles both fought in World War II and graduated from Alcorn Agricultural and Mechanical College. They were both interested in changing the conditions of blacks in Mississippi. After graduating from college, in 1952 Evers went to work for Theodore Howard's Magnolia Mutual Life Insurance Company of Mound Bayou, Mississippi. Howard, who was the founder of the Regional Council of Negro Leadership, introduced Evers to other politically concerned blacks. Evers also joined the Mound Bayou branch of the **NAACP.** As an insurance agent, he had direct contact with rural blacks and understood their challenges and the conditions of their lives. In 1954 Evers was appointed the salaried field secretary of the Mississippi NAACP. Before his appointment the branch had been inactive. Whites were angry with Evers because he was very active in this role, which included his insistence that the state enforce the 1954 *Brown v. Board of Education* ruling stating that segregation was unconstitutional.

It is said that Evers's pressure on the state regarding segregation was the basis for white supremacists attacking him. In his campaign for civil rights, Evers was arrested, beaten, and often threatened. He gave his support to **Martin**

Luther King Jr., who formed the **Southern Christian Leadership Conference** (SCLC) because their ultimate goal of civil rights was compatible with his own. In the early hours of June 12, 1963, Evers was assassinated in the driveway of his Jackson, Mississippi, home. His assassin, Byron De La Beckwith Jr., was tried twice and acquitted in 1964, but on February 5, 1994, he was retried and sentenced to life in prison. Medgar Evers's death caused President **John F. Kennedy,** who would be assassinated five months later on November 22, to take action toward passing a comprehensive civil rights law. Evers's commitment to civil rights in his home state of Mississippi shed light on further injustices in the South and inspired other blacks to claim their citizenship through voting and seeking political office.

Lean'tin L. Bracks

It is said that Evers's pressure on the state regarding segregation was the basis for white supremacists attacking him.

Fletcher, Arthur (1924–2005)

Arthur Fletcher, often referred to as the "Father of Affirmative Action," chaired the U.S. Civil Rights Commission from 1990 to 1993 and was an ardent supporter of the Civil Rights Act of 1991. While in that post, he was critical of President George H.W. Bush for "labeling civil rights legislation as a quota bill." Although he was a Republican, his loyalty to civil rights causes never prevented him from admonishing Presidents Ronald Reagan and George H.W. Bush for failing to support civil rights. During his life, Fletcher was in and out of politics. He was also practically a constant advisor to Republican presidents, becoming well known politically during the Richard Nixon administration, when he was an assistant secretary for wage and labor standards in the Department of Labor. He developed a model for affirmative action and said that it changed the workplace "for the better forever." He also urged corporations to keep the affirmative action movement alive. Fletcher left the Nixon administration in 1971 to head the United Negro College Fund. He long had a zeal for equal economic opportunity and promoted this interest in the firm that he owned and managed, Fletcher's Learning System, Inc. The company created various training materials and guides for maintaining equal business opportunities for minorities.

Jessie Carney Smith

Foster, Marie (1917–2003)

One of the unsung heroines of the Civil Rights Movement, Marie Foster was born October 24, 1917, near Alberta, Alabama, and died September 6, 2003, in Selma, Alabama. Her experiences growing up, including firsthand knowledge of the treatment of the black populace and witnessing the fearlessness of college students, encouraged Foster to confront the system that denied black people their rights. In spite of her advanced education, she was denied the right to register to vote; it took eight years before she could get registered. Once registered, she began to run literacy and citizenship classes and send her graduates to **Southern Christian Leadership Conference** workshops in Savannah, Georgia. Foster was one of the founders of the Dallas County Voters League, which, among other acts, sought to sustain workers negatively impacted by their participation in protests. Foster's influence was so powerful that Judge James A. Hare issued an injunction prohibiting black meetings in groups of three or more in public and banned meetings sponsored by civil rights leaders or groups. She defied these barriers, as well as

threats on her life, and continued her activities. Foster participated in the **Bloody Sunday** March on March 7, 1965. Before the march was halted, she was clubbed severely. In spite of the resulting physical injuries, she was part of the triumphant **Selma to Montgomery march** on March 21, 1965. For the remainder of her life, she continued her fight for equality and voting rights.

Helen R. Houston

Jackson, Luther Porter (1892–1950)

A leading voice in the struggle for racial justice, Luther P. Jackson walked a tightrope of protest and accommodation in Virginia. In so doing, he put his life and that of his family in jeopardy. His struggle preceded the sit-ins and freedom marches of the 1960s and stimulated a social and political awakening that endured after his death. His was considered one of the most powerful voices for African American teachers and politicians, and for the right of blacks to vote.

Born in Lexington, Kentucky, to former slaves, Jackson received undergraduate and graduate degrees from **Fisk University**, a second master's from Columbia University, and a doctorate from the University of Chicago. While at Fisk, he became attracted to the work of George Edmund Haynes, a founding member of the National Urban League who had a deep concern for the welfare of African Americans. Jackson joined the faculty at Virginia Normal and Industrial Institute (later University) in Petersburg, where he remained from 1922 until his death. He established himself as a scholar and an authority on African American history, especially in Virginia. During the 1930s and 1940s, he was a crusader for voting rights for blacks. He organized the Petersburg League of Negro Voters in 1934, which was known later as the Virginia Voters League. Under the auspices of the Southern Regional Council, Jackson expanded his study to examine black voting in the South, published in a special issue of the *New South* (June-July 1948) as "Race and Suffrage in the South since 1940."

Jackson worked with the **NAACP** in promoting voting rights and was fund raiser for the **Association for the Study of Negro** (now African American) **Life and History** . He worked with the Virginia Teachers Association (VTA) and helped to mobilize the association and its members in a drive for salary equalization. He had faith in the ability of teachers to "sow the seeds of racial equality." So concerned was Jackson with voting rights that he brought the matter before VTA meetings and used its publication, the *Virginia Teachers Bulletin,* to further the issue of voting rights as well. Jackson is important for his work in civil rights and liberal initiatives in the South from the 1920s until his death in 1950; afterwards, other activists built on his work and led new civil rights initiatives.

Jessie Carney Smith

Jordan, Vernon (1935–)

Vernon Jordan, a native of Atlanta, Georgia, was educated in the city's segregated public school system and received his undergraduate degree from DePauw University in 1957. With a major in political science and a minor in history and speech, Jordan went on to law school at **Howard University** and received his J.D. in 1960. He actively pursued his interest in civil rights law, which was at the forefront of change during this period. His first position after graduating was as a law clerk in the Atlanta office of prominent civil rights lawyer **Donald L. Hollowell**. Jordan proved his skill and his dedication to the cause of civil rights in a 1960 landmark desegregation lawsuit against the University of Georgia. Jordan, as a part of Hollowell's legal team, conducted careful research in the school records and eventually discovered untruths concerning why Charlayne Hunter and Hamilton Holmes were denied admission to the university. When a federal district court ordered the University of Georgia to admit the students, Jordan received national attention as he escorted Hunter to campus on her first day amidst an angry and violent white crowd of protesters.

Jordan's leadership, abilities, and commitment propelled him into roles that directly impacted the cause for civil rights. In 1962 he was appointed field secretary of the Georgia Branch of the **NAACP**. He led a boycott in Augusta, Georgia, against merchants who refused to serve blacks. In 1966 he became director of the Southern Regional Council's Voter Education Project that set up registration in 11 southern states and offered seminars and information for political participation and for those seeking political offices. Four years later Jordan took a six-month appointment as a fellow at the Kennedy Institute of Politics at Harvard before becoming executive director of the United Negro College Fund (UNCF). Although his time at the UNCF was just over a year, he helped increase contributions to the fund by an unprecedented amount.

On January 1, 1972, Jordan succeeded the late **Whitney Young** as executive director of the **National Urban League**. In this role he provided research information that impacted both planning and policy for black Americans. His report "The State of Black America" became a major resource for public and private viewing. A powerful speaker, he gave lectures, appeared on national programs, and wrote a weekly column. After a 1982 assassination attempt by a white racist, Jordan resigned as director of the Urban League and returned to private practice. He had further opportunity to advise and advocate for civil rights when his longtime friend Bill Clinton was elected President of the United States in 1992. Jordan continues to advocate for civil rights and serves as an advisor to corporate and governmental leaders.

Lean'tin L. Bracks

Jumper, Margie (1915?–2007)

Margie Jumper was a woman of protest who took a stand by sitting down. Nearly 10 years before **Rosa Parks** took a stand against human injustice and the indignity of racial segregation by refusing to give up her seat on a public bus in Montgomery, Alabama, Margie Jumper made a similar public act of defiance in Roanoke, Virginia, while riding on a streetcar in the downtown district on a Sunday in 1946. "No need of letting folks do you wrong," she said. City ordinance in Roanoke at that time prohibited black and white passengers from sitting together. The streetcar was nearly full in the back, where blacks were required to sit, as well as up front, where white passengers sat. "They had those big long seats in the back," she said in an interview. "That's where they wanted us." Jumper sat in the middle of the streetcar for about 10 minutes, until a white passenger entered and asked the conductor to make her move. "It wasn't right, and I had the right to sit there," she said. Jumper was arrested after refusing to give her name and other information. She pleaded guilty to violating the local ordinance, paid a fine, and was quickly forgotten in the history of the Civil Rights Movement. The Roanoke chapter of the **NAACP** remembered her silent protest in 2003, however, and honored her with the Reverend R. R. Wilkinson Memorial Award for Social Justice. Commenting on Rosa Parks's arrest in December 1955, Jumper said, "Maybe she heard about me."

Jessie Carney Smith

Lewis was assaulted several times during his protest activities, yet he continued to put his life on the line for a worthy cause.

Lewis, John R. (1940–)

Since the 1960s John R. Lewis has been a frontline agitator in the struggle for human justice throughout the United States. The **Montgomery Bus Boycott** of 1955 spurred the Alabama native to activism. While a student at **Fisk University** in the 1960s, he learned about the work of **James Lawson**, an activist and divinity school student at Vanderbilt University whose workshops on non-violent techniques were held in fall 1959. He joined the workshops, jointly sponsored by the Nashville Christian Leadership Conference and the Fellowship of Reconciliation. **Septima Clark**, who taught "citizenship school" at **Highlander Folk School**, had Lewis as one of her students as well.

Once trained in non-violent direct action tactics, Lewis became a participant in the Nashville sit-ins, along with students from Fisk, **Meharry Medical College**, American Baptist Theological Seminary (now College), and **Tennessee State University**, on February 13, 1960. That movement, coupled with economic boycotts of white businesses, prompted local white merchants to desegregate their lunch counters by June 1960. In April 1960 Lewis and several other local college students founded the **Student Non-Violent Coordinating Committee** (SNCC). He also joined the **Freedom Rides** that the **Congress of Racial Equality** (CORE) sponsored the next year to protest segregation at interstate bus terminals.

Lewis was assaulted several times during his protest activities, yet he continued to put his life on the line for a worthy cause and continued to practice non-violent methods. He wrote in his autobiography, *Walking with the Wind,* that the Freedom Ride of 1961 "did exactly what we intended. It dramatized the situation of segregation in the South." He added "the rides marked a shift in the temperature of the movement, an upsurge in our aggression." When Lewis was elected chair of the SNCC, he dropped out of school in June 1963; reelected two more times, he became a respected leader in the Civil Rights Movement. He concentrated on the **March on Washington** held on August 23, 1963, and drafted the speech that he would give as speaker for the SNCC. He warned listeners that the march for freedom would continue.

Among the giants of the movement, who included **Whitney Young**, **A. Philip Randolph**, **Martin Luther King Jr.**, **James Farmer**, and Roy Wilkins, Lewis continued to work for the SNCC, particularly in the South. The organization held voter registration drives and worked through the Mississippi **Freedom Summer** and its activities. During the **Montgomery to Selma March** across the Edmund Pettus Bridge on Sunday, March 7, 1965, which was known as "Bloody Sunday," Lewis was attacked again and beaten into unconsciousness. Finally, President **Lyndon B. Johnson** signed the **Voting Rights Act of 1965**. Lewis lost reelection to the SNCC for a fourth term, but he remained active in the Civil Rights Movement. President Jimmy Carter appointed him to direct the ACTION program for volunteers. Elected to the U.S. Congress in 1986, he continued to work for justice for all people. He is a particularly outspoken advocate of public issues that serve the interests of black people.

Jessie Carney Smith

Liuzzo, Viola Fauver Gregg (1925–1965)

A civil rights activist and martyr, Viola Liuzzo was the first woman—and the only white woman—killed during the African American struggle for civil rights and equality. The murder of Jimmie Lee Jackson at the hands of Alabama troopers motivated civil rights leaders to stage a protest march from Selma, Alabama, to the capitol in Montgomery, 50 miles away, which would be led by **Martin Luther King Jr.**, president of the **Southern Christian Leadership Conference**. Jackson's death and the scheduled march from **Selma to Montgomery** prompted Liuzzo to become involved in the modern Civil Rights Movement, too. Although J. Edgar Hoover, the FBI director, portrayed Liuzzo as a northerner, she was a product of the South. The daughter of a coal miner, she was born to Heber Ernest and Eva Wilson Gregg in California, Pennsylvania, a mining town on the Monogahela River, approximately 50 miles from West Virginia. She had lived in Georgia and Ten-

nessee, as well. Liuzzo was familiar with the southern code of Jim Crow and how it relegated African Americans to a second-class status. A woman with a sense of fairness who was concerned about human rights, Liuzzo wanted to be part of a movement that transformed injustice into justice. A 39-year-old wife, mother of five, and student, in 1965 she drove from her home in Detroit to help with the voting rights march in Selma. While giving rides to others after the march, members of the Ku Klux Klan fired bullets through the driver's window of Liuzzo's car, instantly killing her with two shots to the head. The tragedy shocked the nation and President **Lyndon B. Johnson** condemned her slaying on national television. Liuzzo's death gave impetus to the passage of the landmark **Voting Rights Act of 1965**. Memorials in Alabama and commemorations in Detroit honor Viola Fauver Gregg Liuzzo's memory.

Linda T. Wynn

A woman with a sense of fairness who was concerned about human rights, Liuzzo wanted to be part of a movement that transformed injustice into justice.

Malcolm X (1925–1965)

Malcolm Little was born in Omaha, Nebraska, on May 19, 1925. His mother cared for the family and his father was a Baptist minister and president of the local chapter of the Universal Negro Improvement Association (UNIA) founded by **Marcus Garvey**. When Malcolm was six years old, his father was found dead

Malcolm X (AP Photo).

near the local streetcar line. His father's death, although appearing to be a suicide, was thought to actually be a crime perpetrated by the Ku Klux Klan, which despised his work as a Garvey supporter. Malcolm's mother, traumatized by the murder of her husband and her inability to care for her seven children, was eventually institutionalized and her children sent to foster homes. After spending time in several foster homes, at the age of 17 Malcolm moved to Lansing, Michigan, with this half-sister and later spent time in Detroit, Boston, and New York.

After immersing himself in street life, complete with illegal and dangerous undertakings, Malcolm was sentenced to 10 years in prison on burglary charges in 1946. It was in prison that

his purpose and potential were made clear to him through the ideas of the Nation of Islam. Malcolm, who had taken the last name "X," became a national minister in the Nation of Islam in 1952. He spoke directly to the black community, encouraging them to demand their rights as citizens and ultimately recognize the white man as the "devil." Malcolm X spared no words on those blacks who catered to whites at the expense of blacks and the black community. His powerful messages were thoughtful and inspiring, and this brought him national attention from both blacks and whites.

Malcolm X aggressively advocated for the rights of blacks, spoke on national television, and granted interviews to national publications if the Honorable **Elijah Muhammad** sanctioned the meeting. Malcolm X's national attention created some tension within the Nation of Islam, however, while simultaneously keeping the issue of racism and inequality in the forefront of American society. Malcolm was thoughtful, quick-witted, and knowledgeable about a wealth of information. His perspectives were empowering to blacks and squarely placed blame on whites and the systems they initiated to support racist ideology.

Discovering that his mentor and idol Elijah Muhammad had been committing adultery while judging and teaching others to be faithful, Malcolm X left the Nation of Islam after 12 years of service and set out to discover a truth that he had not found there. He started the Organization of Afro-American Unity and later traveled to Mecca in 1964. Returning to the states with a changed sensibility, Malcolm X advocated the condemnation of injustice and inequality and not the condemnation of one group or race. He formed alliances with grass-roots organizations, and had meetings with civil rights organizations and leaders that included **Martin Luther King Jr.** While still using his powerful voice to challenge and bring attention to the denied rights of blacks, Malcolm X was assassinated as he gave a speech on February 21, 1965, in New York City. His journey of self-discovery and his commitment to positive change for his people set an example that offered hope and encouragement for the most downtrodden to the most conservative.

Lean'tin L. Bracks

McNeil, Joseph Alfred (1942–)

A member of the Greensboro Four, Joseph McNeil was born in Wilmington, North Carolina, on March 25, 1942. While a 17-year-old freshman at **North Carolina Agricultural and Technical College** (now State University), he was denied counter service at the Greyhound bus station in Greensboro while returning to campus following Christmas vacation. As he

recounted this experience to his roommate Ezell Blair Jr. (Jibreel Khazan), and friends Franklin McCain and David Richmond, they discussed the reality of being black, the slowness of any significant and sustained change, the need for action, and the point at which a moral man has to stand up and fight injustice. The four students decided they had reached that point and made the decision to emphasize the injustices in an orderly and prayerful manner. Thus, on February 1, 1960, they chose to shop at and then demand counter service at the local F.W. Woolworth store. As a result of their fearless action on this date, four months later the counter was opened to all and the movement swept across the campuses of the South. Following this action, the four students went on to complete their education. McNeil was commissioned a second lieutenant in the U.S. Air Force, where he introduced several diversity programs; he retired from the Air Force Reserves as a Major General and later worked with IBM, and as a commercial banker and stock broker.

Helen R. Houston

Meyzeek, Albert E. (1862–1963)

The integration movement in early twentieth-century Kentucky is partially due to the work of Albert E. Meyzeek, a champion of civil rights causes. He was likely inspired by the activism of his father, John E. Meyzeek, a white Canadian who won two lawsuits against the Indiana School Board, forcing them to abolish segregated schools. As well, his maternal grandfather, John Lott, was an organizer of the Ohio River **Underground Railroad**. As Meyzeek studied law, he learned that the Terre Haute School Board was in violation of the law by maintaining inadequate schools. His protests about this neglect forced a remedy. After teaching at local schools, in 1890 Meyzeek moved to Louisville, Kentucky, and began a stellar 50-year tenure. He was among the black educators who helped to upgrade education for blacks in Kentucky. He was also instrumental in having black schools named for notable African Americans. Among his many initiatives to secure human rights for blacks in Louisville were his drives to desegregate General Hospital, agitation against ordinances permitting segregation on public conveyances, work toward the integration of the University of Louisville, and the founding of a black branch of the YMCA. He also helped found the local Urban League. Meyzeek and others helped to establish the Citizens Amusement Company and the Palace Theater Company when blacks were denied access to local amusement facilities. Meyzeek's drive for racial parity extended to libraries as well. When the Louisville Public Library refused to admit his students, he campaigned to have the Carnegie Library serve black residents. The Western Colored Branch Library, founded in 1907 and opened the next year, is believed to be the first public library opened for blacks in the United States.

Jessie Carney Smith

[Mfume] guided the rejuvenation of the nation's oldest civil rights organization.

Mfume, Kwesi (1948–)

After four consecutive terms representing the Maryland district where he was reared, Kwesi Mfume left his secure seat in the U.S. House of Representatives to assume the leadership of the **NAACP**. As president and chief executive officer, he guided the rejuvenation of the nation's oldest civil rights organization. To increase its visibility, Mfume led the organization's rally and litigation efforts. In doing so, he boosted the NAACP's membership to almost 50,000 and attained its nongovernmental organization status from the United Nations; he simultaneously gained the

respect and admiration of thousands across the world. Born Frizzell Gray, Mfume dropped out of school at 17 after his mother died so he could work and support his three younger siblings. Despite effectively being a teenage father of five, he resumed his studies and obtained his GED at age 23; he graduated from Morgan State University in 1976. Mfume also worked as a popular radio talk show host before serving in the Baltimore City Council from 1978 to 1987 and Congress from 1987 to 1996. As a congressman, he co-sponsored the Americans with Disabilities Act, co-authored the Civil Rights Bill of 1991 and helped to strengthen the Equal Credit Opportunity Law. Declaring that he could do more to advance civil rights outside of Congress, Mfume was unanimously elected as the NACCP's president after leading the **Congressional Black Caucus** as chair in his final term. He led the NAACP for nine years before retiring in 2004.

Crystal A. deGregory

Mitchell, Parren J. (1922–2007)

Parren James Mitchell was the first African American elected to the U.S. Congress from Maryland, and he was a founding member of the **Congressional Black Caucus**. He was also a tireless advocate for economic empowerment initiatives in African American communities. Mitchell was born in Baltimore, the ninth of ten children. His father was a hotel waiter, while older brother **Clarence Mitchell Jr.** became a lobbyist and director of the **NAACP** Washington office from 1950 to 1979. Mitchell graduated from Frederick Douglass High School in 1940, joined the U.S. Army in 1942, received a Purple Heart during World War II, and earned a bachelor's degree from Morgan State College in 1950. He was denied admission to graduate school at the University of Maryland, filed suit, won his case, became the school's first black graduate student, and earned his master's degree in sociology in 1952. Mitchell returned to Morgan State as a sociology professor, and he helped end riots there after **Martin Luther King Jr.** was assassinated in 1968. That same year he ran for Congress and lost, but he won a close election in 1970. Mitchell established "set-aside" programs for African American businesses (a form of affirmative action used by governments in contracting government business, typically by designating a percentage of government contracts or funds to minority-owned businesses), but he was frustrated when investigations revealed improper actions by black and white businesspeople. He retired from Congress in 1986 to chair the Minority Business Enterprise Legal Defense and Education Fund. After suffering a series of strokes, Mitchell died at age 85 from complications of pneumonia in Baltimore.

Fletcher F. Moon

Moore, Harry Tyson (1905–1951)

Before the 1954 *Brown v. Board of Education* decision, **Rosa Parks**'s defiance of Montgomery, Alabama's transit segregation laws, or the June 1963 assassination of **Medgar Evers**, Harry T. Moore labored in Jim Crow Florida on behalf of the **NAACP** and the Progressive Voters League. For 17 years in an era of racial hostility, Moore traveled the backroads of Florida, educating and organizing black Floridians about the injustices perpetrated against them. A teacher, he worked for the Brevard County school system from 1925 until 1946, when his NAACP activities to secure equal pay for black teachers cost him his position as superintendent of the Negro High School. He continued to work for the state branch of the NAACP and focused on not only economic and educational equality but also voter registration and the fair enforcement of laws.

It was Moore's defense of the Groveland Four black youths accused of raping a white woman in Lake County that drew the rage of the Ku Klux Klan upon him and pitted him against Willis McCall, who had a reputation as one of the most ruthless and bigoted sheriffs in the country. In November 1951 two of the Groveland Four were shot, one fatally, while in McCall's custody. Moore demanded that the sheriff be indicted for murder.

On the day of Harry and Harriette Moore's 25th anniversary, December 25, 1951, in Mims, Florida, a bomb placed under their bed instantly ended the life of Harry Moore; his wife, Harriette Vyda Simms Moore, died from her injuries nine days later. At the age of 46, he became the first civil rights martyr, signaling what was to be a long and heart rending line of assassinations in the modern Civil Rights Movement.

Mitchell established "set-aside" programs for African American businesses.

The fatal bombing of the Moores' home was never officially solved. In 2006 Attorney General Charlie Crist released the results of a 20-month investigation into the 1951 Christmas Day murders. At least four individuals were thought to have been directly involved. The investigation, which was led by the Attorney General's Office of Civil Rights in conjunction with the Florida Department of Law Enforcement, drew on extensive circumstantial evidence to indicate that the Moores were victims of a conspiracy by violent members of a Central Florida Klavern of the Ku Klux Klan. Because the four individuals thought to have been involved were deceased, no indictments were brought forth. However, it was believed by those involved with the investigation that, had they been living, an indictment from a grand jury would have been sought.

Linda T. Wynn

Moses, Robert (1935–)

Robert "Bob" Parris Moses was respected for his courageous activism in Mississippi during the early 1960s and for his later efforts to encourage mathematical abilities of African Americans and other minority groups. He used his intellectual abilities to help others empower themselves, regardless of their socioeconomic status. Moses was born in New York City, where his janitor father stressed academic achievement in the family. As a result, Moses graduated from Stuyvesant High School, Hamilton College, and Harvard University, where he earned a master's degree in analytical philosophy. He left a mathematics teaching position to become part of the Civil Rights Movement in the South, after being influenced by **Bayard Rustin**, **Ella Baker**, and other veteran activists. Moses joined the **Student Non-Violent Coordinating Committee** (SNCC) and became field secretary in 1961, working with voter registration projects in rural Mississippi. This dangerous work resulted in his being attacked and arrested several times over the next few years, while several colleagues lost their lives. Moses left the United States in 1966 to avoid the military draft, and lived in Canada and Tanzania. Granted amnesty, he returned in 1977 and planned to complete a doctorate at Harvard, but instead he received a grant from the MacArthur Foundation in 1982 to establish the Algebra Project. Moses expanded the project to various parts of the country, including areas of Mississippi, where he had worked decades earlier for civil rights.

Fletcher F. Moon

Nixon organized the Montgomery Voters' League to help blacks secure governmental assistance.

Nixon, Edgar Daniel, Sr. (1899–1987)

An important agent of change for African Americans in Alabama, E.D. Nixon, as he was called, agitated against racial imbalance for over 40 years. The Montgomery, Alabama, native worked as a sleeping-car porter in Selma and Mobile, and later, with the influence of **A. Philip Randolph**, joined the **Brotherhood of Sleeping Car Porters**. The organization protested racial discrimination against black sleeping-car workers. Nixon had already been involved in local efforts to improve the quality of life for blacks in Montgomery when he joined the union. Though unsuccessful, he fought to build a public swimming pool for blacks, having been prompted to do so when two children drowned while swimming in a draining ditch.

Nixon would go on to build a strong **NAACP** force in Alabama. As state and local president, he established 21 branches and increased local membership from 500 to nearly 3,000. The proposed March on Washington in 1941, which Bayard Rustin and Randolph organized to protest racial discrimination in the defense industry, also brought Nixon into the fold. Although the march never occurred, Nixon was a part of the force that led President Franklin D. Roosevelt to establish the Fair Employment Practices Commission through Executive Order 8802.

In the 1940s Nixon organized the Montgomery Voters' League to help blacks secure governmental assistance. As president of the Progressive Democratic Association, he led a successful campaign to let blacks serve on the local police force. He played a strategic role in the successful **Montgomery Bus Boycott** that began on December 1, 1955, when **Rosa Parks** refused to give her seat to a white passenger. Nixon paid Parks's fine of $100 and called for a boycott of the bus company. The Women's Political Council, however, led a boycott before Nixon's plan could be put in place. It was Nixon, who, along with **Ralph Abernathy** and other leaders, set the groundwork for the extended boycott and a new organization, the **Montgomery Improvement Association** (MIA). **Martin Luther King Jr.** was elected president and Nixon treasurer.

MIA members were indicted for boycott activities, with Nixon the first to be indicted. He surrendered before his arrest, demonstrating to

other members that there was a way to counter-
balance the offensive tactics of white law
enforcement officers. The boycott was highly
successful, received national press, and resulted
in loss of revenue for the bus company. Finally,
by order of the U.S. Supreme Court, the company desegregated its buses, but by then it had lost
65 percent of its business, dismissed drivers, cut
schedules, and increased fares. By December 21,
1956, blacks were seated on the buses in the
place of their choice. After the boycott ended,
Nixon continued to work as a community servant on various commissions. He was appointed
to the U.S. Commission on Civil Rights for the
state of Alabama in 1975 and served as its vice
president. For his long tenure as an activist for
social change, Nixon received over 400 citations
from state and local governments and various
organizations. His Montgomery home is on the
Alabama Register of Landmarks and Heritage.

Jessie Carney Smith

Parks, Rosa (1913–2005)

Rosa Parks (AP Photo).

When Rosa Parks refused to give up her seat
on a Montgomery, Alabama, public bus in
1955, she stood up for generations of African
Americans. While she was not the first to stand
her ground on this issue, the content of her character helped to spark the beginnings of the **Montgomery Bus Boycott**. With Parks as a symbol of
the very best her community had to offer the
world, the boycott's success helped catapult her,
along with then-local minister **Martin Luther
King Jr.**, to prominence. As a result, no other two
names have been as readily associated with the
mid-twentieth century American mass movement
for freedom, justice, and social equality dubbed
the Civil Rights Movement. Parks has been hailed
as the "Mother of the Civil Rights Movement."

Born Rosa McCauley in Tuskegee, Alabama,
Parks was the daughter of James, a construction
worker, and Leona McCauley, a schoolteacher.
Beginning at age six, young Rosa assumed odd
jobs as a field hand on neighboring farms to
supplement her mother's income during the

time her father traveled North in search of
work. His absences soon forced her parents'
separation, and Parks moved with her mother
to Montgomery. She attended the Montgomery
Industrial School for Girls, an all-black private
school where she worked as a janitor in
exchange for tuition. She began high school at
Booker T. Washington High. However, she was
forced to take several leaves of absence to care
for ailing family members, which resulted in her
eventually dropping out. In 1932 she married
barber and civil rights activist Raymond Parks
and worked in various odd jobs, including as a
seamstress. With her husband's encouragement,
Parks completed high school two years later.

Together the Parkses were active members of the Montgomery Chapter of the **NAACP**. Appointed secretary of the Montgomery chapter of the NAACP in 1943, Parks also served as its youth leader. On December 1, 1955, Parks was arrested after refusing to give up her seat on a Montgomery city bus. As the news of her arrest spread through the city's black community, the Women's Political Council and the **Montgomery Improvement Association** (MIA) launched the Montgomery Bus Boycott. For the next year, the MIA used weekly meetings to raise money and organized carpools to keep participants mobilized. Meanwhile, MIA leaders negotiated with the NAACP and Montgomery city officials to legally challenge the city's bus segregation ordinance. After lasting for 382 days, the boycott ended when the courts ruled that the segregation of city bus services was unconstitutional.

Parks was ... the first woman in American history to lie in state at the Capitol.

The Parkses moved to Detroit in 1957 after harassment and threats resulted in the loss of their jobs. She continued her work as a seamstress while promoting civil rights through public speeches; she joined the staff of U.S. Congressman John Conyers in 1965, with whom she worked until her retirement in 1988. Among the numerous awards she received was the Presidential Medal of Freedom in 1999. Following her death at age 92, Parks was placed in the rotunda of the U.S. Capitol for two days, making her the first woman in American history to lie in state at the Capitol, an honor usually reserved for presidents of the United States.

Crystal A. deGregory

Parrish, Charles H., Sr., (1859–1931)

Charles Henry Parrish Sr., who was born into slavery in Lexington, Kentucky, was an active participant in the struggle for civil rights and a founder of the **NAACP** in Louisville, Kentucky. At the age of six, Parrish, along with his parents and two siblings, was granted his freedom. In spite of personal and economic difficulties, Parrish earned an A.B. degree in 1886 and a master's degree in 1889 from Kentucky Normal and Theological Institute (later known as Simmons University) in Louisville, Kentucky. He also earned LL.B. and a LL.D. degrees from Central Law School in Louisville. Parrish was very involved in the black community and was often chosen as a spokesman for issues regarding civil rights. He was called on in 1892 to speak with the Kentucky governor on behalf of the Anti-Separate Coach Movement against racial segregation on trains. He was called on again for his leadership in 1904 as a delegate to the World Sunday School Convention in Jerusalem. In 1913 Parrish, along with other black leaders, formed an NAACP branch in Louisville, Kentucky. He was elected president and served on the executive board until 1920. Parrish also was a member of the Commission on Interracial Cooperation. He was actively involved in community causes and protested against segregation and the city ordinances that supported such practices. As the challenge to segregation continued to intensify, Parrish's stance was considered too moderate. He resigned from the NAACP in 1920 and directed his attention on business in Louisville. His contributions helped to weaken segregation and moved the cause of black civil rights forward.

Lean'tin L. Bracks

Pickens, William (1881–1954)

South Carolina native William Pickens was one of black America's most popular leaders of his time, and from 1915 to 1945 he was an important civil rights leader, as well. After graduating from Yale University and holding teaching positions at various black colleges, he became the first black dean at Morgan College, now Morgan State University. He left his post in 1920 to engage in civil rights activities. Pickens became a founding member of the **NAACP** in 1910 and a successful recruiter for membership. He worked with influential leaders like **James Weldon Johnson**, **W.E.B. Du Bois**, and **Walter White** to mold the NAACP into a potent civil rights organization. As early as 1915, he challenged racial conditions in Memphis. He was appointed assistant field secretary to the NAACP in 1920. Later, when appointed director of branches, he was a liaison between the national office and its branches, many of which he helped to establish. Pickens also investigated lynchings and collected firsthand information on racial discrimination. At the onset of World War I, he persuaded U.S. congressmen to establish an offi-

cers' training facility for blacks at Fort Des Moines, Iowa. He wrote about his experiences with the organization in his memoirs, *The Heir of Slaves* (1911) and *Bursting Bonds* (1923). Pickens continued to publish essays and became a columnist for the **Associated Negro Press**. After leaves of absence from the NAACP and a post with the Treasury Department, he retired and became a lecturer and traveler.

Jessie Carney Smith

Reed, Eugene T. (1923–2002)

A militant leader of the Civil Rights Movement of the 1950s and 1960s, Eugene T. Reed found racism distasteful and favored demonstrations of public anger over the slow pace of integration practiced in American society. His father was the first black full-time dentist

William Pickens (Fisk University).

Robert Purvis (Fisk University).

on Long Island, and his mother commuted to New York City to teach because public schools on Long Island had no black teachers. After graduating from dental school at **Howard University**, the Brooklyn native enlisted in the U.S. Army, served in Germany, and protested the segregated dental clinics that the army provided. After civil rights activist **Harry Tyson Moore** was murdered in Florida on Christmas Day 1951, Reed gave up his dentistry practice to become an activist. He worked with the **NAACP** at local and state levels and headed the state organization from 1960 to 1965; he also served the national organization. Reed was among the militants who criticized the NAACP for the way it handled civil rights issues, and tried to take over the organization. He resigned from the NAACP board in New York State in 1968, following an angry confrontation with members who were moderate in their views. Reed joined the **Freedom Riders**, who fought for integration in hotels and other facilities. He also served on the NAACP's committee that investigated the murders of civil rights workers **James E. Chaney**, Andrew Goodman, and Michael H. Schwerner in Philadelphia, Mississippi. In the 1960s he was a principal organizer of boycotts, pickets, and sit-ins against the segregation that existed in New York City schools.

Jessie Carney Smith

Richmond, David (1941–1990)

David Richmond made American and civil rights history as part of the "Greensboro Four," freshman classmates at **North Carolina Agricultural and Technical State University** (North Carolina A&T) in Greensboro, North Carolina. Their spontaneous sit-in at the city's Woolworth's lunch counter on February 1, 1960, sparked increased student participation in the Civil Rights Movement. Richmond, a Greensboro native, graduated from Dudley High School, where he set the state high jump record. After the actions of the Greensboro Four, Richmond continued business adminis-

tration and accounting studies at North Carolina A&T, later becoming a counselor-coordinator for the Comprehensive Employment and Training Act (CETA) program and working with disadvantaged youths and adults. After receiving death threats, Richmond left Greensboro to live in Franklin, North Carolina, for nine years, but he returned to care for his elderly parents. He had difficulty finding work and became a janitor for the Greensboro Health Care Center. Married and divorced twice, Richmond battled alcoholism and depression, but he managed to reunite with his Greensboro Four colleagues on February 1, 1990, to mark the 30th anniversary of their sit-in. Shortly after his death, Richmond was awarded a posthumous honorary doctor of humanities from North Carolina A&T. On February 1, 1997, a monument was dedicated to him at his unmarked gravesite; a play based on his life was written in 1998. A 2004 documentary film and a 2005 joint congressional resolution also honor Richmond and his colleagues.

Fletcher F. Moon

Robeson, Eslanda (1896–1965)

Eslanda Cardozo Goode Robeson is recognized for her work as a civil rights activist; she was also a manager for her husband, actor and singer **Paul Robeson**. Eslanda Robeson was born in 1896 in Washington, D.C., and died on December 13, 1965. Despite accusations that she was a Communist, leading her to be black listed and denied employment opportunities, during the 1940s Robeson worked as a Pan-Africanist, calling for the liberation from colonial rule of African peoples. As founder and member of the Council on African Affairs, she attended the San Francisco Conference for the establishment of the United Nations in 1945. Robeson was an outspoken critic of American domestic policies on race, as well as of foreign policies that pertained to Africa. She was one of a few protesters who petitioned the United Nations to address the human rights violations of the U.S. government against its own African American citizens. Her travels to Africa encouraged her protests on colonial oppression and fostered an interest in the Soviet Union. Robeson traveled to communist countries, including the Soviet Union and China; her praise of these countries caused the U.S. government to suspect her of being a subversive. Robeson and her husband were questioned by Senator Joseph McCarthy's House Un-American Activities Committee in 1953. She attended the All-African Peoples Conference in Accra, Ghana, in December of 1958. At the conference, Robeson took issue with Europeans speaking on behalf of Africans and questioned the absence of women's voices at the conference. The Robesons moved to the Soviet Union in 1958 but eventually returned to the United States in 1963.

Rebecca S. Dixon

Rustin, Bayard (1910–1987)

Bayard Rustin was a student and advocate of nonviolence. He used his exceptional organizational skills to support the efforts of several civil rights groups. Rustin was reared by his maternal grandparents, Janifer and Julia Davis. His grandmother was a Quaker who passed on her religious beliefs and her sense of commitment to the community to her grandson. While attending City College in New York, Rustin was involved in efforts to free the Scottsboro Boys, who were accused of raping a white woman in Alabama. Rustin became more involved in various causes but he never received a college degree, partly because of a lack of funding. By 1947 Rustin had become a member of the **Congress of Racial Equality** (CORE), and he and colleague George Houser organized the Journey of Reconciliation in 1947 that tested the ban on racial discrimination in interstate travel. This was the first of the **Freedom Rides**, which resulted in Rustin and others spending time in jail. To expand his understanding of pacifism, Rustin spent time in India, studying the philosophy of Mahatma Gandhi, and he used this

knowledge to advise **Martin Luther King Jr.** in 1956 for the bus boycott in **Montgomery, Alabama**. Rustin worked with King while the **Southern Christian Leadership Conference** (SCLC) was being organized, but Rustin's past involvement with the Communist Party and his open homosexuality created controversy and tension from black leadership and outside interests that forced him to resign from the organization in 1960. His contribution was again challenged when he organized the **March on Washington** for Jobs and Freedom in 1963. Rustin's skill as an organizer and planner was exceptional, but the recognition of those efforts was often overshadowed by controversy.

Lean'tin L. Bracks

[Robeson] was one of a few protesters who petitioned the United Nations to address the human rights violations of the U.S. government.

Simkins, Modjeska (1899–1992)

A civil rights activist, Mary Modjeska Monteith Simkins, as she was known, was a central figure in public health and social reform activities for African Americans; she is remembered as the matriarch of South Carolina's Civil Rights Movement. She served in leadership positions in her native South Carolina and at the regional and national levels. She knew gender discrimination early on during her teaching career in Columbia, South Carolina. Simkins had to resign from the school system because married women were forbidden to teach. Afterwards, she directed Negro Work for the South Carolina Anti-Tuberculosis Association (SCATA), and was the state's only full-time African American health employee. In her 11-year tenure she worked with black teachers and physicians, becoming a political activist as a result. She was publicity director for the **NAACP** and in 1939 became one of the founders of the South Carolina Conference of Branches. Simkins was also secretary of the Civic Welfare League, which worked to improve conditions for blacks in Columbia. SCATA fired her in 1942 for refusing to discontinue her work with the NAACP; the result was that she became even more active in civil rights initiatives. Her NAACP activities included a successful push in 1955 for equal pay for black and white teachers in Charleston, South Carolina, and, the next year, in Columbia. Simkins was also involved in the NAACP's most significant case in the state to end segregation in the public schools. The case of *Briggs v. Elliott* became one of the five desegregation cases included in the U.S. Supreme Court's historic *Brown v. Board of Education of Topeka, Kansas* (1954).

Jessie Carney Smith

Steward, William H. (1847–1935)

William Henry Steward, who was active in the struggle for black civil rights, was born to slave parents in Brandenburg, Kentucky. In spite of legal restrictions, Steward attended a private school for his education. He used his education to become a teacher and taught in both public and private colored schools in Frankfort, Kentucky, beginning in 1867, and in Louisville in 1872. Steward was active in the community and in 1875 was named chair of the Board of Trustees of State University in Louisville. He also was the editor and publisher of the *American Baptist* newspaper. Steward was active in the cause for civil rights and worked with other contemporaries such as **Charles H. Parrish**. He looked to **Booker T. Washington** for advice because he was a friend and follower of Washington. Steward joined with Parrish in 1913 to help form the **NAACP** in Louisville; he participated in protests in support of the NAACP

William H. Steward (Fisk University).

and the Commission on Interracial Cooperation. Steward believed that progress for blacks was tied to working with influential whites. This perspective made many of his views moderate, particularly regarding his ideas on segregation. Steward joined Parrish in resigning from the NAACP in 1920, when his moderate views were rejected. In spite of his departure from the NAACP, Steward continued to work for black civil rights and the end of racial segregation.

Lean'tin L. Bracks

Sullivan, Leon (1922–)

Leon Sullivan, the creator of the Sullivan "Principles" that were used to confront discriminatory practices, was born in Charleston, West Virginia, and reared by his grandmother. As a youth, he came to know the harshness of bigotry and was determined to stand against such injustice. After graduating from college, Sullivan spent time in Harlem and had associations with prominent activists such as **A. Philip Randolph** and **Adam Clayton Powell Jr.** In 1950 he became pastor of the Zion Baptist Church in Philadelphia. Recognizing the economic plight of the community and realizing that employment and economic development are crucial for the empowerment of blacks, Sullivan developed projects geared toward confronting discrimination and bigotry. One such project was the organizing of 400 ministers in the city to support a "selective patronage" program. The goal was to boycott any business that had discriminatory hiring practices. Between 1959 and 1963, over 2,000 jobs were gained, and by 1964 that number had doubled. This project was followed by the Opportunities Industrialization Center, which took matters one step further by offering job training. Sullivan's innovative ideas helped to challenge discriminatory practices and supported the community through self-help programs that were emulated all over the nation and abroad. The Sullivan "Principles" are said to be most effective in discriminatory situations and were used in South Africa against apartheid practices.

Lean'tin L. Bracks

Toure, Kwame. *See* Carmichael, Stokely.

Underwood, Edward Ellsworth (1864–1942)

Edward Ellsworth Underwood was born in Mt. Pleasant, Ohio. After completing his education and serving as a licensed minister and teacher, he completed his medical degree in 1891 and moved to Frankfort, Kentucky. While practicing medicine in Frankfort, Underwood was actively involved in community causes. He was a leader in the Anti-Separate Coach Movement in the 1890s, which challenged Jim Crow transportation laws in Kentucky. In 1919 Underwood was one of the founders of the Frankfort branch of the **NAACP** and became its

first elected president. His involvement was not only on the local level but also the state level. He was chair of the Frankfort Inter-Racial Commission and the State Committee of the Inter-Racial Commission. Underwood's leadership reverberated throughout the community. He edited several newspapers including the *Blue Grass Bugle* in 1891, served as president of the State Medical Society, organized and served as president of the State League of Colored Republicans, and was a key delegate to the General Conference of the AME Church in 1920 and 1924 in Kentucky. Underwood's contributions had a direct impact on opportunities for blacks in the segregated society of his time.

Lean'tin L. Bracks

Walker, Wyatt Tee (1929–)

Wyatt Tee Walker is a minister and civil rights activist. He served as pastor of Gillfield Baptist Church from 1952 to 1960 and successfully organized several civil right marches and protests in Petersburg, Virginia. While serving as pastor, Walker was very active in the community and was a member of many of the civil rights organizations in Petersburg. He served as branch president of the NAACP, as a member of the Virginia chapter of the **Southern Christian Leadership Conference** (SCLC), and as state director of the **Congress of Racial Equality** (CORE). Walker organized the "Pilgrimage of Prayer," which protested Virginia's resistance to implementing the federally mandated desegregation of schools. Walker sought guidance and inspiration from Vernon Johns, the former pastor of Dexter Avenue Baptist Church who at that time resided in Petersburg. In August of 1960, Walker was asked by **Martin Luther King Jr.** to take the position of executive director of the SCLC. He replaced interim director **Ella Baker** and served from 1960 to 1964. King was so impressed by Walker's organizational skills that he named him his chief of staff. Walker formulated a highly structured administration that assisted in the organization of the **Freedom Rides** in

1961 and the **Albany Movement** of 1961–1962, and he fully orchestrated the Birmingham, Alabama, campaign in 1963. In 1964 Walker resigned from the SCLC, and Andrew Young succeeded him. Returning to his role as a full-time pastor, Walker maintained his commitment to the community and served as interim pastor of Abyssinian Baptist Church in New York from 1965 to 1966, before serving as pastor of Canaan Baptist Church in Harlem from 1967 to 2004.

Lean'tin L. Bracks

[Young] became one of King's trusted advisors and executive director of the SCLC.

Young, Andrew (1932–)

Andrew Jackson Young Jr., who came to be known as Andy Young, felt a calling in his life and knew he was destined to serve. After receiving a B.S. from **Howard University** in 1951, he earned a bachelor of divinity degree and was ordained in 1955 as a minister in the United Church of Christ. In 1961, when the church started a voter registration drive, Young moved south to Atlanta with his family to serve as the Field Foundation's supervisor. (The Field Foundation was established in 1940 by Chicago banker and *Chicago Sun-Times* publisher Marshall Field; it played a major role in promoting racial integration in the South in the 1950's, and larger foundations later followed its lead). In touring the south and recruiting voters, one of his first recruits was **Fannie Lou Hamer**, who was beaten and terrorized by whites as she fought to gain her civil and political rights. Young also worked with Dorothy Cotton and **Septima Clark**, and for Clark's citizenship

school. The school helped to educate leaders and offered workshops in non-violent organizing strategies. Young at this time joined the **Southern Christian Leadership Conference** (SCLC). The voter registration drive run by the SCLC registered thousands of voters and had a tremendous impact on the political success of the Civil Rights Movement.

Young marched with **Martin Luther King Jr.** during the SCLC's campaign against segregation in Birmingham, Alabama. He became one of King's trusted advisors and executive director of the SCLC. In 1964 Young assisted in drafting the **Civil Rights Act of 1964** and the **Voting Rights Act of 1965**. Young was with King when he was assassinated in 1968. He continued with the SCLC as executive vice president, but later resigned in 1970 to run for the U.S. House of Representatives. Young's impact on racial justice and equality helped to transform conditions in the South. He stepped into the political arena with a continuing focus on civil rights and aid for the less fortunate. Young was reelected twice as representative of the 5th District in Georgia, and in 1977 he was appointed ambassador to the United Nations by President Jimmy Carter. Young resigned in 1979 from his seat as representative after meeting with a member of the Palestine Liberation Organization (PLO), an action that was forbidden by the U.S. government, which considered the PLO a terrorist organization. In 1980 Young was elected mayor of Atlanta and he served two terms. He continues his involvement in all aspects of the political process, is a professor at Georgia State University's Andrew Young School of Policy Studies, and is involved with the Dr. Martin Luther King Jr. Center for Non-Violent Social Change, among other commitments.

Lean'tin L. Bracks

Lynching Victim

Till, Emmett Louis (1941–1955)

Emmett Till was born July 25, 1941, in Chicago, Illinois, and died August 28, 1955, in Tallahatchie, Mississippi. Till, who grew up on the outskirts of Chicago, had just completed the seventh grade when he was sent by his mother to spend a part of summer vacation with relatives in Mississippi. He was unfamiliar with this culture. Swapping stories with the young men there about life in the North and the privileges he enjoyed, he introduced alien concepts to the inhabitants of this poor sharecropping community. He and other young people were in the habit of gathering outside a grocery store to pass the time. Till reportedly did not know his "place" and whistled at a white woman. When recounted, the story seemed to have been exaggerated, but the woman's husband took umbrage anyway. He and his brother kidnapped Till from his bed, pistol whipped him, murdered him, and dropped him in the Tallahatchie River. When Till was reported missing and found in the river, mutilated and tied to a fan, a trial was held. The brothers were acquitted by an all-white jury after just 67 minutes of deliberation. The ruling gained nationwide coverage and outraged the public. Till's death influenced the passage of the **Civil Rights Act of 1957** and added to the impetus of the Civil Rights Movement.

Helen R. Houston

Protest Letter

Letter from Birmingham Jail (1963)

Written by **Martin Luther King Jr.** from the city jail in Birmingham, Alabama, on April 16, 1963, after he was imprisoned for participating in the 1963 Birmingham Campaign, the "Letter from Birmingham Jail" was a response to the criticism of eight local white clerics who four days earlier published a statement entitled "A Call for Unity" in the local newspaper. The writers insisted that "outsiders" such as King, had incited the city's non-violent demonstrations and advocated that local blacks should use the judicial system to remedy their grievances. The authors, who represented several different religious denominations, had written "An Appeal for Law and Order and Common Sense," another public statement released in January of the same year. Their sentiments were not just a criticism of King and his **Southern Christian Leadership Conference** (SCLC) cohorts, but also of the local **Alabama Christian Movement for Human Rights** (ACMHR), which invited King's group to join its ongoing direct action campaign against segregation.

Led by the Reverend **Fred Shuttlesworth**, ACMHR activists, despite facing the rabid racism of Birmingham commissioner of public safety Eugene "Bull" Connor, disobeyed a circuit court injunction against non-violent protest. Jailed for his participation, King penned the now-famous letter as a challenge to the whites who accused Birmingham blacks of being impatient with the city's status quo. Using the opposition's arguments, King defended the use of non-violent protest as necessary to secure equal rights for African Americans. The use of civil disobedience, he argued, was a justified means of objecting to unjust laws and represented a person's moral responsibility to preserve human rights above all laws. The letter has become a part of the Civil Rights Movement cannon. Its statement that "Injustice anywhere is a threat to justice everywhere" remains one of King's most widely quoted adages.

Crystal A. deGregory

Religion

Churches

African American Episcopal Church

The African American Episcopal Church grew in response to the denial of full rights for and disrespectful treatment of black people and their right to worship as they please. Richard Allen and Absalom Jones left St. George's Methodist Episcopal Church, a white congregation in Philadelphia, and formed the Free African Society. Allen organized Philadelphia's Bethel African American Church on July 17, 1794, believing the Methodist practices were more compatible with black people. Today the church is called Mother Bethel Church and is the first black church in America. At a general convention in Philadelphia on April 9, 1816, ministers from several states met and officially formed the African Methodist Episcopal Church, the first black denomination in America. At the convention, Allen was elected the first black bishop. Under his leadership, the denomination, which was concerned with equality of access and treatment, quickly expanded geographically. The church was an advocate of equal rights and treatment for all. Allen sanctioned the inclusion of women in the ministry and authorized Jarena Lee to be an exhorter in the church. The church served as a forum for abolitionists and anti-

Richard Allen, the co-founder of the African American Episcopal Church (Fisk University).

lynching, allowing individuals to use its pulpits to address the issues. It has continued its mission work, educational opportunities, and political involvement in the fight for equality.

Helen R. Houston

287

Churches in the Civil Rights Movement

A key component in the success of the Civil Rights Movement, churches produced not only leadership but also served vital roles as spaces for organizing, strategizing, and training, and as places of refuge during various civil rights activities. The **Southern Christian Leadership Conference** (SCLC) was organized in 1957, primarily with black Baptists, but ministers from other church affiliations were also members. Founding president **Martin Luther King Jr.** was joined by **Ralph Abernathy**, **Andrew Young**, **Fred Shuttlesworth**, **C.T. Vivian**, **James Lawson**, **Joseph Lowery**, **Kelly Miller Smith**, **Jesse Jackson**, and others. Will D. Campbell was one of the few white pastors to actively work for civil rights in the South during the early years of the movement. Some pastors and spiritual leaders from other parts of the country became directly or indirectly involved in the movement as it gained momentum, while others did not participate for a variety of reasons, including their own prejudices.

Many churches have been designated as state and/or national historic landmarks as a result of their role in the Civil Rights Movement.

The "**Letter from a Birmingham Jail**," written by King in 1963, included his critique of fellow spiritual leaders who were unwilling to address problems of discrimination inside and outside of the religious community. In nearly every African American community, one or more churches provided tangible as well as moral and spiritual support to the movement as an extension of its traditional role of service.

The majority of civil rights rallies and mass meetings were held in black churches, generally the largest facilities independently owned and operated by African Americans in a given location. Designated offerings raised during regular church services and community mass meetings were used for direct financial support for various civil rights activities, such as helping jailed demonstrators to make bail and pay other imposed fines. Some churches also encouraged participation and/or membership of their congregations in civil rights organizations, created support networks for students, civil rights workers, and volunteers, and continued civil rights initiatives after media coverage and publicity from major events ended.

Many churches have been designated as state and/or national historic landmarks as a result of their role in the Civil Rights Movement. These include, but are not limited to, the following: Dexter Avenue Baptist (now Dexter Avenue King Memorial Baptist) Church and St. Jude Catholic Church, Montgomery, Alabama; Ebenezer Baptist, Wheat Street Baptist, and West Hunter Street Baptist Church, Atlanta, Georgia; First Baptist Church (Capitol Hill), Nashville, Tennessee; **Sixteenth Street Baptist Church**, Birmingham, Alabama; Brown Chapel African Methodist Episcopal and First Baptist Church, Selma, Alabama; Mount Zion Baptist Church, Albany, Georgia; Butler Chapel African Methodist Episcopal Zion Church, Tuskegee, Alabama; First African Baptist Church, Tuscaloosa, Alabama; Calvary Baptist Church, Oklahoma City, Oklahoma; Bethel African Methodist Episcopal Church, Reno, Nevada; and Mason Temple Church of God in Christ, Memphis, Tennessee.

Fletcher F. Moon

Sixteenth Street Baptist Church

The Sixteenth Street Baptist Church in Birmingham, Alabama, has served as the primary meeting place for the community and as an important part of the planning and events of the civil right activities in the 1960s. The bombing of the church in 1963, which killed four little black girls, was the most tragic of the period. The Sixteenth Street Baptist Church was first constructed as the First Colored Baptist Church of Birmingham, Alabama, in 1873. In 1911 a new building with three stories was constructed. It was designed by the black architect Wallace Rayfield.

With the Supreme Court ruling for *Brown v. Board of Education* in 1954, the South was charged to desegregate its public schools. Sixteenth Street Baptist Church served as the meeting place for marches and protests to impress upon Alabama to implement the ruling. The 1955 **Montgomery Bus Boycott** also pushed the state toward confronting many of its racist and separatists laws and attitudes. The resistance to change was prevalent from the lowest to the highest level of government in Alabama. When two black students—Charlayne Hunter and Hamilton Holmes—tried to register to attend the University of Alabama, Governor George Wallace attempted to deny their entrance by placing himself in front of the doors. Tension continued to mount, and in the spring of 1963 white supremacist groups took an even more aggressive response.

The community of Birmingham had been demonstrating for the end of segregation with the hope that the court-ordered integration of public schools would be implemented. On September 15, 1963, a Sunday morning, three members of the Ku Klux Klan planted nineteen sticks of dynamite outside the basement of the Sixteenth Street Baptist Church. Four young girls dressed in their "Sunday best" were in the basement as they planned to attend the adult service at 11:00 A.M. As other children entered the basement after an earlier youth service, the blast went off. Four young girls, Addie Mae Collins (age 15), Carole Robertson (age 14), Cynthia Wesley (age 14), and Denise McNair (age 11) were killed and 22 others were injured.

This act of violence marked a new low that was condemned by blacks and some whites. At a funeral for three of the girls, **Martin Luther King Jr.** was in attendance and he also spoke before the crowd. This bombing was one of many bombings that had inundated the city over the past decade, but this act of terrorism was the most heinous because it took innocent lives. The nation was shocked at the brutality of the act and those who committed it. It gave America a more intense look at the violence and hatred that blacks in the South had endured. The tragedy placed pressure on Birmingham to address its racial problems and led to the confrontation of racial problems in other Southern cities, too. This tragic event, along with the death of President **John F. Kennedy** two months later, helped the nation to realize and finally pass the **Civil Rights Act of 1964**, which protected blacks' right to vote. By 1977 only one of the individuals who bombed the church was convicted. The Sixteenth Street Baptist Church was declared a national historic landmark on September 17, 1980.

Lean'tin L. Bracks

Leaders

Abernathy, Ralph David (1926–1990)

Ralph Abernathy was born the tenth of twelve children in Linden, Alabama, and grew up during the Great Depression on his family's farm. During his formative years he decided to become a Baptist minister, despite limited exposure to anything beyond his all-black community. After military service at the end of World War II, Abernathy returned to Alabama and became an ordained minister in 1948. Abernathy graduated from **Alabama State College** with a B.S. in mathematics in 1950, and from Atlanta University with an M.S. in sociology the next year.

Abernathy met **Martin Luther King Jr.** in Atlanta, reuniting with him in 1954, when King became pastor of Dexter Avenue Baptist Church, and also at the **Montgomery Bus Boycott** (1955–56). He was the closest associate of Martin

Luther King Jr. during the Civil Rights Movement of the 1950s and 1960s. Abernathy thus became a key leader alongside King, organizing and leading non-violent protests around the country, including the historic **March on Washington** (1963). He helped found the **Montgomery Improvement Association** (1955), the **Southern Christian Leadership Conference** (1957), and the **Poor People's March on Washington** (1968). He was with King at the Lorraine Motel in Memphis on April 4, 1968, when King was assassinated. After King's death, Abernathy tried to continue his work, but only had limited success.

[Abernathy] was the closest associate of Martin Luther King Jr. during the Civil Rights Movement of the 1950s and 1960s.

Abernathy unsuccessfully ran for Congress in 1977 and became controversial in the 1980s after supporting President Ronald Reagan and publishing his autobiography. This 1989 book included unflattering comments about King's personal life, which subjected him to harsh criticism. He died the following year at the age of 64.

Fletcher F. Moon

Agyeman, Jaramogi Abebe. *See* Cleage, Albert Buford, Jr.

Austin, Junius Caesar (1887–1968)

A compelling leader and preacher, Junius C. Austin was an important figure in the African American communities in Pittsburgh and Chicago, where he effected programs that enhanced black community life. A follower of **Marcus Garvey** and the **Universal Negro Improvement League** (UNIA), he was considered a leader of the black nationalist movement. His smooth style and syncopated movements in the pulpit earned him the title "The dancing political preacher."

Austin began his work in Virginia, where from 1910 to 1915 he preached at a sequence of small churches. Between 1915 and 1926, he pastored Ebenezer Baptist in Pittsburgh, became active in civil rights efforts, and was elected president of the local **NAACP**. While there, he advocated black migration from the South to the North, particularly to Pittsburgh. To aid those who migrated, he set up the Steele City Bank and the Home Finder's League—a real estate office. He joined Marcus Garvey's UNIA and supported its focus on black economic self-help. He is pictured with Garvey in his widely reprinted image in a large convertible car as he rode through the streets of New York.

When Austin moved to Chicago, where he remained for over 40 years (1926–1968), he pastored Pilgrim Baptist Church. He continued his work with the NAACP and the self-help movement that Garvey and the UNIA called for early on. He also supported the **Brotherhood of Sleeping Car Porters**. He promoted the "buy black" movement that encouraged blacks to keep their shopping dollars in their own communities. For him, the church "could not afford to ignore the interlocking evils of racism and economic irregularity." Austin built a structure that linked the black church to many community initiatives and stressed the church's economic and political initiatives.

Jessie Carney Smith

Bevel, James Luther (1936–)

J ames Bevel was born October 19, 1936, in Itta Bena, Mississippi. In the 1950s, as an ordained Baptist Minister, he entered American Baptist Theological Seminary in Nashville, Tennessee. Along with other students, he became a participant in the evolving Civil Rights Movement and in the first sit-in protest in Nashville. For a year, he was chair of the Nashville Student Movement. Bevel was one of the founders of the **Student Non-Violent Coordinating Committee** (SNCC) and was its field secretary for Mississippi. He worked with the **Southern Christian Leadership Conference** (SCLC) to protest the trials of freedom riders in Albany, Georgia. He became a member of the SCLC staff as the Alabama Project coordinator in 1963. In this capacity, Bevel's mediating skills were utilized and he became the organizer of SCLC's Birmingham Movement.

Bevel was a forward-thinking man who proposed the **Selma to Montgomery march**. Additionally, he composed freedom songs and was a part of the formation of a statewide coalition of civil rights groups, the Council of Federated Organizations. In 1965, he led the statewide voter registration drive in Alabama. This action aided in the eventual passing of the **Voting Rights Act of 1965**. Following the passage of the **Civil Rights Act of 1964**, **Martin Luther King Jr.**, with whom Bevel had a close association, sent him to head the SCLC and the practice of nonviolence to Chicago. Bevel was not as successful as he had been in the South, however, and began to move in other directions. He worked with the Chicago open housing movement in 1966, the anti-Vietnam War movement in 1967, and the Poor People's Campaign in 1968.

Helen R. Houston

Cleage, Albert Buford, Jr. (1911–2000)

Albert B. Cleage Jr., known as Jaramogi Abebe Agyeman since the 1970s, was born June 13, 1911, in Indianapolis, Indiana, and died February 20, 2000, in Calhoun Falls, South Carolina. He decided to enter the ministry, and after years of study became a minister with the Congregational and Christian Church. He was a vibrant minister, a proponent of black theology and builder of strong congregations. In 1951 he

returned to Detroit as pastor of St. Mark's Community (Presbyterian) Church. Cleage, like his father, was an activist in his field, protesting a white Christianity that did not recognize his humanity. This, and other events of the 1950s such as the Civil Rights Movement and the rise of Islam, as well as his reading from the works of black nationalists, led him to construct a Black Theology for the black community. Cleage argued that Jesus was a black Messiah born of a black Madonna and a black revolutionary. In 1967, while preaching a sermon, he unveiled an 18-foot painting of a black Madonna and child and launched the Shrine of the Black Madonna and the Black Christian Nationalist Movement. He became known as a spokesperson for the people who took a stand for **Black Power**. The Shrines of the Black Madonna spread, and the Shrine established a bookstore to promote black works. Cleage was active in politics, running for office and helping to establish platforms and mentor black politicians.

Helen R. Houston

Clement, George Clinton (1871–1935)

A prominent bishop in the **African Methodist Episcopal Zion Church**, George Clinton Clement agitated for the removal of racial barriers in Kentucky and became an uncompromising race champion. His religious connections and accomplishments led to his selection as editor of the *Star of Zion*, the denomination's journal. He used the journal to promote uplifting messages on race and to encourage his readers to seek black empowerment. For thirteen years Clement was chair of the Federal Council of Churches' Committee on Church and Race Relations, and he later became a member of Louisville's Commission on Inter-Racial Relations. Both groups were deeply involved in civil rights issues and concerns. Clement joined other prominent African American leaders in Louisville, including **Albert E. Meyzeek** and J.A.C. Lattimore, who in 1920 campaigned to defeat a million-dollar bond issue that would

George Clinton Clement (Fisk University).

Alexander Crummell (Fisk University).

have provided the University of Louisville sole use of funds without any provisions for black higher education. Their continued agitation led to the establishment in 1925 of Louisville Municipal College.

Jessie Carney Smith

Crummell, Alexander (1819–1898)

A leading black nationalist of the nineteenth century, Alexander Crummell was involved in the anti-slavery movement throughout his life. His first activist involvement came when he was a boy employed at the American Colonization Society's New York offices. In the 1840s he held unsuccessful pastorates in churches in Providence, Rhode Island, and in New York City. In 1848 he left for England to secure funds for the Church of the Messiah in New York, where he was a pastor. He traveled widely and had a heavy speaking engagement schedule. Crummell's attack on the American Colonization Society secured his role as an orator.

In May 1853 Crummell and his family moved to Monrovia, Liberia, where he was a missionary for the Protestant Episcopal Church of America. He returned to the United States in the spring of 1861 to seek support for African colonization. Meanwhile, he became commissioner for the Liberian government, with responsibility for promoting emigration of blacks from the United States. Crummell traveled widely throughout the United States in 1861 and 1862, lecturing on behalf of the American Colonization Society. He also sought support for Liberia College. He was named to the college's faculty but was dismissed in 1866. A quarrelsome man, Crummell had difficulty wherever he worked and continued to battle authorities. He returned to the United States permanently in 1872, and pastored a church in Washington, D.C., while his national reputation as a thinker and orator continued to grow. The sermons, essays, and lectures that he published provide evidence of his scholarship and dedication to protest.

Jessie Carney Smith

Day, William Howard (1825–1900)

Devoted to the advancement of his race, William Howard Day used his eloquent oratory as well as the various newspapers that he edited or published to denounce the evils of slavery. He became one of the most influential and prominent race leaders of the nineteenth century. Day's work as a civil rights crusader began in 1847. Although very active in the national Negro convention movement, he had a deep concern for the freedom of blacks in Ohio, where he lived. He joined local residents in agitating against legalized discrimination in Ohio, which was provided for in the state's Black Laws that were enacted in 1802 but not repealed until 1849. A reporter for Cleveland's *True Democrat* in 1850, Day used his position there to promote black life. By 1853 he had become a leading public figure in Ohio and elsewhere in the nation. Because he used his personal funds to support his various newspaper ventures, he

William Howard Day (Fisk University).

depleted his financial resources. Health issues forced him to retire to a farm in Dresden, Ontario, where he intensified his concern for racial causes. There he worked in support of educational opportunities for over 50,000 fugitive slaves who lived in Canada. Day returned to the United States in 1863, became a minister, and as superintendent of the **Freedmen's Bureau** schools in Maryland and Delaware continued his support of education for blacks. Among other activities, he reentered the newspaper arena and purchased and edited a local paper that served areas of Pennsylvania, Delaware, and New York, serving as a mouthpiece for African Americans and their cause.

Jessie Carney Smith

Dobbins, William Curtis (1934–1983)

William "Bill" C. Dobbins joined a growing Civil Rights Movement that was sweeping the South and led a movement in Pensacola, Florida, in 1961 to desegregate lunch counters and other businesses. Born in Athens, Alabama, Dobbins, who in 1959 graduated from Gammon Theological Seminary in Atlanta, spent some time in Montgomery while he was in the seminary. While in Montgomery he pastored St. Paul Methodist Church. He lived next door to **Martin Luther King Jr.** and his family, was influenced by King's civil rights activities in Montgomery, and became sympathetic to the cause. Upon graduation, Dobbins became pastor of St. Paul Methodist Church in Pensacola and took an active part in community activities for blacks. In 1960, he began to write a column for the local black newspaper, *The Colored Citizen.* The column, "From Where I Stand," discussed race matters, the black community, and other timely topics. Dobbins also became director of the local **NAACP** Youth Council.

Now fully committed to civil rights, Dobbins and other ministers began to organize protest activities. Joining him was **Charles K. Steele,** who was influential in the Civil Rights Movement in Tallahassee and a minister who was present in that city during the student protest.

As movement leader, Dobbins helped to plan marches on Palafax Street in downtown Pensacola as well as sit-ins at lunch counters in Pensacola. Students from the Youth Council joined the marches and sit-ins. After that, Dobbins identified their next target—downtown stores that refused to hire blacks. So that law enforcement officers would have a cause to arrest the protesters, merchants and the police slipped items in the protesters' pockets, such as batteries and other small objects, and then arrested them for shoplifting. During the sit-ins in Woolworth's, Kress, and Newberry stores, one girl was burned with a cigarette, another sprayed with insecticide, and yet another pricked with a knife.

To further aid the cause, the Pensacola Ministerial Association was formed, held mass meetings to inform the community of the activities planned, and raised money to pay bail, court costs, and fines levied against black protesters. After a boycott of stores around Christmas time, 1961, when merchants lost $25,000 a week, the stores finally relented. During the movement, bomb threats were made to Dobbins's home. When he ran against white opponents for the Florida House of Representatives in 1963, a sniper fired into his home. Fortunately, no one was injured. Later, Dobbins and his family relocated to a church in Sylacauga, Alabama.

Jessie Carney Smith

Farrakhan, Louis (1933–)

For more than three decades Louis Farrakhan has been the beloved and sometimes controversial leader of the African American religious organization the Final Call to the Nation of Islam (NOI). Despite being criticized for comments that are sometimes received as offensive by racial groups, he has remained an ardent advocate for the urban poor since founding the Splinter Group in 1978. A dynamic personality and a charismatic speaker, Farrakhan is widely known throughout the nation and world for his promotion of the organization's black separation and self-reliance platforms. Once recognized as one the most influ-

ential African Americans of his time, he has been featured in numerous American news magazines, and in 1995 he most famously organized the **Million Man March** of more than 1,000,000 black men in Washington, D.C.

Born Louis Eugene Walcott to Sarah Mae Manning Clarke, a native of St. Kitts, Farrakhan was reared in Roxbury, a West Indian neighborhood of Boston, Massachusetts. Despite being a single mother raising two sons, Clarke secured private violin lessons for young Farrakhan. An honor student in two of the city's top high schools, the talented violinist was also a star track athlete and an active Episcopalian. Dubbed "The Charmer" by audiences in Boston's Caribbean nightclubs, he also enjoyed performing to the Calypso rhythms of his West Indian heritage to supplement the family's income. Instead of attending the august Juilliard School of Music, he opted to attend Winston-Salem Teacher's College (now University), a black college in North Carolina in 1950. Married just three years later to the former Betsy Ross, Farrakhan continued to perform as "Calypso Gene," joining the Nation of Islam in the mid-1950s.

Impressed by the spirit of NOI leader **Elijah Muhammad**'s message, he assumed the named Louis X in 1955. That same year, he was appointed a captain in the NOI's security force, known as the Fruit of Islam. Soon after, he was promoted to minister; using the posture of Muhammad and his mentee **Malcolm X**, Farrakhan began to preach to the black underclass. Just as his fame reached its apex in the early 1960s, allegations of improprieties by Muhammad caused serious discord among the two protégés. Farrakhan's role in excoriating Malcolm X, who renamed himself El Haj Malik Shabazz and formed his own non-racist organization, later contributed to suspicions that he was involved in Shabazz's assassination in February 1965.

In May of the same year, Farrakhan was renamed Abdul Farrakhan by Muhammad. He assumed Sabbazz's former position and in 1967 became the NOI's national representative. In spite of his faithfulness, Farrakhan was not

Louis Farrakhan (AP Photo/M. Spencer Green).

named Muhammad's successor upon his death in 1975. The NOI had an estimated 100,000 members at the time, and they were to be led by Muhammad's estranged son, Wallace D. Muhammad. When ideological differences led to the disbanding of the NOI by Muhammad just one year later, Farrakhan revived the Nation and began publishing the *Final Call* in 1979. In less than three decades, he successfully rebuilt the NOI by elevating the role of women, purchasing his mentor's Hyde Park Chicago mansion and the former Temple No. 2 in Chicago, and amassing a membership of several thousand.

Crystal A. deGregory

Fauntroy, Walter E. (1933–)

Over nearly fifty years Walter Fauntroy has made an indelible impact through his ministry and activism in his birthplace of Washington, D.C. His work has ranged from local issues in the Shaw neighborhood where he grew up, national civil rights work with **Martin Luther King Jr.** and the **Southern Christian Leadership Conference** (SCLC), service in the U.S. Congress, and international activism and peace initiatives related to South Africa, India, and other nations.

One of eight children, Fauntroy was born in the midst of the Great Depression. He became aware of racial discrimination early in life, and made it known that he would pursue the ministry to improve conditions in his community. He was encouraged by Charles David Foster, the pastor of New Bethel Baptist Church in Washington, D.C., and given opportunities to preach to the congregation there. Fauntroy was favorably received, and the membership assisted him financially so he could attend Virginia Union University after he graduated from Dunbar High School in 1950. While in college he met Martin Luther King Jr. through mutual friend Wyatt Tee Walker, another future minister and activist.

[Franklin] used biblical stories to draw analogies between the plight of African Americans and the plight of the Hebrews.

After graduating from Virginia Union with a bachelor's degree in history in 1955, Fauntroy continued his studies at Yale University, where he earned a bachelor of divinity degree in 1958. He married the former Dorothy Sims, and shortly after returning to Washington from Yale he became pastor at New Bethel after the death of Foster. Fauntroy became a local civil rights advocate and became the director of the SCLC Washington bureau in 1960. He excelled in logistics, strategic planning, and lobbying for government involvement in civil rights issues, and his access to government officials was critical during such events as the **Freedom Rides** (1961) and the **Albany Movement** (1962). Fauntroy coordinated SCLC involvement in the historic 1963 **March on Washington**, including logistics and preparation for King's landmark "**I Have a Dream**" speech.

After the assassination of **John F. Kennedy** in 1963, Fauntroy continued to lobby for civil rights and voting legislation with the **Lyndon B. Johnson** administration, resulting in the **1964 Civil Rights Act** and the **1965 Voting Rights Act**. His work in coordinating civil rights events continued with completion of the 1965 **Selma to Montgomery March** and 1966 Meredith Mis-

sissippi Freedom March after earlier attempts in these locations were disrupted by violence.

Entering politics as a city councilman in 1967, Fauntroy continued local activism by leading community redevelopment projects, was elected to Congress in 1971, and helped found and chair the **Congressional Black Caucus** for the next twenty years. He was arrested for protesting apartheid in South Africa, lobbied for District of Columbia statehood, and pressed for full voting representation in Congress. After retiring from Congress, Fauntroy continued his ministry and served as chair of the National Black Leadership Roundtable.

Fletcher F. Moon

Franklin, Clarence LaVaughn (1915–1984)

Clarence LaVaughn Franklin, known as "C.L.," was born in January of 1915 in Sunflower County, Mississippi, and died in Detroit on July 27, 1984. Franklin, one of the most charismatic and influential leaders in Detroit, broadcast sermons and music on the radio on Sundays, preached throughout the country, and was one of the first ministers to record his work—76 albums of sermons and gospel songs. (The father of singers Aretha, Erma, and Carolyn Franklin, he would pass down his love of music to his children, too). He used biblical stories to draw analogies between the plight of African Americans and the plight of the Hebrews. The victory of the Hebrews over their enemies gave rise to hope among African Americans who fought the battle for civil rights. Franklin's sermons were not designed for complacency; he encouraged his congregants to see that Christianity is against any ideology that denies the humanity of individuals regardless of color. Thus, they had a responsibility for community involvement and activism. As pastor for over thirty years at New Bethel Baptist Church, he impacted both his congregation and Detroit. He instituted a food ministry, offered financial and legal help for the homeless, conducted a prison ministry, and encouraged church members to register and vote. His pulpit was a forum for black activists; in 1969, members of the Republic of New Africa, a militant organization, were allowed to use the pulpit because Franklin said their goals were the same as African Americans', although their approach was different. He became involved in the Civil Rights Movement and co-organized a freedom march in Detroit in 1963. Franklin was active in the **National Urban League**, **NAACP**, and was on the executive board of the **Southern Christian Leadership Conference**.

Helen R. Houston

Garnet, Henry Highland (1815–1882)

As African Americans in the nineteenth century sought remedies for the ill treatment that they received, Henry Highland Garnet, a leading member of the abolition movement, advocated political action as a necessary alternative. He urged slaves to claim their freedom and urged all blacks to take destiny into their own hands. He was a firm advocate of colonization of Africa from the 1850s forward. An outstanding orator, Garnet fared well along the great black speakers of his time. Born a slave in Maryland, he and his family escaped and finally settled in New York City. When studying at the Africa Free School, he found among the extraordinary students there **Alexander Crummell**, **Samuel Ringgold Ward**, and **James McCune Smith**, who would become important black leaders. He faced racial violence on several occasions, including the time that he and his classmates visited Noyes Academy in New Hampshire on July 4, 1835, and delivered fiery orations at an abolitionist meeting. Afterward, local townspeople destroyed the school and the house where the students stayed.

By May 1840, Garnet was fully committed to abolitionist work and delivered a speech before the **American Anti-Slavery Society** in New York. Garnet entered the Presbyterian ministry and was licensed in 1842. He pastored Liberty Street Presbyterian Church in Troy, New York, from

Henry Highland Garnet (Fisk University).

1842 to 1848. In 1843 he included in his activities an assignment with the American Home Missionary Society, which paid him for his work with abolitionism and temperance. He supported the Liberty Party, which had abolition as one of its major planks. Once a supporter of abolitionist William Lloyd Garrison—who favored moral reform—the two broke their alliance around 1843 because of Garnet's activism. In that year as well, Garnet became one of the eight blacks who founded the American and Foreign Anti-Slavery Society. He was also a prominent member of the National Negro Convention movement and in 1843 gave an electrifying speech at its Albany, New York, conference. In his speech "An Address to the Slaves of the United States in America" Garnet urged slaves to take responsibility for their own freedom, saying that it was better to die free than live a slave.

By 1847 Liberia was a new independent African nation. Garnet, who supported the American

Colonization Society, led the way in encouraging black emigration to that nation. Most blacks, however, condemned the society, were suspicious of its aims and reasons for being, and had little trust for Liberia as well. Garnet's view was that blacks should emigrate to any area that would treat them justly and with dignity. By the mid-1850s, support for black emigration had grown in the black community, yet leaders such as **Frederick Douglass** continued to criticize Garnet because of his position.

When the **Civil War** began, Garnet and other blacks urged the formation of black units and in 1863, he became a recruiter and served as chaplain to black troops in the state of New York. By now Garnet was so prominent that he became a target for white mobs during the draft riots of July 1863; other blacks and leading abolitionists were targeted as well. Fortunately, Garnet escaped the violence again. He continued his pastoral duties at the Fifteenth Street Presbyterian Church in Washington, D.C., and on February 12, 1865, became the first black to deliver a sermon in the chamber of the U.S. House of Representatives. In 1868 he became president of Avery College in Pittsburgh, and in 1870 he returned to Shiloh Church in New York as pastor. After being named minister to Liberia, in 1881 he traveled to Monrovia, where he died in 1882.

Jessie Carney Smith

Grimké, Francis J. (1852–1937)

Francis J. Grimké became a leader among African Americans in Washington, D.C., as pastor of the Fifteenth Street Presbyterian Church. He used his position to fight racism both within his denomination and in society at large. After Grimké graduated from Lincoln University in Chester, Pennsylvania, in 1870, he went on to pursue law and studied one year at the Lincoln University law school and then at **Howard University**'s law school in Washington, D.C. In 1875 Grimké felt the call to the ministry and entered Princeton Theological Seminary, where he graduated in 1878. His first assignment was at the Fif-

Francis J. Grimké (Fisk University).

teenth Street Presbyterian Church. With a congregation of some of the most successful African Americans in D.C., Grimké encouraged them to agitate for civil rights. He was a founding member of the Afro-Presbyterian Council that was devoted to the causes of African American Presbyterians. Grimké had great admiration for Frederick Douglass and came to support many of the ideas of **Booker T. Washington** regarding self-help. He also had great regard for **W.E.B. Du Bois** as a civil rights leader. Grimké was a participant in the call for a meeting that eventually led to the establishment of the NAACP. His focus on civil rights was always tempered by his ministry. He gave a lifetime of service to the church and the community until his death on October 11, 1937.

Lean'tin L. Bracks

Harris, Barbara Clementine (1930–)

A Philadelphia native, Barbara Harris was the first woman to become a bishop in the Episcopal Church. Named a deacon in 1979, she became an ordained priest the next year. Because she was black, a woman, a divorcée, and a liberal social activist, considerable debate surrounded her ordination as suffragan bishop in September 1988, and she was consecrated a bishop on February 11, 1989, making her the first woman to be ordained to the episcopate in the worldwide Anglican Communion. Those who opposed her election protested during the service.

Harris is an outspoken advocate of the rights of minorities, women, and the poor. Her election as suffragan bishop of the diocese of Massachusetts came on September 24, 1988. Harris saw discrimination in the church and joined its journey toward eliminating it. She worked through her church to support the Union of Black Episcopalians (UBE) and its mission to promote blacks throughout the church. She also used the UBE as a vehicle for exercising her social justice ministry and to ensure non-exclusionary participation in her church. Harris's social activism predates her church leadership position. In the summer of 1964, when voter registration drives were prominent in the Deep South, she used her summer vacation to register black voters in Mississippi. On Sunday, March 7, 1965, known as **Bloody Sunday**, she participated in the **Selma-to-Montgomery march** with **Martin Luther King Jr.** and other leaders.

Harris was executive director of the Episcopal Church Publishing Company in 1984 and used its chief publication, the *Witness,* to lash out against racism, sexism, classism, and genderism. Although her work was important to the Civil Rights Movement, she is best known for her activism in the Episcopal church. Harris retired from the church in 2002 but continued to serve part-time as assisting bishop in the Diocese of Washington.

Jessie Carney Smith

Holly, James Theodore (1829–1911)

James Theodore Holly was born October 3, 1829, in Washington, D.C., to free black parents and died in Port-au-Prince, Haiti, on March 13, 1911. As a boy, his family moved in 1844 to Brooklyn, New York, where his brother became involved in abolitionist work and writing for

James Theodore Holly (Fisk University).

Frederick Douglass's *North Star.* At the time, Holly apprenticed as a shoemaker and attended night school. He became associate editor of *Voice of the Fugitive* (1851–1853), which was published in Canada. Holly became affiliated with the Protestant Episcopal Church in 1852 and moved up in the hierarchy: ordained a deacon in Detroit in 1855; ordained a priest on January 2, 1856, in New Haven, Connecticut, and served as rector there until 1861; and on November 8, 1874, he was consecrated as Bishop of Haiti in Grace Church, New York. Holly strove to get support for the emigration of black people to Haiti, but the church refused to help.

Holly attended the National Emigration Convention in Cleveland in August 1856. Attendees included **Martin R. Delany** and William C. Monroe. Different attendees sought varying destinations for emigration, including Africa, South America, and Haiti. It was not until Haiti's President Fabre Geffrard began recruiting black people to emigrate and hired Holly that he began to see his dream come true. Upon setting sail on an overcrowded ship, however, passengers began to die and many of those who ultimately landed soon died as well, including several members of Holly's family. Holly remained in Haiti, zealously working for the cause of Christianity. He became the first head of an independent church in Haiti and the first black bishop consecrated by the American Protestant Episcopal Church. Throughout his career, Holly was involved in fights for black rights and worked towards emigration for blacks, believing that the only way to receive equality was for black people to separate themselves from whites.

Helen R. Houston

Jackson, Jesse, Sr. (1941–)

In the 1960s, Jesse Jackson Sr. emerged as an ally of Civil Rights Movement leader **Martin Luther King Jr.** Appointed to run the **Southern Christian Leadership Conference**'s (SCLC) Operation Breadbasket in Chicago, Illinois, and later becoming its national director, Jackson viewed himself as **Martin Luther King Jr.**'s organizational heir. Passed over for the SCLC's presidency, Jackson founded **People United to Save Humanity** (PUSH) in 1971. Over the course of the following decade, he became increasingly involved in American politics. In 1984 and 1988, Jackson unsuccessfully vied for the Democratic nomination for president of the United States.

Jackson was born to Noah Robinson and Helen Burns, a young unwed mother in Greenville, South Carolina. He was taunted as a child because of his mother's status until 1957, when his mother married. He was adopted by his stepfather and took the surname of Jackson. With the help of his grandmother, he began to overcome his lack of self-confidence in high school. His subsequently stellar academic record and athletic talent earned Jackson a football scholarship to the University of Illinois. Disappointed with the overt racism of the North, Jackson transferred to **North Carolina**

Agricultural and Technical College, an all-black college in Greensboro, North Carolina. While there, he flourished as an athlete and student, was elected student body president, and became a student activist.

Following his graduation, Jackson worked briefly for North Carolina Governor Terry Sanford before enrolling in the Chicago Theological Seminary. Increasingly drawn to political activism, Jackson left the seminary to work for King. In 1966 King chose Jackson to organize Operation Breadbasket and then appointed him national director of the initiative one year later. Catapulted to prominence following his television appearance the day after King's April 1968 assassination, Jackson was suspended from the SCLC as a result of its claim that he was using the organization to further his personal agenda.

As the founder of Operation PUSH, Jackson coined the phrase "I Am Somebody" and became an outspoken critic of South African apartheid, securing his place as a national leader by the mid-1970s. After embracing then-exiled Palestinian leader Yassar Arafat while touring the Middle East in 1979, Jackson began to moderate his political positions during the 1980s. In 1983 he helped secure the election of the first African American mayor of Chicago, Harold Washington. One year later, espousing a platform of expanded civil and voting rights, tax alleviation for the poor, and effective affirmative action programs, Jackson vied for the Democratic presidential nomination. Despite not having the support of most traditional African American leaders and conceding defeat at that year's Democratic National Convention, Jackson's ability to court nearly 3.5 million votes was ground-breaking for African Americans on the nation's political landscape.

Following another unsuccessful bid for the presidency in 1988, Jackson offered his support to the campaign of 1992 presidential candidate Bill Clinton. Having aided the release of Americans in the Middle East and Cuba in the 1980s, Jackson was the first American to bring hostages out of Iraq and Kuwait in 1990. Nine years later, he convinced Yugoslav President Slobodan Milosevic to release three captive NATO soldiers at his side. The same year, Jackson negotiated a ceasefire agreement in Sierra Leone, also successfully negotiating for the release of more than 2,000 prisoners of war. Today, Jackson continues to work for various social, economic, and political rights across the United States and internationally.

Crystal A. deGregory

Johns, Vernon N. (1892–1965)

Vernon N. Johns is considered by some to be the "father" of the modern Civil Rights Movement. One of the movement's early trailblazers, as a pulpiter Johns was noted, along with **Mordecai Johnson** and **Howard Thurman**, as one of the three great African American preachers. The son of William Thomas and Sallie Branch Price Johns, he was born in Darlington Heights, Virginia. His contributions to the modern Civil Rights Movement, however, would later be eclipsed by **Martin Luther King Jr.** and **Malcolm X**, who followed him. He received a B.A. degree from Virginia Theological Seminary and College in 1915 and a B.D. degree from Oberlin College in 1918. The same year that he graduated from Oberlin, Johns entered the University of Chicago, where he was a graduate student in theology.

When African American theologians were not included in the debate regarding issues that ranged from biblical interpretation to social responsibility, and their sermons were not being published, Johns submitted the sermons of Johnson and Thurman to publishing houses. When their manuscripts were rejected, he submitted his *Transfigured Moments*, which in 1926 became the first African American sermon published in John Fort Newton's anthology *Best Sermons*. The first African American to be published in the collection, Johns joined the ranks of well-known theologians such as Reinhold Niebuhr, Henry Sloan, and Willard L. Sperry. That year he delivered his first sermon at

Howard University's Rankin Memorial Chapel and became director of the Baptist Educational Center in New York. A year later, he succeeded Mordecai Johnson as pastor of the First Baptist Church in Charleston, West Virginia.

In 1929 Johns became president of Virginia Theological Seminary and College. Adhering to his rural roots, closeness to nature, and mindful of the needs of his people, while serving as president he founded the Institute for Rural Preachers of Virginia and the Farm and City Club, which attempted to raise awareness on economic issues and understanding between African Americans in rural and urban locales. Johns remained at the Virginia college until his retirement in 1934.

Johns responded with the sermon "It's Safe to Murder Negroes in Montgomery."

After retiring, Johns spent the next ten years lecturing and preaching at colleges and African American, mostly rural, churches. In 1947 he became the nineteenth pastor of Dexter Avenue Baptist Church in Montgomery, Alabama, where he served until 1952. Dexter's congregation consisted mostly of Montgomery's black middle class. In keeping with his social gospel position, Dexter's new pastor was a pioneering proponent of civil rights and he urged his congregation to challenge the city's Jim Crow laws. As one who practiced what he preached, Johns confronted Montgomery's segregated bus seating long before **Rosa Parks** famously refused to move to the back of the bus when he disembarked in protest and demanded a refund, which he received.

After an African American motorist was brutally attacked by police while blacks stood watching, Johns responded with the sermon "It's Safe to Murder Negroes in Montgomery," in which he criticized blacks for not intervening. Because of his unorthodox and country ways, Johns, the church officials, and the congregation often traveled divergent paths. Additionally, because of the tenor of his sermons, which denounced racial segregation, many feared they would come under the fierce scrutiny of Montgomery's white community and local authorities. Given the mood of the times, Johns's advocacy for Montgomery's blacks was seen as dangerous in many ways. Twice he attempted to prosecute white men for the rape of African American girls. He not only protested Jim Crow public transportation rules, but also protested against segregated restaurants.

In 1952, Johns resigned as pastor of the Dexter Avenue Baptist Church. However, his early activism and challenges to the power structure paved the way for Dexter's congregation to receive the Rev. Martin Luther King Jr.'s socially active ministry and for him to take a leading role in the **Montgomery Bus Boycott**. A leading moral force to the Civil Rights Movement, King later described Johns as "a brilliant preacher with a creative mind" and "a fearless man, [who] never allowed an injustice to come to his attention without speaking out against it."

A trailblazer who did not wait on a following in the modern struggle to gain freedom and equality, the Reverend Vernon N. Johns died on June 11, 1965, shortly after delivering a sermon entitled "The Romance of Death," at Howard University's Rankin Memorial Chapel. In 1994 Johns was brought out of the obscure pages of history when a film made for television aired that was based upon an unpublished history by Henry W. Powell of the Vernon Johns Society. Written by Leslie Lee and Kevin Arkadie, *The Road to Freedom: The Vernon Johns Story* was directed by Kenneth Fink, and Kareem Abdul Jabbar served as co-executive producer.

Linda T. Wynn

King, Martin Luther, Jr. (1929–1968)

Arguably the most celebrated black leader of his time, Martin Luther King Jr. rose to his prominence in the late 1950s as the organizer of the 1955 **Montgomery Bus Boycott**. As a local and national organizer, King popularized Mohandas Gandhi's theory of nonviolence to mobilize a mass movement across the American South. His civil rights umbrella organization, the **Southern Christian Leadership Conference** (SCLC), solidified his place as the voice of the American Civil Rights Movement. Awarded the Nobel Peace Prize in 1964, King was posthumously recognized for his lifetime achievements with a national holiday in 1983.

Born Michael King Jr. in Atlanta, Georgia, he was the son of Michael Luther King Sr. and Alberta Williams King. His father was a Baptist minister and both parents were college graduates. He attended the city's public schools and skipped two grades before entering **Morehouse College** at age 15. He was ordained while still an undergraduate student. Following graduation in 1948, King entered Crozer Theological Seminary in Chester, Pennsylvania. He received a bachelor of divinity degree from Crozer in 1951 and his doctor of philosophy in systematic theology at Boston University in June 1955. Three years earlier, King had married Coretta Scott, and the couple relocated to Montgomery, Alabama, in 1954 so he could assume the pastorate of Dexter Avenue Baptist Church.

Once in Montgomery, King became an active member of the local **NAACP** and the Alabama Council on Human Relations. In 1955 King became a leader in the city's boycott on the public bus system to protest the arrest of NAACP secretary **Rosa Parks** and Jim Crow laws. When the boycott ended more than a year later, it was hailed as one of the Civil Rights Movement's earliest grass-roots victories, and it capitulated King to heroic status. Two years later, King founded the SCLC in Atlanta, Georgia. Created to capitalize on the moral authority and organizing strength of black ministers

(From left to right) Rev. Ralph Abernathy, Rev. Dr. Martin Luther King Jr., and Bayard Rustin were the leaders in organizing the Montgomery Bus Boycott in 1955 and 1956 (AP Photo).

and their churches, the SCLC urged social change through non-violent protest.

In 1960 King moved his wife and children to Atlanta, Georgia, where he served as the associate pastor of Ebenezer Baptist Church, where his father was pastor. Inspired by early protests, black college students mobilized a "sit-in" movement in the late 1950s and early 1960s. In October of 1960, King was imprisoned while lending them his support. In 1961 and 1962, King aided activists in the unsuccessful **Albany Movement**. Then, in 1963, King and the SCLC assisted in the protests in Birmingham, Alabama. Nicknamed "Bombingham" because of its numerous unsolved bombings in black neighborhoods, racial violence against activists climaxed with the bombing of the **Sixteenth Street Baptist Church**.

In 1963 King also delivered his famous "I Have a Dream" speech in Washington, D.C., at

the National Mall and was recognized later that year as *Time* magazine's "Man of Year." By the mid-1960s, King's opposition to American imperialism, capitalism, and the Vietnam War had made him an increasingly controversial figure. King was assassinated on April 4, 1968, while standing on the balcony of the Lorraine Hotel in Memphis, Tennessee, where he had come to support a local sanitation workers' strike.

Crystal A. deGegory

King, Martin Luther, Sr. (1899–1984)

Most remembered as the father of slain civil rights leader **Martin Luther King Jr.**, Martin Luther King Sr. helped to inspire his son to enter the ministry. A Baptist minister himself, King was the pastor of Atlanta's famed Ebenezer Baptist Church for more than four decades. King's reach extended beyond the church and touched virtually every facet of black life in the city. His role as president of both the local **NAACP** and the Civil and Political League secured his place as a community leader and a pioneer of the modern Civil Rights Movement.

The first of nine children born in Stockbridge, Georgia, to sharecroppers James and Delia King, he was born Michael King. After moving to Atlanta in 1918, King met Alberta Williams, daughter of then-Ebenezer pastor A. D. Williams. Encouraged by her, he finished high school and enrolled at **Morehouse College** in 1926. The same year he married Williams; he graduated from Morehouse in 1930 and later succeeded his father-in-law as pastor upon his death in 1931. Affectionately referred to as "Daddy King," he had witnessed a lynching as a child and used his pulpit to preach in the black social gospel tradition that had first inspired him to become a minister. His personal acts of dissent and support for civil rights served as a model to his son King Jr. Following his son's assassination, the elder King remained involved in various civil rights causes and served for a time as a Morehouse trustee. One year after his wife's murder in 1974, he resigned his pastorate at Ebenezer. King died of a heart attack at Atlanta's Crawford W. Long Hospital on November 11, 1984.

Crystal A. deGregory

Lafayette, Bernard, Jr. (1940–)

Bernard Lafayette Jr. was born in Tampa, Florida, to Bernard and Verdell Lafayette Sr. After completing high school, in 1958 Lafayette came to Nashville, Tennessee, and enrolled at American Baptist College. Here, he and fellow students **James Bevel** and **John Lewis** came under the influence of people like the Reverend **Kelly Miller Smith**, a professor, civil rights activist, and pastor of the First Baptist Church, Capital Hill. Later in 1958, when Smith established the Nashville Christian Leadership Council (NCLC), which was an affiliate of SCLC, Lafayette began attending workshops on direct nonviolence conducted by the Reverend **James Lawson**. While attending college in 1958 and 1959, he and other students, including Bevel, Lewis, **Marion Barry**, and **Diane Nash**, attended a weekend retreat at **Highland Folk School**, where they were further imbued with the canon and philosophy of direct nonviolence. As a contingent of the **Nashville Student Movement** (NSA), Lafayette and the other students, along with the Reverends Smith and Lawson, began conducting investigational sit-ins at Nashville's segregated restaurants in the late fall of 1959. Because management refused to relinquish the racial segregation customs of the Old South, Lafayette, the NSA and hundreds of students primarily from **American Baptist College**, **Fisk University**, **Tennessee A&I State University**, and **Meharry Medical College** began the **Nashville Sit-in** movement on February 13, 1960.

Later, that spring, Lafayette and a small group from Nashville attended the student conference in North Carolina organized by **Ella Baker**, an experienced civil rights organizer and an SCLC official. During the Easter weekend of 1960, more than 200 students from across the South gathered at Shaw University in Raleigh, North Carolina. This confab gave birth to the **Student Non-Violent Coordinating Committee**

(SNCC) in which members of the NSA played prominent roles, including in the 1961 **Freedom Rides**. Like blacks in Nashville who conducted "freedom rides" by boarding a private Nashville streetcar company's segregated cars and refusing to sit in the "colored section" 95 years earlier, Lafayette and Lewis took similar actions on interstate public conveyances by refusing to leave their bus seats. In 1961 Lafayette participated in the Freedom Rides originally begun by the **Congress of Racial Equality** (CORE), but they aborted the protest because of violence in Anniston, Alabama. The Ku Klux Klan attacked the bus on which Lafayette was riding in Montgomery. The riders, however, continued their journey from Alabama to Mississippi, where Lafayette was arrested and served 40 days in **Parchman Penitentiary.**

In 1962 the civil rights activist served as director of the SNCC's Alabama Voter Registration Project. The following year, Lafayette conducted voter registration clinics in Selma, Alabama. Hired by the American Friends Service Committee in the summer of 1963, he tested non-violent methods in Chicago, Illinois. Later, **Martin Luther King Jr.** selected him to assist in the planning and execution of the direct action program in the Chicago Campaign sponsored by SCLC. Lafayette became SCLC's program coordinator and aided in the planning of the 1968 **Poor People's March on Washington**. While his activism continued, Lafayette received his master's and doctoral degrees from Harvard University in 1972 and 1974, respectively. From 1993 to 1999, he served as president of his alma mater, American Baptist College. He is currently Distinguished Scholar-in-Residence and Director of the Center for Nonviolence and Peace Studies at the University of Rhode Island.

Linda T. Wynn

Lawson, James M., Jr. (1928–)

As a divinity student at Vanderbilt University in Nashville, Tennessee, James "Jim" Morris Lawson Jr. was expelled from the school in the spring of 1960 because of his off-campus involvement in civil rights activities, particularly the sit-in movement. His expulsion created a national embarrassment for the university, sparked debate, and caused repercussions that are still felt today. Lawson was born in Uniontown, Pennsylvania, and graduated from Baldwin Wallace College in 1952. He received his S.T.B. degree from Boston University in 1960. Lawson then transferred from the Oberlin School of Theology to Vanderbilt Divinity School. He had also come to Nashville as a staff organizer for the **Fellowship of Reconciliation**; he was impressed by students in the local black colleges as well as those at Vanderbilt. An intellectual and a minister with impeccable credentials, he had a passion for social justice.

Lawson was jailed early on as a conscientious objector to the Korean War, served as a foreign missionary, studied the philosophies of nonviolence in India, and then returned to Ohio, where he met **Martin Luther King Jr.** during King's visit to Oberlin. In Nashville he had planned to graduate from divinity school in May 1960; meanwhile, he held workshops on nonviolence for students at **Fisk University**, **Tennessee State**, the **American Baptist College**, and **Meharry Medical College**, who then launched a sit-in movement to protest social injustice in the city. They began non-violent civil disobedience at downtown department store lunch counters. In February 1960 the **sit-in** movement peaked; it included white as well as black students. As angry white crowds surrounded the students at their demonstration places, the local press captured their work and portrayed Lawson as an outsider who defied local law to advocate divine laws instead. Their arrest on February 27, 1960, for disorderly conduct and loitering spurred Lawson to define the arrests as simply legal gimmicks to shut down the protests. Despite their defiance of local laws, Lawson spurred them on.

The demonstration occurred at the same time that the executive committee of Vanderbilt's board of trustees met in early March. The committee asked Vanderbilt's chancellor, Harvie

Branscomb, for his views on the matter. Knowing that the conservative-minded board would be distressed over the matter, Branscomb, with the support of the executive committee, decided that Lawson should withdraw from the school or be expelled. He refused to quit and was expelled. When the Lawson Affair, as it was known, reached both the local and national press, Vanderbilt's divinity faculty and some of its students protested in support of Lawson; some faculty resigned as a result. Since the board at first was unwilling to rehire the faculty, the Divinity School dean threatened to follow them. Finally, the board relented and allowed the faculty to withdraw their resignations. Lawson could return if he wished. By this time, Lawson had enrolled at Boston University, where he received his degree; he never graduated from Vanderbilt.

[Lawson's] expulsion created a national embarrassment for the university.

The Lawson affair helped to solidify the sit-in movement as the most effective form of non-violent resistance practiced in the South. The Divinity School at Vanderbilt soon publicly committed itself to racial equality and social justice. Lawson went on to become pastor at Green Chapel Methodist Church in Shelbyville, Tennessee, Centenary United Methodist Church in Memphis, and then Holman Methodist Church in Los Angeles; he served on boards of civil rights organizations, too. Lawson returned to Vanderbilt in 2006–2007 as Distinguished Visiting Professor and Fellow of the Center for the Study of Religion and Culture. The James M. Lawson Jr. Chair was established in his honor.

Jessie Carney Smith

Lowery, Joseph Echols (1924?–)

Recognized as an elder statesman of the Civil Rights Movement in the United States, Joseph Lowery helped **Martin Luther King Jr.** and other ministers create the **Southern Christian Leadership Conference** (SCLC) in 1957. Lowery served as its president from 1977 to 1997, and remained active in the early years of the twenty-first century despite his retirement from full-time ministry. Sources vary as to the year of his birth, but all list Lowery as being born on October 6 in Huntsville, Alabama. His father was a store owner, but Lowery eventually followed in the footsteps of his great-grandfather, who was the first black Methodist pastor in Huntsville. Lowery experienced racism and violence as a teenager, but committed himself to changing the racial situation as an adult. He attended Knoxville College and Alabama Agricultural and Mechanical College, but earned a B.A. in sociology from Paine College in Augusta, Georgia, in 1943. Lowery received his call to ministry and entered Paine Theological Seminary in 1944. During this period he met and married Evelyn Gibson in 1947, was ordained a Methodist minister in 1948, graduated from seminary in 1950, and served as a pastor in Mobile, Alabama, from 1951 to 1961. He met Martin Luther King Jr. through mutual friend the Reverend **Fred Shuttlesworth**, and became a key leader in the Civil Rights Movement. After King's 1968 assassination, the movement and SCLC floundered, but Lowery revived the organization and expanded its work to international human rights issues.

Fletcher F. Moon

Muhammad, Elijah (1897–1975)

As the leader of the African American religious organization the Nation of Islam, Elijah Muhammad was the charismatic leader of thousands. He championed black nationalism and economic self-sufficiency long before its popularization in the mid-1960s and 1970s

Elijah Muhammad (AP Photo/Edward Kitch).

through figures such as **Malcolm X**, one of his most renowned mentees. His militant ideology not only asserted that blacks were the original humans on earth and the superior race, but it elevated the Nation's founder, Wallace D. Fard, to godlike status and Muhammad himself to the mantle of prophet. At the height of his movement, the Nation of Islam had 69 temples or missions in 27 states.

Born Elijah Poole to ex-slaves Wali and Marie Poole, Muhammad worked alongside his sharecropping family until he was 16, when he began assuming odd jobs. After settling in Detroit, Michigan, in 1923, he became a follower of Fard during the 1930s. Along with his brothers, Muhammad embraced Fard's manifesto of black America's African ancestry, as well as his proclamation of Islam as the true religion for black Americans. As a condition of his acceptance, Muhammad denounced his birth name, which the Nation viewed as a slave name given to his ancestors, in exchange for an Islamic name, Elijah Karriem. Despite his increasingly militant posture, he proved to be one of Fard's most trusted aides, which Fard acknowledged by renaming him Elijah Muhammad and appointing him as chief minister of Islam.

Amid the whirlwind of speculation surrounding Fard's mysterious disappearance in 1934, fractures ripped through the movement's leadership ranks in Detroit. Muhammad viewed himself as Fard's heir apparent and reorganized in Chicago at the Southside Temple, then known as Temple No. 2, which he had established in 1932 at Fard's behest. Using the temple as his headquarters, Muhammad began reshaping the movement. Under his militant vision, Fard was elevated to "Allah" and Muhammad assumed the title of "Prophet," which Fard had previously occupied. Once in Chicago, Muhammad organized a Temple of Islam and a newspaper called *Muhammad Speaks,* as well as several community initiatives.

As the owner of grocery stores, apartment buildings, and restaurants, Muhammad's movement encouraged black economic power and popularized its teachings through a local University of Islam, a private school for all ages. The movement's message of economic empowerment, black pride, and self-sufficiency particularly appealed to the community's demographic of young, poor males. Muhammad called on all followers to abstain from alcohol and tobacco, as well as pork and cornbread, and male members were required to seek new recruits to the faith. The Nation also had a strict code of marital fidelity and members were encouraged to improve themselves economically through movement-provided education and training in business enterprises.

Rifts between Muhammad and ambitious followers such as **Malcolm X**, a rising star in the Nation who announced his intention to organize his own group in 1964, regularly challenged Muhammad's control. Speculation about his involvement in Malcolm X's assassination the fol-

lowing year signaled the beginning of the Nation's decline under Muhammad throughout the 1970s. While the power he yielded was frightening to both liberals and conservatives and was habitually the source of police harassment, forms of his movement continued under the leadership of his son Warith Deen Muhammad (who passed away on September 9, 2008), and later reorganized under protégé **Louis Farrakhan**.

Crystal A. deGregory

Powell, Adam Clayton, Jr., (1908–1972)

Adam Clayton Powell Jr. was born November 29, 1908, in New Haven, Connecticut, and died April 4, 1972, in Miami, Florida. Even though Powell's father was the spiritual leader of Abyssinian Baptist Church in New York, he initially had no desire to follow in his footsteps. After a conversion experience in the 1930s, however, he studied and entered the ministry at Abyssinian. He became aware of the social and economic plight of the congregants and the need for change. Powell began working to secure employment for the congregants, but this thrust for justice expanded to a column in the *Amsterdam News* and, later, as Abyssinian's leader to the pulpit. He became active as a political leader, working with and for grass-roots groups to eliminate economic and social inequities. This led to his popularity and to his being elected the first African American to the New York City Council (1941), and, three years later, the first black U.S. Congressman from New York. He began a 23-year tenure in Washington, D.C., where he continued his fight for equal access and became known as "Mr. Civil Rights" because of his strong advocacy for racial equality. His supported the Fair Employment Practice Act and wrote bills to prohibit discrimination in the workplace, including the "Powell Amendment," which denied federal support for any segregated facility and which became part of the **1964 Civil Rights Act**. He authored over 75 pieces of legislation during his congressional career.

Helen R. Houston

Ransom, Reverdy C. (1861–1959)

The African Methodist Episcopal Church had as one of its major leaders Reverdy C. Ransom. Ransom's work for civil rights was challenged by the mass migration of blacks from the South to the North. An Ohio native, he attended Wilberforce University and later Oberlin College. He found black students at Oberlin barred from many aspects of campus life and so helped to organize a protest against that restriction. Ransom had studied for the ministry, and after graduation he was assigned to Allegheny Mission in what is now North Pittsburgh. There he ministered to the need for social services. In 1905 Ransom had been assigned to the Charles Street African Methodist Episcopal (AME) Church in Boston. He became a close ally of **William Monroe Trotter**, who opposed **Booker T. Washington**, his followers, and his views. He joined the **Niagara Movement** that **W.E.B. Du**

Reverdy C. Ransom (Fisk University).

Bois and others organized in 1905. By 1907 he had transferred to New York City, taking with him his militancy about civil rights. Through his life in the ministry, Ransom had many enemies in his church, many of whom opposed his concern for addressing the needs of people from all walks of life, including petty criminals, prostitutes, and derelicts. He became a bishop in the AME Church in 1924, and later became involved in state Democratic politics in Ohio.

Jessie Carney Smith

Shuttlesworth, Fred (1922–)

Born Freddie Lee Robinson in rural Alabama, the Reverend Fred Shuttlesworth was noted for his courage and leadership in Birmingham during dangerous periods of the Civil Rights Movement. He relocated to Cincinnati, Ohio, after several attempts on his life, but continued his ministry and activism until his retirement in 2006, when he needed to recover from brain tumor surgery. He was renamed after his mother married William Nathan Shuttlesworth. As a young man he worked in Mobile, Alabama, where he attended a Baptist church, began giving guest sermons, and then started his career as a pastor in small Alabama churches. Shuttlesworth continued his education with degrees from Selma University, Alabama State College, and Birmingham Baptist College, became pastor of Bethel Baptist Church in 1952, and began local activism in July 1955. After the **NAACP** was banned in Alabama, he founded the **Alabama Christian Movement for Human Rights** (ACMHR) in 1956 and helped found the **Southern Christian Leadership Conference** (SCLC) the following year. Shuttlesworth survived beatings, arrests, jail sentences, home and church bombings, confrontations with segregationist Eugene "Bull" Connor, and fire hose injuries during 1963 Birmingham demonstrations. He also tried to discourage violent 1967 demonstrations in Cincinnati. In 1988 he helped Richard Arrington, Birmingham's first black mayor, to establish a civil rights museum, and

Fred Shuttlesworth (AP Photo).

was honored with a statue when the museum opened in 1992. In his eighties Shuttlesworth served as interim president of the SCLC, and at age 84 he married the former Sephira Bailey.

Fletcher F. Moon

Smith, Kelly Miller, Sr. (1920–1984)

Smith's birth in the all-black town of Mound Bayou, Mississippi, his educational preparation at **Morehouse College** and **Howard Uni-**versity, and his call to the pastorate of First Baptist Church, Capitol Hill in Nashville, Tennessee, paved the way for his significant role as an activist in the 1950s and 1960s Civil Rights Movement in the South. After graduating from Magnolia High School, he enrolled at **Tennessee State University**, where he studied for two years before transferring to Morehouse College. During his academic matriculation at Morehouse, he came under the influence of the college's president, Dr. Benjamin Mays, a social activist and mentor to **Martin Luther King Jr.** After graduating from Morehouse in 1942, he entered **Howard University**'s Divinity School and came under the influence of Howard Thurman, another Morehouse graduate, civil rights activist, and dean of the university's Rankin Chapel. He next completed graduate studies at Howard and became the pastor of Mount Heroden Baptist Church in Vicksburg, Mississippi, where he served from 1946 to 1951. In May 1951, he accepted the pastorate of the First Baptist Church, Capitol Hill, in Nashville, and ultimately rose to the forefront of the city's Civil Rights Movement.

The Reverend Smith's educational preparation at Morehouse College and Howard University under Mays and Thurman, respectively, foretold of his social gospel leanings and his willingness to be in the forefront of bringing down Nashville's wall of racial segregation. Three years after arriving in Nashville, the U.S. Supreme Court handed down its 1954 unanimous decision in the *Brown v. Board of Education* case against school segregation. The following year, Smith joined twelve other parents in a federal lawsuit to achieve desegregation in the Nashville public schools. Smith, who served as president of the Nashville chapter of the **NAACP** from 1956 to 1959, advanced the cause of civil rights among black Nashvillians. As president of the Nashville NAACP, he and the civil rights organization were successful in their voter registration campaign of 1956, as well as efforts to gain fair employment practices. However, Smith and attorney **Z. Alexander Looby** realized that many vestiges of the Old South remained in place throughout Nashville's economic and social milieu.

Smith and the NCLC were in the forefront of organizing the boycott against the city's [Nashville's] merchants.

As a part of the growing Civil Rights Movement throughout the South, in 1957 King and others established the **Southern Christian Leadership Conference** (SCLC); Smith was one of the original 25 members of the executive board, where he served until 1969. In 1958 he established the Nashville Christian Leadership Conference (NCLC), an affiliate of the SCLC, to serve as a direct non-violent paradigm to combat racial segregation. With the NCLC he and **James Lawson** helped organize and support Nashville students in the sit-ins leading to the desegregation of the city's downtown lunch counters, hotels, and theaters. During the Nashville movement, Smith and the NCLC were in the forefront of organizing the boycott against the city's merchants. In his efforts to promote educational and economic parity for black Americans, Smith also founded a local chapter of the Opportunities Industrial Center, Inc., in 1969. That year he was appointed assistant dean of Vanderbilt University's Divinity School. Smith also served on the faculties of Natchez College, Alcorn College, and American Baptist Theological Seminary. In 1983 Smith delivered the prestigious Lyman Beecher Lectures at Yale University. These lectures served as the basis for his final publication, *Social Crisis Preaching* (1984).

Linda T. Wynn

Steele, Charles Kenzie (1914–1980)

"C.K." Steele, as he was called, entered the movement for civil rights when Wilhelmina Jakes and Carrie Paterson, two students from Florida Agricultural & Mechanical University (FAMU), refused to surrender their seat to a white woman on a Tallahassee bus. The only child of Henry L. and Lyde Bailor Steele, his familial ancestry, normative experiences, educational grounding, and intrinsic concept of justice were characteristics that predestined him to be one of Tallahassee's most committed and prominent civil rights activists.

Ordained as a Baptist minister in 1935, Steele earned his undergraduate degree from Morehouse College Interdenominational Theological Seminary in Atlanta, Georgia, three years later. While at Morehouse, Steele discerned that the struggle for social justice must be inculcated into any African American cleric's mission, a deduction his more celebrated colleague and friend **Martin Luther King Jr.** also came to while matriculating at the same institution. As pastor of the Bethel Baptist Church in Tallahassee, and serving as president of the Tallahassee chapter of the **NAACP**, he also became president of the Inter-Civic Council (ICC), which was founded in May 1956 to direct the bus boycott that was begun by black students at FAMU. The ICC's membership included people from all occupations within the community, such as laborers, domestic workers, ministers, professionals, businesspersons, and teachers. Established by Steele and other ministers from the Tallahassee Ministerial Alliance, the ICC coordinated the logistics of the bus boycott. Like the **Montgomery Improvement Association** (MIA), the ICC held mass meetings and organized a carpool. However, it deviated from the MIA, which sought modified seating, by demanding the full integration of passengers on Tallahassee's city buses.

Elected president of the ICC, it was Steele's steadfast fortitude and altruistic advocacy that facilitated the boycott's success. Declaring that blacks in Tallahassee would "rather walk in dignity than ride in humiliation," he and other African Americans persevered despite various legal and financial impediments. Although there were vociferous threats and destruction of property, little physical violence occurred in Tallahassee. This was because of Steele's passionate urging for nonviolence, a position he had advocated since World War II.

Steele's activities in Tallahassee catapulted him to the forefront of the national Civil Rights Movement. Sharing King's philosophy of nonviolence as a means for attaining civil rights for American blacks, in 1956 Steele joined King as a speaker at nonviolence workshops held at the Tuskegee Institute, the annual meeting of the National Baptist Convention, and at the MIA's Institute on Nonviolence for Social Change. A year later he was among those who united with King in Atlanta, Georgia, for the founding of the **Southern Christian Leadership Conference (SCLC)**, and he was elected as the organization's first vice president. Even though SCLC did not conduct a major campaign in Tallahassee, Steele backed the organization's efforts in other localities. In 1962, while King was imprisoned, he led demonstrations during the **Albany Movement**.

After King was assassinated, Steele and the ICC organized a "Vigil for Poverty" in Tallahassee to recognize those who lacked the basic needs to sustain a living. Although not widely known outside of Tallahassee, the labors of the ICC provided hope to those engaged in the freedom struggle. Steele described this engagement as "the pain and the promise" of the civil rights movement. He fervently believed that the power of love and nonviolence would conquer violence, and the promise of the movement would be fulfilled. Diagnosed with cancer in 1977, Steele continued his ministry at Bethel Baptist Church and his activism for civil rights until his death on August 19, 1980. In 2008 Steele's son, the Rev. C.K. Steele Jr., became head of the Southern Christian Leadership Conference.

Linda T. Wynn

Vivian, Cordy Tindell (1924–)

A steadfast supporter of human causes, C.T. Vivian, as he was known, became aware of the power of nonviolence while a student at Western Illinois University. From then on he devoted his life to the cause of human justice. After only two years, the Boonville, Illinois, native left Western Illinois in 1944 and moved to Peoria, where he participated in his first sit-in demonstration. He saw de facto segregation in Peoria and decided to join an integrated group to force restaurants and lunch counters to serve all customers, regardless of race. The demonstrators followed methods used by the **Congress of Racial Equality** (CORE) and sought to raise the consciences of the white community. They were successful in their efforts, and between 1947 and 1948 the demonstrators moved on to desegregate other restaurants in the city.

Steele and the ICC organized a "Vigil for Poverty" in Tallahassee to recognize those who lacked the basic needs to sustain a living.

Vivian was elected vice president of the Peoria **NAACP** and later moved to Nashville, Tennessee, to attend the American Baptist Theological Seminary (now **American Baptist College**). Four years later he joined other ministers in founding the Nashville Christian Leadership Conference (NCLC), which was under the leadership of **Kelly Miller Smith Sr.** The NCLC was a local affiliate of **Martin Luther King Jr.'s Southern Christian Leadership Conference**. Vivian was elected vice president at the organizational meeting and soon joined **James Lawson, James Bevel, Diane Nash, John Lewis, Bernard Lafayette**, and **Marion**

Barry in the **Nashville movement**. As vice president Vivian headed the direct action component while Lawson was in charge of NCLC's Action Committee. They planned workshops to teach Mohandas Gandhi's protest methods.

In November and December of 1959, they put to test Nashville's policies on racial segregation and launched sit-ins at lunch counters at local five-and-ten stores. The lack of media coverage, however, meant that the **Greensboro, North Carolina, sit-in** of February 1, 1960, was the first to receive press coverage. Twelve days later, the Nashville movement was in full swing, and two months after that the successful economic boycott of Nashville's white retail stores was in effect. In Chattanooga, where Vivian moved after the first wave of sit-ins, he was successful in ending segregation in local healthcare facilities. He joined the 1961 **Freedom Rides** and also became active in other campaigns held in Albany, Birmingham, Atlanta, St. Augustine, and Selma.

Williams, an advocate of the direct action approach, led the Bloody Sunday march.

King appointed Vivian to the SCLC executive staff in 1963; he was also national director of affiliates. He was a consultant to the organization's voter registration projects, consumer action projects, non-violent training, human relations, direct action, and other initiatives. Vivian left the SCLC three years later to direct the Urban Training Center for Christian Mission in Chicago, and he taught clergy and other organizational techniques. As coordinator for the Coalition for United Community Action, he led the group into a new organization called Chicago's Black Front. He took his direct action

campaign to the building trade unions to end racism there. The Chicago Plan, which he developed as a result of his work with these unions and united black and Latino gangs, became a model for other cities.

Jessie Carney Smith

Williams, Hosea Lorenzo (1926–2000)

Hosea Williams is well known in Atlanta for his "Feed the Hungry" program. Long before the "Feed the Hungry" campaign, however, Williams was serving African Americans through his work in the Civil Rights Movement. He was born on January 5, 1926, in Attapulgus, Georgia, and died on November 16, 2000. While working as a chemist for the U.S. government in Savannah, Georgia, he became active in the local branch of the **NAACP**. Finding work as a civil rights activist rewarding, Williams moved to Atlanta in 1963 and began working for the **Southern Christian Leadership Conference** (SCLC). One of **Martin Luther King Jr.**'s closest allies, he served as Special Projects Director until 1970. He worked to register black voters throughout the South and to prepare other activists. Williams, an advocate of the direct action approach, led the **Bloody Sunday** march from Selma to Montgomery on March 7, 1965. He served briefly as executive director of the SCLC from 1969 to 1971, and again from 1977 to 1979.

Williams continued to advocate for the disadvantaged by serving as a State Representative for Georgia from 1974 to 1985. From 1985 to 1990, he served as the Commissioner for Dekalb County, Georgia. In the late 1980s, Williams gained national attention when he led protest marches through the all-white and violently hostile Forsythe County, Georgia. He also continued his activism in other ways; in 1970, Williams established his "Feed the Hungry" campaign in Atlanta. This program continues to enjoy success, especially during the winter holidays, and is now led by Williams's daughter, Elizabeth Omilami.

Helen R. Houston

Religious Education

Black Educational and Religious Intellectuals

While they remain for the most part ignored by surveys of the modern Civil Rights Movement, there was a cadre of African American educational and religious intellectuals who made the modern movement possible through their educational leadership, development of an intellectual praxis, and personal mentorship of a generation of college-educated African Americans. In this examination of their contributions to the movement, African American college presidents, deans, and religious leaders emerge as the moral compass for their students and congregants as well as important contributors to the notion of segregation as a moral evil and sin and to the adoption of non-violent resistance. Their ranks include **John Hope**, the first African American president of **Morehouse College** in Atlanta, Georgia; his student **Mordecai Johnson**, the first African American president of **Howard University** in Washington, D.C.; Morehouse alumnus **Howard Thurman**, dean of Howard's Rankin Chapel; and **Benjamin E. Mays**, dean of Howard University's School of Religion and the sixth president of Morehouse College.

Crystal A. deGregory

Hope, John (1868–1936)

Born in Augusta, Georgia, to mixed parentage, Hope graduated from Brown University before beginning his career in academia as a teacher at Roger Williams and Atlanta Baptist colleges. Elected president of Atlanta Baptist in 1906, which was renamed **Morehouse College** in 1913, he assembled a first-rate faculty at Morehouse and mentored a generation of men before assuming the presidency of Atlanta University (later Clark Atlanta University) in 1929. By the time Hope retired as the president of Morehouse in 1931, the future course of More-

house had been set in motion and the fields of African American higher education, as well as civic responsibility and civil rights, already showed signs of his influence. As a race leader, Hope supported the struggle to secure civil rights, as well as public education, improvements in housing, healthcare, and employment opportunities.

Crystal A. deGregory

African American college presidents, deans, and religious leaders emerge as the moral compass for their students and congregants.

Johnson, Mordecai (1890–1976)

A native of Paris, Tennessee, Johnson was the son of a former slave. He attended Roger Williams before graduating from **Morehouse College** in 1911. Appointed to the presidency of **Howard University** in 1926, Johnson secured the federal support necessary to construct new facilities, develop research centers, revamp programs, and increase the faculty salaries. Perhaps most notably, Johnson guided the rejuvenation of the university's schools of engineering, medicine, and law, the last of which would prove indispensable in the building of the modern civil rights movement. Law school professor **Charles Hamilton Houston**'s commitment to training African American lawyers as "social engineers" who utilized their legal expertise to improve the conditions of blacks in America was fully realized due to Howard law school teachers, including Leon A. Ransom and Morehouse alumnus James M. Nabrit, Jr., as well as students such as **Thurgood Marshall** who relied

on Johnson's unwavering backing despite perse-
cution during the 1950s.

Crystal A. deGregory

Mays, Benjamin E. (1894–1984)

More than any other single person, Benjamin E. Mays has been credited with having distinguished **Morehouse College** as a center of intellectual meticulousness, cultural mys-
tique, and social responsibility. During his
weekly chapel hour addresses, Mays repeatedly
imparted his commitment to—and challenge
of—recognizing the dignity of all human beings
and the conflict between actual American social
practices and American democratic ideals to his
students. As the college's sixth president, Mays
helped train a generation of activist-intellectu-
als, including most notably **Martin Luther King
Jr.**, as well as leaders in pivotal localized movements such as the Reverends **C.K. Steele** and
Kelly Miller Smith.

Crystal A. deGregory

Thurman, Howard W. (1900–1981)

Another **Morehouse College** alumnus, Thurman helped create the theological framework for a moral attack on segregation. Thurman, who had been **Martin Luther King Sr.'s**
classmate, worked closely with **Martin Luther
King Jr.** while he was a divinity student at
Boston. Nowhere is his influence on King clear-
er than in the fact that King reportedly carried a
copy of Thurman's book with him when he was
involved in civil rights campaigns. Published in
1949, Thurman's seminal work *Jesus and the
Disinherited* offered an empowering interpretation of the New Testament. His contention that
Jesus's life was lived for the oppressed resonated
so much with his young students that many of
them referred to the book as a required text of
the modern Civil Rights Movement.

Crystal A. deGregory

Sports

Automobile Racing

Scott, Wendell Oliver (1921–1990)

The first African American to win a National Association for Stock Car Auto Racing (NASCAR) event—then known as the Grand National—Wendell Oliver Scott gained fame in the segregated South and the nation in a sport dominated by whites. His racing career was marred by racial incidents and inferior equipment that for many years prevented him from qualifying for races. Still, he was a racer at heart and went on to have a successful career.

Scott was born in the Crooktown section of Danville, Virginia, on August 25, 1921, to mechanic William Scott and his wife, Martha. His maternal side was related to **Muhammad Ali**, Scott's distant cousin. The family relocated to Pittsburgh just before young Wendell entered the first grade. Later, they moved to Louisville to live with his mother's aunt. His mother and his siblings returned to Danville. When he was 18 years old, Scott became a driver for a local taxicab company. After serving as a mechanic and paratrooper in the 101st Airborne, he returned to Danville in 1945 and ran moonshine from illegal stills in the area to the fairgrounds. His "liquor car," as he called it, outran any police car in Danville. In 1949, Scott began to watch races at Danville's Fairgrounds Speedway and became fascinated with the sport. The next year, the racetrack officials expressed an interest in attracting more spectators and asked the local police for any fast black drivers in the area, including any with speeding violations. They recommended Wendell Scott, for they had chased him throughout southern Virginia and knew his racing ability well.

Scott at first ran his "liquor car," but soon bought a used racing car; he was denied entrance into many races, however. Eventually, he was allowed to race and made his debut at the Danville Fairgrounds Speedway. He was the first African American racer in a Dixie Circuit event. While NASCAR did not recognize the Dixie Circuit, Scott won over 80 such events in Virginia and North Carolina, where the Dixie Circuit operated. NASCAR's Modified Division accepted Scott in 1954, and he went on to more victories. Since this division allowed entrants to modify their vehicles, Scott drew upon his mechanical skills to enhance his car. His race, however, still prevented him from securing a sponsor to furnish him a competitive car and enter the Grand National Series, now known as the Winston Cup Series. On several occasions white promoters reneged on their offer to sponsor Scott and provide him with a first-class car. Racial incidents continued as well.

Stock car races, held primarily in the South, attracted drivers who attempted to force Scott off the track while the crowds jeered him. Sometime in the 1960s, he hurried from a race in Birmingham after hostile whites threatened to turn his car over and burn it. Scott won 40 modified racing victories, and in 1959 he won the Virginia State Championship. He qualified for the NASCAR Grand National competition in 1961; after his debut in Spartanburg, he finished in the top 10. His earnings increased, and in 1969 he had his most successful year, earning $47,451. All told, he won $188,000 and raced in 506 events. Scott settled in Danville after his racing career ended and managed the Scott Garage. He died on December 23, 1990. The movie *Greased Lightning,* starring Richard Pryor, is based on Scott's life and career.

Frederick D. Smith

Baseball

Aaron, Hank (1934–)

T hough best known for smashing Babe Ruth's home run record, "Hammerin'" Hank Aaron also deserves recognition for his efforts in the civil rights arena. Aaron participated in the quest for equality on several fronts. The future slugger was born Henry Louis Aaron on February 5, 1934, in Mobile, Alabama. By the time he reached high school, his talent was already evident. While a junior in high school, Aaron began playing semi-professional baseball with the Mobile Black Bears. In 1952, at 18 years old, Aaron signed his first professional contract with the Indianapolis Clowns of the Negro Leagues. The same year, the Boston Braves purchased his contact and sent Aaron to their farm team in Eau Claire, Wisconsin, where he was introduced to integration, finished second in the league in batting, made the league's all-star team, and won the rookie of the year title. The next year, learn-

Hank Aaron (AP Photo).

ing that Aaron was willing to integrate a league from which **Jackie Robinson** had been barred, the Braves sent him to their affiliate, the Jacksonville Suns, where he became the first African American to play in the Sally League.

Despite racial slurs and threats of violence, the young man led his team to a pennant with a league-leading batting title, won the runs-batted-in (RBI) crown, and earned the Most Valuable Player award. Aaron joined the Milwaukee Braves team in 1954. Throughout the following seasons, he performed well. Still, though arguably the best hitter in baseball at the time, superstar status eluded Aaron, perhaps because of his quiet, unassuming demeanor. In spite of his achievements, racial insults continued. During the 1950s, baseball players of color lived and worked within an environment of racial segregation and intolerance. In contrast to his teammates, Aaron was housed with black families, while white players stayed in a hotel. Black players remained on the team bus while teammates ate in restaurants. On one occasion after returning to the black community to collect their personal possessions, Aaron and several black and Latino players were left behind at the airport by teammates who had made the flight with the aid of a police escort. Worse, in Florida in 1958, a young white man harassed Aaron while he was on the road and purposely forced the ball player into a ditch.

As awareness grew that Aaron was closing in on Babe Ruth's home run record, there was an upsurge in the racial abuse, necessitating FBI protection for Aaron and his family. With his 715th home run, he broke Ruth's record on April 8, 1974. Although previously vocal about ethnic injustices within baseball, the new acclaim enabled him to promote even more assertively the need for more African Americans in baseball management positions. The Atlanta Braves named him to an executive position in 1977, empowering Aaron to effect positive changes in baseball. In addition to holding the record for most home runs, Aaron held records for most RBIs, most total bases, and most extra-base hits. His exceptional achievements earned him an induction into the Baseball Hall of Fame in 1982.

Cheryl Jones Hamberg

Bell, James Thomas (1903–1991)

An outfielder for the old Negro Leagues, "Cool Papa" Bell, as he was known, was regarded as the fastest man in professional baseball and one of the most important figures in the Negro Leagues. Bell was born on May 17, 1903, in Starkville, Mississippi, to a farmer named Jonas and his wife, Mary Nicholas Bell. In 1920 Bell, like other blacks of that time, left the impoverished South for urban centers. He settled in St. Louis and became a knuckleball pitcher for a black semi-pro team, the Compton Hill Cubs. In August 1921 he joined the East St. Louis Cubs as a pitcher. Bell signed on with the St. Louis Stars in May 1922, placing him with a major power-

house team in the Negro National League. After he struck out the best hitter in the league, his manager gave him the name that would stick with him for life—"Cool Papa." Bell's pitching career ended in 1924 due to an arm injury; he then became an outfielder. Over the course of his career, Bell played on three of the greatest teams in black baseball: the Stars, the Pittsburgh Crawfords, and the Homestead Grays.

Bell and other players in the Negro Leagues experienced hardships as they traveled in cramped buses or cars that often broke down. Seldom were they served in restaurants, and sleeping accommodations were poor as well. It was racial segregation that kept star players of the Negro Leagues such as Bell from entering mainstream baseball; their stellar records were therefore known for many years only to a few.

Jessie Carney Smith

As awareness grew that Aaron was closing in on Babe Ruth's home run record, there was an upsurge in the racial abuse, necessitating FBI protection for Aaron and his family.

Foster, Andrew (1879–1930)

"Rube" Foster, as he was best known, was a smooth and formidable pitcher, a manager, founder, and administrator of the Negro National League (NNL), the first viable organization for African American baseball players. The NNL functioned at a time when mainstream leagues excluded African Americans. Foster also founded the American Giants, one of black baseball's greatest teams. For his achievements, he became known as "The Father of Black Baseball." Despite his fame, sources still give conflicting information about his birthplace and dates of his activities with baseball teams.

The son of Andrew and Sarah Foster, he may have been born in Calvert, Texas, on September 17, 1879. Young Rube attended church each Sunday morning and played baseball in the afternoons. By age 17 he had left home to play with the Fort Worth Yellow Jackets. Big-city clubs noticed his skill, and in 1901, the six-foot-four-inch tall Foster, who weighed over 200 pounds, pitched against the Philadelphia Athletics. He joined the black Leland Giants, and in 1902 switched to the Union Giants, who were also known as the Cuban Giants. By 1904 he was playing with the Philadelphia Giants; he next joined the Leland Giants in 1906 as manager and player. In 1919 Foster called together owners of black ball clubs and founded the Negro National League. He envisioned a time in which white and black teams would play each other in a World Series. For sharing his talent with players and teaching baseball subtleties to black managers, Foster has been called the world's greatest manager of any race. He died in 1930, before major league baseball in the modern era was racially integrated.

Jessie Carney Smith

Gibson, Joshua (1911–1947)

A right-handed slugger, Josh Gibson was the standard against whom other hitters in black baseball were measured. Called "the Black Babe Ruth," he electrified crowds and was a dominant presence in the batter's box. Gibson was born in Buena Vista, Georgia, to Mark and Nancy Woodlock Gibson. The family moved to Pittsburgh when young Josh had just completed five years of school. He dropped out of school and in 1927 began playing baseball with the Pleasant Valley Red Sox; he then joined a semi-pro boys' team called the Pittsburgh Crawfords. A star batter for the Crawfords, he attracted the attention of the Homestead Grays but was not

signed on as a professional player until the 1930 season. Gibson transformed a good team into a great team and enabled the Grays to win championships. In 1932 Gibson moved to the Pittsburgh Crawfords and became a star among stars on the Crawfords' 1930s teams. Back with the Grays in 1937, he helped to restore that team to dominance in black baseball and helped win the first of the team's nine consecutive Negro National League championships. In 1938 the media promoted integrated baseball. Clark Griffith, owner of the Washington Senators, asked Gibson and Buck Leonard, another powerhouse with the Grays, to discuss with him in his office the possibility of playing for his team, but he made no official offer to the star players. Although Gibson was a fading star by the time **Jackie Robinson** integrated the Brooklyn Dodgers in 1947, he held fast to his vision of playing major-league ball. His dream was never realized. In 1972, however, he became the second player from the Negro Leagues, preceded only by **Satchel Paige**, to be inducted into the National Baseball Hall of Fame.

Jessie Carney Smith

Jackson, Reggie (1946–)

P opularly known as "Reggie," Jackson excelled in baseball, leading his teams to five world championships and 11 division titles. Ranked sixth in home runs (563) when he retired, he also led the league with 2,597 strikeouts in his 20-year career. His performance as a New York Yankee against the Los Angeles Dodgers in the World Series on October 18, 1977, was spectacular. In three consecutive times at bat, he hit three home runs; he batted a .450 average; afterward he became affectionately known as "Mr. October."

Reginald Martinez Jackson was born on May 18, 1946, to Martinez and Clara Jackson in Wyncote, Pennsylvania. When his parents divorced, Reggie remained with his father, while his three siblings left with their mother. By age 13, Reggie was the town's best baseball player and the only black on the Greater Glenside Youth Club's team. While on the team, he encountered racism for the first time. As the team faced the visiting team from Fort Lauderdale, Florida, in the Dixie Series, Reggie's coach pulled him from the game due to his race but failed to explain why he did so. Jackson wrote in his autobiography, *Reggie,* "It was the first time I'd ever come up against anything like that; the first time I ever realized that black was different, that black could be a problem." He went on to perform well in several sports—basketball, football, track, and, of course, baseball.

In 1964 Reggie enrolled at Arizona State University on a football scholarship, but he practiced baseball when he had time. The next year, he joined the university's baseball team. Jackson left college in 1966, having been approached by the major leagues. He joined the Kansas City Athletics minor-league team at its home base in Birmingham, Alabama, and traveled with them throughout the South. Again he felt the sting of segregation: landlords refused to rent an apartment to him, restaurants refused to serve him, and whites threatened him with bodily harm. Jackson played for the Kansas City Athletics (1967), Oakland Athletics (1968–1975, 1987), Baltimore Orioles (1976), New York Yankees (1977–1981), and the California Angels (1982–1986). He then became an advisor, first to the Athletics (1988–1993) and then to the Yankees in 1993. Aaron often spoke out against racism and lobbied teams to hire blacks who were former players as managers, coaches, scouts, and front-office executives. After his retirement, in 1993 Jackson was inducted into the Baseball Hall of Fame. In 1999 he placed Forty-eighth on the *Sporting News* list of "The 100 Greatest Baseball Players."

Jessie Carney Smith

Negro Baseball Leagues

Professional Negro baseball leagues were organized to showcase the talents of African American players during segregation; they

Professional Negro baseball leagues were organized to showcase the talents of African American players during segregation.

became a successful business enterprise, generating millions of dollars in revenue and thousands of jobs for other blacks besides players, coaches, managers, and team owners. Andrew "Rube" Foster, a player, manager, and owner with the Chicago American Giants, developed the Negro National League in 1920 in Kansas City, Missouri. Similar efforts in southern and eastern regions produced the Southern Negro League, Eastern Colored League, East-West League, and other organizations. It was the Negro National League (1920–1931; 1933–1948) and the Negro American League (1937-1960), however, that had the most sustained success. During the heyday of the Negro Leagues, their best teams included the Kansas City Monarchs and Homestead Grays, with legendary players such as pitcher Leroy "Satchel" Paige and home run hitter Josh Gibson. Their all-star games sold out major league venues in Chicago, and the best black players outclassed white major league teams in unofficial "exhibition" games. When Brooklyn Dodgers owner Branch Rickey broke the "color line" by signing **Jackie Robinson** from the Monarchs in 1945, his integration of the major leagues in 1947 ironically signaled the demise of the Negro Leagues. By 1960 top young black players such as **Hank Aaron** and Willie Mays were part of major league teams. Many of the earlier players are now honored in both the Baseball Hall of Fame in Cooperstown, New York, and the Negro Leagues Baseball Museum in Kansas City.

Fletcher F. Moon

Paige, Satchel (1906–1982)

Much of the story of Satchel Paige's life is filled with folklore, but some of his legendary accomplishments are factual. Born Robert LeRoy Paige in Mobile, Alabama, he was the son of gardener John Paige and his wife, Lulu, a washerwoman. He was nicknamed "Satchel" after he attempted to steal a train passenger's satchel. Later, at age 12, he stole toy rings from a store and was sentenced to five years in the Industrial School for Negro Children at Mount Meigs, Alabama. There he honed his skills in baseball. Upon leaving the school, Paige, who had been a pitcher, was encouraged by his coach to concentrate on baseball and take care of his arm. The tall, thin Paige returned home and did menial work near Eureka Gardens, the semi-professional ballpark for the all-black Mobile Tigers. Later he pitched for the club and for other teams as well, including the white minor league team the Mobile Bears. Between 1924 and 1926 he won 30 games and lost one.

Paige made his professional pitching debut in 1926, with the Chattanooga Black Lookouts. He also pitched for the Birmingham Black Barons in 1927 and 1928, and continued to pitch for teams in the Negro Leagues. He played for Nashville's Elite Giants of the Negro Southern League in 1930, then for the Pittsburgh Crawfords from 1931 to 1934 and 1936. In his first game, Paige pitched a victory over the premiere team in the Negro Leagues, the Homestead Grays. With teammates **James "Cool Papa" Bell**, **Josh Gibson**, and others, he led the team to national championships. After he refused to report to the Newark Eagles, to whom his contract had been sold, he pitched for the Mexican League, but returned to the United States due to a sore arm. Paige joined the Kansas City Monarchs for the 1940 season and remained for nine more, becoming their ace player and leading the team to victories over the Grays in the 1942 Negro League World Series. Baseball, however, was still a racially segregated sport; yet white team owners knew that there was a reservoir of untapped talent in the Negro Leagues. Rumors finally circulated that blacks would be allowed to play in the major leagues, and in 1947 **Jackie Robinson** made his debut with the Brooklyn Dodgers, becoming the first to play in a major baseball league.

Paige made his debut in the major leagues in 1948 with the Cleveland Indians; during the pennant drive that year, he became the first African American to pitch in a World Series. He had six victories and one defeat while with the Indians. After playing for several teams, he ended his career in 1967 with the Indianapolis Clowns of the Negro Leagues, and then coached the Atlanta Braves the next season. Page was elected to the Baseball Hall of Fame in 1971, the first Negro Leagues' player to hold that honor. He entered, however, as a Negro Leagues star, which caused a protest over the separate housing of the plaques. After that, he received full membership and his plaque now hangs among all other baseball greats.

Frederick D. Smith

Robinson, Jackie (1919–1972)

As the first African American to play in the major leagues during the modern era, Jackie Robinson was a civil rights pioneer before, during, and after his professional sports career. He differed with activists such as **Paul Robeson** and **Malcolm X** and disagreed when **Martin Luther King Jr.** opposed the Vietnam War, but he generally remained supportive of the Civil Rights Movement. Jack Roosevelt Robinson was born in Cairo, Georgia, the youngest of five children.

His father deserted the family shortly after Jackie was born, but his mother, Mallie Robinson, was a deeply religious woman who relocated to Pasadena, California, in search of a better life for her family. His older brother, Mack Robinson, finished second to Jesse Owens in the 200-meter race during the 1936 Berlin Olympics, while Jackie excelled in several sports at Muir Technical High School, Pasadena Junior College, and the University of California,

Jackie Robinson (Fisk University).

Los Angeles (UCLA). At UCLA Robinson became the first athlete to earn varsity letters in four sports. He was an All-American in football, leading basketball scorer in the Pacific Coast Conference for two years, national track champion in the long jump, and shortstop on the baseball team, but he was forced to leave UCLA in 1941 because of financial issues. Robinson then briefly played semiprofessional football with the Honolulu Bears.

He was drafted into the army in 1942 and sent to a segregated unit in Fort Riley, Kansas, but was eventually commissioned as a first lieutenant in 1943. At Fort Hood, Texas, Robinson was subjected to a court martial after resisting segregation, but he was cleared of all charges and received an honorable discharge in November 1944.

Robinson began his professional baseball career in 1945 with the Kansas City Monarchs in the Negro American League. He quickly earned

respect for his all-around playing skills. Branch Rickey, president of the Brooklyn Dodgers, scouted and interviewed him before deciding that he could endure the hardships he would face in the major leagues. On October 23, 1945, Rickey announced that Jackie Robinson would begin the "Noble Experiment" with the minor league Montréal Royals. In 1946, Robinson married UCLA classmate Rachel Isum.

In 1947, Robinson opened the season with the Brooklyn Dodgers, enduring verbal abuse, death threats, and misgivings among white teammates and opponents. He won the Major League Rookie of the Year award, and in following seasons helped the Dodgers win six National League pennants and the 1955 world championship over the New York Yankees. Robinson retired from baseball in 1956. Six years later he was inducted into the Baseball Hall of Fame.

Robinson was active in Harlem community organizations and helped establish the black-owned Freedom Bank, but he received criticism for involvement with Republican politicians such as Richard Nixon and Nelson Rockefeller. Robinson protested baseball's lack of black managers and executives during his last years. He made a final public appearance at the 1972 World Series in Cincinnati nine days before his death.

Fletcher F. Moon

Walker, Moses Fleetwood (1857–1924)

"Fleet" Walker, as he was popularly known, became one of the first African Americans to play white intercollegiate baseball in 1881, when he was a catcher on Oberlin College's varsity team. His baseball career took him to the Toledo Blue Stockings in 1884, when he became the first African American major leaguer. He felt the sting of racism throughout his baseball career, as racial antipathy and segregation flourished in the late 1800s. In 1887 only seven black players were in the league. Racist taunts, jeers, and threats were commonplace to Walker. In 1883, the Chicago White Stockings' manager refused to plan an exhibition game if Walker and another African American player, George Washington Stovey, were allowed to play. The men were barred from the field, and on that same day the league voted to deny contracts with black players.

Although Walker was never more than a mediocre player, he refused to extend his career by joining all-black teams that invited him to play. Walker, a mulatto, was born to racially mixed parents in Mount Pleasant, Ohio, grew up in Steubenville, and attended Oberlin College. His complexion was fair enough to allow him to move with ease within the white society that he seemed to favor later on, yet his race was well-known in the baseball world. In his 1908 booklet, *Our Home Colony: The Past, Present, and Future of the Negro Race,* he rejected racial mixing and called for African repatriation. In 1904 he purchased the Cadiz Opera house in Steubenville and offered live entertainment and movies to a mostly white clientele. Blacks who attended were seated in the balcony. Although Walker remained bitter due to his treatment in baseball, he continued to mix with whites and to live in white communities.

Frederick D. Smith

Basketball

Abdul-Jabbar, Kareem (1947–)

Abdul-Jabbar's stature can be measured not only by his height and his basketball statistics but also by his legacy as an outspoken civil rights activist. Born April 16, 1947, into a middle-class family, Ferdinand Lewis Alcindor Jr. attended Catholic schools in New York, where he began playing basketball at nine years old. Reaching six feet, eight inches by age 14, the youngster led his high school and his University of California at Los Angeles (UCLA) college teams to championships. In 1964, a life-changing year, the specter of racism intruded on the young athlete's life. During uncharacteristic,

Kareem Abdul-Jabbar (AP Photo/Damian Dovarganes).

lackluster play, a high school coach and mentor wounded him by accusing him of acting "just like a nigger!" That same summer, Alcindor experienced a cultural reawakening when he attended the Harlem Youth Action Project, which was headed Dr. John Henrik Clarke, an eminent black historian. Clarke exposed the youngster to music, art, and journalism. He guided Alcindor to explore African American history and its rich selection of role models, with the intent of providing the teen with an educated perspective—and ultimately inspiration—on the inequalities of black life. The nonviolent speeches of **Martin Luther King Jr.** and the violence of the **Harlem riots** also punctuated that summer. Collectively, these events influenced the shape of Alcindor's future.

Following his junior year at UCLA, Alcindor studied at a New York Islamic mosque and subsequently boycotted the 1968 Olympics to increase awareness in the sports world of the unequal treatment of African American athletes and of the Civil Rights Movement in general. His outspoken support of the black power clenched fist sign used on the Olympic podium by John Carlos and Tommie Smith earned him a bundle of hate mail, while his record-setting college career earned him the first pick position in the NBA draft and a job with the Milwaukee Bucks. With an average of 28.8 points per game, he won the Rookie of the Year title for the 1969–1970 season and led his team to an NBA championship the following year. In 1971, Alcindor legally changed his name to Kareem (generous) Abdul (servant of Allah) Jabbar (powerful). Outstanding, dominant play produced several MVP titles for Abdul-Jabbar during his time in Milwaukee, and he continued to accumulate accolades and awards after joining the Los Angeles Lakers in 1975.

Playing until he was 42 years of age, Abdul-Jabbar perfected his signature shot, the "sky hook." When he retired from the game in 1989, he had scored more points, blocked more shots, played in more games, won more MVP awards, and played in more All-Star Games than any other NBA player. He was inducted into the Basketball Hall of Fame in 1995. After retiring Abdul-Jabbar pursued stints as an actor, scout, sports announcer, and coach. He began to focus on his life-long interests by founding a record label to promote young jazz artists, writing books about history, and "arousing our passions about past injustices and infusing us with strength to fight present ones." Like his high-flying "sky hook," Abdul-Jabbar's life has come full circle.

Cheryl Jones Hamberg

Chamberlain, Wilt (1936–1999)

Born Wilton Norman Chamberlain, Wilt "The Stilt" was one of nine children born to William and Olivia Chamberlain, in Philadelphia. Chamberlain had considered studying law or business at Harvard College. After high school, however, he accepted a basketball and

[Chamberlain] tested numerous restaurants within a 40-mile radius of Kansas City and single-handedly broke down racial barriers in the whole area.

track scholarship from the University of Kansas at Lawrence. On his way to Lawrence, Wilt learned firsthand the bitter facts of racism when he was refused dining room service at a restaurant and then offered a meal in the kitchen. So incensed was Wilt that he tested numerous restaurants within a 40-mile radius of Kansas City and single-handedly broke down racial barriers in the whole area. During his stay in Kansas, Chamberlain was often taunted from the sidelines; he missed several important games when an opponent kneed him in the groin. Chamberlain left college after one year and played with the Harlem Globetrotters during the 1958–1959 season (and again in the summer of 1960). He joined the Philadelphia Warriors in 1959, where he played with such well-known athletes as **Bill Russell**. The Warriors were sold to San Francisco; meanwhile, Chamberlain began to receive recognition as the greatest NBA player ever. He was traded to the Philadelphia 76ers in 1965 and took the team to a world championship in 1967. After a stint with the Los Angeles Lakers from 1968 to 1973, he became player, coach, and part owner of the now-defunct American Basketball Association. Considered one of the greatest basketball players of all time, Chamberlain was elected to the Basketball Hall of Fame in 1978; he was named most valuable player in the NBA four times: 1960, 1966, 1967, and 1968).

Mary N. Hernandez

Lloyd, Earl (1928–)

Earl Lloyd, a professional basketball player and coach known as "Big Cat" and "Moon Fixer," was born on April 3, 1928, in Alexandria, Virginia. He played college basketball at historically black West Virginia State College, where he was known for his strong defense and led the school to two Central Intercollegiate Athletic Association (CIAA) Conference and Tournament Championships (1948 and 1949). He was named All-Conference for three consecutive years (1949, 1950, 1951) and All-American by the *Pittsburgh Courier* for two consecutive years (1949 and 1950). Following college, he was drafted in the ninth round by the Washington Capitols, becoming one of the three black men drafted (Chuck Cooper and Nat "Sweetwater" Clifton being the others). Lloyd became the first of the three on October 31, 1950, to play in the NBA when the Capitols played the Rochester Royals. He was often compared to **Jackie Robinson**, but quickly downplayed this because he said his teammates accepted him.

His racial challenges came from the fans that hurled racial slurs and spit at him, as well as from the problems he had with public accommodations. Following two years in the army, Lloyd played for the Syracuse Nationals in 1952, and was a member of the 1954-1955 NBA National Champions. He thus became the first black player to win an NBA title. In 1956 he was named CIAA Player of the Decade (1947–1956). In 1958 Lloyd was traded to the Detroit Pistons, and he retired in 1960. In 1968 he became the first black assistant coach in the NBA when he was hired by the Pistons; in 1971, he became the first black coach. He was enshrined in the Virginia Sports Hall of Fame (1993), voted to the CIAA's 50 Greatest Player's list, and inducted into the CIAA Hall of Fame (1998). February 9, 1993, was declared Earl Lloyd Day throughout Virginia.

Helen R. Houston

McLendon, John (1915–1999)

John Blanche McLendon Jr. rose from humble beginnings in the small town of Hiawatha, Kansas, to become a legendary basketball coach and gain recognition as the "Father of Black Basketball" for the innovations he brought to the sport. McLendon developed a passion for the game as a youngster, and his determination to learn as much as possible about the sport led him to the University of Kansas, where he studied under James Naismith, the inventor of basketball, and became the first African-American graduate of the university in the field of physical education in 1936. McClendon began coaching high school basketball in Kansas City, then moved to North Carolina College for Negroes (now North Carolina Central University) in 1937, where he demonstrated the excellence of black college basketball by winning championships, as well as a secret game (and victory) against Duke University in 1944. At **Tennessee A&I State University**, McLendon made history with three consecutive National Association of Intercollegiate Athletics (NAIA) championships, between 1957 and 1959, against integrated competition. He also made the social breakthrough of quietly desegregating a downtown hotel in Kansas City, the tournament site. McLendon helped many of the first black players to enter the National Basketball Association (NBA), and eventually became the first African American professional basketball coach with the Cleveland Pipers in 1959. He returned to the college game in 1963, coaching at Kentucky State College and Cleveland State University, where he was the first black head coach at a predominantly white college. McLendon also became the first black to write a book on "fast-break" basketball, coach for the U.S. Olympic team and other international basketball competitions, and represent the Converse athletic shoe company as an international ambassador. In 1979 McLendon was inducted into the Naismith Memorial Basketball Hall of Fame as a "contributor" to the game, an ironic and long-overdue, yet fitting tribute to a basketball giant many referred to as the "Little Coach."

Fletcher F. Moon

Russell, Bill (1934–)

Born February 12, 1934, in Monroe, Louisiana, to Charles and Katie Russell, William Felton Russell was one of, if not *the* greatest, basketball players of his generation. In an effort to escape racism in his home town, his family relocated to Oakland, California, when Bill was nine. He joined the Boston Celtics in 1956 and brought with him a new and winning style. His years with the Celtics were known as the "Bill Russell Era." Through the years Russell was on the receiving end of racist remarks. For example, he overheard a fan in the stands yelling "don't get no chocolate on you." Despite taunts received from those in attendance at the game, Russell continued to prove his excellence on the court. In 1966 Celtics coach Red Auerbach retired and chose Russell to succeed him. Russell retired in 1969. Following the assassination of **Medgar Evers**, Russell held integrated basketball camps in the South, making him the first professional athlete to show an active interest in changing the racist climate there. Russell also visited Africa in 1969 as a U.S. Department of State liaison to teach basketball. In 1974, despite his continuing outspokenness about racial quotas in the National Basketball Association and his personal concerns about its treatment of minority players, Russell was the first black player elected to the National Basketball Hall of Fame. Even so, he protested the election, remembering the Hall's history of racism. Through his efforts, he paved the way for more African Americans to join the organization. The winner of two NCAA championships, an Olympic Gold medal, and 11 NBA world championships, Russell is considered a consummate team player.

Mary N. Hernandez

Wallace, Perry E., Jr. (1948–)

Perry Wallace was the first African American Vanderbilt Commodore to participate in varsity sports at Vanderbilt University and in Southeastern Conference (SEC) basketball. A graduate of Pearl High School in Nashville, Tennessee, he played center on Pearl's basketball team, where he was known for his slam dunks and referred to as the "king of the boards." During the academic year of 1965-66, the first year that the Tennessee Secondary School Athletic Association (TSSAA) allowed African Americans to participate, Pearl romped through district, regional, and state competitions and became the first African American team to win the TSSAA's Boys' State Basketball Tournament. The team posted a perfect season of thirty-one games and a two-year, forty-three game winning streak.

An outstanding player on the team, Wallace was recruited by more than eighty colleges and universities.

An outstanding player on the team, Wallace was recruited by more than eighty colleges and universities. He who won All-Metro, All-State, and All-American honors. The class valedictorian signed with Vanderbilt University in May 1966, which five years earlier, during the **Nashville sit-in movement**, expelled the Rev. **James Lawson**, a student at Vanderbilt's Divinity School. Entering Vanderbilt on an athletic scholarship, Wallace played on the school's freshmen squad because the National Collegiate Athletic Association's (NCAA) regulations barred freshmen from participating on the varsity team. Wallace was joined by fellow teammate Godfrey Dillard, an African American from Detroit, Michigan. During their first year, Wallace and Dillard encountered segregation's flood of hatred at Mississippi State, the University of Tennessee, and Auburn University. Supporting each other, they remained mute about received threats. Later, Dillard suffered an injury and did not go on to play varsity ball.

On December 2, 1967, Wallace stepped on the basketball court and became the first African American student athlete to compete in the SEC. In the midst of burning crosses, waving Confederate flags, and all the bile and hate of the 1960s, the segregationists' odium intensified. He experienced racism at its worst, particularly at SEC schools in Alabama and Mississippi. Cheerleaders led a volley of invective racist cheers. There were threats of beatings, castration, and lynching. He endured physical abuse on the court that referees refused to acknowledge as fouls. Vitriolic crowds harangued, taunted, and threatened Wallace throughout his SEC career. Struggling to stay inbounds between whites who wanted him to fail and African Americans who expected him to be a "superstar," Wallace became the quintessential "organization man." He never retaliated against players who maliciously fouled him. He understood that any perceived misconduct on his part could impede the progress of SEC desegregation. Rather, he executed his plays with precision, passion, and mental adroitness to beat his opponents on and off the court.

Quietly taking the struggles of the modern Civil Rights Movement to the basketball court, as did **Jackie Robinson** to the baseball field, Wallace played a crucial role in desegregating college basketball. In 1970, the first season after he graduated, the universities of Alabama, Florida, Georgia, and Kentucky desegregated their varsity teams; within the next decade, black athletes dominated SEC teams. The first African American to complete four years in the SEC, Wallace ended his tenure as captain of the Vanderbilt varsity team and second-team All SEC.

After earning an undergraduate degree in electrical engineering and engineering mathematics from the Vanderbilt University School of Engineering in 1970, Wallace completed his law degree in 1975 from Columbia University, where he was awarded the Charles Evans Hughes Fellowship.

During the administrations of Presidents Jimmy Carter and Ronald Reagan, Wallace served

as an attorney in the U.S. Department of Justice. A native of Nashville, Tennessee, and the youngest of six children born to Perry E. Sr. and Hattie Haynes Wallace, the SEC basketball pioneer has receive numerous accolades, including induction into the Tennessee Sports Hall of Fame and as an SEC Living Legend honoree. In 2004, Vanderbilt University retired Wallace's jersey, making him only the third athlete in the school's history to receive this honor. In March 2008 he was among those players and coaches featured in the poignant and educational documentary film *Black Magic* that merged sports and society's upheaval during the modern civil rights era. Wallace's experiences at Vanderbilt University and breaking the SEC color barrier heightened his concern about social justice. Currently a tenured professor of law at the Washington College of Law at American University, Wallace specializes in Environmental Law, Corporate Law, and Finance.

Linda T. Wynn

Bowling

National Bowling Association (est. 1939)

Formed on August 20, 1939, in Detroit, as the National Negro Bowling Association (NNBA), this nonprofit organization encourages African Americans to develop their skills in the game of Ten Pins. At the time of its founding, African Americans and other ethnic minorities were denied membership in mainstream organizations, such as the American Bowling Congress (ABC) and the Women's International Bowling Congress (WIBC). The NNBA held its first tournament in Cleveland, Ohio, in 1939. Its membership included teams from Detroit, Cleveland, Columbus (Ohio), Indianapolis, Chicago, and Racine (Wisconsin). Although teams from other parts of the country joined, until the 1950s the league was dominated by bowlers from Cleveland, Chicago, and Detroit. The organization assumed its present name in 1944 and then welcomed people of all races. After pressure from the **NAACP** and the NNBA in the fight for "Equality in Bowling," in 1951, the ABC and the WIBC dropped the racial exclusion clause from their constitutions and whites and blacks competed in the same events. The NBA plays a major role in integrating blacks into the sport of bowling. There are over 23,000 members in more than 100 local chapters across the country and in Bermuda. Over 80 percent of the membership is black. Its slogan is "Promoter of Sportsmanship, Fellowship and Friendship."

Frederick D. Smith

Boxing

Ali, Muhammad (1942–)

Born Cassius Marcellus Clay on January 17, 1942, in Louisville, Kentucky, Muhammad Ali was the first boxer to win the heavyweight title three times. In 1964 he announced he had converted to the Nation of Islam. He studied for three years under **Malcolm X** and took the name Muhammad Ali. He refused to serve in the military for religious reasons and because he believed the war being fought at the time was not in the interest of African Americans. He voiced his opinion on the Vietnam War in his autobiography, *The Greatest: My Own Story* (1975), indicating he had no argument with the Vietcong. As a result, he was convicted of violating the Selective Service Act and sentenced to five years in prison; he appealed the sentence. The U.S. Supreme Court overturned his conviction in 1970; however, he was prohibited from fighting for three and a half years. The response on his conscientious objector stance was varied, but he served as a role model and opened the door for other athletes to take a stand against exploitation. The World Boxing Association stripped him of his titles and the New York State Athletic Commission and other boxing commissions banned him from fighting. He also was forbidden to travel abroad. He never wavered in his religious beliefs, however, and spent the time speaking on college campuses about civil

Muhammad Ali (AP Photo).

rights and justice. The **NAACP** won a lawsuit proving his constitutional rights had been violated, and Ali regained his title. President Jimmy Carter sent Ali on a diplomatic mission to Africa in 1980. In 1985 Ali was sent to Lebanon to try to secure the release of hostages, but was unsuccessful; in 1990, he went to Iraq to promote peace in the region. In 1970, he received the Dr. Martin Luther King Memorial Award for his contributions to equality and human rights.

Helen R. Houston

Armstrong, Henry Jackson, Jr. (1912–1988)

Henry Armstrong Jr., was born in December 1912 in Columbus, Mississippi. The family

[Ali] never wavered in his religious beliefs ... and spent the time speaking on college campuses about civil rights and justice.

moved to St. Louis when he was four. The large earnings boxers made enticed his interest because he wanted to make money to help his family. He began his training at the segregated Young Men's Christian Association (YMCA). Armstrong had his first boxing victory in 1930, when he won the featherweight championship in an Amateur Athletic Tournament. Under the name Melody Jackson, he fought as a professional, lost the first bout and won the second; he changed his name to Armstrong in honor of Harry Armstrong, a former boxer he met at the YMCA and one who was to become his mentor, friend, and trainer. He moved to California and resumed his amateur status. His failure to qualify for the 1932 Olympics led to his turning professional, and he became known as "Homicide Hank." Armstrong has the distinction of holding three titles at once: world featherweight (1937), welterweight (1938), and lightweight (1938), a feat that can never be replicated, since the holding of multiple titles was barred in the 1940s. In 1942, Armstrong found that his manager, Eddie Mead, had mismanaged his monies, and so he returned to the ring until 1945. After suffering from a bout with alcoholism, he became an ordained Baptist minister and helped at-risk youth. In 1956 Armstrong published *Gloves, Glory, and God: An Autobiography.* Having been named fighter of the year by the International Hall of Fame in 1937, his first year of eligibility for the Boxing Hall of Fame was in 1954, and he was promptly inducted. Arm-

strong was also inducted into the Black Athletes Hall of Fame (1975) and named one of the 100 Greatest Black Athletes of the 20th Century. He died in October 1988 in Los Angeles.

Helen R. Houston

Johnson, Jack (1878–1946)

American heavyweight John Arthur "Jack" Johnson flourished during a period in American history when racism against African Americans was common. Some experts call Johnson, who was also called "Lil' Arthur," the greatest fighter ever in his weight class. He was born in Galveston, Texas, the son of Henry and Tina Johnson. He learned boxing skills in bouts with local African American boys and in practice in a local gymnasium. Later, he learned more from Joe Walcott, who won the welterweight title in 1901. Johnson won 57 bouts between 1902 and 1907, having defeated some of the leading black heavyweights, such as Joe Jeannette. In 1905 heavyweight James J. "Jim" Jeffries refused to fight Johnson because he was black. Johnson in 1908 took the title from Tommy Burns in Australia. The boxing world refused to accept his title fully, leading him to fight mediocre contenders just to get recognition. White boxing fans searched for their "great white hope" and in 1910, Jim Jeffries met Johnson in a memorable bout in Reno in which Johnson knocked his opponent out in the fifteenth round. This led to increased racial tensions and fights between blacks and whites. Johnson's marriage to one white woman, and then another, infuriated white Americans, as well. He and his second white wife consequently fled to Canada, where he lived a flamboyant lifestyle. In 1915 Johnson lost his heavyweight title to Jess Willard in Havana, Cuba. In 1954 Johnson was inducted into the Boxing Hall of Fame, and in 1968 the play *The Great White Hope,* which chronicles the search for a white boxer to defeat Johnson, opened on Broadway and starred James Earl Jones.

Frederick D. Smith

Louis, Joe (1914–1981)

Joe Louis Barrow, known as Joe Louis, was born May 13, 1914, in Lafayette, Alabama, and died April 12, 1981, in Las Vegas. He originally learned to fight as a survival strategy. As a young man, Louis pursued boxing, honed his skills, and began to train and box full time. It soon became his profession, and he won the 1933 Detroit Golden Gloves Light Heavyweight Championship. Two years later, he turned professional. He won the heavyweight championship in 1937 and went on to win over fifteen fights. Louis was phenomenal in the ring in spite of the discrimination that he encountered.

The two fights for which he is best known were both against German champion Max Schmeling. In 1936 Schmeling knocked Louis out in the twelfth round. However, two years later when they met again, Louis, to the joy and delight of both black and white Americans, knocked the German out in the first round. To Americans this act represented patriotism, success, and the triumph of democracy over fascism. In 1942 Louis volunteered for the U.S. Army and was assigned to Special Services. He was given the Legion of Merit Award and honorably discharged in 1945. While in the service, he fought exhibition bouts and benefits for the Army and Navy Relief funds. Along with Sugar Ray Robinson and **Jackie Robinson**, he proved to be a force in helping to eradicate the barriers keeping black soldiers out of officer training schools. Joe Louis fought discrimination throughout his life in and out of the ring.

Helen R. Houston

Molineaux, Tom (1784–1818)

Born a slave in the Georgetown section of Maryland, which is now a prestigious section of the District of Columbia, Tom Molineaux became a boxer and defeated another slave, "Black Abe," to win $100 for his master and his freedom. Tom came from a family of boxers: his father, Zachary, was an outstanding boxer and

was said to have founded boxing in America; his maternal grandfather was also a renowned boxer. The Molineauxes, who assumed the name of their owners, relocated to Richmond, Virginia, with their master and his family. Young Tom became chief handyman on the plantation when his father died. He also continued training as a boxer. After he defeated Black Abe, the toughest fighter around and a slave on an

Tom Molineaux (Fisk University).

adjoining plantation, he left the South permanently, moved to New York City, and worked as a porter and then a stevedore. He became a semi-professional boxer in 1800 and in 1809 left for England to further his boxing career. Molineaux came under the tutelage of boxer Bill Richmond, who also conducted a boxing academy. After winning several bouts—and labeled an "unknown" because Londoners did not want it known that their fighters lost to a black—in 1810 he took on Tom Cribb, a recently retired champion. According to Ocania Chalk in *Pioneers of Black Sport,* Molineaux actually won the fight but was "bilked out of his rightful victory." He waited to be dubbed the first black American to become boxing champion in England, but the announcement never came.

Jessie Carney Smith

Cycling

Taylor, Marshall W. (1878–1932)

World champion bicyclist Marshall "Major" Taylor was the first American-born black champion in any sport. He overcame racism in his sport to become the first African American member of an integrated professional team. He had other firsts as well: first black with a commercial sponsor, first black to hold world records, and the first black competitor in an open, racially integrated athletic championship. During his career, Taylor was called "the fastest bicycle rider in the world."

The grandson of slaves, Taylor was born free in Indianapolis to Gilbert and Saphronia Taylor, who, near the time of the **Civil War**, moved from Kentucky to Indiana. While working as horse- and coachman for a wealthy white family named the Southards in Indianapolis, Gilbert Taylor took his young son Marshall to work with him. There he became friendly with the Southards' young son, mixed with his friends, and learned to ride their bicycles. He also became accustomed to the comfort of wealthy life, and the pri-

vate tutor that they provided for him. He learned to speak well and dress well, much to the dismay of his siblings, who soon resented him. When the Southards moved to Chicago, the Taylors refused to allow their son to go. Then, as Taylor wrote in his autobiography, he "dropped from the happy life of a 'millionaire kid' to that of a common errand boy, all within a few weeks."

Taylor had, however, developed excellent skills as a bicyclist and became a trick rider. As he demonstrated his tricks outside a bicycle store, he attracted crowds in the streets. Then he began to work for the bicycle store Hay & Willis, serving as custodian. For this work he received a $35 bicycle and $6 a week. Taylor donned a uniform and was booked to exhibit his tricks and fancy riding. Much to the surprise of his employer, Taylor, then only 13 years old, competed in a 10-mile race that the store held annually and won the race six seconds ahead of the scratch man. He raced again the next year, in the summer of 1892, and came in third in an event for boys under 16.

In 1893 Taylor left the company and worked for another bicycle store, H.T. Hearsey. Taylor taught bicycle riding and regularly won races as well. By now racial prejudice raised its ugly head, as the white, crack riders resented the presence of a black in the events. Tracks in Indianapolis soon barred him from competing. Taylor left Hearsey and joined the firm Munger Cycle Manufacturing Company. There he met racial prejudice again—this time from employees who resented the attention that Munger gave Taylor. Then Munger left the firm, opened a bicycle factory in Worcester, Massachusetts, and hired Taylor.

Taylor made his professional debut in 1896, racing and winning at Madison Square Garden. In 1898 he rode the Sager chainless bicycle faster than anyone in the history of cycling at that time. He became the world champion rider on August 10, 1899, when he raced at Montréal's Queen Park; this made him the first black American champion in any sport and the second black world champion in any sport. Except for the years 1905 and 1906, Taylor had raced almost continuously since 1891. He retired in 1910 when he was just 32 years old. He went on to form the Major Taylor Manufacturing Company in 1914, and between 1913 and 1915 the short-lived Excello Manufacturing Company. Although he had a successful career and lived a comfortable life financially for most of his life, he became impoverished before he died on June 21, 1932.

Jessie Carney Smith

Football

Brown, Jim (1936–)

James Nathaniel Brown was born on St. Simons Island, Georgia. By the time he reached college, he proved that he was talented in several sports. While at Syracuse University, he was the first African American to play in the North-South game in lacrosse; as a sophomore, he scored 15 points per game in basketball; he also ran track, competing in the decathlon and placing fifth nationally. He was denied the opportunity to play football until his senior year, however, and then was the only African American on the team. Despite offers from teams and promoters to box or play basketball or baseball, Brown finally accepted an offer from the Cleveland Browns, where he would remain his entire professional career. In the 1960s and 1970s, Brown and others formed the Black Economic Union, which enabled wealthy African American businessmen to underwrite financial endeavors focusing on teenager education, job training, and rehabilitation. The organization eventually failed, and Brown became the focus of an FBI investigation about it. Ending a successful sports career, Brown branched into acting when Browns owner Art Modell threatened to cut Brown if he did not return to the Browns training camp immediately. In 1971 Brown was inducted into the NFL Hall of Fame, following a career in which he played in the Pro Bowl and led the league in rushing. Two decades later, Brown threatened to withdraw

from the Hall of Fame, citing the continuing neglect of black players. He was also inducted into the College Football Hall of Fame and the Lacrosse Hall of Fame. In addition to his success on the playing field and on the screen, he founded the Amer-I-Can project in 1989 to focus on how to prevent gang violence.

Mary N. Hernandez

[Brown] founded the Amer-I-Can project in 1989 to focus on how to prevent gang violence.

Grier, Rosey (1932–)

Roosevelt "Rosey" Grier began life as the seventh of eleven children born to Joseph and Ruth Grier in Cuthbert, Georgia; he was named in honor of President Franklin Delano Roosevelt. His family endured poverty and hardships, and Grier, already a large youngster by age nine, helped by working in the cotton fields as his father sold produce from a wagon. When Grier was 10 years old, the family moved to Roselle, New Jersey, where he excelled as a defensive lineman on the high school football team. Grier played college football at Pennsylvania State University, where he became an All-American before beginning his professional career with the New York Giants in 1955. He was part of the 1956 National Football League championship team, but also attracted attention for his musical talent before being traded to the Los Angeles Rams in 1963. In Los Angeles, Grier continued to excel in football as part of the "Fearsome Foursome," but also expanded his second career in entertainment as a singer and actor, which he continued after retiring from the Rams in 1968. He became active in community

Rosey Grier (AP Photo).

causes and committed himself fully to African American social issues. Grier served as a celebrity bodyguard for **Robert F. Kennedy**, and subdued Sirhan Sirhan after he shot Kennedy on June 4, 1968. Grier went through an extended period of depression while continuing such varied pursuits as needlepoint, public speaking, and performing, until he became a committed Christian and was ordained a clergyman in 1983. He also became a full-time entertainer who was known as a media celebrity. He hosted his own talk show in 1969, *The Rosey Grier Show*, which featured racial and political issues in its discussions. Grier drew widespread attention again when he provided spiritual counseling to O.J. Simpson shortly after the murders of Simpson's wife and her friend in 1994, overshadowing his other religious and community service.

Fletcher F. Moon

Motley, Marion (1920–1999)

Marion Motley was born June 5, 1920, in Leesburg, Georgia, and died on June 27, 1999, in Cleveland, Ohio. Motley was raised in Canton, Ohio. In 1940 he entered South Carolina State, a black college in Orangeburg. After a year, he transferred to the University of Nevada at Reno (1940–1942). At each institution, he played both as a linebacker and fullback. In 1944 he was drafted into the U.S. Navy and spent most of his service time playing for the Great Lakes Naval Training Station (Great Lakes, Illinois) football team. In 1946 Motley and his teammate Bill Willis became the first black players in the newly formed All-American Football Conference (AAFC) when they signed with the Cleveland Browns, a charter member of the conference. In the four years of the AAFC's existence, Cleveland dominated the championships with the tenacious ground attack of Motley, winning all four and compiling a 47-4-3 record. Motley was the AAFC's all-time rushing leader with 3,024 yards. The Browns joined the National Football League in 1950 when the AAFC went out of business. Motley continued to excel; that year he led the NFL with 810 yards, an average of 5.8 yards per carry, having rushed 188 yards on 11 carries for a total of 17.1 yards-per-carry in one game; he was consequently named to the All-Pro team. The Browns won the NFL title in that year and advanced to the title game in the next three seasons. His brief career (1954) with the Browns ended with a knee injury, and he moved to the Pittsburgh Steelers in 1955. Motley and Willis endured undisguised racism in the NFL, both on the field and off. Officials called back touchdowns and deliberately looked the other way when opponents punched them and stuck their fingers in their eyes. They never complained to officials; as Motley led the team in rushing, however, the attitudes of the officials changed and they enforced the playing rules. When Motley retired, he held a number of Browns club records; he became the second black player to be inducted into the Pro Football Hall of Fame in 1968, and in 1994 he was named to the National Football League's Seventy-fifth Anniversary All-Time Team.

Helen R. Houston

Pollard, Fritz (1894–1986)

A man of courage and ambition, Frederick Douglas "Fritz" Pollard achieved as much in athletics as he did in the area of civil rights. He was the first black to play in the Rose Bowl, the first black head coach and quarterback in the NFL, and the first professional coach to draw players from the black colleges. Pollard was born in Chicago's predominantly white Rogers Park section, where his German-speaking neighbors nicknamed him "Fritz." He was the son of John William and Catherine Amanda Pollard. In 1915 he entered Brown University and joined the football team. He was forced to live alone because no white student would room with him. When Pollard entered the locker room on his first day of practice, he met near silence, then heard a racial insult expressed in a soft southern drawl. He experienced similar humiliation in the shower room, when players filed out as soon as he entered. When on the trolley that took the men from practice to the campus, white players moved back or jumped off rather than ride with him. Pollard was taunted at games with Yale, Harvard, and other schools.

After displaying his talent on the gridiron, however, the likeable Pollard became popular on campus. In 1915 he played in the Tournament of Roses held in Pasadena between Washington State and Brown; he thus became the first African American to compete in the Rose Bowl, as it would be called later. The next year he led Brown to one of its most successful records. Pollard neglected his studies and as a result became ineligible to play in the 1917 season. In 1918 he was named physical director for the army's YMCA at Camp Meade, Maryland, and in late summer he became head football coach at Lincoln University, a black college in Pennsylvania. Pollard played professional football with the Akron Indians in 1919, and in 1920 led the team to a world championship. While with Akron, Pollard endured racial insults and abuse on and off the field and was often a target of unethical play. He and Jim Thorpe became leading players in the American Professional Football Associa-

tion, which in 1922 was renamed the National Football League.

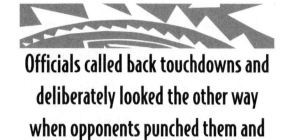

Officials called back touchdowns and deliberately looked the other way when opponents punched them and stuck their fingers in their eyes.

Pollard was named head coach of the team in 1921, the first black to head a major sports team. He retired in 1926 and coached two independent black teams: the Chicago Black Hawks and the New York Brown Bombers. Pollard recruited heavily from the black colleges and built his Brown Bombers into a powerful team. He showed that black athletes were talented enough to play in the NFL and remained a dominant force in the struggle to keep the league integrated; however, no blacks were hired by the teams between 1934 and 1945. In the mid-1930s, he wrote sports articles for the *Amsterdam News* and other black weeklies. He also became an entrepreneur, establishing a black investment company and a booking agency. He was an advocate of the "**Don't Buy Where You Can't Work**" campaign of the Thirties and Forties. Fritz Pollard is among the great black athletes of the past, yet much of his life was shrouded in legend and never recorded in writing. He cared deeply about civil rights issues and racial restrictions and in many instances worked behind the scenes to reach his integrationist objectives. Pollard died in 1986 at the age of 92.

Frederick D. Smith

Tunnell, Emlen (1925–1975)

Emlen "The Gremlin" Tunnell achieved several firsts in sports, while promoting racial parity in coaching and management positions within the National Football League (NFL). Born in Bryn Mawr, Pennsylvania, he was the son of Elzie and Catherine Adams Tunnell. His skill as an athlete was demonstrated early on when he was a star basketball and football player in high school. He enrolled at the University of Toledo and in 1943 played on its basketball team, helping the team reach the National Invitation Tournament finals in New York City. After a stint in the U.S. Coast Guard from 1944 to 1946, he enrolled at the University of Iowa, where he played in the offensive and defensive backfields. From 1948 to 1958, he juggled between offense and defense with the New York Giants; he was the Giant's first African American player; and he became one of the NFL's most outstanding defensive players. While with the Giants, he was nicknamed "Emlen the Gremlin" due to his ability to intercept passes, thus spoiling his opponents' game plans. From 1959 to 1961, Tunnell played with the Green Bay Packers, where he stabilized the backfield. Tunnell played in nine professional bowl games and was four times named an All-Professional. He was the Giant's assistant coach from 1965 to 1973, the first African American in the league to hold that post. The next year, Tunnell became assistant director of professional personnel for the Giants. While in these two positions, he agitated for more African American representation at the top of management; he condemned the NFL teams for their failure to hire blacks as head coaches and as management executives. In 1967 Tunnell became the first black member of the Professional Football Hall of Fame.

Frederick D. Smith

Golf

Elder, Robert Lee (1934–)

Robert Lee Elder was born in Dallas, Texas, to Charles and Sadie Elder, and grew up in Los Angeles. He developed an interest in golf while serving as a caddy, and then let the sport become his most important activity. He met golfer **Ted Rhodes**, who gave him lessons in golf. He turned professional at age 25 and played on the all-black **United Golfers Association** tour circuit, winning the title four times. Elder qualified for the PGA Tour in 1967 but had no corporate sponsor. In fact, for many years his victories came without an endorser. Elder noted the pressure that he faced due to racism, and heard spectators in the galleries call him and other black golfers "nigger" and "boy." He refused to play in certain tournaments due to overt hostility from spectators. On April 10, 1975, Elder became the first black golfer to play in the PGA Masters Tournament. He also played in the 1977 Masters and was as a member of the 1979 U.S. Ryder Cup team. Elder became a record-setter by making his first nine cuts after turning professional. In 1971 controversy surrounded Elder when he agreed to play in the South African Professional Golf Association Championship at the invitation of Gary Player. American civil rights leaders tried to persuade Elder not to participate due to that country's segregationist policies. The South African government agreed that Elder would not be subject to the usual segregation requirements regarding movement around the country. During this period Elder also raised money for a seminary school in South Africa. The South African tournament was the first integrated golfing event in that country, with Elder receiving an ovation from the crowds when he appeared on the course. During his visit to Africa, he also took first place in the Nigerian open tournament. The 1974 Monsanto Open marked the first time Elder won a PGA event.

Mary N. Hernandez

Rhodes, Ted (1913–1969)

A pioneering African American professional golfer, Theodore "Ted" Rhodes was born on November 9, 1913, to Frank and Delta Anderson Rhodes in Nashville, Tennessee. As a preteen, Rhodes began caddying at the all-white Belle Meade Country Club and the Richland Country Club, where African Americans played. Later he played in a number of tournaments sponsored by the United States Colored Golf Association, a national golf association for African American golfers that had conducted tournaments since 1926 that was later renamed the **United Golfers Association** (UGA).

Between 1946 and 1947 Rhodes won six consecutive UGA tournaments, including the Joe Louis Open in Detroit, Michigan. Rhodes was not the first African American golfer, an honor that goes to John Shippen, who played in the 1896 U.S. Open at Shinnecock Hill. However, Rhodes played a key role in advancing the game for African Americans and other people of color. Recognized as one of the first African American professionals in golf, Rhodes, along with fellow black players Bill Spiller and Madison Gunther, filed a civil lawsuit against the Professional Golf Association (PGA) for civil rights violations in 1948. After successfully competing in the Los Angeles Open at the Riviera Country Club, they qualified to play in the Richmond Open in January of the following year. They submitted their entries and were accepted. However, the PGA returned their entries and made reference to their "whites only" clause. Rhodes, Spiller, and Gunther sued the PGA for $315,000 on the grounds that the association denied them the opportunity to make a living in their profession. Before the case was heard in court, the United States Golf Association (USGA) accepted Rhodes's entry into the 1948 Open at the Riviera Country Club in Pacific Palisades, California. In September the trio's lawsuit against the PGA was scheduled to go to court. However, the PGA pledged to stop barring African American golfers from their tournaments before that happened. Notwithstanding, there was a caveat; they could play if tournament sponsors invited them. Rhodes, Spiller, and Gunther believed they had won the concessions they wanted and withdrew the lawsuit. By changing to an "invitation only" arrangement, the PGA sidestepped

its legal and moral responsibilities to let Rhodes and his fellow African American golfers participate in its tournaments.

After a successful year in 1949, when he won consecutive titles in the UGA's National, Rhodes won the Houston National, the Sixth City Open, the Gotham Open, the Ray Robinson Open, and the Joe Louis Invitational. That same year he entered the PGA's tournament in Cedar Rapids, Iowa, which was to be played in August. However, as before, Rhodes's invitation was rescinded when PGA secretary George Schneiter notified him that his invitation was sent by mistake. Later that same year, the PGA reneged on its agreement when the San Diego Open turned down his entry. Covered by the press, the PGA's negative response produced an uproar and caused the PGA to ask heavyweight-boxing champion **Joe Louis** to play. Rhodes, despite being slighted by the PGA, continued to compete on the Negro tour. He won the Negro National Open three consecutive years, beginning in 1949 and repeating this performance again, beginning in 1957.

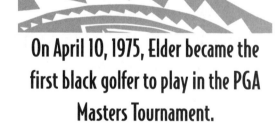

On April 10, 1975, Elder became the first black golfer to play in the PGA Masters Tournament.

After retiring in 1960, Rhodes became a golf instructor. Among his students were African American stars **Lee Elder**, the first black to play in the Masters Tournament at Augusta National (1975); tennis great **Althea Gibson**, the first African American woman to play in the Ladies Professional Golf Association (1964); and Ann Gregory, the first African American woman to play in a national championship conducted by the United States Golf Association (1950) and the U.S. Amateur Championship (1956). The year following Rhodes's retirement, the PGA retracted its "whites only" policy. Golfers **Charlie Sifford**, the first African American PGA Tour member (1962); Pete Brown, the first African American to win a PGA tournament (1964); and **Tiger Woods**, the first person of color to win the Masters (1997) all owe a debt of gratitude to Rhodes. Other African Americans who competed in the PGA included Calvin Peete, Jim Dent, and Jim Thorpe. On July 4, 1969, Rhodes died in Nashville, Tennessee. That same year the Nashville's Metropolitan Board of Parks and Recreation renamed the 18-hole Cumberland Golf Course in his honor. In 1997 Rhodes was inducted into the Tennessee Golf Hall of Fame. The following year the Tennessee Historical Commission built an historical marker commemorating Rhodes's contribution to professional golf.

Linda T. Wynn

A "caucasian clause" in the constitution restricted the PGA from admitting blacks.

Sifford, Charlie (1922–)

After refusing to accept racial segregation on golf courses, in golf associations, and in tournaments, Charles "Charlie" Luther Sifford finally integrated the top golf organization by becoming the first full-fledged African American member of the Professional Golf Association (PGA). The son of Eliza and Roscoe Sifford, Charlie was born in Charlotte, North Carolina. He was introduced to golf while still in school, learning as he and other black youth caddied for white golfers in the nearby links of the Carolina Country Club. He also played at the club on Mondays, when it was closed for practice but available to caddies. Sifford became skilled at the game, much to the dismay of club members, who complained about his game and sought to stop him from playing. After he heard a racial slur aimed at him, he left Charlotte to live with relatives in Philadelphia. There he honed his golfing skills further. After serving in the U.S. Army's 24th Infantry from 1943 to 1946, he returned to Philadelphia and taught golf full time.

As talented as he was, Sifford's progress as a golfer was hampered by the racial barrier, for golf courses, country clubs, and tournaments had not opened their doors to blacks. Nor had the PGA done so. A "caucasian clause" in the constitution restricted the PGA from admitting blacks. Sifford and other leading black golfers, including **Ted Rhodes**, became members of the **United Golf Association**, which was founded in 1925 to serve the needs of black golfers. Their Negro National Open served Sifford well, too; he gained immediate success, winning the championship each year from 1952 through 1956. The purses, however, were small for a professional golfer. Sifford, Rhodes, and other talented black golfers agitated against the prejudicial membership requirement of the PGA. Finally, in November 1961, the PGA changed its constitution and Sifford became the first African American-approved player; in 1964 he was granted Class A PGA membership, and from 1960 to 1974 he placed within the top 60 money winners on the PGA tour. Some courses in the South remained closed to him, though. The PGA, furthermore, could not mandate fair treatment by its spectators, and in 1969 unruly white spectators at North Carolina's Greensboro Open shouted racial epithets at Sifford and threw beer cans at him. Sifford often found the road to success and racial parity lonely and racial harassment frustrating. What bothered him most, however, was the slow pace of integration in the golf world in the mid-1960s. He retired in the mid-1970s, and in 2004 became the first black member of the World Golf Hall of Fame.

Frederick D. Smith

United Golfers Association (est. 1925)

A group of African American doctors from Washington, D.C., who enjoyed the sport of golf and came together to show strength and solidarity, organized the United Negro Golfers Association (UNGA) in a YMCA building located in Washington. Some sources claim that it was initially called the United States Colored Golf Association. On Labor Day weekend 1926, African American golfers from all over the country came together at Mapledale Country Club in Stow, Massachusetts, for the UNGA's first Negro National Open, later known simply as 'The National." The National became a major event for black golfers and was always held the first full week of August. When Mapledale closed, the National was held in other locations in Wisconsin and Illinois. In 1930 the association changed its name to become the United Golfers Association. Racial segregation had restricted black golfers from full access to public courts in Washington and in other cities as well, allowing them to play only on certain days or times, if at all. They were refused entry into white tournaments.

UGA organizers grew tired of the Jim Crow rules in their home town, which forced the doctors to go to New England each summer to play. They realized that the members were lacking skills and needed to upgrade the quality of their play, so they sought ways to make that happen. Early membership included women as well. The association was unable to enroll the majority of the nation's black golfers; its member clubs, however, sponsored most of the UGA-related events. Among the luminaries and athletes who were attracted to the organization were boxing champion **Joe Louis** and pioneering African American golfer **Ted Rhodes**. In the mid-1930s golfing was a betting man's game, and many players depended on the game to make a living by winning bets. Joe Louis was one such player; he sponsored a $2,500 UGA tournament in 1936 and hired black professionals to serve as teachers. The National had a four-year hiatus around World War II, after which it attracted many talented players such as Ted Rhodes, **Charlie Sifford**, **Lee Elder**, Calvin Peete, and Jim Thorpe, who went on to win National titles.

The National's fiftieth anniversary was held in 1976 in San Diego. Although segregation on the golf course had ended years earlier, local officials told the tournament director, Tim Thomas, that the course could not accommodate the large number of players who came. Only intervention from the mayor kept the course open for the black golfers. That was one of the last Nationals held, for the UGA had insufficient funds to continue the event. Membership had declined significantly by the mid-1980s, and the National faded away. Integration in golf had taken its toll on the black golfers' event.

Jessie Carney Smith

United Negro Golfers Association. *See* United Golfers Association

Woods, Tiger (1975–)

An American professional golfer extraordinaire, Eldrick "Tiger" Woods has had an unprecedented career since entering the world of professional golf in 1996. At 21 years of age, Woods, the youngest person to win a major professional golf championship, was the first person of African American—as well as Asian—lineage to win the Masters Golf Tournament. By age 32 he had won 87 tournaments, 65 of which were on the Professional Golf Association (PGA) tour, including the 1997, 2001, 2002, and the 2005 Masters' tournaments; the 1999, 2000, 2006, and 2007 PGA championships; the 2000, 2002, and the 2008 U.S. Open Championships; and the 2000, 2005, and 2006 British Open Championships. In 2001, with his second Masters victory, Woods became the first golfer ever to hold all four major professional championships at the same time.

In the April 14, 1997, edition of *The Augusta Chronicle,* Woods paid tribute to pioneering African American golfers. "I wasn't the pioneer," said Woods. "**Charlie Sifford, Lee Elder, Ted**

Rhodes, those are the guys who paved the way. All night I was thinking about them, what they've done for me and the game of golf. Coming up 18, I said a little prayer of thanks to those guys. Those guys are the ones who did it." Woods's race has often been an issue in a game played predominantly by whites. It was an issue that came to the forefront when, after Woods's first Masters' win, Fuzzy Zoeller referred to him as "that little boy" and urged him not to put fried chicken or collard greens on the menu of the Champions Dinner at Augusta National the following year. To many, Woods's ascendancy to golf prominence is tied to issues of race and ethnicity, as well as to his superior performance on the golf course.

To many, Woods's ascendancy to golf prominence is tied to issues of race and ethnicity.

Racist policies slowly changed to guarantee that African American golfers would not be proscribed from competing on a par with whites. However, the Augusta National Golf Club did not accept its first African American until 1990. In winning the 2000 British Open, Woods became the youngest to complete the career Grand Slam of professional major championships. He ranked fifth behind the likes of Ben Hogan, Gene Sarazen, Gary Player, and Jack Nicklaus. Woods has held the number one position in world rankings for the consecutive weeks and for the greatest total number of weeks. For a record nine times he has been the PGA Player of the Year. The eight-time recipient of the Byron Nelson Award for lowest adjusted scoring, he has tied Jack Nicklaus's record of leading the money list in eight different seasons.

Named the Associated Press's Male Athlete of the year four times, Woods is the only person named *Sports Illustrated* Sportsman of the Year more than once. Woods has written a column for *Golf Digest* since 1997. In 2001, the golfing phenomenon wrote the best-selling *How I Play Golf,* a golf instruction book that in its first edition had the largest print run of any golf book.

Woods was born to Earl (1932–2006) and Kultida "Tida" Punsawad Woods in Long Beach, California, on December 20, 1975. He was given the moniker "Tiger" by his father in memory of his Vietnamese combat friend Nguyen Phong. A child prodigy, Woods began playing golf at age two. It has been said that Woods, who is multiracial (Caucasian, American black, American Indian, and Asian) is credited with bringing about an increased interest in the game of golf. Considering himself a "Cablinasian," a portmanteau he formulated from his multiracial make-up, Woods's masterful athletic and cerebral dominance in the game of golf caused attendance and television ratings to escalate among a diverse, multicultural, and multiracial audience in a sport that was once deemed racially intolerant and restrictive.

Linda T. Wynn

Horse Racing

Horse racing in America took place as early as 1665 in what is now known as Garden City, Long Island, New York. It was not until after the Revolutionary War, however, that owners and trainers realized that, for those who used racing as the betting sport that it became, riders and jockeys were often considered more important than the horse. Most of the jockeys in the American South in 1800 were diminutive slaves who had grown up with horses, built race tacks, and trained and cared for horses. In contrast, jockeys in the North were whites, either migrants from England or coming from local areas. The best black jockey of this early period was "Monkey"

Simon, who around 1806 drew the then-hefty sum of over $100 per ride for himself or his master. Black jockeys were high achievers in what became the most popular sports event in the country. They participated in heralded matches of 1823, 1836, 1876, 1878, and 1883. They became so superior in the sport that, just before the **Civil War**, they were accused of being dishonest, holding back horses during a race, cheating owners, taking bribes, and associating with gamblers—all in an effort to remove them from the tracks. During the war, however, racing in the South nearly stopped, as the horses were needed in the cavalry.

Between 1861 and 1911, the work of the black jockeys was astounding. The most important race of the era occurred at Churchill Downs, where the Kentucky Derby began and continues today as a premiere event. The first "run for the roses" occurred on May 17, 1875, in Louisville. Fifteen horses lined up for the race, with 14 of the jockeys being black. Black jockey Oliver Lewis rode Aristides through to the win, becoming the first jockey of any race to win the Derby. Jockey Isaac Murphy (1861?–1896), who was born Isaac Burns, was the first jockey of any race to win the Kentucky Derby three times: 1884, 1890, and 1891. Like most of the apprentices for a jockey post, Murphy lived at the tracks, slept near the stalls, and became an exercise rider. During the years of the great black jockeys, riders continued to set records. In 1896 the Kentucky Derby distance was reduced from one and one-half miles to one and one-quarter miles. Willie (Willy) Simms (1870–1927) became the first jockey to win at this distance. He also won such well-known races as the Preakness Stakes (1898) and the Belmont Stakes (1893 and 1894). The last of the black American jockeys to ride in a Derby was Jess Conley, who finished third atop Colson, a horse named for black trainer Raleigh Colson. Despite their misfortunes, such as poverty and ill health, these jockeys achieved astounding accomplishments for more than 50 years.

Frederick D. Smith

Olympics

Carlos, John Wesley (1945–) and Tommie Smith (1944–)

Bronze and gold medal-winners at the 1968 Summer Olympics in Mexico City, John Wesley Carlos and Tommie Smith made headlines around the world at the victory stand when they raised their black gloved-covered fists in silent protest, signifying unity and black power. Their gesture became known as the **Black Power** salute, and they became the first athletes to refuse to recognize the American flag and the national anthem at an Olympic event. Their gloves were a pair; thus the men formed an arch, each wearing one glove on the opposite hand. To represent black poverty in America, they wore black socks but no shoes. Silver medalist Peter Norman, a white athlete from Australia, joined their protest by wearing the badge of the Olympic Project for Human Rights, which was initially formed to organize a boycott of the 1968 Summer Olympics. Sports figures often regard the actions of Carlos and Smith as a milestone in America's Civil Rights Movement. Their silent protest received mixed comments, ranging from a sign of disgrace for all Americans to praise for their bravery. During the Olympics, Carlos, of Clarksville, Texas, won a bronze medal in the 200-meter dash; Smith, a Harlem native, won a gold medal for the 200-meter

Their silent protest received mixed comments, ranging from a sign of disgrace for all Americans to praise for their bravery.

dash in the world-record time of 19.83 seconds. The silent protest was documented in an HBO feature titled *The Fist of Freedom*. In 2005 a statue of Carlos and Smith was dedicated at San Jose State University, where they were students at the time of the Olympics.

                                                    Jessie Carney Smith

Coachman, Alice (1923–)

The first African American woman to win an Olympic gold medal in track and field, Alice Coachman set a new record at the Summer Games in London in 1948. She also was the only American woman winner at a track event at the games. Coachman was born in Albany, Georgia, to Fred "Doc" and Evelyn Coachman. Her talent in track and field was noticeable as early as the fifth grade, and she went on to excel at Madison High School under coach Harry E. Lash. Tuskegee Institute (now University) in Alabama recruited her and she continued high school and college studies there, later transferring to Albany State. Albany knew her as the "Tuskegee Flash." Coachman won AAU (Amateur Athletic Union) nationals in running and high jump in 1943, which brought her national fame. For five years she had been the only black on the All-American Women's Team. She and eight other black women joined the American team for the 1948 Olympics in London. Coachman competed in the high jump, reaching 5 feet, 6.5 inches, setting both an Olympic and an American record. When she returned to the United States, a parade and several recognition dinners were held to honor her. She also met with President Harry S. Truman. The nation was still so steeped in segregation and racism, however, that she was forbidden to speak at a recognition ceremony in Albany Municipal Auditorium in Georgia. Major newspapers, however, failed to notice her accomplishment. She is enshrined in eight halls of fame, including the National Track and Field Hall of Fame.

                                                    Jessie Carney Smith

Owens, Jesse (1913–1980)

Born the tenth of eleven children to share-cropper Henry Owens and Emma Fitzgerald Owens in Oakville, Alabama, James Cleveland Owens experienced extreme poverty, poor housing, inadequate food, and no extra money for medical care. As a result, young J.C. endured a variety of childhood health problems, including pneumonia, and rarely attended school because education for black children was nearly nonexistent. Despite their hardships, his mother remained optimistic and convinced her husband to move the family to the North in hopes of better opportunities. In Cleveland, Ohio, Henry Owens and three of his sons found work in the steel mills, and J.C. was able to attend school on a regular basis. On his first day at Bolton Elementary School, his teacher thought he said "Jesse" instead of "J.C." when asked his name. The mistake was not corrected, and the name change stuck.

Jesse Owens (right) shakes hands with another athlete at the 1936 Olympic Games (NBCU Photo Bank via AP Images).

In junior high school Owens met his future wife, Minnie Ruth Solomon, and Charles Riley, a white physical education teacher and track coach. Although Riley continued working with Owens at East Technical High School, Owens credited his father, a county champion runner in Alabama, as being his greatest early influence. He became the only child from his family to graduate from high school, while continuing his athletic activities by breaking the world record in the long jump on May 20, 1933, and tying the world record in the 100-yard dash at the National Interscholastic Championship in Chicago. Owens became a local hero and continued his track career and education at Ohio State University. He did not receive an athletic scholarship, but worked three jobs to earn money to support his family and pay tuition. Owens was prevented from living on campus, forbidden from eating in restaurants serving the campus, was restricted to the balcony section in the only theater that admitted blacks, and could not shower or ride in the same vehicle with his white teammates. He also had academic problems and received little help beyond opportunities to develop public speaking skills.

On the track, Owens broke five world records in 1935, setting the stage for his greatest athletic achievements. In the 1936 Berlin Olympics, Owens became an authentic American hero by winning four gold medals and disproving the rhetoric of black inferiority endorsed by Adolf Hitler, who refused to acknowledge the superiority of Owens and other African American athletes. Along with winning the 100-, 200-, and 400-meter relay races, Owens broke his own world record in the long jump. He enjoyed a hero's welcome in the United States after Berlin, but his fame did not shield him from the same discrimination experienced by other blacks. He was often exploited in track tours and exhibitions, and lost out on other opportunities due to his lack of a college degree. Owens tried several unsuccessful business ventures, but used his celebrity to earn an income as a public speaker; he became politically identified as a Republican and conservative.

Owens came under fire in 1968 for opposing the activism of black athletes during the Olympic Games in Mexico City, and was labeled an "Uncle Tom" for his conservative views. In his first book, *Blackthink*, Owens tried to justify his positions without success. He eventually wrote a second book, *I Have Changed*, which acknowledged the rights of others to protest and indicated that racial problems remain a serious issue in America. Unfortunately, Owens also became a chronic smoker and was diagnosed with lung cancer in 1979. He died in 1980 at age 66 in Tuscon, Arizona, and received numerous posthumous honors and recognitions for his outstanding life and career.

Fletcher F. Moon

Rudolph, Wilma (1940–1994)

The first American woman to win three gold medals in an Olympiad, Wilma Glodean Rudolph was born on June 23, 1940, in Clarksville, Tennessee. The road to Olympic stardom was not easy. Rudolph, who was diagnosed with polio at the age of four, was never expected to walk, much less run. She wore a leg brace and corrective shoe until her adolescent years. Her family took turns massaging her crippled leg every day. Once a week her mother, Blanche, drove 90 miles round-trip to Hubbard Hospital in Nashville, where the young Rudolph received therapy. Because of her family's perseverance and her determination, Rudolph was able to discard her leg brace and corrective shoes by age 12. In four short years, she became a basketball star at the all-black Burt High School. In 1955 she captured the attention of Edward S. Temple, the coach of **Tennessee A&I State University** (now Tennessee State University) women's track team, who invited Rudolph to attend his summer camp. In 1956 she and five other "Tigerbelles" qualified for the 1956 Olympics held in Melbourne, Australia.

Rudolph was the youngest member of the U.S. team; she returned to Nashville with a bronze medal for her efforts in the sprint relay event. Three years later, as a student at Tennessee A&I, she and the Tigerbelles attended the Pan American Games in Chicago, where she brought home a silver medal. The following year, at the 1960 Olympic Summer Games in Rome, Italy, Rudolph won three gold medals and became the first American women to do so in a single Olympiad. She won gold in the 100-meter, the 200-meter, where she set a world record, and the 400-meter relays. It was in the 400-meter relay that she set another world record with fellow Tennessee State teammates Martha Hudson, Lucinda Williams, and Barbara Jones. One of the most popular athletes from the games, the "Tennessee Tornado" emerged as the world's fastest woman. The Italians nicknamed her "La Gazzella Nera" (the Black Gazelle); to the French she was "La Perle Noire" (The Black Pearl).

Rudolph refused to attend a racially segregated event. Consequently, her parade and banquet were the first integrated events in her hometown of Clarksville.

Rudolph paid tribute to **Jesse Owens**, who had been her inspiration and star of the 1936 Summer Olympics held in Berlin, Germany. Governor Buford Ellington, who was elected as an "old-fashion segregationist," planned to head Rudolph's welcome home celebration when she returned home. However, in keeping with the timbre of the times and the civil rights efforts in the city of Nashville, the state of Tennessee, and across the South, Rudolph refused to attend a racially segregated event. Consequently, her parade and banquet were the first integrated

events in her hometown of Clarksville. Rudolph was the 1960 United Press Athlete of the Year and the Associated Press Woman Athlete of the Year. The next year she won the James E. Sullivan Award as the top amateur athlete in the United States and visited with President **John F. Kennedy**. In 1962 Rudolph retired from track and field competition and completed goodwill tours abroad. That same year she was awarded the Babe Didrickson Zaharias Award. She was voted into the National Black Sports and Entertainment Hall of Fame in 1973 and the National Track and Field Hall of Fame in 1974. On December 2, 1980, Tennessee State University named its indoor track after Wilma Rudolph. She was inducted into the U.S. Olympic Hall of Fame in 1983 and honored with the National Sports Award in 1993. The following year, she was inducted into the National Women's Hall of Fame. The recipient of numerous other awards and one of the most celebrated female athletes ever, Wilma Rudolph made an impact on both race and gender in the world of sports. She passed away on November 12, 1994. In 1996, a life-size statue of Rudolph was erected in Clarksville, Tennessee.

Linda T. Wynn

Tennis

American Tennis Association (est. 1916)

America's oldest African American sports organization, the American Tennis Association (ATA), was founded in Washington, D.C., on November 30, 1916. Its founders sought relief for African Americans who had an interest in tennis and whose activities had been hampered by national acceptance of policies and practices that denied blacks access to most activities of the Lawn Tennis Association (USLTA), later renamed the United States Tennis Association (USTA). The organization is the result of a group of African American entrepreneurs, college educators, and physicians who were determined to foster broad interest in a game for people of color, and they thus formed their own tennis circuit. Representatives of more than a dozen black tennis clubs came together on Thanksgiving Day in Washington to found an organization that would foster friendly relations among black tennis enthusiasts and players, improve the standards of the existing tennis clubs, and promote game standards among black players. The ATA agreed to hold a national championship tournament annually, the first coming to Baltimore's Druid Hill Park in August 1917. Tally Holmes (one of the ATA's founders) and Lucy Diggs Slowe were the first to win the men and women's singles respectively. The tournament offered three events: men's and women's singles and men's doubles.

Since racial segregation was still practiced in most hotels in the South where the tournaments were held, several black colleges, including **Hampton Institute** (now University), **Morehouse College**, Central State, and Lincoln University, hosted the championships and offered housing space and tennis courts. Soon the ATA tournament became a highly anticipated social event in the black community, and fashion shows, formal dances, and similar events were held during the week of games. The ATA's first interracial match came in 1940 in an exhibition game in New York's Cosmopolitan Club. Among the world's top players whom the ATA supported were **Althea Gibson** and **Arthur Ashe**. ATA coaches also produced such top professionals as Zina Garrison, Lori McNeil, and MaliVai Washington. The ATA, based in Culver City, California, continues its support of tennis for black people and welcomes to membership people of all racial backgrounds. It also promotes and develops junior tennis players.

Jessie Carney Smith

Ashe, Arthur, Jr. (1943–1993)

Arthur Robert Ashe Jr. was the first of two sons born to Arthur Ashe Sr. and Mattie Cordell Cunningham Ashe in Richmond, Virginia. His father was the caretaker of the city's

Brookfield Park, which was designated for blacks during segregation; they lived on the grounds of the facility. After the death of his mother when Ashe was six years old, he and his younger brother John were raised by their father; Ashe began playing tennis at the age of 11. Ronald Charity, a park instructor, developed Ashe's early talent and potential and introduced Ashe to Robert Walter Johnson, a black doctor from Lynchburg, Virginia, who mentored and trained African American tennis players, including **Althea Gibson**, the first black champion at Wimbledon and other major tennis competitions. With Charity and Johnson's help, Ashe won his first championship in the American Tennis Association's 12-and-under category in 1955. By 1961 Ashe had won the junior tennis indoor singles title twice, so he left Richmond's Maggie Walker High School to train and live with coach Richard Hudlin in St. Louis.

Ashe used his increased visibility to champion civil and human rights causes, particularly protesting the apartheid system in South Africa.

After graduation from Sumner High School as an A student in 1962, Ashe went to the University of California at Los Angeles (UCLA), where he led the tennis team to the collegiate national championship. He also became the first African American to represent the country in the Davis Cup international tennis matches in 1963, before graduating from UCLA with a bachelor of business administration degree in 1966. Ashe served in the U.S. Army from 1966 to 1969, achieving the rank of lieutenant while continuing his tennis career. He won his first major championship, the 1968 U.S. Open, while still ranked as an amateur and turned professional the following year. Ashe used his increased visibility to champion civil and human rights causes, particularly protesting the apartheid system in South Africa, which echoed the segregation he experienced during his early years in Richmond. He helped lead efforts to ban the country from the Davis Cup and other international competitions.

The peak of Ashe's professional career came in 1975, when he defeated Jimmy Connors to become the first African American male Wimbledon champion and was ranked as the number one tennis player in the world. In 1977 he married photographer Jeanne Moutoussamy, but two years later his life changed dramatically after suffering several heart attacks requiring multiple bypass surgeries. The medical challenges forced Ashe to retire from competitive tennis in 1980, but he continued his activism with organizations such as Artists and Athletes Against Apartheid and TransAfrica to the point of being arrested along with other protestors outside the South African embassy in 1985. He also became an author, publishing works like the multi-volume *A Hard Road to Glory: A History of the African American Athlete* in 1988. In addition, he was a public speaker, a teacher at Florida Memorial College in Miami, a sports commentator, and active in charitable activities. As a result of a blood transfusion during his 1983 surgery, Ashe contracted the HIV/AIDS virus. Speculation in the news media eventually caused Ashe to publicly announce his condition to the world on April 8, 1992. He spent the remainder of his life increasing public awareness about HIV/AIDS and working on his memoir, *Days of Grace*, which was completed by literary collaborator Arnold Rampersad after his death.

Fletcher F. Moon

Gibson, Althea (1927–2003)

Gibson was born in Silver, South Carolina, and grew up in Harlem. She would become a tennis champion and a professional golfer. Beginning with her earliest win in tennis in 1942 at the New York State Open, she overcame a history of truancy and disrespect for rules and authority. Boxer Sugar Ray Robinson and his wife convinced Gibson she needed an education. They encouraged her to complete high school and attend college. Others who helped Gibson become a disciplined athlete were Hubert Eaton of Wilmington, North Carolina (with whom she lived during the time she finished her high school work) and Robert W. Johnson of Lynchburg, Virginia. Both Eaton and Johnson were physicians and active in the **American Tennis Association** (ATA).

Gibson began the arduous and difficult task of becoming the first African American to break the tennis color line. She enrolled at Florida Agricultural and Mechanical College (now University) on a basketball and tennis scholarship. She was asked to play in the now-racially integrated National Indoor Championships held in 1949 and sponsored by the all-white United States Lawn Tennis Association (USLTA), but lost in the quarterfinals. Despite her proven talents on the tennis court, having won the ATA championships each year since 1947 (eventually winning nine in a row), Gibson was denied an invitation to play in the USLTA's segregated tournament at Forest Hills, Long Island. Alice Marble, who had played against Gibson, wrote a scathing editorial in the July 1950 issue of *American Lawn Tennis* that focused on the need for the entire sports world to accept the presence of minority players and to judge them by their ability and not skin color. As result, the Orange Lawn Tennis Club in New Jersey invited Gibson to play that year. As well, she was invited to the national championships held at Forest Hills, but lost in the second round.

In 1951 Gibson competed at Wimbledon, becoming the first African American to play in this exclusive international tournament. Although she lost, she continued to hone her skills to the extent that she and her partner won the doubles in the 1956 Wimbledon tournament. That same year she played in 18 international tournaments and won 16. The next year Gibson won the singles at Wimbledon, 6-3, 6-2. She played in four tennis Grand Slams, winning at least one in the Australian national, the French national, Wimbledon, and the U.S. national. Althea Gibson became a hero to such future tennis luminaries as Billie Jean King and **Arthur Ashe**. She also inspired other African women in tennis, including Zina Garrison and **Serena and Venus Williams** during their Wimbledon triumphs. After her retirement from tennis, Gibson began to play golf. Despite criticism by the black press, she continued to strive to bring excellence to the two sports she loved: tennis and golf. She left tennis after 100 tennis victories, and golf after playing in 171 tournaments. She received numerous honors, including induction into the International Women's Hall of Fame in 1980.

Mary N. Hernandez

Washington, Ora (1898–1971)

Ora Mae Washington gained fame as an outstanding athlete in four sports: tennis, basketball, soccer, and golf. Her greatness in tennis led to her comparison to legendary black tennis star **Althea Gibson**, the first black to win a major tennis title. Washington became a pioneering inspiration for young African American women athletes. She developed an interest in tennis at courts in Germantown, Pennsylvania, where a YWCA instructor urged her to learn the game to help overcome the grief over her sister's death. She became so skilled that, by 1924, she won her first national championship in the black American Tennis Association's tournaments, and for 12 years remained undefeated. Washington never warmed up before a game, claiming that she did so as the game progressed. She became the first African American woman to dominate a sport. Both her career and public image were marred by racial segregation, however. While she was 12-year champion in the ATA, Helen Wills Moody, a white player in the

United States Lawn Tennis Association, held a seven-year championship. She refused to meet Washington in a match to determine who was the best player in women's singles. Washington retired from tennis around 1937 and yielded the sport to younger competitors. In basketball she served as team captain of the Germantown Hornets from 1929 to 1930 and became a star center for the *Philadelphia Tribune's* team. Her greatest skill, however, was as a tennis player, where she excelled in both singles and doubles and won 201 trophies. In 1976 she was inducted into the Black Athletes Hall of Fame.

Jessie Carney Smith

Williams, Venus (1980–) and Serena (1981–)

Venus and Serena Williams, the two youngest among five daughters of Richard and Oracene Williams, first developed their talents on the public tennis courts of Compton, California, with their father as their first coach. Venus, who was born in Lynwood, California, began playing at the age of four, while Serena, born in Saginaw, Michigan, started at age three. By the time Serena was five, the sisters were already practicing and playing tennis matches against each other. By the time each of the sisters was 10 years old, they were already winning a number of southern California tennis tournaments in their respective age groups. Their parents made the unusual (and criticized) decision to prevent their daughters from continuing to play junior tennis in favor of a more balanced lifestyle. In 1991 the entire family moved to Palm Beach Gardens, Florida, with financial support from tennis coach Rick Macci, who assisted in the private training of both sisters. Even with this help, Richard Williams continued as the primary coach for his daughters, while their mother home-schooled them and continued raising them in the Jehovah's Witnesses religion.

Venus turned professional in 1994 at age 14, followed by Serena the next year. Serena would become the first of the sisters (and first African

American woman since **Althea Gibson**) to win a Grand Slam championship, which came at the 1999 U.S. Open, but Venus remained the higher ranking player. In 2000 Venus matched another achievement of Gibson's when she won the Wimbledon tournament in London, England. Although she defeated Serena in the semifinals, the two sisters won the doubles championship at the same event. Over the following years, both sisters would be ranked as the number one women's tennis player in the world. Venus has more professional victories, including the first championship match between sisters in a Grand Slam championship since 1884 (the 2001 U.S. Open in New York City, just days before the September 11 terrorist attacks). Serena has won more major championships, defeating her older sister on some occasions. Venus continued to dominate the Wimbledon championship, winning it five times between 2000 and 2008.

The sisters have also been Olympic gold medalists in doubles at the 2000 Games in Sydney, Australia, where Venus also won the gold medal in women's singles; they returned to win doubles in the 2008 Olympics in Beijing, China. The sisters have always been very supportive of each other, even when in direct professional competition. Their father, Richard, refused to be present on these occasions, although he once predicted that Serena would become the better player overall. He has spoken out in defense of his daughters and claimed early on that their critics were racists and jealous. He has called the Women's Tennis Association a close-knit family that embraces its own. As the sisters rose in the tennis world, he also charged that players directed racial epithets toward them. Whenever the sisters sign endorsements, Richard Williams asks the companies to contribute goods to the black community. Away from the court, both sisters have enjoyed lucrative endorsement relationships with sporting goods companies, and pursed interests in fashion design at the Art Institute of Florida. Their sense of style on and off the court has created tension with the tennis establishment and with some of their oppo-

nents, such as their cornrow hairstyles with beads during their early careers, and creative and colorful tennis outfits, often of their own design. Venus is also chief executive officer of V Starr Interiors. Her firm specializes in interior design, while Serena works in fashion, launching her own designer clothing line called Aneres (the reverse spelling of her name).

Fletcher F. Moon

Sports Writer

Lacy, Samuel Harold (1903–2003)

Born in Mystic, Connecticut, Sam Lacy grew up in Washington, D.C., near the old Griffith Stadium where the Washington Senators baseball team played. His intolerance for segregation and racial inequality in the sports world inspired Sam Lacy, sports editor and columnist for the African American Newspapers, to speak publicly about the world of black athletes in the press. He was a strong proponent of desegregating major league baseball, which brought ire from blacks who successfully predicted that the move would end black baseball. In time, integration did destroy the Negro Leagues; quoted in Frank Litsky's article in the *New York Times,* Lacy said "The Negro Leagues were an institution, but they were the very thing we wanted to get rid of because they were a symbol of segregation." Although barred from many press boxes because of his race, Lacy persevered and chronicled **Jackie Robinson's** entrance into major league baseball in 1947, when he joined the Brooklyn Dodgers and became the league's first black player. He held a close friendship with Robinson, **Jesse Owens, Joe Louis,** and **Arthur Ashe.**

Lacy became the first black member of the Baseball Writer's Association of America in 1948 and was inducted into the writer's wing at the Hall of Fame in 1998. He won the J.G. Taylor Association Award for meritorious contributions to sports journalism in that year as well. Lacy's enduring legacy is his pioneering contribution to civil rights and his service as a resource to many African American journalists whom he mentored.

Jessie Carney Smith

Bibliography

Adams, A. John, and Joan Martin Burke. *Civil Rights: A Current Guide to the People, Organizations, and Events*. New York, NY: Bowker, 1970.

Adams, Frank, with Myles Horton. *Unearthing Seeds of Fire: The Idea of Highlander*. Winston-Salem, NC: John F. Blair, 1975.

Adamson, June N. "Few Black Voices Heard: The Black Community and the Desegregation Crisis in Clinton, Tennessee, 1956," *Tennessee Historical Quarterly* 53 (Spring 1994): 30–41.

African American Almanac. 10th ed. Ed. Brigham Narins. Detroit, MI: Gale, 2008.

Ahmann, Mathew H., ed. *The New Negro*. Notre Dame, IN: Fides Publishers, 1961.

Anderson, James D. *The Education of Blacks in the South, 1860–1935*. Chapel Hill, NC: University of North Carolina Press, 1988.

Anderson, Jervis A. *A. Philip Randolph: A Biographical Portrait*. New York, NY: Harcourt, Brace, Jovanovich, 1986.

Anderson, Karen. "The Little Rock School Desegregation Crisis: Moderation and Social Conflict." *Journal of Southern History* 70 (August 2004): 603–636.

Andrews, William L., Frances Smith Foster, and Trudier Harris, eds. *The Oxford Companion to African American Literature*. New York, NY: Oxford University, Press, 1997.

Appiah, Kwame Anthony, and Henry Louis Gates, eds. *Africana: The Encyclopedia of the African and African American Experience*. 3 vols. New York, NY: Oxford University Press, 2005.

Arsenault, Raymond. *Freedom Riders: 1961 and the Struggle for Racial Justice*. New York, NY: Oxford University Press, 2006.

Auerbach, Jerold S. *Unequal Justice: Lawyers and Social Change in Modern American*. New York, NY: Oxford University Press, 1976.

Baldwin, James. *Notes of a Native Son*. Boston, MA: Beacon Press, 1955.

Baraka, Amiri. "Black Art." *The Black Scholar* 18 (January/February 1987): 23–30.

Bardolph, Richard. *The Negro Vanguard*. Westport, CT: Negro Universities Press, 1959.

Barksdale, Richard, and Kenneth Kinnamon. *Black Writers of America: A Comprehensive Anthology*. New York, NY: Macmillan, 1972.

Bass, Jack, and Jack Nelson. *The Orangeburg Massacre*. Atlanta, GA: Mercer University Press, 1984.

Bass, S. Jonathan. *Blessed Are the Peacemakers: Martin Luther King, Jr., Eight White Religious Leaders and the "Letter from Birmingham Jail."* Baton Rouge, LA: Louisiana State University Press, 2002.

Bates, Daisy. *The Long Shadow of Little Rock.* Fayetteville, AR: University of Arkansas Press, 1998.

Bayot, Jennifer. "Joanne Grant, 74, Dies; Documented Grassroots Efforts on Civil Right." *New York Times,* January 15, 2005.

Beals, Melba Pattillo. *Warriors Don't Cry: A Searing Memoir of the Battle to Integrate Little Rock's Central High.* New York, NY: Washington Square Press, 1994.

Becker, Carl L. *The Declaration of Independence.* New York, NY: Knopf, 1942.

Bell, Derrick. *Silent Covenants: Brown v. Board of Education and the Unfulfilled Hopes for Racial Reform.* New York, NY: Oxford University Press, 2004.

Bennett, Lerone, Jr. *Wade in the Water: Great Moments in Black History.* Chicago, IL: Johnson Publishing Company, 1979.

Bentley, George R. *A History of the Freedmen's Bureau.* Philadelphia, PA: University of Pennsylvania, 1955.

Bernard, Jacqueline. *Journey toward Freedom: The Story of Sojourner Truth.* New York, NY: Norton, 1967.

Berry, Mary Frances. *My Face Is Black Is True: Callie House and the Struggle for Ex-Slave Reparations.* New York, NY: Alfred A. Knopf, 2005.

Beschloss, Michael R. *The Crisis Years: Kennedy and Khrushchev, 1960–1963.* New York, NY: Edward Burlingame Books, 1991.

Bethune, Mary McLeod Bethune, "Last Will and Testament," 1955. In *The Rhetoric of Struggle: Public Address by African American Women.* Ed. Robbie Jean Walker. New York, NY: Garland Publishing, 1992. 365–370.

Birnbaum, Jonathan, and Clarence Taylor. *Civil Rights since 1787: A Reader on the Black Struggle.* New York, NY: New York University Press, 2000.

Bittker, Boris I. *The Case for Black Reparations.* Boston, MA: Beacon Press, 2003.

Black Abolitionists Papers, Vol. 4: *The United States, 1847–1858.* Chapel Hill, NC: University of North Carolina Press, 1991.

Blassingame, John W., ed. *The Frederick Douglass Papers.* 5 vols. New Haven: Yale University Press, 1979–1992.

Blaustein, Albert P., and Robert Zangrando, eds. *Civil Rights and the American Negro: A Documentary History.* New York, NY: Washington Square Press, 1968.

Bloom, Harold, ed. *W.E.B. Du Bois.* Philadelphia, PA: Chelsea House, 2001.

Blumberg, Rhoda Lois. *Civil Rights: The 1960s Freedom Struggle.* Boston, MA: Twayne Publishers, 1984.

Bontemps, Arna, ed. *The Harlem Renaissance Remembered.* New York, NY: Dodd Mead, 1972.

Booker, Simeon. *Susie King Taylor, Civil War Nurse.* New York, NY: McGraw-Hill, 1969.

Boyd, Gerald M. "Rights Movement Leaders Gather in Memory of Their Own." *New York Times,* March 24, 1984, 1, 28.

Boyd, Julian P. *The Declaration of Independence: The Evolution of the Text.* Washington: Library of Congress in association with the Thomas Jefferson Memorial Foundation, 1999.

Bradford, Sarah. *Harriet Tubman: The Moses of Her People.* New York, NY: Corinth Books, 1961.

Bradley, David, and Shelley Fisher Fishkin, eds. *Encyclopedia of Civil Rights in America*. 3 vols. Armonk, NY: Sharpe Reference, 1998.

Branch, Taylor. *Parting the Waters: America in the King Years 1954-63*. New York, NY: Simon and Schuster, 1988.

Brinkley, Douglas. *Rosa Parks*. New York, NY: Penguin, 2000.

Brooks, Gwendolyn. *Report from Part Two*. Chicago, IL: Third World, 1996.

Brown, Elaine. *A Taste of Power: A Black Woman's Story*. New York, NY: Pantheon Books, 1992.

Brown, H. Rap. *Die Nigger Die: A Political Autobiography*. New York, NY: Dial Press, 1969.

Brown, Hallie Q., ed. *Homespun Heroines and Other Women of Distinction*. Xenia, OH: Aldine Pub. Co., 1926.

Brown, Linda. *The Long Walk*. Danville, VA: McCain Publishing, 1998.

Brown, Sterling A. *A Negro Looks at the South*. Ed. John Edgar Tidwell and Mark A. Sanders. New York, NY: Oxford University Press, 2007.

———. "Out of Their Mouths." *Reporting Civil Rights: American Journalism 1941–1963*. 2 vols. New York, NY: Library of America, 2003.

Bruce, Dickson D. *Archibald Grimké: Portrait of a Black Independent*. Baton Rouge, LA: Louisiana State University Press, 1993.

Bryant, Nick. *The Bystander: John F. Kennedy and the Struggle for Black Equality*. New York, NY: Basic Books, 2006.

Buckmaster, Henrietta. *Let My People Go: The Story of the Underground Railroad and the Growth of the Abolitionist Movement*. New York, NY: Harper & Brothers, 1941.

Buni, Andrew. *Robert L. Vann of the Pittsburgh Courier*. Pittsburgh, PA: University of Pittsburgh Press, 1974.

Burchard, Peter. *One Gallant Rush: Robert Gould Shaw and His Brave Black Regiment*. New York, NY: St. Martin's Press, 1965.

Burkett, Randall K. *Black Redemption: Churchmen Speak for the Garvey Movement*.Philadelphia, PA: Temple University Press, 1978.

Burkett, Randall K., and Richard Newman. *Black Apostles*. Boston, MA: G.K. Hall, 1978.

Burner, David, and Thomas R. West. *The Torch Is Passed: The Kennedy Brothers and American Liberalism*. New York, NY: Atheneum, 1984.

Burroughs, Nannie Helen Burroughs. "Unload Your Uncle Toms," *Louisiana Weekly*, December 13, 1933. Cited in *Black Women in White America: A Documentary History*. Ed. Gerda Lerner. New York, NY: Pantheon Books, 1972. 551–53.

Burrows, John H. *The Necessity of Myth: A History of the National Negro Business League, 1900–1945*. Auburn, AL: Hickory Hill Press, 1988.

Burton, Vernon. "Race and Reconstruction: Edgefield County, South Carolina." *Journal of Social History* 12 (1978): 31–56.

Califano, Joseph. *The Triumph and Tragedy of Lyndon Johnson: The White House Years*. New York, NY: Simon & Schuster, 1991.

Campbell, Mary Schmidt. *Tradition and Conflict: Images of a Turbulent Decade, 1963–1973*. Exhibition Catalogue. New York, NY: Studio Museum of Harlem, 1985.

Campbell, Stanley W. *The Slave Catchers: Enforcement of the Fugitive Slave Law, 1850–1860*. Chapel Hill, NC: University of North Carolina Press, 1970.

Cantarow, Ellen, and Susan O'Mally. *Moving the Mountain: Women Working for Social Change.* Old Westbury, NY: Feminist Press, 1980.

Carmichael, Stokely, and Charles Hamilton. *Black Power: The Politics of Liberation in America.* New York, NY: Random House, 1967.

Carmichael, Stokely, with Eklwueme Michael Thelwell. *Ready for Revolution: The Life and Struggles of Stokely Carmichael [Kwame Ture].* New York, NY: Scribner, 2003.

Carson, Clayborne. *Autobiography of Martin Luther King, Jr.* New York, NY: Intellectual Properties Management in association with Warner Books, 1998.

———. *Civil Rights Chronicle: The African-American Struggle for Freedom.* Lincolnwood, IL: Legacy Publishing, 2003.

———. *In Struggle: SNCC and the Black Awakening of the 1960s.* Cambridge, MA: Harvard University Press, 1995.

———, David Garrow, Gerald Gill, Vincent Harding, and Darlene Clark Hine. *The Eyes on the Prize Civil Rights Reader: Documents, Speeches, and Firsthand Accounts from the Black Freedom Struggle, 1954–1990.* New York, NY: Penguin Books, 1991.

———, Emma J. Lapsansky-Werner, and Gary B. Nash. *The Struggle for Freedom: A History of African Americans.* New York, NY: Pearson/Longman, 2007.

———, Susan Carson, Adrienne Clay, Virginia Shadron, Kieran Taylor, eds., *The Papers of Martin Luther King, Jr.,: Birth of a New Age, December 1955–December 1956.* Berkeley: University of California Press, 2000.

———, Stewart Burns, Susan Carson, Dana Powell, and Peter Holloran, eds. *The Papers of Martin Luther King, Jr.: Birth of a New Age, December 1955–1956.* 6 vols. Berkeley: University of California Press, 1997.

Chafe, William H. *Civilities and Civil Rights: Greensboro, North Carolina, and the Black Struggle for Freedom.* New York, NY: Oxford University Press, 1981.

Charles, Ray Charles, with David Ritz, *Brother Ray: Ray Charles' Own Story.* New York, NY: Dial Press, 1992.

Cheek, William, and Aimee Lee Cheek. *John Mercer Langston and the Fight for Black Freedom, 1829-65.* Urbana, IL: University of Illinois Press, 1989.

Christian, James Dublin. "Newspapers and the Orangeburg Massacre: Framing a Deadly Encounter." Columbia, SC: University of South Carolina, 2004.

Claiborne, Jack. *The Charlotte Observer: Its Time and Place, 1869–1986.* Chapel Hill, NC: University of North Carolina Press, 1986.

Clarke, Septima. Interview with Grace Jordan McFadden, February 1, 1975. Cited in Vicki L. Crawford, Jacqueline Anne Rouse, and Barbara Woods, eds., *Women in the Civil Rights Movement.* Brooklyn: Carlson Publishing, 1990.

Cleaver, Eldridge. *Soul on Ice.* New York, NY: McGraw-Hill, 1968.

Cleaver, Kathleen, and George Katsiaficas, eds. *Liberation, Imagination, and the Black Panther Party: A New Look at the Panther's Legacy.* New York, NY: Routledge, 2001.

Clegg, Claude Andrew. *An Original Man: The Life and Times of Elijah Muhammad.* New York, NY: St. Martin's Press, 1998.

Clinton, Catherine. *Harriet Tubman: The Road to Freedom.* New York, NY: Little, Brown, 2004.

"Closed Doors." Speech Delivered by Mary McLeod Bethune, ca. 1936, typescript, Bethune Cookman University Archives, Daytona Beach, FL.

Collins, David. *Not Only Dreamers: The Story of Martin Luther King, Sr. and Martin Luther King, Jr.* Elgin, IL.: Brethren Press, 1986.

Conrad, Carl. *Harriet Tubman.* New York, NY: International Publishes, 1943.

Cooper, Anna J. *A Voice from the South: By a Black Woman from the South.* Xenia, OH: Aldine Publishing House, 1892.

Couto, Richard. *Lifting the Veil: A Political Struggle for Emancipation.* Knoxville, TN: University of Tennessee Press, 1993.

Craft, William, and Ellen Craft. *Running a Thousand Miles for Freedom.* London: William Tweedie, 1860.

Crawford, Vicki, Jacqueline Anne Rouse, and Barbara Woods, eds. *Women in the Civil Rights Movement: Trailblazers & Torchbearers, 1941–1965.* Bloomington, IN: Indiana University Press, 1993.

Cronin, Edmund David. *Black Moses: The Story of Marcus Garvey and the Universal Negro Improvement Association.* Madison, WI: University of Wisconsin Press, 1969.

Cross, George Lynn. *Blacks in White Colleges: Oklahoma's Landmark Cases.* Norman, OK: University of Oklahoma Press, 1975.

Crouchett, Lawrence. "Early Black Studies Movement." *Journal of Black Studies* 2 (December 1971): 189–200.

Crouthamel, James L. "The Springfield Race Riot of 1908." *Journal of Negro History* 45 (July 1960): 164–181.

Dallek, Robert. *Flawed Giant: Lyndon B. Johnson, 1960–1973.* New York, NY: Oxford University Press, 1998.

———. *Lone Star Rising: Lyndon Johnson and His Times, 1908–1960.* New York, NY: Oxford University Press, 1991.

Dao, James. "40 Years Later, Civil Rights Makes Page One." *New York Times,* July 13, 2004.

Davidson, James West. *They Say: Ida B. Wells and the Reconstruction of Race.* New York, NY: Oxford University Press, 2007.

Davis, Arthur P. Davis, and J. Saunders Redding, eds. *Cavalcade: Negro American Writing from 1760 to the Present.* Boston, MA: Houghton Mifflin, 1971.

Davis, Leroy. *A Clashing of the Soul: John Hope and the Dilemma of African American Leadership and Black Leadership in the Early Twentieth Century.* Athens, GA: University of Georgia Press, 1998.

Davis, William C. *Look Away! A History of the Confederate States of America.* New York, NY: Free Press, 2002.

Delany, Martin R. *Principia of Ethnology: Origin of Races and Color.* Philadelphia, PA: Harper & Brother, 1879.

Denby, Charles. *Indignant Heart: A Black Worker's Journal.* London: Pluton Press, 1952.

Dennis, Michael. *Luther P. Jackson and a Life for Civil Rights.* Gainesville, FL: University Press of Florida, 2004.

DeVeaux, Alexis. "Bernice Reagan." *Essence* 11 (June 1980): 92–93, 142–150.

Dickerson, Dennis C. *Militant Mediator: Whitney M. Young, Jr.* Lexington, KY: University Press of Kentucky, 1998.

Dierenfield, Bruce J. *The Civil Rights Movement.* New York, NY: Longman Publishers, 2004.

Dittmer, John. *Local People: The Struggle for Civil Rights in Mississippi.* Champaign, IL: University of Illinois Press, 1994.

Douglass, Frederick. *Narrative of the Life of Frederick Douglass, An American Slave.* Boston, MA: Published at the Anti-Slavery Office, 1895.

Doyle, Don H. *Nashville since the 1920s.* Knoxville, TN: University of Tennessee Press, 1985.

Du Bois, W.E.B. *The Autobiography of W. E. B. DuBois: A Soliloquy on Viewing My Life from the Last Decade of Its First Century.* New York, NY: Oxford University Press, 2007.

————. *The Philadelphia Negro: A Social Study.* Philadelphia, PA: Published by the University, 1899.

————. *The Souls of Black Folk: Essays and Sketches.* 21st ed. Chicago, IL: McClurg, 1937.

————. "William Monroe Trotter." [Tribute], Du Bois Papers, Franklin Library, Fisk University.

Duberman, Martin Bauml. *Paul Robeson.* New York, NY: Knopf, 1988.

Due, Tananarive, and Patricia Stephens Due. *Freedom in the Family: A Mother-Daughter Memoir of the Fight for Civil Rights.* New York, NY: Ballantine Books, 2003.

Duncan, Russell. *Where Death and Glory Meet: Colonel Robert Gould Shaw and the 54th Massachusetts Infantry.* Athens, GA: University of Georgia Press, 1999.

Dunnigan, Alice A. *The Fascinating Story of Black Kentukians: Their Heritage and Tradition.* Washington, DC: Associated Publishers, 1982.

Duster, Alfreda M., ed. *Crusade for Justice: The Autobiography of Ida B. Wells.* Chicago, IL: University of Chicago Press, 1970.

Dyson, Walter. *Howard University, The Capstone of Negro Education, A History: 1867–1940.* Washington, DC: The Graduate School, Howard University, 1941.

Egerton, John. "16 Little 'Pioneers' Paved Way." Tennessean, September 9, 2007.

————. *Speak Now against the Day: The Generation before the Civil Rights Movement in the South.* New York, NY: Knopf, 1994.

Eicher, David J. *The Longest Night: A Military History of the Civil War.* New York, NY: Simon & Schuster, 2001.

Eick, Gretchen Cassel. *Dissent in Wichita: The Civil Rights Movement in the Midwest, 1954–1972.* Urbana, IL: University of Illinois Press, 2007.

Ely, James W. *The Crisis of Conservative Virginia: The Byrd Organization and the Politics of Massive Resistance.* Knoxville, TN: University of Tennessee Press, 1976.

Emilio, Luis F. *A Brave Black Regiment: The History of the Fifty-fourth Regiment of Massachusetts Volunteer Infantry, 1863–1865.* 3rd edition. Salem, NH: Ayer Co. Publishers, 1990.

Evans, Rowland, and Robert Novak, *Lyndon B. Johnson: The Exercise of Power.* New York, NY: New American Library, 1966.

Fairclough, Adam. *To Redeem the Soul of America: The Southern Christian Leadership Conference and Martin Luther King, Jr.* Athens, GA: University of Georgia Press, 1987.

Farmer, James. *Lay Bare the Heart: An Autobiography of the Civil Rights Movement.* New York, NY: Arbor House, 1985.

Fehrenbacher, Don E. *The Slaveholding Republic: An Account of the United States Government's Relations to Slavery.* New York, NY: Oxford University Press, 2002.

Field, Ron. *Civil Rights in America, 1865–1980*. Cambridge: Cambridge University Press, 2002.

Fine, Elsa Honig. *The Afro-American Artist: A Search for Identity*. New York, NY: Harcourt Brace Jovanovich, 1973.

"Fisk President Says Sit-Ins Aroused Sympathy." *Nashville Banner,* April 20,1960.

Fleming, Cynthia. *Soon We Will Not Cry: The Liberation of Ruby Doris Smith Robinson*. Lanham: Rowman and Littlefield, 1998.

Foner, Eric. *Free Soil, Free Labor, Free Men: The Ideology of the Republican Party before the Civil War*. New York, NY: Oxford University Press, 1995.

———. *Reconstruction: America's Unfinished Revolution, 1863–1877*. New York, NY: Harper & Row, 1988.

Foner, Philip S., and Robert James Branham, eds. *Lift Every Voice: African American Oratory 1787–1900*. Tuscaloosa: University of Alabama Press, 1998.

———, ed. *The Life and Writings of Frederick Douglass*. New York, NY: International Publishers, 1975.

Ford, Nick Aaron. *Black Studies: Threat or Challenge*. Port Washington, NY: Kennikat Press, 1973.

Foster, Frances Smith, ed. *A Brighter Coming Day: A Frances Ellen Watkins Harper Reader*. New York, NY: Feminist Press, 1990.

Fox, Stephen R. *The Guardian of Boston, MA: William Monroe Trotter*. New York, NY: Atheneum, 1970.

Frady, Marshall. *Jesse: The Life and Pilgrimage of Jesse Jackson*. New York, NY: Simon & Schuster Paperbacks, 2006.

Francis, Charles E. *The Tuskegee Airmen*. Boston, MA: Branden Publishing Co., 1988.

Franklin, Ben A. "5,000 Open Poor People's Campaign in Washington," *New York Times,* May 13, 1968.

Franklin, John Hope. "The Enforcement of the Civil Rights Act of 1875." In *Race and History: Selected Essays 1938–1968*. Baton Rouge, LA: Louisiana State University Press, 1989.

———, and Alfred A. Moss, Jr. *From Slavery to Freedom: A History of African Americans*. 8th ed. New York, NY: McGraw Hill, 2000.

———, and August Meier, eds. *Black Leaders of the Twentieth Century*. Urbana, IL: University of Illinois Press, 1982.

———, and Loren Schweninger, *Runaway Slaves: Rebels on the Plantation, 1790–1860*. New York, NY: Oxford University Press, 1999.

Gabbin, Joanne V., ed., *Furious Flowering of African American Poetry*. Charlottesville: University of Virginia Press, 1999.

Gardell, Mattias. *In the Name of Elijah Mohammed: Louis Farrakhan and the Nation of Islam*. Durham: Duke University Press, 1996.

Garfinkel, Herbert. *When Negroes March*. New York, NY: Atheneum, 1969.

Garraty, John A., and Mark C. Carnes, eds. *American National Biography*. 24 vols. New York, NY: Oxford University Press, 1999.

Garrow, David, ed., *The Montgomery Bus Boycott and the Women Who Started It: The Memoir of Jo Ann Gibson Robinson*. Knoxville, TN: University of Tennessee Press, 1987.

———. *Bearing the Cross: Martin Luther King, Jr., and the Southern Christian Leadership Conference*. New York, NY: Morrow, 1986.

Garvey, Amy Jacques. *Garvey and Garveyism*. New York, NY: Octagon Books, 1978.

Garvey, Amy Jacques, ed. *Philosophy and Opinions of Marcus Garvey*. Vol. 1. New York, NY: Arno Press, 1968.

Gates, Henry Louis, Jr., and Cornel West. *The African-American Century: How Black Americans Have Shaped Our Country*. New York, NY: The Free Press, 2000.

———, and Evelyn Brooks Higginbotham, eds. *African American Lives*. 8 vols. New York, NY: Oxford University Press, 2004.

———, and Nellie Y. McKay, eds. "The Black Arts Movement." In *The Norton Anthology of African American Literature*. 2nd ed. New York, NY: W.W. Norton Company, 2004: 1837–1844.

Gibbs, Mifflin Wistar. *Shadow and Light*. 1902 Reprint. Lincoln, NE: University of Nebraska Press, 1995.

Giglio, James N. *The Presidency of John F. Kennedy*. Lawrence, KS: University Press of Kansas, 1991.

Gilpin, Patrick J., and Marybeth Gasman, *Charles S. Johnson: Leadership behind the Veil in the Age of Jim Crow*. Albany, NY: State University of New York Press, 2003.

Glen, John M. *Highlander: No Ordinary School 1932–1962*. Lexington, KY: University Press of Kentucky, 1988, 2nd ed., Knoxville, TN: University of Tennessee Press, 1996.

Glisson, Susan M., ed. *The Human Tradition in the Civil Rights Movement*. New York, NY: Rowman and Littlefield, 2006.

Goldfield, David R. *Black, White, and Southern: Race Relations and Southern Culture, 1940 to the Present*. Baton Rouge, LA: Louisiana State University Press, 1990.

Goodwin, Doris Kearns. *Lyndon Johnson and the American Dream*. New York, NY: Harper & Row, 1976.

Gordon, Ann D., Bettye Collier-Thomas, John H. Bracey, and others, eds. *African American Women and the Vote, 1837–1965*. Amherst, MA: University of Massachusetts Press, 1997.

Graham, Hugh Davis. *The Civil Rights Era: Origins and Development of National Policy, 1960–1972*. New York, NY: Oxford University Press, 1990.

Gray, Fred. *Bus Ride to Justice: Changing the System by the System. The Life and Works of Fred D. Gray*. Montgomery, AL: Black Belt Press, 1995.

Green, Ben. *Before His Time: The Untold Story of Harry T. Moore, America's First Civil Rights Martyr*. New York, NY: The Free Press, 1999.

Greenberg, Cheryl Lynn. *Or Does It Explode? Black Harlem in the Great Depression*.New York, NY: Oxford University Press, 1991.

Greene, Robert Ewell. *Black Defenders of America, 1775–1973*. Chicago, IL: Johnson Publishing Co., 1974.

Grofman, Bernard, ed. *Legacies of the 1964 Civil Rights Act*. Charlottesville, VA: University of Virginia Press, 2000.

Guy-Sheftall, Beverly. *Daughters of Sorrow: Attitudes toward Black Women, 1880–1920*. New York, NY: Carlson, 1990.

Hair, William Ivy. *Carnival of Fury: Robert Charles and the New Orleans Race Riot of 1900*. Baton Rouge, LA: Louisiana State University Press, 1976.

Halberstam, David. *The Children*. New York, Random House, 1998.

Hamilton, Charles V. *The Struggle for Political Equality*. New York, NY: National Urban League, 1976.

Hampton, Charles. *Adam Clayton Powell, Jr., the Political Biography of a Dilemma.* New York, Macmillan, 1991.

Hampton, Henry, and Steve Fayer, with Sarah Flynn. *Voices of Freedom: An Oral History of the Civil Rights Movement from the 1950s through the 1980s.* New York, NY: Bantam Books, 1990.

Hanley, Sally. *A. Philip Randolph.* New York, NY: Chelsea House, 1989.

Harding, Vincent. *There Is a River: The Black Struggle for Freedom in America.* New York, NY: Harcourt Brace, 1981.

Harrington, Michael. *The Other Americans: Poverty in the United States.* New York, NY: Simon and Schuster, 1962.

Harris, Hamil R. "A Million More." *Crisis* 112 (September/October 2005): 22–25.

———. "Thousands Gather in D.C. for Million More Movement." *Washington Post,* October 15, 2005.

Harris, Jacqueline L. *History and Achievement of the NAACP.* New York, NY: F. Watts, 1992.

Harris, Ron. "Dr. Joseph Lowery: The Man Who's Reinventing SCLC." *Ebony* 35 (November 1979): 53–56.

Hattaway, Herman, and Archer Jones. *How the North Won: A Military History of the Civil War.* Urbana, IL: University of Illinois Press, 1983.

Hedgeman, Anna Arnold. *The Trumpet Sounds.* New York, NY: Holt, Rinehart and Winston, 1964.

Height, Dorothy. *Open Wide the Freedom Gates: A Memoir.* New York, NY: Public Affairs, 2003.

Hill, Oliver W., Sr. *The Big Bang: Brown v. Board of Education, The Autobiography of Oliver W. Hill, Sr.,* ed. Jonathan K. Stubbs. Winter Park, FL: Four-G Publishers, 2000.

Hill, Robert, ed. *The Marcus Garvey and Universal Negro Improvement Association Papers.* Berkeley, CA: University of California Press, 1983–1995.

Hilliard, David, and Donald Weise, eds. *The Huey P. Newton Reader.* New York, NY: Seven Stories Press, 2002.

Hine, Darlene Clark, ed. *Black Women in American: An Historical Encyclopedia.* 2 vols. Brooklyn: Carlson Publishing, 1993.

———, William C. Hine, and Stanley Harrold. *African Americans: A Concise History.* Upper Saddle River, NJ: Prentice Hall, 2004.

Hogan, Lawrence D. *Black National News Service: The Associated Negro Press and Claude Barnett, 1919–1945.* Rutherford, NJ: Fairleigh Dickinson University Press, 1984.

Hogan, Wesley C. *Many Minds, One Heart: SNCC's Dream for a New America.* Chapel Hill, NC: University Press of North Carolina, 2007.

Holmes, William F. "The Arkansas Cotton Pickers Strike of 1891 and the Demise of he Colored Farmers' Alliance." *Arkansas Historical Quarterly* 32 (1973): 107–19.

Holsey, Albon L. "The CMA Stores Face the Chains." *Opportunity* 7 (July 1919): 210–13.

Holway, John B. *Red Tails Black Wings: The Men of America's Black Air Force.* Las Cruces, NM: Yucca Tree Press, 1997.

Honey, Michael K. *Going Down Jericho Road: The Memphis Strike, Martin Luther King's Last Campaign.* New York, NY: Norton and Co., 2007.

Hooks, Benjamin, with Jerry Guess. *The March for Civil Rights: The Benjamin Hooks Story.* Chicago, IL: American Bar Association, 2004.

Horton, Myles, with Judith Kohl and Herbert Kohl. *The Long Haul: An Autobiography*. New York, NY: Doubleday Press. 1990.

Houston, Helen, Tyree J, Miller, et al., eds., *Through a Glass Darkly*. Raleigh, NC: Contemporary Publishing Co., 1979.

"How Effective is Social Protest Art? (Civil Rights)." In Jeanne Siegel, *Artworks: Discourse on the 60s and 70s*. Ann Arbor, MI: UMI Research Press, 1985, 84–95.

Huggins, Nathan Irvin, and Oscar Handlin. *Slave and Citizen: The Life of Frederick Douglass*. Boston, MA: Little, Brown, 1980.

Hunter, Desiree. "Civil Rights Activist Who Joined in Bus Boycott Dies." *Tennessean,* February 24, 2008.

Hunter-Gault, Charlayne. *In My Place*. New York, NY: Farrar, Straus & Giroux, 1992.

Jack, Robert L. *A History of the National Association for the Advancement of Colored People*. Boston, MA: Meador Pub. Co., 1943.

Jackson, Blyden. *A History of Afro-American Literature,* Volume I: *The Long Beginning, 1746–1895*. Baton Rouge, LA: Louisiana State University Press, 1989.

Jackson, Donald W., and James W. Riddlesperger, Jr. "The Eisenhower Administration and the 1957 Civil Rights Act." In *Reexamining the Eisenhower Presidency*. Ed. Shirley Anne Warshaw. Westport, CT: Greenwood Press, 1993.

Jackson, Jesse L. *Straight from the Heart*. Eds. Roger D. Hatch and Frank E, Watkins. Philadelphia, PA: Fortress Press, 1987.

Jacoway, Elizabeth, and C. Fred Williams, eds. *Understanding the Little Rock Crisis: An Exercise in Remembrance and Reconciliation*. Fayetteville, AR: University of Arkansas Press, 1999.

———, and David R. Colburn, eds. *Southern Businessmen and Desegregation*. Baton Rouge, LA: Louisiana State University Press, 1982.

John, Alan. *Dialectics of Black Freedom Struggles*. Chicago, IL: News and Letters, 2003.

Johnson, James Weldon. *Along this Way: The Autobiography of James Weldon Johnson*. New York, NY: Viking Press, 1934.

Jones, Charles E., ed. *The Black Panther Party Reconsidered*. Baltimore, MD: Black Classic Press, 1998.

Jones, Leroi Jones. *Black Magic Poetry, 1961–1967*. Indianapolis, IN: Bobbs-Merrill Co., 1969.

Jordan, Barbara. *Barbara Jordan: A Self-Portrait*. New York, NY: Doubleday, 1979.

Jordan, Winthrop D. *The White Man's Burden: Historical Origins of Racism in the United States*. New York, NY: Oxford University Press, 1974.

Joseph, Peniel E. *Waiting 'Til the Midnight Hour: A Narrative History of Black Power in America*. New York, NY: Henry Holt, 2006.

Karenga, Maulana. *Introduction to Black Studies*. Los Angeles, CA: University of Sankore Press, 1993.

Kellner, Bruce. *The Harlem Renaissance: A Historical Dictionary of the Era*. Westport, CT: Greenwood Press, 1984.

Kellogg, Charles Flint. *NAACP: A History of the National Association for the Advancement of Colored People,* Vol. I. Baltimore, MD: Johns Hopkins Press, 1967.

Kennedy, John F. *Profiles in Courage*. New York, NY: Harper, 1955.

Kilson, Martin. "Political Scientists and the Activist-Technocrat Dichotomy: the Case of John Aubrey Davis." In *African American Perspectives on Political Science*. Ed. Wilbur C. Rich. Philadelphia, PA: Temple University Press, 2007.

King, Coretta Scott. *My Life with Martin Luther King, Jr.* New York, NY: Holt, Rinehart and Winston, 1969.

King, Martin Luther, Jr. *Strength to Love.* New York, NY: Harper & Row, 1963.

———. *Stride Toward Freedom.* San Francisco, CA: Harper, 1958.

———. *A Testament of Hope: The Essential Writings of Martin Luther King, Jr.* Ed. James Melvin Was. San Francisco, CA: Harper, 1986.

———. *Why We Can't Wait.* New York, NY: Penguin, 2000.

———, Sr., *Daddy King: An Autobiography.* New York, NY: Morrow, 1980.

Kirk, John A. *Beyond Little Rock: The Origins and Legacies of the Central High Crisis.* Fayetteville, AR: University of Arkansas Press, 2007.

Klarman, Michael J. *From Jim Crow to Civil Rights: The Supreme Court and the Struggle for Racial Equality.* New York, NY: Oxford University Press, 2004.

Kluger, Richard. *Simple Justice: The History of Brown v. Board of Education and Black America's Struggle for Equality.* New York, NY: Vintage, 1977.

Kohl, Herbert. *She Would Not Be Moved: How We Tell the Story of Rosa Parks and the Montgomery Bus Boycott.* New York, NY: New Press, 2005.

Kurland, Philip B. ed. *The Supreme Court and the Judicial Function.* Chicago, IL: University of Chicago Press, 1975.

Landess, Thomas, and Richard Quinn. *The Politics of Race.* Ottawa, IL: Jameson Books, 1985.

Lanker, Brian. *I Dream a World: Portraits of Black Women Who Changed America.* New York, NY: Stewart, Tabori & Chang, 1999.

Larson, Kate Clifford. *Bound for the Promised Land: Harriet Tubman, Portrait of an American Hero.* New York, NY: Ballentine, 2004.

Lawson, Steven F. *Civil Rights Crossroads: Nation, Community, and the Black Freedom Struggle.* Lexington, KY: University of Kentucky Press, 2003.

———, and Charles Payne. *Debating the Civil Rights Movement, 1945–1968.* New York, NY: Rowman and Littlefield, 1998.

Leckie, William H. *The Buffalo Soldiers: A Narrative of the Negro Calvary in the West.* Norman, OK: University of Oklahoma Press, 1976.

Lee, Chana Kai. *For Freedom's Sake: The Life of Fannie Lou Hamer.* Urbana, IL: University of Illinois Press, 1999.

Lee, J. Kenneth. Interview with Eugene E. Pfaff, Jr., Oral History Collection, Greensboro (NC) Public Library.

———. Interview with Jessie Carney Smith, August 5, 2005.

Lefever, Harry G. *Undaunted by the Flight: Spelman College and the Civil Rights Movement.* Macon, GA: Mercer University Press, 2005.

Leidholdt, Alex. *Standing Before the Shouting Mob: Lenior Chambers and Virginia's Massive Resistance to Public School Integration.* Tuscaloosa, AL: University of Alabama Press, 2008.

Lerner, Gerda. *Black Women in White America: A Documentary History.* New York, NY: Free Press, 1984.

Levine, Robert S. *Martin Delany, Frederick Douglass, and the Politics of Representative Identity*. Chapel Hill, NC: University of North Carolina Press, 1997.

Lewis, David L. *King: A Critical Biography*. Urbana, IL: University of Illinois Press, 1978.

———. *W.E.B. Du Bois: Biography of a Race, 1868–1919*. New York, NY: Henry Holt, 1993.

———. *W.E.B. Du Bois: Fight for Equality and the American Century, 1919–1963*. New York, NY: Henry Holt, 2000.

———. *When Harlem Was in Vogue*. New York, NY: Knopf, 1981.

Lewis, John, with Michael D'Orso. *Walking with the Wind: A Memoir of the Movement*. New York, NY: Simon and Schuster, 1998.

Lincoln, C. Eric. *The Black Muslims in America*. Boston, MA: Beacon Press, 1961.

———, and Lawrence H. Mamiya. *The Black Church in the African American Experience*. Durham, NC: Duke University Press, 1990.

Litsky, Frank. "Sam Lacy, 99, Sportswriter Who Fought Against Racism." *New York Times,* May 11, 2003.

Litwack, Leon F. *Been in the Storm So Long: The Aftermath of Slavery*. New York, NY: Knopf, 1979.

———, and August Meier. *Black Leaders of the Nineteenth Century*. Urbana, IL: University of Illinois, 1988.

Locke, Alain, ed. *The New Negro*. New York, NY: Atheneum, 1980.

Loewenberg, Bert James, and Ruth Bogin, eds. *Black Women in Nineteenth-Century American Life: Their Words, Their Thoughts, Their Feelings*. University Park, PA: Pennsylvania State University Press, 1976.

Lofgren, Charles A. *The Plessy Case: A Legal-Historical Interpretation*. New York, NY: Oxford University Press, 1987.

Logan, Rayford W. *Howard University: The First Hundred Years 1867–1967*. New York, NY: New York University Press, 1969.

———, and Michael R. Winston, eds. *Dictionary of American Negro Biography*. New York, NY: Norton, 1983.

Lovett, Bobby L. "Memphis Race Riot of 1866." *Tennessee Encyclopedia of History and Culture*. Nashville, TN: Tennessee Historical Society/Rutledge Hill Press, 1998.

Lovett, Bobby L. *The Civil Rights Movement in Tennessee: A Narrative History*. Knoxville, TN: University of Tennessee, 2005.

———, and Linda T. Wynn. *Profiles of African Americans in Tennessee History*. Nashville, TN: Local Conference on African American Culture and History, 1996.

Lowery, Charles D., and John F. Marsalek, eds. *Greenwood Encyclopedia of African American Civil Rights*. 2 vols. 2nd ed. Westport, CT: Greenwood Press, 2003.

Lydon, Michael. *Ray Charles: Man and Music*. New York, NY: Riverhead, 2004.

Manis, Andrew F. *A Fire You Can't Put Out: The Civil Rights Life of Birmingham's Reverend Fred Shuttlesworth*. Tuscaloosa: University of Alabama Press, 1999.

Marcuse, Laurence R. "The Adams Case: A Hollow Victory." *Peabody Journal of Education* 59 (October, 1981): 37–42.

Marteena, Constance Hill. *The Lengthening Shadow of a Woman: A Biography of Charlotte Hawkins Brown*. Hicksville, NY: Exposition Press, 1977.

Mason, Gilbert D., and James Patterson Smith. *Beaches, Blood, and Ballots: A Black Doctor's Civil Rights Struggle.* Jackson, Ms: University Press of Mississippi, 2000.

Mays, Benjamin E. *Seeking to be Christian in Race Relations.* New York, NY: Friendship Press, 1957.

McAdam, Doug. *Freedom Summer.* New York, NY: Oxford University Press, 1988.

McCardell, Paul. "Clarence M. Mitchell, Jr." *Baltimore Sun.* February 9, 2007.

McKinney, Richard I., *Mordecai: The Man and His Message: The Story of Mordecai Wyatt Johnson.* Washington, D.C.: Howard University Press, 1997.

McKissack, Pat. *Young, Black, and Determined: A Biography of Lorraine Hansberry.* New York, NY: Holiday House, 1998.

McKnight, Gerald D. *The Last Crusade: Martin Luther King Jr., the FBI, and the Poor People's Campaign.* Boulder, CO: Westview Press, 1998.

McNeil, Genna Rae. *Groundwork: Charles Hamilton Houston and the Struggle for Civil Rights.* Philadelphia, PA: University of Pennsylvania Press, 1983.

McWhorter, Diane. *Carry Me Home: Birmingham, Alabama, the Climactic Battle of the Civil Rights Revolution.* New York, NY: Simon & Schuster, 2001.

Meier, August, and Elliott Rudwick. "The Boycott Movement against Jim Crow Streetcars in the South 1900–1906." *Journal of American History* 55 (March 1969): 756–775.

———. *CORE: A Study in the Civil Rights Movement, 1942–1968.* New York, NY: Oxford University Press, 1973.

Metcalf, George R. *Fair Housing Comes of Age.* Westport, CT: Greenwood Press, 1988.

Mfume, Kwesi, and Ronald Stodghill. *No Free Ride: From the Mean Streets to the Mainstream.* New York, NY: One World, 1996.

Miller, William Robert. *Martin Luther King, Jr.: His Life, Martyrdom, and Meaning for the World.* New York, NY: Weybright and Talley, 1968.

Mills, Kay. *This Little Light of Mine: The Life of Fannie Lou Hamer.* New York, NY: Plume, 1993.

Moore, Jesse Thomas, Jr. *A Search for Equality: The National Urban League, 1910–1961.* University Park, PA: Pennsylvania State University Press, 1981.

Morris, Aldon. "Black Southern Student Sit-In Movement: An Analysis of Internal Organization." *American Sociological Review* 46 (1981): 744–767.

———. *The Origins of the Civil Rights Movement: Black Communities Organizing for Change.* New York, NY: Free Press, 1984.

Mosnier, L. Joseph. "Crafting Law in the Second Reconstruction: Julius Chambers, the NAACP Legal Defense Fund, and Title VII." Chapel Hill, NC: University of North Carolina, 2005.

Muhammad, Elijah. *Message to the Blackman in America.* Chicago, IL: Muhamad Mosque of Islam No. 2, 1965.

Murray, Pauli. *Proud Shoes: The Story of an America Family.* New York, NY: Harper and Row, 1956.

Nash, Diane. "Inside the Sit-ins and Freedom Rides: Testimony of a Southern Student." In Mathew H. Ahmann, ed. *The New Negro.* New York, NY: Biblio and Tannen, 1969.

Navasky, Victor S. *Kennedy Justice.* New York, NY: Atheneum, 1972.

Neal, Larry. *Visions of a Liberated Future: Black Arts Movement Writings.* New York, NY: Thunder's Mouth Press, 1989.

"The Negro Silent Parade." *The Crisis* 14 (September 1917): 241.

Nell, William C. *The Colored Patriots of the American Revolution,* 1855. reprint. New York, NY: Arno Press and the *New York Times,* 1968.

Niven, David *The Politics of Injustice: The Kennedys, the Freedom Rides, and the Electoral Consequences of a Moral Compromise.* Knoxville, TN: University of Tennessee Press, 2003.

Nojeim, Michael J. *Gandhi and King: The Power of Nonviolent Resistance.* Westport, CT: Praeger Publishers, 2004.

Oak, Vishnu V. *The Negro's Adventure in General Business.* 2 vols. Yellow Springs, OH: Printed for the author by The Antioch Press, 1949.

Ogbar, Jeffrey O.G. *Black Power: Radical Politics and African American Identity.* Baltimore, MD: Johns Hopkins University Press, 2004.

Ogletree, Charles J., Jr. *All Deliberate Speed: Reflections on the First Half Century of Brown v. Board of Education.* New York, NY: Norton, 2004.

Olson, Lynn. *Freedom's Daughters: The Unsung Heroines of the Civil Rights Movement from 1830 to 1970.* New York, NY: Scribner's, 2001.

O'Neill, Daniel J., comp. and ed. *Speeches by Black Americans.* Encino, CA: Dickenson Pub. Co., 1971.

"Oration." Delivered by Prof. J. M. Langston, of Howard University, Washington, D.C., at the 15th Amendment Celebration held in Oberlin, OH, May 14th, 1874.

Oshinsky, David M. *Worse than Slavery: Parchman Farm and the Ordeal of Jim Crow Justice.* New York, NY: The Free Press, 1996.

Ovington, Mary White. *Portraits in Color.* New York, NY: Viking, 1927.

Painter, Nell Irvin. *Creating Black Americans: African-American History and Its Meanings, 1619 to the Present.* New York, NY: Oxford University Press, 2006.

———. *Sojourner Truth: A Life, a Symbol.* New York, NY: Norton, 1996.

Palmer, Colin A. *Passageways: An Interpretive History of Black America.* Vol. 1: *1619–1863.* New York, NY: Harcourt Brace College Publishers, 1988.

Parks, Rosa. "Tired of Giving In." The Launching of the Montgomery Bus Boycott." In Bettye Collier-Thomas, and V. P. Franklin, eds., *Sisters in the Struggle: African American Women in the Civil Rights—Black Power Movement.* New York, NY: New York University Press, 2001.

Parks, Rosa, with Gregory J. Reed, *Quiet Strength: The Faith, the Hope, and the Heart of a Woman Who Changed a Nation,* Grand Rapids, MI: Zondervan Publishing House, 1994.

Parris, Guichard, and Lester Brooks. *Blacks in the City: A History of the National Urban League.* Boston, MA: Little, Brown, 1971.

Payne, Charles M. *I've Got the Light of Freedom: The Organizing Tradition and the Mississippi Freedom Struggle.* Berkley, CA: University of California Press, 1995.

Peck, James. *Freedom Ride.* New York, NY: Simon and Schuster, 1962.

Perry, Mark. *Lift Up Thy Voice: The Grimké Family's Journey from Slaveholders to Civil Rights Leaders.* New York, NY: Viking, 2001.

Perry, Regina. *Free within Ourselves: African American Artists in the Collection of the National Museum of American Art.* New York, NY: Pomegranate Artbooks, 1992.

Player, Willa. Interview with Eugene Pfaff, December 3, 1979. "Greensboro Voices, Voicing Observations in Civil Rights and Equality Struggles," University of North Carolina at

Greensboro, http://library.uncg.edu/depts/archives/civilrights/detail-ivasp?iv=115, accessed 30 November 2007.

Player, Willa. Interview with Joan Curl Elliott, 21 January 1991. Cited in *Notable Black American Women*. ed. Jessie Carney Smith. Detroit, MI: Gale Research, 1992.

Pollack, Randi M. "Mrs. Mitchell Prime Force in Civil Rights Battle." *Baltimore Sun,* 16 May 1972, B-1.

Powell, Richard J. *Black Art and Culture in the 20th Century.* London, United Kingdom: Thames and Hudson, 1997.

Powell, William S., ed. *Encyclopedia of North Carolina.* Chapel Hill, NC: University of North Carolina Press, 2006.

Powledge, Fred. *Free At Last? The Civil Rights Movement and the People Who Made It.* Boston, MA: Little, Brown, 1998.

Pride, Karen, and Theresa Fambro Hook, "James Forman, Former Student Civil Rights Pioneer and Defender Reporter, Dies." *Chicago Defender,* January 12, 2005.

Proceedings of the American Anti-Slavery Society at Its Third Decade. New York, NY: Arno Press, 1969.

Pruitt, Anne S., ed. *In Pursuit of Equality in Higher Education.* Dix Hills, NY: General Hall, 1987.

Quarles, Benjamin. *Black Abolitionists.* New York, NY: Oxford, 1960.

———. *Frederick Douglass.* Englewood Cliffs, NJ: Prentice-Hall, 1948.

Rabby, Glenda Alice. *The Pain and the Promise: The Struggle for Civil Rights in Tallahassee, Florida.* Athens, GA: University of Georgia Press, 1999.

Ralph, James R, Jr. *Northern Protest: Martin Luther King, Jr., Chicago, and the Civil Rights Movement.* Cambridge, MA: Harvard University Press, 1993.

Rampersad, Arnold. *The Life of Langston Hughes,* Volume II: *1941–1967, I Dream a World.* New York, NY: Oxford University Press, 1988.

Ransby, Barbara. *Ella Baker and the Black Freedom Movement: A Radical Democratic Vision.* Chapel Hill, NC: University of North Carolina Press, 2003.

Read, Florence. *The Story of Spelman College.* New York, NY: United Negro College Fund, 1961.

Reese, David. *Letters to The Hon. William Jay: Being A Reply to His Inquiry into the American Colonization and American Anti-Slavery Societies.* Kila, MT: Kessinger Publishing, 2007.

Reich, Steven, ed. *Encyclopedia of the Great Black Migration.* Westport, CT: Greenwood Press, 2006.

Richardson, Joe M. *A History of Fisk University 1865–1946.* Tuscaloosa, AL: University of Alabama Press, 1980.

Robbins, Richard. *Sidelines Activist: Charles S. Johnson and the Struggle for Civil Rights.* Jackson, MS: University Press of Mississippi, 1996.

Roberts, Gene, and Hank Klibanoff. *The Race Beat: The Press, the Civil Rights Struggle, and the Awakening of a Nation.* New York, NY: Knopf, 2007.

Robeson, Susan. *The Whole World in His Hands: A Pictorial Biography of Paul Robeson.* Secaucus, NJ: Citadel Press, 1981.

Robinson, Jo Ann. *The Montgomery Bus Boycott and the Women Who Started It.* Knoxville, TN: University of Tennessee Press, 1987.

Robinson, Randall. *The Debt: What America Owes to Blacks.* New York, NY: Plume, 2001.

———. *Defending the Spirit: A Black Life in America.* New York, NY: Dutton, 1998.

———. *Quitting America: The Departure of a Black Man from His Native Land.* New York, NY: Dutton, 2004.

———. *Reckoning: What Blacks Owe to Each Other.* New York, NY: Dutton, 2002.

Rollin, Frank A. *Life and Public Services of Martin R. Delany.* New York, NY: Arno Press, 1969.

Roman, Charles V. *Meharry Medical College: A History.* Freeport, NY: Books for Libraries Press, 1972.

Ross, Barbara Joyce. *J.E. Spingarn and the Rise of the NAACP, 1911–1939.* New York, NY: Atheneum, 1972.

Ross, Rosetta E. *Witnessing and Testifying: Black Women, Religion, and Civil Rights.* Minneapolis, MN: Fortress Press, 2003.

Rouse, Jacqueline Anne. *Lugenia Burns Hope: Black Southern Reformer.* Athens, GA: University of Georgia Press, 1992.

Rout, Kathleen. *Eldridge Cleaver.* Boston, MA: Twayne Publishers, 1991.

Rubel, David. *From Sharecropping to Politics.* Englewood Cliffs, NJ: Silver Burdett Press. 1990.

Rudwick, Elliott M. "Race Leadership Struggle: Background of the Boston Riot of 1903." *Journal of Negro Education* 31 (1962): 16–24.

Ruiz, Vicki L., et al. *Created Equal: A Social and Political History of the United States,* Vol. 2: *From 1865.* New York, NY: Longman, 2003.

Salaam, Kalamu ya. "Black Arts Movement." *The Oxford Companion to African American Literature.* Eds. William L. Andrews, France Smith Foster, and Trudier Harris. New York, NY: Oxford University Press, 1997, 70–74.

Salem, Dorothy ed., *African American Women: A Biographical Dictionary.* New York, NY: Garland Publishing, 1993.

Salvatore, Nick. *Singing in a Strange Land: C.L. Franklin and the Rise of the Black Church in America.* New York, NY: Little, Brown, 2004.

———. *Singing in a Strange Land: C.L. Franklin and the Transformation of America.* New York, NY: Penguin Books, 1998.

Sandler, Stanley. *Segregated Skies: All-Black Combat Squadrons of WW II.* Washington, DC: Smithsonian Institution Press, 1992.

Sayre, Nora. *Previous Convictions: A Journey through the 1950s.* New Brunswick, NJ: Rutgers University Press, 1995.

Scheer, Robert, ed., *Eldridge Cleaver: Post-Prison Writings and Speeches.* New York, NY: Vintage Books, 1969.

Schlesinger, Arthur M., Jr. *Robert Kennedy and His Times.* Boston, MA: Houghton Mifflin, 1978.

———. *A Thousand Days: John F. Kennedy in the White House.* Boston, MA: Houghton Mifflin, 1965.

Schor, Joel Schor. *Henry Highland Garnet.* Westport, CT: Greenwood Press, 1977.

Schuler, Edgar A. "The Houston Race Riot, 1917." *Journal of Negro History* 29 (July 1944): 300–338.

Scott, Emmett J., and Lyman Beecher Stowe. *Booker T. Washington.* New York, NY: Doubleday, 1916.

Sherman, Joan R. *Invisible Poets: Afro-Americans of the Nineteenth Century.* Urbana, IL: University of Illinois Press, 1974.

Sherwood, Henry Noble. "The Formation of the American Colonization Society." *Journal of Negro History* 2 (July 1917): 209–228.

Shockley, Ann Allen. *Afro-American Women Writers 1746–1933: An Anthology and Critical Guide.* Boston, MA: G.K. Hall & Co., 1989.

Simmons, Hortense. "Sterling Brown's 'Literary Chronicles.'" *African American Review* 31 (1997): 443–447.

Simmons, William J. *Men of Mark: Eminent, Progressive and Rising.* Chicago, IL: Johnson Publishing, 1970.

Sklar, Kathryn Kish. *Women's Rights Emerges Within the Anti-Slavery Movement, 1830–1870: A Short History with Documents.* Boston, MA: St. Martin's, 2000.

Smith, Bob. *They Closed Their Schools Prince Edward County, Virginia, 1951–1964.* Chapel Hill, NC: University of North Carolina Press, 1965.

Smith, Elaine M. "Mary McLeod Bethune and the National Youth Administration." *Clio Was a Woman: Studies in the History of American Woman.* Ed. Mabel E. Deutrich and Virginia C. Purdy. Washington DC: Howard University Press, 1980.

Smith, Jessie Carney Smith. *Black Firsts.* 2nd ed. Detroit, MI: Visible Ink Press, 2003.

———, ed., *Encyclopedia of African American Business.* 2 vols. Westport, CT: Greenwood Press, 2006.

———, ed. *Notable Black American Men.* Farmington Hills, MI: Gale Research, 1999.

———, ed. *Notable Black American Men,* Book II, ed. Detroit, MI: Thomson Gale, 2007.

———, ed. *Notable Black American Women.* Detroit, MI: Gale, 1992.

———, ed. *Notable Black American Women.* Book II. Detroit, MI: Gale Research, 1996.

———, ed. *Notable Black American Women.* Book III. Detroit, MI: Thomson Gale, 2003.

———, and Joseph M. Palmianso, eds. *The African American Almanac.* 8th ed. Detroit, MI: Gale Group, 2000.

Stampp, Kenneth M. *The Era of Reconstruction 1865–1877.* New York, NY: Vintage, 1965.

Standifer, Lolita. "Albert Cleage." *Michigan Chronicle,* February 23, 2000, 2.

Stanton, Mary. *From Selma to Sorrow: The Life and Death of Viola Liuzzo.* Athens, GA: University of Georgia Press. 1998.

Sterling, Dorothy. *The Making of an Afro-American: Martin Robinson Delany.* Garden City, NY: Doubleday, 1971.

———, ed. *We Are Your Sisters.* New York, NY: Norton, 1984.

Still, William. *The Underground Railroad: Authentic Narratives and First-Hand Accounts.* Mineola, NY: Dover Publications, 2007.

Taylor, Alrutheus A. *The Negro in South Carolina during the Reconstruction.* New York, NY: Russell and Russell, 1924.

Taylor, Ula Yvette. *The Veiled Garvey: The Life and Times of Amy Garvey.* Chapel Hill, NC: University of North Carolina Press, 2002.

Teipe, Emily M. *Different Voices: Women in United States History.* Redding, California: CAT Publishing, 2007.

Terrell, Mary Church. *A Colored Woman in a White World.* Washington, DC: Ransdell Inc., 1940.

Terry, Wallace. *Missing Pages: Black Journalists of Modern America, an Oral History*. New York, NY: Carroll & Graf Publishers, 2007.

Theoharis, Jeanne, and Komozi Woodard, eds. *Groundwork: Local Black Freedom Movements in America*. New York, NY: New York University Press, 2005.

Thompson, Marilyn." Restoring the Historical Record." *Lexington Herald-Leader* (KY), July 11, 2004.

Thurgood Marshall: His Speeches, Writings, Arguments, Opinions, and Reminiscences. ed. Mark V. Tushnet. Chicago, IL: Lawrence Hill Books, 2001.

Till-Mobley, Mamie, and Christopher Benson. *Death of Innocence: The Story of the Hate Crime That Changed America*. New York, NY: Random House, 2003.

Tindall, George Brown. *South Carolina Negroes, 1877–1900*. Columbia, SC: University of South Carolina Press, 1952.

Torrence, Ridgley. *The Story of John Hope*. New York, NY: Macmillan, 1948.

Truth, Sojourner, and Nell Irvin Painter. *The Narrative of Sojourner Truth: A Bondswoman of Olden Time*. New York, NY: Penguin Books, 1998.

Tushnet, Mark V. *Making Civil Rights Law: Thurgood Marshall and the Supreme Court, 1956–1961*. New York, NY: Oxford, 1994.

Tyson, Timothy. "Civil Rights Movement." *The Oxford Companion to African American Literature*. eds., William L. Andrews, Frances Smith Foster, and Trudier Harris. New York, NY: Oxford University Press, 1997. 147–152.

Ullman, Victor. *Martin R. Delany: The Beginnings of Black Nationalism*. Boston, MA: Beacon Press, 1971.

United States National Advisory Commission on Civil Disorders. *Report of the National Advisory Commission on Civil Disorders*. Washington, DC: U.S. Government Printing Office, 1968.

Waddle, Ray. "Days of Thunder: The Lawson Affair." *Vanderbilt Magazine* (Fall 2002): 36–43.

Walker, Juliet E.K. *The History of Black Business in America: Capitalism, Race, Entrepreneurship*. New York, NY: Macmillan Library Reference USA, 1998.

Walker, LaVerne. "A Mother's Pride, A Daughter's Protest," *The Crisis* 110 (September/October 2003): 56.

Washington, Booker T. "An Address Delivered at the Opening of the Cotton States' Exposition in Atlanta, Georgia, September, 1895." In Carter G. Woodson, *Negro Orators and Their Orations*. Washington, DC: The Associated Publishers, 1925. 580–583.

Washington, Booker T. *My Larger Education*. Garden City, N.Y.: Doubleday, 1911.

———. *The Negro in Business*. 1906. Reprint. New York, NY: AMS Press, 1971.

———. *The Story of My Life and Work*. Naperville, IL: J. L. Nichols & Co., 1900.

———. *Up from Slavery*. New York, NY: Doubleday, 1901.

Waters, Kristin, and Carol B. Conaway, eds. *Black Women's Intellectual Tradition: Speaking Their Minds*. Burlington, VT: Vermont Press, 2007.

Weiss, Nancy J. *The National Urban League: 1910–1940*. New York, NY: Oxford University Press, 1974.

———. *Whitney M. Young, Jr., and the Struggle for Civil Rights*. Princeton, NJ: Princeton University Press, 1989.

West, V. Van, ed. *The Tennessee Encyclopedia of History and Culture*. Nashville, TN: Rutledge Hill Press 1998.

White, Deborah Gray. *Ar'n't I a Woman?: Female Slaves in the Plantation South*. New York, NY: Norton, 1999.

Wiggins, William H. Jr. *O Freedom! Afro-American Emancipation Celebrations*. Knoxville, TN: University of Tennessee Press, 1987.

Williams, Eric E. *Capitalism and Slavery*. Chapel Hill, NC: University of North Carolina Press, 1944. reprint. 1994.

Williams, Juan. *My Soul Looks Back in Wonder: Voices of the Civil Rights Experience*. New York, NY: Sterling Pub. Co., 2004.

Williams, Matt. "City Hopes to Repair Race Divide." *News and Record,* September 14, 2004.

Willis, Miriam DeCosta. *The Memphis Diary of Ida B. Wells*. Boston, MA: Beacon Press, 1995.

Wills, Gary. *Inventing America: Jefferson's Declaration of Independence*. Garden City, NY: Doubleday, 1978.

Wood, Betty. *Slavery in Colonial America, 1619–1776*. New York, NY: Rowman and Littlefield, 2005.

Woodson, Carter G. "The Gibbs Family." *Negro History Bulletin* 12 (October 1947): 3–12, 22.

Woodward, C. Vann. *The Strange Career of Jim Crow*. 3rd ed. New York, NY: Oxford University Press, 1974.

Wynn, Linda T. "The Dawning of a New Day: The Nashville Sit-Ins, February 13, 1960-May 10, 1960." *Tennessee Historical Quarterly* (Spring 1991): 42–54.

———. "The 'Economic Withdrawal' During the Nashville Sit-In Movement" Nashville, TN: Local Conference on African American Culture and History, 2005.

———. "Fiftieth Anniversary of School Desegregation." *Courier* 65, No. 3 (October 2007): 1.

———. "Fiftieth Anniversary of the Brown v. Board of Education of Topeka, Kansas." *Courier* 42, No. 2 (June 2004): 4–5.

———. "Nashville's Streetcar Boycott, (1905–1907)." In *Profiles of African Americans in Tennessee,* Bobby L. Lovett and Linda T. Wynn, eds. Nashville, TN: Local Conference on African American Culture and History, 1996.

———. "Riding through Tennessee: The 1947 Congress of Racial Equality's Freedom Ride, A Journey of Reconciliation." *Courier* 65, No. 1 (February 2007): 4–6.

———. "Tent Cities of Fayette and Haywood Counties, 1960–1962." In *Profiles of African Americans in Tennessee History,* ed. Bobby L. Lovett and Linda T. Wynn, 1996.

———. "Toward a More Perfect Democracy: The Struggle of African Americans in Fayette County to Fulfill the Unfulfilled Right of Franchise." *Tennessee Historical Quarterly* 55 (Fall 1996): 202–223.

X, Malcolm, and Alex Haley. *The Autobiography of Malcolm X*. New York, NY: Grove Press, 1965.

Yee, Shirley J. *Black Women Abolitionists: A Study in Activism, 1828–1860*. Knoxville, TN: University of Tennessee Press, 1992.

Young, Andrew. *An Easy Burden: The Civil Rights Movement and the Transformation of America*. New York, NY: HarperCollins, 1996.

Zaki, Hoda M. *Civil Rights and Politics of Hampton Institute: The Legacy of Alonzo G. Morón*. Urbana, IL: University of Illinois Press, 2007.

Zangrando, Robert L. *The NAACP Crusade against Lynching, 1909 to 1950*. Philadelphia, PA: Temple University Press, 1980.

Zinn, Howard. *SNCC: The New Abolitionists*. Boston, MA: Beacon Press, 1965.

Zinn, Howard. *You Can't Be Neutral on a Moving Train*. Boston, MA: Beacon Press, 2002.

Index

Note: (ill.) indicates photos and illustrations.